# Understanding the Arts

D0166730

John Hospers
*University of Southern California*

Prentice-Hall, Inc., Englewood Cliffs, New Jersey 07632

*Library of Congress Cataloging in Publication Data*

HOSPERS, JOHN 1918–
    Understanding the arts.

    Includes index.
    1. Aesthetics.  I. Title.
BH39.H65 1982      700′1      81–12008
ISBN  0-13-935965-6          AACR2

Printed in the United States of America
10  9  8  7  6  5  4  3  2  1

Editorial/production supervision
    and interior design by Marybeth Brande

Manufacturing Buyer: Harry P. Baisley
Cover design by Frederick Charles, Ltd.

**Front cover:** Paul Cezanne. *Mont Saint-Victoire.* 1904. Philadelphia
    Museum of Art, Philadelphia. Purchased: The George W. Elkins
    Collection. Photographed by Philadelphia Museum of Art.

**Back cover:** El Greco. *The Agony in the Garden.* The Toledo
    Museum of Art, Toledo, Ohio. Gift of Edward Drummond Lib-
    bey.

Prentice-Hall International, Inc., *London*
Prentice-Hall of Australia Pty. Limited, *Sydney*
Prentice-Hall of Canada, Ltd., *Toronto*
Prentice-Hall of India Private Limited, *New Delhi*
Prentice-Hall of Japan, Inc., *Tokyo*
Prentice-Hall of Southeast Asia Pte. Ltd., *Singapore*
Whitehall Books Limited, *Wellington, New Zealand*

# Contents

# Preface

In most American colleges and universities, only a small fraction of the students who enroll in a philosophy of the arts course are majors in philosophy. The readings they are assigned, however, are for the most part written by professors of philosophy in professional journals whose intended readers are other professors of philosophy. The result is that almost all of the readings assigned are quite unintelligible to most of the students, and those who continue the course have few kind words to say for it unless they happen to have an unusually clear and resourceful teacher to guide them through the maze. Even then the benefit derived from the course comes from the teacher, not from the readings.

Most of the students in such a course are likely to be majors in fine arts, literature, music, film, or one of the other arts, who bring with them certain problems arising in the study of their respective fields, which often induced them to enroll in philosophy of the arts in the first place. But in many cases the problems that most interest them never get discussed. Instead they are exposed to an array of other subjects, such as "the ontological status of works of art," which strike them as of no great importance in the pursuit of their own field, and once more they are turned off by what is often their only exposure to philosophy.

It is chiefly as an attempt to remedy this situation that the present book was written. While concerned with philosophical issues, it is designed to appeal to those students of the arts who wish to think clearly about the enterprise in which they are engaged. Specific works of art are constantly used as illustrations, so that the treatment of issues will not be bogged down in abstract formulas and definitions unilluminated by examples.

The book begins with one example, a story by Stefan Zweig, which will be used throughout the book as a kind of peg on which to hang one's aesthetic thoughts.

It is usual to begin books in this field with discussions of "the aesthetic." Since this topic has become immensely more controversial in recent years, a treatment of the aesthetic has been postponed until the last two chapters. The first three fourths of the book is concerned with an exploration of such concepts as art, form, representation, expression, style, and truth, and the problems encountered in such exploration.

# Acknowledgments

Grateful acknowledgment is made to the following persons and publishers who have kindly granted permission to quote from copyrighted works:

**Rudolf Arnheim,** from *Art and Visual Perception* (1974). Reprinted by permission of the University of California Press.

**Monroe C. Beardsley,** from *Aesthetics* (1958). Reprinted by permission of the author.

**Petr Beckmann,** from *Hammer and Tickle*. Reprinted by permission of Petr Beckmann.

**Clive Bell,** from *Art*. Reprinted by permission of G. P. Putnam's Sons from ART by Clive Bell.

**Hector Berlioz,** from *The Memoirs of Hector Berlioz: from 1803 to 1865,* Rachel and Eleanor Holmes, trans., annotated and revised by Ernest Newman. Reprinted by permission of Alfred A. Knopf Inc.

**R. G. Collingwood,** from *The Principles of Art* (1938). Reprinted by permission of Oxford University Press.

**John Dewey,** from *Art as Experience*. Reprinted by permission of G. P. Putnam's Sons from ART AS EXPERIENCE by John Dewey. Copyright 1934; renewed 1962 by John Dewey.

**Robert Frost,** "Stopping by the Woods on a Snowy Evening." Reprinted by permission of Holt, Rinehart & Winston.

**Roger Fry,** from *Vision and Design* and *Transformations* (1927). Reprinted by permission of Mrs. Pamela Diamand and Chatto & Windus, London.

**Theodore M. Greene,** from *The Arts and the Art of Criticism* (Copyright 1940 © 1968 by Princeton University Press): excerpts from pp. 277–278. Reprinted by permission of Princeton University Press.

**A. E. Housman,** from "Eight O'Clock." Reprinted by permission of Holt, Rinehart, Winston and by permission of The Society of Authors as the Literary Representative of the late A. E. Housman and Jonathan Cape Ltd., publishers of A. E. Housman's *Collected Poems.*

**Randall Jarrell,** "The Death of the Ball-Turret Gunner" from *The Complete Poems.* Reprinted by permission of Farrar, Straus, and Giroux, Inc. "The Death of the Ball-Turret Gunner" from RANDALL JARRELL: THE COMPLETE POEMS. Copyright 1945, 1969 by Mrs. Randall Jarrell. Copyright renewed © 1973 by Mrs. Randall Jarrell.

**T. E. Jessop,** from "The Definition of Beauty, vol. 33, (1932–1933)." Reprinted by permission of The Aristotelian Society, London.

**Erwin Panofsky,** from "Style and Medium in Motion Pictures." Reprinted by permission of Mrs. Gerda Panofsky.

**Stephen Pepper,** from *Principles of Art Appreciation* (1949). Reprinted by permission of Harcourt Brace Jovanovich.

**David W. Prall,** from *Aesthetic Judgment* (1929). Reprinted by permission of Thomas Y. Crowell Co.

**Louis Arnaud Reid,** from *A Study in Aesthetics* (1931). Reprinted by permission of Allen & Unwin Ltd.

**Guy Sircello,** from *Mind and Art: An Essay on the Varieties of Expression.* MIND & ART: AN ESSAY ON THE VARIETIES OF EXPRESSION, by Guy Sircello (copyright © 1972 by Princeton University Press; Princeton Paperback, 1978: excerpts from pp. 20–21). Reprinted by permission of Princeton University Press.

**Dylan Thomas,** from "Do Not Go Gentle Into That Good Night." Reprinted by permission of New Directions Press.

**Leo Tolstoy,** from *What is Art?* (1930). Aylmer Maude, trans. Reprinted by permission of Oxford University Press, London.

**Michael Ventura,** from a review of the film "The Elephant Man" (*Los Angeles Weekly,* October 10–16, 1980, p. 11). Reprinted by permission of the Los Angeles Weekly.

**Kendall Walton,** from *The Concept of Style,* Berel Lang, ed. 1979. Reprinted by permission of the University of Pennsylvania Press.

**Stefan Zweig,** *The Royal Game.* Copyright 1944, Copyright © renewed 1972 by the Viking Penguin, Inc. All rights reserved. Reprinted by permission of Viking Penguin, Inc.

# Introduction

## The Royal Game

### BY STEFAN ZWEIG

I

The big liner, due to sail from New York to Buenos Aires at midnight, was filled with the activity and bustle incident to the last hour. Visitors who had come to see their friends off pressed hither and thither, page-boys with caps smartly cocked slithered through the public rooms shouting names snappily, baggage, parcels and flowers were being hauled about, inquisitive children ran up and down companion-ways, while the deck orchestra provided persistent accompaniment. I stood talking to an acquaintance on the promenade deck somewhat apart from the hubbub when two or three flash-lights sprayed sharply near us, evidently for press photos of some prominent passenger at a last-minute interview. My friend looked in that direction and smiled.

"You have a queer bird on board, that Czentovic."

And as my face must have revealed that the statement meant nothing to me he added, by way of explanation, "Mirko Czentovic, the world chess champion. He has just finished off the U.S.A. in a coast-to-coast exhibition tour and is on his way to capture Argentina."

This served to recall not only the name of the young world champion but, too, a few details relating to his rocket-like career; my friend, a more observant newspaper reader than I, was able to eke them out with a string of anecdotes. At a single stroke, about a year ago, Czentovic had aligned himself with the solidest Elder Statesmen of the art of chess, such as Alekhin, Capablanca, Tartakover, Lasker, Boguljubov; not since the appearance of the nine-year-old prodigy, Reshevsky, in New York in 1922 had a newcomer crashed into the famed guild to the accompaniment of such widespread interest. It seems that Czentovic's intellectual equipment, at the beginning, gave small promise of so brilliant a career. The secret soon seeped through that in his private capacity this champion wasn't able to

1

write a single sentence in any language without misspelling a word, and that, as one of his vexed colleagues, wrathfully sarcastic, put it, "He enjoys equal ignorance in every field of culture." His father, a poverty-stricken Yugoslavian boatman on the Danube, had been run down in his tiny vessel one night by a grain steamer, and the orphaned boy, then twelve, was taken in charge by the pastor of their obscure village out of pity. The good man did his level best to instil into the indolent, slow-speaking, low-browed child at home what he seemed unable to grasp in the village school.

But all efforts proved vain. Mirko stared blankly at the writing exercise just as if the strokes had not already been explained a hundred times; his lumbering brain lacked every power to grasp even the simplest subjects. At fourteen he still added with his fingers, and it was only by dint of great strain that he read in a book or newspaper. Yet none could say that Mirko was unwilling or disobedient. Whatever he was told to do he did: fetched water, split wood, worked in the field, washed up the kitchen, and he could be relied upon to execute—even if with exasperating slowness—every service that was demanded. But what grieved the kindly pastor most about the blockhead was his total lack of co-operation. He performed no deed unless specially directed, asked no questions, never played with other lads, and sought no occupation of his own accord; after Mirko had concluded his work about the house, he would sit idly with that empty stare of grazing sheep without participating in the slightest in what might be going on. Evenings, while the pastor sucked at his long peasant pipe and played his customary three games of chess with the police-sergeant, the fair-haired dull-wit squatted silent alongside them and stared from under his heavy lids, seemingly sleepy and indifferent, at the checkered board.

One winter evening, while the two men were absorbed in their daily game, a rapid crescendo of bells gave notice of a quickly approaching sleigh. A peasant, his cap covered with snow, stomped in hastily to tell the pastor that his mother lay dying and to ask his immediate attendance in the hope that there was still time to administer extreme unction. The priest accompanied him instanter. The police-sergeant, who had not yet finished his beer, lighted a fresh pipe preparatory to leaving and was about to draw on his heavy sheepskin boots when he noticed how immovably Mirko's gaze was fastened on the board with its interrupted game.

"Well, do you want to finish it?" he said jocularly, fully convinced that the sleepyhead had no notion of how to move a single piece. The boy looked up shyly, nodded assent, and took the pastor's place. After fourteen moves the sergeant was beaten and he had to concede that his defeat was in no wise attributable to avoidable carelessness. The second game resulted similarly.

"Balaam's ass!" cried the astounded pastor upon his return, explaining to the policeman, a lesser expert in the Bible, that two thousand years ago there had been a like miracle of a dumb being suddenly endowed with the speech of wisdom. The late hour notwithstanding, the goodly pater could not forgo challenging his half-illiterate helper to a contest. Mirko won from him, too, with ease. He played toughly, slowly, deliberately, never once raising his bowed broad brow from the board. But he played with irrefutable certainty and in the days that followed neither the priest nor the policeman was able to win a single game.

The priest, best able to assess his ward's various short-comings, now became curious as to the manner in which this one-sided singular gift would resist a severer test. After Mirko had been made somewhat presentable by the efforts of the village barber, he drove him in his sleigh to the near-by small town where he knew that many chess players—a cut above him in ability, he was aware from experience—were always present in the café on the main square. The pastor's entrance, as he steered the straw-haired, red-cheeked fifteen-year-old before him, created no small stir in the circle; the boy, in his sheep-fell (woolen side in) and high boots, eyes shyly downcast, stood aside until summoned to a chess-table. Mirko lost in the first encounter because his master had never employed the Sicilian defence. The next game, with the best player of the lot, resulted in a draw. But in the third and fourth and all that came after he slew them, one after the other.

It so happens that little provincial towns of Yugoslavia are seldom the theatre of exciting events; consequently, this first appearance of the peasant champion before the assembled worthies became no less than a sensation. It was unanimously decided to keep the boy in town until the next day for a special gathering of the chess club and, in particular, for the benefit of Count Simczic of the castle, a chess fanatic. The priest, who now regarded his ward with quite a new pride, but whose joy of discovery was subordinate to the sense of duty which called him home to his Sunday service, consented to leave him for further tests. The chess group put young Czentovic up at the local hotel where he saw a water-closet for the first time in his life.

The chess room was crowded to capacity Sunday afternoon. Mirko faced the board immobile for four hours, spoke no word, and never looked up; one player after another fell before him. Finally a multiple game was proposed; it took a while before they could make clear to the novice that he had to play against several contestants at one and the same time. No sooner had Mirko grasped the procedure than he adapted himself to it, and he trod slowly with heavy, creaking shoes from table to table, eventually winning seven of the eight games.

Grave consultations now took place. True, strictly speaking, the new champion was not of the town, yet the innate national pride had received a lively fillip. Here was a chance, at last, for this town, so small that its existence was hardly suspected, to put itself on the map by sending a great man into the world. A vaudeville agent named Koller, who supplied the local garrison cabaret with talent, offered to obtain professional training for the youth from a Viennese expert whom he knew and to see him through for a year if the deficit were made good. Count Simczic, who in his sixty years of daily chess had never encountered so remarkable an antagonist, signed the guaranty promptly. That day marked the opening of the astonishing career of the Danube boatman's son.

It took only six months for Mirko to master every secret of chess technique, though with one odd limitation which later became apparent to the game's votaries and caused a sneer. Czentovic never was able to memorize a single game or, to use the professional term, to play blind. He lacked completely the ability to conceive the board in the limitless space of the imagination. He had to have the field of sixty-four black and white squares and the thirty-two pieces tangibly before him; even when he had attained international fame he carried a folding pocket board with him in order to be able to reconstruct a game or work on a problem by visual means. This defect, in itself not important, betrayed a want of imaginative power and provoked animated discussions among chess fans similar to those in musical circles when it proves that an outstanding virtuoso or conductor is unable to play or direct without a score. This singularity, however, was no obstacle to Mirko's stupendous rise. At seventeen he already possessed a dozen prizes, at eighteen he won the Hungarian mastery, and finally, at twenty, the championship of the world. The boldest experts, every one of them immeasurably his superior in brains, imagination, and audacity, fell before his tough, cold logic as did Napoleon before the clumsy Kutusov and Hannibal before Fabius Cunctator, of whom Livy records that his traits of phlegm and imbecility were already conspicuous in his childhood. Thus it occurred that the illustrious gallery of chess masters, which included eminent representatives of widely varied intellectual fields—philosophers, mathematicians, constructive, imaginative, and often creative talents—was invaded by a complete outsider, a heavy, taciturn peasant clod from whom not even the cunningest journalists were ever able to extract a word that would help to make a story. Yet, however he may have deprived the newspapers of polished phrases, substitutes in the way of anecdotes about his person were numerous, for, inescapably, the moment he arose from the board at which he was the incomparable master, Czentovic became a grotesque, an almost comic figure. In spite of his correct dress, his fashionable cravat with its too ostentatious pearl stickpin, and his carefully manicured nails, he remained in manners and behaviour the narrow-minded lout who swept the priest's kitchen. He utilized his gift and his fame to squeeze out all the money they would yield, displaying petty and often vulgar greed, always with a shameless clumsiness that aroused his professional colleagues' ridicule and anger. He travelled from town to town, stopped at the cheapest hotels, played for any club that would pay his fee, sold the advertising rights in his portrait to a soap manufacturer, and oblivious of his competitors' scorn—they being aware that he hardly knew how to write—attached his name to a "Philosophy of Chess" that had been written by a hungry Galician student for a business-minded publisher. As with all leathery dispositions, he was wanting in any appreciation of the ludicrous; from the time he became champion he regarded himself as the most important man in the world, and the consciousness of having beaten all of those clever, intellectual, brilliant speakers and writers in their own field and of earning more than they, transformed his early unsureness into a cold and awkwardly flaunted pride.

"And how can one expect that such rapid fame should fail to befuddle so empty a head?" concluded my friend who had just advanced those classic examples of Czentovic's childish lust for rank. "Why shouldn't a twenty-one-year-old lad from the Banat be afflicted with a frenzy of vanity if, suddenly, by merely shoving figures around on a wooden board, he can earn more in a week than his whole village does in a year by chopping down trees under the bitterest conditions? Besides, isn't it damned easy to take yourself for a great man if you're not burdened with the slightest suspicion that a Rembrandt, a Beethoven, a Dante, a Napoleon, ever even existed? There's just one thing in that immured brain of his—the knowledge that he hasn't lost a game of chess for months, and as he happens not to dream that the world holds other values than chess and money, he has every ground to be infatuated with himself."

The information communicated by my friend could not fail to excite my special curiosity. I have always been fascinated by all types of monomania, by persons wrapped up in a single idea; for the stricter the limits a man sets for himself, the more clearly he approaches the eternal. Just such seemingly world-aloof persons create their own remarkable and quite unique world-in-little, and work, termite-like, in their particular medium. Thus I made no bones about my intention to examine this specimen of one-track intellect under a magnifying glass during the twelve-day journey to Rio.

"You'll be out of luck," my friend warned me. "As far as I know, nobody has succeeded in extracting the least bit of psychological material from Czentovic. Underneath all his abysmal limitations this sly farmhand conceals the wisdom not to expose himself; the procedure is simple: except for such compatriots of his own sphere as he contrives to meet in ordinary taverns he avoids all conversation. When he senses a person of culture he retreats into his shell; that's why nobody can plume himself on having heard him say something stupid or on having sounded the presumably bottomless depths of his ignorance."

As a matter of fact, my friend was right. It proved utterly impossible to approach Czentovic during the first few days of the voyage, unless by rude intrusion, which, of course, isn't my way. He did, sometimes, appear on the promenade deck, but then always with hands clasped behind his back in a posture of dignified self-absorption, like Napoleon in the familiar painting; and, at that, those peripatetic exhibitions were told off in such haste and so jerkily that to gain one's end one would have had to trot after him. The social halls, the bar, the smoking-room, saw nothing of him. A steward of whom I made confidential inquiries revealed that he spent the greater part of the day in his cabin with a large chessboard on which he recapitulated games or worked out new problems.

After three days it angered me to think that his defence tactics were more effective than my will to approach him. I had never before had a chance to know a great chess player personally, and the more I now sought to familiarize myself with the type, the more incomprehensible seemed a lifelong brain activity that rotated exclusively about a space composed of sixty-four black and white squares. I was well aware from my own experience of the mysterious attraction of the royal game, this one among all games contrived by man which rises superior to the tyranny of chance and which bestows its palms only on mental attainment, or rather on a definite form of mental endowment. But is it not an offensively narrow construction to call chess a game? Is it not a science too, a technique, an art, that sways among these categories as Mahomet's coffin does between heaven and earth, an once a union of all contradictory concepts; primeval yet ever new; mechanical in operation yet effective only through the imagination; bounded in geometric space though boundless in its combinations; ever-developing yet sterile; thought that leads to nothing; mathematics that produces no result; art without works; architecture without substance, and nevertheless, as proved by evidence, more lasting in its being and presence than all books and achievements; the only game that belongs to all peoples and all ages and of which none knows the divinity that bestowed it on the world to slay boredom, to sharpen the senses, to exhilarate the spirit. One searches for its beginning and for its end. Children can learn its simple rules, duffers succumb to its temptation, yet within this immutable tight square it creates a particular species of master not to be compared with any other—persons destined for chess alone, specific geniuses in whom vision, patience, and technique are operative through a distribution no less precisely ordained than in mathematicians, poets, composers, but merely united on a different level. In the heyday of physiognomical research a Gall would perhaps have dissected the brains of such masters of chess to establish whether a particular coil in the grey matter of the brain, a sort of chess muscle or chess bump, was more conspicuously developed than in other skulls. How a physiognomist would have been fascinated by the case of a Czentovic where that which is genius appears interstratified with an absolute inertia of the intellect like a single vein of gold in a ton of dead rock! It stands to reason that so unusual a game, one touched with genius, must create out of itself fitting matadors. This I always knew, but what was difficult and almost impossible to conceive of was the life of a mentally alert person whose world contracts to a narrow, black-and-white one-way street; who seeks ultimate triumphs in the to-and-fro, forward and backward movement of thirty-two pieces; a being who, by a new opening in which the knight is preferred to the pawn, apprehends greatness and the immortality that goes with casual mention in a chess handbook—of a man of spirit who, escaping madness, can unremittingly devote all of his mental energy during ten, twenty, thirty, forty years to the ludicrous effort to corner a wooden king on a wooden board!

And here, for the first time, one of these phenomena, one of these singular geniuses (or shall I say puzzling fools?) was close to me, six cabins distant, and I, unfortunate, for whom curiosity about mental problems manifested itself in a kind of passion, seemed unable to effect my purpose. In conjured up the absurdest ruses: tickle his vanity by the offer of an interview in an important paper, or engage his greed by proposing a lucrative exhibition tour of Scotland. Finally it occurred to me that the hunter's never-failing practice is to lure the woodcock by imitating its mating cry, so what more successful way was there of attracting a chess master's attention to oneself than by playing chess?

At no time had I ever permitted chess to absorb me seriously, for the simple reason that it meant nothing to me but a pastime; if I spend an hour at the board it is not because I want to subject myself to a strain but, on the contrary, to relieve mental tension. I "play" at chess in the literal sense of the word whereas to real devotees it is serious business. Chess, like love, cannot be played alone, and up to that time I had no idea whether there were other chess lovers on board. In order to attract them from their lairs I set a primitive trap in the smoking-room in that my wife (whose game is even weaker than mine) and I sat at a chess-board as a decoy. Surely enough, we had made no more than six moves when one passerby stopped, another asked permission to watch, and before long the desired partner materialized. MacIver was his name; a Scottish foundation-engineer who, I learned, had made a large fortune boring for oil in California. He was a robust specimen with an almost square jaw and strong teeth, and a rich complexion pronouncedly rubicund as a result, at least in part surely, of copious indulgence in whiskey. His conspicuously broad, almost vehemently athletic shoulders made themselves unpleasantly noticeable in his game, for this MacIver typified those self-important worshippers of success who regard defeat in even a harmless contest as a blow to their self-esteem. Accustomed to achieving his ends ruthlessly and spoiled by material success, this massive self-made man was so thoroughly saturated with his sense of superiority that opposition of any kind became undue resistance if not insult. After losing the first round he sulked and began to explain in detail, and dictatorially, that it would not have happened but for a momentary oversight; in the third he ascribed his failure to the noise in the adjoining room; never would he lose a game without at once demanding revenge. This ambitious crabbedness amused me at first but as time went on I accepted it as the unavoidable accompaniment to my real purpose—to tempt the world master to our table.

By the third day it worked—but only half-way. It may be that Czentovic observed us at the chess-board through a window from the promenade deck or that he just happened to be honouring the smoking-room with his presence; anyway, as soon as he perceived us interlopers toying with the tools of his trade, he involuntarily stepped a little nearer and, keeping a deliberate distance, cast a searching glance at our board. It was MacIver's move. This one move was sufficient to apprise Czentovic how little a further pursuit of our dilettantish striving was worthy of his expert interest. With the same matter-of-course gesture with which one of us disposes of a poor detective story that has been proffered in a book-store—without even thumbing its pages—he turned away from our table and left the room. "Weighed in the balance and found wanting," I thought and, slightly stung by the cool, contemptuous look and to give vent to my ill humour in some fashion, I said to MacIver, "Your move didn't seem to impress the master."

"Which master?"

I told him that the man who had just walked by after glancing disapprovingly at our game was Czentovic, international chess champion. And I added that we would be able to survive it without taking his contempt too greatly to heart; the poor have to cook with water. But to my astonishment these idle words of mine produced quite an unexpected result. Immediately he became excited, forgot our game, and his ambition took to an almost audible throbbing. He had no notion that Czentovic was on board; Czentovic simply had to give him a game; the only time he had ever played with a champion was in a multiple game when he was one of forty; even that was fearfully exciting, and he had come quite near winning. Did I know the champion personally?—I didn't.—Would I not invite him to join us?—I declined on the ground that I was aware of Czentovic's reluctance to make new acquaintances. Besides, what charm would intercourse with third-rate players hold for a champion?

It would have been just as well not to say that about third-rate players to a man of MacIver's brand of conceit. Annoyed, he leaned back and declared gruffly that, as for himself, he couldn't believe that Czentovic would decline a gentleman's courteous challenge; he'd see to that. Upon getting a brief description of the master's person he stormed out, indifferent to our unfinished game, uncontrollably impatient to intercept Czentovic on the deck. Again I sensed that there was no holding the possessor of such broad shoulders once his will was involved in an undertaking.

I waited, somewhat tensed. Some ten minutes elapsed and MacIver returned, not in too good humour, it seemed to me.

"Well?" I asked.

"You were right," he answered, a bit annoyed. "Not a very pleasant gentleman. I introduced myself and told him who I am. He didn't even put out his hand. I tried to make him understand that all of us on board would be proud and honoured if he'd play the lot of us. But he was cursed stiff-necked about it; said he was sorry but his contractual obligations to his agent definitely precluded any game during his entire tour except for a fee. And his minimum is $250 per game."

I had to laugh. The thought would never have come to me that one could make so much money by pushing figures from black squares to white ones. "Well, I hope that you took leave of him with courtesy equal to his."

MacIver, however, remained perfectly serious. "The match is to come off at three tomorrow afternoon. Here in the smoking-room. I hope he won't make mincemeat of us easily."

"What! You promised him the $250?" I cried, quite taken aback.

"Why not? It's his business. If I had a toothache and there happened to be a dentist aboard, I wouldn't expect him to extract my tooth for nothing. The man's right to ask a fat price; in every line the big shots are the best traders. As far as I'm concerned, the less complicated the business, the better. I'd rather pay in cash than have your Mr. Czentovic do me a favour and in the end have to say 'thank you.' Anyway, many an evening at the club has cost me more than $250 without giving me a chance to play a world champion. It's no disgrace for a third-rate player to be beaten by a Czentovic."

It amused me to note how deeply I had injured MacIver's self-love with that "third-rate." But as he was disposed to foot the bill for this expensive flyer, it was not for me to remark on his wounded ambition which promised at last to afford me an acquaintance with my odd fish. Promptly we notified the four or five others who had revealed themselves as chess players of the approaching event and reserved not only our own table but the adjacent ones so that we might suffer the least possible disturbance from passengers strolling by.

Next day all of our group was assembled at the appointed hour. The centre seat opposite that of the master was allotted to MacIver as a matter of course; his nervousness found outlet in the smoking of strong cigars which followed one after another and in restlessly glancing ever and again at the clock. The champion let us wait a good ten minutes—my friend's tale prompted the surmise that something like this would happen—thus heightening the impressiveness of his entry. He approached the table calmly and imperturbably. He offered no greeting—"You know who I am and I'm not interested in who you are" was what his discourtesy seemed to imply—but began in a dry, business-like way to lay down the conditions. Since there were not enough boards on the ship for separate games he proposed that we play against him collectively. After each of his moves he would retire to the end of the room so that his presence might not affect our consultations. As soon as our countermove had been made we were to strike a glass with a spoon, no table-bell being available. He proposed, if it pleased us, ten minutes as the maximum time for each move. Like timid pupils we accepted every suggestion unquestioningly. Czentovic drew black at the choice of colours; while still standing he made the first countermove, then turned at once to go to the designated waiting-place where he reclined lazily while carelessly examining an illustrated magazine.

There is little point in reporting the game. It ended, as it could not but end, in our complete defeat, and by the twenty-fourth move at that. There was nothing particularly astonishing about an international champion wiping off half a dozen mediocre or sub-mediocre players with his left hand; what served to disgust us, though, was the lordly manner with which Czentovic caused us to feel, all too plainly, that it was with his left hand that we had been disposed of. Each time he would give a quick, seemingly careless look at the board, and would look indolently past us as if we ourselves were dead wooden figures; and this impertinent proceeding reminded one irresistably of the way one throws a mangy dog a morsel without taking the trouble to look at him. According to my way of thinking, if he had any sensitivity he might have shown us our mistakes or cheered us up with a friendly word. Even at the conclusion this sub-human chess automaton uttered no syllable, but, after saying "mate," stood motionless at the table waiting to ascertain whether another game was desired. I had already risen with the thought of indicating by a gesture—helpless as one always remains in the face of thick-skinned rudeness—that as far as I was concerned the pleasure of our acquaintance was ended now that the dollars-and-cents part of it was over, when, to my anger, MacIver, next to me, spoke up hoarsely: "Revanche!"

The note of challenge startled me; MacIver at this moment seemed much more like a pugilist about to put up his fists than a polite gentleman. Whether it was Czentovic's disagreeable treatment of us that affected him or merely MacIver's own pathological irritable ambition, suf-

fice it that the latter's being had undergone a complete change. Red in the face up to his hair, his nostrils taut from inner pressure, he breathed hard and a sharp fold separated the bitten lips from his belligerently projected jaw. I recognized, disquieted, that flicker of the eyes that connotes uncontrollable passion, such as seizes only players at roulette when the right colour fails to come after the sixth or seventh successively doubled stake. Instantly I knew that this fanatical climber would, even at the cost of his entire fortune, play against Czentovic and play and play and play, for simple or doubled stakes, until he won at least a single game. If Czentovic stuck to it, MacIver would prove a gold-mine which would yield him a nice few thousands by the time Buenos Aires came in sight.

Czentovic remained unmoved. "If you please," he responded politely, "you gentlemen will take black this time."

There was nothing different about the second game except that our group became larger because of a few added onlookers, and livelier, too. MacIver stared fixedly at the board as if he willed to magnetize the chess-men to victory; I sensed that he would have paid a thousand dollars with delight if he could but shout "Mate" at our cold-snouted adversary. Oddly enough, something of his sullen excitement entered unconsciously into all of us. Every single move was discussed with greater emotion than before; always we would wrangle up to the last moment before agreeing to signal Czentovic to return to the table. We had come to the seventeenth move and, to our own surprise, entered on a combination which seemed staggeringly advantageous because we had been enabled to advance a pawn to the last square but one; we needed but to move it forward to c1 to win a second queen. Not that we felt too comfortable about so obvious an opportunity; we were united in suspecting that the advantage which we seemed to have wrested could be no more than bait dangled by Czentovic whose vision enabled him to view the situation from a distance of several moves. Yet in spite of common examination and discussion, we were unable to explain it as a feint. At last, at the limit of our ten minutes, we decided to risk the move. MacIver's fingers were on the pawn to move it to the last square when he felt his arm gripped and heard a voice, low and impetuous, whisper, "For God's sake! Don't!"

Involuntarily we all turned about. I recognized in the man of some forty-five years, who must have joined the group during the last few minutes in which we were absorbed in the problem before us, one whose narrow sharp face had already arrested my attention on deck strolls because of its extraordinary, almost chalky pallor. Conscious of our gaze he continued rapidly:

"If you make a queen he will immediately attack with the bishop, then you'll take it with your knight. Meantime, however, he moves his pawn to d7, threatens your rook, and even if you check with the knight you're lost and will be wiped out in nine or ten moves. It's practically the constellation that Alekhin introduced when he played Boguljobov in 1922 at the championship tournament at Pistany."

Astonished, MacIver released the pawn and, like the rest of us, stared amazedly at the man who had descended in our midst like a rescuing angel. Any one who can reckon a mate nine moves ahead must necessarily be a first-class expert, perhaps even a contestant now on his way to the tournament to seize the championship, so that his sudden presence, his thrust into the game at precisely the critical moment, partook almost of the supernatural.

MacIver was the first to collect himself. "What do you advise?" he asked suppressedly.

"Don't advance yet; rather a policy of evasion. First of all, get the king out of the danger line from g8 to h7. Then he'll probably transfer his attack to the other flank. Then you parry that with the rook, c8 to c4; two moves and he will have lost not only a pawn but his superiority, and if you maintain your defensive properly you may be able to make it a draw. That's the best you can get out of it."

We gasped amazed. The precision no less than the rapidity of his calculations dizzied us; it was as if he had been reading the moves from a printed page. For all that, this unsuspected turn by which, thanks to his cutting in, the contest with a world champion promised a draw, worked wonders. Animated by a single thought, we moved aside so as not to obstruct his observation of the board.

Again MacIver inquired: "The king, then; to h7?"

"Surely. The main thing is to duck."

MacIver obeyed and we rapped on the glass. Czentovic came forward at his habitual even pace, his eyes swept the board and took in the countermove. Then he moved the pawn h2 to h4 on the king's flank exactly as our unknown aid had predicted. Already the latter was whispering excitedly:

"The rook forward, the rook, to c4; then he'll first have to cover the pawn. That won't help him, though. Don't bother about his pawns but attack with the knight c3 to d5, and the balance is again restored. Press the offensive instead of defending."

We had no idea of what he meant. He might have been talking Chinese. But once under his spell MacIver did as he had been bidden. Again we struck the glass to recall Czentovic. This was the first time that he made no quick decision; instead he looked fixedly at the board. His eyebrows contracted involuntarily. Then he made his move, the one which our stranger had said he would, and turned to go. Yet before he started off something novel and unexpected happened. Czentovic raised his eyes and surveyed our ranks; plainly he wanted to ascertain who it was that offered such unaccustomed energetic resistance.

Beginning with this moment our excitement grew immeasurably. Thus far we had played without genuine hope, but now every pulse beat hotly at the thought of breaking Czentovic's cold disdain. Without loss of time our new friend had directed the next move and we were ready to call Czentovic back. My fingers trembled as I hit the spoon against the glass.

And now we registered our first triumph. Czentovic, who hitherto had executed his purpose standing, hesitated, hesitated and finally sat down. He did this slowly and heavily, but that was enough to cancel—in a physical sense if in no other—the difference in levels that had previously obtained. We had necessitated his acknowledgment of equality, spatially at least. He cogitated long, his eyes resting immovably on the board so that one could scarcely discern the pupils under the heavy lids, and under the strained application his mouth opened gradually, which gave him a rather foolish look. Czentovic reflected for some minutes, then made a move and rose. At once our friend said half audibly:

"A stall! Well thought out! But don't yield to it! Force an exchange, he's got to exchange, then we'll get a draw and not even the gods can help him."

MacIver did as he was told. The succeeding manoeuvres between the two men—we others had long since become mere supernumeraries—consisted of a back-and-forth that we were unable to comprehend. After some seven moves Czentovic looked up after a period of silence and said, "Draw."

For a moment a total stillness reigned. Suddenly one heard the rushing of the waves and the jazzing radio in the adjacent drawing-room; one picked out every step on the promenade outside and the faint thin susurration of the wind that carried through the window-frames. None of us breathed; it had come upon us too abruptly and we were nothing less than frightened in the face of the impossible: that this stranger should have been able to force his will on the world champion in a contest already half lost. MacIver shoved himself back and relaxed, and his suppressed breathing became audible in the joyous "Ah" that passed his lips. I took another look at Czentovic. It had already seemed to me during the later moves that he grew paler. But he understood how to maintain his poise. He persisted in his apparent imperturbability and asked, in a negligent tone, the while he pushed the figures off the board with a steady hand:

"Would you like to have a third game, gentlemen?"

The question was matter-of-fact, just business. What was note-worthy was that he ignored MacIver and looked straight and intently into the eyes of our rescuer. Just as a horse takes a new rider's measure by the firmness of his seat, he must have become cognizant of who was his real, in fact his only opponent. We could not help but follow his gaze and look eagerly at the unknown. However, before he could collect himself and formulate an answer, MacIver, in his eager excitement, had already cried to him in triumph:

"Certainly, no doubt about it! But this time you've got to play him alone! You against Czentovic!"

What followed was quite extraordinary. The stranger, who curiously enough was still staring with a strained expression at the bare board, became affrighted upon hearing the lusty call and perceiving that he was the centre of observation. He looked confused.

"By no means, gentlemen," he said haltingly, plainly perplexed. "Quite out of the question. You'll have to leave me out. It's twenty, no, twenty-five years since I sat at a chess-board . . . and I'm only now conscious of my bad manners in crashing your game without so much as a by your leave. . . . Please excuse my presumption. I don't want to interfere further." And before we could recover from our astonishment he had left us and gone out.

"But that's just impossible!" boomed the irascible MacIver, pounding with his fist. "Out of the question that this fellow hasn't played chess for twenty-five years. Why, he calculated every move, every countermove, five or six in advance. You can't shake that out of your sleeve. Just out of the question—isn't it?"

Involuntarily, MacIver turned to Czentovic with the last question. But the champion preserved his unalterable frigidity.

"It's not for me to express an opinion. In any case there was something queer and interesting about the man's game;

that's why I purposely left him a chance.''

With that he rose lazily and added, in his objective manner: "If he or you gentlemen should want another game tomorrow, I'm at your disposal from three o'clock on."

We were unable to suppress our chuckles. Every one of us knew that the chance which Czentovic had allowed his nameless antagonist had not been prompted by generosity and that the remark was no more than a childish ruse to cover his frustration. It served to stimulate the more actively our desire to witness the utter humbling of so unshakable an arrogance. All at once we peaceable, indolent seagoers were seized by a mad, ambitious will to battle, for the thought that just on our ship, in mid ocean, the palm might be wrested from the champion—a record that would be flashed to every news bureau in the world—fascinated us challengingly. Added to that was the lure of the mysterious which emanated from the unexpected entry of our saviour at the crucial instant, and the contrast between his almost painful modesty and the rigid self-consciousness of the professional. Who was this unknown? Had destiny utilized this opportunity to command the revelation of a yet undiscovered chess phenomenon? Or was it that we were dealing with an expert who, for some undisclosed reason, craved anonymity? We discussed these various possibilities excitedly; the most extreme hypotheses were not sufficiently extreme to reconcile the stranger's puzzling shyness with his surprising declaration in the face of his demonstrated mastery. On one point, however, we were of one mind: to forgo no chance of a renewal of the contest. We resolved to exert ourselves to the limit to induce our godsend to play Czentovic the next day, MacIver pledging himself to foot the bill. Having in the meantime learned from the steward that the unknown was an Austrian, I, as his compatriot, was delegated to present our request.

Soon I found our man reclining in his deck-chair, reading. In the moment of ap-

proach I used the opportunity to observe him. The sharply chiselled head rested on the cushion in a posture of slight exhaustion; again I was struck by the extraordinary colourlessness of the comparatively youthful face framed at the temples by glistening white hair, and I got the impression, I cannot say why, that this person must have aged suddenly. No sooner did I stand before him than he rose courteously and introduced himself by a name that was familiar to me as belonging to a highly respected family of old Austria. I remembered that a bearer of that name had been an intimate friend of Schubert, and that one of the old Emperor's physicians-in-ordinary had belonged to the same family. Dr. B. was visibly dumbfounded when I stated our wish that he take Czentovic on. It proved that he had no idea that he had stood his ground against a champion, let alone the most famous one in the world at the moment. For some reason this news seemed to make a special impression on him, for he inquired once and again whether I was sure that his opponent was truly a recognized holder of international honours. I soon perceived that this circumstance made my mission easier, but sensing his refined feelings, I considered it discreet to withhold the fact that MacIver would be a pecuniary loser in case of an eventual defeat. After considerable hesitation Dr. B. at last consented to a match but with the proviso that my fellow-players be warned against putting extravagant hope in his expertness.

"Because," he added with a clouded smile, "I really don't know whether I have the ability to play the game according to all the rules. I assure you that it was not by any means false modesty that made me say that I hadn't touched a chess-man since my college days, say more than twenty years. And even then I had no particular gifts as a player."

This was said so simply that I had not the slightest doubt of its truth. And yet I could not but express wonderment at his accurate memory of the details of positions in games by many different masters; he must, at least, have been greatly occupied with chess theory. Dr. B. smiled once more in that dreamy way of his.

"Greatly occupied! Heaven knows, it's true enough that I have occupied myself with chess greatly. But that happened under quite special, I might say unique, circumstances. The story of it is rather complicated and it might go as a little chapter in the story of our agreeable epoch. Do you think you would have patience for half an hour . . .?"

## II

He waved towards the deck-chair next to his. I accepted the invitation gladly. There were no near neighbors. Dr. B. removed his reading spectacles, laid them to one side, and began.

"You were kind enough to say that, as a Viennese, you remembered the name of my family. I am pretty sure, however, that you could hardly have heard of the law office which my father and I conducted—and later I alone—for we had no cases that got into the papers and we avoided new clients on principle. In truth, we no longer had a regular law practice but confined ourselves exclusively to advising, and mainly to administering the fortunes of the great monasteries with which my father, once a Deputy of the Clerical Party, was closely connected. Besides—in this day and generation I am no longer obliged to keep silence about the Monarchy—we had been entrusted with the investment of the funds of certain members of the Imperial family. These connexions with the Court and the Church—my uncle had been the Emperor's household physician, another was an abbot in Seitenstetten—dated back two generations; all that we had to do was to maintain them, and the task allotted to us through this inherited confidence—a quiet, I might almost say a soundless, task—really called for little more than strict discretion and dependability, two qualities which my late father possessed in full measure; he succeeded, in fact, through his prudence in preserving considerable values for his clients through the years of inflation as well as the period of collapse. Then when Hitler seized the helm in Germany and began to raid the properties of churches and cloisters, certain negotiations and transactions, initiated from the other side of the frontier with a view to saving at least the movable valuables from confiscation, went through our hands and we two knew more about sundry secret transactions between the Curia and the Imperial house than the public will ever learn of. But the very inconspicuousness of our office—we hadn't even a sign on the door—as well as the care with which both of us almost ostentatiously kept out of Monarchist circles, offered the safest protection from officious investigations. In fact, no Austrian official had ever suspected that during all those years the secret couriers of the Imperial family delivered and fetched their most important mail in our unpretentious fourth floor office.

"It happens that the National Socialists began, long before they armed their forces against the world, to organize a different but equally schooled and dangerous army in all contiguous countries—the legion of the unprivileged, the despised, the injured. Their so-called 'cells' nested themselves in every office, in every business; they had listening-posts and spies in every spot, right up to the private chambers of Dollfuss and Schuschnigg. They had their man, as alas! I learned only too late, even in our insignificant office. True, he was nothing but a wretched, ungifted clerk whom I had engaged on the recommendation of a priest for no other purpose than to give the office the appearance of a going concern; all that we really used him for was innocent errands, answering the telephone, and filing papers, that is to say papers of no real importance. He was not allowed to open the mail. I typed important letters myself and kept no copies. I took all essential documents to my home and I held private interviews nowhere but in the priory of the cloister or in my uncle's consultation room. These measures of caution prevented the listening-post from seeing anything that went on, but some unlucky happening must have made the vain and ambitious fellow aware that he was mistrusted and that interesting things were going on behind his back. It may have been that in my absence one of the couriers made a careless reference to 'His Majesty' instead of the stipulated 'Baron Fern,' or that the rascal opened letters surreptitiously; anyhow, before I had ground for suspicion, he managed to get a mandate from Berlin or Munich to watch us. It was only much later, long after my imprisonment began, that I remembered how his early laziness at work had changed in the last few months to a sudden eagerness when he frequently offered, almost intrusively, to post my letters. I cannot acquit myself of a certain amount of imprudence, but after all, haven't the greatest diplomats and generals of the world, too, been out-manoeuvred by Hitler's cunning? Just how precisely and lovingly the Gestapo had long been directing its attention to me was manifested tangibly by the fact that the SS people arrested me on the evening of the very day of Schuschnigg's abdication and a day before Hitler entered Vienna. Luckily I had been able to burn the most important documents upon hearing Schuschnigg's farewell address over the radio, and the other papers, along with the indispensable vouchers for the securities held abroad for the cloisters and two archdukes, I concealed in a basket of laundry which my faithful housekeeper took to my uncle. All of this almost literally in the last minute before the fellows stove my door in.''

Dr. B. interrupted himself long enough to light a cigar. I noticed by the light of the match a nervous twitch at the right corner of his mouth that had struck me before and which, as far as I could observe, recurred every few minutes. It was merely a fleeting vibration, hardly stronger than a breath, but it imparted to the whole face a singular restlessness.

''I suppose you expect that I'm going to tell you about the concentration camp to which all who held faith with our old Austria were removed, about the degradations, martyrings and tortures that I suffered there. Nothing of the kind happened. I was in a different category. I was not put with those luckless ones on whom they released their accumulated resentment by corporal and spiritual degradation, but rather was assigned to that small group out of which the National Socialists hoped to squeeze money or important information. My obscure person in itself meant nothing to the Gestapo, of course. They must have guessed, though, that we were the dummies, the administrators and confidants, of their most embittered adversaries, and what they expected to compel from me was incriminating evidence, evidence against the monasteries to support charges of violation by those who had selflessly taken up the cudgels for the Monarchy. They suspected, and not without good reason, that a substantial portion of the funds that we handled was still secreted and inaccessible to their lust for loot—hence their choice of me on the very first day in order to force the desired information by their trusted methods. That is why persons of my sort, to whom they looked for money or significant evidence, were not dumped into a concentration camp but were sorted out for special handling. You will recall that our Chancellor, and also Baron Rothschild from whose family they hoped to extort millions, were not planted behind barbed wire in a prison camp but, ostensibly privileged, were lodged in individual rooms in a hotel, the Metropole, which happened to be the Gestapo headquarters. The same distinction was bestowed on my insignificant self.

''A room to oneself in a hotel—sounds pretty decent, doesn't it? But you may believe me that they had not in mind decenter but a more crafty technique when, instead of stuffing us 'prominent' ones in blocks of twenty into icy barracks, they housed us in tolerably heated hotel rooms, each by himself. For the pressure by which they planned to compel the needed testimony was to be exerted more subtly than through common beating or physical torture: by the most conceivably complete isolation. They did nothing to us; they merely deposited us in the midst of nothing, knowing well that of all things the most potent pressure on the soul of man is nothingness. By placing us singly, each in an utter vacuum, in a chamber that was hermetically closed to the world without, it was calculated that the pressure created from inside, rather than cold and the scourge, would eventually cause our lips to spring apart.

"The first sight of the room allotted to me was not at all repellent. There was a door, a table, a bed, a chair, a wash-basin, a barred window. The door, however, remained closed night and day; the table remained bare of book, news-paper, pencil, paper; the window gave on a brick wall; my ego and my physical self were contained in a structure of nothingness. They had taken every object from me: the watch that I might not know the hour, the pencil that I might not make a note, the pocket-knife that I might not sever a vein; even the slight narcotic of a cigarette was forbidden me. Except for the warder, who was not permitted to ad-dress me or to answer a question, I saw no human face, I heard no human voice; from dawn to night there was no sustenance for eye or ear or any sense; one was alone with oneself, with one's body and four or five inanimate things, rescuelessly alone with table, bed, win-dow, and basin; one lived like a diver in his bell in the black ocean of this silence—like a diver, too, who is dimly aware that the cable to safety has already snapped and that he never will be raised from the soundless depths. There was nothing to do, nothing to hear, nothing to see; about one, everywhere and without interruption, there was nothingness, emp-tiness without space or time. One walked to and fro, and with one went one's thoughts, to and fro, to and fro, ever again. But even thoughts, insubstantial as they seem, require an anchorage if they are not to revolve and circle around themselves; they too weigh down under nothingness. One waited for something from morn to eve and nothing happened. Nothing happened. One waited, waited, waited; one thought, one thought, one thought until one's temples smarted. Nothing happened. One remained alone. Alone. Alone.

"That lasted for a fortnight during which I lived outside of time, outside the world. If war had broken out then I would never have discovered it, for my world comprised only table, door, bed, basin, chair, window and wall, every line of whose scallopped pattern imbedded itself as with a steel graver in the inner-most folds of my brain every time it met my eye. Then, at last, the hearings began. Suddenly one received a summons; one hardly knew whether it was day or night. One was called and led through a few cor-ridors, one knew not whither; then one waited and knew not where it was, and found oneself standing at a table behind which some uniformed men were seated. Piles of papers on the table, documents of whose contents one was in ignorance; and then came the questions, the real ones and the false, the simple and the cunning, the catch questions and the dummy ques-tions, and whilst one answered strange and evil fingers toyed with papers whose contents one could not surmise, and strange evil fingers wrote a record and one could not know what they wrote. But the most fearsome thing for me at those hear-ings was that I never could guess or figure out what the Gestapo actually knew about the goings on in my office and what they sought to worm out of me. I have already told you that at the last minute I gave my housekeeper the really incriminating documents to take to my uncle. Had he received them? Had he not received them? How far had I been betrayed by that clerk? Which letters had they intercepted and what might they not already have screwed out of some clumsy priest at one of the cloisters which we represented?

"And they heaped question on ques-tion. What securities had I bought for this cloister, with which banks had I cor-responded, do I know Mr. So-and-so or do I not, had I corresponded with

Switzerland and with God-knows where? And not being able to divine what they had already dug up, every answer was fraught with danger. Were I to admit something that they didn't know I might be unnecessarily exposing somebody to the axe. If I denied too much I harmed myself.

"The worst was not the examination. The worst was the return from the examination to my void, to the same room with the same table, the same bed, the same basin, the same wall-paper. No sooner was I by myself than I tried to recapitulate, to think of what I should have said and what I should say next time so as to divert the suspicion that a careless remark of mine might have aroused. I pondered, I combed through, I probed, I appraised every single word of testimony before the examining office. I restated their every question and every answer that I made. I sought to sift out the part that went into the protocol, knowing well that it was all incalculable and unascertainable. But these thoughts, once given rein in empty space, rotated in my head unceasingly, always starting afresh in ever-changing combinations and insinuating themselves into my sleep.

"After every hearing by the Gestapo my own thoughts took over no less inexorably the martyrizing questions, searchings and torments, and perhaps even more horribly, for the hearings at least ended after an hour, but this repetition, thanks to the spiteful torture of solitude, never. And always the table, chest, bed, wall-paper, window; no diversion, not a book or magazine, not a new face, no pencil with which to jot down an item, not a match to toy with—nothing, nothing, nothing. It was only at this point that I apprehended how devilishly intelligently, with what murderous psychology, this hotel-room system was conceived. In a concentration camp one would, perhaps, have had to wheel rocks until one's hands bled and one's feet froze in one's boots; one would have been packed in stench and cold with a couple of dozen others. But one would have seen faces, would have had space, a tree, a star, something,

anything, to stare at, while here everything stood before one unchangeably the same, always the same, maddeningly the same. There was nothing here to switch me off from my thoughts, from my delusive notions, from my diseased recapitulating. That was just what they purposed: they wanted me to gag and gag on my thoughts until they choked me and I had no choice but to spit them out at last, to admit—admit everything that they were after, finally to yield up the evidence and the people.

"I gradually became aware of how my nerves were slacking under the grisly pressure of the void and, conscious of the danger, I tensed my nerves to the bursting point in an effort to find or create any sort of diversion. I tried to recite or reconstruct everything that I had ever memorized in order to occupy myself—the folk songs and nursery rhymes of childhood, the Homer of my high-school days, clauses from the Civil Code. Then I did problems in arithmetic, adding or dividing, but my memory was powerless without some integrating force. I was unable to concentrate on anything. One thought flickered and darted about: how much do they know? What is it that they don't know? What did I say yesterday—what ought I to say next time?

"This simply indescribable state lasted four months. Well, four months; easy to write, just about a dozen letters! Easy to say, too: four months, a couple of syllables. The lips can articulate the sound in a quarter of a second: four months. But nobody can describe or measure or demonstrate, not to another or to himself, how long a period endures in the spaceless and timeless, nor can one explain to another how it eats into and destroys one, this nothing and nothing and nothing that is all about, everlastingly this table and bed and basin and wall-paper, and alway that silence, always the same warder who shoves the food in without looking at one always those same thoughts that revolv around one in the nothingness until on becomes insane.

"Small signs made me disturbedly co scious that my brain was not workin

right. Early in the game my mind had been quite clear at the examinations; I had testified quietly and deliberately; my twofold thinking—what should I say and what not?—had still functioned. Now I could no more than articulate haltingly the simplest sentences, for while I spoke my eyes were fixed in a hypnotic stare on the pen that sped recordingly across the paper as if I wished to race after my own words. I felt myself losing my grip, I felt that the moment was coming closer and closer when, to rescue myself, I would tell all I knew and perhaps more; when, to elude the strangling grip of that nothingness, I would betray twelve persons and their secrets without deriving any advantage myself but the respite of a single breath.

"One evening I really reached that limit: the warder had just served my meal at such a moment of desperation when I suddenly shrieked after him: 'Take me to the board! I'll tell everything! I want to confess! I'll tell them where the papers are and where the money is! I'll tell them everything! Everything!' Fortunately he was far enough away not to hear me. Or perhaps he didn't want to hear me.

"An event occurred in this extremest need, something unforeseeable, that offered rescue, rescue if only for a period. It was late in July, a dark, ominous, rainy day: I recall these details quite definitely because the rain was rattling against the windows of the corridor through which I was being led to the examination. I had to wait in the ante-room of the hearing chamber. Always one had to wait before the session; the business of letting one wait was a trick of the game. They would first rip one's nerves by the call, the abrupt summons from the cell in the middle of the night, and then, by the time one was keyed to the ordeal with will and reason tensed to resistance, they caused one to wait, meaningless meaningful waiting, an hour, two hours, three hours before the trial, to weary the body and humble the spirit. And they caused me to wait particularly long on this Thursday, the 27th of July; twice the hour struck while I attended, standing, in the ante-room; there is a special reason, too, for my remembering the date so exactly.

"A calendar hung in this room—it goes without saying that they never permitted me to sit down; my legs bored into my body for two hours—and I find it impossible to convey to you how my hunger for something printed, something written, made me stare at these figures, these few words, '27 July,' against the wall; I wolfed them into my brain. Then I waited some more and waited and looked to see when the door would open at last, meanwhile reflecting on what my inquisitors might ask me this time, knowing well that they would ask me something quite different from that for which I was schooling myself. Yet in the face of all that, the torment of the waiting and standing was nevertheless a blessing, a delight, because this room was, after all, a different one than my own, somewhat larger and with two windows instead of one, and without the bed and without the basin and without that crack in the window-sill that I had regarded a million times. The door was painted differently, a different chair stood against the wall, and to the left stood a filing cabinet with documents as well as clothes-stand on which three or four wet military coats hung—my torturers' coats. So that I had something new, something different to look at, at last something different for my starved eyes, and they clawed greedily at every detail.

"I took in every fold of those garments; I observed, for example, a drop suspended from one of the wet collars and, ludicrous as it may sound to you, I waited in an inane excitement to see whether the drop would eventually detach itself and roll down or whether it would resist gravity and stay put; truly, this drop held me breathless for minutes, as if my life had been at stake. It rolled down after all, and then I counted the buttons on the coats again, eight on one, eight on another, ten on the third, and again I compared the insignia; all of these absurd and unimportant trifles toyed with, teased, and pinched my hungry eyes with an avidity which I forgo trying to

describe. And suddenly I saw something that paralysed my gaze. I had discovered a slight bulge in the side-pocket of one of the coats. I moved closer to it and thought that I recognized, by the rectangular shape of the protrusion, what this swollen pocket harboured: a book! My knees trembled: a *book!*

"I hadn't had a book in my hand for four months, so that the mere idea of a book in which words appear in orderly arrangement, of sentences, pages, leaves, a book in which one could follow and stow in one's brain new, unknown, diverting thoughts, was at once intoxicating and stupefying. Hypnotized, my eyes rested on the little swelling which the book inside the pocket formed; they glowered at the spots as if to burn a hole in the coat. The moment came when I could no longer control my greed; involuntarily I edged nearer. The mere thought that my hands might at least feel the book through the cloth made the nerves of my fingers tingle to the nails. Almost without knowing what I did I found myself getting closer to it.

"Happily the warder ignored my surely singular behaviour; indeed, it may have seemed to him quite natural that a man wanted to lean against a wall after standing erect for two hours. And then I was quite close to the coat, my hands purposely clasped behind me so as to be able to touch the coat unnoticed. I felt the stuff and the contact confirmed that here was something square, something flexible, and that it crackled softly—a book, a book! And then a thought went through me like a shot: steal the book! If you can turn the trick, you can hide the book in your cell and read, read, read—read again at last. The thought, hardly lodged in me, operated like a strong poison; at once there was a singing in my ears, my heart hammered, my hands froze and resisted my bidding. But after that first numbness I pressed myself softly and insinuatingly against the coat; I pressed—always fixing the warder with my eye—the book up out of the pocket, higher and higher, with my artfully concealed hands. Then: a tug, a gentle, careful pull, and in no time the lit-tle book, small in format, was in my hand. Not until now was I frightened at my deed. Retreat was no longer possible. What to do with it? I shoved the book under my trousers at the back just far enough for the belt to hold it, then gradually to the hip so that while walking I could keep it in place by holding my hands on the trouser-seams, military fashion. I had to try it out so I moved a step from the clothes-rack, two steps, three steps. It worked. It was possible to keep the book in place while walking if I but kept pressing firmly against my belt.

"Then came the hearing. It demanded greater attention than ever on my part, for while answering I concentrated my entire effort on securing the book inconspicuously rather than on my testimony. Luckily this session proved to be a short one and I got the book safely to my room, though it slipped into my trousers most dangerously while in the corridor on my way back and I had to simulate a violent fit of coughing as an excuse for bending over to get it under my belt again. But what a moment, that, as I bore it back into my inferno, alone at last yet no longer alone!

"You will suppose, of course, that my first act was to seize the book, examine it and read it. Not at all! I wanted, first of all, to savour the joy of possessing a book; the artificially prolonged and nerve-inflaming desire to day-dream about the kind of book I would wish this stolen one to be: above all, very small type, narrowly spaced, with many, many letters, many, many thin leaves so that it might take long to read. And then I wished to myself that it might be one that would demand mental exertion, nothing smooth or light; rather something from which I could learn and memorize, preferably—oh, what an audacious dream!—Goethe or Homer. At last I could no longer check my greed and my curiosity. Stretched on the bed so as to arouse no suspicion in case the warder might open the door without warning, tremblingly I drew the volume from under my belt.

"The first glance produced not merely

disappointment but a sort of bitter vexation, for this booty, whose acquirement was surrounded with such monstrous danger and such glowing hope, proved to be nothing more than a chess anthology, a collection of one hundred and fifty championship games. Had I not been barred, locked in, I would, in my first rage, have thrown the thing through an open window; for what was to be done—what could be done—with nonsense of the kind? Like most of the other boys at school I had now and then tried my hand at chess to kill time. But of what use was this theoretical stuff to me? You can't play chess alone, and certainly not without chess-men and a board. Annoyed, I thumbed the pages thinking to discover reading matter of some sort, an introduction, a manual; but, besides the bare rectangular reproductions of the various master games with their symbols—*a1-a2, Kt.-f1-Kt.-g3,* etc.—to me then unintelligible, I found nothing. All of it appeared to me as a kind of algebra the key to which was hidden. Only gradually I puzzled out that the letters a, b, c stood for the vertical rows, the figures 1 to 8 for the rows across, and indicated the current position of each figure; thus these purely graphic expressions did, nevertheless, attain to speech.

"Who knows, I thought, if I were able to devise a chess-board in my cell I could follow these games through; and it seemed like a sign from heaven that the weave of my bed-sheet disclosed a coarse checkering. With proper manipulation it yielded a field of sixty-four squares. I tore out the first leaf and concealed the book under my mattress. Then, from bits of bread that I sacrificed, I began to mould king, queen, and other figures (with ludicrous results, of course), and after no end of effort I was finally able to undertake on the bed-sheet the reproduction of the positions pictured in the chess book. But my absurd bread-crumb figures, half of which I had covered with dust to differentiate them from 'white' ones, proved utterly inadequate when I tried to pursue the printed game. I was all confusion in those first days; I would have to start a

game afresh five times, ten times, twenty times. But who on earth had so much unused and useless time as I, slave of emptiness, and who commanded so much immeasurable greed and patience!

"It took me six days to play the game to the end without an error, and in a week after that I no longer required the chessmen to comprehend the relative positions, and in just one more week I was able to dispense with the bed-sheet; the printed symbols, a1, a2, c7, c8, at first abstractions to me, automatically transformed themselves into visual plastic positions. The transposition had been accomplished perfectly. I had projected the chess-board and its figures within myself and, thanks to the bare rules, observed the immediate set-up just as a practised musician hears all instruments singly and in combination upon merely glancing at a printed score.

"It cost me no effort, after another fortnight, to play every game in the book from memory or, in chess language, blind; and only then did I begin to understand the limitless benefaction which my impertinent theft constituted. For I had acquired an occupation—a senseless, a purposeless one if you wish—yet one that negated the nothingness that enveloped me; the one hundred and fifty championship games equipped me with a weapon against the strangling monotony of space and time.

"From then on, to conserve the charm of this new interest without interruption, I divided my day precisely: two games in the morning, two in the afternoon, a quick recapitulation in the evening. That served to fill my day which previously had been as shapeless as jelly; I had something to do that did not tire me, for a wonderful feature of chess is that through confining mental energy to a strictly bounded field the brain does not flag even under the most strained concentration; rather it makes more acute its agility and energy. In the course of time the repetition of the master games, which had at first been mechanical, awaked an artistic, a pleasurable comprehension in me. I learned to understand the refinements, the tricks and feints in attack and defence; I grasped the technique of thinking ahead, planning combinations and riposting, and soon recognized the personal note of each champion in his individual method as infallibly as one spots a particular poet on hearing only a few lines. That which began as a mere time-killing occupation became a joy, and the personalities of such great chess strategists as Alekhin, Lasker, Boguljobov and Tartakover entered into my solitude as beloved comrades.

"My silent cell was constantly and variously peopled, and the very regularity of my exercises restored my already impaired intellectual capacity; my brain seemed refreshed and, because of constant disciplined thinking, even keenly whetted. My ability to think more clearly and concisely manifested itself, above all, at the hearings; unconsciously I had perfected myself at the chess-board in defending myself against false threats and masked dodges; from this time on I gave them no openings at the sessions and I even harboured the thought that the Gestapo men began, after a while, to regard me with a certain respect. Possibly they asked themselves, seeing so many others collapse, from what secret sources I alone found strength for such unshakable resistance.

"This period of happiness in which I played through the one hundred and fifty games in that book systematically, day by day, continued for about two and one-half to three months. Then I arrived unexpectedly at a dead point. Suddenly I found myself once more facing nothingness. For by the time that I had played through each one of these games innumerable times, the charm of novelty and surprise was lost, the exciting and stimulating power was exhausted. What purpose did it serve to repeat again and again games whose every move I had long since memorized? No sooner did I make an opening move than the whole thing unravelled of itself; there was no surprise, no tension, no problem. At this point I would have needed another book with more games to keep me busy, to engage the mental effort that had become in-

dispensable to divert me. This being totally impossible, my madness could take but one course: instead of the old games I had to devise new ones myself. I had to try to play the game with myself or, rather, against myself.

"I have no idea to what extent you have given thought to the intellectual status of this game of games. But one doesn't have to reflect deeply to see that if pure chance can determine a game of calculation, it is an absurdity in logic to play against oneself. The fundamental attraction of chess lies, after all, singly in that its strategy develops in different wise in two different brains, that in this mental battle Black, ignorant of White's immediate manoeuvres, seeks constantly to guess and cross them while White, for his part, strives to penetrate Black's secret purposes and to outstrip and parry them. If one person tries to be both Black and White you have the preposterous situation that one and the same brain at once knows something and yet does not know it; that, functioning as White's partner, it can instantly obey a command to forget what, a moment earlier as Black's partner, it desired and plotted. Such cerebral duality really implies a complete cleavage of the conscious, a lighting up or dimming of the brain function at pleasure as with a switch; in short, to want to play against oneself at chess is about as paradoxical as to want to jump over one's own shadow.

"Well, briefly, in my desperation I tried this impossibility, this absurdity, for months. There was no choice but this nonsense if I was not to become quite insane or slowly to disintegrate mentally. The fearful state that I was in compelled me at least to attempt this split between Black ego and White ego so as not to be crushed by the horrible nothingness that bore in on me."

Dr. B. relaxed in his deck-chair and closed his eyes for a minute. It seemed as if he were exerting his will to suppress a disturbing recollection. Once again the left corner of his mouth twitched in that strange and evidently uncontrollable manner. Then he settled himself a little more erectly.

"Well, then, I hope I've made it all pretty intelligible up to this point. I'm sorry, but I doubt greatly that the rest of it can be pictured quite as clearly. This new occupation, you see, called for so unconditional a harnessing of the brain as to make any simultaneous self-control impossible. I have already intimated my opinion that a chess contest with oneself spells nonsense, but there is a minimal possibility for even such an absurdity if a real chess-board is present, because the board, being tangible, affords a sense of distance, a material extra-territoriality. Before a real chess-board with real chessmen you can stop to think things over, and you can place yourself physically first on this side of the table, then on the other, to fix in your eyes how the scene looks to Black and how it looks to White. Obliged as I was to conduct these contests against myself—or with myself, as you please—on an imaginary field, so I was obliged to keep fixedly in mind the current set-up on the sixty-four squares and, besides, not only the momentary status but to make advance calculations as to the possible further moves open to each player, which meant—I know how mad this must sound to you—imagining doubly, triply, no, imagining sextuply, duodecibly for each of my egos, always four or five moves in advance.

"Please don't think that I expect you to follow through the involutions of this madness. In these plays in the abstract space of fantasy I had to figure out the next four or five moves in my capacity of White, likewise as Black, thus considering every possible future combination with two brains, so to speak. White's brain and Black's brain. But even this auto-cleaving of personality was not the most dangerous aspect of my abstruse experiment; rather it was that with the need to play independently I lost my foothold and fell into a bottomless pit. The mere replaying of championship games, which I had been indulging in during the preceding weeks, had been, after all, no more than a feat of repetition, a straight recapitulation of given material and, as such, no greater strain than to memorize poetry or learn

sections of the Civil Code by heart; it was a delimited, disciplined function and thus an excellent mental exercise. My two morning games, my two in the afternoon, represented a definite task that I was able to perform coolly; it was a substitute for normal occupation and, moreover, if I erred in the progress of a game or forgot the next move, I always had recourse to the book. It was only because the replaying of others' games left my self out of the picture that this activity served to soothe and heal my shattered nerves; it was all one to me whether Black or White was victor, for was it not Alekhin or Boguljobov who sought the palm, while my own person, my reason, my soul derived satisfaction as observer, as fancier of the niceties of those jousts as they worked out. From the moment at which I tried to play against myself I began, unconsciously, to challenge myself. Each of my egos, my Black ego and my White ego, had to contest against the other and became the centre, each on its own, of an ambition, an impatience to win, to conquer; after each move that I made as Ego Black, I was in a fever of curiosity as to what Ego White would do. Each of my egos felt triumphant when the other made a bad move and likewise suffered chagrin at similar clumsiness of its own.

"All that sounds senseless, and in fact such a self-produced schizophrenia, such a split consciousness with its fund of dangerous excitement would be unthinkable in a person under normal conditions. Don't forget, though, that I had been violently torn from all normality, innocently charged and behind bars, for months martyrized by the refined employment of solitude—a man seeking an object against which to discharge his long accumulated rage. And as I had nothing else than this insane match with myself, that rage, that lust for revenge, canalized itself fanatically into the game. Something in me wanted to justify itself, but there was only this other self with which I could wrestle; so while the game was on, an almost manic excitement waxed in me. In the beginning my deliberations were still quiet and composed; I would pause between one game and the next so as to recover from the effort; but little by little my frayed nerves forbade all respite. No sooner had Ego White made a move than Ego Black feverishly plunged a piece forward; scarcely had a game ended but I challenged myself to another, for each time, of course, one of my chess-egos was beaten by the other and demanded satisfaction.

"I shall never be able to tell, even approximately, how many games I played against myself during those months in my cell as a result of this crazy insatiability; a thousand perhaps, perhaps more. It was an obsession against which I could not arm myself; from dawn to night I thought of nothing but knights and pawns, rooks and kings, and a and b and c, and 'Mate!' and castle; my entire being and every sense embraced the checkered board. The joy of play became a lust for play; the lust for play became a compulsion to play, a phrenetic rage, a mania which saturated not only my waking hours but eventually my sleep, too. I could think only in terms of chess, only in chess moves, chess problems; sometimes I would wake with a damp brow and become aware that a game had unconsciously continued in my sleep, and if I dreamt of persons it was exclusively in the moves of the knight, the rook, in the advance and retreat, of the knight's move.

"Even when I was brought before the hearing board I was no longer able to keep my thoughts within the bounds of my responsibilities; I'm inclined to think that I must have expressed myself confusedly at the later sessions for my judges would glance at one another strangely. Actually I was merely waiting, while they questioned and deliberated, in my cursed eagerness to be led back to my cell so that I could resume my mad round, to start a fresh game, and another and another. Every interruption disturbed me; even the quarter hour in which the warder cleaned up the room, the two minutes in which he served my meals, tortured my feverish impatience; sometimes the midday meal stood untouched on the tray at evening because the game made me forgetful of food. The only physical sensation that I experienced was a terrible thirst; the fever of this constant thinking and playing must already have manifested itself then; I emptied the bottle in two swallows and begged the warder for more, and nevertheless felt my tongue dry in my mouth in the next minute.

"Finally my excitement during the games rose—by that time I did nothing else from morning till night—to such a height that I was no longer able to sit still for a minute; uninterruptedly, while cogitating on a move, I would walk to and fro, quicker and quicker, to and fro, to and fro, and the nearer the approach to the decisive moment of the game the hotter my steps; the lust to win, to victory, to victory over myself increased to a sort of rage; I trembled with impatience, for the one chess-ego in me was always too slow for the other. One would whip the other forward and, absurd as this may seem to you, I would call angrily, 'Quicker, quicker!' or 'Go on, go on!' when the one self in me failed to riposte to the other's thrust quickly enough. It goes without saying that I am now fully aware that this state of mine was nothing less than a pathological form of overwrought mind for which I can find no other name than one not yet known to medical annals: chess poisoning.

"The time came when this monomania, this obsession, attacked my body as well as my brain. I lost weight, my sleep was restless and disturbed, upon waking I had to make great efforts to compel my leaden lids to open; sometimes I was so weak that when I grasped a glass I could scarcely raise it to my lips, my hands trembled so; but no sooner did the game begin than a mad power seized me: I rushed up and down, up and down with fists clenched, and I would sometimes hear my own voice as through a reddish fog, shouting hoarsely and angrily at myself, 'Check!' or 'Mate!'

"How this horrible, indescribable condition reached its crisis is something that I am unable to report. All that I know is that I woke one morning and the waking was different than usual. My body was no longer a burden, so to say; I rested softly and easily. A tight, agreeable fatigue, such as I had not known for months, lay on my eyelids; the feeling was so warm and benignant that I couldn't bring myself to open my eyes. For minutes I lay awake and continued to enjoy this heavy soddenness, this tepid reclining in agreeable stupefaction. All at once I seemed to hear voices behind me, living human voices, low whispering voices that spoke words; and you can't possibly imagine my delight, for months had elapsed, perhaps a year, since I had heard other words than the hard, sharp, evil ones from my judges. 'You're dreaming,' I said to myself. 'You're dreaming! Don't, under any circumstances, open your eyes. Let the dream last or you'll again see the cursed cell about you, the chair and washstand and the table and the wall-paper with the eternal pattern. You're dreaming—keep on dreaming!'

"But curiosity held the upper hand. Slowly and carefully I raised my lids. A miracle! It was a different room in which I found myself, a room wider and more ample than my hotel cell. An unbarred window admitted light freely and permitted a view of trees, green trees swaying in the wind, instead of my bald brick partition; the walls shone white and smooth, above me a high white ceiling; truly, I lay in a new and unaccustomed bed and—surely, it was no dream—human voices whispered behind me.

"In my surprise I must have made an abrupt, involuntary movement, for at once I heard an approaching step. A woman came softly, a woman with a white head-dress, a nurse, a Sister. A delighted shudder ran through me: I had seen no woman for a year. I stared at the lovely apparition and it must have been a glance of wild ecstasy for she admonished me, 'Quiet, don't move.' I hung only on her voice, for was not this a person who talked! Was there still somebody on earth who did not interrogate me, torture me? And to top it all—ungraspable wonder!—a soft, warm, almost tender woman's voice. I stared hungrily at her mouth, for the year of inferno had made

it seem to me impossible that one person might speak kindly to another. She smiled at me—yes, she smiled; then there still were people who could smile benevolently—put a warning finger to her lips, and went off noiselessly. But I could not obey her order; I was not yet sated with the miracle. I tried to wrench myself into a sitting posture so as to follow with my eyes this wonder of a human being who was kind. But when I reached out to support my weight on the edge of the bed something failed me. In place of my right hand, fingers, and wrist I became aware of something foreign—a thick, large, white cushion, obviously a comprehensive bandage. At first I gaped uncomprehendingly at this bulky object, then slowly I began to grasp where I was and to reflect on what could have happened to me. They must have injured me, or I had done some damage to my hand myself. The place was a hospital.

"The physician, an amiable elderly man, turned up at noon. He knew who my family were and made so respectful an allusion to my uncle, the Imperial household doctor, as to create the impression that he was well disposed to me. In the course of conversation he put all sorts of questions to me, one of which, in particular, astonished me: Was I a mathematician or chemist? I answered in the negative.

"'Strange,' he murmured. 'In your fever you cried out such unusual formulas, c3, c4. We could make nothing of it.'

"I asked him what had happened to me. He smiled oddly.

"'Nothing too serious. An acute irritation of the nerves,' and added in a low voice, after looking carefully around him, 'and quite intelligible, of course. Let's see, it was March 13, wasn't it!'

"I nodded.

"'No wonder, with that system,' he admitted. 'You're not the first. But don't worry.' The manner of his soothing speech and sympathetic smile convinced me that I was in a safe haven.

"A couple of days thereafter the doctor told me quite of his own accord what had taken place. The warder had heard shrieks from my cell and thought, at first, that I was disputing with somebody who had broken in. But no sooner had he shown himself at the door than I made for him, shouted wildly something that sounded like 'Aren't you ever going to move, you rascal, you coward?' grasped at his windpipe, and finally attacked him so ferociously that he had to call for help. Then when they were dragging me, in my mad rage, for medical examination, I had suddenly broken loose and thrust myself against the window in the corridor, thereby lacerating my hand—see this deep scar. I had been in a sort of brain fever during the first few days in the hospital, but now he found my perceptive faculties quite in order. 'To be sure,' said he under his voice, 'it's just as well that I don't report that higher up or they may still come and fetch you back there. Depend on me, I'll do my best.'

"Whatever it was that this benevolent doctor told my torturers about me is beyond my knowledge. In any case, he achieved what he sought to achieve: my release. It may be that he declared me irresponsible, or it may be that meanwhile my importance to the Gestapo had diminished, for Hitler had since occupied Bohemia, thus liquidating the case of Austria. I had merely to sign an undertaking to leave the country within a fortnight, and this period was so filled with the multitude of formalities that now surround a journey—military certificate, police, tax and health certificates, passport, visas—as to leave me no time to brood over the past. Apparently one's brain is controlled by secret, regulatory powers which automatically switch off whatever may annoy or endanger the mind, for every time I wanted to ponder on my imprisonment the light in my brain seemed to go off; only after many weeks, indeed only now, on this ship, did I pluck up enough courage to pass in review all that I lived through.

"After all this you will understand my unbecoming and perhaps strange conduct to your friends. It was only by chance that I was strolling through the smoking-room and saw them sitting at the chess-board; my feet seemed rooted where I stood from astonishment and fright. For I had totally forgotten that one can play chess with a real board and real figures, forgotten that two physically separate persons sit opposite each other at this game. Truly, it took me a few minutes before I remembered that what those men were playing was what I had been playing, against myself, during the months of my helplessness. The cipher-code which served me in my worthy exercises was but a substitute, a symbol for these solid figures; my astonishment that this pushing about of pieces on the board was the same as the imaginary fantastics in my mind, must have been like that of an astronomer who, after complicated paper calculations as to the existence of a new planet, eventually really sees it in the sky as a clear, white, substantial body. I stared at the board as if magnetized and saw there my set-up, knight, rook, king, queen and pawns as genuine figures carved out of wood; in order to get the hang of the game I had voluntarily to transmute it from my abstract realm of numbers and letters into the movable figures. Gradually I was overcome with curiosity to observe a real contest between two players. Then followed that regrettable and impolite interference of mine with your game. But that mistaken move of your friend's was like a stab at my heart. It was pure instinct that made me hold him back, a quite impulsive grasp like that with which one involuntarily seizes a child leaning over a banister. It was not until afterwards that I became conscious of the impropriety of my intrusiveness."

I hastened to assure Dr. B. that we were all happy about the incident to which we owed his acquaintance and that, after what he had confided in me, I would be doubly interested in the opportunity to see him at tomorrow's improvised tournament.

"Really, you mustn't expect too much. It will be nothing but a test for me—a test whether I—whether I'm at all capable of dealing with chess in a normal way, in a game with a real board with substantial chess-men and a living opponent—for now I doubt more than ever that those hundreds, they may have been thousands, of games that I played were real games according to the rules and not merely a sort of dream-chess, fever-chess, a delirium in which, as always in dreams, one skips intermediate steps. Surely you do not seriously believe that I would measure myself against a champion, that I expect to give tit for tat to the greatest one in the world. What interests and fascinates me is nothing but the posthumous curiosity to discover whether what went on in my cell was chess or madness, whether I was then at the dangerous brink or already beyond it—that's all, nothing else.''

At this moment the gong summoning passengers to dinner was heard. The conversation must have lasted almost two hours, for Dr. B. had told me his story in much greater detail than that in which I assemble it. I thanked him warmly and took my leave. I had hardly covered the length of the deck when he was alongside me, visibly nervous, saying with something of a stutter:

"One thing more. Will you please tell your friends beforehand, so that it should not later seem discourteous, that I will play only one game. . . . The idea is merely to close an old account—a final settlement, not a new beginning. . . . I can't afford to sink back a second time into that passionate play-fever that I recall with nothing but horror. And besides—besides, the doctor warned me, expressly warned me. Every one who has ever succumbed to a mania remains for ever in jeopardy, and a sufferer from chess poisoning—even if discharged as cured—had better keep away from a chess-board. You understand, then—only this one experimental game for myself and no more.''

# III

We assembled in the smoking-room the next day promptly at the appointed hour, three o'clock. Our circle had increased by yet two more lovers of the royal game, two ship's officers who had obtained special leave from duty to watch the tourney. Czentovic, too, unlike on the preceding days, was on time, and after the usual choice of colours there began the memorable game of this *homo obscurissimus* against the celebrated master.

I regret that it was played for only us thoroughly incompetent observers and that its course is as completely lost to the annals of the art of chess as are Beethoven's improvisations to music. True, we tried to piece it together from our collective memory on the following afternoons, but vainly; very likely, in the passion of the moment, we had allowed our interest to centre on the players rather than in the game. For the intellectual contrast between the contestants became plastic physically according to their manner as the play proceeded. Czentovic, the

routinier, remained as immobile as a block the entire time, his eyes unalterably fixed on the board; thinking seemed to cost him almost physical effort that called for extreme concentration on the part of every organ. Dr. B., on the other hand, was completely slack and unconstrained. Like the true dilettante, in the best sense of the word, to whom only the play in play—the *diletto*—gives joy, he relaxed fully, explained moves to us in easy conversation during the early intervals, lighted a cigarette carelessly, and glanced at the board for a minute only when it came his turn to play. Each time it seemed as if he had expected just the move that his antagonist made.

The perfunctory moves came off quite rapidly. It was not until the seventh or eighth that something like a definite plan seemed to develop. Czentovic prolonged his periods of reflection; by that we sensed that the actual battle for the lead was setting in. But to be quite frank, the gradual development of the situation represented to us lay observers, as usually in tournament games, something of a disappointment. The more the pieces wove themselves into a singular design the more impenetrable became the real lay of the land. We could not discern what one or the other rival purposed or which of the two had the advantage. We noticed merely that certain pieces insinuated themselves forward like levers to undermine the enemy front, but since every move of these superior players was part of a combination that comprised a plan for several moves ahead, we were unable to detect the strategy of their back-and-forth.

An oppressive fatigue then took possession of us, largely because of Czentovic's interminable cogitation between moves which eventually produced visible irritation in our friend, too. I observed uneasily how, the longer the game stretched out, he became increasingly restless, moving about in his chair, nervously lighting a succession of cigarettes, occasionally seizing a pencil to make a note. He would order mineral water and gulp it down, glass after glass; it was plain that his mind was working a hundred times faster than Czentovic's. Every time the latter, after endless reflection, decided to push a piece forward with his heavy hand, our friend would smile like one who encounters something long expected and make an immediate riposte. In his nimble mind he must have calculated every possibility that lay open to his opponent; the longer Czentovic took to make a decision the more his impatience grew, and during the waiting his lips narrowed into an angry and almost inimical line. Czentovic, however, did not allow himself to be hurried. He deliberated, stiff and silent, and increased the length of the pauses the more the field became denuded of figures. By the forty-second move, after one and a half hours, we sat limply by, almost indifferent to what was going on in the arena. One of the ship's officers had already departed, another was reading a book and would look up only when a piece had been moved. But then suddenly, at a move of Czentovic's, the unexpected happened. As soon as Dr. B. perceived that Czentovic took hold of the bishop to move it, he crouched like a cat about to spring. His whole body trembled and Czentovic had no sooner executed his intention than he pushed his queen forward and said loudly and triumphantly, "There! That's done with!", fell back in his chair, his arms crossed over his breast, and looked challengingly at Czentovic. At once his pupils gleamed with a hot light.

Impulsively we bent over the board to figure out the significance of the move so ostentatiously announced. At first blush no direct threat was observable. Our friend's statement, then, had reference to some development that we short-thoughted amateurs could not prefigure. Czentovic was the only one among us who had not stirred at the provocative call; he remained as still as if the insulting "done with" had glanced off of him unheard. Nothing happened. Everybody held his breath and at once the ticking of the clock that stood on the table to measure the moves became audible. Three minutes passed, seven minutes, eight minutes —Czentovic was motionless, but I thought I noticed an inner tension that became manifest in the greater distention of his thick nostrils.

This silent waiting seemed to be as unbearable to our friend as to us. He shoved his chair back, rose abruptly and began to traverse the smoking-room, first slowly, then quicker and quicker. Those present looked at him wonderingly, but none with greater uneasiness than I, for I perceived that in spite of his vehemence this pacing never deviated from a uniform span; it was as if, in this awful space, he would each time come plump against an invisible cupboard that obliged him to reverse his steps. Shuddering, I recognized that it was an unconscious reproduction of the pacing in his erstwhile cell; during those months of incarceration it must have been exactly thus that he rushed to and fro, like a caged animal; his hands must have been clenched and his shoulders hunched exactly like this; it must have been like this that he pelted forward and back a thousand times there, the red lights of madness in his paralysed though feverish stare. Yet his mental control seemed still fully intact, for from time to time he turned impatiently towards the table to see if Czentovic had made up his mind. But time stretched to nine, then ten minutes.

What occurred then, at last, was something that none could have predicted. Czentovic slowly raised his heavy hand which, until then, had rested inert on the table. Tautly we all watched for the upshot. Czentovic, however, moved no piece, but rather with the back of his hand pushed, with one slow determined sweep, all the figures from the board. It took us a moment to comprehend: Czentovic gave up the game. He had capitulated in order that we might not witness his being mated. The impossible had come to pass: the champion of the world, victor at innumerable tournaments, had struck his colours before an unknown, a man who hadn't touched a chess-board for twenty or twenty-five years. Our friend, the anonymous, the ignotus, had overcome the greatest chess master on earth in open battle.

Automatically, in the excitement, one after another rose to his feet; each was animated by the feeling that he must give vent to the joyous shock by saying or doing something. Only one remained stolidly at rest: Czentovic. After a measured interval he lifted his head and directed a stony look at our friend.

"Another game?" he asked.

"Naturally," answered Dr. B. with an enthusiasm that was disturbing to me, and he seated himself, even before I could remind him of his own stipulation to play only once, and began to set up the figures in feverish haste. He pushed them about in such heat that a pawn twice slid from his trembling fingers to the floor; the pained discomfort that his unnatural excitement had already produced in me grew to something like fear. For this previously calm and quiet person had become visibly exalted; the twitching of his mouth was more frequent and in every limb he shook as with fever.

"Don't," I said softly to him. "No more now; you've had enough for today. It's too much of a strain for you."

"Strain! Ha!" and he laughed loudly and spitefully. "I could have played seventeen games during that slow ride. The only strain is for me to keep awake at that tempo.—Well, aren't you ever going to begin?"

These last words had been addressed in an impetuous, almost rude tone to Czentovic. The latter glanced at him quietly and evenly but there was something of a clenched fist in that adamantine, stubborn glance. On the instant a new element had entered: a dangerous tension, a passionate hate. No longer were they two players in a sporting way; they were two enemies sworn to destroy each other. Czentovic hesitated long before making the first move and I had a definite sensation that he was delaying on purpose. No question but that this seasoned tactician had long since discovered that just such dilatoriness wearied and irritated his antagonist. He used no less than four minutes for the normal, the simplest of openings, moving the king's pawn two spaces. Instantly our friend advanced his king's pawn, but again Czentovic was responsible for an eternal, intolerable pause; it was like waiting with beating heart for the thunder-clap after a streak of fiery lightning, and waiting—with no thunder forthcoming. Czentovic never stirred. He meditated quietly, slowly, and as I felt increasingly, maliciously slowly —which gave me plenty of time to observe Dr. B. He had just about consumed his third glass of water; it came to my mind that he had spoken of his feverish thirst in his cell. Every symptom of abnormal excitement was plainly present: I saw his forehead grow moist and the scar on his hand become redder and more sharply outlined than before. Still, however, he held himself in rein. It was not until the fourth move when Czentovic again pondered exasperatingly that he forgot himself and exploded with, "Aren't you ever going to move?"

Czentovic looked up coldly. "As I

remember it we agreed on a ten-minute limit. It is a principle with me not to make it less."

Dr. B. bit his lips. I noticed under the table the growing restlessness with which he lifted and lowered the sole of his shoe, and I could not control the nervousness that overcame me because of the oppressive prescience of some insane thing that was boiling in him. As a matter of fact, there was a second encounter at the eighth move. Dr. B., whose self-control diminished with the increasing periods of waiting, could no longer conceal his tension; he was restless in his seat and unconsciously began to drum on the table with his fingers. Again Czentovic raised his peasant head.

"May I ask you not to drum. It disturbs me. I can't play with that."

"Ha, ha," answered Dr. B. with a short laugh, "one can see that."

Czentovic flushed. "What do you mean by that?" he asked, sharply and evilly.

Dr. B. gave another curt and spiteful laugh. "Nothing except that it's plain that you're nervous."

Czentovic lowered his head and said nothing. Seven minutes elapsed before he made his move, and that was the funereal tempo at which the game dragged on. Czentovic became correspondingly stonier; in the end he utilized the maximum time before determining on a move, and from interval to interval the conduct of our friend became stranger and stranger. It looked as if he no longer had any interest in the game but was occupied with something quite different. He abandoned his excited pacing and remained seated motionlessly. Staring into the void with a vacant and almost insane look, he uninterruptedly muttered unintelligible words; either he was absorbed in endless combinations or—and this was my inner suspicion—he was working out quite other games, for each time that Czentovic got around to making a move he had to be recalled from his absent state. Then it took a minute or two to orient himself. My conviction grew that he had really

forgotten all about Czentovic and the rest of us in this cold aspect of his insanity which might at any instant discharge itself violently. Surely enough, at the nineteenth move the crisis came. No sooner had Czentovic executed his play than Dr. B., giving no more than a cursory look at the board, suddenly pushed his bishop three spaces forward and shouted so loudly that we all started:

"Check! Check, the king!"

Every eye was on the board in anticipation of an extraordinary move. Then, after a minute, there was an unexpected development. Very slowly Czentovic tilted his head and looked—which he had never done before—from one face to another. Something seemed to afford him a rich enjoyment, for little by little his lips gave expression to a satisfied and scornful smile. Only after he had savoured to the full the triumph which was still unintelligible to us did he address us, saying with mock deference:

"Sorry—but I see no check. Perhaps one of you gentlemen can see my king in check?"

We looked at the board and then uneasily over at Dr. B. Czentovic's king was fully covered against the bishop by a pawn—a child could see that—thus the king could not possibly be in check. We turned one to the other. Might not our friend in his agitation have pushed a piece over the line, a square too far one way or the other? His attention arrested by our silence, Dr. B. now stared at the board and began, stutteringly:

"But the king ought to be on f7— that's wrong, all wrong—Your move was wrong! All the pieces are misplaced—the pawn belongs on g5 and not on g4. Why, that's quite a different game—that's—"

He halted abruptly. I had seized his arm roughly, or rather I had pinched it so hard that even in his feverish bewilderment he could not but feel my grip. He turned and looked at me like a somnambulist.

"What—what do you want?"

I only said "Remember!" at the same time lightly drawing my finger over the scar on his hand. Automatically he followed my gesture, his eyes fixed glassily on the blood-red streak. Suddenly he began to tremble and his body shook.

"For God's sake," he whispered with pale lips. "Have I said or done something silly? Is it possible that I'm again . . . ?"

"No," I said, in a low voice, "but you have to stop the game at once. It's high time. Recollect what the doctor said."

With a single movement Dr. B. was on his feet. "I have to apologize for my stupid mistake," he said in his old, polite voice, inclining himself to Czentovic. "What I said was plain nonsense, of course. It goes without saying that the game is yours." Then to us: "My apologies to you gentlemen, also. But I warned you beforehand not to expect too much from me. Forgive the disgrace—it is the last time that I yield to the temptation of chess."

He bowed and left in the same modest and mysterious manner in which he had first appeared before us. I alone knew why this man would never again touch a chessboard, while the others, a bit confused, stood around with that vague feeling of having narrowly escaped something uncomfortable and dangerous. "Damned fool," MacIver grumbled in his disappointment.

Last of all, Czentovic rose from his chair, half glancing at the unfinished game.

"Too bad," he said generously. "The attack wasn't at all badly conceived. The man certainly has lots of talent for an amateur."

# 1

# Works of Art

"The Royal Game" is one example of a work of art. Whether or not it is a *good* work of art is a different question: whether it is well put together, whether the actions and the characters are convincing, whether the story has enough variety or unity, whether it is expressive of any dominant mood or feeling, whether it contains any explicit or implicit views on life and the world, and whether any or all of these should be considered reasons for considering it a good work of art, and why—all these questions will be examined later in this book. But before we try to decide whether something is a good work of art, we must decide whether it is a work of art at all.

## 1. WHAT IS A WORK OF ART?

Some might answer by pointing to different things: here is a painting, here is a statue, there is a cathedral, there is a poem, there is a novel. These are all examples of works of art. But in doing this we are just pointing to instances, and we still have not answered the question, "What is it that makes these particular things members of the class 'works of art'?" What is the criterion by which we determine whether or not something is a work of art?

There is one confusion we would do well to eliminate at the outset: sometimes people use the phrase "work of art" in a *descriptive* sense and sometimes in an *evaluative* sense. When someone who isn't accustomed to contemporary art stands looking at some cubist paintings in a museum, he may say, "*That's* not art!" But he isn't really denying that it's art in the descriptive sense; it's painting, good or bad, and paintings are works of art, good or bad. What his remark means is that in his opinion it isn't *good* art, or *worthy* of the honorable title "art." He is denying it the title "valuable art" (evaluative sense) but isn't really denying to it the title "art" (descriptive sense). In this chapter we are concerned only with the descriptive sense; in later chapters we shall pursue the much more interesting and controversial question, "What makes something good art, and why?"

Not everyone agrees on what entitles something to be called a work of art, even in the descriptive sense. We shall now consider the principal views on this question.

1. *A work of art as anything made by man.* The first conception of art employs a fundamental contrast between those things which are made by human beings (one or more) and those that are not. Those that are not—stars, hills, trees—are "natural" objects, and everything else in the world is art (an artifact or the result of human artifice). It was this sense of "art" which the French novelist André Gide was using when he said, "The only unnatural thing in the world is a work of art." By calling it "unnatural," he meant that it was not a natural object but was made by man. So his statement turned out to be, quite deliberately, a tautology: "That which isn't natural (an object of nature) is unnatural (art)."

Good or bad, beautiful or ugly, successful or unsuccessful, they are all works of art, on this definition, if they are made by human beings. Office buildings, coal mines, wastebaskets, garbage dumps, lighthouses—all these are works of art, since all are changes wrought on the face of nature by the activities of man. Some of them were made to satisfy the maker's sense of beauty, but most of them were made to fulfill some practical purpose, either a human need, such as shelter, or a human desire, such as the desire to exhibit something of one's own making.

Simple though this definition appears, some problems arise concerning it.

(a) What about constructions by animals other than man? Are they art? Is a bridge built by a beaver a work of art? a bird's nest? a spider's web? Not if we take the definition strictly, as the work of human beings only. But we could broaden the definition to include all things made or constructed by *sentient beings,* a class that includes birds and beavers as well as people, and in that case these products of animal construction can count as works of art.

(b) Those with a theological point of view sometimes say that *all* things, including stars and trees and animals, are works of art, since, although they were not made by human beings, they were made by God, the Supreme Artist. The universe and everything in it would then be God's works of art. And if one grants the theological premise, this would indeed be true: as human artifacts are to man, so man and animals and plants and planets are to God. Even if we go along with this, however, we will still find it useful to distinguish works of art created by God directly—clouds and stars, hills and human beings—from those very different works of art created by God's first-order creations—human beings—about which we know a great deal more. It is to this latter class that we give the distinctive name "works of art," calling the others "natural objects," or, if we are theologically inclined, "natural objects created by God."

(c) There is also a problem about *how much* change in a natural object is required before it is to be considered a work of art. In most of the arts no problem arises: if we read a poem or novel, there is no doubt that the words were put there in that order by someone; how else would they have gotten there? As Henry Fielding remarks in *Tom Jones,* a freak of nature like a chicken with three legs would not be nearly as astounding as a chicken born with a letter in its belly. If we look at a musical score, with its clefs, key signatures, notes, and measures explicitly indicated, it is perfectly clear that these do not appear there "naturally"—that they were put there by someone. And the same holds true of paintings and sculptures, at least traditional ones. If you see a marble head of Zeus, you can be quite certain that it is the work of a sculptor and didn't come to be in that configuration "accidentally" by the work of the wind and the waves; and the same if you see the visages of four American presidents in the Black Hills of South Dakota.

But now what of cases like the following: a rock isn't a work of art, but what if you drill a hole through it? Is it a sculpture now? (What if it's just the shape you wanted for your "abstract" sculpture, all except for the hole, which is your contribution to an object of nature?) What if you take the rock and put a couple of scratches on it? or your initials? Maybe it's not a sculpture, but is it a work of art, because after all you have made some changes (however minor) on nature's rock? Suppose you do nothing at all to the rock itself but simply change its position relative to other things—you place it on a hilltop and gather little stones around it; you add and subtract nothing to the rocks themselves, only to their positions. Does that make the pattern of rocks a work of art?

The difference between the rock with the hole in it and the rock with the face of Zeus carved in it seems to be only a difference of degree: there was more human interference with a natural object in the case of the Zeus. If the face of Zeus is a work of art, why not the rock with the hole drilled in it? Why not the rock with your initials written on it? Or just your fingerprints? It's true of course that you didn't *make* the rock into which you drilled the hole, but then neither did the sculptor make the rock out of which he carved the face of Zeus. An artist always takes some *preexisting* material and does something to it or with it—he doesn't create the material itself. Only God in Christian theology is said to create *ex nihilo* (out of nothing); even the Greek gods always created as men do, out of preexisting material. So that is not the difference.

There are several possibilities here. (a) We could say that it is a work of art if the natural object (or its arrangement?) has been altered in any way by a human being, however slightly; in that case the rock with your fingerprints on it is a work of art, and a crushed leaf is a work of art because its shape is different as a result of your stepping on it. The trackless jungle would be natural, but the human tracks in the grass would be art.

(b) More plausibly, one could speak of *degrees* of being work of art: we could say that, *to the extent* that one or more human beings intervened in the course of nature, to that extent it is a work of art: thus the marble sculpture of a human face is more a work of art than is the marble piece with only a hole drilled in it, and the one with your initials on it is less a work of art than either. If you saw off a tree trunk and use it as a chair, it is a work of art because, without your interference, there would be a whole tree and not a detached trunk, but yet it would not be as much of a work of art as if you had carved an Indian head on the trunk.

2. *Art as the product of an artistic process.* Many persons, however, have been dissatisfied with the broad definition of a work of art (in the descriptive sense) as anything made or fashioned by man or as being a work of art to the degree that it was man-made. A work of art, let us grant, requires someone to make it; but perhaps this is necessary but not by itself sufficient to make something a work of art. It seems much more plausible to call a painting or poem (even a bad one) a work of art than to call a paper clip or a plastic fork a work of art, even though these too are man-made. Is there any way we can narrow the conception of a work of art, any further distinction we can make among man-made things that does not require us to confer the title "work of art" upon all of them?

One answer that has been given to this question is, "A work of art is the *end-product of an artistic process.*" It is the kind of process that led to the product that determines whether or not the product of that process is to be called a work of art.

In dealing with this definition, it is now necessary to point out an ambiguity in the word "art." When we use the word "art," we ordinarily use the word (and have done so thus far) in the *product* sense: "art" means the *work* of art, the *result* of whatever process brought it into being. But sometimes, when the word "art" is used, we are talking not about the object made but about the *process* involved in making it. This is an example of a fairly widespread phenomenon in language called the "process-product ambiguity." The same word is used to refer both to a process and to the product that results from that process. (We shall see in Chapter 4 how this works in the word "expression.") A person who says "Art is a result of human workmanship," is talking about the product; but someone who says "Art is the *creation* of elements in a medium" or "Art is an activity of self-expression" is talking about the process that (he believes) led to the making of that product. In the sense of "work of art" now under consideration, it is still the product we are discussing, but since it is the product of a specific process, we must now discuss the word "art" as used to refer to that process, whatever it may be.

(a) There are many activities in which people engage that would not be described by anyone as artistic activities. We breathe, but we do so unconsciously, even during sleep; we walk, and though when we first learned to walk we had to concentrate on it, it is now almost as unconscious for us as breathing—we can change its direction consciously but we do not concentrate on every step we take. But now consider the activity of attaching a rivet on an assembly line. We may not want to call that an artistic activity either. Yet it does require a certain *skill*. And when an activity requires skill, we have some inclination to speak of "the art of . . .". There is the art of swimming, the art of darning socks, of blowing bubbles, of eating delicately, of finding out what others are thinking, of creating a disturbance without getting caught, of conning people out of money, and so on endlessly. "Any kind of activity, insofar as it is skilled, is a species of art."[1] The Greeks called it *techne,* from which our word "technique" is derived. Art in the widest of the process senses is any kind of *doing* or *making*: there is the art of growing a vegetable garden, the art of raising healthy dogs, the art of blowing glass, the art of committing burglaries, the art of speed reading, the art of eating corn on the cob without making a mess, the art of driving defensively, the art of freight-hopping, the art of telling people what you think of them without losing your cool, and so on. All are varieties of doing, and all require a certain amount of skill which must be acquired.

Not all of them, however, result in *things* that have come into existence as a result of the activity, and if one insists on art as *making* something by doing it, and not just doing something, then the art-process (in the broad sense we are now considering) occurs only when some thing is made as a result of the activity. Thus, the art of creating a disturbance is indeed doing something, but it does not result in any product made. In the art of freight-hopping, the activity is exerted on a physical thing (the freight train) but does not issue in the production of any physical thing. But in the art of building fences, and carving statues, and preparing dinners, there is something to show for the activity, in the form of a product that is made. In all such cases, preexisting materials were transformed by the activity of making into new combinations that did not exist in that combination prior to the activity of making. The stone existed before, but not the statue; the ingredients of the soup existed before, but not the soup; the wood existed before, but not the fence.

This, then, the doing or the making of anything, is the widest sense of "art" in the process sense—just as anything that is made is the widest sense of "art" in the product sense. But when we speak in daily life of the process of art-creation, we do not usually mean to include as many things as this wide sense includes. We would not usually include the activities of making disturbing noises or hopping freights as instances of the art-process. Let us aim for a narrower process sense and distinguish the art-process in the broad sense just considered from some narrower sense.

[1] C. J. Ducasse, *Art, the Critics, and You* (New York: Liberal Arts Press, 1944), p. 39.

(b) Such a distinction has been made and described by the philosopher of art R. G. Collingwood, and he called it the distinction between *art* and *craft*. Let us suppose that you are a carpenter and that you receive an order for a thousand classroom chairs, with the exact specifications indicated—the kind of wood to be used, the height, width, and so on, and the color they are to be painted. The *end-in-view* (the thousand completed chairs) is already fully known in advance; you have only to provide the *means* toward that end, namely, constructing the chairs in accordance with the specifications. Your activity is that of a craftsman. If you are a good craftsman you will determine in advance what tools you will need, how much wood will be required, and approximately how long it will take you to finish the job—to the extent that you can't do these things you are a sloppy craftsman. And the same is true if what is to be made is more complicated, like a bridge, and requires many workman; the contractor has the blueprints, he knows what is wanted, and his task is to get the product completed in accordance with the specifications as efficiently as possible.

On the other hand, if you are the *designer* of the bridge, you are engaged in the activity of art (again, not necessarily good art, but art); the designer is the creator, and he cannot proceed like the craftsman. He doesn't know when he starts to plan the bridge just what it will look like when it is completed or what every dimension will be—if he did, he would be able to make the blueprint right there and then; the blueprint comes at the end of his creative activity, not at the beginning. He plays around with various ideas that come into his mind, he develops them, rejects various alternatives. Similarly, the poet doesn't know when he begins to write his poem what the final poem will be like, how many words there will be, what the words will be and in what order; if he did, he wouldn't have to go through the creative process, he would only have to write the words down. He has to "play around with the medium," getting ideas as he goes along (and he can't predict when or even whether his ideas will come), usually scratching out some words and substituting others he later finds more suitable. He does not know at the beginning of the process of creating a poem what the completed poem will be like—or even whether there will be one (his inspiration might falter midway, causing him to give it up as a bad job).

> The craftsman knows what he wants to make before he makes it. This foreknowledge is absolutely indispensable to craft. . . . Moreover, this foreknowledge is not vague but precise. If a person sets out to make a table, but conceives the table only vaguely, as somewhere between two by four feet and three by six, and between two and three feet high, and so forth, he is no craftsman.
>
> [By contrast] the poet may get paper and pen, fill the pen, sit down and square his elbows, but these actions are preparatory not to composition (which may go on in the poet's head) but to writing. Suppose the poem is a short one, and composed without the use of any writing materials; what are the means by which the poet composes it? I can think of no answer, unless comic answers are wanted,

such as "using a rhyming dictionary," pounding his foot on the floor or wagging his head to mark the meter," or "getting drunk." If one looks at the matter seriously, one sees that the only factors in the situation are the poet, the poetic labor of his mind, and the poem.[2]

The making of a work of art has little in common with what we ordinarily mean by "making." It is a strange and risky business in which the maker never quite knows what he is making until he has actually made it; or, to put it another way, it is a game of find-and-seek in which the seeker is not sure what he is looking for until he has found it.[3]

It is this feature, then—not knowing the end-product in the beginning, and having to grope your way toward it—that distinguishes the art-process from the craft-process. In this narrower sense of "art-process," not every making counts as art; only the *creative* makings do (again, whether what one creates is good or bad).

But now a problem arises: whether the creator previsions the end in the beginning depends on *to what degree of detail* he is supposed to do this. A person may know when he starts that he is going to write a play, even a play in three acts, and this is *some* degree of prevision though not in very much detail. An artist may prevision his completed work in much more detail. If you read Edgar Allan Poe's essay "The Philosophy of Composition," you will see how in composing his poem "The Raven" he wanted to create certain lilting rhythms that would mesmerize the reader and that the mellifluous word "nevermore" would (he thought) achieve this effect; he thus selected "Lenore" as the name of the central character since it rhymed with "nevermore"; and he used a raven because of its color, the same as the tone of the poem he wanted to write, and also certain somber connotations attaching to the word; and so on. He knew quite a lot about the end-product before he set pen to paper. He didn't know the exact poem, every word in its finished order, of course, else he would have had only to write it down; but he knew a lot more than most people do when they start to write. Does this fact turn Poe's artistry into craftsmanship? And if we consider the poem a good on does our knowledge that he planned it all in a sort of cold-blooded way, somewhat as a carpenter plans how much wood he needs, detract from its merit at all?

The answer seems clear: it doesn't make the activity less creative at all. When Poe thought of the word "Lenore" as a rhyme to "nevermore" and the raven as an appropriate symbol for the poem, he had already in that very act begun the creative process in regard to "The Raven." Some begin writing with a tentative plan already in their minds, and some begin with their minds quite empty; but in both cases they are involved in the activity of creating a poem.

[2] R. G. Collingwood, *The Principles of Art,* Part I (Oxford: Clarendon Press, 1938), pp. 15–16, 20.

[3] H. W. Janson, *History of Art* (Englewood Cliffs, N.J.: Prentice-Hall, 1962), p. 11, quoted in W. E. Kennick, ed., *Art and Philosophy,* 2nd ed. (New York: St. Martin's Press, 1979), p. 174.

The difference is the *degree of specificity* with which the poem is conceived in the poet's mind before he sets pen to paper. In some cases that degree is very high:

> Many of the greatest works of art were executed in accordance with the strictest contracts, how many figures to be shown, where they were to stand, how much gold, how much blue, how much red to be used. Within this rigid framework the painter exerted his genius to create a work of beauty, and he succeeded more often in reaching his goal than many modern artists with a blank canvas and nothing to do but express their own ideas.[4]

Yet even in this case the artist does not know at the beginning of the creative process exactly what the completed work will be like, or even whether there will be one; perhaps he will be unable to go through with the job at all.

Most artists create by physically interacting with their chosen medium: a painter applies paint to his canvas to see whether anything that pleases him will emerge, and a composer sits at the piano trying out various tunes. On the other hand, some, like Mozart, create an entire overture "in their heads" before ever setting pen to paper. Whichever is the case, the activity is creative: he may develop the idea, he may scrap it entirely, he may start over again with something else.

In some cases the designing of the work is done by one individual, and the execution is done by others. The architect designs the bridge, but as a rule he does not build it himself: that is left for others who follow the instructions on the blueprints. The many individuals who actually build the bridge according to the architect's specifications are craftsmen, whose work does require skill (and thus is art in the broad sense of "skill") but who are not creating anything; they are only making (fabricating) something in accordance with the specifications laid down by the architect, who is the creator in the whole enterprise. The designer conceives the bridge, the craftsmen execute his design.

There are many such cases in which the creation is done by one person and the execution by others. When a chef creates a new recipe for a soup or a souffle, he is the creative artist; the thousands of recipe book readers who prepare the dish according to his recipe are simply craftsmen following his instructions. Here again the creating is done by one person, but the actual physical making is done by hosts of other persons all across the land who prepare the dish according to the recipe (although, when they try to improve on his recipe, *they* are being creative). When a fashion designer designs a new dress, his activity is creative; when a thousand sewing-machine operators in the dress factory make the dresses in accordance with the designer's specifications, they are engaged in craft, but are not involved in the art-process.

In other cases, the two functions are combined in the same person. Michelangelo conceived in his mind the statue of Moses, but he also did the

---

[4] John Walker, *The National Gallery of Art* (New York: Harry Abrams, Inc. 1974), p. 548.

physical work of carving in stone to make the sculpture. Seurat conceived the idea of creating certain paintings according to a pointillist technique, but he also painted with his own hands the work that resulted from his creative ideas. Both activities are of course indispensable: without a prior conception there would be nothing to execute, and without execution the idea would remain simply that, an idea in the artist's mind, and no completed product that others could see and enjoy. As a rule in painting and sculpture, both activities are embodied in the same person, who is both artist and craftsman, both conceiver and maker.

The literary artist (poet, dramatist, novelist, etc.) is the one who conceives the work in his mind, and he is also (as a rule) the person who writes down the words with his pen. In literature there is no special difficulty in the execution: anyone who can write or type can set down the words as they occur to him. Penmanship, as well as typewriting, are crafts which most people learn at an early age, unlike painting and sculpting. If the novelist dictates his work to someone else, who then writes it down, or if he utters the word into a tape recorder, he is still the artist who creates the novel, and we do not consider the novel any the less his creation, as we would in the case of a sculptor who described to someone his "idea for a sculpture," even in great specific detail, but didn't bother to sculpt it. Why the difference? It is not merely that the art of chiseling in stone is something much more difficult to do (for most people) than is that of writing. The difference lies largely in the fact that the *appearance* of the final product—the sculpture, the painting—counts a great deal with us; it is after all what we have to look at and on which our estimate of the work is based. But in the case of literature the appearance of the final product is incidental, as long as we can read it: it is not the appearance of the words on the page that we enjoy; it is the thoughts and feelings in our minds that are generated by the words. How the words appear on the printed page is incidental; how the painting or sculpture looks to the eye is not.

In music, the artist is again the person who created the symphony; ordinarily he is the same person who writes the notes of the symphony on score paper, but even if he is not (Frederic Delius was blind and paralyzed in his later life and dictated his score to an assistant, who wrote it down), he is nevertheless the creator of the music, and the man who wrote the score from the composer's dictation is not.

What of the composer who conceives of the main melodies of his composition, as well as their development, but leaves the orchestration to his subordinates? Can he be said to leave the execution to others? Yes, but he is also leaving part of the creative endeavor to others: what instruments of the orchestra are to carry which melodies and their accompaniments is part of the design or conception of the work. Such a composer is not only leaving the execution to others, he is leaving an important portion of the *creative* endeavor (the artistic process) to others.

The matter is more complex with an art in which many people cooperated to produce the final product, such as film. Is the person who first conceived in his mind the idea for a new film the artist, and all the rest—the director, the script writer, the set designers, the cameramen, and so on—merely executants? No, they too were creative in *their* activities, albeit subsidiary to the original creator's general plan: the script writer had to create ideas for the script, just as in the case of the poet; the set designers created ideas for the scenes before the camera, just as in the case of the painter and architect. All were creative in their own special areas, and all were (as a rule) involved in executing the ideas by making or rearranging physical things. They were all involved in some creative activity, and they were also involved in the execution of these creative ideas—along with many other persons who were simply following orders by painting furniture, moving it around, changing sets, and so on and had nothing to do with creating the movie but were involved only in its execution.

For a product to exist, then—be it a bridge, a painting, a statue, a novel, a symphony, or a film—there is required (a) a creative process in which the idea for the completed product is conceived and developed (this is the artistic process) and (b) execution of the creative ideas on some physical materials (the crafting process). Only the first involves creative artistry, but the second is also required in order for a work of art (good or bad) to come into existence which can be observed and appreciated by other people. If the second process does not take place, there is nothing that can be observed and appreciated, and we do not yet have a work of art (only "the idea for one").

But now we must ask, "What things that are called art by our first definition (anything man-made) would *not* be called art by our second definition?" It could well be that nothing whatever is excluded. It's true that no artistry is involved (only craft) in the making of a thousand classroom chairs or paper clips or plastic forks; but, just as in the case of the bridge, someone first had to *design* them, and even though the creative activity required for this may be minor compared with the creation of a symphony or a cathedral there would appear to be some creative activity involved nonetheless. In principle the classroom chairs are no different from the bridge: the furniture designer who designed the chairs probably viewed the possibilities, had some ideas for designing the chairs, scrapped some of them and hit upon others, altered his plans until he hit upon a design acceptable to him— all of which characterizes the artistic process as much as designing a bridge or a cathedral. So it seems that there could be just as many objects classifiable as works of art according to the second definition as according to the first: even if the execution of the plan involved no creative activity, the inception of the plan did so. However minor the creative activity involved, it is still sufficient to classify the completed thing(s) as art by the second definition.

But now another problem confronts us: in distinguishing creative activity, in which we work our way to the completion of an idea but don't know its details at the outset, from craft, in which we do know all this with precision in advance, we are distinguishing craft from creativity in general, not just *artistic* creativity. But it seems obvious that not all creative endeavor is artistic and that not all products of creative endeavor would be called works of art. When a scientist is engaged in devising a theory about the nature of subatomic particles, or when a mathematician is in the process of devising a theorem, aren't these activities too creative? The physicist and the mathematician do not know at the beginning of their speculations how they will end, or even in what direction they will go, until they have arrived there. If the artist "doesn't know what he's going to say until he's said it," it is equally true that the scientist doesn't know what his theory will be, in detail, until he has conceived it. The activities in both cases are creative; they just occur in different fields of endeavor.

How then shall we narrow our concept of the art-process still further, so as to enable us to talk about the art-process *as opposed to* the (equally creative) scientific process? If they are not the same, how are they to be distinguished from each other?

The answer now seems plain enough: when a scientific theory is created, the result of the creative activity is a scientific theory, which can be set down on paper and evaluated by other scientists. When a work of art is created, the result of the creative activity is a different sort of thing, a work of art. But now what is the meaning of the phrase "work of art"? Art is not, apparently, the result of just any activity, for that would include the results of unconscious activities like breathing and so on; neither is it the result of any skilled activity, for then the craft of producing a thousand classroom chairs to advance specifications would be art; neither is it the result of just any *creative* activity (as opposed to craft), for we find as much of this in science, mathematics, and other areas which we distinguish from art, since we do not classify mathematical and scientific treatises as works of art.

One way in which to answer this question would be to introduce the term "aesthetic" and say that works of art are aesthetic objects, or have aesthetic qualities, and that the others do not. But to introduce the term "aesthetic" at this point would raise more questions that it solves. When we do have a rendezvous with this term, it will have to be a lengthy one (Chapters 8 and 9). Besides, it won't do to say that only the arts have aesthetic features. If elegance, neatness, economy of means, and so on are aesthetic features, as most people take them to be, then these occur also in mathematics and science: the neatness and elegance of a proof has a "lean, clean" aesthetic character, even if the argument is fallacious and the "proof" establishes nothing. No, we shall try to concentrate on the *kind of object* which is created and see whether we can limit "works of art" in that way.

There is a difference, however, somewhat vague though understood by everyone, between those humanly created objects which are made to be contemplated or enjoyed *for their own sakes,* not as means toward some further end (these are called "fine arts"), and those which are made primarily for some useful purpose, to fill some need other than the need for enjoyment itself (these are called "useful arts"). There isn't much you can do with a poem except read it and enjoy it if you can; there isn't much you can do with a work of music except listen to it and try to enjoy it also. But much as you may enjoy the appearance of certain glass tumblers, baskets, automobiles, and so on, they are first and foremost practical or useful arts, and the result of practical or useful activities: tumblers are made for one to drink out of, baskets to put things in, automobiles to drive in (a beautiful automobile that won't run isn't of much use). This is the difference between what have traditionally been called the "fine arts" and the "useful arts."

Since we are concerned more with things we can enjoy for their own sakes than with things whose enjoyment is incidental to some practical activity, we shall concentrate on the fine arts to see in what ways they are alike and in what ways they are different.

This difference will concern us in the next section; meanwhile, there is one more view to consider about what distinguishes art from nonart.

3. *The institutional theory of art.* In 1917 the painter-sculptor Marcel Duchamp, calling himself for this occasion Mr. Mutt, took a urinal, named it "Foundation," and exhibited it in an art museum. He had neither designed nor constructed the object exhibited, but the purpose was to *make* it a work of art *by the act of exhibiting it.*

> Whether Mr. Mutt with his own hands made the fountain or not has no importance. He *chose* it. He took an ordinary article of life, placed it so that its useful significance disappeared under a new title and point of view (and) created a new thought for that object.[5]

It was not his designing or making the object that made it his work of art, for he did neither; it was his *placing it on display* in a certain context (an art museum). The artist is the person who is responsible for displaying the work (it could be the museum director); and the same object which was not a work of art before becomes one through the act of being exhibited in the requisite context.

But does anything that is publicly displayed thereby become art? If the plumbing salesman shows his wares to you in your house to try to make a sale, are the plumbing fixtures art? No, says the theory, because they lack the *institutional setting* required to make something art. What exactly is this institutional setting? The institution is not a formal one like a government or a university; it is rather an informal and vaguely delineated institution called the *artworld.* And who or what makes up the artworld? This again is a vaguely delineated class: there are the people who go to plays, the people who go to

[5] Marcel Duchamp, Beatrice Wood, and H. P. Roche, *The Blind Man,* 2nd issue (May 1917), quoted in *Marcel Duchamp,* ed. Anne D'Harnoncourt and Kynaston McShine (New York: Museum of Modern Art and Philadelphia: Philadelphia Museum of Art, n.d.), p. 283.

concerts, the people who go to museums, the people who read poems and novels, and so on (it isn't clear whether, for example, people who buy antiques at swap meets are part of the artworld). All these groups together constitute the artworld.

Now within the artworld, there are people who (like premiers of state) are empowered to confer the status of art on things of their choice. A museum director, perhaps under the persuasion of a well-known artist like Duchamp, takes a piece of driftwood which was neither designed nor made by any human being and exhibits it alongside man-made sculptures, thus emphasizing its likeness to them, and indicating by his act that the object should be viewed in much the way a sculpture is. And thus, once the piece of driftwood is exhibited, it *becomes* a work of art, even though it has not been altered in any way since it was picked up on the beach. It becomes a work of art by a kind of act of baptism, just as a person through immersion is baptized into the realm of the "saved." The status of art is conferred on an object through the informal activity of the institution called the artworld. Without that institutional framework nothing whatever is a work of art. That is why the plumbing salesman's wares are not art when they are exhibited for sale in your house—they lack the institutional setting; "Duchamp's action took place within the institutional setting of the artworld, and the plumbing salesman's action took place outside of it."[6]

What if you take the piece of driftwood and display it in your living room, perhaps with a few small spotlights under it to highlight its contours? This may be a borderline case, but it could be made out that you are like the museum director and you are exhibiting the driftwood in your living room much as the museum director might exhibit it in a museum.

Are the paintings of Betsy the chimpanzee to be considered works of art? On the first definition of art they are, provided we include sentient beings besides man as makers. On the second definition they presumably are not, since it is likely that Betsy painted hit or miss and did not go through an "artistic process." On the present definition we would have to say, "It all depends on the institutional setting." When displayed at an anthropological museum, they would not be art, but if displayed in a museum of fine arts, they would be. Why the difference? One institutional setting is congenial to conferring the status of art and the other is not. Betsy's [paintings] would remain her paintings even if exhibited at an art museum, but they would be the *art* of the person responsible for their being exhibited. Betsy would not (I assume) be able to conceive herself in such a way as to be a member of the artworld and, hence, would not be able to confer the relevant status."[7] (Would she confer it, or the museum director? and if the art institute director, why not the field museum director?)

[6] George Dickie, *Art and the Aesthetic* (Ithaca, N.Y.: Cornell U.P., 1974), p. 38.
[7] *Ibid.,* p. 46.

And thus hundreds of things, such as Brillo boxes, tomato soup cans, paring knives, notebooks, hatracks, packages of cigarettes—all become works of art by being displayed in the appropriate institutional setting. All these things, being man-made, are already art by the first definition, but they become art according to the present (institutional) definition by having the *status* of art conferred upon them by their being shown in the proper context. Indeed, there are many more far-out cases than this: a horse was cut into little pieces and exhibited, thus becoming art; a grave was dug behind the Metropolitan Museum in New York and christened a work of art by the digger. A glass tumbler is a work of art when exhibited in your living room, but not when used for drinking in the kitchen.

There were paintings in ancient Egypt which were never exhibited at all, but entombed with the Pharaohs to accompany them on their journey to the next world. Were they not works of art because they were never exhibited? Presumably—although it could be replied that in the institutional setting of ancient Egypt the act of conferring the status of art was made by the artists, or the pharaohs, in a different way—not by being exhibited to the general public, but only to one chosen person, the pharaoh—much as the choicest paintings would hang not in the Louvre but in Louis XIV's private quarters. But what of the vast array of paintings that are not exhibited and have never been, but lie unnoticed in cellars and attics? Should one say they are art because they could or *might* be exhibited? But, then, what couldn't?

Also, it is not clear what "exhibit" means when works other than paintings and sculptures are involved. Is a symphony "exhibited" when it is performed? Is it not art during periods when it is not performed? And if it has never been performed, is it not then a work of art? Is a poem "exhibited" when it is being read? Are literary works the sort of thing that are exhibited at all? or does reading them aloud to an audience constitute an exhibition? or does writing the poem on a piece of paper so that other people *could* see it constitute "exhibiting" it?

There are so many counterintuitive consequences of this definition—such as the connection of a work of art with exhibition to the artworld, and a thing's not being a work of art until it has been displayed, and the artist's being the person who showed or displayed it rather than the one who created it—that one is inclined simply to scrap the definition entirely. But one should be aware of the context in which this way of conceiving of art arose: it arose only in connection with visual arts, and it arose only when things like driftwood, jade and other precious stones, as well as "ready-mades" like Brillo boxes and soup cans, began to find their way into museums. If you think some enterprise worthy enough to call for laudatory language, and if you think that calling it "art" is indeed an example of such language, then you will devise a definition of "art" in such a way as to include the things you like (or want to call attention to) within the definition. That, surely, besides a certain iconoclasm, is the genesis of this bizarre departure from the more traditional ways of conceiving something as art. It would seem much more "natural" to say of pieces of driftwood and precious stones that they are *not* art but, rather, natural objects which are placed in a context in which one is more inclined to look at them in a different way; this would have avoided all the paradoxes of the institutional theory. But if one wants badly enough to call something art, and the thing doesn't qualify by more traditional definitions, then one simply devises a new definition so as to incorporate the things one likes into the category one values.

## 2. CLASSIFYING THE ARTS

Among the things that human beings have made, there are some which are primarily objects of practical use, such as hammers and nails, chairs and tables, automobiles and airplanes. These are sometimes called objects of *practical* or *useful* art. Automobiles are primarily designed and constructed as a convenient means of transport; houses are built to be lived in; glass tumblers are made to drink from; lamps are designed to give light; and so on.

But there are also objects of human creating and making which don't seem to have any such practical use at all; they are made to be enjoyed, to be appreciated, to be looked at or heard or read. These are sometimes called the *fine* arts. As we have already observed, there isn't much that you can do with a piece of music except listen to it and, it is hoped, enjoy it; and there isn't much you can do with a poem except read it. It's true that one could use a Rembrandt painting to hide a crack in the wall, but an object that provided no enjoyment or satisfaction to look at, such as a pine board, could hide the crack just as well. The main reason for the very existence of these objects of "fine art" is for them to be enjoyed and appreciated.

Something may be in the category of fine art and not be a success: it may be ugly, repellent, awkward; it may have missed the boat on artistry and yet be an object of fine art. A bad poem is certainly no more a work of "useful art" than a good one is.

Often a work of art, or a type of work, will have one foot in both classes. Although automobiles are designed primarily for locomotion, and one wouldn't usually pay much money for a car that won't run, still cars—some cars—are also found enjoyable just to look at; and it may be that the choice of which car to buy is made as much because on the basis of its pleasing appearance as its being mechanically efficient. Although glasses are made for drinking, there is a difference between Swedish cut glasses and dime-store tumblers in the satisfaction it gives one to just look at them. We may select a table for its stark angles and simplicity of design as much as for its utility as a thing on which to eat or write.

But these are man-made things which *primarily* serve a practical function.

In general this may be true of architecture too: homes and garages primarily serve everyday practical functions. But is a cathedral or a temple something primarily to be worshiped in or primarily to be looked at and enjoyed? People find them to be worthwhile for both reasons. Some of them serve no religious function now, though they once did: the Parthenon was originally a temple to the goddess Athena, although its designers could hardly have been ignorant of its value as an object of beauty, worth contemplating apart from any use to which it could be put—too many things, like making pillars rounded so that they would look straight from a certain angle, had to have been done intentionally. Still, it once *had* a religious function; today the Greek gods have passed from the scene, and we contemplate the Parthenon solely as an object of beauty, to be enjoyed and admired; that is the way in which it operates in our experience now.

One cannot plausibly say that all works of art which we view with admiration today were created solely or even primarily to satisfy our taste for the beautiful. Many temples were built primarily or entirely as places of worship. By his own account, Lucretius wrote *De Rerum Natura* to convert his readers to Democritean materialism, Dante wrote *The Divine Comedy* to convert his readers to Catholicism, and Milton wrote *Paradise Lost* "to justify the ways of God to man." It hardly behooves us to say they were liars and that this wasn't really what they were trying to do; but it also seems to us that they wrote memorable lines of poetry and that they did this not incidentally or accidentally but on purpose.

We simply have to distinguish between their original *intent*—which in the case of most artists, who are long dead, we know little or nothing about—and the way in which their artworks function in our experience today. If we defined "fine art" as art which was *intended* by its creator(s) to be enjoyed or appreciated, we would be faced with questions about what the artist really intended which we are usually in no position to answer. It seems on the whole much wiser to define "fine art" as art which, whatever its original intent, is regarded primarily as a "thing of beauty." What motivated the creators when they created is for the most part lost in the mists of history; how we respond now to their creations is not. We therefore distinguish fine arts from useful arts on the basis of how we experience them, not on the basis of how the creator of these works intended them.

There are many ways in which the fine arts could be classified. For example, we could distinguish those arts which have, or can have, a subject-matter (the sculptured bust of Napoleon, the painting of Napoleon, the novel or play or film about Napoleon) from those arts which do not, such as music and architecture. (Whether music can ever have a subject-matter will be discussed in Chapter 3.) Or we could classify them as *spatial* or *temporal* arts: painting, sculpture, and architecture are spatial arts, since the object exists "out there" in space, all of it at every moment that the object exists, whereas music and literature are temporal arts—the parts of the work succeed one another in time, and you have to begin at a certain place, proceed in one direction, and end at a certain place (you can't do it backward). Some arts, such as film, include both spatial and temporal elements: each frame of the film exists whole at any given moment and can be viewed like a painting, but the film as a whole has to be shown in temporal succession and in a certain order (not mixing up reel 4 with reel 5, for example). In this case the film *can* be run backward—in reverse succession—but the film was not designed to be seen backward, and the results are not usually any more rewarding than trying to read a novel backward, word by word, from the last page to the first.

The most fruitful way in which to distinguish the arts is through the nature of their *medium*. The arts can be classified most precisely by the medium in which they are created, which separates them from each other and determines their possibilities and their restrictions.

1. *Visual arts.* Painting, sculpture, and architecture are visual arts; so are most of the useful arts—automobiles, lamps, tables, dishes, baskets, and so on, which all appeal to us through the sense of sight. Without vision we would be quite lost in trying to appreciate these arts. Some visual arts appeal not only to the sense of sight but to the sense of touch also, such as sculpture, but much as we might like to touch the smooth white marble of the statue, we are not usually permitted in a museum to do so. Even here, however, touch is at best an auxiliary to sight: if you are approaching the statue for the first time and had to choose between seeing it and touching it, you would probably decide that you would get the most out of seeing it. Painting, sculpture, and architecture are different from one another in many ways, but clearly they are all (at least primarily) visual arts.

Sometimes the word "art" is used synonymously with "visual art." The Department of Art, or the School of Fine Arts, in most colleges and universities, means painting and sculpture and sometimes architecture, but not music or literature. Yet music and literature are as much art, and fine art, as the visual arts are, and when we speak of "art" or "the arts" in courses in philosophy of art, these terms are never restricted to the visual arts alone.

2. *Auditory art.* This includes music in all its forms. The medium of music is sound, just as that of the visual arts is sight. Sounds are divided into (a) noises, which when emitted have many frequencies at once, and (b) tones, which are primarily on one frequency—for example, middle C plus its overtones. Traditionally, music has been defined as combinations of *tones* or, more accurately, tones plus rests. But the invention of such things as electronic music, where one could not say that there is one tone emitted at any given moment, may have made this traditional definition a bit too narrow. Still, it would hardly do to include all sounds (noises as well as tones) as music: we would not call things like ordinary conversation, screams, foghorns, and thunderclaps music. Even bird songs, at least most of them,

seem to belong in the category of noises rather than tones: if you hear a bird song, can you say what note the bird is singing, or in what key? Music hardly exists in nature at all; it is man-made instruments that produce sounds of a definite pitch. Have you ever heard a chord of the sixth of seventh in nature?

Tones must also be distinguished from *notes*. The notes are visual notations on a written score; *they* are not what you hear when you go to a concert. Notes are simply a detailed set of cues which tell the players what tones to play on their instruments and when. If the performers had perfect memories, they would not need the written score. The notes are visual, and tones are auditory—and music of course is an auditory art.

Sometimes a person who is accomplished at reading a score—such as a conductor of orchestras—doesn't need to hear the orchestra playing the tones at all. Does this show that for such a person music is not an auditory art? Clearly not: what the conductor can do is read the notes and then *imagine* the sounds in his mind. He can imagine the sounds from reading the score, whereas most people have to actually hear the sounds. The difference here is between imagined sounds and physically heard sounds, not between sounds and something visual such as notes.

3. *Literary art.* Where in all this does literature belong? Is literature a visual art when one reads the poem or novel from the printed page and an auditory art when one reads the words aloud?

Works of literature are sometimes read aloud, and in poetry especially the effect is often enhanced if one hears the sounds of the words. (Even if one reads silently, one can *imagine* the sounds of the words—although many readers say that they don't do even this.) Still, literature is not to be classified as an auditory art—its auditory aspect is fairly incidental. The medium of music is sounds (or tones), and the medium of literature is *words*—some would prefer to say words and sentences. A spoken word is not just a sound (in this case, a noise), it is a sound *with a meaning;* and to appreciate a work of literature it is absolutely necessary to understand what the words mean. When you know what the word sounds like, you still haven't understood the meaning of the word. Imagine hearing a poem read aloud in a language you do not understand; you may get a certain amount of emotional response, as I once did hearing Katina Paxinou reading Euripides in classical Greek, but that was because she was an actress and was able to project emotion through her voice. One still can't understand what she was saying unless one knows what the words mean. Learn the sounds of a foreign language without knowing the meanings of any of the words, and see if you can appreciate a poem in that language!

In music it is the sounds themselves, in their various complex combinations, which you appreciate when you appreciate the musical composition; but in literature the heard sounds are *vehicles* for the *meaning,* and without knowing the meaning of the words one cannot go far toward appreciating the poem. The sounds in a poem sometimes reinforce the sense, but without knowing what the words mean you do not even know that the sound of the poem is suited to the sense, since you do not yet know what the sense is. The sound of a poem *without the meaning* is comparatively poverty stricken aesthetically, and if poetry were to be construed simply as an art of sound (with no meaning), poetry would virtually have to go out of business—it couldn't stand the competition with music. "Murmuring" and "murdering" are almost identical sounds, but they carry very different effects in a poem because their meanings are different. "Murmuring" is a pleasant sound to roll off the tongue, and if "murdering" doesn't seem so, it is because we know what this word means, and we react to the meaning more than to the sound. "Sleep within a gloomy grot" and "Peep within a roomy cot" are very similar in sound, but far from similar in meaning.

Is literature then a visual art? No more than it is an auditory one. Usually we read works of literature silently, by looking at the printed page, which of course is a visual object. When blind persons read in Braille, reading is not a visual activity but a tactual one. But just as in reading aloud, seeing the printed marks on the page helps us not at all unless we identify them as words and know what the words mean. In fact, what the words look like on the printed page is even less important that what the words sound like when uttered aloud. In rare cases it may be of some auxiliary interest, as when E. E. Cummings's poem about a cross is written on the page in the shape of a cross. But appreciation of poems is not appreciation of the way the words look on the page. If a critic were to write, "This is a bad poem, because it is written in small, hard-to-read type (or cramped handwriting) on yellowed paper, so thin that the words on the opposite page show through," we would say at once that it was not the poem that he was criticizing; he was saying something about the visual layout. But a poem, whether in large type or in small type, in black ink or purple ink, printed or typed or penned on paper or on the blackboard or on a granite slab, is still the same poem as long as we have the same words in the same order. If it's hard to read, this is the fault of the printer or the book designer, but not of the poet.

If literature is not an auditory art and not a visual art, what then is it? It is neither—it has sometimes been called a *symbolic* art because its medium is words, and every word in a language is a sound (or printed mark) that is a symbol of something else, namely, its meaning. A word is not merely a sound, like the wind whistling past the window, but a sound (or printed mark) to which a meaning has been given by the users of the language; to appreciate "murmuring" as a word and not merely as a sound, you have to know what the English word "murmuring" means. We can't appreciate a poem without grasping the meaning of the words any more than we can appreciate music if we are deaf or painting if we are blind. And meanings are grasped not by the senses, but by the mind—the senses (sight and sound) are only vehicles for grasping what is not itself sensory, the meanings of the words. That is why literature has been called an *ideosensory* art, as opposed to music and visual arts, which are *sensory* arts.

In literature the medium is not and cannot be regarded as purely sensory. Words, phrases, sentences are not mere sounds, but sounds appointed to be an operative as vehicles of determinate images and meanings and of the emotional evocations of these. The auditory aspect offers many possibilities of design, but all this various form and texture of sound-pattern has to be contributory to or concordant with the burden of ideas which is the inalienable essence of the words. The so-called pure poetry desired by some of the moderns is not poetry, not literature, because its medium is not words but simply sounds; nor is it even music, for music is minimally a pattern of musical sounds, different both sensorily and physically from spoken sounds. Important, then, as sound-beauty may be in verbal art, it is subordinate; its whole office is not to present itself, but to introduce and reinforce a system of images and meanings and emotions; and since images and meanings and emotions are the distinctive stuff and life of human experience, verbal beauty is indefeasibly humanistic; not only properly but inescapably ideal, representative, expressive and evocative—. . . inescapably related to that system of needs, interests, and evaluations which make us practical and moral beings.

This is not the case in painting. Here the medium can be apprehended in its purely sensory aspect without mutilation. It can stand alone entire. It is not a necessary part of color, line, and space to represent, express, or evoke. *The sensory medium itself has a beauty all its own.* Certain colors sit quietly side by side, others enhance each other; certain lines are graceful, directive, and organizing; certain masses are mutually supporting, coherent. These are the specific excellencies of color in its spatial setting, its own aesthetic aspect. With nothing more than these, a picture is beautiful, and so too is an evening sky. . . . In no case is it necessary to know what a color-object stands for in order to appreciate its own beauty; as beautiful it is non-significant. I could still apprehend beauty in a sunset even if I did not know it to be a sunset, and without contemplating it imaginatively as the death-moment of day, as an emblem or monition of our mortality, or as an intimation that a passing so gorgeously attended is not extinction but translation. Paint may be used to represent, but the mere representing of things will not make beauty unless the things are beautiful. When what is represented is not centrally a visual thing, but some fragment of life's joy or pathos, itself perhaps beautiful, we have a *supervenient* beauty, that of the subject of the painting, not of the medium, of the painting as paint.

If then, painting and the other visual arts, and probably music too, may be beautiful quite apart from what they represent or express, there is a beauty distinct from that of which alone literature is capable. To approach painting, sculpture, architecture and music from the side of literature and require there what is always to be found here, is to overlook the nature of the difference between the two kinds of media—one of which may, the other of which may not, forego all representational or expressive character. A word ceases to be a word and therefore loses the beauty of a word when its signification and significance are not apprehended; a color is most a color when apprehended apart from what it may happen to represent, and then most reveals its own beauty.[8]

[8] T. E. Jessop, "The Objectivity of Beauty," in *Introductory Readings in Aesthetics,* ed. J. Hospers (New York: Macmillan, 1969), pp. 279–280.

And thus literature, the ideosensory art, is distinguished from the sensory arts, the visual and the auditory. It should be added at once, however, that even the sensory arts require not only the senses, but the receptive mind of the hearer which sifts out the multiplicity of sensory stimuli and organizes them. Try your favorite symphony or sonata on your pet dog or cat; no matter how often you play it, the pet will not appreciate it as music at all. It's not that dogs and cats can't hear—they can hear better than you or I do—but, rather, that they lack the mental capacity to integrate the multiplicity of auditory sensations which reach their ears. It's not that animals lack minds but, rather, that their minds seem directed solely to practical purposes such as physical survival and (in the case of pets) affection gathering; they cannot make sense of a series of sounds which serves no practical purpose for them. But let them hear a meowing sound just outside the door, and they will act accordingly at once.

For that matter, when you first heard what is now your favorite symphonic composition, it probably didn't make much sense to you—it came to you as a confused welter of sounds, with perhaps a few melodies standing out amidst the chaos; then on the second hearing the chaos became a little more ordered, on the third hearing you perceived connections and relations you had not grasped before, and so on, until you became thoroughly familiar with it. The mind, not only the senses, had done their work.

The same holds true of the visual arts. Having sight is as necessary for appreciating painting and sculpture as having hearing is necessary for appreciating music; but in both cases the condition is necessary, not sufficient. A mind is required to organize the data of the senses. Animals have little or no ability even to recognize two-dimensional representations of three-dimensional objects. You point to a dog on the television screen and your dog looks around bewildered—he can't recognize what's on the screen as the representation of a dog—though often if a dog barks on television, your dog recognizes it as a bark (a poor mechanical imitation of one) and sometimes barks in response, in bewilderment, only half convinced, as if unable to decide what sort of creature the bark is coming from. And of course there is much more to the appreciation of painting than the representation of objects: appreciation of line and color, masses and planes, a prevailing mood of somberness or gaiety—these and many other things we appreciate in paintings are lost on animals, not because they can't see (though most mammals are nearly color-blind to many of the colors we see), but because they cannot integrate their visual perceptions in the required way.

All arts, then, require the activity of a mind in response to the data of the senses; and all arts require some sensory input. But in visual arts and music, this sensory input (sights, sounds) *itself* constitutes the things we appreciate and enjoy, whereas in literature the sensory input, the sound of the words or the sight of them on the page, is only a *vehicle* for the apprehension of meanings, and only after these meanings have been understood can we appreciate the poem, not as a succession of sounds but as a poem, a highly organized and emotionally charged succession of words. In visual arts and music the sight and sound directly generate our response; in literature the sight or sound of the words is rarely considered beautiful itself: the response occurs only when the words are understood and (in their interrelations) appreciated.

The words in a poem are rather like the notes (not the tones) of a musical score: we have to interpret the notes in order to produce the required tones, and it is the tones and tonal combinations that are appreciated; in literature we have to interpret the written marks before us as vehicles of meanings, and only then can the poem be appreciated. In the visual arts, there is (or can be) an "object of beauty" before us, in music, not an object but a succession of beautiful sounds; but in literature there is on the page no succession of beautiful marks—there is no "object of beauty" out there at all. When we find a poem beautiful, we are moved by (a) the succession of words, not just their sounds and their rhythms, but the complex juxtaposition of their meanings, and (b) the world of the poem created in our minds as a result of the apprehension of these meanings.

> Ah, love, let us be true
> To one another! for the world, which seems
> To lie before us like a land of dreams,
> So various, so beautiful, so new,
> Hath really neither joy, nor love, nor light,
> Nor certitude, nor peace, nor help for pain;
> And we are here as on a darkling plain
> Swept with confused alarms of struggle and flight,
> Where ignorant armies clash by night.

> (Matthew Arnold, from "Dover Beach," 1867)

4. *Mixed arts.* Finally, there are arts that combine two or more of the first three. The arts of performance are usually mixed arts. Drama as read is a form of literature, but drama as performed is partly literature (the text) and partly the sights and sounds of the characters on stage, the sets, the lighting, and so on. Ballet and dance are primarily visual spectacles (you go to *see* a ballet) but the musical accompaniment is also important. Opera combines music, words, and the visual aspects of staging and performance, though in opera the music almost always predominates: the plot can be silly and even the words can be rather insipid or prosy, but most operagoers don't mind much as long as the music is strong. Movies also combine all three, as a rule: they are shown on the screen, and have to be seen; there are spoken words and musical background, which are auditory; and since what is spoken is not mere noises but words, there is also a literary aspect to film (the script). Having a good script is usually the most important single ingredient in a film; without it, not all the labors of actors and directors can come to much; however, there are some films that are memorable as much for their visual effects as for their

story line; in *The Informer,* for example, as the various shapes emerge from the night fog and back into it again, almost every frame of the film can be viewed as if it were a painting.

Another way of classifying the arts would be by dividing them into (a) arts that are performed and (b) arts that are not. Music, drama, ballet, and dance are all arts of performance. Most people don't read the musical score; they hear the music performed by vocalists and instrumentalists. Sometimes we just read the play, but usually in doing so we imagine it as being performed; even when we don't, drama is still an art of performance, and we miss a dimension of it by reading it instead of seeing a performance. (Shakespeare is handled in one way by the English department, in another way by the drama department, because the drama department is primarily interested in performance and the English department is primarily interested in the lines to be performed.) Film, too, is a performing art, but, unlike drama, one doesn't perform it in front of an audience, one performs in front of a camera, and what the audience sees is projections on the screen of performances that have already taken place when the work is viewed by the audience.

In all performing arts, we distinguish between the *primary* artist, or originating artist, and the *secondary* artist, or executing artist. Beethoven, the primary artist, wrote the piano concerto, and Horowitz, the secondary artist, performs it. Both contribute something to the final outcome, and different performers will place their own individual stamp on the work. The character of Hamlet was created by Shakespeare, the primary artist, but performed in various ways by secondary artists such as John Gielgud, Laurence Olivier, Michael Redgrave, and Nicol Williamson. Although the contribution of the primary artist is doubtless more important, since without it there would be nothing to perform, the performance is also essential to the final effect.

In painting and sculpture, and in architecture, the artist himself physically constructs the object which is the work of art. In architecture, the one who designed it may not be the same person as the one(s) who built or constructed it, but the point is that what we, the observers, see is the final product of their efforts; it is the work of art itself. But in music, drama, ballet, opera, and so on, the audience does not see or hear directly what the creative artist did: the audience doesn't usually look at the musical score of the opera—only a few music students sitting in the opera house with pen-type flashlights do that. We experience the music *through* the activity of the performers. What the creator (primary artist) did in these arts is to provide a kind of *recipe* for the performance of the work of art, much like the chef who creates the recipe for a soup but doesn't himself prepare the soup: if the soup is being prepared simultaneously in a thousand restaurants, this would be impossible. In the same way, the musical composer could not possibly supervise all the performances of his compositions.

Where in all this does literature fit in? Is literature a performing art? Sometimes a poem is read aloud to an audience, and one might call this a performance of the poem by the reader. But most of the time one reads poems, and certainly novels, silently to oneself, and it surely seems that only the reader and the novelist are involved, just as when you look at a painting, only you and the painter (no performer) are involved. Still, they are different: when you look at the painting you are looking directly at the work of art itself (what would it mean to perform a painting?); but when you look at the page of the novel, it would appear that you are not: as we have just seen, the ink marks on the printed page aren't the work of literature; not even the sum of the ink marks on all the pages of the ten thousand copies of the novel are "the novel." We seem to have on the page of the novel something more like the written score of a symphony: the one is a recipe for the novel, the other is a recipe for performing the music.

A recipe for the novel—doesn't that mean a recipe for *performing* the novel? When you read the novel silently, aren't you performing the novel *to yourself* just as the trained conductor can look at a musical score for the first time and decide instantly whether the symphony is worth performing, because he is performing it to himself, hearing the notes performed "in his mind" even if not with his physical ear?

Perhaps, but the phrase "performing it to oneself" is not quite accurate. People who specialize in reading musical scores often hear no sounds, they don't even hum to themselves; they read slower parts faster than the music might go, and nobody could read a fast and complicated piece at a speed that equals that of the music. Instead of saying that the musician performs the music to himself (there are too many dissimilarities with actual performance for this), it seems preferable to say that he is simply *score reading*.

Perhaps reading literature, too, then, is like reading a score, only in this case the score consists of words instead of notes. The difference could then be described by saying that in music it is usual to physically perform the work, whereas in literature one customarily doesn't.

> Literature has the logical character [of] a performing art, but one in which in practice we frequently, though far from invariably, confine ourselves to score reading. We read to find out how the performance will go and are then content.[9]

Are we always doing this when we read anything—not a work of literature, say, but a textbook? Is that score reading too? It could be so called, but with an important difference. Although we usually read a poem silently, we do evaluate it partly by how it *would* sound if it *were* spoken. We would not criticize a textbook because when read aloud the sounds would not be pleasant of alliterative or enjoyable to hear rolling off one's tongue, but we do take

---

[9] J. O. Urmson, "Literature," in *Aesthetics,* eds. George Dickie and Richard Sclafani (New York: St. Martin's Press, 1978), p. 339.

these things into consideration in the case of poetry. Thus, reading poetry is somewhat *like* reading a score, and we evaluate what we see on the printed page partly by how it *would* sound if it were performed, even though we do not customarily go ahead and do the performing.

Is film an art of performance? Yes, actors perform—on a sound stage (or on location) rather than on the stage of a theater. If you sit through a movie twice, have you seen two performances of the film? That depends on what you take the word "performance" to mean. You have certainly sat through two *showings* (or screenings) of the film; but when we speak of a performance we usually have in mind a *live* performance, and of this there was only one (though there may have been many rehearsals), and it occurred at the time that the actors played their parts in front of the camera in the final shooting of the film, the one that became incorporated in the completed film.

## The Problem of Translation

Literature, and all the mixed arts that include literature as a component (drama, opera, film), face one problem that the other arts do not: the problem of translation. The medium of literature is words; words are symbols for things, actions, processes, relations, and so on in the world; a language is a system of such symbols; and different groups of people throughout the world use different systems of symbols. So when a person who knows only French wants to read a poem in English, he has a problem. This problem does not exist in the other arts: you don't have to learn a new language in order to appreciate French painting or German music.

One solution to the problem would be, every time you want to read something in a foreign language, to learn that language. Many people have learned Homeric Greek in order to read Homer in the original, and Attic Greek to read Greek drama, and Italian to read Dante. Often they report that it was well worth the trouble. Still, learning a new language every time is a laborious and time-consuming procedure, and one can't do it indefinitely without using up a large slice of one's life. And so the second solution is to read translations of these works into a language with which you are familiar.

One also pays a high price for adopting the second solution, because so much is lost in translation. People may read a translation and "think they are getting the same thing" that the poet wrote, but they are almost always missing more than they know, often so much that the translation is hardly worth reading. "Why don't they make better translations then?" The problem is not usually that there are no good translations—some are probably as good as can ever be made; the problem lies in the very nature of the enterprise of translation. Let us consider some of the main difficulties involved in translating literature into another language.

1. *Words considered apart from their meanings.* (a) *Word sounds.* Although the sounds of words are auxiliary to their meanings, word sounds can be important, particularly in poetry. When a word is translated into another language, the word sound in the language into which it is translated is usually very different from the original. "Dog," "chien," "Hund," and "canus" all refer to dogs, but the sounds are very different, and their effects in a line of poetry would be quite different. When Homer describes a battle in the *Iliad,* the words are highly cacophonous, matching the cacophany of battle (that is, words are used onomatopoetically); when the same scene is translated into English there is virtually no cacophany at all, and so at least one poetic effect is lost. If the sea could speak, it would probably prefer to be called *thalassa,* as Homer did, rather than by the insipid-sounding noise 'sea'."

(b) *Word rhythms.* Words in certain combinations can create a regular (or irregular) rhythm which can be an important element in the poetic effect. In Byron's poem *The Destruction of Sennacherib,*

> The Assyrian came down like a wolf from the fold,
> And his cohorts were gleaming in purple and gold,
> And the sheen from their spears was like stars on the sea,
> As the blue wave rolled nightly down deep Galilee . . .

the visual description can be translated into another language (if it has the right words) but the regular mesmerizing rhythm cannot: if you want to preserve the rhythm in another language, you have to do violence to the words. A word of two or three syllables in English may translate into a one-syllable word in French or a six-syllable word in German; and even if this were to occur only once in a stanza it would utterly destroy the rhythm. A poem is a delicate structure, easily toppled by one extra syllable, one cacophanous sound in a mellifluous context, one pause in the rhythm where it should be continuous; and this sort of thing is likely to happen not once but many times in the translation of even one stanza. Much more is thereby lost than when we try to perceive the exotic coloration of a tropical garden in a faded black-and-white print. Shakespeare translates comparatively well into German, which like English tends to be sibilant and expansive, but not at all well into French, which is short, precise, clipped, with every word standing as naked as every tone on the piano in a Mozart piano concerto.

(c) *Word rhymes.* When the poem in the original language has rhyming lines, and the translator tries to make it rhyme in translation also, the result is usually disaster. (Look at some of the rhymed translations of Dante's *terza rima* stanzas.) The metaphors are lost, the meaning is utterly distorted, and every effort goes toward producing a rhyme at any cost. Byron's couplet in *Don Juan*

> 'Tis strange the mind, that very fiery particle,
> Should let itself be snuff'd out by an article.

may not be sublime poetry, but what charm it has comes from the interesting rhyme at the end of the lines. What other word could be found to rhyme with "particle" but "article"? And into what possible language would any translation of "particle" and "article" yield a rhyme?

2. *The meanings of the words.* These might seem to be the easiest of all to translate. You see *chat* in French, you translate into the English "cat," and nothing is lost, at least as far as the meaning of the word is concerned. The trouble is, however, that when we turn from ordinary nouns like "cat," which denote a rather definite range of physical objects that can be pointed to, to abstract nouns, as well as to many verbs, adverbs, prepositions, and conjunctions, there are no longer such equivalencies. French and Greek prepositions are much more elastic in their meanings than are most English ones, and when we confront a Greek preposition like *epi* it is often not clear whether we should translate it as "on," "beside," "near," "around," or something else. Or the meaning in the original may be quite narrow and precise, more so than that of any word in the language into which we are doing the translating; so we give the nearest approximation, which may not be near at all, and greatly distort or flatten out the original meaning, though it's the best we have at our disposal in the language. Sometimes when this happens we simply prefer to leave the word untranslated, as we often do with the German word *Weltanschauung,* which has no English equivalent. But in poetry it would be a disaster to do this. Many musical words have been imported into English from Italian, and culinary words from French, so that for all practical purposes *cuisine* has become an English word.

The problem is much greater when we translate into English from ancient languages than from modern Indo-European languages. Not many abstract terms in ancient Greek have the same meaning as their usual English translations; the translated term is so far off the mark, and hence so misleading, that the student must learn the Greek words themselves because no English translation will do: consider such Greek words as *arete, kalon, mimesis, mithexis, hamartia, episteme, doxa, techne,* and countless others. Schopenhauer wrote in his essay "On the Study of Latin" that one of the great values of learning Latin—and the same applies to classical Greek—is that the mind is forced into new ways of conceiving and thinking; the conceptual net is different, and we are forced to rethink our concepts. To a much greater extent, then, than most people suspect, the meaning of a word or phrase in language A does not carry over into language B, thus making accurate translation impossible.

3. *The connotations of the words* (or the "overtones of meaning," sometimes called the "secondary meanings," of the words). The English word "sea" names any large body of water. If the word, especially in the context of a poem, triggers reactions when you hear or read it, it is not because of the uninspiring sound of the word, or because it means a large body of water, but because of what the word suggests to your mind: the calm sea, the stormy sea,

the moonlit sea, the Arctic sea, the tropical sea, and so on—these associations
are what capture the imagination and make "sea" an effective word in poetry.

> The sea is calm tonight.
> The tide is full, the moon lies fair
> Upon the straits;—on the French coast the light
> Gleams and is gone; the cliffs of England stand,
> Glimmering and vast, out in the tranquil bay.
> Come to the window, sweet is the night-air!
> Only, from the long line of spray
> Where the sea meets the moon-blanched land,
> Listen! you hear the grating roar
> Of pebbles which the waves draw back, and fling,
> At their return, up the high strand,
> Begin, and cease, and then again begin,
> With tremulous cadence slow, and bring
> The eternal note of sadness in . . .

(Matthew Arnold, "Dover Beach," first stanza.)

Try to capture the subtlety of that—the word sounds, the irregular pulsing
rhythm, the quick stops followed by the stately consonant-rich lines, and most
of all the complex interrelations of suggested meanings of word after
word—in any translation, and you have some idea of the magnitude of the
problem of translation.

At least the connotations of the word "sea" and its translated equivalents
are comparatively uniform from one language to another; the sea captures the
imagination everywhere. But this is not always so. Often, for example, the
emotional impact of a phrase will be very great in one language and almost
nonexistent in another although they are literal equivalents. Try translating
the French expression *mon dieu* into the English "my God." "My God" is, or
was until recently, considered profanity, but the French expression is so
commonplace and unemotional that even the most devout use it without ac-
cusations of profanity. While the literal sense of the phrase is preserved in
translation, its emotional impact is changed. Or consider a novel in which one
woman calls another one a cat. In English (and some other languages) this has
very definite connotations: the one is calling the other untrustworthy, two-
faced, cold, calculating. But in a language in which only the primary meaning
(domesticated quadruped) carries over and all this secondary meaning is lost,
the whole point of the imprecation too is lost. Think of the connotations of
the animal names which we sometimes apply to people: snake, mouse, insect,
wolf, fox, lion, tiger, walrus, weasel. Some of these secondary meanings are
shared in other languages, some partially, some not at all. One wonders in
how many languages the old definition of an assistant dean, "a mouse training to be a rat," would retain its barb.

All these factors tend to work against one another, with the result that if
you are translating a work from one language to another, you have to make
some painful choices. If you want an accurate translation as far as meanings

go, you'll have to forget about the sounds of the words, their rhymes, their rhythmic flow in translation, and their various connotations. If you want to capture as much as possible of the word connotations, you will often have to forget about the more literal (primary) meanings and the sound values as well. If you want to capture the rhythm of the original, you may have to neglect everything else.

And if you want to recreate the sound of the original, you'd better forget about the whole enterprise. When Alexander Pope translated Homer's *Iliad,* it came out in neatly and elegantly rhymed couplets. But then "Pope's Homer is not Homer, but Pope." When the Lang, Leaf, and Myers translation appeared late in the nineteenth century, it was justly praised as the most nearly accurate rendition that could be given; nevertheless, to us it sounds stilted, whereas the original was much more easy-going and conversational. To correct this defect, translations into the English vernacular started to appear, which did capture this aspect (often at the expense of the text), but as English slang expressions changed, the vernacular translations themselves soon became dated. Unfortunately there is no solution to this problem, since there is no way in which a translation can duplicate the original even on one front, much less on all fronts at once.

Perhaps the best translations of works of literature are those that attempt to hold intact the connotations of the original words, in all their complex interrelations. At least these may succeed in capturing the imaginative sweep and feeling-tone of the original, even though in nonequivalent words. For that reason the best translation of the *Odyssey* may be that of T. E. Lawrence, for, though it takes liberties time and again with word meanings, it does capture that sweep, and the elegant, measured, yet unstilted lines in English seem, as far as this is possible, to match the pulse, rhythm, stateliness, and imaginative quality of the Homeric saga in Greek. The good translator of poetry must himself be something of a poet, creating in the language of the translation something that is a poem in its own right rather than simply a translation of something else. Louis Untermeyer's translations of the lyric poems of Heinrich Heine are excellent for this reason. The emotional quality captured in the translations seem invariably to be the same one that pervades the original poem; yet a student of second-year German, asked to translate Heine's lines into English with the greatest possible accuracy, would probably get an "F" if he came up with Untermeyer's translation.


The Arts and the "Lower" Senses

In the classification of the arts, nothing has been said about the so-called "lower" senses of smell, taste, and touch. Why have these not been included?

The data of these senses certainly does enter into our appreciation of nature, sometimes as much as the data of sight and sound.

If there is a beauty of August nights, or beauty in the rareness of a June day, or the fresh loveliness after rain, if there is ripe and languorous beauty in the mist and mellow fruitfulness of autumn, or a hard, cold beauty of glittering winter frosts, such beauty is not all for the eye and ear. . . . The saltiness of the breeze is as integral to the beauty of the sea as the flashing of the fish or the sweep of the gulls or the thunder of the surf or the boiling of the foam. . . . The beauty of flowers is enriched by fragrance, the beauty of Catholic ceremonials by the odor of incense.[10]

The "lower" senses also figure in our appreciation of the practical or useful arts. In cookery, the taste of the meal is of fundamental importance, and the visual appearance of the dinner on the table is auxiliary. The smell is also important—in fact much of what we take to be the taste is really smell: if your nose is clogged with a cold, you can tell the difference between onions and potatoes by their appearance and felt texture (touch) but not by their taste. But in the fine arts the "lower" senses seem to play a very small part. They do play a little: we have already observed that it would be better to be able to touch the marble statue than only to see it, though a person born blind who could *only* touch it would miss most of what we find beautiful in it. And, as Prall says, "organ tones depend without question, for even their strictly aesthetic effect, at least in part on the feelings not due to hearing and ears, but stirred by quite other bodily processes." But in the appreciation of fine art their role seems to be minor; and there are no fine arts of *just* smell or taste or touch, the way painting is visual and music auditory. Why is this? Is it just prejudice or snobbery on our part? or is there a reason why no arts of smell, taste, or touch have emerged?

One suggested reason is that human beings are not as sensitive to smells and touches as they are to color and sound. Most animals live in a smell universe and identify each other more through smell than through vision; people are not sensitive to any but a small fraction of the smells that most animals can detect. Human beings and birds, among all living creatures, seem to have the most strongly developed sense of sight. But birds have no visual arts; and most animals are more sensitive to sound than most people are, yet they do not appreciate music.

It has been suggested that the "lower" senses are "too close to our bodies," too intimately connected with organic needs. We can see and hear things a long way off, but we can't taste anything unless it is actually touching the palate—though we can sometimes smell things quite a distance away. Yet the palate, says Prall, "is no more internal than the ear, and the taste of strawberries is no more a function of the human body than their color or their shape." It is true, however, that the "lower" senses are more intimately connected to organic needs: we usually eat when we are hungry; when we are very hungry the food smells and tastes wonderful, but the moment the edge is off our hunger we enjoy it less, and when we are satiated we can hardly bear to taste, smell, or even see the food any more. Nature has implanted our sense of

[10] D. W. Prall, *Aesthetic Judgment* (New York: Crowell, 1929), pp. 65, 67. Reprinted in John Hospers, ed., *Introductory Readings in Aesthetics* (New York: Free Press, 1969).

hunger in response to an organic need, and when the organic need has been satisfied our reactions to the taste and smell stimuli changes completely: desire is quickly replaced by revulsion. Also, we can both look at the same apple but we can't both eat the same apple; the act of consumption, which is necessary to appease our hunger, destroys the very object we are appreciating.

Although all this is true, it does not fully explain the comparative absence of the "lower" senses from the arts, especially the fine arts.

> It is not their intimate connection with our vital bodily processes and motions that makes tastes less characteristically aesthetic than sounds or colors or shapes. Part of the appreciation of form itself, as in jars or vases, is without question incipient motions or motor tendencies in our own bodies; and the beauty of the morning is in part the freshness of our vital functioning as well as of our perceptive faculties. . . . We usually consume what we taste but not what we see or hear . . . [but] we do not need to consume and absorb it in order to taste it, though, as with tobacco or incense, we sometimes appreciate its savor best by passing the smoke of its destruction intimately over the organs by which we apprehend it. Such distillations of beauty are common enough even with roses or lavender, with the resin of pines or the oil of bays. It is only accident, then, that bodily consumption is the means to the full aesthetic flavor of objects, and this without any relation, either, to biological needs or interests. Appetite is not hunger. . . . We could be nourished by our food perfectly well, though our senses were anesthetized. And in any case the perception of tastes or odors is never the devouring of them. We devour the *substance,* not the *quality.* And the smell of boiled cabbage, as of blooming roses, is a distinctly discriminated and easily remembered quality, eternally a quality to delight in or be offended by, were all the cabbages in the world consumed, all the roses dead forever.[11]

Perhaps, then, the difference lies in the fact that the data of the "lower" senses are extremely transitory and evanescent: the dinner smells good, and a few minutes later its attractiveness is gone. But the same consideration applies to other senses also: "Nothing," says Prall, "is more transitory than sound. And what is more transitory than beautiful expressions upon human faces, or than beautiful young human bodies themselves?" The smell of a particular rose is transitory, and so is the rose itself, which dies at the end of the season; but is our favorable response to the smell of roses in general (not one particular rose) any more transitory than our response to the sight of roses in general? Human beings everywhere and always seem to enjoy them both.

It is true, of course, that great works of art are *enduring* sources of enjoyment—one can return to them again and again—but perhaps no more than the smell and sight of roses, or the sight of the night sky besprinkled with stars. And even here there are limits: if you have a mountaintop home, at first the sight is inspiring, but after a while you become so accustomed to it that you hardly notice it, and it is only occasional visitors who will "ooh" and "ah" the view from your living room. Even great works of art are subject to "aesthetic fatigue": if you have already heard your favorite musical composi-

[11] *Ibid.,* pp. 51, 60–61.

tion thirty times today, you probably won't care to hear it again just now; if you've seen the same painting hanging above your fireplace for years, you may well want to vary the scene by hanging another in its place, even if only temporarily; much as you enjoy *Hamlet,* you won't want to see a performance of it every week.

The true reason for the difference, says Prall, lies elsewhere:

> Smells and odors do not in themselves *fall into any known or felt natural order or arrangement,* nor are their variations defined in and by such an intrinsic natural structure, as the variations in color and sound and shape give rise to in our minds. Hence our grasp of them, while it is aesthetic very clearly, since they may be felt as delightful, is the grasp in each case upon just the specific presented non-structural quality, which is as absolutely different, unique, simple, and unrelatable to further elements intrinsically through its own being, as anything could be. *One smell does not suggest another related smell close to it in some objective and necessary order of quality or occurrence or procedure, nor does one taste so follow another.*
>
> There are apparently more or less compatible and incompatible smells and tastes, but there is no clearly defined order of smells and tastes, or any structure of smells and tastes in which each has its place fixed by its own qualitative being.
>
> Tastes may be subtly blended, and so may odors. Cooks and perfumers are in their way refined and sensitive artists, as tea-tasters and wine-tasters are expert critical judges. But such art and such criticism have no intelligible, or at least so far discovered, *structural or critical principles,* simply because the elements they work with have neither intelligible structure nor apparently any discoverable order in variation.[12]

If you start with middle C on the piano, playing the white keys only one at a time, C D E F G A, numerous times in succession, you could soon drive your neighbors crazy. Why? Because in this succession of tones a felt tension is set up: once you have got to A, the series "demands" to be resolved by continuing to the C octave; only then can we relax again, after the "resolution" of the series. There is in music an extremely precise relation among tones, some of which are experienced as bland (C–G–C), some as consonant (C–E–G), and some as dissonant (C–D). We may not know the physics of these relationships, such as the number of vibrations per second of each tone, but we experience them so strongly that when the singer sings even a shade flat, the experience is painful in the extreme. It is not merely that there *exists* a precisely ordered series of tones, but that this order is *felt* by human beings, and without this felt order of tonal relationships the thousands of tonal combinations we find in music would not affect us as they now do.

To a certain extent there is a felt order in the "lower" senses too: there are relations which

> must be at least dimly discerned by any artist if he is to use the materials of beauty at all. But there is no such system of smells and tastes, and what relations

[12] *Ibid.,* pp. 62–63. Emphasis added.

and contrasts we do notice in such matters seem fairly arbitrary and accidental: apples with pork perhaps, and perhaps not sour wine with sweets; certain blendings of tea and of spices, certain combinations toned into each other with sugar, or toned in general with garlic; but no structure, or any very clear general principles.[13]

There may indeed be as definite a physical basis for our perceptions of smells, tastes, and touches as there is for sights and sounds (there probably is), but this makes no difference to us as experiencers as long as there is no *felt* ordering of the data of these senses. That is why there are no "smell symphonies" analogous to the "sound symphonies" we have. First there is one smell, then another, then another (or group of smells presented simultaneously), but there is no one that leads "naturally" or "inevitably" to another—no accumulation, no resolution, no climax. There is not much more than a before and after. Should the odor of the rose come before that of the lily, or after? Should the feel of velvet come before or after, or in combination with, the harsh feel of emory? Does the one "demand" the other, the way in which a profusion of warm colors demands a cool color for contrast or the way in which a dissonance demands resolution into an assonance?

Works of fine art, especially those that have endured through the ages, are all works of very great formal complexity. And through this complexity, an enormous variety of feeling-tones can be conveyed. As we shall see in coming chapters, great works of fine art can be expressive of an incalculable diversity of human moods and feelings, can transform our responses to the world around us and the world within us, and can reveal features of life and the world. It is questionable whether arts of smell, taste, or touch, if they existed, could do this. What they could do is give us novel kinds of sensory titillation, the kind of thing we get from some paintings which give us novel and titillating combinations of colors or forms which tease the eye and nothing more.

> Chefs, perfumers, and upholsterers, who produce the means of sensory pleasure for others, are not rated as the torchbearers of culture and inspired creators. . . . If music, patterned sound, had no other office than to stimulate and soothe our nerves, pleasing our ears as well-combined foods please our palates, it might be highly popular, but never culturally important. Its historic development would be too trivial a subject to engage many people in its lifelong study, though a few desperate Ph.D. theses might be wrung from its anecdotal past under the rubric of "social history." And music conservatories would be properly rated exactly like cooking schools.[14]

The fine arts are important in the emotional and intellectual enrichment of human life, and this is something of which smells, tastes, and touches by themselves do not seem to be capable.

[13] *Ibid.,* pp. 64–65.
[14] Susanne Langer, *Feeling and Form* (New York: Scribners, 1953), p. 54.

## 3. THE MEDIA OF ART

There is a tale about an ancient emperor who promised the court painter a handsome fee for painting a likeness of him, the emperor. The painter did so and was rewarded. The emperor then asked him to paint the emperor's favorite horse; again the painter succeeded brilliantly and was even more generously rewarded. Then the emperor demanded that he paint the sound of the emperor's trumpet; but try as he would, the painter could not, and he was beheaded.

It is, of course, impossible in a visual medium to depict sounds. If an artist attempts to do what is impossible, of course he cannot succeed. But sometimes an artist attempts to do in one medium what is better done in another, or something which in the medium he chooses is strained or awkward or overly limited. In this case one attempts to describe what each art, in its given medium, can do best. This attempt was made by the eighteenth-century aesthetician Gottfried Lessing in his book *Laokoön*. Lessing confined himself to the relation between visual art and literary art, and his message was that each was capable of different things and that neither should attempt to achieve the effects best achieved by the other. The statue of Laokoön, a Trojan priest killed with his two sons by sea serpents after warning the Trojans against the wooden horse, is the first of many examples he gives to illustrate his thesis.

In visual art, the entire work is present before us at every moment of time; since there is no temporal succession, there is no change—whatever knife-edge of time is selected for representation, that moment is frozen into eternity in the painting or statue. Accordingly, said Lessing, that one moment must be chosen with great care. No matter how long we look, Laokoön will not change his expression. Most moments will soon become boring or embarrassing or painful to look at, such as a picture of you snapped when you are speaking and your mouth is open. We would expect Laokoön, who is being strangled to death by serpents, to have his face distorted in pain, and an expression of unending pain on someone's face soon becomes hideous to look at. Lessing says that the unknown sculptor who did the *Laokoön* knew in this respect exactly what he was doing. He knew that a distorted grimace would soon become repellent to the viewer, and so the sculptor in carving Laokoön's face muted the expression of pain. A work of sculpture, Lessing believed, should be a thing of beauty, and even the depiction of pain should not blemish his achievement of creating beautiful faces and bodies. The sculptor of Laokoön did not allow his work to be blemished in this way.

But when the Latin poet Vergil describes the tale of Laokoön in *The Aeneid*, he does not work under these limitations.

> When Vergil's Laokoön screams, does it occur to anyone that a wide-open mouth is necessary in order to scream, and that this wide-open mouth makes the

face ugly? . . . He who demands a beautiful picture here has failed to understand the poet.

There is nothing to compel the poet to compress his picture into a single moment. He may, if he so chooses, take up each action at its origin and pursue it through all possible variations to its end. Each variation which would cost the sculptor a separate work costs the poet but a single pen stroke; and if the result of this pen stroke, viewed by itself, should offend the hearer's imagination, it was either anticipated by what has preceded or is so softened and compensated by what follows that it loses its individual impression and in combination achieves the best effect in the world.

While the sculptor was right in not permitting Laokoön to cry out, the poet has done equally well in having him do so.[15]

The poet can describe the characters and incidents in temporal succession, which the sculptor cannot do; moreover, in Vergil the scene is described, not shown, and this also makes a great difference. When a scene, however horrifying if we were to see it before our eyes, is described in poetry, its effect can be muted through the softening of our mental images of it or canceled out through the beauties of poetic language.

A work of visual art can show a person who is in motion, but it cannot depict the motion. A temporal art such as literature, however, can do so. ("Architecture is frozen music.") But literature, on its part, should not (said Lessing) attempt to duplicate the effects of visual art by describing the visual features of a scene in great detail: no amount of description can compete with the actual *showing* that painting and sculpture can provide. Literature is ideally equipped to describe *temporal succession* of scenes and actions, but when the author tries to describe in detail what an object or scene looks like, the action stops. Here, says Lessing, Vergil made a mistake: he described the shield of Achilles, for example, in great visual detail. Homer had done it better in the *Iliad:* he described the shield in the process of its construction, the selection of the materials, its being forged in the fire by Vulcan, and so on; and thus the thing that literature is best equipped to handle, temporal succession, is never lost in Homer.

Just as that which can be shown in visual art is not something that the poet should attempt to duplicate, so the poet should not describe a scene in such a way that the painter or sculptor could give a representation of it from the poet's description. Someone could paint the shield of Achilles in detail from Vergil's description of it; in this respect Milton did better—in *Paradise Lost* he captured in his description the mood and atmosphere of hell, but he did it poetically, not visually, and as a result a painter who tried to paint a picture of hell based on Milton's poem would find that he had very few clues to go by. According to Milton, hell is pervaded by "not light, but rather darkness visible." How would a painter paint that? Poetically this is a powerful and pregnant image; but visually it gives nothing that anyone could paint. And this,

[15] Gottfried Lessing, *Laokoön* (Indianapolis: Bobbs-Merrill, 1962), pp. 23–24.

says Lessing, is exactly as it should be: each art is best equipped to do one kind of job, and when one art-form tries to achieve the effects best achievable by another, the result is at best awkwardness and at worst disaster.

Lessing subtitled his book "An Essay in the Romantic Confusion of the Arts." Living at the inception of the Romantic era, he thought that Romantic poets were attempting to ape the effects of painting by describing nature in great visual detail. If Lessing were alive today, he would be many times more shocked than he was by Romantic poetry. He would probably insist that movies, being a temporal art with no restrictions on change or type of location (unlike the stage), should *move* and that, where there is no action, there should be no movie. He would probably say that music is a temporal art which is nonrepresentational and, hence, that program music, which attempts to represent scenes and objects, and often static ones at that, is a total mistake—that representation should be left to representational arts.

That different arts do different kinds of jobs is hardly disputable. In view of this fact, a scene or story which is the subject of one art-form often needs to be changed considerably in order to be adapted to the requirements of another art-form. Consider Thomas Mann's famous story *Death in Venice* and the motion picture made by Visconti from that story. Each does something quite different. The story can only describe what Aschenbach looked like and spoke like, and how Venice looked and smelled in the midst of the plague. We are left, following the cues in Mann's words, to construct the scenes in our imagination. But the film can *show* us—there it is before our eyes; we don't have to imagine it. Is this to the advantage of the film? Does it justify people in saying "I don't think I'll read the book, I'll wait to see the movie"? Hardly, for (1) many people would prefer to imagine the scenes and persons in their minds rather than having it "thrown into their faces" by visual confrontation. And there are other things the story can do that the film cannot: (2) The story can go into the minds of the main characters and tell us what they thought and felt; the film cannot do this, but can only show us the visual appearances of the characters' faces and gestures and their words, and leave it to us to infer what their inner feelings are. The storywriter thus has "inner access" to his characters which no visual artist has. Also (3) the author can give us his reflections on the person or scene being described, in his own right, not merely through the speech of his characters. (Fielding does this constantly in *Tom Jones,* and this very important part of the novel, one of its most charming features, could not be included when the book was made into a film.) Even if the author does not give us his reflections on the scene or person, he can "slant" the depiction through his choice of words in characterization. (This could also be done in a film *if* there was an unseen voice on the soundtrack narrating and commenting; but many believe that this device is uncinematic—that the film's task is to *show* and that the characters may comment but not the author.) (4) The literary artist can also create effects impossible to visual art through his choice of words, the rhythm and cadence of his language, and his use of metaphor and other literary devices, none of which are available to the visual artist.

Although drama and film are more alike than most arts, there is a considerable mediumistic difference between them. For example, in the play you are in the living presence of the actors and can to some extent react with them and get a response, whereas in a film, which is "canned," this is impossible. In a play on stage there are severe limitations to what kind of actions and scenes can occur, such as crossing the ocean by boat or plane, whereas in a film there is no problem with such things. (When a film sticks to one set, it's a fairly sure bet that it was taken from a stage play and filmed without much alteration.) In transferring a story from one medium to another, it is doubtless wise advice to make such changes as are required to adapt it well to the new medium: Olivier's *Henry V* was changed considerably in adapting it to film, and the film was better for it. It is probably also wise *not* to adapt at all when the transfer cannot be made effectively: for example, "The Royal Game" is so "internal" a story that it would probably make a bad movie (the real action goes on inside people's minds), just as Henry James novels are ill suited for cinematic treatment. Good novels and plays don't necessarily make good movies; and conversely, a thoroughly indifferent and inconsequential novel or story can be made into an excellent movie if the writer and director have enough imagination to adapt the literary work to the cinematic medium: they can add to the drama a kind of immediacy, say, in the confrontation between characters, that does not occur in literary art, in which the characters and setting have to be "made alive" through our imagination on the basis of the text; in the film the order of events may have to be changed, incidents added that come off well in visualization, static scenes deleted, and the entire sequence of events kept flowing in constant shifting motion.

Thus fidelity to the novel may be a mistake in cinema: one would have thought that Fielding's novel *Tom Jones* could never have been made into a satisfactory film because so much of the novel's effect arises from the many little essays "to the gentle reader" interspersed through the narrative as well as the delights of literary style. And indeed this literary aspect cannot survive in the film; but the film adopts quite different devices, unique to the medium of cinema, to achieve much the same effect. Instead of a tongue-in-cheek essay on how the author would prefer to refrain (out of concern for the reader's modesty) from relating the next sexual escapade of our hero, but is nevertheless required to relate it all the same out of concern for the truth, in the film, Tom Jones, while starting to undress, throws his hat over the lens of the camera so that the film audience will be spared the sight of another such escapade.

Both drama and film have actors, set designers, directors, and producers, and it might have been expected, during the early development of film around the turn of the century, that the new art of cinema would derive its materials primarily from the stage. Yet the two are entirely different media. No better illustration of Lessing's principle could be found than the difference between drama and another art-form Lessing could never have foreseen, the cinema. As the critic Erwin Panofsky puts it in his classic essay "Style and Medium in the Motion Pictures," drama is essentially literature enacted, while the central feature of cinema is not words but *motion*. Even when the camera focuses on an unmoving object such as the Rock of Gibraltar, the camera moves, and the spectator watches as if through the lens of the camera.

> In a theater, space is static, that is, the space represented on the stage, as well as the spatial relation of the beholder to the spectacle, are unalterably fixed. The spectator cannot leave his seat, and the setting of the stage cannot change. . . . But, in return for this restriction, the theater has the advantage that time, the medium of emotion and thought conveyable by speech, is free and independent of anything that may happen in visible space. Hamlet may deliver his famous monologue lying on a couch in the middle distance, doing nothing and only dimly discernible to the spectator and listener, and yet by his mere words enthrall him with a feeling of intensest emotional action.
>
> With the movies the situation is reversed. Here, too, the spectator occupies a fixed seat, but only physically, not as the subject of an aesthetic experience. Aesthetically, he is in permanent motion as his eye identifies itself with the lens of the camera which permanently shifts in distance and direction. And as movable as the spectator is, as movable is, for the same reason, the space presented to him. Not only do bodies move in space, but space itself does, approaching, receding, turning, dissolving and recrystallizing as it appears through the controlled locomotion and focusing of the camera and through the cutting and editing of the various shots—not to mention such special effects as visions, transformations, disappearances, slow-motion and fast-motion shots, reversals and trick films. This opens up a world of possibilities of which the stage can never dream.[16]

Even the invention of the sound track does not change the fact that a moving picture, even when talking, remains a picture that moves, and not a piece of writing that is enacted. "It remains a series of visual sequences held together by an uninterrupted flow of movement in space."

Many consequences flow from this difference in medium. One is that

> good movie scripts are unlikely to make good reading and have seldom been published in book form; whereas, conversely, good stage plays have to be severely altered, cut, and, on the other hand, enriched by interpolations to make good movie scripts. In Shaw's *Pygmalion,* for instance, the actual process of Eliza's phonetic education and, still more important, her final triumph at the grand party, are wisely omitted; we see—or, rather, hear—some samples of her gradual linguistic improvement and finally encounter her, upon her return from the reception, victorious and splendidly arrayed but deeply hurt for want of recognition and sympathy. In the film adaptation, precisely these two scenes are not only supplied but also strongly emphasized; we witness the fascinating activities in the laboratory with its array of spinning disks and mirrors, organ pipes

[16] Erwin Panofsky, "Style and Medium in the Motion Pictures," in *Aesthetics,* eds. Dickie and Sclafani, p. 354.

and dancing flames, and we participate in the ambassadorial party, with many moments of impending catastrophe and little counter-intrigue thrown in for suspense. Unquestionably these two scenes, entirely absent from the play, and indeed unachievable upon the stage, were the highlights of the film; whereas the Shavian dialogue, however severely cut, turned out to fall a little flat in certain moments. And wherever, as in so many other films, a poetic emotion, a musical outburst, or a literary conceit (even, I am grieved to say, some of the wisecracks of Groucho Marx) entirely lose contact with visible movement, they strike the sensitive spectators as, literally, out of place.[17]

What, then, are we to say about Lessing's principle of the irreducible distinctness of the various arts? That one medium can do what another medium cannot do at all is clear enough; that one can do what another can do but not as well is also plain. Still, there may sometimes be reasons why it should be done anyway, and there seems little point in making an unalterable dogma out of Lessing's principle and letting it stand in the way of a possibly worthwhile goal. Not everyone who wanted to was able to see the stage play *Long Day's Journey into Night* by Eugene O'Neill, and so it was made into a film so that the performances could be immortalized on celluloid. No attempt was made to change anything in the play for cinematic purposes; it was simply a stage play recorded on film. It is true that the resulting product was static and unsuited to the medium of film, but as long as members of the audience got from it what they wanted, performances which they were unable to see live, the transcription had achieved its purpose and no one was the loser. One's objection would not be to this kind of enterprise but, rather, to another kind, in which a film is made from a stage play and the action seldom moves from the set, whereas a few imaginative touches might have successfully adapted the play to the very different medium of film. *The Petrified Forest* and *Watch on the Rhine* are two of many examples. On the other hand, there are films which are limited to one set which *are* suited to the medium of film, for the camera constantly moves from one expressive face to another, letting us see the emotions registered on the faces in close-ups such as we could never obtain on the stage. Two outstanding examples of this are Sidney Lumet's *Twelve Angry Men,* which takes place entirely in a jury room, and Carl Dreyer's *The Passion of Joan of Arc,* which is a study in the faces of Joan of Arc and her jury of interlocutors.

## 4. THE EXISTENCE AND IDENTITY OF WORKS OF ART

1. *The existence of works of art.* Under what conditions can it be said that a work of art exists? When does it cease to exist? Is a work of art always, or ever, a physical object? How much change can it endure while still remaining the same work of art?

[17] *Ibid.,* p. 356.

Let us begin with the simplest case, works of visual art—painting, sculpture, architecture. Here is El Greco's painting, *The View of Toledo,* on the wall of the Metropolitan Museum of Art in New York. The painting has a definite span of existence in time: it came to exist when El Greco finished painting it, and it will cease to exist only when it is destroyed. There are many copies of this painting all over the world, but only one original; copies can be had quite cheaply, but the original commands a very high price. If the painting were burned, El Greco's painting *The View of Toledo* would no longer exist, though copies of it would still exist, so we would still have some idea of what the original looked like—but not a completely adequate idea, since no copy ever made has yet totally duplicated the original.

The same considerations apply to the other visual arts. If someone melted down Brancusi's *Bird in Flight,* that work of sculpture would no longer exist, though the metal from which it was made would still exist. If the cathedral at Chartres were to be bombed, there would be no more Chartres cathedral but a pile of rubble; only photographs would give us some idea (a very incomplete one) of the original.

Now let us turn to music. We speak of Beethoven's Ninth Symphony as if it were an object like the painting or sculpture. And of course there was, and still is, the original manuscript of the symphony written in Beethoven's own hand, with all his corrections on it. But we do not value the original manuscript, or consider it "the original" of the symphony, in the same way we do the painting. Why is the case of music different? After all, the original Beethoven manuscript too would command a high price and would be valued by historians and Beethoven scholars. But it would not be valued in the same way: the Beethoven manuscript is not itself the object of beauty, although the original El Greco painting is. We would get no experience of beauty from looking at the Beethoven manuscript, only perhaps a feeling of reverential awe because we were touching the same pieces of paper that Beethoven himself once touched. We are moved not by *seeing* the (not very pretty) manuscript but by *hearing* the Beethoven played in accordance with the set of instructions provided by the manuscript.

But that is all the manuscript is, a set of instructions. For the purpose of playing the symphony correctly, any copy that is readable will do as well (or better, since printed copies are more easily readable that is Beethoven's manuscript). The manuscript contains the *notes,* but music is something *heard,* and thus is not notes but *tones;* and any set of notes that will enable an orchestra to produce those tones will suffice. Moreover, different orchestras, with different conductors, will take that same set of notes and interpret it differently: some orchestras will take forty-five minutes to complete the performance of the *Eroica,* and others will take fifty minutes. The secondary artists (conductor, soloists, orchestra) determine how the performance will sound, within the limits prescribed by the notes in the score.

The painting exists continuously: it is there all the time, although it is not being viewed all the time. Does the music exist continuously? The score does, but the score is not the music, only a set of instructions for producing the music. When then can we say the music exists? Only when it is being performed? That is the only time that the sound waves actually exist—though of course we can also hear the sounds, with some distortion, in a *recorded* performance. But even so, the sounds of actual or recorded performances are not being heard all the time; and so, it would seem, the music exists *discontinuously*—it doesn't exist during the times when there is no performance. In fact there are some works of music that have been composed and have never been performed at all; must we say then that such compositions have never existed?

Such a conclusion seems very strange. If someone asked whether a certain obscure work of music by Dufay was still in existence, and we said to him, "No," meaning that it was not being performed at the moment, he might well reply, "You mean the score (or all copies of the score) have been lost?" Only if this were so would he admit that the composition in question no longer exists. When, in daily discourse, we ask whether a composition still exists, we do not mean thereby to ask whether it is being performed at that moment (whether the sound waves of it exist at that moment); we mean to ask whether all copies have been lost.

This, however, is strange too: the music is not the notes but the tones; the tones exist only when they are being emitted by the musical instruments (the tones exist discontinuously); and yet, we say, the music exists all the time, as long as all copies of the score are not destroyed or lost. How do we solve this puzzle?

To solve it, we must recognize that, when we ask whether this musical composition still exists, we are not asking whether the tones are at that moment being emitted somewhere, in spite of the fact that music is tones and not notes. Rather, we are asking whether the *conditions for reproducing the tones* still exist, so that the tones *can* still be played even though they are not at the moment being played. We are asking not whether the series of tones (and rests) that constitutes the composition is being played, but whether the series of tones is *reproducible*. And the usual condition for their reproducibility is the score; with the score we can play the symphony again, so "it still exists." In fact, even if all copies of the score were destroyed, and someone, such as the composer himself if he is still alive, remembers the entire score note for note, then he could write it down again and the composition would not be lost after all, for the tonal series would still be reproducible.

Thus, even if the original Beethoven manuscript were destroyed, we would not consign his symphony to the same fate as long as there were other copies of the score, or if by some other means the score could be reconstructed. But if the El Greco painting were destroyed, we would say that this work of art had been destroyed, since the original painting is, unlike the musical score, the object of our enjoyment. (What would we say if there existed copies of the painting which were indistinguishable from the original? We would still say that the painting had been destroyed, but could then add, "But don't worry—we have copies that are just as good.")

What about scores of ancient Greek or Egyptian musical compositions which we have but can't read? With these we are in the same position as we were with Egyptian hieroglyphics before the discovery of the Rosetta stone. Does that music exist today? "Well, yes," we might say, "in a way: the score does, but thus far nobody can read it so as to produce the music."

Now what of literature? The original manuscript of "The Royal Game" exists, along with the rest of Zweig's posthumously collected papers. But even if this manuscript had been lost or destroyed, we would not hesitate to say that the work is not lost, for there are thousands of printed copies of it in existence. And as long as we can read it, one copy is as good as another. Like the musical score, the manuscript itself is not the object of aesthetic interest: aesthetic interest occurs only if we can read the manuscript (or printed copy) and thus experience the story as it unfolds. All manuscript copies of Shakespeare's plays have been lost, but we do not on that account say that Shakespeare's plays have been lost. In some cases, like the Homeric poems, many centuries elapsed before there were any written copies (there was no written language in Homer's time), but the Homeric sagas were memorized word for word and repeated from generation to generation, thus preserving these poems for each new generation—probably with numerous changes along the way. Literature then, though unlike music in not being an art of performance (unless you want to say that you perform it to yourself every time you read it), is like music as far as the status of the original manuscript is concerned. The poem, like the musical composition, still exists as long as it is, by some means or other, reproducible word for word.

What of the dance? Dance, like music, is an art of performance. It is only while it is being performed that we can appreciate and enjoy the dance; between performances we can only remember it, unless we have a videotape of it. If dance had a precise score like music, then the case of the dance would be just like that of music. Scores for dances have recently been worked out, so that a person who had never seen a certain dance performed could discover from the dance score which steps and movements each dancer would perform at every moment of the performance. But of course the series of steps and movements is not all there is to the dance: the score cannot tell us with what precise gestures, for example, each movement was made. To some extent this is true of music too: before the invention of the metronome the composer could not tell us exactly how fast or slow he wished the music to be performed, and the score cannot tell us even today with exactly what dynamics (loud or soft) the score is to be performed, and no score can tell us with exactly what nuances of touch the instrument is to be played: Horowitz, Schnabel, and Serkin can all follow the score to the letter and yet the same composition sounds different when played by each of them. This feature is much more widespread in performances of a dance, because there is no way of scoring the dance (at least not yet developed) which is anywhere nearly as precise as musical scores can be. Thus, we can say that "the dance still exists" even though the original dancers are dead and no visual record has been kept of their performance, as long as there is a written score; but in saying this it must be remembered that dance scores are very far from enabling us to reproduce the dance precisely.

A certain performance of a work may be lost (and no longer exist) even though the composition of which it is a performance is not lost. Berlioz, Wagner, and Mahler were reportedly excellent conductors of their own music (as well as the music of other composers), and many of us would give a great deal to have recordings of these performances, but since recording had not been invented at that time, these immortal performances are now lost to us forever. Fortunately, the compositions of which there were performances have been preserved and can be reproduced in performances today, though not exactly as their composers performed them. Some of Martha Graham's dance performances have been recorded on sound films, so that later generations can see (and hear) her dances; but if this had not been done (and it still hasn't been done with all her dances), her performances, though not the dances performed, would have been forever lost to succeeding generations.

In arts of performance, we distinguish the work that is performed from the performance of it; the performance may be bad though the composition is good, and there can also be good performances of trivial or banal compositions. Besides the work and the performance, however, we can distinguish also the *production* of the work. There is the Gielgud production of *Hamlet,* which ran through many performances nightly; there is the Olivier production, which was very different, and which also ran through many performances; and so on. A production can be witnessed only through some performance or other, and a production may be lost if no performance of it was recorded (on film or tape), even though the play itself is preserved because of its reproducibility through the text. Performances of a work may be so different from one another, even if exactly the same text (script) is employed, that it is often worthwhile to have a visual record of more than one production of the same play, just as it is worthwhile to have more than one conductor's performance of a musical composition.

2. *The identity of works of art.* "When is it *the same* work of art that exists?"—that is, how many changes, and what kind of changes, can a work of art undergo and still be considered the same work of art as before?

If we change one note in the score of a melody, is it still the same melody? On reflection it is likely that we would have to say no: the change of a D to a D sharp may alter the character of the whole melody. It is no longer melody A, but melody B, which resembles melody A except for that one note. Now, what if instead of changing one note we transpose the entire melody into a different key? Here we would say, "It's the same melody, only played in a different key." In the transposition case, most listeners won't even know the difference—unless they try to sing it.

Why the difference? The difference lies in the fact that a melody is a series of *tonal relationships*. When a melody is transposed into a different key, the system of tonal relationships is preserved intact; but when a note in the melody is changed, say, the second note, that second note's relationships to the other notes has been altered, and the entire melody has been tampered with, distorted (perhaps in some cases for the better, but distorted from the original melody nonetheless).

Is it still the same musical composition if it's a theme-and-variations composition and one of the variations is omitted? If one asks, "Is it the same composition—yes or no?" we would have to say no, for the omitted variation was indeed a part of the original composition; but to be more precise, we might say, "It's the Brahms *Variations on a Theme by Haydn* minus the fifth variation." Is it still the same composition if a theme assigned in the score to the English horn is given to the French horn instead? Here we would be inclined to say yes, for although the sound quality is now different, the system of tonal relationships remains unchanged. (Often the main third movement theme from Mahler's Third Symphony, assigned to the flugelhorn, is played by the trumpet instead, since most orchestras don't have flugelhorns, but we don't hesitate to say that it's Mahler's Third that is being performed.) What if the composition is played at a much faster tempo than the composer's instructions specify? Then we would probably say that it's the same composition but played very fast—the tempo has been tampered with but not the system of tonal relationships. (It is not clear how far we would go with this: if you play a 33 r.p.m. record at 78 r.p.m., it is so incredibly faster that it is hardly recognizable as the same composition.) The same could be said of changes in dynamics (loud and soft, crescendo and diminuendo, accelerando and ritardando): a conductor can take considerable liberties with these without being accused of not playing the same composition, because though some parts of the composition are performed much louder that we may think proper, the system of tonal relationships specified in the score has not been interfered with. (When you play the 33 r.p.m. record at 78 r.p.m., not only is it much faster, but it is much higher in pitch; still, you might be able to recognize it as the same composition, incredibly distorted.)

Is it the same painting after time has paled its original vivid colors? Important though color is in painting, we would be more inclined to say that it's still the same painting than if any of the color boundaries (shapes) had been changed, though in both cases the difference between the present painting and the original painting might be considerable. Now suppose that we have a painting by Alfred Ryder which is practically falling to pieces, and the only way we can preserve it at all is to attempt to restore it. Is it still the same painting? Again, if we had to answer yes or no, we would have to say no—"part of the painting is new." Or we might say "It's the Ryder painting, partially restored so as to resemble the original one as closely as possible." When a vandal in the Rijksmuseum in Amsterdam slashed holes in Rembrandt's *Night Watch* some years ago, the painting was painstakingly restored so as to be practically indistinguishable from the original (prevandalized) painting. Is it still the *Night Watch*? "Not exactly," we might say, even though we might not be able to tell the two apart. "It's the *Night Watch* as restored, not as it was originally." And if we have only part of an ancient piece of sculpture, and the rest of it was lost, we may say we have the work of sculpture, but if we are careful we shall say that in fact we have only a part of one.

Is it the same poem if we take out a word or phrase and substitute another one? This is like changing the melody: it is a direct tampering with the text. The poem is *this* series of words in exactly *this* order, and if that is changed, we have a different poem, just as in the case of the melody. Suppose, however, that we italicized a word that was not italicized in the original text. That would be something of a distortion, but not enough on the whole to make us call it a different poem. If the lines were spoken at the speed of light, though every word were there, we would blame the performer for a dizzyingly rapid performance but would not be able to accuse him of altering the play, since there was still the same succession of words in the same order. If through his performance the actor gave what we thought was the wrong emphasis to the play—if, for example, through his facial expressions, gestures, and word emphases he gave the character of Hamlet a Freudian interpretation—we might castigate him for his performance (at least if we thought the Freudian interpretation was unjustified), but if he kept the lines intact we could not accuse him of rendering something that was not the play (only of "violating its spirit"). If, however, he omitted many of the lines Shakespeare assigns to Hamlet, we would have to say, if we were careful, that the performance was of Shakespeare's original play *Hamlet,* but in an abbreviated version.

Whether we are talking about works of art or anything else, questions of the form "When is it still the same X?" and "When is it no longer the same X?" admit of some elasticity in their answers. Is it still the same table if I scratch it? Yes, it's the same table, but with a scratch on it. Is it still the same table if I repaint it a different color? Yes, it's the same table (the same pieces of wood, put together in the same way), but repainted. Is it still the same table if I replace every piece of wood in it, one by one, with fiberglass? No, now I have a different table—the table I had was wood and this one isn't. But at what point did it become a different table? Surely it wasn't a different table when I replaced one wooden leg with a fiberglass leg! There is a "slippery slope" here, and no clear point at which I could say, "*Now* it's not the same table any more." I might give a careful answer, such as "It's not *quite* the same table any more, since one of the original legs has been replaced." Or I might, after I have replaced each part, say, "You know, I have a different table now—but I can't honestly say when it stopped being the same table and became a different one." Or I might say, if the fiberglass table was of the same structure and dimensions as the wooden one, and I took structure rather than materials as the criterion of sameness, "It's the same table as it was before—exactly the same, only now it's made of fiberglass."

Similar exercises could be performed—and we have performed some of them—in regard to works of art. What the discussion has brought out, however, is that we regard some features of works of art as more capable of being tampered with than others while the work retains its identity (is still the same work): we can change the instrumentation but not the notes; we can change the tempo or emphasis in a poem or musical composition but not the text; the painting can be allowed to fade somewhat, but we mustn't tamper with its formal features. This at least tells us something of the importance of form in art—which is the subject of Chapter 2.

3. *Works of art: physical or mental*? One more aspect of the existence of works of art needs to be discussed briefly. Must all works of art exist in physical time and/or space?—in visual arts, as physical objects; in music, as physical score followed by physical sound waves (performance); in drama and dance, as physical text followed by physical audio and visual phenomena (performance); in literature, as physical text with no (physical) performance?—or can something exist as a work of art in the mind only?

Most philosophers of art would insist that a work of art must have some kind of physical existence—that there must be a *physical continuant,* in Stephen Pepper's terminology, something that persists in the physical world, either the work of art itself (the painting, statue, or building) or the text (musical score, written poem). The reason is that only in physical existence is their public, or interpersonal, *accessibility.* You may have a beautiful dream, but even if it is a dream *of* a work of art, the dream is not itself a work of art, because nobody else can have your dream—quite apart from any questions about whether you have made or constructed it (the general requirement for anything's being a work of art) or whether it is something that happens to you. For the same reasons, hallucinations, however beautiful, cannot be works of art, for unlike objects in the physical world, they are not "publicly accessible." A work of art, even if it isn't publicly visible and tangible like paintings and statues, must at least be publicly reproducible, like musical compositions and dances which can be performed from a score. The physical existence, be it objects or sound waves or whatever, is the only *anchor* that makes it possible to say truly that you and I and others are in the presence of *the same* work of art, even though it is of different performances.

The only art of which it is plausible at all to say that it exists "in the mind" is literature. Literature, unlike music and performed drama and dance, has no performance in the usual sense. In music the score is the set of instructions for a performance, and the music is the sounds we hear; but when you read a novel or poem you have the written text or score but at least no visible performance. If there is one, it goes on in your mind, or in your imagination: you imagine the scene the novel describes, and each mind will imagine it differently. And so, one might say, if the score isn't the music, but only a set of instructions for the performance of the music, then the written text isn't the novel either, but a set of instructions for imagining (or performing in your mind) the novel. And if the written text isn't the novel, where does the novel exist except in the reader's mind? (The music at least exists in the sounds of the physical performance.)

In the case of literature, this conclusion is highly plausible. But even if it is accepted, we must admit that even in the case of literature there is a physical continuant—the written text, there on the page—which unifies our various mental construals or interpretations and assures us that, however different our images or impressions may be, it's still *Tom Jones,* a novel written by Fielding, that we are reading or thinking about. In dreams we do not even have that much.

Some persons, however, have gone on to assert a far more radical thesis: that *all* works of art exist only in the mind. First, there is the creative activity of the artist in originating the work; second, there is the physical artifact—the painting or sculpture out there; third, there is the apprehension of this artifact, which takes place in the mind of the consumer (viewer, reader, listener). The second item, the artifact, is only a *means toward an end,* namely, of putting a certain complex set of experiences into the mind of the consumer. The "real" painting, however, does not exist until a perceiving mind views the painting and imaginatively interprets it, and only then does it exist as a work of art—in the mind of the viewer, not as pigments on a physical canvas which are incorrectly spoken of as the painting.

If this is simply a move calculated to emphasize how important the perceiving and interpreting mind is to the appreciation of any and all works of art, the point may be granted at once: without a mind there would be no appreciation of art, since it takes a mind to appreciate anything. But if it is taken literally, to assert that the "real" painting isn't out there at all but in the mind only, then it seems to be little more than a piece of semantic sleight-of-hand. It comes to nothing more than a new recommendation for the use of language, particularly the word "real." Everything is as it was before; only the verbal descriptions are different. In ordinary discourse, we say that what's out there is the painting and that what occurs in your mind is the *response* to the painting. This seems clear enough, and true in the ordinary meanings of the terms. But now a new mode of describing the situation is suggested: the painting isn't out there at all, only the artifact is (but that's not the "real" painting); the painting is what's in your mind when you look at the artifact (in which case the painting, not just your reaction to it, varies from moment to moment and day to day); and the customary distinction between the work of art and the response to the work of art collapses entirely, for the response (or set of such responses over a period of time) now *is* the work of art itself!

"This way madness lies," unless one recognizes the maneuver for what it is, a semantic trick which changes nothing in the world, only our descriptions of the world.

As if this were not enough, some philosophers, such as Berkeley, have gone even further and have held that not only does the creative activity of the artist go on in his mind, and not only does the response of the viewer go on in his mind, but the allegedly physical artifact (the statue) is also in the mind! But of course if everything that exists is in the mind (your mind, my mind, God's mind, or whoever's), then to say that something is in the mind distinguishes nothing from anything else. It is like saying that there is only one color in the world, blue, but then we have to distinguish red-blue, green-blue, yellow-blue, white-blue, and even blue-blue. But in that case nothing is added by saying that everything is blue: within that category we still have to make the same perceived distinctions that we made before. Nothing is added, that is, except terminological awkwardness, and confusion for the unwary. Indeed, one might say to all this, "If you say that everything without exception is in the mind, so be it. But within that one great category, the mind, which everything is in, we still have to distinguish the artifact (the painting), from one's response to it; for how can one deny that different people have varying responses to the same object? So, under a different rubric, we still have to make the same distinctions that we made before."

## 5. ENJOYING, UNDERSTANDING, AND APPRECIATING WORKS OF ART

If someone says that he likes or enjoys a certain work of art, this carries no implication that he comprehends what is going on in it. If we play for him the Brahms Piano Concerto No. 2 and afterward ask him "Wasn't that an exciting passage in the second movement when the first pieces of thematic material wind down and are replaced by a different set?" and he looks blankly at us, not having been aware of any such change at all, we may still believe that he "enjoyed it," but doubt that he truly appreciated it. Some people say, "Sure I like classical (as if through the last twelve centuries that were all *one type* of music), and I like rock, and I like country western, and . . .". But are these paragons of enjoyment, with the enviable capacity to enjoy every musical sound they hear, profound or trite, imaginative or humdrum, really aware of what they're hearing, if they haven't even noticed the most obvious things about it and remember nothing afterward unless it is something blatant like a sudden thunderclap or a cowbell in the music? Are they really *listening* to the music instead of just *hearing* it (listening is active, hearing is passive, just as looking is active, seeing is passive), passively allowing the cascades of sound to penetrate their eardrums? They seem to be like the person who says, "I like all diamonds, real and imitation"—in which case they have not much power of discrimination among (real or alleged) diamonds.

There is a story about a Chinese student recently arrived in America, who was taken to a concert. Asked afterward whether he enjoyed it, he said, "I enjoyed it all." "But what composition did you enjoy most?" "The first one." His hosts smiled, thinking that he was referring to "The Star-Spangled Banner" and that he was trying to show his allegiance to his newly adopted country. But that wasn't what he meant at all. He was referring to the tuning up of the instruments before the playing of the first piece.

Maybe he *did* enjoy everything played at the concert, but, we would add, he certainly didn't understand much. So let us substitute "understand" for "enjoy" and see what happens. On reflection, it seems that "just understanding" isn't what we want any more than "just enjoying." The term "understand" has an intellectualistic flavor; a person may understand a work of art without having any vital experience of it. If he *merely* understands it, that's not enough: we want him to *enjoy* it also.

Nor is it clear, especially in some of the arts, what "understand" means. In the case of literature, the most intellectual of the arts, its meaning is the clearest: at first we didn't understand Eliot's *The Waste Land* at all, but now, having read what some critics had to say about it, and various interpretations of the poem, and having read some of the background material such as Weston's *From Ritual to Romance,* we now know what some of the obscure references were to, and we can begin to make sense of the poem; we are better able to understand it now than before. Whether we enjoy it after all this is something else again.

What does it mean, however, to "understand" a musical composition? Not the cultural background, not the life of the composer, not the conditions of its composition, but the music itself? We can't say "We must understand what the music *means,*" because unlike literature, which is composed of words which have meanings, musical tones have no meanings: if you play a melody for someone and are asked "What does it mean?," you can only reply with something like "Don't look for meanings, the way words have meanings— just savor the melody!" So what is it to understand not "the music's meaning" but the music itself?

A person would not be said to "understand" the music if he didn't *notice* at least some of the things which, musically, were going on in it: here is a change of tempo, there is a chord in the minor third, here a repeat, there a pizzicato, there a theme from the first movement reappearing in the second movement in altered form. . . . But do we have to be acquainted with the elaborate technical terminology of music to notice these things? In that case, only trained musicologists can understand music. No, there are other ways of indicating that we notice certain things: we can stop the player at a certain point, where the bass chord drops half a tone and modulates the composition into a new key, and ask "That's what I mean; what's that called?" A music teacher can soon pick up on whether a student is noticing things in the music even if he lacks the words for it.

There is one misunderstanding about "understanding" that needs to be corrected. Understanding a work of art involves at least an ability to *analyze* elements in it, in their relation to each other; and the word "analyze" is viewed with fear or disdain by many people who are devoted to the arts. "To analyze," they say, "is to take apart, to dissect, to cut to pieces. When you have dissected a frog in the zoology lab, you have before you the pieces of what *was* a frog, but you don't have the functioning living organism before you any more. In the same way, when you analyze a work of art you take it apart, and when you've taken it apart you may know everything that's in it, but you are left with a bunch of dissected pieces and you no longer have the living work of art before you." The analogy with the frog, however, is misleading; might it not as well have been that of a clock, with the repairman's taking the clock apart only to put it together again better than it was before? If fact both analogies are defective, for they involve physically taking a thing (frog or clock) apart, and this is not what happens when you subject a work of art to analysis. The analysis here is intellectual, not physical: you do not literally take anything apart at all, you notice features and relations in it that you failed to notice before, but the *work of art itself is unchanged by your activity,* unlike the frog, which *is* changed by your dissection of it. The change is not in the work of art but in you: first you didn't notice things in it, now you do; at first you were ignorant, now you have knowledge. What you've done is not really dissecting at all; it's rather like shining a light on it so you can see it better. Understanding it is not literally taking it to pieces, but shining a light on it. Instead of preventing you from appreciating it, you are now in a position to appreciate it more than before.

The fact remains, however, that we can understand without appreciating. On a tour of the Greek islands I ran into a graduate student in archaeology and art history who understood just about everything there was to understand about ancient Greek temples and statues; not only did he know history, he was expert at precise ruin identification, and he could reel off the reasons for his (invariably correct) identifications. But there was no evidence that he cared much about any of it or that it was anything but intellectually interesting detective work for him. This would seem to be a clear case of understanding without appreciation.

Not just enjoyment, then, not just understanding, but *appreciation*—is that the word we want? Perhaps. But what is it to appreciate a work of art? In daily life appreciation implies some kind of gratitude: "I appreciate what you've done for me." The word may not, of course, carry that same implication in artistic contexts; let us try to see what the main implications of it are.

If I say sincerely that I enjoy it, I really can't be mistaken, unless I am misusing the word "enjoy"—much as a person can't be mistaken in saying that he's seeing blue in his field of vision, unless he's confusing blue with green or some other color. But surely I *can* be mistaken in thinking that I truly appreciate a work of art—I can think I appreciate it when I don't, and I may later come to realize this. If I appreciate it, let's grant that I enjoy it, but what *more* is required for appreciation? Here the obvious answer will be suggested: "Understanding it. You may enjoy it but not understand it, but if you enjoy it *and* understand it, you appreciate it. Appreciation of a work of art is enjoyment plus understanding."

It does seem that "I appreciate X" seems to hover somewhere between "I enjoy X" and "I understand X." Yet it is not a halfway house between them, or a combination of them, for several reasons:

On the one hand, the requirement seems to demand too much. To appreciate a Bach organ fantasia, I have to do more than just enjoy it (I can do that when I use it as background music for getting to sleep), but do I have to understand it? If so in what way and to what extent? If it means that I have to know every musical device that goes into this highly complex work, as a musicologist does, surely I don't have to be able to do all that in order to appreciate it! Can't many members of an audience genuinely appreciate a musical composition without having the musicologist's capacity to analyze it in detail? Surely we can appreciate it with a very *incomplete* understanding of Bach's endless ingenuity?

On the other hand, the requirement seems not to demand enough. Here is a person who "enjoys just anything"—and here is a shoddy hastily-put-together piece of trash. The person will enjoy it, and while still "enjoying all" he may even come to understand it, at least well enough to realize what an ill-constructed contrivance it is; he may have no respect for it as a work of art and yet be like the person who sees a movie every night, saying "I like all movies—good, bad, and indifferent." He enjoys it, he understands it, but we would not say that he appreciates it. Why not? Because, unlike the other two, "appreciate" is a *value* term: when you use it, you presuppose that there is something there that is worthy of appreciation. "I understand this lousy poem" is in no way puzzling; neither is "I enjoy this lousy poem" (we conclude only that he is indiscriminate in his enjoyments); but "I appreciate this lousy poem" surely is. Can you appreciate when there's nothing worth appreciating? In this respect "appreciate" used in artistic contexts *is* like its use in moral contexts: if I say "I appreciate what you did for me" when I know you did nothing for me, is it appreciation? In moral contexts the use of the term presupposes that you have done something worth appreciating; and in artistic contexts it presupposes that the work of art contains something worth appreciating. Since "appreciate" has a value component which "enjoy" and "understand" do not have, its meaning can hardly be a combination or a running together of the other two.

As with so many other terms, "appreciate" has no clearly fixed meaning in ordinary discourse. The result is that, when we try to fix it more precisely, and still remain faithful to ordinary usage of language, we run into trouble—the term is just too slippery. Perhaps then we can prepare the ground for the question to be discussed in the next section—what conditions are necessary for appreciating a work of art?—by trying a few alternative formulations.

We might ask, "What conditions are required for approaching or coming at a work of art?" Here there is no reference to appreciation; but now the question is not clear: approaching a work of art for what purpose? to enjoy it? to understand it? to write a report on it? to while away an hour? to let it make us fall asleep? to enable us to glean from it a psychological or sociological generalization about human behavior? to try to fathom what was going on in the artist's unconscious mind?

Or we might ask, "How can we most effectively gain the *maximum total experience* of the work of art?" But total experience of what kind? Anything, as long as it's massive or intense? Perhaps you can get maximum experience out of a song by having an orgasm every time it's played. "But that's not primarily an experience of the *song.*" Let's change the example then: you may get a maximum total experience of a work of art if it expresses a point of view with which you enthusiastically agree—but does this agreement, total though it may be, mean that you appreciate the work that much more? Might not your agreement even stand in the way, by preventing you from searching out other details of the work which you might have appreciated if you hadn't concentrated exclusively on the aspect of agreement?

The term "appreciate" has entered the arena again, so let us qualify it and ask our question again: "Under what conditions can we best *aesthetically* appreciate a work of art?" The qualifying adjective will enable us to eliminate some things: it will help to make it clear that we are not considering the novel as social or political theory, or history, or propaganda, or as a treatise on morals, or as something you'd better read if you want to keep up with the Joneses, or something that will help you in your job, or make you more scintillating at parties, or more *gemütlich* in a small company of friends, since the term "aesthetic" does not cover, but rather precludes, all of these things. This formulation seems to be clearly an improvement; the trouble with it is that it is not clear at this point (and according to some writers, never will or can become clear) *exactly* what the qualifying adjective "aesthetic" includes or precludes. It is hoped that this will become clearer in subsequent chapters. Meanwhile, let us ask, "What conditions are required for the aesthetic appreciation of works of art?"—assuming one thing, that we have in mind works which are worthy of appreciation, else the very term "appreciation" would be misplaced.

## 6. CONDITIONS FOR THE APPRECIATION OF ART

One extremely direct and simple answer to the question "What conditions are required for the aesthetic appreciation of works of art?" is "None at all, outside the work of art itself." To appreciate a work of art, you look at it, listen to it, read it (as the case may be), and then do it again, again, and yet again, carefully and as perceptively as you can. All you need is *reexposure.* Great works of art tend to be those to which you can return with pleasure and profit again and again, though not for the same qualities each time: often you will enjoy it for some particular quality or qualities for a time, then come to enjoy other qualities of it that you hadn't suspected were there. A work of art is like a constellation rather than a single star; as one star dims, others shine forth more brightly. To appreciate the work, then, you simply "get into it" by exposing yourself to it repeatedly. In less complex works of art you don't need much or any repetition, and there's nothing wrong with enjoying superficial works for relaxation, but the enduring works of art are those that continue to be interesting and challenging after often-repeated exposure. You don't need to read books about the work, you don't need to delve into its history or cultural background, you need only to look/listen/read more, savoring it, appreciating it more each time until a saturation point is reached.

This view, for rather obvious reasons, is sometimes called *isolationism.* It is a refreshing change from courses you may have had in art history in which you had to memorize endless facts about the period, the artist's life, his works and their dates of creation or publication, and you were tested on your knowledge of facts quite extraneous to the work of art rather than on your appreciation of the work of art itself. (But how *would* a teacher test a student on how much the student appreciated it?) What you do instead of all this is to keep your senses and your mind alert and return to the work itself for whatever it has to offer. Knowledge of background facts may, in fact, distract your attention from the work. Nothing will suffice but focusing on the work itself—a task often more difficult to follow through, but more rewarding in the end, than picking up background facts about the work. At least this view is a healthy counterpoise to excessive emphasis on historical facts so constantly emphasized in courses of visual art, literature, music, and theater. Tests in high school literature classes are often more about the poet than about the poems—which raises in the inquiring student's mind the question, "Why is the poet's life so important? Isn't what makes the poet important his poetry? So why shouldn't the emphasis be on that?" A good question indeed, to which many teachers would find it difficult to supply a satisfactory answer.

When you want to introduce someone to a musical composition that means so much to you that you want to share it, what do you do? You play it in his or her presence, and if it is a complex work you play it again and yet again. Gradually a few clear chords or melodies begin to emerge from the chaos, and as one theme is developed and leads into another which is in turn developed, your hearer comes to grasp this and is pleased or moved or awed by it, wants to hear it again, can't get it out of his head, and you say to yourself "At last it's grabbed him!" without his ever having learned a single fact about the composer or the conditions under which the composition was created.

That is the way it often works in music, but this method—reexposure and no more—doesn't always work. Suppose the work is a very difficult one, like

Joyce's *Ulysses* or *Finnegan's Wake.* Or suppose it is a painting, such as Dürer's, heavy with symbolism, which you can't interpret without going outside the painting—the painting itself may offer you no clues. Then you need to call in outside help. The view opposed to isolationism, called *contextualism,* says that you should always appreciate the work of art *in its context*—the context of its artistic heritage and traditions, of the life of the artist, of the era in which he lived. Let us consider the main sources of outside help you might call upon to enhance your appreciation of the work.

1. *Other works of art.* Sometimes focusing your attention on *other works of art,* either by the same artist or in the same genre or artistic tradition, may enhance your appreciation of this work. When you listen to one of Mozart's piano concertos your appreciation may be enhanced by comparing it, even subconsciously, to one or more of the twenty-six other piano concertos he wrote: you then hear this one in the context of the others. You compare this work by Tintoretto or Matisse or Picasso with other paintings they did before or after. You may appreciate Beethoven symphonies and quartets if you are acquainted with earlier works in the same genre by Haydn and Mozart and see how Beethoven's developed from theirs—and how his in turn developed into those of Schubert, Brahms, and Mahler. T. S. Eliot, in his essay "Tradition and the Individual Talent," has gone so far as to say that each work of art that appears must be seen against the entire set of preceding works in that tradition and that our experience of all the other works is changed, however slightly, because of the appearance of this one.

Sometimes it is not merely convenient, but quite essential, to be acquainted with other works, especially preceding ones. When you read Milton's *Lycidas,* it is assumed not only that you are acquainted with Latin pastoral poetry, to see what changes Milton has wrought on this genre, but that you have to be acquainted with some of Vergil's *Georgics,* since Milton makes explicit reference to these in his poem and the allusions cannot be fully understood unless one has read Vergil.

2. *Facts about the medium.* Besides knowing other works of art, it is often helpful to know certain facts about the artistic medium in which the artist worked. In literature, of course, you have to know the language; to read Chaucer you have to know Middle English—the translations into modern English are all vanilla flavored and have lost most of their "punch." If you know something about pipe organs in Bach's day, or the pianoforte in Mozart's, you will understand what the limitations as well as the virtues of these instruments were, and why the composers did or did not do certain things in composing these works. If you know that Gothic cathedrals were built stone on stone, as opposed to the construction method of most modern buildings, which are supported from within by structural steel, you will know why certain things could not be done by medieval cathedral builders, and how marvelously they did do with the limited technology at hand. Whether you actually appreciate the works more when you know these things, or whether

have only gleaned background material which helps to explain why they did what they did, is of course a disputable (and disputed) point.

A dramatic illustration of the importance of knowledge of the artistic medium is provided in this example of the Gibbs façade of the cathedral of St. Martin-in-the-Fields.

> In order to understand not merely its profound influence, but also it in itself, we need to see it as a solution to a problem which had for fifty years exercised English architects: how to combine a temple façade or portico with the traditional English demand for a west tower. If we omit this context, much in the design is bound to seem willful or bizarre.[18]

But some would disagree about the necessity of this external knowledge. Many would say that they prefer simply to look at the cathedral in isolation of any context, to examine it again and again, and ask themselves, "Do I find it beautiful or not?" They would relegate the historical and mediumistic considerations to "the historians and architects who want to do that sort of thing" or to those who enjoy tracing the historical influences on the building at which they are looking. Still, if they insist in limiting their activities in this way, there is surely a dimension of understanding and appreciation that they are missing: partly the technical problems that the artists in successive generations solved, and partly the appreciation of the art-object *in* its historial context, in relation to the entire tradition of which this work is a part. The isolationist approach has sometimes been called the "thin" way of appreciating art, the contextualist the "thick" way. Each has its rewards; but unfortunately those who engage in for the one kind of appreciation have a tendency to be ignorant of the rewards of the other.

3. *The time in which the artist lived.* "To appreciate a work of art, we must view it in the context of its time," not in the context of other works of art merely, but in that of history and historical influences. To appreciate the plays of Aeschylus, don't we have to know something about Greek religion and culture? To appreciate Chaucer's *Canterbury Tales,* don't we have to know something about English society of that period, and the role of friars, pardoners, reeves (sheriffs), nuns, and so on in Chaucer's time? Such facts about the period are not parts or aspects of the appreciation but are (or are believed to be) *necessary conditions* for appreciation.

But not all examples are equally convincing. To appreciate the *Laokoön* statue, must we first be acquainted with the Laokoön legend? To appreciate the *Paradise Lost* of Milton, must we be aware that Milton was acquainted with the new Copernican astronomy but nevertheless employed the older Ptolemaic astronomy instead, because the references he constantly made to classical literature and mythology were steeped in it? To appreciate

---

[18] Richard Wollheim, *Art and Its Objects* (New York: Harper and Row, 1968), p. 62.

Shakespeare's plays, do we have to know a great deal (or anything) about the English Renaissance, the era of Queen Elizabeth I, in which they were created? Must one know something about Dutch history at the time of the great Dutch painters to appreciate their paintings? How much must one know about the doctrines of Christianity to appreciate medieval and Renaissance religious paintings and sculptures?

There are cases in which, it would seem, we need to know nothing at all: to appreciate the chamber and orchestral music of Haydn and Mozart, what do you have to know about the social, economic, and political conditions of central Europe during that period? It is difficult to escape the conclusion that total ignorance of these facts about the period would not prevent one from appreciating their music. Thus the need for knowledge of the historical background would appear to vary from case to case; what holds true for some cases need not for all. To appreciate a work of music, it is less important to be acquainted with the wars and political turbulences of the time than it is in the case of historical novels.

In general, however, it must be observed that we come to works of art with a certain background of knowledge, which we do not forget or lay aside as we peruse the work of art. We come to the reading of novels by Dickens, Arthur Conan Doyle, Virginia Woolf, and Galsworthy with a certain amount of background knowledge of what London was like at the time described in the novels; and many allusions in the novels will be lost on us if we do not have that knowledge. We are not told in the stories about Sherlock Holmes that the era of the automobile had not yet arrived and that Holmes had to do his investigations either on foot or with benefit of a cab horse. Such knowledge is simply *presupposed*: not everything can be explained in the novel itself—some facts must be assumed to be already known to the reader.

But what facts, and how many? How much "general background" should be presupposed and already known to the reader before he can fully grasp the work. Some say, "The information must not exceed that which an amateur of the arts would naturally bring with him."[19] In that case, the *Cantos* of Ezra Pound, which presuppose much more than that—bits of obscure knowledge which few people in the world have, plus acquaintance with some twenty languages which are used in the *Cantos* without benefit of translation—would be criticized because they presuppose too much knowledge on the part of the reader. Yet it won't do to say that none at all is required; some such knowledge almost always is. Perhaps we can subject the matter to what economists call a "cost-benefit" analysis: if you have to bone up on a lot of information that you don't already have before you come to a work of art, it had better turn out to be worth the trouble! When James Joyce said that a reader of his works, to fully understand them, would have to spend his entire life reading these works, he was placing an enormous burden on his reader

---

[19] *Ibid.,* p. 63.

and apparently assuming that after all the time and labor spent the prize at the end of the road would be worth it.

4. *The artist's life.* If sometimes knowledge about the age in which the artist lived is necessary, is not knowledge of his biography at least relevant? To appreciate Milton's *On His Blindness,* should one know that Milton himself was blind? or that Beethoven was deaf when he wrote the last quartets? Should one know whether Van Gogh's *Portrait of His Room* was in fact his room? Should one know in reading Byron's poetry that Byron was himself involved in the Greek war for independence? Anthologists of literature do seem to assume that knowledge of the author's life is important, for they always include biographies of the authors before presenting selections from their works. But is this assumption justified?

You have read "The Royal Game." Did you know that it was Zweig's last published work? that in addition to his earlier stories, such as *Amok,* he also wrote biographies of Balzac, Ibsen, Erasmus, Freud, Marie Antoinette, and others? that having opposed Austria's entrance into World War I, he left Austria, returning later to his war-ravaged homeland, only to find Nazism building up in Germany and himself (a Jew) a sure victim if Hitler conquered Austria? that he then left for England, left England in 1939, came to the United States, and sailed for Brazil to make a new home for himself and his wife at the age of sixty? but that in spite of his exhilaration while writing "The Royal Game," he became discouraged and feared that he would be unable to adapt once again to a new country with unfamiliar customs and language, so immediately after he had written it and his wife had sent the carefully typed copy to his New York publisher, he shot her (at her request) and then himself? Very well—now that you know, does this knowledge make any difference to your appreciation of the story? or does it only add a dimension to your conception of the author who created it? (Appreciating *him* as a human being and appreciating the *story* he wrote are, of course, two different things.)

Many will say that no knowledge of the artist's life is ever necessary for appreciation—it's one of those many things that's interesting to know about, for purposes of satisfying one's curiosity about what kind of person created these works, but unnecessary for appreciating the work itself. We know almost nothing for sure about Shakespeare's life (only enough to say with G. B. Shaw that if the plays weren't written by Shakespeare they must have been written by someone else with the same name), but even if we knew nothing at all about it, would this fact prevent us from appreciating his plays and poems to the full? If you tell people before they read Fielding's novels *Tom Jones* and *Joseph Andrews* that Fielding was a lawyer, they may say to you after reading the novels, "It certainly helped me to know that!"—but I didn't know it till *after* I had read the novels, and as far as I can see it didn't inhibit my appreciation at all. We are tempted to believe that knowing about Van Gogh's life greatly enhances our appreciation of his paintings; but if tomorrow morning we were to see headlines, "Big Hoax Uncovered! Paintings Alleged to Be by Van Gogh Not Painted by Their Purported Author,'' would it really make any difference, as long as we still had all the paintings?

We know nothing at all about the lives of most artists in antiquity; does this inhibit appreciation of their work (granted that we know something about the period)? We admire today the grace and expressiveness of figures drawn on cave walls by prehistoric men more than fifty thousand years ago; we know nothing about the artists, nor are any of their biographies likely to appear in print; does this fact close off our appreciation of their works? Are we any the worse off for this biographical ignorance?

One might go further and say that biographical knowledge as often as not gets in the way of appreciation. When we know some facts about the artist's life, we tend to read them into the work—but shouldn't we see in the work only what's there? Worse still, people often *substitute* knowledge of the artist's biography for appreciation of the work itself. Instead of listening to the late quartets of Beethoven with the great care that they require, people think of the deaf Beethoven and "feel so sorry for him, what a pity it was that it had to happen to him." To read a biography is usually easy and pleasant and makes good cocktail party conversation; it even gives others the impression that we appreciate the works when we have only a nodding acquaintance with them; and it often helps to keep up with the Joneses. But it is not the artist but the works of art he created which are the object of appreciation; if the artist's life were filled with struggle to realize his artistic ideals against great odds, that is the object of a very different kind of appreciation. That Berlioz had to endure extraordinary hardship is a fact that moves one deeply on reading his biography, but does it enhance one's appreciation of his music? Must one be content with appreciating his music less if one doesn't know about his struggles?

There is, however, one special aspect of the artist's life that requires separate consideration: the artist's intentions with regard to his work. Even if knowledge of his life history isn't necessary, isn't it necessary to know what his intentions were with regard to each work he created?

5. *The artist's intentions.* The German poet Goethe said that there were three and only three criteria for evaluating works of art: (a) What was the artist trying to do? (b) Did he do it? (c) Was it worth doing? Presumably the first of these questions can be answered only by knowing something about the artist. Don't you have to know what his intentions were before you can judge whether he succeeded in fulfilling them? Can one blame him for failing to do something he had no intention of doing in the first place?

Yet, of the vast majority of works of art that we possess, created from ancient times to the present, we have no record of what the artist's intentions were; we have only the work of art. We tend to conclude that he intended to do just what he did do, that every brush stroke was intentional, inasmuch as he put it there, that nothing went wrong, and that the work of art fulfilled his intentions entirely; if in some cases that is not true, we have no present way of knowing it. We judge by the product we see before us.

Even if we discover that some feature of the work of art was intentional, but we believe it was a disaster, we don't on that account praise the work in accordance with Goethe's criteria, saying "I guess it's all right, he intended to shock us by inserting that raucous dissonance in the last measure of his *Requiem Mass,* and he did, so he fulfilled his intentions." If we chastise an author for writing trash, and he says, "But I *intended* to write trash," this doesn't make his novel any better. If the prima ballerina takes an awkward fall during the middle of her dance, and she later says she intended to do it all the time "just to vary the diet," we do not on that account justify the inclusion of the fall in the performance; whether she did it intentionally or not, it marred the performance. If she was suffering from a sprained ankle that evening, we may *excuse* her, but we still do not rate her performance any higher.

Conductors often say that they performed the piece a certain way because they "believed that this was the composer's intention." As a rule they have no knowledge of the composer's intention. There is always some latitude in the performance of a work of music (tempo, dynamics, light or heavy touch, mood generated) even if the conductor follows the score religiously; and the fact is that while paying lip service to the composer's intentions he conducts the piece in whatever way *sounds the best to him.* Consider the phrase that introduces the second subject in the first movement of Beethoven's Symphony No. 5:

> In the exposition section, Bars 59–62, it is in E flat, and is given to the horns, but in the development section, Bars 303–06, it is in C major and is given to bassoons. Most conductors now assign the second passage, like the first, to the horns, without hesitation. Why? It is argued that if Beethoven's horns had had valves, so that they could play in both keys, instead of being limited to one, he would have let them do so; hence, the decision is based upon an appeal to intention. But the ground of this appeal is not intention; it is the supposition that, had Beethoven been free to choose, he would have recognized, as we do, that the phrase is better when played on the horns, more solemn and momentous. We don't decide what should be done after deciding what Beethoven wished, but the other way round.[20]

In one of John Donne's *Elegies* a bereaved wife mourns the death of her husband, who has been killed trying to climb a mountain:

> Thy soul hovers
> O'er the white Alp, alone . . .

and knowing what we do about the attitude toward mountains in the seventeenth century, it seems highly probable that the intended effect is one of ter-

---

[20] Monroe C. Beardsley, *Aesthetics* (New York: Harcourt Brace, 1958), p. 23.

ror; mountains were not then viewed as scenic wonderlands for hiking and vacations, but as barriers to transport and sources of great danger. But then, two hundred years later, came the Romantic movement, and mountains were no longer viewed in the same way. As the reader now reads the lines, he or she shudders not in terror but in delight, with pleasant titillations of the spine. Do we rule out this reading because it was probably contrary to Donne's intention in these lines? If we rule it out, it is because it disturbs or spoils the mood unity of the rest of the poem (or for some other such reason), not because Donne's intentions were not fulfilled in the new interpretation. Readers, conductors, actors, and other performers usually interpret a passage in accordance with what they consider its *best* interpretation (the interpretation that makes the passage or the work of art as a whole come off best), which may or may not be the one that the artist intended.

Generations of critics have praised Titian's famous painting *Sacred and Profane Love* for the exquisite way in which the theme of sacred versus profane love is exemplified in the painting of two women, one clothed and one nude. "How beautifully he carried out his intention!" Centuries later historians discovered that the title was not given the painting by Titian at all but by an unknown copyist long after Titian had painted it. As if this were not enough to make them blush, it also developed that the copyist considered the nude woman to represent sacred love and the clothed woman profane love—exactly the reverse of what the later critics assumed. Doubtless there is a lesson here for those who had expatiated on how well Titian had carried out his intentions. (Of course, he could have illustrated the theme of sacred versus profane love in the painting, even without intending to.)

"But sometimes we have to know the intention, else the work remains opaque to us." The author of highly obscure modern poetry has a poem published in a poetry magazine. Even after repeated readings with great concentration, nobody can make head or tail of it; it is unintelligible to every critic that tries. Meanwhile, the poet has tipped off a few of his friends as to "what he really meant by it," and these friends write learned commentaries in critical journals explaining "what the poem really means." It seems that in this case we would never have known "what the poem really means" unless we had the author's statement of what *he* meant by his obscure sentences.

Two comments, however, are in order: (a) Yes, and perhaps we don't know even now. Maybe the gibberish hasn't any meaning at all. The mere fact that such-and-such is what the author said he *intended* the lines to mean doesn't prove that this is what they *do* mean. If I accept your invitation to dinner and don't show up, and you later say to me "But you said you were coming," and I reply "When I said that, I meant that I was *not* coming," does that let me off the hook? Regardless of what *I* meant, the sentence I uttered to you was "I am coming," and that is what the sentence meant. In a poem what we usually want to know is what the lines in the poem mean (to those who read the work at the time of its creation), not what the author intended them to mean. (b) When no examination of the lines, however painstaking, yields any intelligible meaning, but we have to go outside the poem to the poet's (real or alleged) intention, we may well consider this an artistic defect. We feel that there should be some clues in the lines themselves as to how they are to be construed. Simply taking the author's word for it (or that of his friends who have been tipped off) will not suffice if we, on going back to the lines, cannot find in them the meaning he says he intended. What he intended to put there is one thing; what he actually put there is another.

The matter of intentions however, is not yet at an end. There are certain kinds of artworks, such as parodies, that seem to create a special problem. Prokofieff's *Classical Symphony* is a parody of a Mozartian classical symphony; Prokofieff in his symphony appears to twit and make gentle fun of the neat precision and elegance of Mozartian symphony. But to judge something as a parody, don't we have to know that Prokofieff intended it to be one? Presumably a parody is intentional; if we give his symphony low marks for not being a truly "classical symphony," and he tells us that he never intended it to be a classical symphony but a parody of one, and that we have been judging it by the wrong standards, shouldn't we stand corrected? Don't we have to admit that we must first know his intention before we are in a position to evaluate the work?

This is a more troublesome case, but the outcome need be no different than before. Regardless of what the composer intended, we can say, "Judged as a classical symphony, this may have defects; but judged as a parody of a classical symphony, it's excellent." If the symphony were to be discovered and performed many centuries from now, and all record of Prokofieff's intentions lost, the symphony could still be enjoyed and the judgment of it could be the same as the one just given. What *is* necessary, or at least helpful, to know before listening to Prokofieff's symphony is not Prokofieff's intentions but what the traditionally classical symphony is like. To appreciate a parody you have to know what kind of thing it is that is being parodied; but this is to be acquainted with one or more previous works of art, not the artist's intentions.

Here is a ponderous moralistic Victorian novel, deadly serious in its tone. Reading it, however, we suspect that it may be intended as a parody of a Victorian novel. We may never know whether or not it was so intended. So we say, "Judged as a serious Victorian novel, this is ponderous, pretentious, etc.; judged as a parody, it is brilliant." And this may well be true whether it was intended as a parody or not.

This is not to say that we should turn a deaf ear to the author's own statement of intentions. If the work is difficult or obscure, any clue to its interpretation, or various possible interpretations, will be welcome, *whether they come from the author or from someone else*. If the author tells us what he intended his poem to mean, and his suggested interpretation "stands up" (is borne out by the text) when we examine the poem again, we may well accept his suggestion with thanks. But we may do exactly the same with a suggestion that comes from a critic who is not the author. Once the work of art is in the public world, it is, so to speak, public property over which the artist has no longer any special title. Suggestions for its interpretation by others may be more fruitful than his suggestions. When T. S. Eliot was asked how to interpret certain obscure passages in his poems, he would refer the inquirers to F. O. Matthiesen's book *The Achievement of T. S. Eliot:* "He can do that sort of thing better than I can." There is no reason why the artist should necessarily be the best interpreter of his own work, particularly if he hasn't looked at it since it was created and critics have been poring over it constantly. Brahms was not very adept at conducting his own works before an audience; he usually had his friend, the violinist Joachim, conduct it instead, saying that Joachim could "bring out his (Brahms') intentions better." A work of art may be greater, or may hold out richer potentialities of performance or appreciation, than the artist himself was aware when he created it.

When the English poet A. E. Housman wrote a poem celebrating the anniversary of Queen Victoria's reign, concluding with the couplet

> Get you the sons your fathers got,
> And God will save the Queen,

the critic Frank Harris congratulated Housman on having written such a masterful spoof on the Queen. Housman replied with some indignation that it wasn't a spoof at all, that he loved the Queen, and that the poem was intended seriously. Harris still didn't accept Housman's interpretation of his own poem, saying, "How was I to know that someone steeped in a savage disgust of life could take pleasure in outcheaping Kipling at his cheapest?" Harris believed that his interpretation was better than Housman's own; but many readers would give preference to Housman's own interpretation *because,* they say, Housman was the author and thus was in a special position to comment on his own poetry.

In Day's eighteenth-century poem *The Parliament of Bees* there occur the lines

> When of a sudden, listening, you shall hear,
> A noise of horns and hunting, which shall bring
> Actaeon to Diana in the spring . . .

and two hundred years later T. S. Eliot writes of

> The sound of horns and motors, which shall bring
> Sweeney to Mrs. Porter in the Spring . . .

Is Eliot's couplet to be read in the light of the earlier poem? In view of their similarity, is the later one to be taken to refer to the earlier one? Is the question to be decided by discovering whether Eliot *intended* his lines to hark back to the earlier ones—whether he intended to presuppose in the reader of his poem a knowledge of the earlier poem?

> A reader's response to a work will vary with what he knows; one of the things which he knows and with which his responses will vary is what the author had in mind, or what he intended.[21]

Gerard Manley Hopkins wrote a poem entitled "Henry Purcell" in which the phrase "fair fall" occurs, and Hopkins himself later wrote, "One thing disquiets me: I *meant* 'fair fall' to mean 'fair (fortune be) fall': it has since struck me that perhaps 'fair' is an adjective proper and in the predicate and can only be used in cases like 'fair fall the day,' that is 'may the day fall, turn out fair.' My lines will yield a sense that way indeed, but I never meant it so." In a case like this, writes one critic, "knowledge of an author's avowed intention in respect of his work exercises a *coercive influence* on our apprehension of it."[22] (emphasis added) And then he asks, "When doesn't it?"

Never, some would respond. But many would disagree: if they are isolationists, they will say the poem is defective if it requires external knowledge (such as of the author's intentions) to decipher it; if they are contextualists, they may say that, although the author's intention (when it is known) is worthy of consideration, it may be no *more* worthy of consideration than the remarks of literary critics and readers who may have spent much more time with the author's works than the author himself has and may give helpful suggestions that the author never thought of.

In any case, there are examples which *seem* to show the relevance of the artist's intention but actually appeal to something else. (a) When Keats wrote the famous lines, "Beauty is truth, truth beauty," many readers are puzzled that Keats could have identified as one two such different concepts. To make sense of the line, isn't it relevant (even necessary) to know that what Keats meant by the term "beauty" is construed as knowing Keat's *intentions* at all but, rather, as knowing the meaning of the word (either in common use then, or in use among a special group of scholars or critics)? (Remember that the poem isn't just the words, but also the meanings of the words.) In that case this example would fall under the heading of "knowledge of the medium," not "knowledge of the artist's intentions." (b) And when someone asks "Are the metaphors in Othello's soliloquy which begins 'Steep me in poverty to the very lips' deliberately inappropriate so as to suggest the disorder of Othello's mind?" one is not inquiring as to what Shakespeare's intentions were (what he would have said if he had been asked what he meant) but, rather, whether the lines if construed in that way would make the entire passage more coherent or

[21] Frank Cioffi, "Interpretation and Intention in Criticism," in *Philosophy Looks at the Arts,* 2nd ed., ed. Joseph Margolis (Philadelphia: Temple U.P., 1979), p. 315.

[22] *Ibid.,* p. 317.

consistent, or intelligible. But again, in that case, in spite of the intentionalistic word "deliberately," the question only *seems* to be one about intention.

Let us conclude with a somewhat different kind of case. Most great poems,
plays, novels, musical compositions, paintings, cathedrals, and so on cannot
be fully appreciated at one sitting—they are too complex and subtle and require repeated exposure to them. But most films can be fully grasped at one
viewing, in fact they tend to be a bore if one is forced to see them a second
time. (A very small percentage, those we call "great films," which turn up
year after year in art theaters, can be enjoyed over and over again.) Now suppose someone says, "You have to understand that films, which are almost
always made for commercial purposes, were *intended* to be fully assimilated
at one sitting, and not to be seen twice. If you condemn films for not containing as high a percentage of great art as other media do, you're blaming a cat
for not being a dog: films weren't intended to be as profound or complex as
the other arts."

Most of us already know this fact about films. But suppose we didn't; being ignorant of the intentions behind them, would we then be drawn into
mistaken judgments about them? Not for lack of knowledge of intention. We
would watch, say, several hundred films made between 1930 and 1980, then
compare them with works in other media created since the Renaissance, and
make judgments such as "There are fewer great films than great symphonies"
and "It takes longer to appreciate most symphonies than most films." And
*wouldn't these judgments be true*?

It would also be true that most films were made with different intentions,
but that fact would not alter the truth of these judgments one iota. To explain
why they were made as they were, we would have to know the makers' intentions; but to describe the films, to interpret them, and to evaluate them, we
would need to make no reference at all to intentions. We may praise an artist
for his noble intentions, but we evaluate works of art for what they are, not
for what they were intended to be.

It is worth noting that we often *seem* to be talking about an artist's intentions when in fact we are talking not about his intentions but about his work.
"The poet's intention is these first stanzas was to establish a mood," we say;
but we may know nothing whatever about his intentions, and we may merely
be noting that the first stanzas do establish a certain mood. "The poet wasn't
sincere," we may say, when (the poet being long since dead) we have no way
of ever discovering whether or not he was sincere at the time: what we are
describing, however, is a feature of the poem, such as that the serious tone of
one part of it is not consistently upheld throughout and that a serious subject
is treated elsewhere in the poem in a trivial or facetious way. In such cases,
statements that are ostensibly about the poet's intention are actually about
features of the poem.

On the other hand, we may actually be talking about the artist's intention, using the work of art as (perhaps our only) *evidence* of that intention. Whether the work itself supplies any reliable evidence of that intention is, to say the least, highly disputable. It is all too easy to say that the artist's intention was this or that, when all we have is the work of art and the artist is no longer around to give the lie to our statements.

Sometimes critics distinguish between the intention *of* the poet and the intention *in* the poem.[23] But such locutions are extremely misleading: poem's don't have intentions, poets do. Intentions characterize poets, not poems; if it is features of poems we are talking about, it is wise to describe those features and not mislead our listeners into thinking we are talking about poets' intentions.

## EXERCISES

1. (a) "This piece of driftwood is a nice piece of sculpture." Is this statement a contradiction in terms? According to what theory of art is it, and according to what theory is it not, a contradiction? (b) If a pot of paint accidentally spilled onto the canvas and the painter said, "That makes it better" and left it that way, is the resulting product any the less a work of art than it was before?

2. Would the following count as works of art? Why or why not?

   a. the Great Stone Face

   b. abstract designs produced by a computer

   c. the faces of four presidents on Mt. Rushmore

   d. a bush transplanted from the forest to a large pot in the living room

   e. When the sculptor Branchusi had completed his abstract sculpture *Bird in Space* and it was imported into the United States, the customs authorities refused to call it a work of art (in which case it would enter duty free) because it did not represent any object.

   f. In Paris, Yves Klein's model climbed into a tub of blue paint and impressed her "pose" on a white canvas.

   g. Robert Rauschenberg's *The Bed* (1962) consisted of the artist's own blanket and pillow which he sprayed with color.

   h. Wladislaw Hasior uses only rubbish from which to construct ornaments.

   i. Maholy-Nagy tried to execute an art object by issuing directions over the telephone, so as to "avoid all individual intervention" in the work.

3. "A person already known as an artist (sculptor) buys 120 bricks and, on the floor of what advertises itself as an art gallery, arranges them in a rectangular pile, two bricks high, six across, and ten lengthwise. He entitles it "Bricks." Across town a bricklayer's assistant at a building site takes 120 bricks of the very same kind and arranges them in the very same way. Is the first pile of bricks a work of art, the second not?" (W. E. Kennick, *Art and Philosophy,* p. 116.)

[23] Henry David Aiken, "The Aesthetic Relevance of Artists' Intentions," *Journal of Philosophy,* Vol. 52, No. 24 (November 24, 1955).

4. Evaluate the following as a work of art. "There was a 'solemn installation' of an 'invisible sculpture' behind the Metropolitan Museum of Art. The installation consisted in digging a grave-sized hole and filling it in again. 'It is really an underground sculpture,' said its conceiver, Claes Oldenburg. 'I think of it as the dirt being loosened from the sides in a certain section of Central Park.' The city's architectural consultant, Sam Green, commented on the proceedings: 'This is a conceptual work of art and is as much valid as something you can actually see. Everything is art if it is chosen by the artist to be art. You can say it is good art or bad art, but you can't say it isn't art. Just because you can't see a statue doesn't mean that it isn't there.'" (Quoted by Monroe Beardsley, "The Aesthetic Point of View," in *Contemporary Philosophic Thought,* eds. Howard E. Kiefer and Milton K. Munitz, Vol. 3.)

5. Assess the following definitions: "A work of art is

   a. anything that is a candidate for appreciation."

   b. anything that its creator calls art."

   c. anything that the viewer thinks of as art."

   d. anything that current art theory calls art."

   e. anything that is presented as art."

   f. anything that is indexed or catalogued as art."

6. Now consider these more sophisticated versions.

   a. Anything is a work of art if it is an artifact, a set of the aspects of which has conferred upon it the status of candidate for appreciation by some person or persons acting on behalf of a certain social institution, the art-world (George Dickie). (For example, if a painting by Betsy the chimpanzee is exhibited in Chicago's Field Museum of Natural History, it is not art; but if it is exhibited a few miles away at the Chicago Art Institute, it is. It all depends on its institutional setting.)

   b. What makes the difference between a Brillo box and a work of art consisting of a Brillo box is a certain theory of art. It is the theory that takes it up into the world of art, and keeps it from collapsing into the real object which it is (Arthur Danto). For example, the Brillo box would not have been art fifty years ago, but it is now because art-theory has changed so as to include such things.

7. Could the following be considered works of art, and why?

   a. your private fantasies.

   b. geometrical theorems you've worked out.

   c. a tree that you have grown from a seed, with weeding, fertilizing, and watering.

   d. a litter of pups you have raised from birth when their mother died.

   e. an oyster shell you found on the beach and placed on the mantel of your fireplace.

   f. an empty canvas on which some paint accidentally fell, causing blotches and other formations that you find pleasing.

8. Some years ago an Australian poetry magazine published "some poems by a brilliant new poet." The critics praised them. Later it was revealed that the words of the "poems" had been drawn at random from a glass bowl. (a) Could these be poems, since there was no poet? (b) Now that you know how

the "poems" were made, does this change your opinion of them? Were the critics necessarily mistaken?

9.  "The notion of the artworld is unclear. . . . Do you belong to it? Does a professor of aesthetics belong to it? Do regular museum visitors belong to it? Does the custodian of an art museum belong to it? Or the director's secretary? Or the director's assistant? . . . [Perhaps] the important thing is knowing whether someone is *acting on behalf of* the artworld in the way required by the definition. But is it any easier to determine who is doing this than it is to determine whether someone belongs to the artworld?" (W. E. Kennick, *Art and Philosophy*, p. 115.) Is there, in your opinion, any clear way to decide this question, and why?

10. A George Price cartoon "shows an archaeologist, who has just opened an ancient Egyptian tomb, aiming his flashlight at a wall that, in addition to the expected paraphernalia of hieroglyphs and depictions of gods, holds an exact duplicate of Whistler's famous *Arrangement in Gray and Black,* No. 1 (popularly known as Whistler's Mother)." (W. E. Kennick, *Art and Philosophy,* p. 172.) Would we have two (qualitatively indistinguishable) works of art or one? Would Whistler's painting be a copy of the ancient painter's?

11. Do you have to be able to play, or understand, chess in order to appreciate "The Royal Game"? If you are a "chess freak," will the story mean more to you? Will you be able to appreciate the story more?

12. On translation,

    a.  You have now read "The Royal Game" in English translation from the original German. Would you be able to tell that it was a translation if you hadn't been told?

    b.  If you can, read the story in German and report whether the translation still seems just as good to you as it did before.

    c.  Should foreign language films be offered dubbed in English or with written titles? Give reasons pro or con.

    d.  Should opera be performed in the original language or in English translation? Can you say in general or does it vary from case to case? on what does it depend?

13. Wordsworth wrote five different versions of his *Lyrical Ballads.* Should we accept the last version as the definitive one because it represents "his final intention"?

14. Imagine a poem ten times as difficult to interpret as the most difficult one by T. S. Eliot. Wouldn't we have to know the poet's intentions in order to be able to interpret such a poem?

15. "It is a well-known fact that knowledge of the circumstances surrounding the composition of a work enhances the audience's appreciation. . . . It is because of this that program notes, radio comments, and music appreciation courses are in such demand. To secure such knowledge is one of the important tasks of musical research." (Hans Tischler, "The Aesthetic Experience," *Music Review,* 17 (1956), 200; quoted by Monroe Beardsley, in "The Aesthetic Point of View.") Do you agree, and why?

16. Do you agree or disagree with the following comments on the relation of film to music? "Film is to sight what music is to sound. Most directors treat film merely as prose. They show one thing, then another, then another, and the

sequence shapes into a story, a movie. The form is fundamentally literary. Used well, it is a good, honest style for filmed story-telling, and excellent works of film-as-heightened-prose have been done by its great practitioners, Howard Hawks, John Huston, Sam Fuller, Godard, to mention a few. But at its highest, the nature of film is closer to music, because in film one needn't focus on one thing at a time, as most "prose" directors do; one can be simultaneous, as music is—and as Griffith and Fellini and Welles and *The Elephant Man's* David Lynch know. The nature of film is also closer to music than even to painting or still-photography, simply because film *moves,* and so can have motifs, refrains, major and minor themes interweaving at the same time, in background and foreground, and cadenzas, triots, duets, solos, full choruses and codas. Watching a film is a musical version of seeing—heightened seeing, as music is heightened sound—and to watch a great film is to know the rhythms and harmonies of seeing. (Michael Ventura, in *Los Angeles Weekly,* October 10–16, 1980, p. 11.)

17. Can an interpretation of one work by an artist be supported by citing *other* works by the same artist? Can you resolve some doubt about the meaning of one novel by Conrad by citing another of his novels and then saying "The same man who wrote this novel could never have intended the meaning you suggest in *that* one"?

18. Can one legitimately use previous drafts of the poem or novel as evidence that such-and-such was the author's intention when the work itself is not clear?

19. When Kipling is accused of being racist because of an epithet he uses in referring to an Indian native, are we to infer that Kipling had a racist attitude or only that the speaker (in his poem *Loot*) had this attitude? (Cioffi remarks: "How is this issue to be decided? By an appeal to the text? Isn't it rather our sense of Kipling which will determine the side we come down on? A sense built up not only from the other tales but from his autobiography and other sources as well? Don't these throw a 'field of force' round the work? If it had been written by someone else wouldn't this make a difference to our apprehension of it?")

20. Can an author be mistaken about his own intention? (What does the word "slow" mean in the first line of Goldsmith's poem *The Traveller:* "Remote, unfriended, melancholy, *slow.* Goldsmith said it meant "tardiness of locomotion," but Samuel Johnson contradicted him: "No sir. You do not mean tardiness of locomotion. You mean that sluggishness of mind that comes upon a man in solitude.")

# SELECTED READINGS

1. Principal anthologies of contemporary aesthetics and philosophy of art currently in print:

DICKIE, GEORGE, AND RICHARD SCLAFANI, eds. *Aesthetics: a Critical Introduction.* New York: St. Martin's Press, 1978.

HOSPERS, JOHN, ed. *Introductory Readings in Aesthetics.* New York: Free Press, 1969.

KENNICK, W. E., ed. *Art and Philosophy,* 2nd ed. New York: St. Martin's Press, 1979.

LEVICH, MARVIN, ed. *Aesthetics and the Philosophy of Criticism.* New York: Random House, 1963.

MARGOLIS, JOSEPH, ed. *Philosophy Looks at the Arts,* 2nd ed. Philadelphia: Temple Univ. Press, 1979.

RADER, MELVIN M., ed. *A Modern Book of Aesthetics.* 5th ed. New York: Holt, 1979.

WEITZ, MORRIS, ed. *Problems in Aesthetics.* New York: Macmillan, 2nd ed. 1970.

VIVAS, ELISEO, AND KRIEGER, MURRAY, eds. *The Problems of Aesthetics.* New York: Rinehart, 1953. (Articles reprinted in these anthologies will henceforth be referred to by the names of the editors.)

2. Histories of aesthetics:

BEARDSLEY, MONROE C. *A History of Aesthetics from Classical Greece to the Present.* New York: Collier-Macmillan, 1963.

GILBERT, KATHARINE AND HELMUT KUHN. *A History of Aesthetics.* New York: Macmillan, 1939.

NAHM, MILTON C., ed. *Readings in Philosophy of Art and Aesthetics.* Englewood Cliffs, N.J.: Prentice-Hall, 1975.

SESONSKE, ALEXANDER, ed. *What Is Art? Aesthetic Theories from Plato to Tolstoy.* New York: Oxford Univ. Press, 1965.

3. *What Is A Work of Art?*

AAGAARD-MOGENSEN, LARS, ed. *Culture and Art.* Atlantic Highlands, N.J.: Humanities Press, 1976.

COLLINGWOOD, ROBIN G. *The Principles of Art.* Oxford: Clarendon Press, 1938.

DANTO, ARTHUR. "The Art World," *Journal of Philosophy,* 61 (1964).

DICKIE, GEORGE. "Defining Art," American Philosophical Quarterly, 6 (1969).

DICKIE, GEORGE. *Art and the Aesthetic.* Ithaca, N.Y.: Cornell University Press, 1974, Chapter 1.

GALLIE, W. B. "Art As An Essentially Contested Concept," *Philosophical Quarterly,* 6 (1956), 97–114.

KHATCHADOURIAN, HAIG. "Family Resemblances and the Classification of Works of Art," Journal of Aesthetics and Art Criticism, 28 (1969).

MANDELBAUM, MAURICE. "Family Resemblances and Generalization Concerning the Arts," *American Philosophical Quarterly,* 2, (1965).

MARGOLIS, JOSEPH. *Art and Philosophy.* Atlantic Highlands, N.J.: Humanities Press, 1979, chapters 2–5.

MITIAS, MICHAEL. "The Institutional Theory of the Aesthetic Object." *The Personalist,* 58 (April 1977).

MORAWSKI, STEFAN. *Inquiries Into the Fundamentals of Aesthetics.* Cambridge: M.I.T. Press, 1974, Chapter 2.

PEPPER, STEPHEN. *The Work of Art.* Bloomington: Indiana University Press, 1955, chapter 1.

SCLAFANI, RICHARD. "Art As A Social Institution: Dickie's New Definitions," *Journal of Aesthetics and Art Criticism,* 32 (winter 1973).

SILVERS, ANITA. "The Artworld Discarded," *Journal of Aesthetics and Art Criticism,* 34 (1976).

WEITZ, MORRIS. "The Role of Theory in Aesthetics." *Journal of Aesthetics and Art Criticism,* 15 (Sept. 1956), 27–35. Reprinted in Margolis, Rader, and Weitz.

YANAL, ROBERT J. "The Institutional Theory of the Aesthetic Object: a Reply to Michael Mitias." *The Personalist,* 58 (April 1977).

ZIFF, PAUL. "The Task of Defining A Work of Art," *Philosophical Review,* 62, (1953).

4. The Media of Individual Arts:

*A. Painting*

ARNHEIM, RUDOLF. *Art and Visual Perception.* Berkeley: University of California Press, 1954.

BARNES, ALBERT C. *The Art in Painting.* New York: Harcourt Brace, 1937.

GROSSER, MAURICE. *The Painter's Eye.* New York: Mentor Books, 1951.

LANGER, SUSANNE. *Feeling and Form.* New York: Scribners, 1953, chapters 5–6.

LESSING, GOTTFRIED. *Laokoön.* New York: Liberal Arts Press, 1962. Also in Everyman Library edition.

PANOFSKY, ERWIN. *Studies in Iconology.* London: Oxford University Press, 1939.

WOLFFLIN, HEINRICH. *Principles of Art History.* New York: Dover Publications (no date; English translation first published 1932).

*B. Sculpture*

ADRIANI, BRUNO. *Problems of the Sculptor.* New York: Nierendorf Gallery, 1943.

READ, HERBERT. *The Art of Sculpture.* New York: Pantheon Books, 1955.

RINDGE, AGNES. *Sculpture.* London: Payson and Clarke, 1929.

RODIN, AUGUSTE. *Art.* Many editions.

*C. Architecture*

LECORBUSIER. *Towards A New Architecture.* New York: Payson and Clarke, 1927.

PARKER, DEWITT. *The Analysis of Art.* New Haven: Yale University Press, 1926, chapter 5.

RICHARDS, J. M. *An Introduction to Modern Architecture.* Baltimore: Penguin Books, 1953.

SCOTT, GEOFFREY. *The Architecture of Humanism.* London: Constable, 1914.

WITTKOWER, RUDOLF. *Architecture Principles in the Age of Humanism.* New York: Columbia University Press, 1965.

WRIGHT, FRANK LLOYD. *Modern Architecture.* Princeton: Princeton University Press, 1931.

*D. Music*

COKER, WILSON. *Music and Meaning.* New York: Free Press, 1972.

COPLAND, ARRON. *What To Listen For In Music.* New York: McGraw-Hill, 1939.

MEYER, LEONARD. *Explaining Music.* Berkeley: University of California Press, 1973.

TOCH, ERNST. *The Shaping Forces in Music.* New York: Criterion Music Corp., 1958.

TOVEY, DONALD F. *The Forms of Music.* New York: Meridian Books, 1944.

*E. Literature*

FORSTER, E. M. *Aspects of the Novel.* New York: Harcourt Brace, 1937.

ROSENTHAL, M. L., AND A. J. M. SMITH. *Exploring Poetry.* New York: Macmillan, 1955.

STEVENSON, CHARLES L. "On 'What Is A Poem?'" *Philosophical Review,* vol. 66.

URMSON, J.O. "Literature," and MONROE C. BEARDSLEY, "Philosophy of Literature," in G. Dickie and R. Sclafani, eds., *Aesthetics.* New York: St. Martin's Press, 1978.

WELLEK, RENE, AND AUSTIN WARREN. *The Theory of Literature.* New York: Harcourt Brace, 1942.

*F. Drama*

BENTLEY, ERIC. *The Life Of the Drama.* London: Methuen, 1965.

FERGUSON, FRANCIS. *The Idea of A Theater.* Princeton: Princeton University Press, 1949.

MORGAN, CHARLES. "The Nature of Dramatic Illusion," in Susanne K. Langer, ed., *Reflections On Art.* New York: Oxford University Press, 1961.

*G. Motion Picture*

ARNHEIM, RUDOLF. *Film As Art.* Berkeley: University of California Press, 1957.

CAVELL, STANLEY. *The World Viewed.* New York: Viking Press, 1971.

EISENSTEIN, SERGEI. *The Film Sense.* New York: Harcourt Brace, 1942.

KRACAUER, S. *Theory of Film.* New York: Oxford University Press, 1960.

MANVELL, ROGER. *Film.* Baltimore: Penguin Books, 1946.

PANOFSKY, ERWIN. "Style and Medium in the Motion Picture," *Critique,* I, 3, (1947). Reprinted in Weitz and in Dickie & Sclafani.

5. Contextualism and appreciation:

AIKEN, HENRY D. "The Aesthetic Relevance of the Artist's Intentions." *Journal of Philosophy,* 52 (1955).

CIOFFI, FRANK. "Intention and Interpretation in Criticism." *Proceedings of the Aristotelian Society,* 64 (1963–1964). Reprinted in Margolis.

HUNGERLAND, ISABEL. "The Concept of Intention in Art Criticism." *Journal of Philosophy,* 52 (1955).

KUHNS, RICHARD. "Criticism and the Problem of Intention." *Journal of Philosophy,* 57 (1960).

VIVAS, ELISEO. "Contextualism Reconsidered." *Journal of Aesthetics and Art Criticism,* 18 (1959).

WIMSATT, W. K., AND MONROE C. BEARDSLEY. "The Intentional Fallacy." *Southern Review,* 45 (1946). Reprinted in Margolis and Weitz.

WIMSATT, W. K., AND MONROE C. BEARDSLEY. "The Affective Fallacy." *Southern Review,* 57 (1949).

# 2

# Form in the Arts

There are many things in a painting that we can appreciate. We can appreciate the vividness of its color, the way in which the color harmonies or color contrasts tease the eye, the way in which various curves or figures complement one another here and there throughout the painting, the piling up of masses in this sector to balance a large dominant mass in another, its lean spare uncluttered look, the clean elegant lines that lead our eyes toward the central object of attention in the painting. All these things have to do with what is *presented* to our eyes directly from the canvas—*mediumistic* features. They do not refer beyond themselves to anything else; although some of the qualities are more subtle than others, and may not be experienced till you have looked long and often, they are all there on the canvas to be seen, and seeing them requires no knowledge of objects in the world outside the painting.

But there are other features as well: if the painting is *representational* (that is, representing of people or things), we can appreciate the quality of the representation, the character revealed in the faces, their emotional expressions; we can appreciate not only the emotion registered in the faces, but the emotional quality or feeling-tone of the painting as a whole—calm and subdued, disturbed, melancholy, or carefree; we may also find in the painting *symbols,* in which case we may try to discover that things outside the painting they symbolize (the halo as a symbol of holiness). The painting may even be a vehicle for certain *ideas* which are supposed to be communicated in it. All

100

these features point beyond the painting to things and qualities in the life outside art. These are sometimes called *life-values*.

A simple example may help to clarify the distinction. A circle or oval in a painting is *pre*sented for our attention—the shape is there, on the canvas. If the painting is representational, however, the circular shape may be the representation of a balloon, a globe of the earth, the top of a wastebasket or lampshade, a cantaloupe, or any of hundreds of other things. These things are not presented on the canvas but are *re*presented. The canvas contains a circle, but it does not contain a cantaloupe—it contains only the two-dimensional shape that is a representation of a three-dimensional cantaloupe.

Sometimes this difference is described as the difference between "form" and "content." But this way of putting it is so misleading that it would be wise to rid our talk of this piece of jargon. Form, as we shall see shortly, is not the only mediumistic element in works of art, and, the term "form" will turn out to be multiply ambiguous. As for content, the word means "everything that is in it"—just as the contents of a bucket is everything that's in the bucket; and if so, content would include form as a part of itself! Instead of talking about a "form-content" distinction, it would be much clearer to talk about the difference between *mediumistic* elements and *transmediumistic* elements. The mediumistic elements (sensuous and formal) will be discussed in this chapter; the principal transmediumistic elements—representational, expressive, and ideational—will be discussed in successive chapters.

## 1. SENSUOUS ELEMENTS

The simplest kind of appreciation occurs when we take pleasure in the way in which an object appears to the senses. Some substances are "naturals" for this kind of enjoyment: ivory, jade, gold, marble. It is not that we find these things economically valuable—that of course is a different matter—but that we simply find them pleasant to see and to touch, quite apart from any use to which they can be put. It may be an object of fine art, such as a marble statue; it may be an object of useful art, such as a pot, a chair, a precious stone in a ring; or it may be something in nature, such as a leaf, the snow under one's feet, the ice on a lake. Much of our enjoyment of nature is of this kind: the touch of alabaster, the smell of roses, the taste of wild berries.

Once we appreciate *combinations* of colors, either in nature or in visual art, we are already appreciating relationships, that is, form. But before we get to combinations, like the design of the stripes on a tiger, we may enjoy singly the elements of which the design is composed, such as the wonderful color called "cerulean blue" that comes out of the painter's tube and is sometimes seen in a late-afternoon Mediterranean sky.

We can also appreciate sounds in this way. When we enjoy even a simple melody we are already into form, since a melody is a system of tonal relationships; but without having yet arrived at melody, we can enjoy the sensuous qualities of a single tone—its pitch, its loudness, its tone quality (timbre). Although most of our appreciation of music is as an interplay of forms, tones can be enjoyed for themselves other than in combination. I once thought I had tired forever of Ravel's *Bolero* until I heard it played with the saxophone as the principal solo instrument; the notes played were exactly the same as before, but the peculiar sound quality of the saxophone, which seemed so appropriate to the sensual quality of the composition, made it possible to endure one or two more hearings. The poignant and almost wailing quality of the English horn in its long solo in the Prelude to Act 3 of Wagner's *Tristan und Isolde,* with its overpowering sense of impending doom, could not be duplicated by any other instrument; even with every note the same, the auditory quality and the resultant effect are quite different.

In the art of sculpture the sensuous quality of the medium is very important. Sculptures of living things are often made out of wood, itself an organic substance, rather than from inanimate materials like cement or stone; the sensory qualities, both visual and tactual, are quite different. Rodin allowed copies of his sculptures to be made out of many kinds of material with diverse sensory qualities, apparently believing that as long as the resulting shape was the same it didn't much matter what the statue was made of; but this view of sculpture is no longer widely entertained in the twentieth century.

## 2. FORMAL ELEMENTS

During the first few minutes of listening to a symphonic composition, you may have noticed the way in which the conductor kept all the sections of the orchestra playing in harmony with each other; a few details may have stood out in your mind, such as a few staccato blasts from the trumpets or the gentle glissando of the strings. But something else will have begun to be noticeable: a pattern of development. After a brief introduction, a musical theme will have emerged, which was thrown like a ball from one section of the orchestra to another with a few changes, after which a distinctively different bit of thematic material emerged. The composer has made certain moves—now what is he going to do with them? where will he go from here? The situation is rather like that of a chess game after each player has completed his first few moves. You now wait to see what he does with the material he has introduced. In short, you have become aware of *form.*

When we talk about form in the arts, we are talking about the *relationship* of the parts or elements to each other, the *organization* of the parts into a whole; one might describe the form of a work of art as the way it is organized or put together. We shall try to be more precise about the meaning of the term "form" as we proceed. Meanwhile, to give a feeling for the concept, and gradually work our way into it, we shall consider several criteria—formal criteria—for judging works of art, which have come down through the ages and are almost as old as theory of art itself.

Let us begin with the requirement of *unity,* a concept that has figured prominently in discussions of art from Aristotle's *Poetics* to the present. A work of art must "hang together," "be of one piece," "be a single totality," not like a collection of beads on a string. We can see most easily what is involved in unity by considering its opposite: imagine a play in which there is a main plot and a subplot but in which the two plots never get connected in any way; none of the characters in the one story ever meet any of those in the other, nor do they ever refer to one another. Such a play would be condemned for lack of unity—it might do as two separate plays, but (except in name) it does not come off as one play.

"The Royal Game" has unity. The first part is about one of the two important characters, the second about the other. The story *almost* loses its unity for a while: half way through Part 2, in the long disquisition of Dr. B, we can't help wonder "How is all this going to connect with the chess game we started with?" But suddenly we see the connection when we learn about the book; the unity we thought lost has been restored, and in Part 3 the strands of the story are all tied together.[1]

The requirement of unity can be made more specific by considering this twofold test: (1) Everything that's necessary must be there, and (2) Nothing that isn't necessary may be there. Admittedly the test is somewhat vague; one may ask "Necessary for what?" Different readers may have different ideas about what the story should do or accomplish. Nevertheless, let us ask of "The Royal Game," is everything necessary there? Is there anything that you think should have been included but wasn't? Second, does everything that *was* included belong there? Was there anything irrelevant, anything that you think could have been dispensed with, without damaging the effect of the story? And is there anything that should have been there but wasn't?

It is always possible for two people to agree about general principles but disagree about the particular case: philosophers of art talk about the general principles, and critics apply them (not always consciously) to individual works of art. Some of you might have thought that "The Royal Game" was too detailed, that there was too much characterization for sustaining the plot, that perhaps the description of Dr. B's imprisonment might have been shortened. Others will insist that every detail given adds depth and richness to the story, that the details are very well chosen and heighten our involvement in the lives of the characters. Some readers object to the passages of comment inter-

---

[1] See Exercise 2 and the end of the chapter.

spersed in the narrative, such as the description of chess—"mechanical in operation yet effective only through the imagination; bounded in geometric space though boundless in its combinations; ever-developing yet sterile; thought that leads to nothing; mathematics that produces no result; art without works; architecture without substance . . ."—while others will assert that this adds a depth and philosophical dimension to the story. Doubtless there will always remain a measure of unresolved disagreement about these things: some readers, who want a story always to move fast, will be annoyed at the accumulation of details, whereas others will value this very feature as adding to the vividness and richness of the characterization and the depth of impact of the story.

To take a more familiar case, some readers object to the grave-diggers' scene in Act 5 of *Hamlet* as being irrelevant and disturbing the unity: the characters appear in that one scene only, and sometimes the play is performed (in shortened version) without that scene, with no apparent injury to the plot. On the other hand, it could be replied that "plot isn't everything," that the scene adds depth and is important for setting the mood of the closing act of the tragedy, with its constant preoccupation with death and dying, and that the effective setting of this mood is good enough reason for saying that the scene belongs there, and is better in than out.

The concept of unity is better spelled out if we now add a qualifying adjective, *organic*. A woodpile has a kind of unity—the unity of a collection; you can often remove a piece of wood and leave the rest as it was. Organic unity, as the name suggests, is the kind of unity that is present in a living organism, such as the human body. The various organs in an organism are not *independent* of one another, but are *interdependent;* they work together and cannot function separately. The ideal of organic unity is for every part to be necessary for the functioning of each of the others. No organism, of course, is as completely an organic unity as this. The stomach won't work without the liver, and the liver without the intestines, and none of them will long function without the heart. But it would be an exaggeration to say that your toenail is as necessary to the functioning of your body as your heart is. Some parts, such as the earlobe, can be rather easily dispensed with, some can be dispensed with only with difficulty, others can't be dispensed with at all while the organism remains alive.

Works of art can be more nearly complete organic unities than any organism probably is. It seems really to be true that in some works of art, if you changed even a small part of it you would ruin the whole thing, and often that you would render it much less valuable than it was. Not only can you not omit a line in one of Shakespeare's sonnets, if you omitted a phrase or a word, or substituted a word of your own for another word, you would disfigure the whole poem. It is just *this* combination of words, in just *this* order, that is required—nothing more and nothing less; it is perfect as it is, and any change will either wreck it or disfigure it. Can you change a single word in Dylan Thomas's lines on death?

> Do not go gentle into that good night.
> Old age should burn and rave at close of day.
> Rage, rage, against the dying of the light.

Or try translating it into a foreign language—or even giving a prose summary of it in English!

The same principle applies in the other arts. Try changing one color expanse in a Mondrian painting or the position of one vertical or horizontal line; or just one of those tortured lines in the garment of Christ in El Greco's *Agony in the Garden,* or for that matter one of the rocks in the garden that seem equally agonized. Or try to change one note in the score of a melody; the entire character of the melody is altered. In the famous main theme of the final movement of the Beethoven Ninth Symphony, if you changed the second note, F sharp, to an E, you would reduce a stirring, majestic, and noble theme into a lullaby.

If you take an entire work of art and not just a small section of it like a musical theme, you will usually find that most works of art are not as highly unified as all that. When you have a very long work, such as an epic poem, a novel, or an opera, it is unlikely that the loss or change of one word or note (unless it is in a very crucial place) is going to undo the whole thing; many audiences wouldn't even notice the difference. But in a fairly short work, the principle of organic unity may very well be exemplified to a greater extent than in any biological organism. There is such a delicate balance, the entire work depends so much on each part's being just as it is and where it is, that if you changed one detail all the others would be affected—much as the removal of the kingpin of the arch results in the collapse of the whole arch.

A second principle of form is an expectable counterpoise to unity: namely, *diversity,* or *variety.* The longer a work of art, the more diverse the elements within it. Unity is easy to achieve if there is no diversity: a blank white wall has unity, but it doesn't repay your concentrated attention very long. To remain interesting over a span of time, a work of art must not only be unified, but it must contain a good deal of variety ("difference") within it, held, as it were, in suspension. All great works of art are more complex than they may first appear; and one evidence of this is that, the more you hear/see/read them, the more dividends they yield—you missed most of what was in them the first time round, and would never have dreamed how much you would get out of them by attending to them again and again. We can have this experience because of the extraordinary amount of variety or diversity to be found in works of art. The eighteenth-century English aesthetician Francis Hutcheson put it this way in 1725:

The figures which excite in us the ideas of beauty seem to be those in which there is uniformity amidst variety. There are many conceptions of objects which are agreeable upon other accounts, such as grandeur, novelty, sanctity, and some others. . . . But what we call beautiful in objects, to speak in the mathematical style, seems to be in a compound ratio of uniformity and variety.[2]

And in our own century Roger Fry writes,

The first quality that we demand will be *order,* without which our sensations will be troubled and perplexed, and the other quality will be *variety,* without which they will not be fully stimulated. . . . Unity of some kind is necessary for our restful contemplation of the work of art as a whole, since if it lacks unity we cannot contemplate it in its entirety, but we shall pass outside it to other things necessary to complete its unity.[3]

Often the two criteria are incorporated into one formulation, that of *unity-in-variety* or *diversity-in-unity.* A work of art seems always to be walking a tightrope between unity and diversity. If you invent a melody, and don't know what to do with it, you may just repeat it (A, A) or even repeat it again (A, A, A), thus retaining unity at the expense of diversity. Finally the repetition of the same thing becomes simply boring. (This is what happens to many promising songwriters who can think of a good melody but then don't know what to do with it.) But if you follow one melody with another, and that one by still another, and so on (A, B, C, D), you have achieved diversity all right, but sacrificed unity: there is nothing to connect all these different melodies together into one composition—they are more like a variety of different beads which are united only by the fact that they are placed together on the same string.

Somehow you have to achieve both variety and unity at the same time. It is not without reason that the theme-and-variation device has been so popular: you have a main theme, and then you vary it in different ways, but the variations are always related to the main theme; thus you have both unity (one theme) and diversity (different variations on it). In sonata form, you have one or two or even three main themes, developing each in turn, combining or otherwise integrating them into each other—again achieving unity and diversity at the same time.

If you are comparatively unacquainted with music and want to listen to a simple example of unity-in-variety which will teach you more than any verbal exposition, listen several times to the third movement of Haydn's String Quartet No. 82 (Op. 77, No. 2), which begins with one main theme, then varies it in different ways but never departs far from it, but when it returns it

[2] Francis Hutcheson, *An Inquiry into the Origin of Our Ideas of Beauty and Virtue.* First published in London, 1725; several subsequent editions.

[3] From Roger Fry, "An Essay in Aesthetics," in *Vision and Design* (London: Chatto and Windus, 1920). Emphasis added.

is altered in subtle ways for having passed through the variations; and even when the theme is restated at the end in its original form, one hears it now in the light of the variations through which it has traveled. Most movements in quartets, concertos, and symphonies are more complex than this, for they play with two or more main themes rather than just one—that is why the Haydn movement is a good one to begin with.

Other musical works, while still preserving unity-in-variety, proceed along entirely different developmental lines. Consider, for example, Symphony No. 7 of Sibelius (the entire work is in one movement); at first it seems confusing and quite unintelligible, with an occasional bit of melody emerging from what seems to be a general mist or fog of inchoate orchestral background, then returning to chaos again, with another fragment of melody drifting in and disappearing again, and so on, proceeding with increasing pace and intensity as if toward the vortex of a whirlpool, until in the last few minutes all these scattered fragments which seemed not at all unified at the beginning come together and are integrated with one another in a conclusion of great dramatic power. At first there was only diversity, but in the end it was all unified.

In "The Royal Game" there is, of course, a great deal of diversity—the details of action and characterization pile on one another thick and fast. Yet all, or at least most, of it serves the final unity; like many other literary artists, Zweig was merciless with himself in omitting any detail that seemed to him even on the borderline of irrelevance. But not all readers will resolve the tension between unity and diversity in the same way; some want unity at any (or almost any) cost, some want diversity even if not all of it is incorporated into a final unity. Greek tragedies are relatively short, and considering their brevity they contain a good deal of diversity, but every detail that cannot be incorporated into the unity is scrupulously pared away. Shakespeare's tragedies, which are many times longer, contain a much wider range of diversity. Some would say that all or most of the disparate elements come together in the end, all the better for the greater diversity; others would say, particularly against the background of classical dramas, that Shakespeare's plays are in the end lacking in unity and that, while we get much more "fullness of life" from Shakespeare because of the enormous diversity of characters and situations, we pay a price in lessened unity.

As Aristotle pointed out in the *Poetics,* the first systematic study in theory of art, some art-forms or genres are "by their nature" less unified than others. The epic or saga, to use Aristotle's example, can excusably be much less unified than can something as brief and concentrated as a Greek tragedy. In the *Odyssey,* for example, the plot wanders considerably: first we have the various wanderings of Odysseus, then the adventures of Telemachus, then Odysseus' wife Penelope, and though they all come together in the end, and there are no loose strings there, there are still chapters that aren't much related to other chapters and that could even have been omitted without apparent loss to the remainder of the work.

Diversity at the expense of unity is perhaps illustrated best in the picaresque novel, which is a series of adventures united only by the one main character to whom it all happens. *Don Quixote* is a kind of *reductio ad absurdum* of the picaresque novel—a long chain of comparatively unrelated incidents, in which many could be omitted with no visible damage to the remainder—which is why many readers find the picaresque novel to be artistically defective. Other readers, however, will insist that the whole range of incidents is required to give *Don Quixote* its full and elaborate characterizations, the impression of the chaos and senselessness of the world in which the characters act, and the "richness of life" that results from the endless details of scenes, stories, characters, and (sometimes) author's comments.

Often, as in music, there is one *dominant theme* around which the remainder of the work (or movement) centers—sometimes two such dominant themes. In painting some easily recognizable pattern (a group of lines or a shape) is selected and then varied—but the theme must be recognizable through all its variations.

In Fra Angelico's *Madonna* there is a pair of such themes that interweave and reappear all over the composition. We may pick them up from the curtain which the angels are holding up behind the Madonna. The pattern of this curtain consists of a row of circles alternated with a row of forms consisting of two pairs of straight lines set crosswise like a little grill. Take the circle and the grill as the two *themes* (noticing incidentally the strong linear contrast between them), and observe how they are echoed in variations all through the picture. The circle reappears varied in size in the halos, in the neck-lines, wristbands, and girdles of the angels and the Madonna, in the shapes of their heads. Arcs and elongations of the circles are taken up in the folds and edges of the Madonna's gown and the curtain and the mat, and in the ends of the cushion on which she is sitting. Circles will even be found in the centers of the contrasting grill theme.

Now follow the grill. It reappears on the mat in the form of alternate red and black squares. The alternation of red and black squares on the mat, incidentally, is a variation of the alternation of *red* circles and *black* grills on the curtain. The theme reappears in the half square formed by the angels' arms at right angles to each other, holding up the curtain. It comes out in a central position in the crossed arms of the Madonna. The child's arms form right angles, so does the Madonna's knee and some of the folds in her gown and in the drapery about her.

Just imagine the squares of the mat turned into fleurs-de-lys or violets, and you will see why Fra Angelico made them squares. Go over the picture form by form and imagine some unrelated form in its place, and you will see why the artist was drawn to variation of a theme. He was avoiding confusion. And he was not making exact repetitions of his theme, because he was avoiding monotony. Imagine the grills of the curtain repeated in the mat, or imagine little circles there. These would be passable but not nearly as interesting as the squares. Fra Angelico knew his squares felt right, whether he consciously knew they were variations of the grill pattern or not.

The power of theme-and-variation to keep away monotony is well illustrated in this example. There are practically no limits to the amounts of material that can be kept interesting by this principle. The only limit lies in the selection of a theme which must be simple enough to be taken in quickly and recognized in its variations. But its variations may become as intricate as desired so long as a relationship to the theme is still felt. In fact, there is a very intricate development of the circular theme in the conventionalized plant form developed within the circles on the drapery behind the Madonna.[4]

In this as in most paintings, the unity sought is the unity of the work of art as a whole. The same is true in most stories, novels, and dramas, where we are propelled ever forward toward the conclusion; again the unity is of the work as a whole. In music, by contrast, most of the unity is to be found within each movement, but often there is little or nothing to tie one movement in with the next one. Would you really have "suspected something wrong" if you heard the second movement of Brahms' First Symphony interchanged with the second movement of his Second Symphony? If you already know these symphonies, of course you will detect the change at once. But suppose you had always heard it that way, would you have said, "Something is wrong—this movement belongs in the other symphony"? When thematic material from one movement reappears in another movement, then of course you would detect it soon enough; but usually this is not what happens, and each movement comes to be almost like a complete work of art in itself, detachable enough from the rest of the composition so that you could hear it without the other movements and still appreciate it. Sometimes there is an overall "unity of mood"—Brahms' First Symphony is dramatic, the Second Symphony is lyrical and singing—without any thematic material from earlier movements reappearing in later ones. There can be works of overpowering impact, such as the Symphony No. 2 (*Resurrection*) of Mahler, which is almost a "musical potpourri" of five movements with no very great relation to each other; there is unity within each movement but not much (yet some) overall unity. However, we must be careful about this; in Mahler's Sixth Symphony, for example, there is an overall unity, but it comes home to one only after repeated careful hearings, for the composition is complex, subtle, and multitextured, and many unifying details are so submerged in the powerful cascades of sound that they easily escape one's attention.

Some critics have held that, other things being equal, the more diversity a work of art can contain without sacrificing the unity, the greater is that work of art. Thus, it would be said, *Macbeth,* one of Shakespeare's most concentrated and unified plays (which we have today only in a shortened and somewhat garbled version), is greater than any of his sonnets, because, though both are unified, *Macbeth* contains a greater diversity of elements. Whether or not this is true, however, just as much a matter of dispute as

---

[4] Stephen C. Pepper, "Aesthetic Design," in *Principles of Art Appreciation* (New York: Harcourt Brace, 1949). The Fra Angelico painting is in the National Gallery of Art, Washington, D. C., and is reproduced on the front cover of the companion volume to this work, John Hospers (ed.), *Introductory Readings in Aesthetics* (New York: Free Press, 1969), pp. 61–77. Passage quoted is from pages 53–54 of Pepper's book.

whether unity should be sacrificed to attain greater diversity. It does seem to be true, however, that a work of great simplicity—unified but containing little diversity—will, as a rule, soon exhaust its capacity to keep us interested; consider for example most jukebox tunes, popular today and forgotten tomorrow. At the other extreme, diversity can go too far, even for readers with very retentive memories: a novel two thousand pages long may be a good novel, but it will very likely be more noteworthy for its diversity than for its unity: it is extremely difficult to keep any work of that length before the mind as one whole. Unity is often at odds with diversity—there is a constant tension between the two. When the one is strong, the other tends to be inhibited or curtailed.

Not all portions of a work of art are equally important. Some are indispensable, and others could be changed without damage to the rest. For example, in Robert Frost's "Stopping by the Woods on a Snowy Evening," let us delete the second and third stanzas; the poem now reads

> Whose woods these are I think I know.
> His house is in the village though;
> He will not see me stopping here
> To watch his woods fill up with snow.
>
> The woods are lovely, dark and deep,
> But I have promises to keep,
> And miles to go before I sleep,
> And miles to go before I sleep.

These are the important lines of the poem; the poem thus truncated lacks amplitude, but it is not greatly changed. The middle could have been filled out in various ways, other than the lines that now constitute it, without altering the rest of the poem.

> Consider some of Frost's intermediate lines: "Between the woods and frozen lake/The darkest evening of the year." "The only other sound's the sweep/Of easy wind and downy flake." These are obvious fillers, padding. They sketch in the scenery and provide atmosphere and mood. This is their function. But other lines could perform this function quite as well.[5]
> There is a place for slack lines. Such troughs allow the major lines and images to assert their full value and give reign to the free play of the imagination.[6]

It could even be argued that such a high degree of unity, in which every part is necessary to the whole and no part, however small, could be changed or deleted with impunity, would not be desirable: it might become too op-

---

[5] Catherine Lord, "Unity with Impunity," *Journal of Aesthetics and Art Criticism,* Vol. 25 (fall 1967), 105.

[6] Catherine Lord, "Organic Unity Reconsidered," *Journal of Aesthetics and Art Criticism,* Vol. 22 (spring 1964), 267.

pressive, there would be no breathing space, nothing would stand out. In this light, Henry James's dictum than in every part of a novel there must be something of all the other parts may not even be a counsel of perfection as much as an ideal that does not merit full realization.

In his classic book *The Craft of Fiction,* Percy Lubbock criticizes Tolstoy's *War and Peace* for not being an organic unity: it doesn't have a unified subject. There are actually, he says, two novels here: one is about the human cycle of youth, maturity, and old age in a small group of men and women and their families; the other is the epic of an imperial Napoleonic war and the invasion of Russia. Each of these alone, he says, could have made a great novel. But the two loosely carried along together produce a failure. Nevertheless one could object to this:

> From the point of view of a rigorous organicist, Lubbock is absolutely correct by definition. But from a broader perspective, as a masterly sample of real life and human relations over a wide landscape, vividly exposed with the delights and fascination of verisimilitude, and the contrasts of mood and scene, and the intensification of catharsis—would the novel really have been aesthetically better in the straightjacket of a perfect organic whole?[7]

Another formal principle, closely related to unity but still distinguishable from it, is *development,* or evolution. It occurs primarily in temporal arts—literature, music, film—in which each part succeeds another one in time rather than in the arts of space, where all parts are present simultaneously. In the arts of time, the first part leads into the next, and that in turn into the next, and so on to the end. Acquaintance with each part is necessary for appreciating what follows it; each later part carries within it, so to speak, the accumulated impact of everything that has preceded. Thus you could not, in a five-act play, exchange a scene from Act 2 with a scene from Act 4; if you could, what would be the significance of everything that had gone on in between? To appreciate the present moment, one needs the entire past that has preceded it. The dramatic climactic scene of "The Royal Game" would be quite unintelligible without the careful laying of the groundwork in all the previous incidents. Read by itself without the preceding pages, the last couple of pages would be incomprehensible and quite without impact. You can't "skim off the cream" of a work of art by viewing or hearing just the climax or the conclusion, for it has the cumulative effect that it does only because everything that led up to it was just what it was. (If a person can enjoy a movie entering during the last thirty minutes, and seeing the earlier parts the next time round, what can be said for the movie? or the viewer?)

In Chapter 3 we shall discuss the importance of the formal principle of

[7] Stephen C. Pepper, review of Harold Osborne's *Aesthetics and Art Theory, Journal of Aesthetics and Art Criticism,* Vol. 29 (summer 1971), 545.

development in determining what kinds of actions and characters should be represented in works of narrative art.

## Meanings of "form"

The criteria just described should give some idea of what philosophers of art and art critics are talking about when they mention form, or formal features, of works of art. Form has to do with the many ways in which a work of art is organized or put together, with the way the various parts or elements are *related* to one another. Every complex object, and every collection of objects, has to have *some* form or other—its parts must be related in some way. If you throw a bunch of marbles out of a bag and roll them on the floor, they are going to form some kind of pattern, however complex or chaotic; and whatever arrangement they fall in is their form. Most such arrangements, of course, are of no particular interest aesthetically; what aestheticians are interested in is the *aesthetically desirable* (or "good") arrangements. And that is what unity, variety, development—and other suggested criteria we have not yet mentioned—are all about.

But now we must make a distinction. The form of a work of art can be divided into (1) structure and (2) texture.

Structure is the work's *overall* form—"form in the large," so to speak. The criteria we have been discussing are all structural criteria, because they have to do with the large-scale relations of parts in the *entire* work (or sometimes, as in some musical compositions, the entire movement). For example, the structure of the first movement of Mozart's G Minor Symphony, No. 40 (K. 540), is as follows:

I. Exposition: a-1, a-1; a-2; bridge passage; b-1, b-1; b-2; bridge passage; c-1, c-1; c-2; c-3.

II. Development: d-1; d-2; d-3; returning passage.

III. Recapitulation: a-1, a-1; a-2 (extended); bridge passage; b-1, b-1; b-2; bridge passage; c-1, c-1; c-2; coda.

But that first melody, a-1, the first building block of the structure, itself has parts or component notes. It is only one element (molecule) in the structure, but when you examine it, the molecule is composed of atoms. You might have two movements with the same structure as outlined, but with entirely different melodies a-1, a-2, and so on, and the result would be a symphonic movement quite different from Mozart's. The structure would be the same, but the two movements would be different because the texture would be different. Texture is form-in-the-small; it has to do with the relations of the more minute ("microscopic") parts to one another. If one melody begins on C and goes up to E and G and then high C, and another melody begins on C and goes up to E flat, A flat, and then high C, they are quite different in texture, although in either case they would count as a-1, the opening melody or theme of the movement. In the main theme of the last movement of the Beethoven Ninth Symphony, already discussed, whether the melody goes from F sharp–F sharp–G–A . . .(as now) or F sharp–E–F sharp–G is a matter of immense importance in the character of the melody and indeed of the whole movement, but in the diagraming of the structure it would appear, in either case, simply as a-1.

Structural units are like stones that can be made into a building, a wall, a barbecue pit, and countless other things; the stones are the same, but what they form is different. Differences in texture are like having different kinds of materials of which the building blocks are made: stone, brick, wood, clay, and so on.

Suggested criteria of form almost always have to do with structure. Unity, variety, development, and balance or proportion characterize the entire work (or movement) and have to do with structure. General criteria about texture seem to be impossible to give. What general rule of composition says that you should stick to F sharp for one more note rather than go down to E and then back up to F sharp again? Thus, although texture is immensely important, it is extremely difficult to set down general rules for it. We shall return to this in Chapter 7.

The distinction between structure and texture is not a sharp one. It can be stated quite clearly in music, since there is a rather clearly defined unit, a theme or melody, of which the structure consists of its development and the texture consists of its inner parts (or "infrastructure"). In literature the distinction is less sharp because there is no clearly defined unit to use: shall it be a stanza, a paragraph, a line? Although the distinction is vague, it can still be made: whether this word should be followed by that word is a matter of texture; whether this stanza or chapter jars upon the overall unity, when considered in relation to the other stanzas or chapters, is a matter of overall structure. In visual arts it is even more difficult to find a unit: how large or how small a segment of the painting must it be to count as texture? Your best practical test will be this: if your interest is in a part or portion of the work, like the head of the statue or the folds of the Madonna's cloak in Fra Angelico's painting, your interest is in texture; but if you are concerned with the painting as a whole, to determine whether a certain formal quality is present overall, your interest is in structure.

A further distinction must now be made: that between *abstract* form and *individual* form. When we speak, in logic, about the form of an argument, we are always talking about abstract form—about a certain structure that an argument has. Thus, any argument of the form

If A then B
If B then C,
Therefore,
If A then C

is valid, regardless of what the A's, B's, and C's are, "If all men are mortal and if Socrates is a man, then Socrates is mortal" and "If all mammals are four-legged and all dogs are mammals, then all dogs are four-legged" are both valid arguments because they have exactly the same logical form. It is in this sense, "abstract form," that we speak of the sonata form in music and the sonnet form in poetry: works in these "forms" all have the same *kind* of structure. They don't, however, have the *same* structure: the Mozart movement outlined earlier has a different structure from most other symphonic movements, but since it shares with many other movements the feature of exposition–development–recapitulation, it has, along with the others, the abstract form of the sonata.

But isn't the structural outline of the Mozart movement given also an abstract form, since, as we already indicated, different movements might possess exactly that same structure? Yes, it too could be called an "abstract form," only *less* abstract (that is, more specific); but form consists of texture as well as structure, and even if the structures were the same, the textures of the two movements would be different, since the themes which constituted the building blocks of the structure would be different.

When we talk about the form of a work of art, we mean both its structure and its texture. Since at least one of these (and usually both) is different in each work of art, each work of art has a different *individual* form: the form (structure and texture together) of no two works of art is identical. When you talk about the form of a work of art in sufficient detail, every work of art has a different form, that is, a different individual form. If two works of art had exactly the same structure and texture, they would be identical works of art.

## 3. FORMALISM IN THE ARTS

Thus far nothing has been said about the importance of form in the arts, in comparison with other characteristics of art. The theory of art known as *formalism,* however, says that form is all-important. To the question "What makes *good* art?" the formalist replies, "Form alone." To the question "What features of a work of art are relevant to a judgment of aesthetic value upon the work?" the formalist replies, "Formal features are the only ones that are relevant"; that is, *nothing* else matters, nothing else is required. Form is not only necessary, it is sufficient.

### Formalism in painting

Criteria we have already discussed, such as unity, have been championed since ancient times without any of its champions' declaring that formal considerations were the only ones to be considered in evaluating works of art. The modern art critic Clive Bell, in his book *Art* (1914), does make this claim, at least for the visual arts; yet he does not explicitly subscribe to any of the specific criteria of form already discussed. There is only one criterion he does discuss, which he says is *the* one and only test of good art wherever and whenever it occurs, and that is the presence of a quality in works of art which he calls "significant form."

What then is this quality, this significant form? The name is certainly misleading, for although the quality Bell has in mind is significant in the popular sense of being *important* (as in "This is a significant development"), it is not significant in the literal sense of *signifying* anything. According to Bell, the world of art and the world of life are utterly divorced from one another, and the features we should find valuable in a work of art are not those we find valuable in the world outside art, not even in nature. The valuable quality in art—significant form—signifies nothing, represents nothing, reproduces nothing that exists in the world of nature or human life. What counts is what is *pre*sented on the canvas, never a *re*presentation of anything.

Most people, says Bell, are totally mistaken in their approach to art. They treat pictures much as if they were photographs; they judge art by its resemblance to reality. "Instead of going out on the stream of art into a new world of aesthetic experience, they turn a sharp corner and come straight home to the world of human interests. For them the significance of a work of art depends on what they bring to it; no new thing is added to their lives, only the old material is stirred." But they have been looking for the wrong thing; the unique experience they could get out of art comes not from its likeness to anything in the world but from its difference from it. What is worthwhile in art comes not from any connection between what is in art and what is in the world.

Nevertheless most painting through the ages has been representational: it has contained representations of people, buildings, landscapes, skies, water. Is this a condemnation of this entire body of visual art? No, says Bell,

> Let no one imagine that representation is bad in itself. A realistic form may be as significant, in its place as a part of the design, as an abstract. But if a represen-tative form has value, it is as form, not as representation. The representative elements in a work of art may not be harmful; always they are irrelevant. For to appreciate a work of art we need bring with us nothing from life, no knowledge of its ideas and affairs, no familiarity with its emotions. Art transports us from the world of man's activity to a world of aesthetic exaltation. For a moment we are shut off from human interests; our anticipations and memories are arrested; we are lifted above the stream of life. The pure mathematician rapt in his studies knows a state of mind which I take to be similar, if not identical.[8]

We do need, in the appreciation of visual art, (1) a sense of form and color and (2) a knowledge of three-dimensional space.

---

[8] Clive Bell, *Art* (London: Chatto and Windus, 1914), pp. 25–26.

This bit of knowledge, I admit, is essential to the appreciation of many great works, since many of the most moving forms ever created are in three dimensions. To see a cube or a rhomboid as a flat pattern is to lower its significance, and a sense of three-dimensional space is essential to the full appreciation of most architectural forms. Pictures which would be insignificant if we saw them as flat patterns are profoundly moving because, in fact, we see them as related planes. If the representation of three-dimensional space is to be called "representation," then I agree that there is one kind of representation which is not irrelevant.[9]

Representation may help us "get into" a painting, but its value as art is never its value as representation. In fact, says Bell, it can be dangerous, both for painters and for viewers:

A painter too feeble to create forms that provide more than a little aesthetic emotion will try to eke that little out by suggesting the emotions of life. To evoke the emotions of life he must use representation. Thus a man will paint an execution, and, fearing to miss with his first barrel of significant form, will try to hit with his second by raising an emotion of fear and pity. But if in the artist an inclination to play upon the emotions of life is often the sign of a flickering inspiration, in the spectator a tendency to seek, behind form, the emotions of life is a sign of defective sensibility always. It means that his aesthetic emotions are weak or, at any rate, imperfect. Before a work of art people who feel little or no emotion for pure form find themselves at a loss. They are like deaf men at a concert. They know that they are in the presence of something great, but they lack the power of apprehending it. They know that they ought to feel for it a tremendous emotion, but it happens that the particular kind of emotion it can raise is one that they can feel hardly or not at all. And so they read into the forms of the work those facts and ideas for which they are capable of feeling emotion, and feel for them the emotions that they can feel—the ordinary emotions of life. When confronted by a picture, instinctively they refer back its forms to the world from which they came. They treat created form as though it were imitated form, a picture as though it were a photograph.[10]

So much for the negative aspect. Significant form has nothing to do with representation of things in the world, or of expression of the emotions of life (love, hate, joy, sadness), or of the ideas of men in relation to reality. It has to do with formal properties of the painting, and these only. But which formal properties? There are billions of formal combinations possible in a painting—for instance, having a set of twelve half-inch-long ovals in the left-hand corner and nothing at all in the rest of the painting. But not all such combinations would be considered aesthetically worthy—the one just described, for example; in fact very few of them would be. What then distinguishes those combinations of colors and shapes and masses which exhibit the praiseworthy quality of "significant form" from that vast majority of formal combinations that lack it?

[9] *Ibid.*, p. 27.
[10] *Ibid.*, pp. 28–29.

No answer is given to this crucial question, at least not in words, because according to Bell, and his formalist colleague Roger Fry, no answer *can* be given in words. What they attempt repeatedly to do is to show us paintings and then point out features of these paintings, to try to *show* us the quality they have in mind; but the quality itself they take to be indefinable. You can show examples of it to others and hope that they will grasp what you are talking about, but you cannot define it in words, only "ostensively" (by showing).

Before we reject the entire view out of hand, saying "This sounds like a copout," we should remind ourselves that what Bell says of "significant form" is surely true of many words and phrases in language. You cannot define "red" for me in such a way that if I have never seen it your definition will lead me to recognize it when I do see it. You can point to it, and if I am not blind or color-blind I shall see what color it is you mean; but if I do not see it for myself, I shall never know what the color you are pointing to looks like. The same is true of "inner" sensations: I will never know what it feels like to be afraid, if I have never felt fear myself, no matter how much you may try to explain it to me in words. The fact that a word cannot be defined verbally (by means of other words) is not by itself an objection to its introduction into the language. Indeed, some words must be definable by other means than words, else how would we have learned our very first words?

Still, there is a problem with significant form that does not exist with red. We look at the same portion of the same object and you thus teach me—by showing—the meaning of the word "red." But if you point to some lines in a painting and say "That's significant form," and I see nothing but a series of colors and shapes, I still have not learned the meaning of the expression "significant form."

Perhaps the answer lies not in pointing to the lines in the painting but in trying to describe, or somehow elicit, a certain kind of emotional *response* to the painting. And, indeed, Bell says that the presence of significant form in a painting gives rise to a very special kind of response, which he calls "the aesthetic emotion." "By 'significant form,'" he says, "I mean arrangements and combinations that move us in a particular way." Very well—what way? By evoking us the aesthetic emotion. And what is the aesthetic emotion? One answer we get is that it is the emotion we feel in response to a quality of the object called significant form. But this answer of course is entirely unhelpful: A is defined in terms of B, and B is defined in terms of A.

However, Bell does say some things about "the aesthetic emotion" which may give an idea of what it is like—it cannot be defined any more than can significant form, but at least it can be described sufficiently so that we know where, in the area of feeling-experience, to seek it. Let us not expect too much: after all, is there *any* emotion whose nature you can communicate to someone else if that person has never experienced it? It is an experience of great intensity; the experience has nothing to do with the objects or emotions of life; and it is a response to the combinations of lines and colors in works of visual art; and we can experience it only when seeing works of art. Most people never reach this high eminence; with them, "only the old material is stirred." For most people, seeing a painting is associational: it triggers memories, recognition of objects and events, but nothing fundamentally different from what they experience in the world around them. Most people live in

> the snug warm foothills of humanity. It is a jolly country. No one need be ashamed of enjoying himself there. Only no one who has ever been on the heights can help feeling a little crestfallen in the cozy valleys. And let no one imagine, because he has made merry in the warm tilth and quaint nooks of romance, that he can even guess at the austere and thrilling raptures of those who have climbed the cold, white peaks of art.[11]

If that doesn't ring a bell, what more can be said? One can turn to *examples,* as Bell does constantly in *Enjoying Painting* and *Landmarks in 19th Century Painting,* and Fry in *Transformations* and *Vision and Design,* and try to help us see (or feel) the quality from the description of the examples.

Fry first examines a number of paintings in which the psychological appeal—its subject-matter and its effect upon us—is strong, the story being told is vivid and dramatic (e.g., Brueghel's *Christ Carrying the Cross*), but the formal qualities are largely absent; such paintings he calls "literary" as opposed to "plastic," since he believes that the depiction of such events is better handled by works of literature than by painting. Then he examines some paintings which, though they do have subject-matter taken from life, are noteworthy for their formal achievements more than for their representational ones. For example, on Daumier's *Gare St. Lazare* (a painting of the central Paris railroad station),

> the first impression . . . is of the imposing effect of the square supports of the arcade, the striking and complicated silhouette of the man to the right, the salience of the centre figure so firmly planted on his feet, and the contrast of all this with the gloomy space which retires to the left, and finally the suggestion of wide aerial spaces given by the houses glimpsed to the right . . .
> The ample block made by the colonel's figure creates the chief salience and divides the space left to right satisfactorily—or nearly so, for I find myself always wondering whether it should not be a little further to the left for perfect balance; nor is it after all quite big enough as volume to fulfill the function it has to perform. For this it should be fused more closely with some other mass to the left instead of being, as it is, rather sharply cut off from the light on the pious father, whose forms, thus cut into, are rather meagre and insignificant. And this failure in plastic completeness seems actually due to Daumier's desire to bring out more clearly this particular dramatic incident . . .
> One of the hardest plastic problems of such a scene is due to the fact that human beings are all of about the same height and that a crowd produces a rec-

---

[11] *Ibid.,* pp. 32–33.

tangular mass which it is very difficult to relate significantly with the architectural setting. Daumier was clearly conscious of this . . . and the seated peasants are an excellent device to break this monotony, as is also the space left between them and the colonel which invites the eye to break into the too monotonous mass by a diagonal receding movement. [12]

There is more, but let us turn to Fry's analysis of one of Poussin's minor paintings, *Ulysses Discovering Achilles Among the Daughters of Lycomedon:*

First the curious impression of the receding rectangular hollow of the hall seen in perspective and the lateral spread, in contrast to that, of the chamber in which the scene takes place. This we see to be almost continuously occupied by the volumes of the figures disposed around the circular table, and these volumes are all ample and clearly distinguished but bound together by contrasted movements of the whole body and also by the flowing rhythm set up by the arms, a rhythm which, as it were, plays over and across the main volumes. Next, I find, the four dark irregular openings at the end of the hall impose themselves and are instantly and agreeably related to the two dark masses of the chamber wall to right and left, as well as to various darker masses in the dresses. We note, too, that the excessive symmetry of these four openings is broken by the figure of one of the girls, and that this also somehow fits in with the slight asymmetry of the dark masses of the chamber walls. So far all our interests have been purely plastic. What the picture is about has not even suggested itself. . . . We are not likely to get much for our pains. The delight of the daughters in the trinkets which they are examining is of such dull conventional elegance that they remind me of the desolating effect of some early Victorian children's stories; nor is Ulysses a more convincing psychological entity, and the eager pose of his assistant is too palpably made up because the artist wanted to break the rectangle and introduce a diagonal leading away from the upright of Ulysses. Finally, Achilles acts very ill the part of a man suddenly betrayed by an overwhelming instinct into an unintentional gesture. Decidedly, the psychological complex is of the meagrest, least satisfactory, kind, and the imagination turns from it, if not with disgust, at least with relief at having done with so boring a performance. We return to the contemplation of the plasticity with the conviction that our temporary excursion into the realm of psychology has led us nowhere. But on the other hand our contemplation of plastic and spatial relations is continually rewarded. We can dwell with delight on every interval, we accept the exact situation of every single thing with a thrilling sense of surprise that it should so exactly satisfy the demands which the rest of the composition sets up. How unexpectedly, how deliciously right! is our inner ejaculation as we turn from one detail to another or as we contemplate the mutual relations of the main volumes to the whole space. And this contemplation arouses in us a very definite mood, a mood which . . . has nothing whatever to do with psychological entities, which is as remote from any emotions suggested by the subject, as it would be if I listened to one of Bach's fugues. Nor does the story of Ulysses enter into this mood any more than it would into the music if I were told that Bach had composed the fugue after reading that story. . . . The story of Achilles was merely a pretext for a purely plastic construction. [13]

[12] Roger Fry, *Transformations* (London: Chatto and Windus, 1926), p. 17.
[13] *Ibid.*, pp. 20–22.

Sometimes it is the psychological or dramatic value of the paintings that appeals to the painter's contemporary audience, but if his painting endures through the ages it is usually because of the formal qualities, appreciation of which requires no knowledge of a particular time or place. For El Greco's contemporaries there was a strong psychological appeal in his paintings: "those moods of extravagant pietistic ecstasy . . . those abandoned poses, those upturned eyes brimming with penitential tears . . .". Today it is not these features that make us return again and again with satisfaction to the works of this great Spanish master, but rather that El Greco had an over-mastering sense of form, and the formal satisfaction that can be gleaned from his paintings is immense. The life-values have "evaporated," to use Fry's expression, but the formal values endure through time. Formal values are the ones that all works of great art have in common, no matter when or where they were created.

> When Mr. Okakura, the government editor of *The Temple Treasures of Japan,* first came to Europe, he found no difficulty in appreciating the pictures of those who from want of will or want of skill did not create illusions but concentrated their energies on the creation of form. He understood immediately the Byzantine masters and the French and Italian primitives. In the Renaissance painters, on the other hand, with their descriptive preoccupations, their literary and anecdotic interests, he could see nothing but vulgarity and muddle. The universal and essential quality of art, significant form, was missing, or rather had dwindled to a shallow stream, overlaid and hidden beneath weeds, so the universal response, aesthetic emotion, was not evoked. It was not until he came on to Henri Matisse that he again found himself in the familiar world of pure art.[14]

Once in a great while there is a painter who possesses an unusual ability to render *both* formal and psychological values; according to Fry, Rembrandt is an example of this. He analyzes such paintings of Rembrandt as *Parable of the Hidden Talent* and *Christ before Pilate* to show that both kinds of features occur in high degree; and when this happens, says Fry, a *tension* is set up between them. "How can we keep the attention equally fixed on the spaceless world of psychological entities and relations, and upon the apprehension of spatial relations? What in happens is that we shift our attention backwards and forwards from one to the other," in a kind of polarization of attention. "I do not know," concludes Fry, "whether the world would not have gained had Rembrandt frankly divided his immoderate genius into a writer's and a painter's portion and kept them separate."

The fact that a painter's works are entirely representational tells us nothing one way or the other about whether he is a formalist; he may use representation in order to enhance form, or simply use it as "a peg to hang his form on." Consider what the painter Marc Chagall says about his own work:

[14] Clive Bell, *op. cit.,* pp. 36–37.

Please defend me against people who speak of "anecdote" and "fairytales" in my work. A cow and a woman to me are the same—in a picture both are merely elements of a composition. In painting, the images of a woman or of a cow have different values of plasticity—but not different poetic values. As far as literature goes, I feel myself more "abstract" than Mondrian or Kandinsky in my use of pictorial elements. "Abstract" in the sense that my painting does not recall reality. . . . In the case of the decapitated woman with the milk pails, I was first led to separating her head from her body merely because I happened to need an empty space there. In the large cow's head in *Moi et le Village* I made a small cow and a woman milking visible through its muzzle because I needed that sort of form, there, for my composition. Whatever else may have grown out of these compositional arrangements is secondary.[15]

On the other hand, when a painter's work is nonrepresentational, one should not assume that he is a formalist. Consider what Mondrian says about his own work:

Impressed by the vastness of nature, I was trying to express its expansion, rest, and unity. At the same time, I was fully aware that the visible expansion of nature is at the same time its limitation; vertical and horizontal lines are the expression of two opposing forces; these exist everywhere and dominate everything; their reciprocal action constitutes "life" . . .[16]

One might object to this, of course, by saying that the painter's works are formalistic even though he himself eschewed formalism: his intention to do X doesn't assure that he has achieved X, and it is we as observers of his work who can determine what he has achieved, regardless of what he intended to achieve or said that he achieved. If viewers of his works find the principal value or the only value of his works to lie in interesting formal combinations, then that is what he achieved, regardless of what he, the painter, said or intended.

Still, in Mondrian's case it is far from clear that the bulk of critical comment would classify his work as formalistic. Consider the following comment:

Mondrian's abstractions are exercises in optical balance. Around an imaginary center the primary colors black, red, and yellow, to which he limited his palate, are carefully equalized in their placing, values, intensity, and amount. Thus the eye is drawn equally over the whole picture's surface. This gives the effect of dynamic movement held in tension.[17]

Is this a comment on Mondrian's work as formalistic? If the answer is not clear, this may be because it is not entirely clear what range of comments is to

[15] Marc Chagall, quoted in "An Interview with Marc Chagall" by James Johnson Sweeney, *Partisan Review,* Winter 1944, 90.

[16] Piet Mondrian, "Toward the True Vision of Reality," pamphlet published by the Valentine Gallery, New York, No date.

[17] John Walker, *The National Gallery of Art* (New York: George Abrams, Inc. 1974), p. 604.

be counted as "formalistic." If a painter's work is characterized by "dynamic movement held in tension," is this a formal feature, or a "life-value" which is achieved through, or by means of, the combination of forms?

That works of art present complex combinations of forms, few would deny. That works of art do *only* this, that their sole value as art lies in this, only formalists would contend. Here, for example, is a typical statement (one of thousands) about painting, in this case the works of Renoir, which implicitly denies the formalist thesis:

> His painting catches the spirit of youth and springtime and vitality; he sees and draws forth the joyous and glamorous in the world. . . The ornamental motif in evidence in Renoir is so fused with the structural elements that an enriched plastic form emerges. The picture sheds light upon what is represented, and this revelation of the world has a value which, though in the strict sense illustrative, is truly plastic or pictorial, not at all "literary."
>
> . . .So far as there is appeal to such sentiments as sorrow, pity, wonder, awe, irony, contempt, a painting may be termed an illustration, though not in any derogatory sense. Confusion of values arises only when the spectator is moved, not by what the artist shows him, but by what he does *not* show him—the historical event.[18]

Indeed, the majority of painters—and their audiences—throughout history have not been exclusively interested in form:

> If the artist is interested *merely* in the "pure" formal relations of the human face, if he is interested, that is, simply in the general emotional values of plastic forms and their relations, he is not painting a *human* face at all. His subject-matter is merely a general arrangement of plastic forms, which, as it happens, bears some resemblance to a human face. It is not a matter of the psychological factor being "emphasized" less; it is a case of the psychological factor not existing at all for the artist. But it is a strained and unnatural attitude.
>
> Of course the painter is interested in the expressiveness of visual *forms*. But he is interested in their *expressiveness*. The forms are "significant." And what does a human face express more definitely than human character? Surely the artist has more before him than "lines, planes, and volumes." Surely, if he is not ridden by theories, he is interested in character. Not the disembodied, purely mental character which is the object of the psychologist, but, once again, character plastically expressed in a face which interests him. If this interest can in some sense be called dramatic, it will not be true to say that the "dramatic" painter will give emphasis to ultra-plastic values, in the sense of values outside and independent of the plasticity. Rather, psychological values will become apprehended plastically.[19]

Louis A. Reid has attacked the formalism of Bell and Fry, denying Fry's allegation that, when there are formal ("plastic") elements in a painting and

[18] Albert C. Barnes, *The Art in Painting* (New York: Harcourt Brace, 1937), p. 25.

[19] Louis Arnaud Reid, *A Study in Aesthetics* (London: Allen & Unwin, 1931), p. 321.

also dramatic (representational) elements, there is a tension set up between them. This may be the case at the beginning of one's appreciation, but after a while the two elements tend to *fuse* in our experience, as two metals fuse under intense heat. This view has been called the *fusion theory*.

It is not that we are interested in two things, side by side. . . . When I look aesthetically at Verocchio's *Colleoni* I am not in the least interested in the character which the gentleman on the horse originally possessed. Yet I cannot but feel braced up and inspired by the intense vigor of character which is embodied in every inch of horse and man. Or when I see the fresco (in the Arena Chapel at Padua) of *Joachim Retiring to the Sheep-fold,* it may be that my first interest is psychological, or it may be that it is plastic (in my own case it was the latter). But in a full appreciation I cannot possibly cut out one or other element. *In the whole, each becomes transformed.* There is not, when the experience is complete and mature, psychological interest *and* plastic interest. There is just the plastic-psychological expressiveness of the forms of the dignified old man with head bent, enwrapt in his mantle, in contrast to the different plastic-psychological expressiveness of the naïve-looking shepherds who come to meet him.[20]

Fry said that in representational painting the representational values "evaporate"—they soon lose their interest—remember his examples of El Greco and Poussin. Reid replies that this indeed tends to be true when the two remain separate, when the two are not "fused": "It is only where there are elements of external allusion and mere illustration, that psychological elements will tend to 'evaporate.'"

Mr. Fry, I think, is sometimes guilty of seeking after a too great simplicity of aesthetic experience. The aesthetic experience is (even when "pure") a complex experience and, even when much psychological fusion occurs, a complexity of meaning remains. This complexity must be fused and unified aesthetically, but aesthetic fusion does not mean the disappearance of the parts. The aesthetic fusion, or assimilation or unification of parts, must simply be accepted as a fact which is irreducible.

To say all this is not to deny that the emphasis in different works may be on different things, or that in the same work the focus of our interest may not shift about. Indubitably the focus does shift. This does not mean the same thing as that of which Mr. Fry is speaking when he speaks of the "shifting of attention." In poetry the images and ideas may be an accompaniment of the delightful words; or the ideas and images may be the focus, and the sound of the words their accompaniment. In representative painting we may now be interested in the character-aspect . . . and now in the formal aspect. . . . But the "shifting" is not from *mere* "dramatic," *mere* "psychological interest, to *mere* formal interest. It is only, if the experience be an aesthetic one, an emphasis on aspects of a whole, in which one aspect modifies and colors the others.[21]

[20] *Ibid.,* p. 321.
[21] *Ibid.,* p. 324.

A fusion is not like a mixture; when two elements are mixed, they retain their own distinctive properties; but when they are fused (chemically combined, as it were), like hydrogen and oxygen in water, we have a new complex of properties in which the elements are no longer separable. As Reid says in a later work,

> Watch yourself actually appreciating this picture—in relation of the grey moonlit house to the green shadows in contrast to the almost black background, the way the shadows lick, like tongues, over the grass slopes in front of the houses, the way in which the complex details of the patterns weave into a whole with a kind of liquid unity—and you find it is quite impossible to distinguish between the experience of the painted shapes, and their meaningfulness; their meaning is embodied in them. In contrast to this, other symbols are not only clearly distinguishable from their meanings but are separable from them. The sentence is separable from the proposition.[22]

Indeed, it may be only when such a fusion of elements occurs that the most worthwhile experiences of art are attained.

> To create an effective pattern of line and color is something; if line and color are made instrumental to massiveness, to distance, to movement, that is an important addition; if the dynamic masses in deep space are so composed and interpreted as to render the spirit of place in landscape, as in Claude or Constable, of religious elevation, as in Giotto, of drama and power, as in Tintoretto, of poignant humanity, as in Rembrandt, the total result attains or approaches the highest summits of artistic achievement.[23]
>
> Take from Mozart his gaiety suddenly breaking off into solemnity, from Watteau his sensual melancholy, from Chardin his love of common things . . . and you will no doubt be left with valuable relations of pure form, but you will no longer have Mozart, Watteau or Chardin.[24]

As a historical phenomenon, formalism was a useful movement. It was a reaction against the nineteenth century's exclusive emphasis on the details of what is represented in works of art. It called the public's attention to a vitally important aspect of works of art which most people had ignored or failed to make themselves aware of. But as the whole account of what is valuable in works of art, it is incomplete: it has swung the pendulum too far the other way. It considers irrelevant both the representational and symbolic content of works of art, which is manifestly there to be appreciated, and the humanly expressive character of works of art as well. These aspects of art will be discussed in the ensuing chapters.

[22] Louis Arnaud Reid, *Meaning in the Arts* (London: Allen & Unwin, 1969), pp. 70–71.

[23] Albert C. Barnes, *The Art in Painting* (New York: Harcourt Brace, 1937), p. 49.

[24] Charles Mauron, *Aesthetics and Psychology* (London: The Hogarth Press, 1935), pp. 27–28.

Formalism in music

That formal qualities are the sole criterion of merit in a work of art is a view that has been applied not only to visual art but to music. Clive Bell himself, though he disclaims any expertise in music, has this illuminating passage about his view of music:

> Sometimes, at a concert, though my appreciation of the music is limited and humble, it is pure. Sometimes, though I have a poor understanding, I have a clean palate. Consequently, when I am feeling bright and clear and intent, at the beginning of a concert for instance, when something that I can grasp is being played, I get from music that pure aesthetic emotion that I get from visual art. It is less intense, and the rapture is evanescent; I understand music too ill for music to transport me far into the world of pure aesthetic ecstasy. But at moments I do appreciate music as pure musical form, as sounds combined according to the laws of a mysterious necessity, as pure art with a tremendous significance of its own and no relation whatever to the significance of life; and in those moments I lose myself in that infinitely sublime state of mind to which pure visual form transports me. How inferior is my normal state of mind at a concert. Tired or perplexed, I let slip my sense of form, my aesthetic emotion collapses, and I begin weaving into the harmonies, that I cannot grasp, the ideas of life. Incapable of feeling the austere emotions of art, I begin to read into the musical forms human emotions of terror and mystery, love and hate, and spend the minutes, pleasantly enough, in a world of turbid and inferior feeling. At such moments, were the grossest pieces of onomatopoetic representation—the song of a bird, the galloping of horses, the cries of children, or the laughing of demons—to be introduced into the symphony. I should not be offended. Very likely I should be pleased; they would afford new points of departure for new trains of romantic feeling or heroic thought. I know very well what has happened. I have been using art as a means to the emotions of life and reading into it the ideas of life. I have been cutting blocks with a razor. I have tumbled from the superb peaks of aesthetic exaltation to the snug foothills of warm humanity.[25]

"Sounds combined according to the laws of a mysterious necessity"—that is what music is, according to Bell. This "mysterious necessity" has nothing to do with the representation of scenes from life or the expression of the emotions of life; to appreciate music one must put all such things out of one's mind. After a certain succession of tones in a melody, a certain tone is "called for" to follow it and other ones are not; what more can one say? Can *you* say, he might challenge us, what makes even a simple melody good or bad? or what makes the melodies from Mozart's *Magic Flute* perennially captivating and moving, whereas most melodies are easily forgettable? Are there any general rules that you could lay down? Isn't "sounds combined according to the laws of a mysterious necessity," however mysterious, about as definite as you can get?

[25] Clive Bell, *op. cit.*, pp. 30–32.

The two nineteenth-century writers who defended most systematically the tenets of musical formalism, and whose writing is of undiminished value to this day, are Edmund Gurney, whose great work *The Power of Sound* came out for musical formalism in 1880, and Eduard Hanslick, whose shorter and better known *The Beautiful in Music* appeared in its final edition in 1894. Most of the pages in both books are devoted to showing why the value of works of music is not related to the expression of feelings—a matter we shall discuss in Chapter 4. Most of the "punch" of what these writers have to say will have to wait until the topic of expression is treated in that chapter. The formalist thesis, the only one of relevance here, is that "in music our attention is centered on forms which are for us the unique inhabitants of a perfectly unique world, disconnected from the interest of visible things.[26]

"The ideas which a composer expresses are primarily of a purely musical nature, " says Hanslick (*The Beautiful in Music,* Chap. 3). Music is, in Hanslick's phrase, a *moving arabesque;* it is the auditory analog of a kaleidoscope in which the patterns constantly shift and move, except that in music, unlike the visual kaleidoscope, they generate momentum and move toward climax and resolution. The combination of "sounds combined according to the laws of a mysterious necessity" gives us, in Gurney's phrase, a "peculiarly musical beauty," which inhabits a world apart, and draws none of its powerful effects from the objects and emotions of life. To put it in the modern jargon, music is *autonomous*—sufficient unto itself, drawing and requiring nothing from outside it for its appreciation—and not *heteronomous,* which it would be if in order to appreciate it one had to draw on nonmusical experiences.

Late in life the nineteenth-century painter James MacNeill Whistler changed the names of many of the paintings he had painted. His famous *Portrait of His Mother* became entitled *Harmony in Grey and Black;* one of his many Battersea Bridge paintings became *Harmony in Grey and Gold,* and so on—to take the viewer's mind off the subject-matter and concentrate it on the form alone. He wrote:

> Why should I not call my works "symphonies," "arrangements," "harmonies," and "nocturnes"? . . . My picture *Harmony in Grey and Gold* is an illustration of my meaning—a snow scene with a single black figure and a lighted tavern. I care nothing for the past, present, or future of the black figure, placed there because the black was wanted at that spot. All I know is that my combination of grey and gold is the basis of that picture.
>
> The great musicians knew this. Beethoven and the rest wrote music—simply music; symphony in this key, concerto or sonata in that . . .
>
> Art should be independent of all clap-trap—should stand alone, and appeal to the artistic sense of eye or ear, without confounding this with emotions entirely foreign to it, as devotion, pity, love, patriotism, and the like. All these have no

[26] Edmund Gurney, *The Power of Sound* (London: Smith, Elder & Co., 1880), p. 340.

concern with it and that is why I insist on calling my works "arrangements" and "harmonies."[27]

## Formalism in literature

Formalism is a position virtually impossible to hold in regard to literature. The very medium of literature prohibits it: the medium of literature, as we have seen, is not simply sounds, or marks on a page, it is words, and words are sounds or marks with meanings. These meanings of course are taken from the life outside art; even when we use words to describe works of art, such as "sad" or "joyous," these describe feelings we have had in response to life-situations, long before we ever discovered works of art. And thus literature, as Jessop remarked (page 48), is "indefeasibly humanistic," fully imbued with life and its values.

One can, indeed, admire the formal elements in a poem, drama, story, or novel; but far from being the *only* thing of interest in the work of literary, form is seldom even the *main* thing. The structural and textural features of "The Royal Game" are very impressive; but the powerful developmental drive toward the climax and conclusion is not appreciated as form alone, but as the drive toward the climax and conclusion of a *narrative*. An analysis of the formal elements alone gives us, as it were, only the shell.

Since for Bell the aesthetic emotion is a response to an aspect of art that has nothing at all to do with life-values, it is inevitable (if he is to be consistent) that he should consider literature to be outside the domain of what is properly called "aesthetic." And for Fry, as we have seen, to call painting "literary" is a term of condemnation, for the "literary" (descriptive, illustrational) painting tries to make painting do, à la Lessing, something that literature can do far better (except that for Lessing what visual arts do best is depict objects in space, whereas for Fry it is not the depiction of objects at all but the presentation of formal relations that it is best equipped to do), and only distracts us from what painting *can* give us, complex and subtle and endlessly rewarding relations of form.

It is not surprising, then, that the doctrine of formalism has never been extended to include literature—or those mixed arts that include literature, such as drama and film. Attempts have been made to regard poetry as "an art of pure sound," but even if the poem is Poe's *The Bells,* it is not the pure sound that affects us, but the fitting of the sounds to the meanings: would "the tintinnabulations of the bells" have any effect on you as pure sounds, with no knowledge that it's bells about which the poet is talking?

Clearly, then, literature cannot be placed in formalism's ballpark. Not even poetry can: one must appreciate not only the "sensuous surface" and

---

[27] James MacNeill Whistler, *The Gentle Art of Making Enemies* (London: W. Heinemann, 1890), pp. 126–128.

whatever formal qualities the poem may have, but "beneath" or "beyond" the form, one must grasp the primary and secondary meanings of the words. Whether the same holds true for painting and music as well, whether formalism is an acceptable view even for those arts in which it has been most strongly maintained, is a subject that will recur in various contexts in the next two chapters.

## 4. STYLE

Form is not the same thing as style. There is some confusion on this point, since both form and style are popularly associated with the "how" of saying or expressing something, whereas the "content" is supposed by contrast to be concerned with "what" is said or expressed. We have already described the misleadingness of the "form-content" distinction. Nor does form have to do with the "how"—it has to do, as we saw, with the relationships among the parts or elements of a work of art. What must be clarified now is what style is. There are various views about the nature of style. Let us begin with one that became popular during the Romantic period in the nineteenth century.

1. *Style as a manifestation of the artist's personality.* "Style is the man," is a famous epigram of Buffon. Like most epigrams it cannot be taken literally: style is not literally a man, but the view is that the style of a person's art is a *manifestation* of the artist's personal characteristics. Just as a person's manner (style) of walking and gesturing is a reflection of his personality, so are his artistic creations. Eugene Véron wrote in 1878,

> Read a page of Demosthenes and of Cicero, of Corneille and of Racine, of Lamartine and of Victor Hugo. However slight may be your literary perceptions, you will at once notice that no two of them sound the same. Apart altogether from subjects or ideas, which may be identical, each one had an air, an accent, which can never either be confounded or replaced. In some of them we find elegance, finesse, grace, the most seductive and soothing harmony; in others, a force and élan like the sound of a trumpet . . .[28]

A unique style manifests a unique individual; mediocre style manifests mediocre individuals:

> Why have mediocre artists no style? For the same reasons that they are mediocrities. The particular characteristic of mediocrity is commonness or vulgarity of thought and feeling. . . . The mediocre artist thinks and feels like the ordinary run of mankind, and has nothing to separate him from the crowd. He may have a manner, an ensemble of habits of working peculiar to himself; but he can have no style in the accurate sense of the word. Facility is not style; for

[28] Eugene Véron, *L'Esthetique.* Chapter reprinted in Melvin M. Rader (ed.), *A Modern Book of Aesthetics,* 5th ed. (New York: Holt, Rinehart, & Winston, 1979), p. 56.

style is really a product, a reverberation . . . from the soul itself, and can no more be artificially acquired than can the sonorousness of bronze or silver be acquired by lead. Style, which is a simple reflection of the artist's personality, is naturally found in the work of every artist who possesses any personality. The indescribable quality, the *je ne sais quoi* . . . is precisely the assemblage of qualities, the condition of being and temperament, which caused Rubens to see things differently from Rembrandt. The two extracted from one and the same object emotions widely different, though congenial to their respective natures. [29]

It is undoubtedly true that an artist's personal characteristics may be reflected in his works of art, just as it is reflected in his habits of speech, gestures, and facial expressions. Still, to say that style simply *is* a reflection of the artist's personality seems at best an overstatement. Can you infer, by viewing an artist's work, whether he was cruel or affectionate toward his wife, or whether he drank to excess, or even whether in his personal life he was proud or humble? Perhaps such inferences are too specific: but what *can* one infer about the artist just from his work, other than that he was industrious enough to have completed the works that he did complete? Certain compositions, such as those of Mozart in one period of his life, may radiate happiness, and one would naturally infer that Mozart was happy at the time he wrote them—but he wasn't; it was the most miserable period of his life. The composition of music was presumably an escape from all this, but one could not infer any personality trait of his from the nature of his compositions. His style may even have characteristics *opposite* to his personality: both primary artists and (most of all) secondary artists such as actors, may be dashing and heroic in the roles they play but utterly dull and unheroic in their personal lives. An artist may be utterly chaotic and undisciplined in his daily affairs, but bring a high degree of order and discipline to his art, and to his art alone. His "artistic personality," what is exhibited in his artistic creations, may be quite at odds with his day-to-day personality as it reveals itself to those who are living with him under the same roof. What often happens is that we *already* know something about the artist's life and personality, from reading biographies or program notes, and then read these characteristics back into his work. If we do not already know independently about his personality traits, it is extremely unsafe to infer them from his works of art alone.

Nor was it always the case that artists attempted to show their individual characteristics in their work. Medieval composers were not supposed to exhibit their individual peculiarities in their work, but to submerge themselves in the artistic tradition of the time and follow its conventions to the letter. That is one reason why it is harder to distinguish one composer's work from another in music of this period. Surely this does not show that these composers in their personal lives differed less from one another in their personality traits than composers do today. Yet if style is (a reflection of) the man,

---

[29] *Ibid.,* pp. 56–57.

that is the conclusion we would have to draw. And what of the builders of cathedrals working on the same structure for centuries, all in the same Gothic style, their individual contributions quite indistinguishable from each other? All had the same style; but surely they were not all similar people.

Instead of saying that style is a reflection of the artist's personality, one might more plausibly say that it is—to some degree, and with exceptions—a reflection of his basic attitude(s) toward reality, the general feeling-tone of his life. But even if something like this is true, it is hardly a *definition* of style. It doesn't tell you what style *is;* rather, it is an empirical generalization about the correlation of an artist's personality with the style of his artistic creations. But all this, of course, still leaves "style" undefined.

2. *Style as a means of identification of artists (style as "signature").* In the first novel, *Swann's Way,* of his seven-volume series *Remembrance of Things Past,* Marcel Proust describes the experience of a child in a Paris apartment expecting to be taken out on a picnic that day but the sky looking as if it will rain:

> The day grew dark. My mother said that it might clear again, that one burst of sunshine would be enough, but that more probably it would rain; and if it rained, of what use would it be to go to the Champs-Elysees? And so, from breakfast-time, my anxious eyes never left the uncertain, clouded sky. It remained dark. Outside the window, the balcony was grey. Suddenly, on its sullen stone, I did not indeed see a less negative color, but I felt as it were an effort toward a less negative color, the pulsation of a hesitating ray that struggled to discharge its light. A moment later the balcony was as pale and luminous as a standing water at dawn, and a thousand shadows from the iron-work of its balustrade had come to rest on it. A breath of wind dispersed them; the stone grew dark again, but, like tamed creatures, they returned; they began, imperceptibly, to grow lighter, and by one of those continuous crescendos, such as, in music, at the end of an overture, carry a single note to the extreme fortissimo, making it pass rapidly through all the intermediate stages, I saw it attain to that fixed, unalterable gold of fine days, on which the sharply cut shadows of the wrought iron of the balustrate were outlined in black like a capricious vegetation, with a fineness in the delineation of their smallest details which seemed to indicate a deliberate application, an artist's satisfaction, and with so much relief, so velvety a bloom in the restfulness of their sombre and happy mass that in truth those large and leafy shadows which lay reflected on that lake of sunshine seemed aware that they were pledges of happiness and peace of mind.[30]

Many people who have read widely in the world's literature would be able to identify this rather quickly as a passage from Marcel Proust. Why? "Because nobody else writes like that!" would be the obvious reply. What can we infer from the passage about the author? Perhaps that he was a very sensitive person, that he knew enough about music to liken the lightening sky to

[30] Marcel Proust, *Swann's Way,* Scott-Moncrieff translation, Modern Library edition, pp. 511–512.

an analogous change in music, and a few similar things, which might all equally characterize other writers besides. But these things are not what enables us to identify Proust as the author; it is characteristics of the work, not inferences to the man, that enable us to do this.

We can do the same in any art-medium when we come to be familiar with it. "That's Beethoven!" we exclaim after hearing just a few measures, even if we have not heard this work of Beethoven before. We don't need to know anything about Beethoven the man to do this, but we do need to be already acquainted with *other* works by Beethoven. If we have heard some of his symphonies and concertos, and then hear the *Leonora, Egmont,* or *Coriolanus* overtures for the first time, we would bet a lot of money that this overture is by Beethoven, and we would be right. Similarly we could say, "That painting is by Seurat—nobody else paints in just that way."

Sometimes, of course, the feeling of being sure deceives us: we think that one person was the artist, and it turns out to be another. Most of us find it difficult to tell the difference between late Haydn and early Mozart. And if we have heard only early- and middle-period Beethoven works, we might not be able, on first hearing, to identify the late quartets (Op. 127–135) as being by the same composer. The same might well be true of Picasso because of his many changes in style during his long artistic career. Even when we have the strongest feeling of certainty we may be mistaken; perhaps instead of "knowledge" we should say we have made an "educated guess."

Still, when we are right almost all the time, as some people are, it is not coincidence: there must be a reason. What are the features which enable us (or some people) to make such accurate judgments? It seems to be, as Véron says, an "indescribable quality, a *je ne sais quoi*." But that doesn't tell us much; can we do better? In Beethoven there is a certain relentless driving energy. That goes a little way, but compositions by other composers have driving energy too, yet they are recognizably different from Beethoven's. If we know musical terminology, we can perhaps go further: for example, Sibelius has a penchant for fourths rather than for thirds. But that too would be only the beginning. We would usually end up with a fairly long list of characteristics, and even this would not suffice unless the presence of just this group of characteristics was distinctive of the work of *this* composer, as opposed to all others.

3. *Style as objective features of the work of art.* Defining style as a means of identifying the work of a certain artist would seem to be putting the cart before the horse. We can, very often, identify the artist from examining (hearing, seeing, reading) his work. But why is this possible? What enables us to do this? It is the fact that the work of artist A has a group of characteristics or features which are lacking in the work of artist B. It is those features, then, whatever they are, which constitute his style; and the ability to identify the artist by noticing those features is the result, or consequence, of the presence of those features. It is the features which make the identification possible that

are important, not the identification itself. It is because the features differ from artist to artist that we can perform such identifications.

What, then, constitutes an artist's style? Let us now attempt to define style as *recurrent features of texture and structure*. It is the word "recurrent" that is of most importance here. It's not "in the artist's style" unless the feature is one (or more) which occurs in many, or even all, of the artist's works. It is because the same features recur in different works by the same artist that we can identify the artist; similarly, it is because the same features recur in works by different artists in the same tradition that we can identify works as being in that tradition (such as baroque).

It is especially in the subtle textural details—just such as Veron described as distinguishing pairs of authors from one another—which are extremely difficult to describe precisely and in detail in words, that we can distinguish, for example, Seurat from Pisarro, Shakespeare from Marlowe, Shelley from Keats, Schubert from Beethoven. Tschaikovksy is simple and direct, Brahms is involuted and tortuous, Richard Strauss and Mahler can both be bittersweet, but Mahler has a way (for example) of sustaining one long note on one instrument while meanwhile the orchestra shifts almost imperceptibly from one key to another beneath it and suddenly we are in a different emotional universe—and, in context at least, often that enables us to distinguish Mahler from Strauss all by itself.

In his fiction, including "The Royal Game," Stefan Zweig has an unfailing structural tightness: no unresolved details, everything moving inexorably toward a climax, nothing "thrown in for kicks." These structural features characterize other authors as well. But in Zweig there are also prominent textural features, much harder to describe: there is a fullness and amplitude, nothing merely outlined or skeletal as in Hemingway; at the same time there is a penetration, an "instinct for the jugular" when it comes to the selection of descriptive details. (All this is textural rather than structural because it need not characterize the work as a whole, but individual parts or passages—in this case, almost every single line in the story, but *each* individual line; structural features such as overall unity and development do not characterize each individual line.) There is also an almost instant momentum, which quickly sustains the narrative at a high level of intensity, so that we feel with virtually every paragraph we read as if we are being connected to, or "zapped" by, high-voltage electricity. Probably even this more extended description will apply to the work of other authors as well; and if so, it does not identify Zweig uniquely: if you had read only the description but not the stories, you would not be able to identify the work of Zweig by means of it. This shows, however, only that the *description* is not yet adequate, not that the features of Zweig's work which constitute his style are not sufficiently distinctive. Since many readers *can* correctly identify his authorship without knowing it in advance, it is reasonable to conclude that there are still more recurring features which these readers are able to recognize but which, owing to insufficient analysis or the inability to express these subtleties in words, have not gotten themselves incorporated into the description.

The concept of style, of course, applies to all the arts: in all arts there are recurrent features of structure and texture. But there is a special problem about style in literature because literature operates on two levels: there are (a) the words and sentences themselves—the sounds of the words individually and in combination, the rhythm and cadence of the lines, the alliterations and the onomatopoeia, the consonances and dissonances; there are also (b) the meanings, both primary and secondary, of the words and sentences, for which the sounds or printed marks are merely vehicles. There are distinctive and recurrent features of an author's work in both these dimensions. Hemingway's work can often be identified by both (a) the textural qualities of his prose ("crisp, short, sharp") and (b) his recurrent treatment of certain themes, such as the proud competent he-man conquering nature. (Some critics would include only the first of these as stylistic features; others would include both.)

There is a prevalent confusion in this connection. Since in literature there are sentences, and sentences can be used to *say* things, it is assumed that style is independent of meaning, that style has to do with "not what is said, but how it is said." But the distinction is not so easy as that; how it is said cannot easily be separated from what is said, for you cannot change *how* you say something without also changing *what* you say (you have to use different words). Style is not independent of meaning, it is inextricably bound up with meaning.

There are certainly pairs of sentences which do not differ in style but do differ in meaning: "She bought coats and dresses" and "She bought coats and hats" have different meanings, but no discernible difference in style—but of course it's only one sentence: the two passages from which the sentences have been excerpted might well differ in style.

The problem is to find pairs of sentences (or passages) which do differ in style but do not differ in meaning. A prose translation of Shakespeare's "Canst thou not minister unto a mind diseased?" might be "Can't you wait on a lunatic?" These certainly do differ in style; but don't they differ in meaning also? Does the prose rendition really "say the same thing" as the line of poetry? Does "mind diseased" mean exactly the same as "lunatic"? It may, in one sense: that any evidence that would confirm or disconfirm the sentence "He is a lunatic" might also confirm or disconfirm the sentence "He has a diseased mind" (even this much is not obvious, depending on exactly what meaning one attaches to these vague terms); but when one includes the range of secondary meaning, it becomes obvious that they are quite different, and one could not substitute the one for the other in every context in which they occur.

Suppose you wish to tell someone who is with you in some cooperative venture that together you must plunge forward, for now is the time, and if you wait the venture will not succeed. Now compare what you just said with what Brutus says in Shakespeare's *Julius Caesar* (Act 4, scene 3):

> There is a tide in the affairs of men
> Which, taken at the flood, leads on to fortune;
> Omitted, all the voyage of their life
> Is bound in shallows and in miseries.
> On such a full sea are we now afloat;
> And we must take the current when it serves,
> Or lose our ventures.

Now, can you honestly say that you and Shakespeare said the same thing, but just "said in different ways"? It is not merely that Shakespeare used different *words,* but words express different *thoughts;* surely the thought in the Shakespeare passage is much richer than in the bare sentence preceding it. It is true that they have to do with the same general *subject matter;* but the description and elaboration of that subject matter is quite different in the two examples.

Or suppose, as an Englishman, you feel a surge of patriotism for your native land. When Shakespeare wrote (*King Richard II,* Act 2, scene 1)

> This royal throne of kings, this scepter'd isle,
> This earth of majesty, this seat of Mars
> This other Eden, demi-paradise,
> This fortress built by Nature for herself
> Against infection and the hand of war,
> This happy breed of men, this little world,
> This precious stone set in the silver sea,
> Which serves it in the office of a wall
> Or as a moat defensive to a house,
> Against the envy of less happier lands,
> This blessed plot, this earth, this realm, this England . . .

was he saying, but in different words, merely that "England's a great place"? One might say that they "reflect similar sentiments" or some such thing; or that they are in the same general ballpark; still "England's a great place" is an abysmally poverty-stricken rendition of the lines of poetry.

Almost no two words in a language have *exactly* the same meaning (both primary and secondary). Since a word is a symbol for a meaning, you can't change the symbol (word) without changing the meaning at the same time. Even using the same words in a different order changes the meaning: "They had children and got married" is different from "They got married and had children" in that the first sentence suggests (but not the second) that they had the children first. Admittedly short sentences are not enough to enable us to pick up much in the way of differences of style, but even there they occur:

"I am here" and "Here I am" don't have entirely the same meaning—"I am here" suggests that I have been long awaited or searched for. One could be challenged, then to try to find two passages in literature which say *exactly* the same thing in two different ways; to try to find a difference in style where there is no difference in meaning. In view of the apparent impossibility of doing this, one must conclude that the two are inextricably interwoven and that "the style of a literary work consists of the recurrent features of its *texture of meaning.*"[31]

4. *Style as a manner of making.* That style is a feature of works of art themselves has seemed to many so obvious as to be beyond dispute. Nevertheless, it has not remained undisputed. According to a still different view, style characterizes not objects themselves but *ways of doing* things. "Style," writes the art historian E. H. Gombrich, "is any distinctive, and therefore recognizable, way in which art is performed or an artifact made, or ought to be performed and made."[32] "Styles of works of art," writes Kendall Walton, "are to be understood in terms of the notion of styles of *action.* Specifically, attributing a style to a work involves, somehow, the idea of the manner in which it was made, the act of creating it."[33] Thus, we speak of what style a painting is *done* in; and we speak of styles of pain*ting* or wri*ting*—the processes, rather than the products of such processes. When something is not a product of human action, we do not speak of them as having styles, even though they have distinctive characteristics, even expressive characteristics.

What is the style of a tulip, or an alpine meadow, or a pristine lake in the high Sierras? Are the Grand Canyon and Yosemite Valley in the same style or different ones? Sunsets in the tropics are very different from sunsets in the Arizona desert, and Arizona sunsets in January differ from Arizona sunsets in June. But are these differences stylistic? . . . It is beginning to look as though human action has something to do with all style attributions. . . . A wide range of very important "aesthetic" qualities of works of art are not to be found in natural objects. Poems and paintings are sometimes witty, or morbid, or sophisticated, but it is hard to imagine what a witty tulip, or a morbid mountain, or a sophisticated lake would be like. A sunset can hardly be sentimental, or unsentimental for that matter, even though a realistic painting of the sunset might be a paradigm of sentimentality. The lines in a drawing may be sensitive, or bold, or carefree, but one hesitates to attribute these qualities to similar lines in nature. Could the pounding of a surf be pompous or exuberant or passionate or bombastic or energetic, as a performance of a Rachmaninoff Prelude might be? It is rarely appropriate to describe natural objects as ponderous, deliberate, neurotic, anguished, pretentious, profound, flamboyant, expressive, or reserved.[34]

[31] Monroe C. Beardsley, *Aesthetics* (New York: Harcourt Brace, 1958), p. 222.

[32] E. H. Gombrich, "Style," in *International Encyclopedia of the Social Sciences* (ed. David Sills), New York: Macmillan, 1968.

[33] Kendall Walton, "Style and the Products and Processes of Art," in *The Concept of Style,* ed. Berel Lang (Philadelphia: University of Pennsylvania Press, 1979), p. 46.

[34] *Ibid.,* p. 46.

But if the style of a work has to do with the way in which it *was* made, we have a problem: in most cases we were not there to watch the work being created, and so we really do not know how it was made. Sometimes we can *infer* it with some probability—for example, that Van Gogh used rough brush strokes—but sometimes we cannot do even that. This problem, however, is avoided by saying something different; not that the style of work depends on how it *was* made, but how, judging from the work of art before us, it *appears* to have been made. Even if it really wasn't made a certain way, if it appears to have been so made, it has a certain style, and the style depends on how it appears to have been made. "If we should discover that one of Daumier's drawings was not done by Daumier at all but rather by a machine run by a computer, or in some other way, we would (probably) still feel comfortable saying that it was in the *style* of Daumier."

For example,

> the sounds of a musical performance seem to listeners to have been made by actions of banging, scraping, blowing, singing, and so on. And they sound as though these actions were performed vigorously or gently, carefully or with abandon. Usually the sounds we hear are in fact made in pretty much the manner they seem to have been. But let us consider just how the sounds sound, the impression they give of how they were made (even when we don't see the performers), regardless of whether the impression corresponds to the reality. There can be no doubt that much of the emotional impact of music depends on what activities sound to the listener as though they are going on. It is with reference to these apparent activities what we describe melodies or passages of music as tender, nervous, raging, flowing, energetic, and that we characterize musical performances as sprightly or bombastic or timid or ponderous.[35]

The style of a work of art is a matter of not how it was actually made but how it *appears* to have been made. "To be in a flamboyant, sentimental, or timid style is to appear to have been created in a flamboyant or sentimental or timid manner."

Similarly, a painting often gives strong impressions of the physical behavior of the painter, for example, Van Gogh's paintings with their visible brush strokes. And in literature one often has a strong impression of the kind of choices the author made concerning his writing: it is *as if* he wrote with intense conviction, or in the heat of passion, whether or not he actually did, and this impression determines what we shall describe as his writing style.

But sometimes the painting gives little or no indication of how the work even *appears* to have been created. Leonardo da Vinci's paintings leave very few clues as to their artist's physical activities. Shall we say then that such painters have no style? Moreover, there are many aspects of what we call style that do not seem to be covered by any account of how the work appears to have been made. In Romantic painters, it isn't so much how they applied (or

---

[35] *Ibid.*, p. 53.

appear to have applied) paint to canvas that determines their style, but what kinds of features, including mood and tone, keep turning up their works. And this takes us back to style as recurrent features of structure and texture.

As for literature, unless we have the original manuscript before us with some words in heavy pencil (for example), we have very little idea of the physical operations by which the work was written: for example, whether it was penned or whether the manuscript was typewritten. When we speak of style in literature, we aren't talking about *that* at all. We are talking about recurring features of the work, recurring themes, recurring details of texture: "In the study of the arts, works—not institutions or people—are the primary data; in them we must find certain characteristics that are more or less stable. . . . A distinguishable ensemble of such characteristics we call a style."[36]

There may be no one thing to which we always refer when we call something a style: sometimes it may indeed refer to the process by which the work appears to have been created, but even when we talk about this we are led back to features of the product, especially those which are recurrent.

## EXERCISES

1. "You can change every component in [a melody] by playing it at a different pitch or on a different instrument, but it remains the same melody. But it must be apprehended as a single impression. If you play the ten notes of a melody to ten different hearers, or if you change the order of the notes, the melody is lost. If you play it in bits to a hearer who knows it, he will hear the bits *as fragments of a melody,* not as several small melodies. The melody as a whole has a character of its own distinct from that of the notes or fragments which compose it. Yet the notes and fragments, *heard as parts of that melody,* acquire a perceptually different character from the character which they possess if heard in isolation or as parts of a different melody." (Harold Osborne, the chapter on organic unity in his *Aesthetics and Art Theory*.)

   Do you agree with the author that organic unity, thus conceived, is the central feature of all art?

2. With regard to the unity of "The Royal Game," consider the following possibilities:

   a. Is the rather long characterization of the history of Czentovic as a stupid lout essential to the story?

   b. Take a comparatively minor character such as MacIver. Does he add anything to the story? Could he have been omitted entirely without damage to the whole? The story would be *different,* of course, if he were not in it; the question is not whether it would have been different but whether it would

[36] James S. Ackerman, "Style," in Ackerman and Carpenter, *Art and Archaeology* (Englewood Cliffs, N.J.: Prentice-Hall, 1963), p. 164.

have been more unified if he had been omitted. What does he add? Could the story have been altered without damage by deleting him?

    c. Consider a segment of the plot development, such as Dr. B's discovery of the book. How is this prepared for? Does the author tantalize us too long with suspense concerning the nature of the book? Is his distress after seeing what the book is about too lengthily described?

3. In Dewitt Parker's essay, "The Problems of Aesthetic Form," in his *Analysis of Art,* he discusses *balance* as a formal feature for visual arts as an analog of development in the temporal arts. There must be, he says, a balance between the right and left halves of a painting: not perfect symmetry, but nevertheless a fairly equal "weight" on both sides of the painting. Factors such as distance of a certain shape from the center, its color, its size, and the object represented all count in determining the weight on one side of a painting. In recent visual art, however, the concept of balance has been pretty much neglected or forgotten. How important, and why, does balance seem to you as a formal feature in visual art?

4. Edgar Allan Poe contended that a poem must express emotion. But emotions cannot be sustained for a long time. Therefore, he said, a long poem is only a series of lyrics connected by passages of prose. Do you consider the following case a counterexample to this allegation? "What if the constituent lyrics, separated from the parent frame, should pine and die? *Lear* is a play from which hardly three consecutive lines can be extracted and kept alive. No 'great speeches'; no 'Tomorrow and tomorrow and tomorrow' or 'To be or not to be'; nothing detachable, nothing quotable or declaimable in isolation; no slackening of dramatic pressure; everything comes from the situation and must in turn be applied to it. Passages almost unbearably intense, like 'I tax you not, you elements, with unkindness. I never gave you kingdom, call'd you children,' and 'What, have his daughters brought him to this pass?' are cold and dull—the poetry washes out of them—unless we are thinking of the speaker and of all that has happened to him. *Lear* is the great example of a seamless dramatic entity." (Arnold Isenberg, "Cordelia Absent," in his *Aesthetics and the Theory of Criticism,* p. 127.)

5. "Shakespeare is the very last dramatist whose plays one would normally describe as integrated wholes. On the contrary, it is the critics' prior conviction of the greatness of the plays which has driven them to search for principles of integration. To say that these plays are great because they are integrated is to put the cart before the horse." (Hans Eichner, "The Meaning of 'Good' in Aesthetic Judgments," *British Journal of Aesthetics,* Vol. 3 (October 1963), 316.) Rather, he says, Shakespeare's plays are more like epics, in which irrelevancies and even meanderings that are not tied to the whole often occur—and such vast profusion and richness of detail would not be possible if Shakespeare had stuck to the ideal of unity. Do you agree? Do you see more unity in his work than that?

6. Roger Fry, in "The Artist and Psychoanalysis," speculates on why it is that certain combinations of forms in visual art are moving and strike us as "profound," "revealing," and so on, whereas others are simply dull and nonsignificant: "It is not a mere recognition of order and interrelations; every part, as well as the whole, becomes suffused with an emotional tone. . . . The emotional tone is not due to any recognizable reminiscence or suggestion of the emotional experiences of life; but I sometimes wonder if it nevertheless does not get its force from arousing some very deep, very vague, and *im-*

*mensely generalized reminiscences.* It looks as though art had got access to the *substratum* of all the emotional colors of life, to something which underlies all the particular and specialized emotions of actual life. . . . Or it may be that art really calls up, as it were, the *residual traces* left on the spirit by the different emotions of life, without however recalling the actual experiences, so that we get an *echo* of the emotion without the limitations and particular direction which it had in experience.'' Do you think he is onto something here?

7. Do the following pairs of statements ''say the very same thing'' in different words? What does this tell you about the relation of style to meaning?

   a. He ate the food rapidly.
      He wolfed down the food.

   b. Would you please leave?
      Get out of here!

   c. He killed her.
      He murdered her.

   d. You are our Creator.
      Thou art our Creator.

   e. After the rain, there were numerous political assassinations . . .
      They shot the six cabinet members at half past six in the morning against the wall of a hospital. There were pools of water in the courtyard. There were wet dead leaves on the paving of the courtyard. It rained hard. All the shutters of the hospital were nailed shut. One of the ministers was sick with typhoid . . . .(Ernest Hemingway, *In Our Time,* pp. 399–400.)

8. In ''An Essay on Aesthetics'' in his book *Vision and Design,* Roger Fry makes an observation which some readers believe to be at odds with his artistic formalism. Do you believe it is?

# SELECTED READINGS

ABELL, WALTER. *Representation and Form*. New York: Scribners, 1936.

ACKERMAN, JAMES S. "Style," In J. Ackerman and Rhys Carpenter, *Art and Archaeology*. Englewood Cliffs, N.J.: Prentice-Hall, 1963.

BARNES, ALBERT C. *The Art in Painting*. New York: Harcourt Brace, 1937.

BELL, CLIVE. *Art*. London: Chatto & Windus, 1914.

BELL, CLIVE. *Since Cezanne*. London: Chatto & Windus, 1922.

COKER, WILSON. *Music and Meaning: A Theoretical Introduction to Musical Aesthetics*. New York: Free Press, 1972.

DICKIE, GEORGE. "Clive Bell and the Method of *Principia Ethica*," *British Journal of Aesthetics*, 10, (1970).

EISENSTEIN, SERGEI. *Film Form: Essays in Film Theory*. New York, 1949.

EKMAN, ROSALIND. "The Paradoxes of Formalism," *British Journal of Aesthetics*, 10, (1970).

ENKVIST, NILS. "On Defining Style," In John Spencer (ed.), *Linguistics and Style*. London: Oxford University Press, 1964.

FRY, ROGER. *Transformations*. London: Chatto & Windus, 1926.

FRY, ROGER. *Vision and Design*. London: Chatto & Windus, 1920.

GOMBRICH, E. H. *Norm and Form*. London: Phaidon Press, 1964.

GOTSHALK, D. W. "Form," *Art and the Social Order*. Chicago: University of Chicago Press, 1947, pp. 108–126.

GREENOUGH, HORATIO. *Form and Function*. Berkeley: University of California Press, 1947.

GURNEY, EDMUND. *The Power of Sound*. London: Smith & Elder, 1880.

HADOW, W. H. "Outlines of Musical Form," in *Studies in Modern Music* (2nd series). New York: Macmillan, 1907, pp. 32–56.

HANSLICK, EDUARD. *The Beautiful in Music*. New York: Liberal Arts Press, 1957.

ISENBERG, ARNOLD. "Formalism," *Aesthetics and Theory of Criticism*. Chicago: University of Chicago Press, 1973, pp. 22–35.

LANG, BEREL (ed.). *The Concept of Style*. Philadelphia: University of Pennsylvania Press, 1979.

LOVE, GLEN, AND MICHAEL PAYNE. *Contemporary Essays on Style*. Glenview, Ill.: Scott, Foresman & Co., 1969.

MEAGER, RUBY. "Clive Bell and Aesthetic Emotion," *British Journal of Aesthetics*, 5, (1965).

McLAUGHLIN, THOMAS. "Clive Bell's Aesthetic: Tradition and Significant Form," *Journal of Aesthetics and Art Criticism*, 35 (1977).

OSBORNE, HAROLD. *Aesthetics and Criticism*. London: Routledge & Kegan Paul, 1955.

PARKER, DEWITT. "The Problem of Aesthetic Form," in *Analysis of Art*. New Haven: Yale University Press, 1926.

PEPPER, STEPHEN. "Aesthetic Design," in *Principles of Art Appreciation*. New York: Harcourt Brace, 1949. Reprinted in Hospers.

POLE, DAVID. "The Excellence of Form in Works of Art." *Proceedings of the Aristotelian Society,* 1970-1.

PRALL, D. W. *Aesthetic Judgment*. New York: Crowell, 1929.

REID, LOUIS ARNAUD. *A Study in Aesthetics*. New York: Macmillan Publishing Company, Inc., 1931, pp. 312-25.

REISER, MAX. "Problems of Artistic Form: The Concept of Art," *Journal of Aesthetics and Art Criticism,* 27 (1969).

RITCHIE, BENBOW. "The Formal Structure of the Aesthetic Object," *Journal of Aesthetics and Art Criticism,* 3, (1945).

ROTHSCHILD, LINCOLN. *Style in Art*. New York: Thomas Yoseloff, Inc., 1960.

SHAPIRO, MEYER. "Style." In *Aesthetics Today,* ed. Morris Philipson. Cleveland: World Publishing Co., 1961.

STAMP, KENNETH M. "Unity as A Virtue," *Journal of Aesthetics and Art Criticism,* 34, (1975).

STEELE, BERYL LAKE. "A Study of the Irrefutability of Two Aesthetic Theories," in William Elton (ed.), *Aesthetics and Language*. Oxford: Blackwell, 1954.

STOKES, ADRIAN. "Form In Art: A Psychoanalytic Interpretation," *Journal of Aesthetics and Art Criticism,* 18 (1959).

WEITZ, MORRIS. *Philosophy of the Arts*. Cambridge: Harvard University Press, 1950, chapters 1-3.

# 3

# Representation in Art

Formalists say that all you should look at when you see a painting is lines and colors, shapes and masses, and (as Bell added) an awareness of when what is represented is three-dimensional objects—but not the nature or quality of those objects themselves. Whether this figure is a cow or a woman, said Chagall, doesn't matter at all; these are just excuses for having a form of that size at that spot.

But many viewers, while grateful to formalists for making them sensitive to formal relations, will object that there is much more to painting and the other visual arts than that. A painting can *represent* people and objects; it can *express* moods, feelings, emotional qualities; it can *symbolize* abstract qualities. We shall come to grips with each of these concepts in turn.

The circle in a painting doesn't *represent* a circle, it *is* a circle, but it can represent a balloon, or an orange, or any number of other round things, and if we had seen only paintings and not physical objects in the great outside world we would not know what the shapes in a painting represent. One can try to view it only as a circle, and try not to notice what it represents, but since most paintings throughout history have been representational—they have represented something or the other—the feat of not noticing what it is is not only psychologically difficult or impossible, but (many would say) undesirable: that this is an orange in a still-life and not a balloon is a fact not to be ignored. All theories of the proper function of art through the eighteenth century were theories of art as some kind of representation or other.

142

The most time-honored view of what the function of art should be is that art should in some way "represent reality." "Art is imitation"—from Plato through the eighteenth century countless variations were set forth by critics and philosophers of art on this general theme. There was a great deal of disagreement about *how* art should represent reality and *what* sorts of things should be represented, but virtually all theories started from this general format.

The Greek word *mimesis,* from which the English word "imitation" is derived, is usually translated as "imitation." In view of twentieth-century connotations of the word "imitate," the translation is misleading, since what we today call imitation is usually a relation of one artist's work to that of a previous artists: "Imitate? Whose work does he imitate?" "This man's work is quite unoriginal—it's largely an imitation." What was meant by the traditional theory is not a relation of one artist's work to another's but of an artist's work to nature, or the world, or "reality"; and this relation we ordinarily describe not by speaking of imitation, but of representation.

## 1. REPRESENTATION IN VISUAL ART

There are many aspects of the world that cannot be rendered in visual art: tastes, smells, sounds, touch sensations; these can be *suggested* but not directly represented. For that matter, inner states—thoughts, attitudes, feelings—cannot be rendered either except as they are present in the faces and bodies that are represented visually.

What then should visual arts represent? One might well reply, anything that can be rendered visually. Anything and everything—no limitations. Whether what is represented is real or imaginary, regal or humble, ennobling or revolting, anything that can be rendered visually is within the purview of painting, sculpture, and architecture.

1. *Photographic realism.* Nevertheless, there have been many attempts to limit the scope of what should be represented in the visual arts. The simplest theory is one which has been officially espoused by many painters, that painting should "show it like it is"—that objects represented in paintings should look just like the objects we see in nature, at least as seen by the human eye. On this theory, it was considered a mark of painterly excellence if a portrait of someone were drawn so accurately that one could not only recognize the person from the portrait, but one could discern how many wrinkles that lady had on her face or how recently she had cut her fingernails. Murals of hanging fruit were considered praiseworthy if the grapes were painted so realistically that the birds would pluck at them, mistaking them for real grapes.

Such an ideal could really not be fulfilled. No one would be likely to confuse a painting of a house with a house; the painting is obviously two dimensional whereas a real house is three dimensional, and what you see on canvas looks more like daubs of shiny paint than like any physical object. It is not likely either that the birds were deceived by two-dimensional representations of three-dimensional objects. The differences are simply too great.

In any case, one could well ask whether such an ideal was worth fulfilling. If the painter ever had any obligation to show us the way in which things look to the human eye, such an obligation would surely be rendered obsolete by the invention of photography, which can do that sort of thing much better than painting could ever hope to do. Nor does the history of painting through the ages confirm the view that painters show us the world as it appears to our eyes: not only do the objects not look all that much like those we see in nature, the picture is *composed* in a way that scenes in nature are not, so as to present us with a pleasing array of forms. That is to say that not all paintings are very *realistic:* realism in painting is only one ideal among many, and most painters do not adhere to it very closely. Realism is a matter of degree (this painting is more realistic than that one), and the degree of realism is a function of two principal factors:

(a) Absence of *distortion*: Distortion is putting in details that aren't there. If you draw a figure having six toes instead of five, or elongate someone's neck to a length that no human neck has in relation to the body (à la Modigliani), you are distorting, you are representing things as having features that they do not have in real life. There is often a point in doing this, but it is nevertheless a departure from realism. One might not wish to see colored statues and prefer them to be monochromatic, yet people's skins are not monochromatic, so representing them as if they were one uniform color—particularly when it's white or silver, which the flesh of no human being is—is a departure from realism. All painters indulge in what is called ''necessary distortion'': they may start to copy a scene from nature, but either to satisfy their sense of form, or to emphasize some aspect of the natural objects before them, they distort: they add a tree here, they put this one in a different place to achieve balance or contrast, they intensify a color there. All this may add to the formal unity or the thrust and power of a painting, but, still, to the extent that this is done it is not realism.

(b) Absence of *abstraction*: Abstracting is the omitting of details that are there. Even if a painter does not distort, he inevitably abstracts. To abstract is to take away, to remove, to omit features which are present; and no painter can include them all, nor would he wish to. Consider the real-life apple in all its fullness. Now consider a sculpture of the apple: although three-dimensional as the apple is, it lacks some of the characteristics of the real apple—it is not made of the same substances, it is (probably) not edible, it is (probably) monochromatic. Now consider a painting of the same apple: the painting is two dimensional whereas the real apple is three dimensional, so the third dimension has been abstracted from the picture. If the painting is colored, it still doesn't have all the complex color gradations over every inch of its surface that the real apple does. (The more it retains them, the more realistic the painted apple is.) If the painting is a "primitive," the representation of the apple is all of one uniform color, and this is a considerable abstraction from reality. And if it is a line drawing, the color of the apple isn't shown at all—only the shape of the circumference is. The further we go with abstraction, the further we get away from realism, until finally we reach the point where there is nothing left that is recognizable as an apple: in the line drawing, if the shape goes, so does any representation of an apple. The limit of abstraction is nonrepresentation.

There are some problems about defining "realism" in terms of these two characteristics. How much detail must be present for a representation to be realistic? As much as the human eye can see? (Other animals have different optical equipment and presumably see things very differently.) In much Dutch painting there is such atmospheric clarity that one can see details of objects long distances away that no unaided human eye can discern; is that being realistic? If an object were represented on canvas with thousands of details such as can be discerned only through a powerful microscope or telescope, would that be more realistic or less? If the painter showed every blade of grass on a lawn, presumably this would be more realistic than if he showed only a green mass; but what if he showed it as it would look through a telescope, or an electron microscope, or X rays, or radar?

Such issues might be decided simply by stipulating that something is realistically depicted if it is represented as looking the way it looks to the normal human eye without magnification. This is somewhat vague, since the same thing even at the same distance and in the same light will often look different to different eyes, even those classified as "normal." What the champion of such a view may have in mind is rather that things should be depicted as they appear in a good color *photograph*. Indeed, it might seem that photography would be the ideal art form according to this view. If so, it may be worth pointing out that photographs are often not very realistic either. Every photographer knows many "tricks of the trade" which will make things look different from (and people more flattering than) their "appearance to the normal eye." Every photographer will first "compose" a picture by moving furniture and props and focusing the camera in a certain direction, so as to obtain the most pleasing design. Lights can be combined and otherwise manipulated so as to emphasize some objects or angles and deemphasize others, change the colors of objects, alter their texture, and so on. Much also depends on what film is used: no color film yet devised makes things look quite the same color they do to most human eyes. One can also get varying effects by changing the time exposure, lenses, and f-stops. Considerable trickery can also be employed in the developmental process, such as rubbing portions of the negative while it is in the developing tank, or underexposing the whole thing. One can superimpose one negative on another and thus get effects like that of King Kong reaching his huge paw into Fay Wray's hotel bedroom. That "the camera doesn't lie" is true in one sense: the lens does not distort the image presented to it; but much can be done between the scene and the image to make the one fail to correspond to the other. In every other respect, the photograph can lie—that is, mislead—almost as much as one desires. Sometimes the complaint "That photo doesn't look like me" may be attributable to the fact that most people have too flattering a conception of how they look; but it may also often be true. Also, one reads a good deal into or out of the photograph: if you see an up-to-date photograph of someone you haven't seen for ten years, your first thought may be "How he's aged!," but if you have seen him every day during that time you will probably notice hardly any change at all, and the photograph will not strike you that way because the day-to-day changes were imperceptible.

Curiously, the ideal of realism has sometimes been appealed to in painting when the objects in the painting are represented as completely different from the way in which they appear to the human eye. Roger Fry remarks,

Ordinary people have almost no idea of what things look like—so that oddly enough the one standard that popular criticism applies to painting, namely, whether it is like nature or not, is one which most are, by the whole tenor or their lives, prevented from applying properly. The only things they have ever *looked* at being other pictures, the moment an artist who has looked at nature brings to them a clear report of something definitely seen by him they are wildly indignant at its untruth to nature. . . . Monet is an artist whose chief claim to recognition lies in the fact of his astonishing power of faithfully reproducing certain aspects of nature, but his really naîve innocence and sincerity were taken by the public to be the most audacious humbug, and it required the teaching of men like Bastien-Lepage, who cleverly compromised between the truth and an accepted convention of what things looked like, to bring the world gradually round to admitting truths which a single walk in the country with purely unbiased vision would have established beyond doubt.[1]

It is undoubtedly true, as Fry says, that most people are not very careful observers of nature and that they miss a thousand details like the purple in the shadows, which painters have trained themselves to see. Most people, Fry says, "read only the labels on the bottles" and see objects just enough to identify them as belonging to this or that class, and then look at them no further. They see just enough to enable them to get along. The painter, with the trained eye, sees much more. Doubtless this is true, but this fact does not make paintings which show such details realistic: certain details may be there which correspond to features of the world, but that does not make the entire painting realistic by the criteria of realism explained above.

2. *Representing reality.* If it is suggested that the painting should repre-

[1] Roger Fry, *Vision and Design* (London: Chatto and Windus, 1924), pp. 25-26.

sent things, not as they *look,* but as they *really are,* we are in still worse trouble. Suppose someone were to tell you to imagine (or draw) a tree, not as it looks but as it "really is": but you can't even imagine how it "is" without imagining some looks or other—for example, it must have some shape and some color. And after centuries of epistemological arguments philosophers have still come to no agreement on whether the colors we see show things "the way they really are": if the colors we see depend, as they do, on our optical equipment, for example, on the rods and the cones of the retina of the human eye, then not only would animals with different optical equipment see things differently (and color-blind persons too), but it is far from clear that color is really a quality of objects at all: perhaps color is only of our visual sensations when light strikes an object and light waves impinge on the retina of the eye and are somehow "conveyed" through the optic nerve to the brain. Phrases like "as it really is in itself" are full of pitfalls, as every student of philosophy knows.

3. *Representation of universals.* According to Plato's theory of forms (incorrectly called the theory of ideas), the artist cannot show us reality at all, but only gives us the representation of a representation ("an imitation of an imitation").

Every object has many qualities: it is large, round, red, and so on. One way of putting this is to say that every object *instantiates*—in an instance of—the qualities: this object is red (it instantiates the quality redness), but many other objects also are instances of "redness." This tree is an instance of "treeness" (whatever combination of qualities something has to have in order to be a tree), but every tree in the world also instantiates this complex quality. Plato believed that these qualities, or *universals,* had some kind of objective existence in reality and that the actual things we see around us—actual trees, actual people—are simply instantiations of the objectively existing qualities treeness and humanness (humanity). These objectively existing universals were called *the Forms.* There has been endless dispute to this day as to exactly what kind of status Plato meant to ascribe to *the Forms,* but one could put the matter simply by saying, for an object to be red, there must first be redness for it to be.

What, then, are the objects depicted by the visual artist? They are imitations of imitations. Beds are instances of the form "bed" (or bedness), and when a painter paints a bed he is imitating (representing) a particular bed. The bed is a representation of the Form, and the painting of a bed is a representation of a particular bed. The painting of a bed is a representation of a representation, at second removed from the Form itself. But this is all that a painter or sculptor can do. His work is at second remove from Reality, which is the Form.

One can see how a painting of a bed could be considered a representation of a particular bed, but how is a particular bed a *representation* of a Form? A

Form, being an abstract entity, has no visual properties and thus cannot *look* like anything at all; and a particular bed cannot look like a Form, so how can it be said to "represent" the form?

4. *Representation of perfect particulars.* Sometimes, however, especially in his earlier dialogues, Plato spoke of "the forms" as if they were some special kind of *particular thing:* when speaking of "the form of a horse," he appeared to be thinking of a *perfect* horse, with all the defects of actual horses omitted, a horse superior to any horse actually existing in the world, a perfect example of the species. Since all horses we come across have some imperfections, such a perfect specimen of the species does not exist on this planet; but it exists "out there in reality" nevertheless, and it is this that the painter represents: what he represents is not some imaginary object existing in his mind only, but something which exists somewhere in the realm of the real, on which the painter can fix his vision, and represent in paint. In this sense, what is represented is not strictly a universal but a *super-particular,* a particular thing which embodies a combination of qualities that is considered superior to those qualities possessed by any actual thing existing on this earth.

Even granted the metaphysical assumptions of their theory—that there is something existing as an ideal, not in one's mind, but objectively in the real world—there are still problems. There will still be considerable differences of opinion on which combination of qualities in a thing constitute perfection: presumably a perfect horse will be healthy and strong; but will the perfect horse be large, or small, or medium sized? Will it be full of driving energy, pride, high spirits, or more passive and benevolent in demeanor? Whatever qualities constitute perfection in a species, it *is* possible for visual arts to represent a particular specimen that is without blemish and "perfect" in a way that no horse that exists or even existed is perfect. Indeed, Greek painting and sculpture often attempted to do this: statues are of men and women who are, at least as physical specimens, more perfect—better proportioned, for example—than any individual one ever encounters. In this sense, much art depicts what is *better* than, or *superior* to, the reality we see with our senses when we confront specimens in the actual world. (In literature, too, an author may attempt to depict a perfect man or woman—physically perfect, or even morally perfect—such a man or woman as he has never encountered in life.) This, then, is an ideal of representation in art that has often been held as a theory and often been achieved, or at least approached, in artistic practice. This ideal is being used every time an artist portrays his characters as "better than life," "larger than life," "nobler than life," and so on.

Aristotle is the classical exponent of this kind of view. Each species of things in nature, according to his view, is "striving" to achieve perfection—to realize its potentialities in a perfect thing of that type or class. The acorn can become a perfect oak tree, but it is prevented from realizing this by many circumstances: during its period of growth it can get too much heat or not enough, too much moisture or not enough, a storm may stunt or distort its branches, and so on. Although it is striving (not necessarily consciously) to achieve the perfection peculiar to its species, it seldom or never achieves this. But even if this perfection is not realized in nature, it can be achieved in art, and one of art's purposes is to try to depict such idealized individuals. Thus art can achieve what nature itself never realizes, the "perfect form of each species."

> The painter's work is understood to include the study of examples of the species, comparing them in their imperfections, learning finally to see what nature is trying to achieve. This is not the common form but the perfect form, reached by a process of thought that is both generalization and idealization.[2]

5. *Representing the typical.* Still other ideals of representation have been held. In the eighteenth century the view was prevalent that the artist should represent the *species* rather than the *individual.* Only individual objects can be depicted, though of course each individual is a member of some species. But, according to one popular theory, what should be depicted are the *essential* characteristics of the species, not the *accidental* characteristics—in other words, those characteristics which all members of the species or class have in common, not those that some individuals happen to have but which are not essential to their belonging to the species.

The question is, what do "essence" and "essential" mean? Normally an essential characteristic is one that is *defining* of the class of things in question. But the view that art should present only the defining characteristics cannot stand up. No depiction can be of *only* the defining characteristics. Dogs come in various colors, for example, and color is not a defining feature of dogs, since a creature can be a dog and yet not be white, or brown, or black, and so on; yet any dog depicted must have some color or other. So whatever is depicted, it must be more than the characteristics that are defining of the species.

According to another version of this view, the painter or sculptor should depict those features which *regularly* or *typically* occur, not the extraordinary or freakish ones. If a certain dog has a purple patch on its back, this should not be depicted, because this is not a regularly recurring feature of dogs, or of any subclass of dogs (collies, shepherds, poodles, etc.). However, white dogs, black dogs, brown dogs, and so on occur with regularity and may be depicted, even though having any of those colors is not defining of dogs or of any species of dogs.

There would be considerable difference of opinion on what a *typical* shepherd dog, a typical collie, a typical armadillo is supposed to look like, perhaps as much disagreement as to what an *ideal* dog or armadillo would look like. In any case, it would be difficult to provide any reason *why* an artist

[2] F. B. Blanshard, *Retreat from Likeness in The Theory of Painting* (New York: Arno Press, 1945), p. 37.

should render the typical (don't we see enough of these already?) unless, again, art is supposed to be a carbon copy of nature.

6. *Representing the individual.* According to other theories, what art should try to capture is not that which is common to all members of the species, or even typical of them, but that which is unique to *this individual object.* If an artist depicts a tree, he should show *this* tree in all its uniqueness and individuality, emphasizing the *differences* between this tree and all other trees. On this view, the departure from the photographic ideal would be not that the tree should be idealized (an idealization of nature), but that it should highlight and emphasize whatever features are *peculiar to* this tree—the gnarls in the trunk of this tree, the peculiar way in which the foliage grows as opposed to other trees, even those of the same species.

All this, and many other variations on the theory of art as representation that we have mentioned, may seem strange to modern readers. The whole tendency of visual art in the twentieth century has been away from them. Indeed, much of modern art is not representational *at all.* Sometimes we have simply combination of lines and colors, as in Mondrian; sometimes we have clashing planes and strange forms which, like figures on Rorschach tests, may *suggest* objects but which cannot be said to *represent* any identifiable objects at all. If the whole idea that visual art must represent has been abandoned, it is not surprising that there is little interest any longer in speculations on what *kinds of* representation should be attempted.

## Criteria of representation

We have yet to ask an all-important question with regard to representation: what makes something, A, in a work of art a representation of something else, B, in the world outside the work of art? Are there any clear criteria by means of which we can say whether something is a representation of something else? Let us consider several possibilities.

1. *The artist's intention.* "What makes you think that that's a bust of Socrates?" "That's what the sculptor said he was doing." "Why do you say that this strange bunch of squiggles on the canvas is a portrait of Winston Churchill?" "Because the painter in undertaking the job said in my presence that it was his announced intention to paint Churchill—that's how I know what it is."

A child is drawing something with a pencil, composed only of dots and lines connecting some of the dots. This dot, he says, stands for himself; that dot stands for his father; a third dot stands for Aunt Emma; and so on. Well, if he says it does, then it does, doesn't it? we are inclined to ask. That dot stands for Father because he says it does. If he changes his mind and says it stands for Uncle Joe instead, then until further notice that dot stands for Uncle Joe. You couldn't tell just by looking at the dots, of course; but the child explains what is to represent what, and that tells us. Doesn't it?

There seems to be some plausibility in this. We may well go along with the child's game and may even ask, "What's your father doing standing next to Aunt Emma, since they never see each other?" The criterion for what represents what seems to be a stipulation to that effect made by the person doing the drawing.

Still, one is inclined to go only so far with this. If a child draws what he says is an apple and it doesn't look like an apple at all but does look like a pear, we may say, "No, that's not an apple, that's a pear." In this case, we are not using his statement of intention as the final word on what the drawing represents. If the drawing is of whatever the artist says it is, you make him infallible about what it is he's drawing. Does saying make it so? If he says it's a sheep but everybody who sees it says it's a cow, must one say it's still a drawing of a sheep? Wouldn't we say instead that he intended to draw a sheep, but failed?

2. *Causal history.* If you saw the painter at work from the beginning to the end of the process of painting a portrait, and you saw Mrs. Smythe sitting there hour after hour, as the painter first looked at her, then at his canvas, did a few strokes, then looked back at her and did some more strokes, and so on, you might say when it is completed that this *is* a portrait of Mrs. Smythe—you know because you saw her sitting for the portrait and saw the painter at work, even if the completed work didn't look much like her. But if the painting looked like nothing you have ever seen, not a human being, not even an animal, but an indecipherable assortment of clashing lines and planes, would you still say with the same confidence that it was a portrait of Mrs. Smythe—not merely that it was intended to be, but that it was? If it looked like a dead flea, would you still say it was a portrait of Mrs. Smythe?

Not the intention of the artist, but the causal history of the work of art through all its stages (including who if anyone sat for it), is one suggested criterion for who or what is represented. Photography would seem to be the most obvious illustration of this view. Ordinarily a photograph would be said to represent Westminster Abbey because the photographer was facing Westminster Abbey when he snapped the picture. He may not have photographed it intentionally: he may have thought the building was something else, or he may have pressed the shutter without intending to. Still, it was a photograph of the Abbey, wasn't it, whether he knew it or not? In other words, there was a

causal sequence between some "original scene" (what the camera was originally pointed at) and the photograph, considered as an end-term in that sequence. The Photograph P, that is to say a certain piece of shiny paper, showing a distribution of light and dark patches, resulted—so the story goes—from a camera's being pointed upon a certain occasion at Westminster Abbey, thus allowing a certain sheaf of light rays to fall upon a photo-sensitive film, which was subsequently subjected to various chemical and optical processes ("developing" and "printing") so that at last *this* object—the photograph in our hands—resulted. . . . P portrays S, in virtue of the fact that S was a salient cause-factor in the production of P.[3]

But now suppose the history of the photograph is as described, but the final outcome is a uniform gray blur (you didn't have the camera focused). Is this uniform gray blur still a representation of Westminster Abbey? Should we call it an "unusual view" of Westminster Abbey, or a blurred view, or no view at all? Does it make no difference at all what manner of object this "causal sequence" yields?

3. *Resemblance.* But surely, one might say, the answer to the question "What makes A a representation of B?" is obvious. "A is a representation of B if it resembles, or looks like, B—at least if it does so *enough*. It is not what the artist intended it to be, nor who sat for it, for whether A sufficiently resembles B, that is the deciding factor."

Using this criterion, we can divide representation into two types, *depiction* and *portrayal.* Grant Wood's *American Gothic* represents a man and a woman, clad in midwestern American farmer garb, with the representation of a church in the background. What is represented is (as far as we know) not some particular man or woman, but simply *a* man and *a* woman and *a* building (persons or objects of a certain kind). What is depicted is always a creature or thing *of* a certain kind (a ballerina, a Conestoga wagon, an otter).

But works of art may contain representations in another sense: a *specific* person may be *portrayed,* such as Napoleon or Winston Churchill; or a specific animal, such as my pet dog; or a specific thing, such as Westminster Abbey. Gilbert Stuart's famous painting of George Washington is a depiction of a man with such-and-such a facial expression and such-and-such clothing, but it is also a portrayal of a specific man, George Washington. When a person is depicted in a painting, it may or may not be a specific person: when it is, it is a portrait or portrayal of that person. (You can have depiction without anyone's being portrayed, but you cannot have portrayal without depiction.) Many famous paintings we see in galleries were probably portraits of specific individuals living at the time, though in many cases we do not know this—we see only that this is a depiction *of* a woman of royalty, clad in such-and-such garments, and so on.

How do we know what it is that is being depicted? By what it looks like. A depicts a B if A looks more like B than it looks like a member of any other class of things. This is a depiction of a German shepherd dog if it looks more like a German shepherd dog than it looks like a member of any other class of things. Similarly A portrays B if A looks more like B than it looks like anyone

[3] Max Black, "How Do Pictures Represent?" in E. H. Gombrich, H. Hochberg, and Max Black, *Art, Perception, and Reality,* (Baltimore: Johns Hopkins Univ. Press, 1970), p. 101.

(or anything) else: this is a portrait of Winston Churchill if it looks more like Churchill than it looks like anyone else.

A special problem arises in the case of depictions and portrayals of fictitious beings. Here is a painting that depicts a unicorn, but you can't say that it looks like a unicorn because no unicorns exist or ever did exist; how can you compare the painting with something that never was? Here we say, not that it is a picture *of* a unicorn (there never were any "in reality"), but that it is a *unicorn-picture.*(The unicorn is contained in the picture and doesn't exist in the world outside.) How do we know it is a unicorn-picture and not a centaur-picture? By comparing it with previously existing unicorn-pictures and noting the resemblances. How do we know that the first picture was a unicorn-picture? We compare the unicorn-picture with *descriptions* of unicorns in myths and sagas to see whether the object in the picture matches the description. And where did the first unicorn-picture come from? Presumably, from the imagination of the author of the tale or, if it first appeared in visual art, the artist who first drew it.

In the case of Napoleon there is no such problem: even though Napoleon is now dead and we can't directly compare the portrait with Napoleon, we have some indication of what he looked like from portraits drawn at the time, as well as descriptions of him; in any case he did exist, so it is possible, in principle if not in actual fact, to compare an existent A with an existent (or once existent) B. The problem is no different with a portrait of a private in Napoleon's army: we never heard of the man and we haven't the faintest idea what he looked like, but since he existed, someone did know—perhaps the portrait painter did. But in the case of a portrait of Zeus no comparison of the portrayed Zeus with the real Zeus is possible, since there was no real Zeus. (In the case of Napoleon we speak of *real* portrayal; in the case of Zeus and other nonexistent beings, we speak of *nominal* portrayal.) In the case of Zeus, unlike that of Napoleon, it doesn't even make sense to ask whether it is an *accurate* portrayal. What we can do, as in the depiction of unicorns, is compare this painting with other Zeus portraits, as well as literary descriptions, remembering that those other portraits, or descriptions, or at least the first of them, were not drawn from reality but were inventions of man's mind.

But how, in the case of nominal portrayal, can we fulfill the requirement of portrayal, namely, that A looks more like B than like anyone else? Since there was no B, we say that it looks like previous Zeus-portrayals, or matches descriptions in literary Zeus-portrayals; and since these vary somewhat, we keep the requirement elastic by saying something like this: that this Zeus-portrayal has no important characteristics that are *incompatible* with previous Zeus-portrayals (as it would, for example, if it portrayed Zeus as a woman, or as having five legs, or feathers). In cases of unimportant incompatibility, such as the color of his eyes, we would probably say that it is not significant enough to prevent this representation from being a Zeus-portrait; but there would probably be borderline cases, such as a depiction similar to the previous ones except that this one shows him with webbed feet, where we would be doubtful whether it should be called a Zeus-portrayal or not. We will give the painter the benefit of the doubt, but there are nevertheless cases in which, on the basis of our own previous knowledge of Greek sculpture or literature, we would say, "No, that's not Zeus, it's Poseidon."

Apart from nominal portrayal, there are problems with defining representation (depiction and portrayal) solely in terms of resemblance.

(a) Resemblance is a symmetrical relation: if A resembles B, then B resembles A as well. So if a painting of Churchill is a representation (portrait) of him because it resembles him, then, since Churchill also resembles the portrait, Churchill must also be a representation of the portrait.

(b) Even if this difficulty is taken care of, we are disinclined to say that every A that resembles B represents B. If a natural rock formation looks (at least from a certain angle) exactly like Napoleon, does that make it a representation of Napoleon?

(c) Many representations don't resemble their originals very much. A painting of Churchill doesn't look nearly as much like Churchill as it does like another painting of Churchill, or perhaps a photograph of Churchill. Paintings most closely resemble other paintings, not objects in the world. Yet we don't say that the one painting represents the other one, or the photograph. In fact it is more likely that a portrait of Churchill resembles a portrait of Churchill's cousin more than it resembles Churchill himself, yet we call the portrait a representation of the man Churchill, not of the portrait of his cousin.

The fact is that paintings don't look like their originals all that much. The figure in the painting doesn't move in perspective as we change our angle of vision, as it always does when we are looking at real people from different angles.

> As we shift our position with respect to the canvas, we do not get the systematic changes in appearance that would occur if there really were a live (person) in the indicated position: a painted canvas does not even produce as much "illusion" as a mirror. Furthermore, the presented visual appearance is "frozen," it does not show the slight but perceptible changes to be seen in even a "still life," and so on.[4]

Besides, most observers see brush-strokes and similarly painterly devices in paintings which at once make them look different from the people the paintings ostensibly represent.

Drawings and cartoons are often of real and recognizable people, but sometimes resemble them very little indeed. When a president of the United States is shown in a cartoon as a sheep or hawk or wolf or snake, the representation certainly looks more like the animal than like a human being, and yet

---

[4] *Ibid.*, p. 115.

he (the president himself) is a human being. How then do we recognize him as a president—unless of course there is an inscription in the cartoon *saying* that it's the president, in which case we are not *shown* it but simply *told* it? We recognize him by certain resemblances: some familiar facial configuration, some gesture, or perhaps something in the context (he is sitting in the Oval Office), makes us realize that this is a representation of the president. (It's a donkey, but it sits in the Oval Office and has Carter's teeth.) Isn't it the resemblance after all that does the trick, even if the resemblance is often not very great?

The answer probably is that we do rely on resemblance—even small resemblances in the right places may be enough—but that we do not do so *exclusively.* Suppose, for example, that there are any number of Greek temples which are pretty much alike, and we couldn't tell from seeing a rather impressionistic painting of a Greek temple which specific one, if any, it portrayed: all we could say from looking at it is that it is a depiction of a Greek temple. But if the painter indicated, through the title given to the painting, that this was supposed to be a certain temple on a certain hill in Athens, and the painting indeed looked as much like that temple as like any other (though lacking many of the characteristics of the real temple), then we might well allow that it was after all a portrait of this particular temple: we would give the painter the benefit of any doubt.

Or suppose that a certain painting, a portrait, looks very much like Mr. A but, also, looks just as much like Mr. B. We then learn that Mr. A was a sitter for the portrait and that the painter painted him from life. Would that information not incline us to agree that it is after all a portrait of Mr. A? perhaps not a good portrait, but a portrait of Mr. A nonetheless?

All this leads us to conclude that in practice we don't use just one criterion, but all of them; although resemblance is normally the main one, we do use the others, and they sometimes make a difference to what we decide.

Resemblance, though the most powerful of the three criteria in actual practice, is also the one that is the most troublesome. To say that A resembles B is much too simple; what if A appears to Jones to resemble B, but doesn't appear so to Smith? We constantly say such things as, "No, I don't think she resembles her sister at all; she looks much more like her cousin Martha." Perhaps we have to be content not with "A (objectively) resembles B" but "A *seems to X* to resemble B, and A *seems to Y not* to resemble B but to resemble something else, C, much more." In other words, perhaps resemblance is a *relational* characteristic, so that we have to specify not only the two allegedly resembling things, A and B, but the person, X or Y, *to whom* A appears to resemble B.

Consider first a simple example, a picture of a stairway. Looked at one way, it looks like a stairway going up; but when we look again we see it as a stairway going down. In the familiar duck-rabbit illusion, the same figure seen at one time looks like a duck, and at another time like a rabbit. "Which is it really?'' Neither—or both; it has the wherewithal for being seen as both. The ink blotches in the Rorschach test are deliberately designed not to look very much like any one kind of thing but to contain suggestions for being seen as any of many different kinds of things—that is why "what one sees the blotches as" is so psychologically revealing. The person who, for example, sees most of the blotches as representations of bats will say that these pictures depict bats, since they look to him more like bats than like anything else. But "X looks like Y" is not a complete statement; the complete statement would be "X looks like Y *to Z.*" And what it looks like depends on the background, habits, expectations, and unconscious conflicts of the person who is doing the looking.

E. H. Gombrich, in his monumental work *Art and Illusion,* has argued in great specific detail that there is no such thing as *the innocent eye,* processing the "raw data" of the senses and emerging with an image of the thing "as it is." Rather, everything we see is "filtered" by the mind, which organizes and interprets the data in certain ways, and the painter paints with certain modes of organization already "programmed" in his mind.

People don't perceive the same object in the same way. Even when there is no *sensory* defect such as color-blindness, people organize the data of their senses in different ways (Gestalten) depending on their past habits, their emotional predilections, their tempermental bias. An aborigine from the wilds of Australia, on first coming into your room, will not see this object as a chair and that one as a table: he has never seen these things before and, if he classifies them at all in his mind, it will be according to a schema unknown to us. A baby will not see the object in your hand as a pen but (perhaps) as a "smooth biteable." Even though the objects seen will be perceived according to the same classificatory system, as with two Frenchmen, the "emotional thrust" of their drawings will be quite different: when Millet painted a certain sunny field in southern France, it appeared calm and serene, but when Van Gogh painted the same field from the same angle in virtually identical conditions of light, his painting was very different, with rough brush strokes, full of passion and vividness and violence.

A person's past history will partly determine the way in which he paints or draws: a person who has been cowed into submission all his life will, in "painting it as he sees it," do it quite differently from a person who is self-confident and serene. Not only one's past experience, but one's expectations, will alter how one sees it and how one paints it: to a woman who has experienced rape and fears it in the future, a tree stump in a forest at twilight may look menacing, like a threatening man, and she would draw it with an air of ominousness, while a person who saw it only as an ordinary tree stump would be likely to paint it without these emotional projections. When people look at the night sky and are asked to group the stars into constellations, trying to find objects (such as animals) which the patterns of stars (however slightly) resemble, different persons will group the stars into patterns into different ways, just as different persons will interpret the various shapes in Rorschach tests as the shapes of very different creatures. To one person the clouds will assume one kind of configuration, to another person a very different one.

In Egyptian sculpture, the gods are depicted as ferocious human beings with large heads and savage power. Did the Egyptians who sculpted these works "see" them in this way? The Greeks, who were on much more familiar terms with their gods, saw them as ordinary human beings (better physical specimens than most people are, but otherwise not particularly different), and they depicted them in that way. But the Egyptians depicted domestic scenes, ordinary people, cats, and so on very realistically. So it seems likely that they painted and sculpted the gods with deliberate distortion, in order to communicate some conception of their power and ferocity.

Many painters used Derwentwater in the English lake district as their model. So did the Chinese painter Chiang Yee. But his drawing of it makes it look like a Chinese landscape. Did he see it that way, or did he deliberately paint it that way to make it look Chinese? We do not know, but one thing seems clear: that differences in vision, and consequent differences in drawing and painting, are not merely the result of such individual differences among painters. They are also, and usually to a much larger degree, the result of differences in the *artistic tradition* in which various painters are embedded.

Consider Dürer's 1515 woodcut depicting a rhinoceros. We look at it and notice how little it looks to us like a rhinoceros. Perhaps, we think, this is because Dürer had never seen a real rhinoceros. But in 1789 James Heath, who had seen one, made an engraving of a rhinoceros which he claimed was a "true representation." It is somewhat different from Dürer's, but it still seems to us a very inaccurate depiction of a rhinoceros. The fact is that is has ever so much more resemblance to Dürer's woodcut than it does to a rhinoceros; or, if we object that a real rhinoceros is three dimensional and a woodcut representation of it isn't, we can make the same point by saying that it doesn't look much even like a *photograph* of a rhinoceros. In general, paintings and woodcuts of creatures resemble previous paintings and woodcuts more than they do the real creatures they are supposed to be representing. In his depiction of a rhinoceros, Heath was not "following nature" as much as he was following the conceptual schemes of earlier artists. Whether Heath thought he was giving a "true representation" or not (and apparently he thought he was), the fact is that his woodcut owes more to previous representations than to nature.

"The letterpress of a German woodcut from the sixteenth century," writes Gombrich (p. 79), "informs us that we here see 'the exact counterfeit' of a kind of locust that invaded Europe in menacing swarms." But the locust looks like no locust we have ever seen; it has more of the aspect of a horse with wings. Indeed, "the zoologist would be rash to infer from the inscription that there existed an entirely different species of creatures that has never been

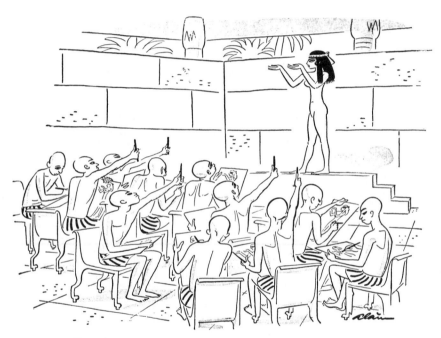

Drawing by Alain; ©1955 The New Yorker Magazine, Inc.

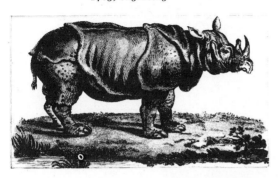

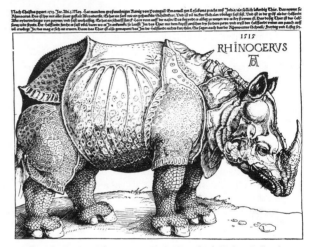

Albrecht Durer. *Rhinoceros.* 1515. Woodcut. (Print Collection,
Art, Prints and Photographs Division, The New York Public
Library, Astor, Lenox and Tilden Foundations.)

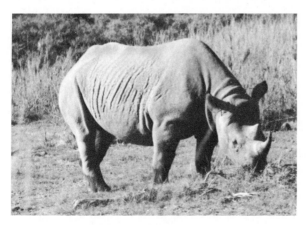

African rhinoceros.
(Photograph courtesy
of Elizabeth Lange.)

**159**

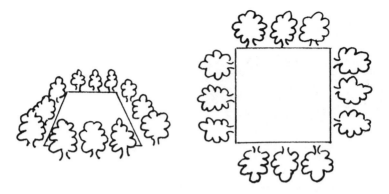

Renaissance and Egyptian drawing of square pond

recorded since. The artist had again used a familiar schema, compounded of animals he had learned to portray, and the traditional formula was illustrated. Perhaps the fact that the German word for locust is *Heupferd* (hay horse) tempted him to adopt a schema of a horse for the rendering of the insect's prance.''

> Even Dutch genre paintings that appear to mirror life in all its bustle and variety will turn out to be created from a limited number of types and gestures, much as the apparent realism of the picaresque novel or of the Restoration comedy still applies and modifies stock figures which can be traced back for centuries. There is no neutral naturalism. The artist, no less than the writer, needs a vocabulary before he can embark on a 'copy' of reality. . . . Without some starting point, some initial schema, we could never get hold of the flux of experience. Without categories, we could not sort our impressions.[5]

There is, says Gombrich, no such thing as the innocent eye. The way we see things now, as well as the way we draw them, is the result of our background, training, experience, emotional predilections, and, most important of all, the artistic schema to which we are accustomed. To us it is easy to decipher a photograph: "that's a picture of me, and that's my dog standing beside me." It is difficult for us to believe—though it is true—that primitive people don't recognize photographs of themselves until they have learned how to look at them—much as dogs who look at Lassie on the television screen don't recognize what they see as the representation of a dog. One first has to "learn the code": savages can and do learn it; apparently dogs never do. In a famous statement of Sir Winston Churchill,

> We look at the object with intent regard, then at the palette, and thirdly at the canvas. The canvas receives a message dispatched usually a few seconds before

[5] E. H. Gombrich, *Art and Illusion* (Princeton: Princeton Univ. Press, 1961), p. 88.

the natural object. But it has come through a post office en route. It has been transmitted in code. It has been turned from light into painting. It reaches the canvas a cryptogram. Not until it has been placed in its correct relation to everything else that is on the canvas can it be deciphered, is its meaning apparent, is it translated once again from mere pigment into light. And the light this time is not of Nature but of art.[6]

Consider perspective drawing, for example, the drawing of a square pond with trees around it. We would probably draw it much as it appears in Figure 3, but the Egyptians drew it much as it appears at the right; each would consider his own way of doing it the correct way. We might remark that a photograph would show it as it appears on the left; but this would not impress the Egyptian who drew it as it is on the right. For his part,

the Egyptian might criticize the perspective drawing as follows: "The picture is all wrong and very confusing! The shape of the pond is distorted. It is an irregular quadrilateral rather than a square. In reality the trees surround the pond symmetrically and meet the ground at a right angle. Also, they are all of equal size. In the picture some of the trees are in the water, some outside. Some meet the ground perpendicularly, others obliquely; and some of them are taller than others." If the Westerner retorted that the Egyptian's own pond was acceptable only as an airplane view and that all the trees were lying flat on the ground, the Egyptian would find this impossible to see and hard to understand.[7]

"Each style aims at a faithful rendering of nature and nothing else, but each has its own conception of Nature."[8] But does this make the whole business of drawing entirely subjective? Is there no such thing as true or false representation, no such thing as accuracy or inaccuracy in depiction? Remember that photographs are sometimes used as evidence in court: yes, that is Jones, and he is holding a smoking gun in his hand, and the victim is on the ground in front of him . . . and so on. Specialists can often get information from photographs that neither the subject nor the photographer were aware of. Similarly, can't we say that the photograph of the rhinoceros gives us more true *information* about the structure of the animal than does Heath's highly inaccurate portrait of a rhinoceros? There are features that every rhinoceros has that the photograph also shows, that the woodcut lacks, and features that the woodcut shows that neither the photograph nor the rhinoceros itself presents to us. And surely we can say that the spatial relation of the parts of a human face are more accurately represented in a photograph than they are in some Matisse and Picasso paintings and thus that the photograph *resembles* a human face more than a (distorted) painting does: if a

[6] *Ibid.,* p. 39.
[7] Rudolf Arnheim, *Art and Visual Perception* (Berkeley: Univ. of California Press, 1957), p. 96.
[8] Gombrich, *Art and Illusion,* p. 19.

Martian saw the painting and concluded that human faces were like that, he would be mistaken—he would have received false information.

New departures in painting, such as impressionism, did not have to be content with the subjectivistic comment, "Well, that's how *I* see it," though that may have been true enough.

> There *is* such a thing as a real visual discovery; and there is a way of testing it despite the fact that we may never know what the artist himself saw at a certain moment. Whatever the initial resistance to impressionist paintings, when the first shock had worn off, people *learned to read them.* And having learned this language, they went into the fields and woods, or looked out of their window onto the Paris boulevards, and found to their delight that the visible world *could* after all be seen in terms of these bright patches and dabs of paint. The transposition worked. The impressionist had taught them, not, indeed, to see nature with an innocent eye, but to explore an unexpected alternative that turned out to fit certain experiences better than did any earlier painting.[9]

The question "Is reality like that?" invites all kinds of metaphysical puzzles and speculation, most of which are of little interest or relevance to artists or students of the arts. But the questions "Can I see it that way?" and then "Is it rewarding, satisfying, pregnant with possibilities for future vision, to see it that way?" are much more fruitful to ask; and we can, in the course of time, after trying different ones, give answers to them from our own developing experience of the arts.

It is doubtless true that when we look at certain paintings we can see nature anew and notice aspects we never noticed before. When we look at a number of Cézanne landscapes, and then go out of the museum and look at the trees in the courtyard, they may all look to us like trees painted by Cézanne. This does not show, however, that what he painted was all "really there"; it only shows that what Cézanne saw we too can see—that we *can* look at the world in that way, that we can share his vision and be enriched by it, and we can do this without making claims that he "saw it as it really is." For we can be enriched by the vision of other painters too, which are totally different from his, and did they too "see it as it really is"—even if they paint trees in ways that conflict with one another? Is it not enough that we can and do share their way of looking at the world, without claiming also that one or more of these represents "the way things really are"?

The fact is that each landscape painter is trying to capture something different; each brings out certain aspects of things, emphasizing some, playing down or deleting others, inventing here, imagining there, all to enrich our total experience—and the painter, not limited by the lens of the camera, is in a position to provide that enrichment much more than even the best

[9] *Ibid.,* p. 324.

photograph. Consider how different painters treat the same general subject, trees:

> Theodore Rousseau is preoccupied in his careful drawings and paintings with the multiplicity of leaves and the intricacy of leaf, bark and branch patterns. The oak is one of his favorite subjects . . . .Corot, in his later style, emphasizes the softness of the foliage and the way in which it seems to melt into the surrounding atmosphere. Birches and willows are his favorite subjects. Henri Rousseau, unlike Corot, takes pains to delineate each individual leaf and delights in constructing patterns of leaves in which each leaf exists as a stiff, relatively self-contained object. Tropical vegetation lends itself to such treatment, and this is one reason . . . for Rousseau's love of tropical forests. Cézanne, in his treatment of trees as of other perceptual objects, is interested in their three-dimensional solidity and, particularly in his later years, in the manner in which they contrast visually with their background . . . .Witness the strength of his trunks, the dynamic thrust of his branches, the manner in which his foliage relates itself to its supporting branches, and the way in which his trees exist as individual entities in three-dimensional space. He is also interested in the endless play of light and shadow, and of warm and cold color, which trees in the sunlight so clearly manifest. André Derain resembles Cézanne in many ways, but . . . he emphasizes the sinewy, tensile, almost rubbery character of the twisting branches. Matisse . . . is always primarily interested in two-dimensional decorative character of perceptual objects. His trees . . . are represented less for their own intrinsic character than as occasions for, and aids to, the creation of an interesting pictorial design. Yet even Matisse catches some of the flair and sweep of tree trunks and branches.[10]

And that is only one of many ways of looking at these landscape paintings. Here is a very different one, of Cézanne, developed by Bernard Berenson and described here by R. G. Collingwood:

> His landscapes have lost almost every trace of visuality. Trees never looked like that; that is how they feel to a man who encounters them with his eyes shut, blundering against them blindly. A bridge is no longer a pattern of color . . . it is a perplexing mixture of projections and recessions, over and round which we find ourselves feeling our way as one can imagine an infant feeling its way, when it has barely begun to crawl, among the nursery furniture. And over the landscape broods the obsession of Mont Saint-Victoire, never looked at, but always felt, as a child feels the table over the back of its head.[11]

Can we perceive objects in nature in these ways? Indeed we can, though usually not until after the painter has shown us the way. Do objects as we ordinarily see them look to us the way these painters depict them? No, and that is why an acquaintance with their works extends our vision of the world and is

---

[10] Theodore M. Greene, *The Arts and the Art of Criticism* (Princeton: Princeton Univ. Press, 1940), pp. 277–78.

[11] Robin G. Collingwood, *The Principles of Art* (Oxford: The Clarendon Press, 1938), p. 144.

not merely a reduplication of it. Art is, after all, not a carbon copy of nature; if it were, we could well say, "Forget the carbon copy, give me the original." If looking at paintings is more rewarding to many persons than looking at nature itself, this may be because art is not an imitation of nature but an *imaginative transformation* of nature, and the transformation that the artist gives us is often more satisfying than the original that presents itself to our vision. When Turner showed one of his landscapes to a lady, she exclaimed, "But I never saw a sunset like that!" and he replied, "Madam, don't you wish you could?"

What are we to say, finally, of the value of representation in visual art? Formalists, as we have seen, find it to be irrelevant to the appreciation of art; they admire many representational works, but not because of their representations. At the other extreme, some may find some works of interest solely because of the representations they contain. Others may find the fusionist view—that the representational and formal elements should not only be adapted to each other but that in one's experience of art they tend to fuse into one—to be more acceptable than either of the extremes. What would Cézanne's work be without the mastery of form? But at the same time, what would Cézanne's work be without the very special and unique way in which he represents things in the world of our experience?

When Clive Bell was praising the development of the great nineteenth-century painter Georges Seurat from interest in representation to exclusive interest in form, he wrote,

> In *La Baignade* there are still indications of muscles, and I have seen a study for one of the seated figures wherein the muscles are fully and very beautifully rendered; and if in such a picture as *Chahut* (1890) he has reduced muscles to their simplest geometrical equivalents that is not because he could not draw muscles with the best—or worst, but because by eliminating details he sought to give his design an easily apprehended intensity which would have been lost in a multiplicity of complicated forms . . . .Think of the processional movement of those figures, those cylinders, in *La Grande-Jatte:* here is an art nearer to architecture than to painting as understood and practiced in 1886 . . . .
>
> Few painters can have felt more passionately than Seurat; none perhaps has compressed his feelings more pitilessly. Every twist he gave the vice meant, at the first pang, the sacrifice of some charming quality; but every sacrifice was rewarded in the end by added intensity. Turn from his grand hieratic compositions to his studies of sea and shore at Grandchamp and Honfleur: all the familiar charm of sand and water has been squeezed out, but in exchange we are offered subtleties of tone—or rather of relations of tones—which I think I am right in saying had never before been rendered. . . . By the remorseless suppression of all those enchanting harmonies by which the Impressionists ravished and still ravish us, Seurat has contrived to reveal relations, to touch chords, I will not say more moving, but rarer and more acute.[12]

[12] Clive Bell, *Landmarks in Nineteenth Century Painting* (London: Chatto and Windus, 1927), pp. 200-203.

Yet there are viewers who value the very same "familiar charm of sand and water" in Seurat's work as much as, or more than, formal "architecture" of his later work, just as there are those who find the early representational works of Mondrian as much worth treasuring as the more famous, angular, and totally nonrepresentational work. There is an additional element also, the expressive quality, which must also be considered in the assessment of art; but we shall be concerned with this in the next chapter.

## 2. REPRESENTATION IN LITERATURE

What kinds of characters and actions should literature represent? One answer is, "anything and everything"—no exceptions, no qualifications, as long as it's real. Literature should describe simply a *slice of life*—unadorned, unchanged, unfiltered. One should "tell it like it is," or "give it straight, with nothing added or subtracted."

Such a view was held by the late nineteenth-century novelist Emile Zola and set forth in his book *The Experimental Novel.* The novel he envisions

> no longer interests itself in the ingenuity of a well-invented story, developed according to certain rules. Imagination has no longer place, plot matters little to the novelist, who bothers himself with neither development, mystery, nor denouement. He does not intervene to take away from or add to reality. He does not construct a framework out of whole cloth, according to the needs of a preconceived idea. You start from the point that nature is sufficient, that you must accept it as it is, without modification or pruning; it is grand enough, beautiful enough to supply its own beginning, its middle, and its end. Instead of imagining an adventure or complicating it, of arranging stage effects, which scene by scene will lead to a final conclusion, you simply take the life study of a person or group of persons, whose actions you faithfully depict. The work becomes a report, nothing more; it has but the merit of exact observation.[13]

The novelist becomes an observant reporter of the human scene, not its interpreter and never its judge:

> The novelist is but a recorder who is forbidden to judge and to conclude. . . . The facts are thus; experiment tried in such and such conditions gives such and such results; and he stops there; for if he wishes to go beyond the phenomena he will enter into hypothesis; we shall have probabilities, not science. . . . He himself disappears, he keeps his emotion well in hand, he simply shows what he has seen. Here is the truth; shiver or laugh before it, draw from it whatever lesson you please, the only task of the author has been to put before you the true data. . . . One cannot well imagine a chemist becoming incensed with a zote,

[13] Emile Zola, *The Experimental Novel* (New York: The Cassell Publishing Co., 1894), pp. 123–124.

because this body is injurious to life, or sympathizing with oxygen for the contrary reason. In the same way, a novelist who feels the need of becoming indignant with vice, or applauding virtue, not only spoils the data he produces, for his intervention is as trying as it is useless, but the work loses its strength; it is no longer a marble page hewn from the block of reality; it is matter worked up, kneaded by the emotions of the author, and such emotions are always subject to prejudices and errors.

We teach the bitter science of life, we give the high esteem of reality. Here is what exists; endeavor to repair it. We are but savants, analyzers, anatomists; and our works have the certainty, the solidity, and the practical applications of scientific works. I know of no school more moral or more austere.[14]

Let us grant, at least for the moment, that the novelist should not moralize. There are still many problems with Zola's account, which attempts to reduce the role of the novelist to that of experimental scientist:

1. *The need for selection.* Even if the novelist presents "the truth," he cannot present "the whole truth" any more than the witness in court can possibly tell "the whole truth" which he swears an oath to tell. From among the infinite subject-matter possibilities in the world, he must select some subject, some series of human events. He must begin his story somewhere, and end it somewhere; and whatever he selects will already give some indication that he considers what he has selected for treatment as more interesting, more significant, or more important than all other subjects he could have selected but did not.

Even within the range of what he does select, he must omit most of the details; if, for example, he selects as his subject a year in the life of some historical person, he will not describe how often he urinated or what food the person ate at every meal, or in what way the fork was conveyed from the plate to his mouth with every mouthful. Not only would the story become a colossal bore, but it would take forever in the telling; no lifetime, however long, would be enough to tell it. He must select, select, and then select some more, and even if he takes as his subject the career of some actual person, and doesn't have to invent details, he must rigorously select from the total. Presumably he will make a selection which will, at the least, *unify* his work. As Aristotle said in the *Poetics* (section 8), "The story, as an imitation [representation] of action, must represent one action, a complete whole, with its several incidents so closely connected that the transposal or withdrawal of any one of them will disjoin and dislocate the whole. For that which makes no perceptible difference by its presence or absence is no real part of the whole." This is, of course, a formal requirement; but life reported raw does not meet any such requirement of form. No life history has all its segments as closely intertwined as that, and it is the author who will have to select and organize his material in such a way as to achieve it.

One can hardly accuse a motion picture of failing to be photographic; yet

[14] *Ibid.,* pp. 125–126.

everything depends on what the camera focuses on, how, how long, and in what context. In the film *Night Must Fall,* after a headless victim has been discovered, and as the characters are wondering who committed the deed, the camera focuses on a hat box; the audience immediately concludes, what the characters do not yet know, that the hat box contains the severed head. The camera *says* nothing, but the conspicuous selection of this detail at this point does the job of revealing to the audience a detail which in other films would have been left a mystery till the end. Similarly an author reveals countless details and withholds or submerges others.

2. *Stylistic coloration.* Not only the details he selects, but the manner in which he presents them, will "color" his account. No two authors selecting exactly the same details of the same person's life would describe them identically. Just as the same stretch of ocean, at the same moment, will look different when one photographs into the sunlight than what it does when one photographs with the sun behind one, so the same set of incidents will leave a different impression and have a different thrust and impact depending on how the author marshals and organizes them and the way in which he describes them. The same incident, described by four different people, would give a very different impression—not necessarily as different as the four versions of the murder in the film *Rashomon,* but the account would be colored by what details the different people observed. Even if they were told to concentrate on certain details and ignore others, their accounts would have different emphases, depending on their interests and conceptions of significance; the events would be organized into different patterns. Each of the reporters would have a different manner of presentation, which alone would give different impressions of the attitude of the observer and the emotional impact of the scene of each one. Style, as we have seen, is not independent of meaning, but meaning includes secondary meaning, and different observers, no matter how accurate and uninvolved they tried to be, would use words with differing secondary meanings, resulting in a different feeling-tone. Whereas one would say, "He murdered her in cold blood," another might say, "He smiled, aimed the pistol, and shot her," whereas still another would say, "He took the gun in his hands and fired; the bullet left the gun and implanted itself into her brain two inches above her eyes"; and so on. Even the simplest incident would be reported differently: if one little girl says, "I saw my father," and the other, "I saw my daddy," this tells us a great deal about the probable attitudes of each one toward her male parent. Since most words have a great deal of secondary meaning packed into them, there is no way, if one is using language at all, to avoid this consequence.

An author will betray his sympathy for certain characters and lack of sympathy for others, not only by the actions he describes them as performing, but by the manner in which he describes them, reserving certain adjectives for one character and nearly synonymous adjectives with a different secondary meaning for another. If there is no innocent eye in visual art, there is no innocent eye—or should one say no innocent pen—in literature. Sir Arthur Quiller-Couch defined literature as "life seen through a temperament"—and there is no way, even if one could wish, to keep the temperament out. One of the founders of the American school of "literary realism," William Dean Howells, who defined realism in literature simply as "truthful presentation of material," selects (among all possible subjects) the rise of an American industrialist in *The Rise of Silas Lapham,* and although he remained fairly detached from the action and never commented on it as author, there is little doubt that he treats his character on the whole with sympathy.

In film, the "manner of selection" will not be the selection of words (except for the script) but the selection of devices such as close-ups, camera angles, camera motion, dissolves, and so on. Since the viewer sees the action through the lens of the camera, he sees only what the camera chooses to reveal, from the angle that it chooses to reveal it. What is revealed (or not revealed), and when, can make or break the movie. An instructive example occurs in the following criticism of a scene in Stanley Kubrick's film *The Shining:*

> There's a shot of Shelley Duvall snooping around the writing table of her author-husband Jack Nicholson to see what he's been working on for weeks. The camera is behind the table, low, and her head comes into view over the top of the typewriter. It's not only a new angle on a commonplace action, it heightens the sense of illicit peering. Then this feeling of scared intrusion into her husband's madness—the evidence is in the machine and in finished pages—is blown away when Kubrick shoots Nicholson's discovery of her intrusion with Nicholson in the foreground, watching her in the background. Because we see him seeing her, we're not scared when he speaks. If the camera had been on Duvall and his voice had cut in, Kubrick would have peaked the suspense that the opening shot of the sequence had begun.[15]

3. *Necessary invention.* Besides the main character is usually imaginary—not taken directly from life, though he may have been a pastiche of various persons taken from life. Even so, the author's own imagination selected details, decided which to emphasize, in what order the events were to occur, how they were to be propelled toward a climax. Even when a novelist takes as his subject-matter the life of an actual person, he not only must select the most significant incidents and tell them from a point of view, but he will almost always find it necessary to *invent* scenes that never took place—partly for formal reasons (continuity, unity, progression, climax) and partly to bring out the nature of the characters and the conflicts: a good invented scene, such as a confrontations scene at a crucial point in the characters' history, can often do that a thousand times more than any actual scene, however selectively reported.

[15] Stanley Kaufmann, *The New Republic,* June 14, 1980, p. 26.

Just as painting is not photography, literature is not reporting. A novelist or storywriter can take practically any news story, or series of events in history, and make them far more dramatic and compelling and insightful by eliminating some details, changing others, inventing scenes to bring out character, propel the action forward, and make them fall into a dominant pattern. Just as nature seldom processes a picture, so actual biography seldom brings forth a good story unaided. In life two people may never, for example, have a direct dialogue on their fundamental attitudes toward life, and if one were restricted to reporting what actually happened, one could not include such a scene; the good novelist, however, could devise one, bringing out at one stroke the fundamental drives and motives of the respective characters and adding tension and excitement into the narrative. Most conversations in life are insufferably dull and hardly bear recording. A murder trial may be exciting, but a stenographic report would be extremely dull if one reads an unabridged transcript; much of the material is boring, much of it irrelevant to any significant action, and the climaxes occur, it at all, in the wrong places. Even a mediocre storywriter by a few deft touches could make it far more exciting as a story, even if he were not concerned with overall significance.

Shakespeare borrowed most of his plots from previous plays and, in his historical dramas, from history; but although he was on the whole quite faithful to history, he knew when to change history and when to leave it alone. If Shakespeare had followed history, Hotspur in *Henry IV Part I* would have died by the end of the first act; but since there were reasons for making him a principal character, he kept Hotspur alive until the play was nearly over, which made for more interesting drama though not more accurate history.

The moral of the tale is plain: neither visual art nor literary art is just a "slice of life." Nor is any art a carbon copy of life. Just as one is always at least subconsciously aware in viewing a painting of the painter who painted it—why did he put these heavy brush strokes here? why that figure in the left corner?—so in reading a story one knows that the words did not fall into that order by themselves and that their selection and ordering is the work of the author, who guides and shapes them purposively. And just as one cannot imagine the visual world as seen from *nobody's* point of view, one cannot imagine the human scene depicted by the author without the "human equation" present—even detachment (as in Flaubert) is an attitude. Literature could not be created, even if one desired it to be created, by an author without attitudes and feelings, a mental set, a background of habit patterns, conflicts and ideals, which imbue his creations. If this is so, we need speculate no further about Zolaesque ideals for literature. Not only did Zola never achieve it himself in his own novels, not only would it have been a mass of raw undigested material if he had done so, but there is no way he *could* have done so. One must see the world through *some* eyes or other, and the novelist's eye is no more innocent than the painter's.

Elements of Literary Representation

In all narrative fiction—novels, short stories, plays (including poetic drama)—several elements are present.

(1) There is *plot,* or the series of events described. Aristotle considered plot the most important of all the elements in a narrative: Literature, he said, is a description of action, and everything else is incidental.

(2) There is *character:* someone must perform the actions, and the initiators of actions are the characters. If the characterization is too thin, the reader does not usually care enough about the characters to care what happens to them; if we can imaginatively identify with the characters, the action—what they do or what happens to them—will matter to us. On the other hand, there are many novels, such as those of mystery and detection, in which "what happens next" is what the reader mainly cares about, and the character is not described any more fully than would enable the reader to pigeonhole him in his mind as "a good guy" or "a bad guy." At the opposite extreme, some stories are primarily character sketches, with nothing much happening to the character; here our attention is riveted almost exclusively on the character with little attention to action.

(3) There is the *setting*—the physical circumstances in which the drama is laid—the stage on which the action is set. Usually the setting is auxiliary, but not always: in Thomas Hardy's *Return of the Native* one might say that the central character is not a person at all but Egdon Heath, the place where the action occurs and whose nature sets the tone for the action and gives special life to the characters. The entire first chapter is given over to a description of the heath, and only in the second chapter do we encounter characters or action.

(4) There is sometimes a *theme,* or underlying idea, which is illustrated by the action. Not all narratives have this—some are just an interesting story and no more—but others have a moral, a point the author is trying to illustrate through the action.

Many of the distinctions already made in visual art can be applied also to literary art. Although representation in literature is through description in words and not through direct visual presentation, we still speak of the representation of characters, objects, and events in literature. Most literary genres contain characters and, unlike visual arts, their actions are through time, though some, such as love poems, contain no plot or characters at all, unless one takes the author of the poem (the speaker) to be the solo character. We can distinguish depiction and portrayal just as in visual art: in a novel there is depiction of (for example) five people lost in the jungle after a plane crash and what happens to them. There can also be a portrayal of specific persons, such as Napoleon and Kutuzov, the opposing generals in the War of 1812, in Tolstoy's *War and Peace.*

The world is populated with *persons;* works of literature contain *characters*. Even if the character is based on the life of a historical person, he appears as a character in a novel. Napoleon and Kutuzov were persons, but they are characters in Tolstoy's novel. When the literary genre is biography, however, the subject is a person, not a character. The difference is that in a biography there is an implicit claim to factual accuracy: if the biography of a man describes him as doing something which in fact he never did, the biography can be faulted for inaccuracy; and so can a chronicle or history book. But in a novel, even a historical novel, the author is at liberty to invent scenes out of whole cloth and attribute to the character actions and conversations which never took place, or which no one (including the author) knows whether they took place as described. The novelist is first a fiction writer and only second (and then only occasionally, when the novel has a historical basis) a reporter of historical facts. Shakespeare's historical plays are based on the lives of kings of England, but Shakespeare distorts history when it suits his purpose and makes them speak lines of poetry which it is safe to say they never uttered.

The author is, of course, the person who wrote the novel. But even when the novel is told in the first person, the author is not to be identified with the *speaker* or *narrator* of the novel. In some of Joseph Conrad's novels, written in first person, the narrator answers to the name of Marlowe: Marlowe is the narrator although Conrad is the author—thus serving to detach the narrator (and his life and views) from the author. In "The Royal Game," although the author is Stefan Zweig, we are not told who the narrator is—whether he is or is not to be identified with the author; and in this case it probably does not matter, since nothing in the story turns on it. *Huckleberry Finn* was written by Mark Twain (Samuel Clemens), but it is told in the first person and the narrator is Huckleberry Finn himself, though his words views are often at variance with Mark Twain's views. Not only is Huckleberry Finn the narrator but he is also the principal *character* in the novel and chief participant in the action. (Sometimes the narrator is a passive spectator reporting the action, as he is for the most part in "The Royal Game," except when he interviews Dr. B.) Sometimes, on the other hand, the narrator is indistinguishable from the author, as in Fielding's *Tom Jones,* when the narrator at the beginning of each section gives the reader a gently humorous sermon on manners and morals, which are presumably (though not necessarily) those of the author, Fielding, himself.

Characters in literature can be portrayed in varying degrees of detail and depth. Sometimes a character portrayal in a novel, story, or play is so detailed that the reader feels by the time he has finished reading that he knows the character "inside out." Such are called *three-dimensional* characters. Usually only a few main characters in a novel are three-dimensional, sometimes just one; in some novels, where plot is emphasized to the exclusion of character, no character at all may be three-dimensional. Most characters are portrayed much less thoroughly: only a few significant traits are described, usually enough to make the character credible and to sustain the action, but not enough to constitute an in-depth character presentation. These are called *two-dimensional* characters.

With respect to characterization, the literary artist has a great advantage over the painter and sculptor: he can describe the character acting through an extended period of *time*. (So, of course, can film.) He is not limited to the description of speech and actions; and he can assume the mantle of omniscience and describe to us what is going on in the character's mind, what he is thinking and feeling, what his attitudes, intentions, and motives are. But in a drama, where everything is depicted through speech and action on the stage, he cannot do this, but must give us an insight into the character entirely through representation of behavior. (This is true even in a dramatic tour de force like O'Neill's *Strange Interlude* and *Mourning Becomes Electra,* in which the audience is supposed to know what the characters' real motives and feelings are by the *sotto voce* asides which they utter, which the audience can hear but the other characters supposedly cannot.)

Many novelists, such as Dostoyevsky, seldom or never avail themselves of the novelist's privilege of entering directly into the minds of his characters; although his characterizations are among the most profound in literature, he describes their speech and behavior in detail, and we get the character portrait entirely from these. One of the great short story writers, Katherine Mansfield, describes "minimal cues" in the characters' behavior, never once telling us directly what they feel or think; yet so telling is the description, with such a feeling for significant detail, that when a man and a woman meet after ten years and have tea together, it is perfectly plain after ten pages of trivial tea-talk that he no longer really cares but that she still cares very deeply; but it is all done through description of speech and behavior. Nevertheless, a character described "from the inside" as well as from the outside (through behavior and speech) can also be extremely effective, though it is limited by most novelists and storytellers to one or a very few major characters; the other characters are presented entirely "from the outside."

## 3. REPRESENTATION IN MUSIC

We have seen how visual arts and literature can be said to represent persons, things, and events in the world. Can music be representational also?

The vast majority of musical compositions make no such attempt. Songs often tell stories and operas always do, but in these mixed arts it is the words that tell the stories. But what about music unaccompanied by words?

There are numerous musical compositions which their composers have devised specifically to *tell a story*. Berlioz's *Sinfonie Fantastique,* Dukas's *The*

*Sorcerer's Apprentice,* and numerous tone-poems by Richard Strauss, such as *Don Quixote, Ein Heldenleben, Till Eulenspiegel's Merry Pranks, Don Juan,* and so on. Other musical compositions tell no stories but do have *descriptive titles,* and the music is intended to illustrate in some way the subject indicated by the title: Debussy's *Nuages* and *Fêtes,* for example, and Delius's *Song before Sunrise, Summer Night on the River, Paris, Sea Drift,* and many others. Some would say that only the first of these two groups is properly called program music, since only members of the first group tell a story or relate a sequence of events. But it may be useful to discuss the second group as well, to see what connection there is between the music and the subject-matter indicated by the title.

In program music there is assumed to be a "natural" relation, as opposed to a conventional relation, between the music and the program—specifically, a relation of *resemblance.* The resemblance should be great enough so that we can "perceive the connection" between the two, much as we can look at a representational painting and say, "That's a woman and two children in front of a log cabin," without having been told this in advance. Our question is; "Does program music provide any such resemblance between the sounds of the music and the alleged subject of the composition?"

1. *Musical representation of other sounds.* If painting can make us more sensitive to what the world looks like, can music make us more sensitive to what the world *sounds* like? If painting can cause us to see the world in new ways, can music make us hear the world in new ways? Painting certainly cannot show us what things sound like, and it would seem equally hopeless for music to show us what things look like.

Can music duplicate any of the sounds of nature? Certainly it cannot do so with any exactness, since in nature we find almost entirely *noises* (sounds with no definite pitch), whereas the sounds emanating from musical instruments (with a few exceptions, such as drums) are *tones* (sounds with a definite pitch). There is no sound in nature that could be mistaken for the tones emanating from pianos or violins or flutes or trombones. As for musical harmonies, probably no one has ever heard a musical chord in nature. And as for melodies, the only instance that comes to mind are bird songs, and even these, at least most of the time, cannot be tied to a musical scale.

> The systematic succession of measurable tones which we call *melody* is not to be met with in nature, even in its most rudimentary form. Sound phenomena in unassisted nature present no intelligible proportions; neither can they be reduced to our scale. Just as little as melody, do we find in nature . . . *harmony* in a musical sense, the simultaneous occurrence of certain notes. Has anybody ever heard a triad, a chord of the sixth or seventh in nature? Harmony, like melody, is an achievement of man, only belonging to a much later period.[16]

[16] Eduard Hanslick, *The Beautiful in Music* (New York: Novello, Ewer & Co., 1891), pp. 144–145.

In general, the analogy between painting and music seems to break down. Music appears to give us little if any added insight into the sounds of nature as painting does into the sights of nature. Who can say that the study of music has enriched his conception of the sounds in nature in the way the study of painting has enriched his conception of the sights of nature?

Toward the end of Vaughn Williams's *Sinfonia Antarctica,* there is a depiction of a snowstorm (at least an intended depiction) by a wind machine which is added to the regular instruments of the orchestra. As program music goes, it does sound remarkably like what it was supposed to depict. This is perhaps as good a case as one could find of the sounds emanating from the orchestra resembling the sounds of nature. Another example that might be suggested is Debussy's tone-poem *La Mer,* intended to capture the sounds of the sea (we shall discuss the sights in a moment): while composing it Debussy spent weeks at the French seaside, studying the rhythms of the waves as they crashed against the rocks. In the tone-poem there is no great resemblance to the actual *sounds* of the sea, but there is some resemblance to the *rhythms* of the sea.

> In the galloping of the horse, the clack of the mill, the singing of the blackbird and the quail, there is an element of periodically recurring motion in the successive beats which, when looked at in the aggregate, blend into an intelligible whole. . . . But the point in which natural rhythm differs from human music is obvious: in music there is no independent rhythm; it occurs only in connection with melody and harmony expressed in a rhythmical order. Rhythm in nature, on the other hand, is associated neither with melody nor with harmony.[17]

Even when the resemblance is considerable, it is not usually great enough so that one would have guessed the subject without first knowing the title. Even if one hears the composition repeatedly, one is usually unable to get it right. I have at various times played a recording of *La Mer* (especially the last section, "The Dialogue of the Wind and the Waves") to persons unfamiliar with the work and asked them to guess the title. The answers were various: a thunderstorm, a fight in a barroom, a railway train going through a tunnel. Only when I revealed the title did the person usually exclaim, "Of course!" and after that it seemed obvious—but it had not seemed obvious before. If the sound of A (the music) resembles the sound of B (some sound in nature), it apparently does so no more than it also resembles C, D, and E (other sounds in nature). This is very different from painting, in which it is usually quite clear and unambiguous what objects are being represented.

But most programmatic titles do not refer exclusively to sounds; in fact, more titles are visual than auditory. Even *La Mer* itself is generally supposed to "convey" to us the sight and feel of the sea as well as its sounds.

2. *Musical representation other than sounds.* How, one might well ask, can music represent sights or smells or tastes or anything other than sounds? It

[17] *Ibid.,* pp. 145–146.

would seem that it cannot represent these at all—but it depends on how loosely we use the word "represent." If we use it as we did in discussing visual arts—depiction-subjects and portrayal-subjects—then we must admit that music cannot represent that which is not sounds at all, any more than painting can represent that which is not sights. Nevertheless, although we might not wish to call it representation, there are certain *intersensory similarities* among the data of sense. For example, you can have sharp pointed objects and sharp staccato sounds; the word "sharp" applies to them both. One could object that the word "sharp" here is ambiguous and doesn't mean the same in the two sentences; still, the two senses aren't unrelated—if one knew what a sharp object was and heard someone talking about a sharp sound, he might well guess, without having been told, what kind of sound was meant. Although no one would probably guess the title of Debussy's *Nuages* (Clouds), it is true that the succession of musical sounds that constitute this composition have a light, airy quality, and move in tenuous, indeterminate ways, as if floating (the sounds are not tied to any one key for long), like cumulus clouds. There may also be a certain appropriateness in the title "Reflections in the Water," which Debussy gave to one of his piano compositions. Reflections in water do not make sounds, so if sounds can be like only other sounds the composition would have to consist of nothing but silence in order to fit its title. But when a tone in the treble is immediately paralleled by the same tone in the bass clef, repeatedly, this succession is reminiscent of a parallelism of sights when one sees some scene in nature and then sees the same scene reflected in still water.

The trouble is that, if we say A represents B because A is similar in some way to B, we shall probably have to say that A also represents C and D and E because it has some similarities to these as well.

> If we allow that music signifies [represents] every mental process to which it is iconic [which it resembles], then, since many qualitatively different mental processes may have the same kinetic pattern, musical signification is bound to be incurably ambiguous. A long crescendo, as in Ravel's *Bolero,* might signify bursting with joy or blowing your top.[18]

Thus far we have been pursuing possible resemblances between musical compositions (or passages) and things, qualities, and events outside music. Someone might object, however, that to do this is to pursue the wrong path: "The tone-poem by Debussy represents the sea *because he gave it that title*—that's all he needed to do to make the one represent the other." In other words, there need be (according to this view) no natural relation of resemblance between the two, but only a *stipulation* by the composer, given in the title, of what the composition shall stand for. To take this line is to abandon all need for resemblance: "A represents B because the composer said so?" "And if he had changed the title of *Nuages* (Clouds) to *Bryce Canyon at*

---

[18] Monroe C. Beardsley, *Aesthetics* (New York: Harcourt Brace, 1958), p. 336.

*Sunset,* then that's what the composition would have represented?" At this point he might say yes, if he found the new title equally appropriate; but if it was something wildly inappropriate like "Tornado over Kansas" (while the composition itself is the epitome of calmness), he would at least hesitate—for at this point he would come to see that, however elastic the business of giving musical titles, there must be *some* relation perceivable between the title of the piece and what it represents, and that merely stipulating will not do; some relation between A and B must exist, and it cannot be created by an act of stipulation.

Most listeners probably do not take titles all that seriously; at any rate, they need not: if they find that the title doesn't fit, or distracts their attention, they may be able to enjoy the composition more by not thinking of the title at all. All that the title does, as a rule, is to *channel one's responses* to the composition along a certain line, which would not have occurred without being given the title. After knowing the title of *La Mer,* one associates it from then on with the sea; and it is for each listener to say for himself whether doing this enriches this total experience of the composition or not. Many listeners believe that *all* compositions would be better off without titles, since the title tends to distract one's attention away from the composition and its internal structure and into the wild, woolly realm of mental associations: "How is this pattern of sounds like clouds? I enjoy the composition but I don't see the connection with clouds—perhaps I'm missing something," and so on. Anything, they say, that takes our attention *away* from the composition itself, *toward* something else which lies outside it, is better dispensed with. "To say to the painter that he should copy nature," said Whistler, "is to say to the composer that he should sit on the piano."

Whether one prefers to retain or to dispense with such titles, it seems advisable to say that music is *not* a representational art. We can associate passages of music with certain things outside, and passages of music may to a degree resemble certain qualities of things in the outside world, but none of this is tantamount to saying that the music *represents* it. How can a series of sounds be "a musical portrait of Don Quixote" in the way that we have a literary portrait in Cervantes's novel, where his actions and characteristics are fully *described?* How can music describe? How can a series of sounds portray a duchess, for example, in the clear and unambiguous way that a pictorial representation of her does? How, for that matter, can it do so *at all?* How would one refute someone who said, "How can you tell it's a duchess? or a cat? or nothing at all?"

If we applied to musical representation the same criteria we do for representation in visual arts and literature, we would see that the whole idea of "musical representation" collapses completely: we have an A associated with a B (thanks to the title) in a listener's mind, but that doesn't show what the composition is *about* (or that it is "about" anything at all), any more than a picture is about my childhood experiences because I think of those experiences every time I see the picture. Music is not the *re*creation of anything—music is an art of pure *creation,* of combinations of sound that are unlike anything that existed in the world before those sounds were created by the composer.

If the composer has attached a program to the combination of sounds he created, nothing need be said against this, provided that the listener can take or leave it as he chooses. Program music, as Ernest Newman remarked, must still be *music;* and if it is bad music, it cannot escape condemnation just because it has a program. The relation of the program to the music is not even as intimate as that of a tail to a dog, in which the dog does the wagging, not the tail; it is rather like that of a garment to the body which it covers—the body may be enhanced by this particular garment, but if the garment does not suit the body that wears it, then the garment can be discarded or replaced with no resulting injury to the body.

## 4. SYMBOLS IN THE ARTS

To represent is one thing, to symbolize is another. The circle above the Madonna's head *represents* a halo; the halo *symbolizes* divinity. We have discussed what is involved in representation; what is involved in being a symbol?

The words "sign" and "symbol" are used in so many different ways that it would take a long time to untangle them all, and most of the overlapping senses in which these words are used have nothing specifically to do with the arts.

Anything whatever, A, is said to *mean* something else, B, if A stands for B in some way or other. The word "cat" means a certain species of domestic animals. A small circle on the bottom line of the treble clef means a whole note, the E above middle C. A certain kind of ring means that someone is telephoning you, another that someone is at the door. Ordinarily A is more accessible, but B is what we are primarily interested in, and we use the A as (in one way or another) an indicator of B. These As that stand for Bs have been classified in many ways, into (for example) signs, symbols, and signals, with unending controversies about how each of these terms is to be used and why.

Since our present concern is with the arts, it will fortunately be unnecessary to go into these various niceties. What is important for our purposes, however, is to distinguish those cases in which the standing-for is *natural* from those in which it is *conventional.*

Some regular correlations between certain As (events, processes) and Bs occur in nature quite independently of human wills; they would exist even if no human beings existed. Some of these are *causal* relations: the combined action of the sun and moon causes tides, the sun causes the earth to have warmth and light, sexual intercourse causes offspring to come into existence, storms cause trees to fall down. Some of them are *signs* to us that something else is about to occur: dark nimbus clouds are signs that rain is coming, a twister in the sky means that a tornado is approaching, a falling barometer means that a storm is on the way. These too occur independently of human volition, and human beings *discover* in these cases that A is a sign of B, but they do not *make* A a sign of B. This is true even of objects made by man: a certain kind of motor noise is a sign that the fanbelt is broken; although cars are made by man, the fact that the noise is a sign of a condition is the result of the operation of laws of nature independently of man. Again, some As in nature *resemble* some Bs; the reflection of trees in a clear pond resemble the trees that are reflected.

Sometimes the relation between A and B is conventional rather than natural: the relation between the word "cats" and cats is conventional, and other languages use quite different words for the same animal. The relation between the tone middle C and the note middle C on the score is conventional, and there are other systems of musical notation which do not place middle C half way between a bass and a treble clef. Chimes ringing between the acts at a theater mean that the curtain for the next act is about to rise—we could have used other ways of indicating the same thing.

Often the relation between A and B is determined by convention, but the convention itself has some natural basis. Consider the American twenty-five cent piece. That this coin, with its particular insignia, is legal tender of the United States was brought about by convention, through act of Congress. The eagle represented on one face of the coin has a natural relation (resemblance) to eagles, at least enough for us to recognize this represented creature as an eagle without being told. The fact that the eagle was used as a symbol of the United States was again the result of convention, but the fact that this convention was adopted was the result of some shared qualities between eagles and the nation they signify: qualities such as strength, courage, tenacity. (These need not be *actual* qualities either of the eagle or of the nation, but at any rate they must be qualities popularly believed to be true of them, and thus imputed to them, truly or falsely. Foxes need not be cunning, or snakes duplicitous, or lions courageous, or mice meek. Machiavelli's statement "The prince must be both a lion and a fox" is understood even if the qualities of courage and cunning do not belong to lions and foxes, respectively. A weasel or a mosquito would not have been as appropriate a symbol.)

There is no universally agreed-upon definition of the word "symbol," even in the arts. But we come quite close to its actual usage and cover most of the cases in which symbolism has been imputed to objects in works of art, if we explore the cases in which there is a convention by which A stands for B, while yet at the same time there is some natural basis for the convention. The picture of an eagle not only represents (depicts) an eagle, the eagle by virtue of its qualities becomes a *symbol* of the United States. The cross in the Christian tradition—not the word "cross" but the thing, cross—is a symbol of suffering in Christian art as well as Christian tradition, the connection being, of course, the crucifixion of Christ on the cross. In Christian art the sheep is a symbol of discipleship: this symbolism seems appropriate in view of certain qualities of sheep, such as following a leader, though other creatures might have sufficed just as well. White symbolizes purity: if something white exhibits no stain it is probably clean. The flat gilt background in Christian paintings is a symbol of eternity; this one is more nearly conventional, and one would be unlikely to guess it, but still seems more appropriate than, for example, a horse.

In the film *Lost Horizon* (the original 1937 film, not the 1974 remake), there is a scene in which the High Lama of Shangri La dies.

> The writer and director of the movie could have simply left the camera on the Lama, allowing us to see his breath cease and his eyes close. Instead, they chose (with no great originality, of course) to let the camera rest upon a candle flickering before an open window. We watch the flame flicker as a cold gust of air fills the curtain and lets it fall, and then we see the flame go out. We know that the Lama has died. But more than that, we are presumably made to feel countless suggestions about the connection between the soul and flux and change, warmth and light, impermanence and yet eternalness of fire.[19]

The sputtering and going out of the candle are here a symbol of the extinction of life. This is not because human deaths are regularly accompanied by candles going out; nor is the symbolism the product of a convention, as in the case of a flag at half mast. Nevertheless, "the maker of the movie could use the extinction of the candle to signify death without fear of misunderstanding, because the going out of a flame easily suggests—that is, reminds us of, makes us think of—dying."[20]

But why does the one make us think of the other? It would seem that there is a sufficient *analogy* between the two processes to provide a natural basis for the symbolism: the candle burns, then sputters in the wind, then burns brightly again for a moment, then sputters again as a stronger wind arises, and this time goes out. Life too ebbs with much the same variations and is finally extinguished.

What does the symbol *add* to our experience of the film? Our thoughts, attitudes, and feelings are *transferred* from one thing to another and become, so to speak, "cross-fertilized" by the intertwining. There is, according to Mrs. Hungerland, "a transference of trains of thought and the accompanying attitude and feelings . . . from one object to another. If I begin to think and feel about a man, in certain respects, as I did about my father, and to treat him as I treated my father, then he becomes a father-symbol to me. Analogously, . . . when we transfer trains of thought and the related attitudes and feelings from one object to another, a symbol is established."

[19] Everett Carter, quoted in Isabel Hungerland, "Symbols in Poetry," *Poetic Discourse* (Berkeley: Univ. of California Press, 1958), pp. 136–137.

[20] Isabel Hungerland, *op. cit.,* p. 137.

But this model does not appear to fit all cases, for many symbols in art are not as "natural" as this. To realize what complex symbolism can occur in painting, of which most modern viewers are quite unaware, every student of the arts should read Erwin Panofsky's essay "Symbolism and Dürer's Melancholia," an analysis of one painting by Dürer. To most viewers today the painting seems to be simply a representation of an assortment of people and animals gathered about; but to viewers at the time the painting was created, it was the symbolism that they were most aware of.

> Melancholia typifies Theoretical Insight, which thinks but cannot act; the ignorant infant, making meaningless scrawls on his slate and almost conveying the impression of blindness, typifies Practical Skill which acts but cannot think. . . . Theory and practice are thus not "together," as Dürer demands, but thoroughly disunited; and the result is impotence and gloom.[21]

The planet Venus in the painting symbolizes the sanguine temperament, moist and warm like air; Mars symbolizes the choleric temperament; the Moon symbolizes the melancholic temperament. Saturn also symbolizes the mind, Jupiter the soul, and so on.

This symbolism, though there is some natural basis (in some cases), strikes us today as almost wholly conventional, and it "means" very little to us, unless we are immersed in scholarship dealing with Dürer's time. In his day most viewers were acquainted with this symbolism, and their experience of the paintings was much richer than ours is likely to be, because they connected the object with what it symbolized almost as surely as we connect the dab of paint with the object we take it to represent.

Symbolism occurs also in music which is to be distinguished sharply from program music, which attempts to represent some scene or story. In much music prior to the eighteenth century, even compositions that are quite popular today, there is elaborate symbolism of which listeners today are not aware, though at the time it was written it was both intended by the composer and grasped by the audience. In Bach's *B Minor Mass,* in the "Credo" the constantly moving bass symbolizes the constancy and solidarity of the church's faith, and in the duet of the "Credo," "Et in unum Deum," the overlapping phrases symbolize the unity of Father and Son.

To symbolize distance,

> when the text reads "so far," Bach writes an interval in which the tones are widely spaced. . . . Here Bach writes an augmented or diminished ninth. Similarly with the words "wandered far and wide."

[21] Erwin Panofsky, *The Life and Art of Albrecht Dürer* (Princeton: Princeton Univ. Press, 1955), pp. 156–171. Reprinted in Morris Weitz (ed.), *Problems in Aesthetics,* 2nd ed. (New York: Macmillan, 1970); passage quoted is on p. 480.

, "Night and darkness" is symbolized by downward intervals, "deepest abysses" in the basses. Sometimes Bach used the diminished ninth to symbolize, not distance, but anger and horror, on account of that chord's harmonic sharpness. Or again, Bach regularly uses a fugue to symbolize divine law, and all Biblical passages in Bach's cantatas which are of dogmatic importance are set in fugue or canon form. The trumpet symbolizes the divine majesty. The chorale melody occurs ten times (e.g., in "And Thou Shalt Love the Lord Thy God") as a mystical allegory of the number ten. [22]

None of this is programmatic: it does not attempt to *represent* anything but, rather, to *symbolize* various qualities. In the opinion of musical scholars—just as in the Dürer example—modern listeners miss a great deal by being unaware of this symbolism.

When we recognize the five-fold complexity of meaning [in the Bach cantata] and hear it as a simultaneous musical unity, we experience a feeling of immense richness. As we listen, it is as though we were perpetually leaping from one meaning to another. This multiplicity in unity, this combination of spiritual and purely aesthetic pleasure, appears to me unique in its intensity. [23]

To modern listeners, however, it does not strike us as "natural" enough—not as natural, certainly, as the representational relation of Debussy's *La Mer* to the sea.

In Romantic music, which is more easily accessible to listeners today, one of the most instructive examples of symbolism is Wagner's unique opera tetralogy *Der Ring das Nibelungen*. In this enormous work, a kind of sixteen-hour symphony with voices, there are more than four hundred main musical themes, or *leit-motifs*. Each of them stands for some person or some quality. There is the theme of Siegfried, of the god Wotan, of Alberich, of Hagen, and a host of other characters, and the leit-motif announces the person's entrance and occurs sometimes when the character is referred to or even thought of by someone on the stage. Other themes symbolize qualities: there is the leit-motif of the Ring, of Greed, of Hate, of Love, of Death, of Fate. These themes are conventional in that one has to learn them, much as one learns the words of a foreign language; yet once one knows what they are, one feels a certain appropriateness to them (at least to most of them), that the theme "fits" the thing, quality, or character in a way that another one would not. The leit-motif of love is in the violins, lyrical and melting; the Siegfried theme is extroverted, heroic, assertive; the theme of the Curse is a series of descending tones on the trombones that seem to end in an abyss; the theme of Siegfried's death is mournful yet savage, with muted trombones and repeated pairs of

[22] Manfred Bukofzer, "Allegory in Baroque Music," *Journal of the Warburg and Courtauld Institutes,* Vol. 3 (1939–40), pp. 2–3.

[23] *Ibid.,* p. 18.

drumbeats reverberating through the Rhine Valley. As the drama progresses, the various themes interact and intermingle, and each successive scene in each opera absorbs into itself the themes already introduced in previous scenes and previous operas in the series. This makes for an increasingly dense musical texture, often with several themes occurring at once in different parts of the orchestra, and by the time we get to the last act of the last opera (*Götterdämmerung*), as many as twenty leit-motifs enter with subtle variations in the course of two minutes. All this adds enormously to the power of the opera. One can hear it just as music, without knowing the musical symbolism, but then one misses a whole dimension of appreciation: the juxtaposition of the various themes, together with the listener's recollection of their context as they appeared in previous scenes, adds enormously to the felt significance of the scene; without the symbolism much of this effect would be lost.

In one scene, in the two-hour first act of *Götterdämmerung,* the villain Gunther assumes the disguise of Siegfried and comes to Brunnhilde on the rock by night. The fires on the mountaintop flicker ominously, hinting that something menacing is in the wind; by the light of the fires we see the figure that looks like Siegfried, and from Brunnhilde's words of affection we see that she does not perceive any deception; the orchestra emits a confused jangle of sounds, full of ominous warning and mounting terror, but then through it all we hear clearly the theme of Gunther, not the theme of Siegfried. *We* know, though *she* does not. It is one of the most terrifying moments in opera, perhaps in all art. But the full effect would have been quite impossible without knowing the symbolism. You have to master Wagner's musical vocabulary, but once you know it, the progression of events in the *Ring* cycle is a revelation to the listener.

Not all things that we count as symbols in the arts, however, function in the same way. The candle sputtering and going out symbolizes death even though it occurs only once; and although the halo as a symbol of divinity occurs in many paintings, it would have been a symbol even if only one painter had chosen to use it. But especially in the temporal arts, there are objects which *become* symbolic by their *repetition* or *repeated occurrence* in important contexts; without recurrence no one would think of them as symbols at all. The primary symbol in Tolstoy's novel *Anna Karenina* is that of the train—although on its first appearance in the novel the train does not strike us as symbolic.

> At the beginning of the novel, Anna meets the man who will be her lover, Vronsky, on the Moscow-St. Petersburg express. As they meet, there has been an accident; a workman has been killed by the train coming in to the station. This is the beginning of Anna's doom, which is completed when she throws herself under a train and is killed; and the last we see of Vronsky is in a train, with a toothache; he is being seen off by a friend to the wars. The train is necessary to the plot of the novel, and I believe it is also symbolic, both of the iron forces of

material progress that Tolstoy hated so and that played a part in Anna's moral destruction, and also of those iron laws of necessity and consequence that govern human action when it remains on the sensual level.[24]

The train becomes invested with more significance on each appearance in the novel, and its emotional significance becomes woven into the story. It acts as a kind of *recurring prop* in the narrative.

One could read the novel through without its ever occurring to the reader that the train is a symbol. What then is added if we view it as a symbol? For one thing, it acts as a *unifying* element in the story—it ties the story together. More important, it lends it great *affective* significance: many things we associate with trains—their power, their strength, their impersonality—are associated also with those aspects of the story that occur in connection with this central prop. If you still think the train is only a train and not to be construed as a symbol (after all, Tolstoy never mentions that it is to be taken as a symbol, and no one suggests that trains in *other* novels or dramas or paintings are to be taken as symbolic), there is no way of proving it. There is no established conventional base here as there is in our examples from painting—but there is a considerable difference in the way the novel will appear significant to us. Compare it with this case: is the whale in *Moby Dick* simply a whale (a represented object) or is it also a symbol of evil?

To become a symbol, an object in a work of art must take on a strong *affective quality*—either developed within the work of art itself, as in *Anna Karenina*, or in the relation of the work of art to something outside it, as in the case of the candle, where the similarity (or analogy) was already present and had only to be taken up and used. The degree of "naturalness" of the symbol, however, varies considerably: if the natural basis is slight, the conventional base must be well established, and if the conventional basis is absent (as in *Anna Karenina*), the natural basis must be, or become, strong and powerful. But there appears to be no one formula that will cover all cases of symbolism in the arts.

A word of caution about symbols is in order. There is a tendency, especially in literature courses, to look for disguised symbolism everywhere, and to make the detection by the student of hidden symbols a kind of test of the sensitivity of one's reading. But while it is admirable to find things that are present but lie hidden, it is less admirable to "discover" what is not there. Works have been written, for example, to demonstrate that *The Odyssey* contains an elaborate symbolism of the Freudian type—the wanderings of Odysseus symbolize the oedipal return of the wanderer to the womb of mother, and so on. In all such speculations, one alternative is seldom discussed: that *The Odyssey* is simply a good story, with no symbolism in it at all. One would have to

[24] Mary McCarthy, "Settling the Colonel's Hash," *Harpers,* February 1954, pp. 72–73.

decide the merits of each case individually, of course; but meanwhile one would do well to keep in mind that the study of literature offers many rewards other than opportunities for recondite symbol hunting.

## 5. MEANING IN THE ARTS

In a way all the topics we are discussing could be incorporated under the general heading of "meaning." The word is simply too broad; it is also extremely ambiguous, as C. K. Ogden and I. A. Richards amply showed in their trail-blazing work, *The Meaning of Meaning* (1920), in which they isolated sixteen *principal* sense of the word "meaning." Thus when one asks, "What does a work of art *mean*?" the question is crying out for classification. Before a question can be answered, we must know specifically what the questioner is asking. And that is far from obvious in the present case.

Anything in the world—call it A—can "mean" anything else—call it B—in some way or other; the only thing A cannot do is mean itself: the meaning of A has an essential reference to something beyond, or other than, A.

A shape in painting can mean something in the sense of *representing* it: that's a woman, that's a tree. Something in nature can mean something in the sense of being a *sign* of it: the dark clouds are a sign of rain. Something can mean something by *convention:* by convention, the word "cat" stands for a certain species of domestic animal—other languages have other words for it. Something can mean something else in the sense of being a symbol of it—a natural symbol for light and warmth such as the sun; a conventional symbol such as a flag flying at half mast; or, what is commonly found in the arts and are the most artistically fruitful, symbols with both natural and conventional elements, such as the cross symbolizing suffering.

Since the medium of literature is words, and words (unlike mere noises) have meanings, else they would not be words at all, and since words have a penumbra of "secondary meaning" as well as their primary meaning, the question "What does it mean?" arises most frequently in the case of literature, especially in the case of poems which we find obscure and difficult to understand: what complex of secondary meanings unites them, which can act as a key to unlock them, or make them intelligible to us? Sometimes, to discover this we must know not only what meanings the words or sentences carried at the time they were written, but also what secondary meanings can be extracted from them so as to make them all together maximally coherent within the poem. The same kind of problem can confront us when we look at a Dürer painting as if it simply contained represented objects, without knowing the symbolism attached to each: this again, as we have seen, is another kind of "discovery of their meaning." Sometimes a work of art contains more than one "level of meaning": on one level, Matthew Arnold's "Dover

Beach'' is about going to Dover Beach and watching the coast of France; at another level, it is a philosophical reflection concerning loss of faith in a secular age.

Sometimes people believe that they can "unlock the secrets" of a work of art by discovering "hidden meanings" in it everywhere, whereas only a persistent reexposure to the work of art will make it come alive to them. A person who seldom listens to music wonders what you are getting out of repeatedly listening to the Siegfried Funeral Music from *Götterdämmerung*—to him it's all "sound and fury, signifying nothing"; and you tell him about the story of Siegfried and his death and the various leit-motifs involved in this section of the opera, and he says, "Why didn't you say so in the first place, now I know what it *means*," whereas the truth is that he may get as little out of the *music* as he did before. Artists themselves, unless they are trying to impress their audiences or make their works appear momentous when they are not, are not as a rule deluded by this sort of thing:

> It was customary to ask Robert Frost on his lecture tours whether the last lines of "Stopping by the Woods on a Snowy Evening" were a reflection on death. Did he mean, in other words, that the desirability of death was offset by the more onerous duties in the here and now? To which Frost always replied "no." The lines, he said, described a man stopping his carriage to view a field newly filled with snow before going on into town. Picasso is similarly reported to have denied that his painting of a red bull's head depicted the dangerous emergence of Fascism. What his painting showed, he maintained, was the head of a red bull. Faulkner, who was always suspicious of academics, is said to have replied to the suggestion that the spotted horse in *As I Lay Dying* referred to the morally blemished nature of man: "Well, I wouldn't know, I never had much education."[25]

Works of art, as we have seen, may sometimes be construed as containing meanings that the artist did not intend, and of which he had no awareness when he wrote. Nevertheless, the constant "search for hidden meanings" smacks of mystery-mongering, as well as a tendency to take shortcuts to the full appreciation of works of art, allowing the quick-and-easy memorization of a few "This stands for that"'s to substitute for the longer, more difficult, but in the end far more rewarding process of becoming acquainted with the idiom of that particular art-form and then, through repeated exposure, allowing the work of art to seep into one's consciousness, working its way gradually into the status of something valued and treasured quite apart from considerations of "this means that."

One could, of course, say that a work of art "means" to a particular consumer whatever *effects* it has on that consumer at that time—and consequently that if its effects on him are enriched through time, then its meaning is

[25] H. Eugene Blocker, *Philosophy of Art* (New York: Scribners, 1980), pp. 223–224.

*ipso facto* enriched; and that if the effects of a work of art on two consumers is markedly different, then it "means" different things to them. One can indeed speak this way, probably quite harmlessly, but we already have a word for this, namely, "effects," and it seems pointless to duplicate it by the use of a second word ("meaning") for the same thing. If we mean "effects," it would seem preferable to say "effects."

The important point is that the effects of a work of art can be wrought *only* by *that* work of art; it cannot be rendered by a statement, a summary, a synopsis, or a description. Students in a course in history of the novel who don't read the novels but read instead a book such as *100 Greatest Novels Condensed* may get the bare bones of the plot and may even be able to pass an examination, but they will not have obtained the induplicable experience of reading the novel for themselves. If one of Haydn's eighty-two string quartets were to be lost, the loss would be irreparable in that nothing in the entire world could substitute for the experience of that work; no descriptions, however ecstatic, by people had heard it could achieve the effect wrought by the quartet itself. Since each work of art is unique, no description of it will suffice, else Dante and Jonathan Swift might have written a tract instead of affording us the rich experience of reading *The Divine Comedy* and *Gulliver's Travels*. In this respect the composer Jan Sibelius was right when, having played a recording of his Fifth Symphony for a guest who then asked "But what does it mean?" he did the only thing appropriate under the circumstances: he turned on the machine and played it over again.

## EXERCISES

1. Picasso said, "There is no abstract art. You must always start with something. Afterward you can remove all traces of reality." Do you agree?

2. Flaubert said, "In literature there are no such things as beautiful subjects. . . . One can write about any one thing equally well as about any other." Do you agree? (He also said, "I would like to write a book about nothing.")

3. Do the following comments by John Walker have to do with representation? Since they are not formalistic, how would you describe them? (John Walker, *The National Gallery of Art*, pp. 302, 516, 586, 508.)

   a. "Vermeer among all Dutch artists is unrivaled in his mastery of optical reality. In his painting just so much detail is included as can be seen from a normal distance, not by focusing the eye successively on objects or in any instant of time, but with a steady gaze. Similarly in his treatment of tone relations there is a perfect consistency with what we actually see. No other painter has been able to maintain such subtle distinctions of color in different planes of light, or to extend this organization of tone into such depths of shadow."

b. "Seurat accurately recorded what he was painting, but he carefully selected the exact locale from which he was to paint."

c. "If I were asked to choose the greatest portrait painter of the 20th century, I would unhesitatingly pick Modigliani. For he has solved beyond any of his contemporaries the basic problem of portraiture: how to represent the human face both as a likeness of an individual and as an element of formal design."

d. Cézanne's aim was "to discover a means of transcribing the weft of color that in nature covers and yet indicates mass, and to find a way of conveying an impression of space without destroying these color relations. . . . he wished to show the trees and the walls of cottages not only as the colored patterns of light and shade which would have satisfied an impressionist painter, but also to communicate the perception of their volume, the dense mass of the foliage, and the solidity of the buildings. . . . Instead of allowing the colors to fade into a misty background, the conventional method of suggesting recessions, he wanted to maintain a chromatic intensity even in the distance." (*The House of Père Croix*)

4. "To say that a novel is realistic is to characterize the novel negatively rather than positively. It is to say that the characters and events do not contravene any known laws of science or well-established common-sense generalizations about people and events. We can characterize the true-to-life only by reference to the *absence* in a work of fiction of implausibilities which would cause our sense of reality to rebel. . . . A realistic novel can be said to give us an illusion of reality in the sense that it, but not an unrealistic novel, could be mistaken for a true story." (D. D. Todd, "Henry James and the Theory of Literary Realism," in *Philosophy and Literature,* p. 97.) Discuss.

5. We have described realism in painting as nondistortion and nonabstraction. What would constitute realism in film? Does William Dean Howells's literary definition "truthful presentation of material" work? Or does realism mean "just take out a movie camera and start shooting"? If there are more realistic and less realistic films, how would you describe the difference?

6. In literature the author's selection of words, as well as his ordering of them, "colors" his account, so that we would get two quite different (and equally accurate) literary descriptions of the same scene. Now consider by what means two filmings of the same event might differ. Read the following description of the first few moments of David Lynch's film *The Elephant Man* (by Michael Ventura in *Los Angeles Weekly,* October 10–16, 1980, p. 11) and (a) discuss how other directors might have done it, (b) consider in what sense if any the term "realism" is applicable, (c) consider whether Lynch's way of depicting the scene described in any way "reveals his personality."

"After a brief, dream-like opening, the first realistic shot is a close-up of Anthony Hopkins, as Dr. Treves . . . in a top hat, obviously (by the sounds all around him) in a large crowd. This face is haunted and intense and a little frightened. That is the face of the film, and this first shot is like a strong minor chord being struck. Then the camera pulls back, without cutting, changing a close-up smoothly into a long tracking shot while Hopkins walks through the crowd, searching for something with piercing eyes. The sounds intensify, the crowd is teeming, you see that you are in a carnival, the tracking shot sucks you in. With the tight close-up changing to a tracking shot full of visual and audio noise, already you have lost distance and objectivity—lost control. The rhythm, the music, has swept you up.

"And exactly when that is happening: *cut,* at an odd angle, to a banner on the tent with the word "Freaks"—for just long enough to read it, then cut again back to the crowd. *But: now* you are at the height of a child, looking through a lot of elbows and shoulders, and Hopkins, who has been your anchor, disappears. The visual mood is that of a kid who's been separated from the grown-up's all important hand in a frightening crowd. Now you *are* lost, and the rhythm and key have changed drastically through the change of angle and the loss of Hopkins. The visual music is telling you, subliminally, that you are in a world where no hand can be held for long. You are already a bit scared, and you don't know why. Nor is anybody tricking you into unease; for it is this *world* that is scary, and not some monster within it.

"Without a cut, Hopkins suddenly appears in the *background,* suddenly popping above everyone else's head—you know that he must have elbowed through the crowd and gone up some steps, but there are a lot of shoulders between you and him, and he's disappearing into the tent. Your whole visual impulse is to shove through the crowd and follow him (grab his hand). It is brilliant. Without directly calling attention to anything, in a few brief moments the film has infected you with its rhythms, and started several important themes, and given you the impulse to follow with your eyes wide open, though you don't know what to expect. Because not to follow is worse, is to be left in this body-music of abdominal regions all around you—the truth is, you'd rather see the monster."

7 . In the following examples, is A a symbol of B? if so, is it natural, conventional, or what?

| A | B |
|---|---|
| a. red | blood |
| b. red | courage |
| c. black | death |
| d. yellow | cowardice |
| e. white | purity |
| f. springtime | resurging life |
| g. halo | holiness |
| h. the moon | romance |
| i. the sun | light |
| j. hand-clapping | applause |
| k. trumpet-sound | regal majesty |
| l. sackcloth | humility |
| m. lion | strength |
| n. wolf | predatoriness |
| o. mouse | meekness |
| p. the stars and stripes | U.S.A. |

8. Whether or not you believe that music can be representational, can music have "nationalistic" qualities? We speak of Smetana's and Dvorák's music as "Bohemian," Mussorgsky's and Rimsky-Korsakov's music as "Russian" or "Slavic," and we mean more than that their music originated in those

countries; we are saying something about the qualities of the music. What do you think it is? Does "Russian music" reflect in any way the distinctive qualities of the Russian people? Or is it rather that there are certain musical idioms originated by composers like Mussorgsky and Smetana which were carried on by their followers in the same nation and thus became identified with those nations? (Is all music composed in Russia, such as Tschaikovsky's, "Russian"? And what would it mean to say that a work of music has a "German" quality?)

9. In the film *The Deer Hunter* there are set in Vietnam scenes in which characters are playing a game of Russian roulette with each other. There is no evidence that such games were played during the American involvement in Vietnam. The director, Michael Cimino, said that the roulette game was a symbol of the uncertainty of each man's fate in wartime. Do you agree that the device should be called a symbol? Why?

10. Evaluate the following statements about meaning, bringing out vaguenesses or ambiguities in the word "meaning":

    a. Every work of art is pregnant with meaning.

    b. Don't look for meanings in music, just listen.

    c. If a work of art doesn't mean anything to you, you're not getting anything out of it.

    d. Every work of art has meaning, but its meaning is different for every member of its audience.

11. Suppose that someone says to you, "It is well known that in his last years Gustav Mahler was greatly preoccupied with death, and that after the onset of his heart condition the dread of a premature death was always with him. In his very last work, the Tenth Symphony, there is a kind of primal scream heard toward the end of the first movement and again in the finale—a nine-note dissonant chord (for full orchestra) ending with a high A on the trumpet; and in the closing measures of the work, there is an agonized upward-leaping sigh (from C to A flat) in the strings. In view of what we know about Mahler's life at that time, and after repeated listening to this symphony, we may safely conclude, though Mahler himself said nothing about it, that these passages symbolize death." How would you respond, and why?

# SELECTED READINGS

ABELL, WALTER. *Representation and Form*. New York: Scribners, 1936.

ARISTOTLE, *Poetics*. (Many editions.)

ARNHEIM, RUDOLF. *Art and Visual Perception*. Berkeley: Univ. of California Press, 1957.

BARNES, ALBERT C. *The Art in Painting*. New York: Harcourt Brace, 1937.

BEARDSLEY, MONROE C. "The Limits of Critical Interpretation." In Sidney Hook, ed., *Art and Philosophy*. New York: New York University Press, 1966.

BERNHEIMER, RICHARD. "In Defense of Representation." In *Art: a Bryn Mawr Symposium*. Bryn Mawr, Pa.: Bryn Mawr Press, 1940.

BOWERS, DAVID. "The Role of Subject-matter in Art." *Journal of Philosophy,* 26 (1939).

BUKOFZER, MANFRED. *Music in the Baroque Era*. New York: Norton, 1947.

BUKOFZER, MANFRED. "Allegory in Baroque Music." *Journal of the Warburg and Courtauld Institutes,* 3 (1939–1940).

BUTCHER, S. H. *Aristotle's Theory of Poetry and Fine Art*. 4th edition. London: Oxford Univ. Press, 1923.

COKER, WILSON. *Music and Meaning*. New York: Free Press, 1972.

GOMBRICH, E. H. *Art and Illusion: a Study in the Psychology of Pictorial Representation*. Princeton: Princeton Univ. Press, 2nd ed., 1961.

GOMBRICH, E. H., JULIAN HOCHBERG, AND MAX BLACK. *Art, Perception, and Reality*. Baltimore: Johns Hopkins Univ. Press, 1972.

GREENE, THEODORE M. *The Arts and the Art of Criticism*. Princeton: Princeton Univ. Press, 1940.

HERMEREN, GORE. *Representation and Meaning in the Visual Arts*. Lund, Sweden: Berlingska Poktryckereiet, 1969.

HULME, T. E. *Speculations*. New York: Harcourt Brace, 1924.

HUNGERLAND, ISABEL. "Iconic Signs and Expressiveness." *Journal of Aesthetics and Art Criticism,* 3 (1945).

ISENBERG, ARNOLD. "Perception, Meaning, and the Subject-matter of Art." *Journal of Philosophy,* 41 (1944). Reprinted in Vivas and Krieger.

KAPLAN, ABRAHAM. "Referential Meaning in the Arts." *Journal of Aesthetics and Art Criticism,* 12 (1954).

LANGER, SUSANNE K. *Philosophy in a New Key*. Cambridge: Harvard Univ. Press, 1942.

LUBBOCK, PERCY. *The Craft of Fiction*. New York: Scribners, 1955.

MANNS, JAMES W. "Representation, Relativism, and Resemblance." *British Journal of Aesthetics,* 11 (1971).

MEYER, LEONARD. *Music, The Arts, and Ideas.* Chicago: Univ. of Chicago Press, 1967.

PLATO. Republic. (Many editions.)

PRALL, D. W. *Aesthetic Judgment.* New York: Crowell, 1929.

PRICE, KINGSLEY. "Is a Work of Art a Symbol?" *Journal of Philosophy,* 50 (1953).

STEVENSON, CHARLES L. "Symbolism in the Non-representational Arts." In Paul Henle (ed.), *Language, Thought, and Culture.* Ann Arbor: Univ. of Mich. Press, 1958. Reprinted in Hospers.

REID, LOUIS ARNAUD. *A Study in Aesthetics.* London: Allen and Unwin, 1931.

REID, LOUIS ARNAUD. *Meaning in the Arts.* London: Allen and Unwin, 1969.

WALTON, KENDALL. "Categories of Art." *Philosophical Review,* 79 (1970). Reprinted in Margolis.

WALTON, KENDALL. "Pictures and Make-believe." *Philosophical Review,* 82 (1973). Reprinted in Kennick.

WHISTLER, JAMES MACNEILL. *The Gentle Art of Making Enemies.* London: W. Heinemann, 1890.

ZOLA, EMILE. *The Experimental Novel.* New York: Cassell Publishing Co., 1894.

# 4

# Art and Expression

If art is not primarily representation, not of "nature as it is" or of "nature as it ought to be," not of actual particulars in nature or of an ideal "form" or "essence" or of anything at all that exists in the world outside the artist, what then is it? One answer suggests that we have been looking in the wrong place—at the outer world, rather than the inner; art is an *expression* of the artist's inner world of feelings, emotions, attitudes, and this, not representation, is what art is all about.

But what is expression?

## 1. EXPRESSION AS A PROCESS

The basic meaning of "expression" is the *outer manifestation of an inner state*. We are acquainted with expressive behavior from our earliest years: a person expresses joy by smiling or laughing, sadness by crying, anger by his tone of voice, tension by the way in which he speaks and walks and the tautness of his mouth, and so on. These are just the ways in which people behave when they feel certain emotions or moods, and so the behavior comes to be seen as expressive of those emotions or moods.

In the popular sense of the term, all these are undoubtedly instances of expression. Yet if we are to discuss expression in a way that is of relevance to the arts, we shall have to go beyond this popular sense. John Dewey, in his highly influential book *Art as Experience,* says of expression,

> Not all outgoing activity is of the nature of expression. . . . There are storms of passion that break through barriers and that sweep away whatever intervenes between a person and something he would destroy. There is activity, but not, from the standpoint of the one acting, expression. An onlooker may say "What a magnificent expression of rage!" But the enraged being is only raging, quite a different matter from *expressing* rage. Or again, some spectator may say "How that man is expressing his own dominant character in what he is doing or saying." But the last thing the man is thinking of is to express his character; he is only giving way to a fit of passion. Again the cry or smile of an infant may be expressive to mother or nurse and yet not be an act of expression to the baby. To the onlooker it is an expression because it tells something about the state of the child. But the child is only engaged in doing something directly, no more expressive from his standpoint than is breathing or sneezing—activities that are also expressive to the observer of the infant's condition. . . . As far as the act itself is concerned, it is, if purely impulsive, just a boiling over.[1]

What then distinguishes this "boiling over" from expression proper?

While there is no expression, unless there is urge from within outwards, the welling up must be clarified and ordered by taking into itself the values of prior experiences before it can be an act of expression. And these values are not called into play save through objects of the environment that offer resistance to the direct discharge of emotion and impulse. Emotional discharge is a necessary but not a sufficient condition of expression.

There is no expression without excitement, without turmoil. Yet an inner agitation that is discharged at once in a laugh or cry, passes away with its utterance. To discharge is to get rid of, to dismiss; to express is to stay by, to carry forward in development, to work out to completion. A gush of tears by bring relief, a spasm of destruction may give outlet to inward rage. But where there is no administration of objective conditions, no shaping of materials in the interest of *embodying* the excitement, there is no expression. What is sometimes called an act of self-expression might better be termed one of self-exposure; it discloses character—or lack of character—to others. In itself, it is only a spewing forth.

At first a baby weeps, just as it turns its head to follow light; there is an inner urge but nothing to express. As the infant matures, he learns that particular acts effect different consequences—that, for example, he gets attention if he cries, and that smiling induces another definite response from those about him. As he grasps the meaning of an act at first performed from sheer internal pressure, he becomes capable of acts of true expression. The transformation of sounds, babblings, lalling, and so forth, into language is a perfect illustration of the way in which acts of expression are brought into existence and also of the difference between them and mere acts of discharge. . . . An activity that was "natural"—spontaneous and unintended—is transformed because it is undertaken *as a means to a consciously entertained consequence.* Such transformation marks every deed of art.[2]

[1] John Dewey, *Art as Experience* (New York: Minton, Balch & Co., 1934), p. 61.
[2] *Ibid.,* pp. 61–62.

The difference lies in this, that an act of discharge *lacks a medium,* whereas expression is always through a medium. "Instinctive crying and smiling no more require a medium than do sneezing and winking."

> Etymologically, an act of expression is a squeezing out, a pressing forth. Juice is expressed when grapes are crushed in the wine-press;. . . lard and oil are rendered when certain facts are subjected to heat and pressure. Nothing is pressed forth except from original raw or natural material. But it is equally true that the mere issuing forth or discharge of raw material is not expression. Through interaction with something external to it, the wine press, or the treading foot of man, juice results. . . . It takes the wine-press as well as grapes to express juice, and it takes environing and resisting objects as well as internal emotion and impulsion to constitute an *expression* of emotion.[3]

The unpressed grapes, in the case of the artist, are the materials of his art—the painter's paints, the sculptor's stone or wood, the poet's words; the wine-press is the activity of the artist, grappling with the resisting medium which he must bend to his will (else the grapes would go down the chute unchanged); the result of the interaction of these two, the juice, is the work of art. Only through such an interaction of the artistic materials with the resistant artistic medium does the work of art emerge.

The notion that art is not the representation of something "outer" but the expression of something "inner" seems very natural to students of art in the twentieth century and often seems so obvious that it is simply taken for granted. But prior to the Romantic movement in the arts it would not have seemed familiar at all. When Wordsworth, at the beginning of the Romantic movement in English poetry, wrote, "Poetry is an overflow of powerful feeling," such an idea was much more revolutionary than it now appears to us. If you had asked Bach what he was doing as he sat down with a score to compose, he would certainly not have replied, "I am engaged in an act of expression" or "I am expressing my feelings"; he might even have wondered what expression or feelings had to do with the whole enterprise of art-creation. He would have been much more at home with such an answer as "I am plying my trade" or "I am creating new combinations of sounds," with no reference at all to feelings. But the idea of art as an expression of inner states through a medium in the nineteenth century changed the entire direction of aesthetic theory.

Nor is it "just anything" that art expresses. Art is, according to the Romantic tradition, specifically concerned with the expression of feelings, emotions, attitudes—the *affective* life of man. "But don't we express *ideas* too?" one may ask. Typically, in the sciences one expresses ideas and in art one expresses feelings. Scientists do not ordinarily produce works of art, but their activity is certainly not precluded by Dewey's definition of expres-

[3] *Ibid.,* p. 64.

sion—an activity, in this case the use of language, "is undertaken as a means to a consciously entertained consequence." And indeed ideas are expressed in art as well, especially in literature, whose medium is language. But though ideas may be expressed in the arts, many works of art are quite lacking in ideas (we speak of "musical ideas," but this just means a musical theme which gets developed, a series of tones, not ideas in the more usual sense of that term). At any rate, art's special function has to do not with the life of ideas but with the life of man's feeling, with joy and pain and tension and peace in all their manifold varieties, with inner experiences "directed outwards" through a medium and culminating in an object, the work of art.

"Art," wrote Eugene Veron in his book *L'Esthetique* (1878), " is the manifestation of emotion, obtaining external interpretation, now by expressive arrangements of line, form or color, now by a series of gestures, sounds or words governed by particular rhythmic cadence."

## Croce's Theory of Expression

A famous exponent of one form of expression theory is the Italian philosopher Benedetto Croce (1866–1952).

The popular view of the artist is that he is a *technician*—that he has mastered the technique of handling his medium (paints, stone, etc.) and that this is what distinguishes him from other people. According to this view, he is a craftsman like the blacksmith, the cabinet maker, and the bridge builder. But, says Croce, this view is entirely mistaken: the artist can indeed be a craftsman dealing with a physical medium, but only *after* he gets his artistic ideas. Technical skill in one's medium can be learned by almost anyone with training and practice; it can be taught in schools, and most persons, if they have no physical or mental handicap, can learn to paint or sculpt or compose music. But all this is only *externalization*—putting one's ideas on paper or canvas. It tells one nothing about *how to get the ideas*. What the public naïvely thinks is the distinctive characteristic of the artist—his skill in handling a medium—is only incidental to the task of the artist. What the public takes for artistry is what any dunce can learn if he goes to art school long enough. "Renoir can draw and I can't—that's the difference between us," reflects this popular view.

But if skill in handling his chosen medium is not the distinguishing feature of the artist, what is? It is his ability to have *artistic ideas*—or, as Croce calls them, *intuitions*. Artists differ from other people, not in that they can skillfully wield a brush or a chisel, but in that they have artistic intuitions which most of us never have. One paints, not with his hands, but with his brain; it is the painterly vision that counts—the fact that, in his imagination, he can *see* configurations of shapes and colors that others could never think of.

Michelangelo said, "One paints, not with the hands, but with the brain." Leonard shocked the prior of the Convent of the Graces by standing for days together gazing at the "Last Supper," without touching it with the brush. He remarked of this attitude: "The minds of men of lofty genius are most active in invention when they are doing the least external work."[4]

People think that all of us ordinary men imagine and intuit countries, figures, and scenes like painters and bodies like sculptors; save that painters and sculptors know how to paint and carve such images, while we bear them unexpressed in our souls. They believe that anyone could have imagined a Madonna of Raphael but that Raphael was Raphael owing to his technical ability in putting the Madonna upon canvas.

Nothing can be more false than this view. The world which as a rule we intuit is a small thing. It consists of little expressions, which gradually become greater and wider with the increasing spiritual concentration of certain moments. They are the words we say to ourselves, our silent judgments: "Here is a man, here is a horse, this is heavy, this is sharp, this pleases me," and so on. It is a medley of light and color, with no greater pictorial value than could be expressed by a haphazard splash of colors, from among which one could barely make out a few special, distinctive traits. This and nothing else is what we possess in our ordinary life; this is the basis of our ordinary action. It is the index of a book. The labels tied to things take the place of the things themselves. These indexes and these labels suffice for small needs and small actions.

When, after having given a rapid glance at anyone, they attempt to obtain a real intuition of him, in order, for example, to paint his portrait, then this ordinary vision, that seemed so precise, so lively, reveals itself as little better than nothing. What remains is found to be at the most some superficial trait, which would not even suffice for a caricature. The person to be painted stands before the artist like a world to discover. . . . The painter is a painter, because he sees what others only feel or catch a glimpse of, but do not see.[5]

These intuitions do not usually burst upon the artist in one flash. As a rule, they begin with what William James called "a big blooming buzzing confusion": a glimpse here, a spark there, a relation perceived, a promising avenue developed. A fragment of melody floats into the composer's mind from he knows not where; it interests him, it seems promising, he works on it; perhaps he gives it up again until some other fragment, or development of the first, comes into his mind, and then he begins seriously to develop these fragments into some coherent whole. Promising avenues are explored, blind alleys tried and cast aside, much setting aside occurs and then returning to it afresh, and long periods of gestation in the unconscious—and finally the composition is completed to his satisfaction—we have the "final artistic intuition." It is not so much the having of initial intuitions that matters—most of us have had ideas for stories—but his ability at "working through" the initial ideas into a completed work of art.

The entire process just described occurs in the realm of the artist's ideas (in-

[4] Benedetto Croce, *Aesthetic,* 2nd ed., Douglas Ainslie translation (New York: Farrar, Straus & Co., 1922), p. 10.

[5] *Ibid.,* pp. 10–11.

tuitions); it all goes on "in the composer's head." Of course, after the bits of melody (and so on) are conceived in his head, he probably (as an aid to memory) writes them down on score paper. Most composers create with score paper before them, to put down their intuitions after they have them—and often a piano as well, to see how their ideas sound—just as most painters sit at an easel, since "playing around with the physical medium" often help them to get new painterly ideas. But the main artistic activity goes on in the artist's head: the painter can paint with his hands only if he has the ideas in his head, even if the ideas in his head come to him only after he has experimented with his hands. Experimenting with the physical medium can help in the process of arriving at intuitions; and after the intuitions are there, the creation of an external object in physical space (the "externalized intuition") is only a technical matter—often difficult indeed, especially in sculpture and architecture—but a matter of skill (technique) nevertheless, something that can be taught and learned, unlike the ability to have the artistic ideas in the first place.

When the artist has before his mind the "final artistic intuition," the mental image of the completed work of art as it will be when externalized, his creative process—his intuiting process—is complete. Normally, he then externalizes it, so that he doesn't have to rely on his memory; more often still, he externalizes bit by bit all the time, even while he is getting his ideas—he adds to the score, erases some items, adds to the score again in response to his developing intuitions; only in rare cases such as Mozart does the completed work of music appear "in his mind's eye," note by note. Similarly, the painter and sculptor externalize all along, but the externalization—a matter of skill or technique—is what it is because the artistic intuitions in his mind develop as they do. If the poet has created a short poem, he may hold it in his memory without writing it down for a long time, or he may never do so at all—but even though his poem exists only in his mind, the process of intuition is already complete, even though the process of externalization (writing the poem on paper) has not yet occurred. An external object is needed only so that other people—readers, viewers, hearers—can capture and share the intuition of the artist; for, lacking extrasensory perception, there is no way that the intuition can go from the artist's mind to the viewer's mind without the intermediary physical object (artifact).

When the artistic intuitions are being born in the artist's mind, he is doing what is called *expressing himself.* And when the intuitions have been completed—when the "final artistic intuition" has been created—then the *process of expressing* is also complete. The artist may or may not yet have externalized anything, in physical paint or stone or words, for other people to see. *That* is no part of the intuitive-expressive process. Here we have the nub of Croce's view—that the process of intuition and the process of expression *are one.* They are two descriptions of the same thing. When you work up those scattered fragments of melody into a completed sonata, you are engaging in the process of expression—"to yourself" of course; expression is always to yourself, not for the benefit of other people. No audience is needed for this, and any interruption of this characteristically lonely process would be destructive (as when someone knocked on the door while Coleridge was creating his poem "Kubla Khan" and he never finished it.) Intuition-expression is an "encounter of the alone with the alone."

What is it that has been born in the artist's mind? Not emotions merely; there may indeed be emotions, but more often than not these yield nothing; under the impetus of emotions, or perhaps without them, the artist intuits bit after bit of his work-to-be always *conceived in the medium* of paints, or stone, or words, or musical sounds. The artistic ideas are always conceived *in the medium;* if they have not reached that stage, they are not yet *artistic* intuitions. The test of whether one is having artistic ideas is not "What feelings or emotions are you having?" but "What items have you created *in* the artistic medium?" Croce says,

> Just as one who is deluded as to the amount of his material wealth is confuted by arithmetic, which states its exact amount, so he who nourishes delusions as to the wealth of his own thoughts and images is brought back to reality when he is obliged to cross the *Pons Asinorum* of expression. Let us say to the former, count; to the latter, speak; or, here is a pencil, draw, express yourself.[6]

Thus, if one claims to be a great poet, but "just can't think of the right words," he is not a poet at all; he might have the makings of one, but he has no *poetic* intuitions unless he has thought of *the words of the poem* in their proper order; artistic intuitions are always *in the artistic medium.* There are no "mute inglorious Miltons," for if they are mute, they are not poets at all and certainly not Miltons. However rich and wonderful a person's inner life may be, he is not an artist unless he has artistic intuitions—that is to say, ideas cast *in* the artistic medium. There are probably thousands of people who have rich emotional lives, for every one who ever creates a work of art worth looking at twice.

## Collingwood's Theory of Expression

The British philosopher of art Robin G. Collingwood (1889–1943) is very much in the tradition of Croce, though with some special twists. He agrees with Croce that the popular idea of the artist is mistaken; that the distinctive feature of the artist is intuition-expression, not externalization; that once the activity of intuition-expression is complete the work of art has been created and has only to be externalized; and that the creation of a work of art, all occurring in the artist's mind, is an encounter "of the alone with the alone" to which all other persons are outsiders.

[6] *Ibid.,* p. 11.

What is different in Collingwood is his account of the relation of the artist to emotion. The creation of art has something to do with emotion, says Collingwood. What does the artist do with emotion? Nothing is more familiar, or more true, than to say that he *expresses* it. But what is it to express an emotion?

> When a man is said to express emotion, what is being said about him comes to this. At first, he is conscious of having an emotion, but not conscious of what this emotion is. All he is conscious of is a perturbation or excitement, which he feels going on within him, but of whose nature he is ignorant. While in this state, all he can say about his emotion is: "I feel . . . I don't know what I feel." From this helpless and oppressed condition he extricates himself by doing something which we call expressing himself . . . . As unexpressed, he feels [the emotion] in what we have called a helpless and oppressed way; as expressed, he feels it in a way from which this sense of oppression has vanished. His mind is somehow lightened and eased. [7]

Expression is a matter of making clear the exact nature of one's emotions to oneself. One cannot say in advance what one's expressive process will yield; if one is a poet, one may know that it's going to be a poem (perhaps not a good one), but one doesn't know in advance the exact words that the poetic intuition will take—that is, one doesn't know what words, in what order, the completed poem will contain. If one did, one would have only to write them down, and thus one would be spared the "divine agonies" of creation: what word belongs here? what is the proper image at this point? how can I get this thought into iambic pentameter? and so on. The artist doesn't know what he's going to say until he has said it, doesn't know what he's going to express until he has expressed it. The words (or whatever) as they finally appear ("completed artistic intuition") are the poem, but one doesn't know what those will be until one has completed the creation of the poem.

Dewey distinguished expression of emotion from *discharge* of emotion; Collingwood distinguishes expression from something at the opposite pole from discharge, namely, the deliberate *arousing* of emotion in others. Arousing is a means to an end: one uses the words (or whatever) as a means toward arousing emotion in others—one does this in moral or religious tracts, and in political oratory. The speaker is not exploring his own emotions; in fact he may feel nothing at all himself; he is not concerned with his own emotions, he is solely concerned with arousing emotions in other people.

Expression is not at all like this: expression is always a solo process, it is always "to oneself." In expressing, one doesn't need other people around. Expression is a coming-to-consciousness about one's own emotions: it is not directed at an audience. If a poet expresses his feeling by writing a poem, then others who read it *overhear* what he was expressing. (John Stuart Mill said

---

[7] Robin G. Collingwood, *The Principles of Art* (Oxford: The Clarendon Press, 1938), pp. 109–110.

that poems are not heard, they are *over*heard.) Their position is rather like that of eavesdroppers on his process of expression. It is possible that

> the expression of an emotion by speech may be addressed to someone; but if so it is not done with the intention of arousing a like emotion in him. If there is any effect we wish to produce in the hearer, it is only the effect which we call making him understand how we feel. But . . . this is just the effect which expressing our emotions has on ourselves. It makes us, as well as the people to whom we talk, understand how we feel.
>
> Until a man has expressed his emotion, he does not yet know what emotion it is. The act of expressing it is therefore an exploration of his own emotions. He is trying to find out what these emotions are. There is certainly here a directed process: an effort, that is, directed upon a certain end; but the end is not something foreseen and preconceived, to which the appropriate means can be thought out in the light of our knowledge of its special character. Expression is an activity of which there can be no technique.[8]

Nor can expression be a means toward a preconceived end. If the end is the completed work of art, there can be no means toward achieving that, for a means is something whose nature we know in advance, prior to achieving the end. I want to send a book in the mail (end), and I package, address, and stamp it (means). I make a hundred identical bookshelves to fill an order; I know in advance, if I am a good technician, exactly what each one must be like, its dimensions, its composition, its color. I "know the end in the beginning," else I could not exert my skill (techne) in realizing the end. But in art I do *not* know the end in the beginning: I do not, as a poet, know what words will constitute the poem after I have completed it. Once I have the words in my mind, I can of course write them down; but there is no means I can undertake for getting the words in my mind.

> The description of the unwritten poem as an end toward which his technique as a means is false; it implies that before he has written his poem he knows, and could state, the specification of it in the kind of way in which a joiner knows the specification of a table he is about to make. This is always true of a craftsman; . . . [but] the artist has no idea what the experience is which demands expression until he has expressed it. What he wants to say is not present to him as an end toward which means have to be devised; it becomes clear to him only as the poem takes shape in his mind, or the clay in his fingers.[9]

Comments on Croce and Collingwood on Expression

1. *Art and technique.* Croce and Collingwood are both opposed to "the technical theory of art." It is certainly true that, unlike the skilled craftsman, the artist does not "know the end in the beginning"—he doesn't know exactly

---

[8] *Ibid.,* pp. 110–111.
[9] *Ibid.,* pp. 28–29.

what the completed work will be like until he has completed it, at least "in his mind's eye" (he may know after he has the poem in his head what words he will *write down,* but that is externalization, not intuition-expression).

Still, one may ask, isn't there always something we could call "the technical aspect of art"? A pianist may perform imaginatively and expressively but to do this he must first be the master of piano technique—he must know how to play the notes, often difficult and rapid combinations of them, and do it well; there is technique as well as art in playing.

Moreover, technique may apply not only to the secondary artist but to the primary artist as well: not only to *playing* the notes but to *creating* them. The composer must know his harmony and counterpoint; he learns certain "tricks of the trade," for example, how to create the arpeggios so as to get the effect one wants; as a poet, one gets better at rhyming and alliteration as one's poetic experience matures; and so on. We speak not only of the pianist's technique at playing, but of Brahms's technique in piano composition. Technique alone does not make an artist—one can have marvelous technique, exercised upon nothing worth hearing—but although technique is not a *sufficient* condition for good performance or creation, it is surely a *necessary* condition. It is true, of course, that what many performers and creators lack is not technique but any artistic ideas on which to exercise that technique.

2. *Separation from the physical medium.* It has been charged that the Croce–Collingwood view is too "mentalistic": it emphasizes what goes on in the artist's mind rather than the physical artifact—and admits the artifact as a necessary and perhaps unfortunate requirement for getting artistic ideas into the minds of the audiences. Externalization appears to be of importance only in relation to an audience. But, one may ask, isn't externalization important to the artist himself—even in his "encounter of the alone with the alone"? If there were no audience and he knew there never would be, might he not still want to paint—not only as a way of getting new ideas, but just to have something down on canvas, not merely "in his mind"? Wasn't Dewey correct in constantly emphasizing the importance of the *physical* medium?

In any event, Croce and Collingwood did not commit the error of which they have most often been accused: of emphasizing the artist's state of mind as opposed to his intuitions. Remember that an emotion, however powerful, is not an artistic intuition (idea); only words or paints or musical tones and so on are items in the artistic medium—and until *these* have been created by the artist, even if only "in his mind," there *is* no work of art. The words of the poem may not yet be in the physical medium (on paper), but there is no poem until they have been *conceived* in the medium—that is, it must be *words* that the poet has in his mind, not *emotions.*

3. *Intuitions and emotions.* At this point, however, there is a difference between Croce and Collingwood. Collingwood speaks constantly of emotions, Croce almost never. In Croce, the process of having intuitions is the process of expressing—and there is no indication that in his view it has to be *emotions*

that are expressed. In Croce, it would seem, there is really no need for emotions at all: a few melodies pop into the composer's head, then some more, he works with them, develops them. . . . In all this there may be no emotions. Emotions are apparently not even like technique, a necessary condition for successful creation. As long as the composer creates good compositions, why need he have emotions at all? T. S. Eliot wrote, "Poetry is not a turning loose of emotion, but an escape from emotion" ("The Sacred Wood"); and later, "The emotions of a poet may be simple, crude, and flat." Richard Strauss wrote, "I work very coldly, without agitation, without emotion even. One must be completely master of oneself to organize that changing, moving, flowing chess-board, orchestration. The mind which composed *Tristan* must have been as cool as marble."[10]

Strauss would certainly not say that *he* was expressing emotions when he was creating; does that make him less of a composer? Must not one, in an important sense, be *free of* emotion, at least free of being under the strong influence of some emotions like grief and remorse (even extraordinary joy?) in order to be able to create such formal complexities as a symphony or a mural? Wordsworth himself said that in poetry one had "emotion *recollected in tranquillity*"; does it have to be even recollected emotion? Shouldn't his mind be cleansed of emotions entirely, at least during the time he is creating? Isn't emotion more of a disturbing and distracting influence?

Croce could accept all this with equanimity; he speaks only of getting artistic ideas (intuitions), and thus expressing oneself, without making any claims about emotions. But Collingwood is in a different position. He speaks of what it is to express an emotion, as opposed to arousing it; he speaks of feeling an inner turbulence, then through expression feeling calm, and so on. In Collingwood's case one cannot delete from the account all reference to emotions. And in his case at least the need for talking about emotions as an essential ingredient of the artistic process could be questioned. It is not at all clear what Collingwood would say to the Richard Strauss quotation.

4. *Expression vs. creation.* Regardless of what is the status of emotions in art, what can be said regarding the creation of art as a process of *expression* (whether of emotions or not)? One can agree with Croce's account of the coming-into-being of works of art as that of getting artistic intuitions—but isn't that enough? Need one also say that the process of getting intuitions *is also* the process of *expressing*?

The *creation* of art consists in combining the elements in the medium (words, or tones, or colors and shapes on canvas, etc.) in ways that did not exist before. This, one may say, is what artistic creation *is,* regardless of what mental processes may *cause* it or what accompaniments or effects it may have. One can call this creation the acquiring of artistic intuitions—this appears to

---

[10] Richard Strauss, *Autobiography* (1926), p. 409. Quoted in Harold Osborne, *Aesthetics and Criticism* (London: Routledge & Kegan Paul, 1955), p. 162.

be another way of saying the same thing. But is there any necessary connection between all this and *expression*—whether of emotions or not?

One could argue as follows: It is possible that, *when* an artist creates, he *also* expresses his emotions; for example, as Collingwood says, he may feel tense and unsatisfied before his creation is complete, and calm and fulfilled afterward; or he may have felt frustrated and worked out his frustration by composing, or painting or writing, and after he has the thing the way he wants it his frustration has been dissolved. He may have expressed his emotions *by* creating a work of art, but how does this show that his special activity in creating a work of art *is* the activity of expression? Hasn't the scientist who develops a complex theory and finally "gets it right" also expressed his feelings in this way? Yet no one could call the creation of a scientific theory simply an act of "emotional expression"—that's not what the scientific theory *is*.

Scientists evaluating his theory would not be concerned one way or another about any of his mental states, including whether or not he had expressed his inner urges by creating his theory. We who are on the consumer end of works of art, are we not in the same position? Unless we are interested in the biography of the artist, do we really care whether he expressed himself in some way, for example, relieved his frustration or anger or tension by creating the work? His psychoanalyst might care what feelings he expressed by creating a work of art, but to us as readers or hearers it hardly matters whether he first felt frustrated and then fulfilled, or first tense and then calm, or whether what was unclear in his mind became gradually clarified, enabling him to continue creating the work.

Perhaps we should say, then, that the *creation* of a work of art is one thing, and the *expression* of emotions is another—something which may or may not *accompany* the process of creating the work. In that case, it would not be true to say that the creation of the work *is* the expression of emotions or of anything else; expression would simply have no place in the account.

Further, one could ask, is it plausible to believe that what the artist is always doing *qua* artist is expressing emotions (or expressing anything else)? When Shakespeare was writing, was he expressing his emotions? If so, he managed to keep it a dark secret what those emotions were: we experience in his plays the emotions of various characters, but nowhere is there anything we can safely identify as Shakespeare's own emotions. This doesn't show of course that he didn't have them, or even that he wasn't expressing them by writing plays, but it does make it very dubious to say that the act of artistic creation always and necessarily *is* the process of expressing emotions.

Indeed, the expression of emotions seems to have no closer a connection with the creation of art than with the creation in science or mathematics or technology. All the remarks Collingwood makes to describe the creation of art would also fit these other kinds of creation. What then does the expression of emotions have specifically to do with art?

But, one might object, we have got it all wrong. The connection between art and emotion is more intimate than this. It is true that we can express emotions *by* creating in mathematics or science, or creating a scene or an uproar or a disturbance, or anything else. But when we talk about artistic expression we are not talking about expressing emotions *by* creating something; we are talking about expressing emotions *in* something—the work of art itself. The emotion in the artist is indeed irrelevant to anyone but his friends, family, and psychiatrist; but the emotion that he *put into the work of art* is not. It is the emotion in the work of art, not in the creator of it, that matters.

But once we have said this much, we are no longer talking about expression as a part of the *process* of creating works of art; we are now talking about expression as a part or aspect of the *product* of the act of artistic creation—namely, the work of art itself. And this is a different, and more important, subject, to which we shall turn, in Section 3.

## 2. EXPRESSION AS COMMUNICATION OF FEELING

We have not quite done with expression as a process. There are those who have thought that expression is not a solo process, but requires the response of an audience for its completion. Ordinary language is a means of communicating ideas. Emotions can be communicated through gestures and body language, but, it is alleged, the most effective way to communicate emotions is through art: art is the most powerful vehicle by which emotions can be communicated from person to person. The most famous champion of this kind of view was the novelist Leo Tolstoy. The activity of art, says Tolstoy in his book *What Is Art?*

> is based on the fact that a man receiving through his sense of hearing or sight another man's expression of feeling, is capable of experiencing the emotion which moved the man who expressed it. To take the simplest example: one man laughs, and another who hears becomes merry; or a man weeps, and another who hears feels sorrow. A man is excited or irritated, and another man seeing him is brought to a similar state of mind. By his movements or by the sounds of his voice a man expresses courage and determination of sadness and calmness, and this state of mind passes on to others. A man suffers, manifesting his suffering by groans and spasms, and this suffering transmits itself to other people; a man expresses his feelings of admiration, devotion, fear, respect, or love, to certain objects, persons, or phenomena, and others are infected by the same feelings of admiration, devotion, fear, respect, or love, to the same objects, persons, or phenomena.
>
> And it is on this capacity of man to receive another man's expression of feeling and to experience those feelings himself, that the activity of art is based.
>
> If a man infects another or others directly, immediately, by his appearance or by the sounds he gives vent to at the very time he experiences the feeling; if he causes another man to yawn when he himself cannot help yawning, or to laugh or cry when he himself is obliged to laugh or cry, or to suffer when he himself is suffering—that does not amount to art.

Art begins when one person with the object of joining another or others to himself in one and the same feeling, expresses that feeling by certain external indications. To take the simplest example: a boy having experienced, let us say, fear on encountering a wolf, relates that encounter, and in order to evoke in others the feeling he has experienced, describes himself, his condition before the encounter, the surroundings, the wood, his own light-heartedness, and then the wolf's appearance, its movements, the distance between himself and the wolf, and so forth. All this, if only the boy when telling the story again experiences the feelings he has lived through, and infects the hearers and compels them to feel what he has experienced—is art. Even if the boy had not seen the wolf but had frequently been afraid of one, and if wishing to evoke in others the fear he had felt, he invented an encounter with a wolf and recounted it so as to make his hearers share the feelings he experienced when he feared the wolf, that would also be art. And just in the same way it is art if a man, having experienced either the fear or suffering or the attraction of enjoyment (whether in reality or in imagination), expresses these feelings on canvas or in marble so that others are infected by them. And it is also art if a man feels, or imagines to himself, feelings of delight, gladness, sorrow, despair, courage, or despondency, and the transition from one to another of these feelings, and expresses them by sounds so that the hearers are infected by them and experience them as they were experienced by the composer.

If only the spectators or auditors are infected by the feelings which the author has felt, it is art.

To evoke in oneself a feeling one has experienced, and having evoked it in oneself by means of movements, lines, colors, sounds, or forms expressed in words, so to transmit that feeling that others experience the same feeling—this is the activity of art.

Art is a human activity consisting in this, that one man consciously by means of certain external signs, hands on to others feelings he has lived through, and that others are infected by these feelings and also experience them.[11]

Many artists, while not presenting their views in such explicit detail as Tolstoy, have nevertheless believed, or by their remarks about their works led their readers to think they believed, not that expression is a process originated and completed by the artist himself in the creation of his work, but that it is a "two-way deal" involving both the artist and his audience.

But it is not always clear exactly what is being asserted: (1) Is it that an audience is necessary to the act of expression (or the act of creation)? This seems quite implausible: hasn't the artist "expressed himself" in his work if he completes it to his own satisfaction, even if the next moment he should find himself alone on the planet? or if his newly completed work were to be destroyed before anyone else had a chance to see it? (2) More frequently, the view is not specifically about expression at all; what is asserted rather than being the relation between the artist and his audience is that of *communication of feeling*—that whatever experience the reader has should be the same, or

---

[11] Leo Tolstoy, *What Is Art?* (Aylmer Maude translation) (London: Oxford Univ. Press, 1928), Chapter 5. Reprinted in W. E. Kennick, ed., *Art and Philosophy* 2nd ed. (New York: St. Martin's Press, 1979), pp. 36–37.

similar in every detail, to the experience the artist had when he created his work. If this is the view, some objections to it can be made:

1. *Knowing what the artist felt.* How do any of us know exactly what the artist felt at the time of creation? In most cases the artist is dead, and even if he is alive he cannot tell us. But perhaps, it is said, the best indication of how he felt was not what he said but *the work of art itself* which he left us. Even in this case, however, it is usually impossible to infer anything safely about the artist's experiential states. Does anyone know what Shakespeare felt when he wrote *As You Like It*? Does a reading of the play tell us? Should it? If two people disagreed on this, how would we determine which was correct?

Not only is there usually no way of telling, but, one might add, there is no *need* to know. Can't we appreciate a work of art just as much without knowing what was going on in the artist's mind? In fact, don't we usually have to appreciate most works of art without any such knowledge? If we knew how Zweig felt when he created "The Royal Game," would this help in our appreciation of the story?

2. *Experiences of artist vs. consumer.* Why should the mental state of the consumer (listener, viewer, reader) be identical to, or even similar to, that of the artist in the process of creation? There is a vast difference between the experience of *creating* something and the experience of *appreciating* it after it has been created by someone else. There are countless problems that arise for an artist during the process of art-creation—some of them purely technical problems, such as how to sculpt a human figure from a recalcitrant block of marble—which the person who is on the consuming end of the work of art need not worry about at all: he may appreciate the fact that it was done, but he need not have the experience of doing it. The creator may work with great rapidity, like Mozart, or he may agonize through the whole process of creation, like Brahms; but this aspect of the work, the hearer, who listens only to the completed product, need not share. The "divine agonies of creation" are something the creator undergoes; the consumer need not reduplicate that experience—the experience of hearing the work may be divine, but he need not go through the agony. If it took the composer a year to get a lilting scherzo just right, the listener can enjoy the scherzo without going through the inner turmoil that it took to produce it. It would be difficult to find a reason why the *aesthetic* process, experienced by the consumer, should match the *artistic* process, undergone by the creator of art.

3. *Tests of communication.* If the test of a work of art is whether it "communicates feeling," must not something also be said about (a) whether the feeling in question is worth communicating and (b) whether it is *well* communicated? Tolstoy, for example, insists on the *sincerity* of the artist; but a person can be totally sincere and yet express himself awkwardly, his work may even be ludicrous. Nor is spontaneity enough: after a few "spontaneous" performances we may yearn for a well-rehearsed one. If the boy telling his tale of

his encounter with the wolf doesn't tell it *well,* is it still art, no matter how sincere and spontaneous? He may have these qualities and the result may come to nothing. Tolstoy says it must also be "infectious." But many works may be coldly calculated and not at all deeply felt, like Edgar Allan Poe's "The Raven" (read Poe's essay "The Philosophy of Composition"), and yet quite infectious in evoking strong feelings in the reader.

4. *Meaning of "communications."* It is far from clear what "the communication of feeling" means. Usually one relies on a series of metaphors. "The artist *transmits* his emotion to the audience." But what is the test of transmission? When a letter is transmitted by the postman from the writer to the receiver, the same physical object which was sent at one end was delivered at the other. We also speak of a message being transmitted even when the physical object is not, for example, a Western Union telegram; and of electrical current being transmitted through a wire, and here the same subatomic particles do not enter at one end and exit at another, as they do when water is transmitted through a pipe. But is *emotion* transmitted? Suppose that the poet felt emotion X–131 and that the reader, on reading the poem, felt emotion X–131. No such emotion existed in the interim; it disappeared in one place and popped up in another. Would we then be justified in saying that the artist had communicated this emotion to his reader?

"The artist *conveys* his emotion to the audience." I can convey an object from point A to point B by carrying it, or putting it in my car and driving it to B; water can be conveyed through a pipe; and so on. But what is it to convey emotion? If a certain feeling appears here (in the artist) and later there (in a reader), does that constitute proof that it has been "conveyed"? For perhaps the artist has *deposited* his emotion in the work of art, as a dog deposits his bone in the ground, for the reader to experience when he comes across the poem. It is clear that the artist has, in a sense, deposited his *work* in the world by publishing it or exhibiting it, but has he done the same with the *emotion*? The emotion that he felt when he created, or before—something that inspired him to create? the emotion he wants the audience to feel?

If this kind of view is to have any plausibility at all, we must take it to mean not the emotion (if any) that he felt, but the emotional quality that he *embodied in the work of art* (even if he was unaware of doing so), for the audience to recognize, to enjoy, and to appreciate. But in that case the emotional quality need not even be his own—it was his own only in the sense that he created the work of art which contains or embodies this quality. And then we are back with a conception of art which has already been discussed—not the emotion of the artist (it is not the emotion of artists that makes works of art great), not the emotions of the audience (these may vary enormously, depending on one's temperament and mood of the moment), but with the effective quality which the work of art itself possesses, quite independently of how it got there.

## 3. THE WORK OF ART AS EXPRESSIVE

When we say that the adagietto movement of the Mahler Fifth Symphony is sad, with an unutterly lost and lonely sadness, we are not talking about what Mahler felt or of any other activity he was involved in. We are not talking about any aspect of his artistic *process* at all, but about his artistic *product:* we are saying that the movement itself, or at least part of it, has this quality.

But how can a musical composition, or any other work of art, be sad? *People,* and perhaps animals, can be sad; inanimate objects such as stones and works of art cannot. If they really were sad, perhaps, as E. F. Carritt once remarked, we should "try to cheer the poor things up."

Of course works of art cannot *literally* be sad. When we say that the melody is sad, we are ascribing sadness to it *metaphorically,* just as we do when we say that the sky is gloomy, by which we surely don't mean that the sky *feels* gloomy. When we say "That was a sad occasion" (e.g., a funeral), we are not saying that the occasion itself was or felt sad, but only that it was the kind of event that can normally or usually cause those involved in it to feel sad; and gloomy skies are skies that make people inclined to feel gloomy. It's not that they have the quality themselves, but that their presence tends to *evoke* that quality in the minds of conscious beings.

Let us apply this approach to statements about emotional qualities in art: "A (a work of art or part or aspect of it) expresses B (some feeling-quality or feeling-tone) = A tends to evoke B (at least usually or normally)."

Tempting as this simple view is, it simply will not suffice as an account of the affective qualities (feelings, emotions, moods) that people attribute to works of art.

Consider a melody or musical passage you would describe as sad or melancholy. Does it always, or even usually, cause you to *feel* sad? Do grief-stricken works of art, such as a Lament in poetry or music, cause you to feel grief? If so, why would one want to have such experiences? Ordinarily people don't like to feel sadness or grief, and they avoid it when they can.

The problem of how the same emotion that is unpleasant in life can be pleasant in art has been a recurring challenge to philosophers. We know what "the problem of evil" in theology is: how could a benevolent God create a world so full of evil? A corresponding "problem of evil" in philosophy of art is: how can that which is unpleasant in life be found pleasant in art? For example, tragedy deals with situations of death, malevolent fate, fear or terror at one's precarious position in the universe; if it did not, it would not be tragedy; yet the *experience* of tragedy is not an unpleasant one, else we would not come back to the experience or wish to have it repeated.

One possible answer is that we regard with sufficient psychological *distance* so that its contemplation does not disturb or distress us as it does when it impinges on our personal lives:

If there are states of mind that are full of displeasure, it is grief and fear. But in music strong experiences of beauty, colored by pleasure, are connected with these very states. . . . How can things that are deeply displeasing in reality be pleasant to meet in art?

The explanation that is probably best starts out from the view that in art reality has a distance to us. The perfect funeral music and the musical clatter when the gates of hell are opened give us sensations that are of the same kind as our sensations in connection with grief and fear. That is why we say that it is grief and fear that this music expresses. But by the distance from reality the sensations at the funeral march of the symphony or the "Tuba Mirum" of the [Berlioz] *Requiem* are softened. They do not then reach the intensity that creates displeasure, the displeasure that colors the real grief and fear. Instead pleasure arises . . . . The distance to reality means that we can take part in the funeral procession without mourning, stand before the risk of being sentenced to eternal punishment when Christ returns and not feel the least panic, take part in the wild hunt with the damned hunter of César Franck [*Le Chasseur Mauduit*] without risking anything or even sweating. This distance is fundamental and belongs to the conditions of art. In a corresponding way we listen to so-called "happy" music without ourselves being happy *about* anything, we only enjoy the music.[12]

To others is seems somewhat less than plausible that we should attribute the difference to felt *distance.* Isn't the terror of the Berlioz "Tuba Mirum" movement or the panic of the "Deus Irae" in the Verdi *Requiem* just as immediate, just as intense, just as heart-quickening as any experience of terror or panic in real life? Perhaps then the difference is best described in this way: in life, experiences of grief and sadness are always *tied to particular events,* such as the death of a loved one, which evoke the sadness or grief; because we do not like loved ones to die, we do what we can to avoid the situations which produce the emotion. But the sadness of music (and art in general) are not like that: we can experience the emotion *without* the situation that in life would bring it on; we experience it in detachment from a life-situation, and abstracted from that occasion we can enjoy and savor it: we get the frosting, so to speak, without having to eat the unappetizing cake. Whatever the true account is of the difference, we can at least distinguish *life-sadness* from *art-sadness*: we do not seek to cultivate the first, but we may well cultivate the second.

It is still something of a mystery *why* the experience of sadness, with or without the life-situations that give rise to it, should be sought, or experienced as pleasant. Some people don't like to hear sad music—they say that it makes them sad and that they have enough sadness in their lives already. Other people don't mind sad music at all; in fact they may prefer it to happy music, not because they are masochists who seek unhappy experiences, but because in some strange way the hearing of sadness as expressed in music actually makes

[12] Ingemar Hedenius, "On the Musically Beautiful," in *Contemporary Aesthetics in Scandanavia,* ed. Lars Aagaard-Mogensen and Goran Hermeren (Doxa Publishing Co., Lund, Sweden, 1980), pp. 63–64.

one feel not sad but happy. In that case, however, the statement that sad music is music that makes one *feel* sad is false, since hearing the music makes one feel not sad but happy.

Others would say that when we hear music we call sad we do not *feel* sadness, we *imagine* sadness. But this view has problems of its own. When you hear sad music, *do* you imagine sadness? And what is it like to imagine sadness? If imagining in any way involves "having an image," how do you have an image of sadness? You can have a visual image of hills and streams and an auditory image of sounds heard in childhood, such as the sound of a freight-train whistle in the far distance; but an image of sadness? What does it look/sound/smell like?

Another problem with the view that a work of art expresses what it evokes is that the same work may evoke all sorts of different mental states in different people, or even in the same person at different times. Works of art have a tremendous variability in what experiences they evoke. A work of art that makes one person feel tense may make another person feel calm; a poem that makes you feel inspired may make me feel melancholy. The same work of art may make me experience one feeling at one time and another one at another time: I may be exhilarated upon hearing a composition, but if I have already heard it twenty times that day I shall probably feel tired or bored by the twenty-first exposure.

The fact is that what is *expressed* may not at all be similar to what is *evoked*. Aristotle, in his theory of catharsis, believed that witnessing the performance of a tragedy should evoke the emotions of pity and fear; but are pity and fear what is expressed in tragedies? What feeling is evoked depends on thousands of factors having to do with your physical health, you mental set at the time, previous exposure to the work of art, whether you are in the mood for it, whether you are receptive to this kind of work on this day at this hour, and so on. In fact, one could argue that the feeling that is evoked is very seldom that one that is expressed.

> A face expressing agony inspires pity rather than pain; a body expressing hatred and anger tends to arouse aversion or fear. Again, what is expressed may be something other than a feeling or emotion. A black and white picture expressing color does not make me feel colorful; and a portrait expressing courage and cleverness hardly produces either quality in the viewer.[13]

One could reply to all this by making a distinction: the fact that I feel listlessness or boredom *when* hearing the composition doesn't show that I hear them *in* the composition. Even when I am bored, I do not attribute the boredom to the composition, or for that matter to the composer, but only to myself. And a composition may make me feel sad for all kinds of extraneous reasons: a happy piece may make me sad because it reminds me of my lost

[13] Nelson Goodman, *The Languages of Art* (Indianapolis: Bobbs-Merrill, 1969), pp. 47–48.

love. But then it is clear that the sadness is mine, not the composition's; I do not say that the piece is sad just because I feel sad when I hear it. I am perfectly able to distinguish between what I feel *when* I hear the piece (and this, depending on circumstances, could be practically anything) and what qualities I hear (or seem to hear) *in* the piece.

But if this is so, we are back where we started: we do not judge what is expressed by what is evoked in us. We judge whether "A expresses B" not by what we feel when we hear it but by what qualities we attribute to the composition itself. We say that the Mahler "adagietto" is sad—it's a piece of sad music, regardless of whether we feel (or imagine) sadness when we hear it. So we are back with our original question: what is the meaning of saying that the work of art is sad? And once we have said it, how do we determine whether it is true?

When we say that A expresses B, we do not mean that A evokes B; we mean that in some way A *has* the quality B; we attribute the sadness to the music, not to ourselves (if we also feel sad when we hear it, that is another and separate issue—of what is evoked, not what is expressed).

"Well, what we mean is not that we feel sad when we hear it, but that the composer has expressed *his* sadness . . .". But we have already seen the pitfalls of this account in discussing the process sense of "express." Perhaps the process of artistic creation is not a process of expression at all; and even if it is, it may not be the expression of emotions or feelings. Besides, do we need to know what the composer felt at the time? Some of Mozart's most joyful compositions were written during a period of extreme sadness and depression in his life: a happy composition does not imply a happy composer. If we heard the composition and knew nothing about his life, we might say, "He was expressing his great joy in this composition," and yet this would be false, since he experienced no joy at all during this period. Most important, we have to distinguish again between "He expressed his feelings *by* creating the composition" (he was frustrated, then satisfied and fulfilled) and that he expressed feelings *in* the composition—for in this latter case, once again, we are talking about feelings as being in the work of art, not in the composer. If you wanted to verify the statement that a certain composition is joyous, you wouldn't go to the composer's biography to find out whether he felt joyous at the time, you would examine the composition itself; if you decide that the composition is joyous, it will be no less so if you then discovered that he felt no joy at all; you might find it "strange" or surprising, but the fact remains that what he felt is one thing, and what you attribute to the music is another thing.

When we hear a composition, we do not merely experience combinations of sounds, and when we see a painting, we do not merely experience combinations of shapes and colors; sounds and colors are *percepts*—they are what we perceive with the senses—and one of the most remarkable things about art is that *in art all percepts are suffused with affect,* or feeling-tone. Not merely that when we see or hear X we feel Y, but that we perceive X as *having* the quality Y. It is not geometrical shapes we see first, it is the *expressive quality* of those shapes:

> Expression can be described as the primary content of vision. We have been trained to think of perception as the recording of shapes, distances, hues, motions. The awareness of these measurable characteristics is really a fairly late accomplishment of the human mind. Even in Western man of the twentieth century it presupposes special conditions. It is the attitude of the scientist and the engineer or of the salesman who estimates the size of the customer's waist, the shade of a lipstick, the weight of a suitcase. But if I sit in front of a fireplace and watch the flames, I do not normally register certain shades of red, various degrees of brightness, geometrically defined shapes moving at such and such a speed. I see the graceful play of aggressive tongues, flexible striving, lively color. The face of a person is more readily perceived and remembered as being alert, tense, concentrated rather than as being triangularly shaped, having slanted eyebrows, straight lips, and so on. This priority of expression, although somewhat modified in adults by a scientifically oriented education, is striking in children and primitives. . . . The profile of a mountain is soft or threateningly harsh; a blanket thrown over a chair is twisted, sad, tired.[14]

All these are examples of what is called *natural expressiveness*. There are gestures, bodily behavior, and facial configurations that go with one kind of mental state but not another. If you are tense, others can "see your tension" in your body and your facial lines, which are *expressive* of tension. If you are in a nasty mood today, others can know this from your behavior—they may even know it before you do, and your pet dog can even detect it, and the dog avoids you while you are in this mood. Your behavior, your facial configuration, your tone of voice, all are *expressive* of your mood—and if others are observant, your behavior *reveals* to them what that mood is.

Ordinarily the behavior is expressive of the mood or emotion you actually feel—that is how the connection between the mood and the behavior was established in the first place. But it need not be so in every case: you may be an actor or actress on a stage, and you may express anger or rage or frustration or benevolence, and yet not feel any of these things yourself. You may be so "caught up in the act" that you do feel them, but if you have to repeat the performance every night at 8:30 for a year, it is unlikely that you feel them every time—you may even feel cool as a cucumber while you go through the motions. Nevertheless, your face and gestures and bodily movements are *expressive* of the kind of mood or emotion you wish to communicate to your audience. They are no less expressive of anger because of the fact that you don't at the moment feel the anger yourself. That certain gestures and behavior are expressive of anger is just an objective fact.

What has all this to do with works of art? Works of art, too, contain expressive features. Certain passages of literature are angry or indignant or

---

[14] Rudolf Arnheim, *op. cit.*, Chapter 10. Reprinted in John Hospers, ed., *Artistic Expression* (New York: Irvington Books, 1971), pp. 219–220.

tense—you can tell from the words used and the rhythm of the lines; and for this it doesn't matter whether the author felt angry or not. Horizontal lines in a painting are calm, relaxed, peaceful; jagged lines are tense and disturbed. This is not simply conventional—we didn't learn it that way and come to accept it as dogma; if we had been told that relaxed body movements are expressive of anger, we would soon learn from our own experience that this was not so. The horizontal position, for human beings at least, is the position of rest and sleep and the position from which we cannot fall down. The connection between restfulness and horizontality is neither accidental or coincidental; it is there in all human beings, since we tend to rest most in this position, and we are all subject to gravitation. It might be different for chickens who sleep while standing on their roosts, but even they are subject to gravitational pull from the ground while perched in their elevated position.

And so it is only "natural" that when we see a painting such as Tintoretto's *Christ Walking on the Water,* in which the horizontal lines of the quiet sea predominate, that we should attribute to this picture such qualities as calm, serenity, and peace. Similarly, a lightning bolt in a painting is the very opposite of calm and peace, not only because we know that lightning goes with storms and can strike human beings but because *the jagged lines themselves* have the quality of tension and disturbingness.

> A steep rock, a willow tree, the colors of a sunset, the cracks in a wall, a tumbling leaf, a flowing fountain, and in fact a mere line or color or the dance of an abstract shape on the movie screen, have as much expression as the human body, and serve the artist equally well. In some ways they serve him even better, for the human body is a particularly complex pattern, not easily reduced to the simplicity of shape and motion that transmits compelling expression. Also it is overloaded with non-visual associations. The human figure is not the easiest, but the most difficult, vehicle of artistic expression.[15]

Such depictions in visual art bring out the expressive qualities of objects in the world—they are a far cry from "self-expression."

> The method of self-expression plays down, or even annihilates, the function of the theme to be represented. It recommends a passive, "projective" pouring-out of what is felt inside. On the contrary, the method discussed here requires active, disciplined concentration of all organizing powers upon the expression that is localized in the object of representation.[16]

This "primacy of expression" is important for those who teach, and for those who learn, the visual arts:

> If expression is the primary content of vision in daily life, the same should be all the more true for the way the artist looks at the world. The expressive qualities

---

[15] *Ibid.,* p. 222.
[16] *Ibid.,* p. 221.

are his means of communication. They capture his attention, through them he understands and interprets his experiences, and they determine the form-patterns he creates. Therefore the training of art students should be expected to consist basically in sharpening their sense of these qualities and in teaching them to look to expression as the guiding criterion for every stroke of the pencil, brush, or chisel. In fact many good art teachers do precisely this. But there are also plenty of times when the spontaneous sensitivity of the student to expression not only is not developed further, but is even disturbed and suppressed. There is, for example, an old-fashioned but not extinct way of teaching students to draw from the model by asking them to establish the exact length and direction of contour lines, the relative position of points, the shape of masses. In other words, students are to concentrate on the geometric-technical qualities of what they see. In its modern version this method consists in urging the young artist to think of the model or of a freely invented design as a configuration of masses, planes, directions . . .

This method of teaching follows the principles of scientific definition rather than those of spontaneous vision. There are, however, other teachers who will proceed differently. With a model sitting on the floor in a hunched-up position, they will not begin by making the students notice that the whole figure can be inscribed in a triangle. Instead they will ask about the expression of the figure; they may be told, for example, that the person on the floor looks tense, tied together, full of potential energy. They will suggest, then, that the student try to render this quality. In doing so the student will watch proportions and directions, but not as geometric properties in themselves. These formal properties will be perceived as being functionally dependent upon the primarily observed expression, and the correctness or incorrectness of each stroke will be judged on the basis of whether or not it captures the dynamic "mood" of the subject.[17]

That objects have certain expressive properties is, we have said, an objective fact about them. If a painter could not rely on the peacefulness of horizontal lines—if it were just a matter of whim, or caprice—what could he count on by way of response to his painting? For that matter, if bright and warm colors did not tend to "come forward" in a painting, and cool or pastel colors to recede into the background, if there were no such tendency or it just happened hit-or-miss, sporadicaly and not regularly, how would he go about composing his color combinations? Such tendencies are, as we say, "objectively there."

The same can be said of music. Certain passages of music are *restless*, for example, and again this is no accident:

A person says that he feels restless. A description of what it feels like to be restless might include references to such things as increased rate of breathing and heartbeat, unsteady organics in the region of the diaphragm, tapping of the feet or fingers, inability to keep still, etc. It requires no great knowledge of music to appreciate the fact that much the same kind of movements may easily be produced in musical phrases. Staccato passages, trills, strong accents, quavers, rapid accelerandos and crescendos, shakes, wide jumps in pitch—all such devices conduce to the creation of an auditory structure which is appropriately described as restless.[18]

---

[17] *Ibid.*, pp. 221–222.
[18] Carroll C. Pratt, *The Meaning of Music* (New York: McGraw Hill, 1931), p. 198.

Returning at last to sadness, does not the same principle apply again? If we said, "Sad music is characterized by slowness, by downward-tending in pitch, by no great leaps in pitch, by legato rather than staccato . . ." and left it at that, a person might reply, *"You say* that these things go with sadness; but that's just your opinion—I say they don't. Now prove me wrong!" If you associate sadness with qualities ABC, and he with DEF, where do you go from there? But if we show him that certain patterns or configurations in music (A) are "naturally expressive" of certain affects (B), then we have, so to speak, *anchored* our position in facts of reality. There is, after all, a connection between people's behavior when they are sad and the kind of music we call sad. "Sad music has some of the characteristics of people who are sad. It will be slow, not tripping; it will be low, not tinkling. People who are sad move more slowly; and when they speak, they speak softly and low."[19]

Not all of the features that we associate with sad music can be accounted for in this way. The slowness undoubtedly can, since people in a state of grief do tend to move more slowly. Try playing a slow melody that is supposed to be played on a 33 r.p.m. phonograph record at a 78 r.p.m. speed, and see if it still sounds sad to you! In fact, can you think of any music you would call sad that is also fast? But slowness is not all, of course; the avoidance of skips and jumps is also part of it. What about the prevalent notion that sad music is in the minor key? Here is a strictly musical feature that resists translation into emotional terms. Is this association coincidental, since so much sad music is in the major key and so much nonsad music in the minor key? Perhaps, but there does seem to be a *tendency* for music in the minor key to be characterized as sad. Probably this is because the minor chord (A–C, or C–E flat), entirely by itself and without any notes being played before or after, has a kind of sad or melancholy quality to it. But it is far from clear *why* this is the case. Prior to the Renaissance, this same chord was perceived as a dissonance and was, therefore, avoided. It seems, then, that at least one of the characteristics of music that tends to make us hear it as sad is not accounted for on the analysis of "natural expressiveness."

When we say that the association of A (a part or passage of a work of art) with B (a type of affect) is an objective fact, we do not of course mean that the affective quality is a quality *intrinsic* to the passage, that is, an internal property: what is, strictly speaking, in the melody is a succession of tones, not emotions. The opposite of "intrinsic" is "relational," and the emotional quality of certain bodily movements is clearly relational: that is, the bodily movements of an angry person are *related* to his anger—his anger is not intrinsic to the movements, though the movement is (correctly) perceived as an angry movement. Similarly, the sadness of the music is not literally in the notes or the tones; nevertheless, owing to the similarity of aspects of the music to aspects of the movements of human beings, the melody is (correctly)

[19] O. K. Bouwsma, "The Expression Theory of Art," in Max Black, ed., *Philosophical Analysis* (Ithaca, N.Y.: Cornell Univ. Press, 1950). Reprinted in John Hospers, ed., *Artistic Expression;* passage quoted is on p. 249.

perceived as sad, for it does, objectively, have at least some of the features of people who are sad.

There is a further twist that may be given the theory of expressive properties, which has been presented recently by Guy Sircello. It has to do with what are called "artistic arts." For example,

> We might say of Poussin's *The Rape of the Sabine Women* . . . that it is calm and aloof. Yet it is quite clear that the depicted scene is *not* calm and that no one in it, with the possible exception of Romulus, who is directing the attack, is aloof. It is rather, as we say, that Poussin calmly observes the scene and paints it in an aloof, detached way.
>
> Brueghel's painting called *Wedding Dance in the Open Air* can be aptly if superficially described as gay and happy. In this case, however, it is surely the occasion and the activities of the depicted peasants which are happy. Perhaps the prominent red used throughout the painting can be called "gay." The faces of the peasants, however, are neither happy nor gay. They are bland, stupid, and even brutal. It is this fact which makes the painting ironic rather than gay or happy. Yet there is certainly nothing about a peasant wedding, the dull peasants, or their heavy dance which is ironic. The irony lies in the fact that the painter "views," "observes," or depicts the happy scene ironically.
>
> William Wordsworth's sentimental poem "We Are Seven" . . . is quite obviously not *about* sentimentality. It purports simply to record the conversation between the poet and a child. Neither the child nor the poet . . . is sentimental. The child matter-of-factly reports her firm conviction that there are still seven members of her family despite the fact that two of them are dead. The poet is trying, in a rather obtuse and hard-headed sort of way, to get her to admit that there are only five. But the little girl is made to win the point by having the last word in the poem. She is thus made to seem "right" even though no explicit authorization is given to her point of view. By presenting the little girl's case so sympathetically, Wordsworth (the poet who wrote the poem, not the "character" in the poem) treats the attitude of the little girl, as well as the death of her siblings, sentimentally.[20]

With these examples, are we back again to expression in the process sense? Surely not. We have no idea from the works of art what feelings the artist had or whether he expressed them. Our judgment in each case is confirmed by examining the work of art itself; and surely the features described are an overall expressive quality—not of the characters but of the work of art as a whole. It isn't that Poussin *views* the rape of the women with detachment, but that the painting itself *has* an aloof quality. It isn't that Brueghel views the scene with a certain attitude (how do we know whether he did? and if he did, does it matter?), but that the irony is to be found in the picture—in the clash between the happy spirit of the wedding dance and the dull brutal faces of the peasants. It isn't that Wordsworth the man feels a certain way toward his subject (how do we know how he felt?) but that the mood of the poem itself is one of sym-

---

[20] Guy Sircello, *Mind and Art* (Princeton: Princeton Univ. Press, 1971), pp.19–21.

pathy with the little girl, even though it is recognized that she is mistaken. All these examples are interesting and provocative, but they do not take us from expressiveness as a quality of the work of art to expression as a process, in spite of the process language ("He viewed the scene with aloofness . . .") that is used to describe it.

There are several problems, however, which should now be mentioned:

1. *The inadequacy of expression-words.* Expression-terms like "sad," "melancholy," "joyous," "triumphant," and so on are not very precise in describing what we mean. No two states of sadness even in the same human being are exactly alike; they always differ to some extent in their exact feeling-quality. We call them both "sad" only because, though they differ from each other, they are similar enough to one another to fall under the same general term, "sad"—just as two human beings may differ in size, weight, appearance, skin color, and bodily dimensions of all kinds, yet we classify them both as human beings because they share certain qualities in common that distinguish them from apes and elephants.

When we are talking about physical objects and their physical qualities, we can subclassify these general terms as far as we wish: there are not only quadrilaterals but squares, parallelograms, rectangles, parallelopipeds, and so on. There are not only trees, but deciduous trees and evergreen trees, and within these two classifications there are thousands of subvarieties of trees, each of which is named and classified. How can we tell whether you mean the same kind of tree or rectangle that I do when I use the same word? By pointing to the object, or a picture of it. But in the case of emotions we have no such outside check. There is *some* check: the mother may say to her daughter, "It's not love you're feeling, it's only infatuation," and she may be right, for she may be a closer observer of the daughter's behavior than the daughter herself is, and the daughter may not be in much of a position to classify what she feels (she feels what she feels, but she may not be able correctly to *conceptualize* what she feels under a general heading). But if two people stand before the same picture in a museum and neither is exhibiting any overt behavior, how are you to determine exactly *what* the other person is experiencing? Even if the other person uses words to describe his or her feelings, the words may not correctly classify the feelings experienced. If I experience a peculiar kind of inner ecstasy whenever I see a certain painting by Picasso, and I want to share this experience with you, and I take you to the museum and lead you in front of the picture, you may feel utterly bored and hide this fact out of politeness. "Now you know what the Picasso-emotion is like!" I say triumphantly; but you experience nothing of the sort. "Oh," you may say under your breath, "you mean it's a kind of boredom."

It has sometimes been suggested that instead of the one word "joy" we should devise a million words, each naming a different subclass or species of joy. Thus we could say I am now experiencing joy-18472, as opposed to what I experienced yesterday, joy-29385. But even if you could make such distinctions within your own consciousness and had a totally reliable memory, how would you communicate to other people what kind of joy you were feeling. How would others know what specific state of consciousness you had in mind when you used the term "joy-18472"? Assuming that you had the word and used it consistently in the same way, how, in the absence of precise behavioral accompaniments, would you communicate to others what you meant, or discover, if they used the same word, whether they meant by it the same qualitative emotional state that you did?

Thus we seem doomed to using the same emotion-words we have now, and if we want to be more precise, we say "The joy I experienced was the joy of suddenly hearing some wonderful piece of unexpected good news," and hope that when our hearer gets good news he feels the same way we do. Yet even this is not very precise: joy-at-good-news-1 is still different from joy-at-good-news-2.

When we go from ordinary life-experiences to art, these difficulties are compounded. The slow movement of the Mozart Quintet K. 515 is quite different in its emotional quality from the slow movement of the K. 516 Quintet; both could be described as sad, or melancholy, perhaps even heart-rending, but there is no way *in words* to distinguish the sadness of the one from the sadness of the other. All we can do is say "Listen to both movements, then again, then yet again" and hope that when they hear the two movements they will understand the difference. The difference certainly does not come out in calling them both sad; even if we said the one was the sadness of loneliness and the other the sadness of grief long ago remembered, it wouldn't be precise enough: the sadness of one grief long ago remembered is still different from the sadness of another grief long ago remembered.

That is undoubtedly why Mendelssohn wrote, "What any music I like expresses for me is not feelings too indefinite to clothe in words, but *too definite*. If you asked me what I felt on the occasion in question, I say, the song itself precisely as it stands. And if, in this or that instance, I had in my mind a definite word or definite words, I would not utter them to a soul, because words do not mean for one person what they do for another; because the song alone can say to one, can awake in him, the same feelings it can in another—feelings, however, not to be expressed by the same words."[21]

2. *Cultural variations in expressiveness.* Aside from the problem of finding the right words to describe our feelings (in life, but even more in art), there is the fact—or seeming fact—that "natural expressiveness" does vary somewhat from culture to culture, even from person to person. How universal, for example, is the following account of the expressive characters of various colors?

> The vegetable covering of the normal foreground is not for the most part . . . of direct significance as food or danger or other vital condition. It af-

[21] Quoted in Edmund Gurney, *The Power of Sound* (London: Smith, Elder & Co., 1880), p. 357.

fords shade and at the same time reflects the sun's rays with less loss of brightness than do distant objects. It is in no way an exciting fact, but a harmless and agreeable one. Those plants that are important as food, and those dangerous as poisons, are in neither case especially represented as a class by the color green. The green vegetable covering of the earth is just the normal fact of existence. Psychologically, then, we would expect green to appear as a feeling of quiet cheerfulness. Who does not feel this to be in fact the character of green?

No other color can compare with [red] in the systematic way in which it stands for the dramatic crises of life, among all the higher animals. It is not merely that arterial blood, the central life-fluid, is of that color. We have to remember also that from the standpoint of vision it is chiefly by its color that blood is identified. Otherwise it cannot by sight be distinguished from water or other common fluids. Outside of vegetation nothing in nature probably is so readily and safely to be identified by its mere color as is the blood of the higher animals. But the identification of blood is the knowledge that edible flesh is at hand, or that foes or friends or members of the pack or the animal itself are in danger or pain. Blood is interwoven with success in the hunt, with consuming of the prey, with combat, and with being one's self, in person or in the group, preyed upon. Here are nearly all the great instinctive emotions, social solidarity, everything save sex, which depends visually upon form rather than color, and otherwise chiefly upon hearing and smell. What is life for a higher animal but a shedding of blood and a struggle to conserve his own or that of certain of his neighbors? If the color of blood is not to excite and move the higher animal, the remaining colors ought to put him to sleep! What, psychologically, do we find? That red is precisely the most dramatic and stirring of colors; that it lacks the light-hearted gaiety of yellow, the sunshine color; the cold intensity of white, the snow-and-cloud color; the quiet cheerfulness of green; the gentle affectionate quality of blue; and possesses as no other color, the quality of excitement or activity. There is no other color which it is so necessary to take seriously.[22]

There is a large measure of agreement on these things and yet a considerable disagreement on details. The conclusions arrived at also presuppose a certain environment: people living in the temperate zones may feel as the author describes about green, but not people in the Arctic zones for whom white is the constant color of the ground (snow) and green the occasional and exciting exception.

Thus far we have spoken of expressiveness as if it were entirely the product of *association*: red is dramatic because of its association with blood, horizontal lines with restfulness because of their association with sleep, and so on. But this may not be the whole story: maybe it is true that "all percepts are suffused with affect" but that not all affect comes via association. Some writers believe that certain colors, lines, or other visual or auditory percepts are in some way *intrinsically* expressive of certain qualities, even prior to (or without benefit of) association with pervasive qualities in nature.

We may associate pink with sentimental persons, with pink dresses and pink decorations and pink chocolate boxes. . . . The trumpet and the drum have mar-

[22] Charles Hartshorne, *The Philosophy and Psychology of Sensation* (Chicago: Univ. of Chicago Press, 1934), pp. 253–256.

tial associations. Yet, though in fact these associations always do come into play in our apprehension of colors and sounds, it is certain that there is a residue of non-associative meaning. It is indeed probable that in many cases the colors and sounds have come to possess the associations *through their intrinsic suggestiveness* rather than by the reverse process. Their effects cannot be entirely due to association. A certain kind of crude pink comes to have vulgar associations *because something in pinkness itself* jars upon us . . . The trumpet and the drum come to have martial associations because their quality, as apprehended through our organisms, suggests in itself "martial" meaning.

Straight lines express the "values" of directness, unwaveringness, or what can be called, in rather feeble language, rectilinear efficiency. Horizontal lines suggest—and not, I think, through association only—stability and balance; vertical straight lines in a picture or a landscape or a building suggest a different kind of stability. . . . Some curves suggest grace, or fluidity, or, again, vigor. Others suggest uncertainty and hesitation.[23]

May it not even be that the strong, vivid, dramatic expressive quality of red depends not only on primordial associations with red things in nature such as blood but on certain ways in which the color red impinges on the retina of the human eye? Perhaps there is a neurological component, as well as an associational component, to the full story.

In spite of all this, not everyone is agreed that certain percepts are "naturally" expressive of certain affects, whether by universal human association or otherwise. Some of the observations about color (where white is the standard background of the earth instead of green, for example) would tend to confirm this claim. Doris Humphrey, the dancer, writes,

> I've had to advise everybody how to express anxiety, alarm, and endless other emotional states. They may have felt these things, but the movements for them are complete strangers.
>
> There are many feelings which can be expressed in so many ways that there is really no pattern for them. For example, hope has no shape, nor do inspiration, fear, or love.[24]

And over a century ago the musicologist Edmund Gurney wrote,

> It is often found that music which wears a definable expression to one person, does not wear it or wears a different one to another, though the music may be equally enjoyed by both. For instance, the great "subject" of the first movement of Schubert's B-flat trio represents to me and many the *ne plus ultra* of energy and passion; yet this very movement was described by Schumann as "tender, girlish, and confiding.[25]

[23] Louis Arnaud Reid, *A Study in Aesthetics* (London: Allen & Unwin, 1931), pp. 76–77, 83. Emphasis added.

[24] Doris Humphrey, *The Art of Making Dances* (New York: Rinehart & Co., Inc., 1959), pp. 114, 118.

[25] Edmund Gurney, *op. cit.,* p. 342.

This was the same point that Hanslick had in mind more than a hundred years ago in describing what we might call the *relativity of expressiveness*. If people say that a certain bit of music has a definite kind of expressiveness, said Hanslick,

> let them play the theme of a symphony by Mozart or Haydn, an adagio by Beethoven, a scherzo by Mendelssohn, one of Schumann's or Chopin's compositions for the piano, anything, in short, from the stock of our standard music. . . . Who would be bold enough to point out a definite feeling as the subject of any of these themes? One will say "love." He may be right. Another thinks it is "longing." Perhaps so. A third feels it to be "religious fervor." Who can contradict him? Now, how can we talk of a definite feeling being represented, when nobody really knows *what* is represented? Probably, all will agree about the beauty or beauties of the composition, whereas all will differ regarding its subject.[26]

The translation uses the term "represent," but since we have used "represent" in a somewhat narrower sense, to cover depiction-subjects and portrayal-subjects, and these are not being discussed here by Hanslick, it would be preferable to substitute the word "express."

Hanslick also reminds us that the kind of expressed quality we attribute to the musical passage will depend on the era in which we live and that in the historical context of other works of art we shall be inclined to change our attribution of expressive qualities to a given piece of music:

> How many compositions by Mozart were thought by his contemporaries to be the most perfect expression of passion, warmth, and vigor of which music was capable. The placidity and moral sunshine of Haydn's symphonies were placed in contrast with the violent bursts of passion, the internal strife, the bitter and acute grief embodied in Mozart's music. Twenty or thirty years later, precisely the same comparison was made between Beethoven and Mozart. Mozart, the emblem of supreme and transcendent passion, was replaced by Beethoven, while he himself was promoted to the Olympic classicalness of Haydn. The *musical* merit of the many compositions which at one time made so deep an impression, and the aesthetic enjoyment which their originality and beauty still yield, are not altered in the least by this dissimilar effect on the feelings of different periods.[27]

For many listeners, such remarks will clinch the point about the relativity of expressiveness. Yet one cannot be sure: our words for expressive qualities are so crude (compared with our words for physical objects), and the associations in people's minds with different expression-words are so varying, that it could well be—and surely is often the case—that our experiences of a certain passage do not differ nearly as much as the words we use to describe our experiences.

---

[26] Eduard Hanslick, *op. cit.*, pp. 43–44.
[27] *Ibid.*, p. 25.

The feelings experienced by human beings are endlessly various, and only a very few, such as love, fear, anger, etc., have received names. The immense majority of them cannot be referred to by name because they have received none.
Only a few feelings . . . have names. They are feelings which are closely connected with typical, recurrent situations in life, and are usually accompanied by overt and easily recognizable modes of behavior. The terms "the emotions" and "the passions" designate principally those standard, labelled feelings, and indeed those feelings primarily as out of the aesthetic status, that is to say, as mere accompaniments or incidents of practical endeavor of one sort or another. But to one such named feeling, there are a thousand that have received no name, but which are none the less real experiences of the very same general sort.[28]

Thus, many of the differences in description may not be indicators of real differences in the experience itself. This is even true of color perceptions: we agree fairly well on clear cases of red, orange, and yellow, but if you take a color in the region between red and orange or between orange and yellow, there will be considerable disagreement about what color name to apply to it. If this is true of colors, where our labeling techniques are more precise, how much more will this not be true of moods and feelings? What one person calls fear, another calls terror; what one person calls longing, another calls yearning. Besides all this, there is another consideration: when you take an entire movement from a musical composition (never mind the whole piece) and ask someone what its prevailing mood is ("Is the last movement of Tschaikovsky's *Pathètique* Symphony despairing?") you may get different answers because the feeling-quality shifts constantly from measure to measure, and a passage in the movement which strikes one person as more significant or typical may not strike another person in the same way, so they will *appear* to differ in their responses because each one has in mind a different passage in attempting his description. Probably no one would describe the expressive quality of the last movement of Schubert's C Major Symphony (No. 9) as dour, mournful, or somber; yet, depending on the passage one has in mind, reports would differ: some would call it glad and joyous, others triumphant and heroic, others as full of driving energy, and so on. There would probably be more agreement about specific passages—of a few measures—than about the expressive quality of the movement as a whole, since these are constantly shifting about and replacing one another like quicksilver.

Hanslick, however, does not rest his case with the contention that the expressive qualities of music are relative to the listener; his thesis is much more radical than this: he claims that musical compositions can have no *emotionally* expressive qualities at all: they can give us *motion,* but not *emotion.* Just as, in representation, music can convey to us the *rhythms* of horses' hooves on cobblestone but not the *sounds* of the horses' hooves themselves (no musical instrument can produce that sound), so music can express only the *kinetic* (motion) qualities that *accompany* emotions, but not the emotions themselves.

[28] Curt J. Ducasse, *The Philosophy of Art* (New York: Dial Press, 1929), pp. 195-196.

Expressionists have waxed lyrical on how music expresses the whispering of love or the clamoring of ardent combatants:

> The whispering may be expressed, true; but not the whispering of love; the clamor may be reproduced, undoubtedly; but not the clamor of ardent combatants. Music can reproduce phenomena such as whispering, storming, roaring, but the feelings of love and anger not at all. Definite feelings are unsusceptible of being embodied in music.
>
> The feeling of *hope* is inseparable from the concept of a happier state that is to come, and which we compare with the actual state. The feeling of sadness involves the notion of a past state of happiness. These are perfectly definite ideas or conceptions, and in default of them . . . no feeling can be called "hope" or "sadness," for through them alone can a feeling assume a definite character. On excluding these conceptions from consciousness, nothing remains but a vague sense of motion which at best could not rise above a general feeling of satisfaction or discomfort. The feeling of love cannot be conceived apart from the image of the beloved being, or apart from the desire and the longing for the possession of the beloved. It is not the kind of psychical activity but the intellectual substratum, the subject underlying it, which makes it love. Dynamically speaking, love may be gentle or impetuous, buoyant or depressed, and yet it remains love. . . . Music can express only those qualifying adjectives, and not the substantive, love, itself. . . . Music may be described by terms such as graceful, gentle, violent, vigorous, elegant, fresh; all these ideas being expressible by corresponding modifications of sound. What part of the feelings can music represent, if not the subject involved in them? Only their *dynamic* properties. It may reproduce the motion accompanying psychical action, according to its momentum: speed, slowness, strength, weakness, increasing and decreasing intensity. But motion is only one of the *concomitants* of feeling, not the feeling itself. Music cannot reproduce the feeling of love, but only the element of *motion,* and this may occur in any other feeling just as well as in love.[29]

Music cannot express the feeling, but only its dynamic (kinetic) properties, says Hanslick. But what if a kinetic property A is regularly correlated with a feeling-state A$^1$? Then we could move from the dynamic property A to the feeling-state A$^1$ and still attribute the feeling-state (by association with the dynamic property) to the music. Thus we could go from a certain kind of glissando in the strings to (for example) tenderness. The case would still not be lost.

But this, according to Hanslick, is just what we cannot do. The same feeling-state may have very different dynamic properties: "love may be gentle or impetuous, buoyant or depressed, and yet it remains love." But, one may reply, we do distinguish kinds of love in music: gentle love from impetuous love, for example. Still, how do we know that it is love and not other emotion that may also have this same dynamic property? Love may be impetuous or tender, but so may filial concern. But even to speak of tenderness at all may be going too far for Hanslick: if tenderness is admissible, why not sadness?

[29] Eduard Hanslick, *op. cit.,* pp. 40–41.

Yet it is only the dynamic accompaniments of the emotion, not the emotion itself, that can be rendered in music, he says. If only the dynamic properties can be rendered, it would seem, from the near unanimity of persons in response to at least *some* music, that some dynamic properties do regularly go with some kinds of feeling. Everyone, even those comparatively untutored in music, say without prompting that a certain melody is "very sad"—and how could this be unless it had certain dynamic properties (such as slowness, and others already discussed) that are indicators of sadness, much as wolf tracks are indicators of a wolf, and of not something else?

### Expressiveness and Artistic Value

Granting all that has been said about expressiveness in the arts, one might ask, So what? How does a work's or passage's being expressive make it a better work of art than it would have been otherwise? Both Gurney and Hanslick argued that expressiveness makes no difference to musical value.

1. Suppose, says Gurney, that we set down the score of a number of admittedly great or beautiful melodies, and just underneath them the score of other melodies (perhaps of our own invention) differing from them only very slightly in rhythm and tone relationships, which are at once felt to be trivial, dull, or banal. Yet the affective quality of the pairs may be the same: the members of the first pair are both sad, those of the second pair both tense, the third pair both graceful or scintillating, and so on. If the expressive character has not changed (between the first and second members of each pair) and yet the artistic value has, what can the expressiveness have to do with the value of the music? As Hanslick puts it, "In every song, slight alterations may be introduced which, without in the least detracting from the accuracy of expression, immediately destroy the beauty of the theme"[30]—which would be impossible if the expressiveness constituted all or even a part of the beauty of the theme.

This still does not show that expressiveness is not one of the criteria determining the beauty of the piece; if Gurney's observations are correct, it only shows that expressiveness is not *all* that makes for musical excellence.

2. "In an immense amount of beautiful music the element of definable expression is absent; or present only in such vague and fragmentary ways that, in describing the phenomena under that aspect, we seem to get about as near the reality as when we attempt descriptions of things in the vocabulary of some unfamiliar foreign language . . ."[31]

This may be true if one is talking about *definable* expression; but, as we have seen, most expressive qualities we find in works of art cannot be ac-

[30] *Ibid.,* p. 65.
[31] Gurney, *op. cit.,* p. 339.

curately named owing to the inevitable poverty of our emotion-vocabulary. So it is possible that the pieces he values are expressive, but not *describably* ("definably") so. We all know, says Hanslick, of many compositions of exquisite beauty which have no definable expressive quality—such as Bach's Preludes and Fugues. But if so, this doesn't show that they have no expressive quality, only that they do not have a *definable* expressive quality—a point which may easily be admitted.

3. "Take twenty bits of music," says Gurney, "each presenting the same definable character, such as melancholy or triumph. Now if the stirring of this emotion is the whole business of any one of these tunes, how is anybody the richer for knowing the other nineteen? . . . In reality, of course, each of them is an individual, with a beauty peculiar to itself, and each is, to one who loves it, a new source of otherwise unknown delight."[32]

This, however, does not show the irrelevance of expressiveness: the twenty bits of music may all be expressive of gentle melancholy—but each one may do it in a different way, so none duplicates the other; so one can well be "richer" for knowing the other nineteen.

4. "If I find twenty bits of music beautiful and indescribable, and one bit beautiful and pathetic [full of pathos], it is unreasonable to say I enjoy the last (which I don't enjoy at all more than the others) *because* it is pathetic."[33]

And this is true enough; but I may still enjoy the other twenty just as much, not because they lack expressiveness, but because they lack *definable* expressiveness, that is, an expressive quality which I can capture in words. This doesn't show that it *is* because of the indefinable expressive quality that it is beautiful, of course; but neither does it show that it is not—only that it is not because of a *definable* expressive quality.

5. Why, says Gurney, should expressiveness be any more an indicator of beauty in a tune than it is in a face? A face can be expressive without being beautiful; so can a tune.

This argument assumes that expressiveness is not an indicator of beauty in a face. But many would contend that it is; in fact many would say that a beautiful face *is* one that is expressive. In any case, there may be a false analogy here: what holds true of a face may not hold true of a tune.

6. It is not the inability to give the expressive quality of a name that is so important, it is the growing impression of the *irrelevance* of the whole enterprise of finding an expressive label for it to the quite different enterprise of finding or discovering the source of its musical beauty. The heart of the matter lies elsewhere: "If one forces himself to try to give a name to the character of the successive sentences or phrases in a page of a sonata, though this one as compared with that may be more confident, or more relaxed, though we may

[32] *Ibid.,* p. 342.
[33] *Ibid.,* p. 340.

find an energetic phrase here and a leading phrase there, a capricious turn in close proximity to a piece of emphatic reiteration, etc., *our interest seems to lie in something quite remote from such a description*; and it is only by a sort of effort that we perceive whether or not the musical current has been colored by occasionally floating into the zone of describable expression."[34] We evaluate a tune quite independently of whether we can find a descriptive term for it; and even if we do find one, such as "poignant," we have not even begun to explain why we find the tune beautiful. Even after we have determined its expressive quality, we seem, as he puts it, to be as far from explaining why the tune is beautiful as a heap of clothes scattered over the floor explains the living beauty of face and form.

7. Hanslick argues that "the beautiful tends to disappear in proportion as the expression of some specific feeling is aimed at." Opera is one of several examples he uses. The expressive character of the arias in opera is designed to match the emotions being expressed in the lines the character is singing. Pure music, an interplay of forms, wants to go on its way serenely independent of such shifting expressiveness, but tied as it is in opera to the expression of emotions in the characters, it must constantly try to match in the music the feelings expressed in the words. The result is that it "reduces the opera, as it were, to a constitutional government whose very existence depends upon an incessant struggle between two parties equally entitled to power. It is from this conflict, in which the composer allows now one principle and now the other to prevail, that all the imperfections of the opera arise. . . . The principles in which music and the drama are grounded, if pushed to their logical consequences, are mutually destructive."[35] Pure music pushes one way, the requirements of expressiveness another. Yet it is possible for opera to surmount this inherent difficulty: "In Mozart's operas there is perfect congruity between the music and the words," but this is because "even the most intricate parts, the finales, are beautiful if judged as a whole, quite apart from the words." Mozart had the sense always to subordinate the expressive requirements, drawn from the characters and plot, to the purely musical requirements.

One often does feel in opera the very thing which Hanslick points out. Yet the irrelevance of expressiveness is not thereby established. Often the music itself has its own expressive character, quite apart from the dramatic action of opera whose expressive features it is supposed to match at every stage of the action.

8. In opera at least, music is dominant; in film it is usually subsidiary. Film music usually does not stand up very well alone, as it is composed primarily to accompany the scenes being shown on the screen. Yet, it would seem that, if any music can be expressive of feelings and moods, film music can: the film

---

[34] *Ibid.*, pp. 336–337.
[35] Hanslick, *op. cit.*, pp. 49–50.

composer is told, "I want two minutes of sadness and pathos. Then after that, a change of mood—first I want music that's threatening, then uncertainty, doubt, rising hope. Oh yes, and at the end I want two and a half minutes of triumphant music as the hero and heroine march into the sunset." The composer creates this music to order, and it does have these qualities. If it does have these qualities, but doesn't (by common consent) have much value as music, then this is a clear example of the one divorced from the other.

A determined expression-theorist could try to rebut even this charge. He might say that the music has these qualities in a very crude or superficial way, done without much subtlety, sophistication, or imagination. He might say that the expressiveness is not achieved with the imaginativeness in film music that it is in other music, and that music specifically designed to accompany verbal effects is not likely to have expressive qualities of the subtlety that other music can have. He might say, in other words, that whereas the music does express these qualities, it does not as a rule *express them well*. The wrath of the thunderstorm in the film *Rebecca* does not express wrath or anger as well as does the "Deus Irae" of the *Requiem* of Berlioz or Verdi.

And, he will continue, that's the nub of the matter. The Verdi *Requiem* is a great work of art, partly because it expresses each successive emotion so superbly—the wrath of the "Deus Irae," the sublime tenderness of the "Sanctus" and "Offertorium," the hope and exultation of the "Hosanna." That it expresses these qualities (however poor our names for the qualities) is one of the reasons, at least, why we treasure the *Requiem* so highly. Of course, as Hanslick says, it must stand up as music, quite apart from its expressive qualities (whatever counts as "standing up" here). But, as between two compositions which do thus "stand up," if one of them does not express or only inadequately or superficially expresses these gamuts of human emotion, whereas the *Requiem* does, then of the two the *Requiem* is the greater achievement. But exactly *how* music of such incredible complexity can be created so as to express such a gamut of these fundamental human emotions remains a deep mystery. Even Verdi could probably not have told you how he did it—but through his successive intuition-expressions, he did it, and we have the living proof before us every time we hear his *Requiem*. But in the end we shall probably have to agree with Herbert Spencer's dictum that "to explain why certain groups of notes are fitted or unfitted for purposes of expression, seems impossible."[36]

## EXERCISES

1. Wordsworth defined poetry as "an overflow of powerful feeling." Could you tell from reading this poem by him, "Composed upon Westminster

[36] Herbert Spencer, *Facts and Comments* (New York: Crofts, 1902), p. 75.

Bridge, September 3, 1802,'' whether he had powerful feeling? whether he was expressing himself? whether the poem was expressive? Is the expression theory in any way helpful in reading the poem?

> Earth has not anything to show more fair:
> Dull would he be of soul who could pass by
> A sight so touching in its majesty:
> This City now doth, like a garment, wear
> The beauty of the morning; silent, bare,
> Ships, towers, domes, theatres, and temples lie
> Open unto the fields, and to the sky;
> All bright and glittering in the smokeless air.
> Never did sun more beautifully steep
> In his first splendour, valley, rock, or hill;
> Ne'er saw I, never felt, a calm so deep!
> The river glideth at his own sweet will:
> Dear God! the very houses seem asleep;
> And all that mighty heart is lying still!

2. "Great artists know or believe that they are inspired from something outside themselves. Why should we suppose them to be deceived? . . . The artist's creativeness conceals from us his real passivity. Every artist is in his degree like Shakespeare, who was a reed through which every wind from nature or human nature blew music." (Samuel Alexander, *Beauty and Other Forms of Value,* p. 74.) Comment.

3. "The music of Carlo Gesualdo, Prince of Venosa, can be seen simplistically as a reflection of his tortured life. He is famous for having had his wife and her lover murdered (though contemporary opinion seems to have criticized him only for not carrying out the deed personally), and the rest of his life was dismally unhappy. He maltreated his second wife, saw the death of their only child, and lived in continual painful ill health. Is it any wonder, then, that his music should be so anguished, so chromatic, so powerfully pessimistic?" (Review of a Gesualdo recording in *High Fidelity,* December 1980, p. 79.) (a) Does Gesualdo's being unhappy in any sense "explain" his music? Is it that if he had not experienced sadness there would have been no sadness to express in his music? (b) Being sad is surely not a sufficient condition for creating sad music (most sad people don't create at all); is it a necessary condition? If he had had a different life, could he not have created the music that he did? (c) He was sad and his music was sad; does it follow that his music expressed his sadness?

4. Theories of artistic expression usually describe the expression process as one in which the artist begins with the "germ of an idea" (sometimes called an "incept") and develops it until he has reached his "final artistic intuition," having no exact prevision at the beginning of what the completed work will be like. This Beardsley calls the "propulsive theory." But there is a very different kind of theory, according to which what guides the artist from the beginning of his creative process is a vision of the end-product, only the vision is vague and obscure at the beginning and only becomes clarified and filled out as the creative process proceeds. This he calls the "finalistic theory." (See Monroe C. Beardsley, "On the Creation of Art," *Journal of Aesthetics and Art Criticism,* 23 (1965), 291–304.)

a. What actual difference if any do you think there is between these theories? Could you tell by watching an artist at work, or by creating a work of art yourself, which theory is correct for that particular case?

b. If the "finalistic theory" came to be accepted, would this render unacceptable the expressionists' account of artistic creation discussed in this chapter?

5. "The artist doesn't know what he's going to express until he's expressed it." Is this self-evident to you, or could it be false? "If artists only find out what their emotions are in the course of finding out how to express them, they cannot begin the work of expression by deciding what emotion to express." (Monroe Beardsley, "On the Creation of Art.") Presumably Collingwood would assent to this. But "After the artist has expressed his emotion, and come to experience it clearly, how does he know it is the same emotion he started with? He cannot compare them, since the other was unknown to him. How does he know that the emotion he feels now is not a new and different emotion—an emotion that is perhaps felt as the *effect* of the finished work, rather than its cause?" (Beardsley) Is this objection fatal to Collingwood? Need the artist be able to compare them?

6. "The whole concept of *clarifying* an emotion is itself very obscure. I have a suspicion that when Bruckner finished one of his enormous symphonies, his emotions were no more clear to him than they were at the start. . . . They are big emotions; anyone can see that. But clarity is hardly the word for them." (Beardsley, "On the Creation of Art.") What do you make of Collingwood's insistence that in the expression-process the artist is "clarifying his emotions to himself"?

7. "Assuming—rightly—that it is possible in at least some cases for one to know what he is going to do, one *can* know that he is going to paint a picture, say, and not write a poem or compose a symphony; *can* know that he is going to paint a seascape, say, and not a portrait or a still-life; *can* know that he is going to paint a seascape of Honfleur, say, and not one of Antibes or Monhegan Island—and all this before he has actually painted it. But, it will be replied, although he can know *in general* what he is going to do (create) before he has actually done it (created it), he cannot *quite* know, *fully* know, know *exactly,* know *to the minutest detail* what he is making until he has actually made it. . . . But we could continue to specify to any assignable degree of specificity the description of what our painter is going to do, and I do not see that we must in principle arrive at a point beyond which it is logically impossible for him to know what he is going to do. The burden of specifying that point is on those who claim that there is one." (W. E. Kennick, "Creative Acts," in *Art and Philosophy,* p. 175.) Discuss.

8. "Is there anything in poetry comparable to the expressiveness of single tones or colors like red and blue and yellow? To this, I think, the answer must be, little or nothing. Almost all the expressiveness of single words comes from their meaning. At all events, the sound and meaning of a word are so inextricably fused that, even when we suspect that it may have some expressiveness on its own account, we are nearly incapable of disentangling it. As William James has remarked, a word-sound, when taken by itself apart from its meaning, gives an impression of mere queerness." (DeWitt Parker, *The Principles of Aesthetics,* p. 198.)

9. Which of the following, if any, do you think music can express, and why? Hope, fear, longing, despair, rage, gentleness, doubt, youthfulness, tension, disbelief, humor. (See Alan Tormey, *The Concept of Expression.*)

10. Most "program notes" are singularly unhelpful in enabling us to appreciate the work of art. If the following example is in any way an exception, why do you suppose this is? It concerns the Quintet for Piano and Strings, by Ernest Bloch.

"Very few works of music come to mind which display such an intensity of emotionality as the Quintet. From the first suppressedly brooding notes of the first movement through to the hushed, dark resolutional coda of the last, the work runs the gamut of emotions and drama, but its singular passionate energy never flags. The music never relaxes; it becomes quiet or it broods or it despairs, but always behind the momentary mood there runs a pulsing movement impelled ever forward by a single motive power. . . . With an almost-respiring rise and fall, quiet, beautiful episodes accelerate themselves like the beating of a heart under stress." (Edward Cole, notes on Ernest Bloch's Quintet for Piano and Strings, MGM record E–3239.)

11. What is there about Handel's music which might lead you to describe it as "square" rather than (for example) "round"? (See Charles L. Stevenson, "Symbolism in the Non-representational Arts," in *Language, Thought, and Culture* ed. Paul Henle, and reprinted in J. Hospers, ed., *Introductory Readings in Aesthetics.)*

12. When the expressiveness is not of the music alone but of a song (music plus words), how much do the words contribute to whatever expressive quality you attribute to the song? Would the music be expressive without the words? would it be expressive of the same qualities, or do the words guide you in determining what the expressive qualities are? Try it on several vocal compositions and determine the answer for yourself. (First try it without knowing what the words mean, then try it after you know.) Richard Strauss's *Four Last Songs* are good specimens to begin with, as are almost any songs by Schubert and Brahms. (Hanslick uses the example of an aria from Gluck's *Orfeo,* in which the singer sings "I have lost my love" and imbues the aria with an air of melancholy, and then he tries to show that exactly the same melody would be equally fitting for the words "I have found my love." Do you agree?)

13. Can music be *religious?* Handel wrote many oratorios which have no religious subject and many more that do, such as *The Messiah, Saul, Solomon,* and *Israel in Egypt.* Does the religious character commonly attributed to the music arise from the music, or from the words alone, or from both together? Would the same melodies (such as "He was despised and forsaken . . .") be equally suitable to a text that had no religious content? ("But even if Handel's music isn't religious, Palestrina's is . . .".)

14. Are there any expressive qualities in "The Royal Game"? If so, how would you describe them?

# SELECTED READINGS

## A. On Artistic Creation

ALEXANDER, SAMUEL. *Beauty and Other Forms of Value.* London: Macmillan, 1933. Ch. 4.

BEARDSLEY, MONROE C. "On the Creation of Art." Journal of Aesthetics and Art Criticism, 23 (1965), 291–304. Reprinted in Rader.

COLLINGWOOD, ROBIN G. *The Principles of Art.* Oxford: Clarendon Press, 1938.

CROCE, BENEDETTO. *Aesthetic.* Ainslie translation. 2nd ed., New York: Farrar, Straus & Co., 1922.

DEWEY, JOHN. *Art as Experience.* New York: Minton, Balch & Co., 1934.

GHISELIN, BREWSTER (ed.). *The Creative Process.* Berkeley: University of California Press, 1952. (Also in Mentor Books.)

GLICKMAN, JACK. "Creativity in the Arts." In Lars Aagaard-Mogensen (ed.), *Culture and Art,* 1976. Reprinted in Margolis.

GOLDWATER, ROBERT, AND MARCO TREVES, eds. *Artists on Art.* New York: Pantheon Books, 1945.

HOSPERS, JOHN. "The Croce-Collingwood Theory of Art." *Philosophy,* Vol. 31 (1956).

KENNICK, WILLIAM. "Creative Acts." In W. Kennick, *Art and Philosophy.* St. Martin's Press, 1979, pp. 163–185.

KOESTLER, ARTHUR. *The Act of Creation.* New York: Macmillan, 1964.

MAITLAND, JEFFREY. "Creativity." *Journal of Aesthetics and Art Criticism,* 34 (1976).

PALMER, ANTHONY AND ANDREW HARRISON, "Creativity and Understanding." *Proceedings of the Aristotelian Society,* Supplementary Vol. 45 (1971), 73–121.

ROTHENBERG, ALBERT AND CARL R. HAUSMAN (ed.). *The Creativity Question.* Durham, N.C.: Duke University Press, 1976.

TOMAS, VINCENT (ed.). *Creativity in the Arts.* Prentice Hall, 1964.

TOMAS, VINCENT. "Creativity in Art." *Philosophical Review,* Vol. 67 (1958). Reprinted in Kennick.

VIVAS, ELISEO. *Creation and Discovery.* New York: Noonday Press, 1955.

## B. On Expression

ARNHEIM, RUDOLF. *Art and Visual Perception.* University of Calif. Press, 1957, Chapter 10.

ARNHEIM, RUDOLF. "The Gestalt Theory of Expression." *Philosophical Review,* 56 (1949).

ARNHEIM, RUDOLF. "The Priority of Expression." *Journal of Aesthetics and Art Criticism*, 8 (1949).

BENSON, JOHN. "Emotion and Expression." *Philosophical Review*, 76 (1967).

BERNDTSON, ARTHUR. *Art, Expression, and Beauty*. New York: 1969.

BOUWSMA, O.K. "The Expression Theory of Art." In Max Black (ed.), *Philosophical Analysis*. Ithaca, N.Y.: Cornell Univ. Press, 1950.

BUFFORD, SAMUEL. "Susanne Langer's Two Theories of Art." *Journal of Aesthetics and Art Criticism*, 30 (1972). Reprinted in Dickie and Sclafani.

GOTSHALK, D.W. "Aesthetic Expression." *Journal of Aesthetics and Art Criticism*, 13 (1954).

HANSEN, FOREST. "Langer's Expressive Form—an Interpretation." *Journal of Aesthetics and Art Criticism*, 28 (1968).

HARTSHORNE, CHARLES. *The Philosophy and Psychology of Sensation*. Univ. of Chicago Press, 1934.

HOSPERS, JOHN (ed.). *Artistic Expression*. New York: Irvington Books, 1971.

HOSPERS, JOHN. "The Concept of Artistic Expression." *Proceedings of the Aristotelian Society*, 55 (1954–5). Reprinted in Weitz and Hospers.

HUNGERLAND, ISABEL C. "Iconic Signs and Expressiveness." *Journal of Aesthetics and Art Criticism*, 111, pp. 15–21.

ISENBERG, ARNOLD. "Perception, Meaning, and the Subject-matter of Art." *Journal of Philosophy*, XLI (1944).

ISENBERG, "The Technical Factor in Art." In his *Aesthetics and the Theory of Criticism*. Univ. of Chicago Press, 1973, pp. 53–69.

KANDINSKEY, WASSILY. "The Expressiveness of Colors." *Documents of Modern Art*, Vol. 5, George Wittenborn, Inc. New York., n.d.

KIVY, PETER. *The Corded Shell*. Princeton, New Jersey: Princeton University Press, 1980.

LANGER, SUSANNE K. *Feeling and Form*. New York: Scribners, 1953.

LANGER, SUSANNE K. *Problems of Art*. Baltimore: Johns Hopkins Press, 1958.

MEYER, LEONARD. *Emotion and Meaning in Music*. Univ. of Chicago Press, 1956.

NAHM, MILTON. "The Philosophy of Aesthetic Expression, the Crocean Hypothesis." *Journal of Aesthetics and Art Criticism*, 13 (1955).

PRATT, CARROLL C. *The Meaning of Music*. New York: McGraw Hill, 1931.

SIRCELLO, GUY. *Mind an Art: An Essay on the Varieties of Expression*. Princeton Press, 1971.

TILGHAM, BENJAMIN R. *The Expression of Emotion in the Visual Arts*. The Hague, 1970.

TOMAS, VINCENT. "Creativity in Art." *Philosophical Review*, 67 (1958).

TORMEY, ALAN. *The Concept of Expression*. Princeton Univ. Press, 1971.

ZINK, SIDNEY. "Is the Music Really Sad?" *Journal of Aesthetics and Art Criticism*, 19 (1960).

# 5

# Truth in the Arts

One of the features of the arts for which it is valued is *truth*. There is much disagreement on how important truth is in the arts, and also in what ways it occurs. Since the notion of truth has its most obvious application to literature, we shall consider that first, and then consider how it applies to the other arts.

When someone writes a biography of a historical person, the author of the biography need not tell the *whole* truth, but he must tell *the* truth about the person whose life he is describing. If he makes a factual error and says that Napoleon was at a certain place at a certain time when in fact he wasn't, his credibility as a biographer is in question, and other historians will pounce upon him to point out his inaccuracy: they will criticize him because some detail(s) of his account are not *true*. But the storyteller usually makes up his characters—they are fictitious—so how could any question of truth arise?

> No one could report truly that Charlotte Brontë died in 1890; that she wrote *Villette* before *Jane Eyre;* that she was tall, handsome and a celebrated London hostess. No biography of Charlotte Brontë could contain such a statement and remain a biography. For what is truly said of Charlotte Brontë must be controlled by what she was and what happened to her. But Jane Austen was under no such restraints with Emma Woodhouse. For Emma Woodhouse was her own invention. So she may have any qualities and undergo any adventures her author pleases.[1]

[1] Margaret Macdonald, "The Language of Fiction," in Joseph Margolis, ed., *Philosophy Looks at the Arts,* 2nd ed. (Philadelphia: Temple Univ. Press, 1979), pp. 431–432.

When we read that Tom Jones ran off to London, is the statement true or false? Since Tom Jones is a fictitious character who never existed (many others with the same name did, but not the Tom Jones that Fielding was describing), one is tempted to say that it is false—that all statements about fictitious characters are false. A storyteller is giving a tissue of lies, he is making up a tale, "telling a yarn"—and isn't that lying? Not only is he saying what's false, but he is *intentionally* saying what's false, and that's what a lie is—an intentional falsehood.

The "falsity theory," however, has a strange consequence. If we say that the statement "Hamlet sailed for England" is false because there never was a Hamlet in the first place, what then are we to say of the statement "Hamlet did not sail for England"? Is that statement then true? On the contrary, it's as false as the first one, according to the theory, for the same reason, that Hamlet did not exist. But in logic if a statement is false, its contradictory must be true.

The usual reply to this is that the second statement does not contradict the first, for they both are compound statements, "There was a person Hamlet" and "This person sailed for England (or did not sail for England)." The second statement *presupposes* the truth of the first one, and if the first one is not true, the second one has no application. And in this case of course the first statement is false, so the matter of truth or falsity of the second does not arise. (Similarly, "The king of France is bald" and "The king of France is not bald" both presuppose what is false, namely, that there is a king of France.)

Still, all this seems to miss the point. We don't usually accuse novelists and dramatists of being liars; neither do their tales mislead us concerning the facts. Every child knows that "it's just a story" and goes along with it. The whole thing is a kind of "let's pretend" game: we know there are no witches, but in *Hansel and Gretel* we pretend there is, and simply do what Coleridge called "the willing suspension of disbelief," which to the reader of fiction may provide great dividends in satisfaction.

In fact we may go further: *in* the "let's pretend" game, certain things are true and others not. *In* certain literary works, it is true and not false that Hamlet sailed for England, that Tom Sawyer ran away from home, and that Ivan Karamazov was a religious skeptic. Every child can tell you that *in the story of Hansel and Gretel* it is *true* and not false that there is a witch.

But now a problem arises: what is the relation between what's in the story and what's "in the world out there"? One might first be tempted to say that there is no relation at all, since the story comes out of the author's imagination; but still, when we read a story with characters who fascinate us, and they behave in certain ways that seem to us very plausible, we find ourselves making remarks such as "How true"! Thus, even though the characters may be fictitious, there is something about them that in some sense or other has to do with truth. Our task now is to track this down. The task will not be a simple one, since words "true" and "truth" don't always operate in the same way.

# 1. TRUTH TO HUMAN NATURE

There is one area in which truth has seemed to many people to be very relevant indeed to the enterprise of literature, and that is human characterization. Nathaniel Hawthorne said that the novelist must always be "true to the human heart." Each character introduced must be "true to human nature," to the way in which people think and act and feel. And since "truth to" means "fidelity to," what the statement comes to is that characters in literature must possess fidelity to the behavior and motivation of people in the real world.

Let us pursue this view in more detail: *Human nature* is the subject of the poet, the novelist, the storywriter, the dramatist, in a way that no other subject-matter is. And although astronomical and geological and even historical truth may be safely ignored in evaluating the achievement of a literary artist, the insight he gives us into human character cannot. His account of human beings must in some way possess *truth*. Even when his literary work does not state or suggest any general truths about human nature, it must be somehow *true to* human nature.

This kind of view goes back to Aristotle, who in three trenchant sentences in his *Poetics* set the stage for the controversy. According to Aristotle, history gives us only "particular truths" (this man did this, then he did that, etc.), but literature gives us "*universal* truth." Since it is typically the sciences that give us universal truths ("All bodies are subject to gravitation"), how can it be said with any plausibility that the arts do, or even a specific art such as literature? "Poetry," said Aristotle, "is a more philosophical and a more serious thing than history; for poetry is chiefly conversant about universal truth, history about particular truth. In what manner, for example, any person of a certain character would speak or act, probably or necessarily—this is universal; and this is the object of poetry. But what Alcibiades did, or what happened to him—this is particular truth."[2]

But universal statements do not often occur in works of literature. Indeed, there are very few universal statements about human nature that can be made—at least in the present state of psychology. What can we say about what *all* persons would do or think or believe or feel, since persons behave, think, and so on so differently? We can't even say "Everyone becomes angry when insulted," "Everyone gets bored or irritated when lectured to for a long time," for there are some people who don't.

Let us then try a more qualified formulation in which the statements are still universal: "Every person of a certain *kind* or *class* acts, feels, and so on a certain way, in response to a certain kind of situation." For example, irritable people are irritated when crossed, nonirritable people are not. People of

[2] Aristotle, *Poetics,* 1451-b.

235

happy temperament are not easily made unhappy by misfortune, other people are. But these are very nearly if not actually tautologies, and utterly trivial: if you are irritable, you will be easily irritated—but that's a definition of what it *is* to be irritable: so the statement comes to this: "If one is easily irritated, one is easily irritated." If we say that a person of a certain kind or type or class will do so-and-so under certain circumstances, and then under those circumstances it turns out that he doesn't do so-and-so, we can always say that he didn't after all belong to that class or type.

Some critics have believed—and have argued that Aristotle believed—that literature should depict characters who are *representative* of (typical of) a certain *class:* warriors, shopkeepers, housewives, frustrated suitors, cuckolds, power-hungry madmen, and so on. There are, of course, many ways in which one could divide up the human race, many different systems of classification; the same individual may be at once a husband, a stockbroker, a redhead, a lodge member, and so on, but, one could say, however one classifies, that the individual should be *typical,* or *representative* of, the class in question.

But once this view has been stated, it will be difficult to find any good reasons for holding it: why, after all, should a character portrayed in literature be typical of any class at all? Why shouldn't one say instead they should be individual, unique, induplicable, not representative at all? Of what class is Hamlet typical? Is he typical of any class of persons? He would seem to be by any standard a most untypical character, and so are most of Shakespeare's major characters.

We would hardly find it desirable for the major characters in fiction to be *type* characters—characters who merely represent a certain type, and nothing else. Type characters are characters who possess the features common to all other members of the type or class, with few or no features that *individualize* the character and distinguish him from other members of the same type. Such characterizations quickly degenerate into *stereotypes,* like the butlers in English novels who walk in, say a few deferential words, and walk out again, and one never knows anything else about them. Literature would be very dull if each character merely typified some type or class, without being (as the major characters in literature are) through and through an individual. A gallery of great characters in literature—Hamlet, Dmitri Karamazov, Faust, Becky Sharp—is very far indeed from being a series of "reports of typical cases." If it were, we could say, "here's a typical wastrel" or "here's a typical businessman" and praise the characterization simply for its typicality. And we do not usually do this: there is doubtless no individual in the world who is *merely* representative of a type, without individualizing features, and when a character in fiction is simply a type character, we consider this a defect in characterization unless the character is so minor that it doesn't matter.

"How a person of a certain character would speak or act, probably or necessarily—this is universal," said Aristotle. Let us try again to clarify this statement in such a way as to retain the universal and yet admit as much individuality and uniqueness as the characters of great fiction possess. Take a specific action of a specific character in fiction: let us say that *any* person who possesses the particular combination of characteristics ascribed to this character in the novel or drama *would* (probably or necessarily, as Aristotle says) act (or say, or think, or feel, etc.) what the novel portrays him as doing *in* the specific set of circumstances described. This formulation preserves the universality—"*any* person . . ."—and yet can accommodate any amount of individuality, since the circumstances in which people act, and the combination of features present in every person, are always different.

For example, we often criticize a characterization in fiction because "he is made to act out of character"; that is, we do not believe that a person such as the author describes *would* do (or feel, etc.) what the author makes him do. He is made to kill someone, and from all we have learned about him thus far we do not believe that a person such as has been described so far would kill anyone, at least in the circumstances in which he is described as doing so. And when this happens, we say of that characterization that it is *not true to human nature,* that is, that it is not in accord with the way in which *such* a person in *such* circumstances *would* behave. Or, if we have a highly motivated character who sacrifices everything to achieve a certain goal, and then when he is in sight of the goal he walks away from it for no apparent reason, we are critical of the characterization. This is not because some people in real life don't sometimes walk away from the goals when the goals are within sight of attainment. Some people do—some people are afraid of success and the responsibilities that go with it. But if this fictional character is to be one of these, the author must have convinced us through his characterization thus far that this is in fact one such character—and of course not everyone is. What we must believe is not that *all* people would behave so-and-so, or that all members of a certain class of people would behave so-and-so, but that any person with *just these* character traits in just *this* situation (both internal and external) *would* behave in the way the author describes him as behaving. (And, of course, there may be in the real world no actual person with just this combination of traits acting in just his situation.)

The criterion can even be used to account for sudden characterlogical changes. If there were a novel describing the life of St. Paul, and we come to Saul's conversion on the road to Damascus, after which his behavior is markedly different from everything that had gone before, the novelist, to make this sudden change plausible to the reader, would have to convince us through his prior characterization, not that *any*one would have undergone such a sudden conversion but that Saul *was* a person who might "do a sudden flip-flop." In retrospect we must be able to say "I should have known that something like that would happen in such a situation to a person with such a makeup."

In any situation, there are usually a number of things that a person might do: one could seldom say that a person who has been characterized by traits A, B, C, D would *necessarily* do act X in circumstances C. Aristotle himself says "necessarily *or probably.*" It would be preferable not even to be as stringent as this, but to add *"or plausibly."* That is, the author through his characterization must have made it plausible (credible or believable) that this character would act as he is portrayed as acting. Often, in the light of the characterization given, a person would just as probably do B as A—he might never do C or D, but A and B would be about equally plausible in view of the characteristics and circumstances thus far presented. In the circumstances described, a lady might accept a man or on the other hand she might turn him down; both might be equally plausible, but she would definitely not do a third thing, such as kill or maim him. Even in a full three-dimensional characterization, we do not have to know so much about a character as to be able to predict his every action. If we did, we would know more about the character than any person ever knows about another, or even about himself; and such a narrative with such a degree of predictability would contain no surprises. Perhaps we should be able to say afterward, "I should have known that he'd do something like that," but we are not in a position to say this in advance.

Fictional characters resemble real characters in many ways—in their ways of acting, in their fundamental motivations—for if they did not, we would not be able to understand them or identify imaginatively with them. How would we understand a character who was not motivated by love or hate or envy or affection or fear or anger or any other human emotion? Even when the character is a stoat or a weasel (as in Kenneth Grahame's *The Wind in the Willows*), it is only *biologically* an animal—psychologically it is a human being, and if it were not, we could not understand it. When at the beginning of Kafka's *Metamorphosis* a man changes into a beetle, he is still *psychologically* a man, trying to adjust himself to his sudden inconvenient change of species. Human nature is something the literary artist cannot tamper with very much, else he would leave his audience in a state of total incomprehension.

Still, this does not mean that characters should be carbon copies of persons in real life. Even though every character has only such characteristics as actual human beings possess, they may occur in *different combinations* in the fictional character than they do in any actual person. Thus, works of fiction may still be creations more than *re*creations, because, although they deal with the same building blocks, they erect them into new and unique combinations. There is in all the world no person exactly like Hamlet; and so the character depicted by Shakespeare is an addition to the world, not a duplication of it. And when you put this unique character in a unique *situation,* such as no human being may ever have been in, you have a new *character-plus-situation,* and you can now speculate as to what such a person in such circumstances would do. Even so, however, you must remain convinced that such a person in such circumstances *would* plausibly behave as this character is represented as behaving.

One cannot tell, by this criterion, whether a certain action by a certain character is "true to human nature" by examining the action in isolation from the character who performs it. A lady storywriter is said to have had her story rejected by a magazine publisher because in the story a writer shoots her editor. The editor complained that this was too far-fetched to be plausible and rejected the story. Furious, the lady storywriter took out a pistol and shot her editor dead on the spot: "I'll show you how implausible it is!" she cried as she pulled the trigger. But what did her action prove? Not what she apparently meant it to: the fact that she, the writer, shot her editor in no way shows that a *different* person, such as the character in her story, would plausibly also have done so. There are very few kinds of actions that someone, somewhere, sometime hasn't performed, but that doesn't show that *you,* or A or B or C, would do it. What the author has to make plausible in a story is that a person like the character in the story would do it, *in* the given circumstances.

Most characters in stories, novels, and dramas are what E. M. Forster called "two-dimensional characters," characterized sufficiently to be believable, but not very fully, not enough so that the reader comes to know them well. (See pages 171–72). When a character appears briefly a couple of times in a novel, there is no need to go in for a full characterization. It is only the major characters who are "three-dimensional characters," whose actions and thoughts and motivations are described in detail, and it is usually only these three-dimensional characters (and not even all of these) who are described "from the inside"—whose inmost thoughts and feelings are described to us directly by the writer. Because we have such a detailed account of the behavior—and sometimes the inner experiences—of these three-dimensional characters, we often feel that we know them more intimately than we know most people in the real world, such as next-door neighbors with whom we may have chatted for years; and we feel this for good reason, since we have witnessed their behavior in situations of crisis and been party to their innermost thoughts and feelings.

Two-dimensional characters have most of their characterization missing, but this is not considered a defect when the character is a minor one in the story; it is rather a defect when Dostoyevsky devotes a full chapter to the life and background of a minor character who never turns up in the story again. But the two-dimensional character is lacking in fullness because of *omission*—many things about the character that would have been true to human nature had they been included but the author chose not to—rather than because of *commission,* which would consist of implausible actions or motivations ascribed to the character. The latter, if it were done, would be a violation of truth to human nature.

What we look for in novels and poetry is truth about what we may call the human heart. If, as we read, we are convinced that this is how a human being could feel and has felt, however misguidedly, then we have poetic or imaginative truth. And to be convinced of this we must recognize the feeling as one of which we ourselves are capable, had our circumstances been different. We must feel the seeds of it, however unhappily stifled, however heroically weeded out, to have been once within our own hearts.[3]

A problem arises, however, in this connection: what is it that counts? whether a person like the one described *would* have done the deed in the circumstances described or whether we *believe* or *feel* that he would? We may believe a person like the character described in a novel would have done the act described or plausibly might have done it, but may we not be mistaken in thinking so? Indeed, we may be mistaken in this as in most other judgments. When Dostoyevsky gave his fictional account of the pathological gambler, the majority of readers, unfamiliar with such persons, were unbelieving. And yet Freud, in his little book *Dostoyevsky,* remarks that Dostoyevsky gave an accurate character portrait of the pathological gambler (in this case, characteristics marked by all such persons), down to the most minute detail; apparently the readers were in error in thinking that the characterization was implausible, for it was in fact accurate down to the last detail. A child may not believe, on reading an adult novel, that a man would sacrifice so much to gain the favors of a woman, but that does not change the fact that some men would, and do; and when the child becomes an adult he will understand that the storywriter was right.

We should distinguish clearly between the plausibility of a *character* and the plausibility of *events*. The events occurring in the career of Don Quixote are extremely implausible, but the character of Don Quixote still "rings true." Granted the existence of such a wacky character, we could well believe that he would do the things described, embarking time after time on utterly foolish and futile heroic exploits. (And this may be so, in spite of the fact that the novel may have been a spoof of the picaresque novel, "doing it in " at one stroke through fanciful exaggeration.) Many events in science-fiction novels are (as far as we know) empirically impossible, but this does not disturb us as long as the characters are recognizable human beings with recognizable human motives. Even spacemen, when they appear in sci-fi novels and films, are human in their motivations: in the film *The Day the Earth Stood Still* the Venusians come to earth in order to prevent people from massacring one another in a nuclear way—a highly human and understandable motive. Spacemen in literature, like animals in literature, must still be human beings under the skin; we have no other means by which to understand them.

But if literature can or should be true to human nature, then, it would seem, literature encroaches on the province of one of the empirical sciences, psychology. Now, psychology at its present stage is more interested in perception and white rats and animal conditioning than in the characteristically human traits explored by novelists and dramatists. In fact, if one is interested

---

[3] E. F. Carritt, *What Is Beauty?* (Oxford: The Clarendon Press, 1930), pp. 32–33.

in human nature, some good advice might be "Observe yourself and others carefully; read great novels and plays, read biography; but don't bother with psychology—you learn very little about human nature from that, except special branches like abnormal psychology and psychotherapy."

Many people, in the interests of simplicity and tidiness, will prefer to make a complete separation of the *arts* on the one hand and the *sciences* (including psychology) on the other. Still, the two do seem to impinge on one another, as Freud's remark about Dostoyevsky seems to indicate. The two domains do not seem to be two separate circles, but two circles that intersect in one area, namely, where human nature is concerned. But the aims of the two are still different, even when they enter the same arena, human behavior and motivation: the psychologist, like all scientists, is not concerned with individual cases except as material for generalizations and *laws* (physics and chemistry have many established laws, and psychology, thus far, very few). But the novelist need not be interested in generalization at all: he is drawing a character portrait of *this particular* character; he may be suggesting, in effect, *"this* characterization is true to human nature," but he does not normally generalize about what other characters, whom he does not describe, would be like, or into what scientific classifications they would fall. Also, the novelist does not usually proceed by canons of scientific method; perception of human nature is much more "intuitive." He feels from his own nature and observation of others that this is the way such-and-such a person would act in the given circumstances. He is less like the animal psychologist, who can tell you many true propositions about the behavior of animals but may be able to manage none of them, than like the animal *trainer,* who may not have articulated his knowledge of animals into the form of general propositions, but who "has a feel" for animals, "knows how their behavior goes," and is usually much better able to tell you what this particular animal, whom he knows well, is going to do.

The importance of "truth to human nature" in works of literature, however, has often been questioned. Let us consider some of the standard objections to see whether they may make us more skeptical about the importance of psychological truth in literary characterizations.

1. *Life as copying fiction.* There is a famous remark of Oscar Wilde that, rather than life's providing the originals which are then represented (with some alterations) in fiction, it is fiction which provides the originals, of which the actual persons in real life are the copies.

As an ironic remark, or a typical Wildean exaggeration, this remark does indeed have some point. There are no exact originals for complex characters like Hamlet, Julien Sorel, and Monsieur Swann. But, then, it was never claimed that there would be. Each characteristic is recognizable from life, but the *combinations* wrought in fictional characters may be different from any combination to be found in any person in the actual world.

A characterization in literature can, indeed, be so lifelike and vivid that when we encounter certain people in the real world they seem to us like imitations of a character created by a novelist: we first read of Don Quixote in Cervantes, and when we see a person somewhat like him in life we turn to the novel as the source of the type: the original of the type is to be found in the novel, with people in life reminding us of the novel we would never even have thought of the "Don Quixote" type.

Still, creative though Cervantes undoubtedly was with respect to his central character, he was abstracting certain features—wild romantic exaggeration, attacking imaginary enemies—from people in life. The plain fact is that there were *first* people in the world, and only much later was there fiction. We first find that people are motivated as we ourselves are, by fear, love, revenge, and so on, and then we construct characters who are motivated in these ways—not the other way round. The basic originals are in life; secondary originals then occur in fiction, which in turn people in life may resemble.

2. *Depth of knowledge required.* One might question, just the same, whether a character in fiction needs to be judged by truth to human nature, especially when this demands more than "common sense garden-variety" knowledge of people. Most people, for example, know nothing about the behavior of hebephrenic schizophrenics, and if one such person is depicted in a novel, should the reader be able to evaluate the characterization with psychological accuracy? Freud pronounced Dostoyevsky's character portraits of psychotics to be clinically accurate; but, one might say, this is all right as case histories in abnormal psychology class, but is it really needed for the general reader? Such character portraits may *be* true to human nature, but must such detail of psychological portraiture be *recognized* as such by the reader? If you have read books on abnormal psychology, can you appreciate literature more? (This is not a rhetorical question: one might well say "Yes, I now understand people better, not only in life, but also in fiction.")

Suppose, for example, that a character in a novel comes to hate women for the rest of his life because he had a mother who was a "nagging bitch" who turned him against all women. But suppose it is discovered by psychology that this condition has an entirely different origin, a mother who overprotects and emotionally smothers her son. Does the characterization in fiction have to be in line with the discoveries of psychology? Is it not enough that the motivations in fiction be *plausible* to the reader without having to be psychologically accurate? And in that case the next question is, plausible *to whom?* to just any reader? To a child almost any kind of motivation may seem quite plausible. Must we then relativize the criterion of truth to human nature—adjusting it to read "to the person who is doing the reading"? or "to a reasonably well-educated person in the culture of the time"?

If a person finds the characterization plausible, he will obviously not fault the story's characterization, even if it were unacceptable to a trained psychologist or psychotherapist. A psychotherapist might find the characterization full of holes: he might allege, with excellent evidence, that nobody of all the thousands of people he had ever come across had behaved in *that* way and that, on the basis of what is currently known about the genesis of a certain kind of dementia, no one ever could. But the layman might not know this and find the characterization above reproach. Since *he* finds no holes in it, he is satisfied, though someone who knows much more about psychology is (with good reason) very much dissatisfied with the characterization.

*Should* the layman be dissatisfied? It all depends on what one wants or expects in reading fiction. If one wants simply to be entertained, one can be entertained (at least our layman can) by the superficial as well as, or better than, by the profound. If one wants to gain knowledge from reading fiction, specifically if one wants deeper insight into human nature, then it would be well for him to be informed that what he takes for truth to human nature (what such a character would probably do in the circumstances described, etc.) is not so at all.

3. *"True but unconvincing."* The previous objection was that a work of fiction might be satisfactory although its characterizations were not true to human nature. The present objection is the reverse: that the characterizations may be unsatisfactory although true to human nature. "True" though it is, we still find it unconvincing, or "it's sterile, dead, lifeless"—or any of a series of similar objections.

> The author might rebut us by saying that the fault is ours, not his, and that were our experience wider, our judgment would be different. And now he produces case after case from real life of persons behaving just as he has his characters act in such situations. He shows us passages in obscure volumes of abnormal pyschology, latinized references from erotic orientalia, transcripts from police blotters in Balkan capitals in the nineteenth century . . . . Somehow the fault remains with the author. . . . Had he convinced us, he would not have had to produce examples, and indeed we might remain persuaded by the argument (as in a Gedanken experiment) even though no instances were to be found. Similarly, a narrative must persuade us, and, if it fails in this, the fact that there are characters who so behave in no sense vindicates the narrative aesthetically.[4]

There can be numerous reasons for this. A fictional portrait may be true but boring or described with endless but insignificant detail. Also, it may simply be superficial—that is, guilty of omission rather than commission: it is "true as far as it goes," but it doesn't go far enough to make the character come really alive.

A character in a mystery novel may have only one characteristic known to the reader, that someone has offended him and he is out for revenge. This is true enough to human nature; the trouble is that this feature alone is not enough to flesh out a characterization. As a characterization, at this stage, it is still a failure, though not lacking in psychological truth as far as it goes.

[4] Arthur Danto, "Imagination, Reality, and Art," in *Art and Philosophy,* ed. Sidney Hook (New York: New York Univ. Press, 1966), p. 226.

But, then, no one would be likely to allege that truth to human nature in such a superficial exhibition of it as this is *sufficient* to make something a good characterization; the most that would be claimed is that a certain degree of truth to human nature (more, surely, than occurs in the superficial characterization just described) is *necessary*.

4. *Is psychological truth necessary?* Why need a character have plausible motives at all? What's wrong with unmotivated acts in fiction, even if they don't occur in life? Imagine, for example, a plot "in which a 'mad' (gratuitous?) act is performed at the beginning by a person carefully established as a routine, conventional chap, whose reasons and purpose remain a mystery, however the other characters seek to plumb it, throughout the book."[5]

This could well happen; but would it be a merit or a defect? It is one thing for a character's acts to be unmotivated; it is another thing for the character's motives to remain a mystery to the reader—that is simply a case of the motivation's never becoming *known,* which is a different case entirely from that of having no motives or having no plausible motives. What, then, of motives that never become known to the reader? It happens quite frequently in fiction, including many of the classics, for example, Greek tragedies. (In Greek tragedy, unlike, e.g., Elizabethan tragedy, plausibility of characterization did not count for much, and most characters are much closer to being stereotypes than in modern tragedies.) Consider two stories or novels or dramas virtually identical, except that in one of them the characterization is clear and the motivation (however complex and subtle) is plausible and understood by the reader, and that in the other, it remains a mystery—there is never a clue as to why the protagonist did what he did. As between these two, there can surely be little doubt that the first is a better novel or story than the second. If the second is still a good work of literature, it is surely in spite of the lapse in characterization rather than because of it.

It is true that in art almost anything can be given up if there is a payoff in the enhancement of some other feature(s). For example, (a) physical laws can be suspended with impunity in a story if something important or interesting is to be gained by doing so. It won't do, in a novel about slum life in New York, to have a character escape from a knife fight in an alley by suddenly flying through the air like Batman. But in a science-fiction novel, for example, the suspension of laws of nature, or some of them (never all of them at once), as in the spate of recent films about E.S.P., may be what makes the story interesting, or challenging, or thought provoking. Laws of nature are suspended in novels whose main characters are animals (as in countless Disney stories), since animals do not talk and reason as people do; they are animals biologically but human beings psychologically. (b) Even when there is no suspension

---

[5] Mortimer Kadish, "The Dogma of the Work of Art Itself," in *Art and Philosophy,* ed. Sidney Hook, p. 216.

of laws of nature, enormous *improbabilities* in sequences of events are admitted if some important effect or point can thereby be achieved. Such improbabilities dominate the novels of Thomas Hardy and reflect his view of the world. The bumbling idiocy of the character portrayed by Peter Sellers in the *Pink Panther* films, which through a series of outrageous coincidences always turns out favorably for him, is so wildly implausible that no one would believe in such continuous runs of luck; yet in the films it doesn't bother us at all: we take the implausibilites of plot as given, and this makes the comic outcomes possible. We pay the modest price of suspension of disbelief in order to get some enjoyment. And if we accept the improbabilities in the plot, the characterization of Detective Clouzot itself is plausible enough.

(c) Why not, then, violate plausibility of characterization also, if some point is thereby made or something interesting or exciting results from doing so? The answer seems to be the same as before: go ahead and do it, if there is a payoff in doing so. Devise, if you can, a character who undergoes deep-seated characterological changes every week or every day (as actual human beings never do), so that one never knows what to expect in each new bit of behavior. But there is a limit to all this: as we get farther and farther away from the feeling and motivations we are familiar with in people around us, the characterization starts taking on an air of remoteness and unreality: we cannot empathize with such a character or care what happens to him. (We continue to care about the man turned beetle in Kafka's *Metamorphosis* only because he continues to be *psychologically* human all the time, with feelings of hurt, resentment, and helplessness.) And very soon we reach the area of unintelligibility. Once we start to tamper in any fundamental way with human nature—not through omission, but commission—we encounter problems we never have with a material world that is contrary to laws of nature. Suppose there are Venusians in our story who know no anger or resentment or hurt of any kind; very well, one is tempted to say, let's try it and see what happens. But *other* features of human nature must remain intact if we are able to grasp this wrench in human characterization. Indeed, it is difficult to imagine even *this* change carried through consistently—a character who neither shows nor knows fear or anger and is indifferent and unresponding when attacked, even while he is being hacked to pieces? Can we really understand such a creature?

If we depart very far from human nature as we know it, we become not only unable to empathize but unable to grasp even remotely what makes the character tick. We have, after all, only our own human nature to go by; we do not even know dog nature or cat nature from the inside, and that is why novels about dogs and cats must treat their animal characters as psychologically human, not as canine or feline. Once we depart far from this sole compass we have, our own human nature, we are totally lost in a sea of unintelligibility.

5. *Imaginary worlds*. It has been objected that characters in fiction, many of them at least, are not denizens of our world, but of an imaginary world;

they belong in that world, not in ours, and should not be judged by the standards of plausibility in ours.

> In terms of counterparts, Lady Macbeth, or Oedipus, or Phaedra, or the Baron de Charlus are perhaps unduplicated. Who knows such people in real life? Next to them, people are pale and adimensional. They have a life of their own, and it is this to which we refer, I believe, when we speak of the reality of a character, or the reality of the world created by the fiction master: the world of Combray, or of Chandrapore, or even of Alexandria or Dublin. These are worlds *alongside* the real world, not worlds which have the world itself as model. The gift consists in making it appear as though one were adding to the world, rather than reflecting it. Questions of plausibility or implausibility arise only when this gift fails.[6]

One could say, indeed, that, besides the actual world, Planet Earth which we all inhabit, there are countless *possible worlds* presented to us in works of fiction. They may have some features in common with the actual world—as we have just seen, unintelligibility results when characters and their motivations stray too far from the human world we know—but they are not to be judged by standards of conformity to this world. Thus we have the world of Proust's novels, and the characters in that world are to be judged by—by what? It is not at all clear how indeed they *are* supposed to be judged. By their conformity to the laws of *that* world? by psychological laws? And how do we know what these are? And how can we understand the characters, much less empathize with them, to the extent that they are alien to the only world we know? It is much more plausible to say that such characters do belong to this world, though with some aspects intensified and other aspects sliced off, and that they are so vividly portrayed in certain aspects, with no portrayal at all in other aspects equally or more familiar to us, that they seem "strange," "otherworldly," "far out." But the same point must be repeated: that when we stray far from actual human nature, a wall of unintelligibility stops us cold.

Perhaps one could make a case, however, for a portrayal of human beings "not as they are, but as they *might be*" (perhaps in some more advanced age or in a more just society). In his book *Beethoven,* J. W. N. Sullivan remarks that in Beethoven's late quartets we have a "striving of the human spirit" toward what it might be but has never yet attained. Sullivan's formulation creates many problems when talking about music (e.g., how can it portray anything at all?); his remarks have a much readier application to literature. Fiction might be able to depict human potentialities which have never yet been realized—portrayals of people or actions that far transcend anything that actual human beings have ever yet done or achieved. Yet, I suggest, these actualizations of potential must be seen as being possible in the light of the characters' present potential. It must still be plausible, on the basis of their

---

[6] Arthur Danto, *op. cit.,* p. 223.

presently discernible characteristics, to believe that "they have it in them" to attain such heights. Without such a qualification as this, the characterization would be anchorless, and the situation would be describable by such phrases as "anything goes now," "one characterization is as good as another" (since there's nothing to judge by), and "it's deuces wild."

## Truth in Nonliterary Art

Does the concept of "truth to human nature" apply to arts other than literature?

It applies as obviously to film as it does to the literary arts, and not merely because of the literary aspect of film (the script). There was characterization through visual action, without words, in silent films, and often such characterizations were very insightful and penetrating. Film is unique in having *two* channels for depicting human nature: it can *show* people in action and can also, like literature, portray their speech through the sound track. We often criticize characterizations in films, just as we do in stories and plays, for being superficial, out of character, inadequately developed, distorted, implausible, not the way people would act, and so on.

Does "truth to human nature" apply to painting and sculpture? Yes, since there is in these arts representation of characters. But such depiction is much more limited, since we cannot in these arts trace the development of a human being *through time*. A series of paintings could do so, but each painting would be a static representation, incapable of movement in time. Most characterizations in painting are not very profound—visual arts are usually on the trail of other values—but the element is often present. One has only to look at the series of self-portraits by Rembrandt to be aware of the deep humanity of the sitter, the faces showing character development, the increasing effect of suffering on the lines of the face. And when Velasquez presented Pope Innocent X with his portrait of him, showing him not as a saint but as a hardened man of the world, the Pope commented sadly, "Too true! too true!" "A surpassing masterpiece, such as Velazquez's great Portrait of Pope Innocent X," writes Gombrich, "never looks arrested in one pose, it seems to change in front of our eyes as if it offered a large variety of readings, each of them coherent and convincing."[7]

The concept of truth to human nature does not appear to be applicable to nonrepresentational arts, such as music and architecture. Since no character representation occurs in these arts, there can be no faithful representation of character, or unfaithful either. Opera, a mixed art, can have this feature, though its characterizations are usually rather two-dimensional owing to the dominance of the musical ingredient in opera. Listeners desire operatic

---

[7] E. H. Gombrich, in Gombrich, Hochberg, and Black, *Art, Perception, and Reality* (Baltimore: Johns Hopkins Univ. Press, 1970), p. 42.

characterizations to be plausible as far as they go, even when the situations depicted are absurd or ridiculous. But only rarely does opera provide any great depth of characterization: if Verdi in adapting Shakespeare's *Macbeth* and *Othello* for opera had attempted to capture all the subtleties of Shakespeare's character portraits, the opera would have had to be at least a dozen hours long. The primary ingredient in opera is music, and characterization is usually incidental.

## 2. TRUTH AND SETTING

So much for the characters. But what of the world which they inhabit, the stage on which their actions are set? Is this the real world or not? Tom Jones is an imaginary character, and so of course are the actions attributed to him; but what of rural England in the early eighteenth century, in which the action is set? If the author had described in the novel the hero climbing a 10,000 foot mountain a hundred miles to the west of London, wouldn't we take this as a defect, a mistake? Wouldn't people quite correctly point out that there is no such mountain and that the author was guilty of a gross factual inaccuracy? And isn't the setting as a matter of fact the real England of that time, so that from reading the novel we pick up quite a bit of information about English life in the eighteenth century?

There are, to be sure, novels whose setting is wholly fanciful, taking place in imaginary kingdoms that do not resemble any existing on the earth, such as in Swift's *Gulliver's Travels* and Tolkein's *Lord of the Rings*. Even here, however, the same laws of nature apply as to the world we know. The setting is not *wholly* imaginary. Nevertheless, there is a difference between those works of fiction whose setting is the real world and those taking place in a fanciful world. Coleridge, among others, distinguished literary works of *fancy* from those of *imagination*.

> When the imagination withdraws itself from the conscious labor of creation into the contemplation of a world to the reality of which it is indifferent, and when it exercises its processes for their own sake, it is no longer *imagination*, but *fancy*. . . . It is true, of course, that we can imagine for the sake of imagining; and no doubt there is a natural pleasure to be found in playful indulgence of the imagination. But such is not the imagination of which Coleridge is speaking. . . . What the imagination makes is the world to which it adapts itself in all its activities. It is only when it relaxes from this task that it becomes indifferent to reality, and enjoys itself in fancy. The works of fancy supply a release from the serious business of living, a playful enjoyment of that to the reality of which we are indifferent; the works of the imagination, on the contrary, compel a strong sense of the real world.[8]

[8] D. G. James, *Scepticism and Poetry* (London: Allen & Unwin, 1937), p. 48.

Most works of fiction are strongly "tied to the real world." A novelist has a certain degree of "novelistic license," but if Tolstoy had described the Battle of Borodino (in *War and Peace*) as having taken place in a conspicuously different way from the way in which it occurred in history, his treatment would have evoked criticism; if he had said, "After all it's only an imaginary world I was creating, including an imaginary War of 1812," the critic could have responded, "But by having Napoleon and Kutuzov as characters, and declaring the setting to be that of Russia in 1812, and by describing the Battle of Borodino and others explicitly, you were *committing* yourself to at least a considerable degree of historicity in so doing. If you wanted the setting to be an imaginary world, you should have invented different settings and different place names." It is precisely because there is this *implicit claim to historicity* that we can learn quite a lot about the War of 1812 from reading Tolstoy's novel.

The view that in fiction we are confronted not only with imaginary characters but with a totally imaginary world is seldom or never true. Unless we receive signals to the contrary, the world the novelist describes is the real world of the time and place that is depicted. Much of the effect of this historical novel depends on recognizing the Russia of the novel as the real Russia of the time and, not only that, on knowing that the descriptions of it are true. Indeed, much of the background is not even filled in the novel, since the reading audience was assumed to have some acquaintance already with Napoleon, Kutuzov, and the facts of the 1812 war.

Even in works of fiction in which there are no historical characters, the reader assumes that the world of the novel is like the world outside, unless there are special clues to the contrary. When Arthur Conan Doyle writes about London in the Sherlock Holmes stories, it is the real London, not some fictitious city that happens to have the same name, that is the background of the story. And if the setting is 1880, it is London of that period in which we are to imagine the events taking place. Even Baker Street is not fictitious, and we assume that it is Baker Street as it appeared at that time. What is fictitious is the main characters and their actions, and of course Holmes's address *on* Baker Street. Everything else belongs to the real London of 1880, not to some fictitious world invented by the author. If in the novels we were told something markedly contrary to fact, such as London in 1880 had only a thousand residents, or that it had a year-long tropical climate, or if airplanes suddenly appeared in the story, we would consider this a lapse on the author's part even though the work is "a work of fiction." We do not insist that the story contain detailed true descriptions of London at the time but that it not include any glaring historical falsities. If, for example, we were told in a novel that Germany won World War I or II, we would infer at once that we were dealing with some fantasy and not an ordinary work of fiction.

The author produces an imaginary world by specifying only a few clues, which we readily supplement for ourselves; and we supply what is needed from our memory of the actual world. The memories appealed to are of two kinds: (1) general knowledge of the kinds of things and persona and places and happenings that the actual world contains; and (2) particular knowledge of actual events, etc., in the actual world. What the author does, and invites us to do, is not to imagine the world *de novo,* but to suppose that the actual world that we know is modified in certain specified respects. It is only because we are able to suppose that everything not specified as being different is just as it is in the actual world that we are able to imagine worlds of such continuity that we are able to make sense of the tales told of them.[9]

It is true that not all of the description is historically accurate, because some of the characters Tolstoy describes as participating in the war were fictitious characters invented by him. "Russia as the setting for the Rostovs differs from the Russia which Napoleon invaded, which did *not* contain the Rostovs. . . . Tolstoy did not create Russia . . . yet one might say that Tolstoy did create Russia-as-the-background-to-the-Rostovs. . . . The mention of realities plays a dual role in fiction; to refer to a real object and to contribute to the development of a story."[10]

Indeed, a great deal of information about the historical setting in a novel or drama is *presupposed* by the author. Tolstoy does not tell us in detail what Russia was like in 1812, but we in our imagination fill in much of the background from our general knowledge of the period. We assume that the Russia described is the real Russia of the time, unless the author provides some clues to the contrary. Similarly, we assume that, when Sherlock Holmes (an imaginary character) is described as roaming the streets of London, it is the same London as existed at the time in which the novel is set.

Sometimes the reader has to know a considerable amount of detail about the historical setting, not given in the novel itself, if he is to comprehend some of the details of the action. In one of Agatha Christie's novels (I forget which), one clue to the murder is provided by the fact that a certain character is assumed to have received a certain letter in the 8:30 P.M. London delivery. There aren't 8:30 P.M. deliveries any more, but there were then (six mail deliveries per day); and if you mailed a letter from High Holborn at noon it was quite certain to reach Westminster in the 8:30 P.M. mail. Many assumptions in solving the murder were questioned in the novel, but never this one. The reader would certainly find this very puzzling if he did not know a fact which the author assumed her readers to be acquainted with, namely, that the British postal service at that time was prompt, regular, and quite predictable. Another example: aren't we expected to know, in reading Henry James's *The Turn of the Screw,* that a headmaster would not have expelled a boy whose father was not only rich but a prominent donor to the school, except for some

---

[9] Francis E. Sparshott, "Truth in Fiction," *Journal of Aesthetics and Art Criticism,* Vol. 26 (fall 1967), p. 4.

[10] Margaret Macdonald, "The Language of Fiction," in Margolis, *op. cit.,* p. 435.

very extraordinary and compelling reason? and without James telling us this in so many words?

The setting of most novels, then, is the real world at some particular time and place. However, many critics have a tendency to speak of "the world of the work of art," as if each author created a different world, and indeed each different work of art involved the creation of a different world. The God-centered world of Dante's *Divine Comedy,* for example, is light years away from the atomistic world ("particles in a void") of Lucretius in *De Rerum Natura.*

> The poet sees the world in a certain way; thus has his imagination created it, and thus is it real to him. . . . The world as it is represented is the poet's world; and in so far as his poem is successful, he will make it the reader's world by compelling his vision upon him. And this is so whether the poet be a Lucretius or a Wordsworth. In great poetry we at once receive and create and imaginative vision of the world; a new world becomes acutely present to us, or, as Coleridge says, the poet makes us creators, after him, of such a new world.[11]

Thus, it is claimed, Shakespeare created for us in his various plays a variety of different *worlds:* there is the world of Hamlet, the world of Macbeth, and so on. In a remarkable essay "The Othello Music," the literary critic G. Wilson Knight contrasts the "world" of *Othello* to the world of *King Lear:* the world of Othello, with its "alabaster heavens," is measured, finite, ordered, and this comes out most of all in the character of the imagery predominant throughout the play:

> Like to the Pontic sea,
> Whose icy current and compulsive course
> Ne'er feels retiring ebb, but keeps due on
> To the Propontic and the Hellespont,
> Even so my bloody thoughts, with violent pace,
> Shall ne'er look back, ne'er ebb to humble love,
> Till that a capable and wide revenge
> Swallow them up.
>
> (*Othello,* Act 3, scene 3, 453)

In utter contrast to this, the world of *King Lear* is unbounded, chaotic, fragmented, wild and disorderly, as is the imagery that prevails throughout the play;

> Blow, winds, and crack your cheeks! rage! blow!
> You cataracts and hurricanes, spout
> Till you have drench'd our steeples, drown'd the cocks!
> You sulphourous and thought-executing fires,

---

[11] D. G. James, *op. cit.,* p. 63.

Vaunt-couriers to oak-cleaving thunderbolts,
Singe my white head! And thou, all-shaking thunder,
Smite flat the thick rotundity o' the world!
Crack nature's moulds, all germens spill at once,
That make ingrateful man!

(*King Lear,* Act 3, scene 2, 1)

The constant stream of animal imagery, the storm, the wild character of the terrain, intensity of the most primeval passions shooting forth in speech after speech, all tend to bear this out.[12]

The difference between the two plays, exhibited conspicuously but not exclusively in the imagery, is quite remarkable and is hardly subject to question once one has studied it (the study of it is one of the richest rewards of reading critical works on Shakespeare). The question, however, is whether this difference should be described in such a way as to commit us to saying that in King Lear we are in a different *world.* Is this description not itself a figure of speech? Isn't the setting in both plays, literally, *the same* world (one in Venice, one in England)? with all people subject to love and hate and envy and the same law of gravitation? Isn't the remarkable way in which the plays differ is the ambience, the mood, the tone—not so much the physical world, but the total *affect?*

What then of the difference between Dante and Lucretius? Isn't Dante's world, containing Hell, Purgatory, and Heaven, all of which Dante believed constituted part of the real universe, quite different from the world of Lucretius, which didn't contain any of these realms? Indeed, the universe *as envisaged by* these two writers differs enormously—not just in mood, but in geographical details. Milton's world in *Paradise Lost* and *Paradise Regained* was a Ptolemaic world, with the earth at the center and the sun, moon, stars, and planets all encircling it (although Milton himself was familiar with the new Copernican astronomy), which is quite different from the heliocentric solar system with which we today are familiar and which is presupposed in countless works of science fiction. Different works, then, embody different views of the universe, but their starting point is the real world we all know, including the real people who inhabit it.

## 3. TRUTHS ABOUT THE ARTIST

Let us now investigate another area in which the topic of truth arises. Sometimes, from reading a work of literature, we *make inferences* (infer statements) about the author of the work, or about the culture in which the

---

[12] See also Wolfgang Clemen, *The Development of Shakespeare's Imagery* (New York: Hill & Wang, n. d.).

author worked, about who influenced him, and so on. The statements are not made in the work of literature, yet we make them with considerable confidence after reading the work of literature. We believe that the work of literature "tells us something" about its author, even if it doesn't say so in so many words, and critics constantly make inferences from literary works to the beliefs of the author, the author's attitudes, feelings, behavioral tendencies, and the like. Indeed, this is one of the favorite indoor sports of literary critics.

When we are in the presence of someone speaking, we not only hear what he says, we note his facial expression, gestures, bodily stance, and so on. When we read a work of literature, we have *only* the written word to go by. There is, then, much less basis for making inferences about the writer than about the speaker. Yet there is some. We receive a letter from a friend, and we conclude that the author was angry, or disturbed, or depressed, when he wrote it. We infer this from the *tone* of the letter, the selection of words, the rhythm of the lines, and so on. Reading a series of letters from someone may tell us a good deal about the author.

If we can do it with letters, so, it would seem, we can do it with novels, plays, and poems. We constantly make inferences from the written word about the nature of the author—for example, that he was very much interested in some subjects but relatively little in others; that he had a heroic concept of human life; that he was a keen observer of details; that he hated hypocrisy and cant; and so on. And when asked what is our evidence, we point out features of the works that he wrote.

Still, we should be very careful about making inferences from the work to the author. Many people have inferred, from the fact that Shakespeare's sonnets were addressed to a man, that Shakespeare was homosexual; but one might equally infer, from the fact that the great bulk of his work (the plays) never refer to the subject, that he was not. Either inference is surely unsafe. Some have made the inference from passages in his work, especially *Hamlet,* that Shakespeare had an oedipal conflict (not Hamlet, but Shakespeare himself). Some have inferred from the fact that *Othello* deals with a racially mixed marriage that Shakespeare was sensitive to race relations; but there is in the plays no particular evidence of this, and race has very little to do with the action of the play. The fact is that we know very little about the details of Shakespeare's life aside from the composition of the plays and that anyone who tries to make inferences from his work to his views or his feelings or attitudes or motivations is utterly frustrated by the attempt. The *characters* in Shakespeare's plays eloquently present many different views; but these are the characters' views, and there is no evidence that they are also Shakespeare's views. To know what Shakespeare's views were, we would need *external* evidence—from biographies, witnesses, friends who knew him, and so on—and of this we have practically nothing; and the *internal* evidence, from the plays themselves, fails to provide it.

There are two important factors in literature that tend to block inferences from work to author, which do not operate in letters. First, we must remember the difference between the *author* and the *speaker*. This is obvious in the case of a character in a play or novel; the character speaks and his views need not be the views of the author—the author is simply *presenting* a character, not speaking through his voice. Even when the novel is written in the first person, we must not assume that it is the author speaking. *Huckleberry Finn* is written in the first person, but the teller of the tale (the speaker in the novel) is not Mark Twain but Huckleberry Finn himself. Huckleberry Finn has mental anguish about whether the slave Jim should be returned to the South, but Twain himself would have had no such anguish—and we know this, not from the novel, but from external evidence about Twain's beliefs on slavery.

Even when the author tells the story in the first person, we should not identify the speaker with the author. Perhaps the author is just "putting us on," detaching himself from his views from the tale he is telling. He may well present views which are not his own. In *Tom Jones,* Henry Fielding introduces each section of the book with a little humorous essay expressing views on life, chance, and destiny; since these are not put in the mouth of a character, we tend to assume that this is Fielding himself speaking. But why need we assume this? Why not say that there is an unnamed speaker, the teller of the tale, who stands back and reflects on the tale he is telling, but that this speaker need not be identical with the author? The speaker in "The Royal Game" is unnamed—it need not be Zweig, the author. Perhaps it is some imaginary narrator that he invented for the occasion, just as he invented the characters in the story; and the thoughts expressed by the narrator may not coincide with the author's own any more than the thoughts of the characters do.

Second, we must keep in mind the distinction between *saying* something and *asserting* it. That life is a dome of many-colored glass was *said* by Shelley in his poem "Epitholamian"; but are we warranted in saying that Shelley was *asserting* this in his poem? Many things can be said, particularly by an author of a literary work, that are not really being *asserted* by him. And if they are not being asserted by him, there is no ground for saying that he believed them. At least the work itself provides no such grounds—to find them, we have, once again, to go to external evidence.

But aren't there some cases in which we have good grounds for inferring that an author had a certain belief, even without external evidence? Consider the case of Tolstoy in *War and Peace.* Even if we ignore the last seventy-five pages, in which the narrative was ended and he presents an essay on the philosophy of history, aren't we sure what his views on history were—through which characters he treats sympathetically, the way in which he "rigs" the action, and so on? Let us try to ignore the fact that we already know from external sources what his views on history were. Suppose we have only the novel (without the essay). Again, the speaker, the teller of the tale, need not be identified with the author; and the fact that something was *said* does not show that it was *asserted*. Maybe the philosophy expressed by the speaker, as well as by certain characters, is also "part of the act." We cannot even safely infer, without external evidence (which we have in this case), that Harriet Beecher Stowe was an opponent of slavery. It is possible that she was a "white supremacist" who was offered a million dollars to present the views of the other side. She, the author, need not have been the narrator; and the things said in the novel may not have been asserted. That such a view is ridiculous is evident to us because we know from external evidence what her views were. With these points in mind, it will be well to exercise great caution in making inferences, from *internal* evidence alone, to the beliefs, attitudes, emotions, or motivations of the author.

The same considerations apply to the other arts as well. Making inferences from work of art to artist is extremely popular in program notes and museum brochures. If we are given the artist's own testimony that he believed so-and-so or felt so-and-so, and the artist was a generally trustworthy person, we can infer with some probability that he really did believe or feel so-and-so. But this is external evidence; what can we infer about the artist from the work of art only? Can we infer from the fact that a composer wrote many joyful compositions that he was a joyful person, of happy temperament? Not at all: a happy composition does not imply a happy composer. We cannot safely make such an inference at all.

Consider again prehistoric drawings on cave walls 50,000 years old. We know nothing about the artists or their mental states, and we shall never come across their autobiographies (they had no written language). We can say things about their artistic styles—this we recognize *in* the drawings, we do not infer it *from* the drawings. What can we infer about the artists just *from* examining the drawings? Can you think of any one inference you could make with safety?

Suppose we have no external evidence at all about the creator of a given work. What can we infer, just from the sculpture or painting or musical composition alone? The things we can safely infer are all fairly trivial: that he was *able* to create this work (since he did create it), that he not only had the capacity to do so but followed it through to completion, that he was probably interested in it, though it is possible that he was bored by it and did it for money, and so on. We cannot even infer with certainty that he "believed in" what he was doing. Evidence of an artist's thoughts or feelings must, in general, be obtained from external evidence.

According to the contemporary novelist Ayn Rand, it is not through the discovery of biographical facts about the artist that the reader or viewer "establishes contact" with him. Rather, what is communicated about the artist to the audience is something too instantaneous, and too unconscious, to be called an inference. What is noninferentially picked up by the reader or viewer is what she calls the artist's *sense of life*—something to be distinguished sharply from the artist's philosophical views, even those he was consciously attempting to express in his work.

> Art "tells us something" about the artist by communicating to us the artist's *sense of life*. A sense of life is not the same as a philosophy of life: it is not set forth explicitly in statements: "a sense of life is a pre-conceptual equivalent of metaphysics, an emotional, subconsciously integrated appraisal of man and of existence."[13]
>
> Regardless of the nature or content of an artist's metaphysical views, what an art work expresses, fundamentally, under all of its lesser aspects, is: "This is life as *I* see it." The essential meaning of a viewer's or reader's response, under all of its lesser elements, is: "This is (or is not) life as I see it."
>
> It is the artist's sense of life that controls and integrates his work, directing the innumerable choices he has to make, from the choice of subject to the subtlest details of style. It is the viewer's or reader's sense of life that responds to a work of art by a complex, yet automatic, reaction of acceptance and approval or rejection and condemnation.[14]

For example, an ancient Greek sculptor, "who presents man as a god-like figure is aware of the fact that men may be crippled or diseased or helpless; but he regards these conditions as accidental, as irrelevant to the essential nature of man—and he presents a figure embodying strength, beauty, intelligence, self-confidence, as man's proper, natural state."[15] By contrast, "if one saw, in real life, a beautiful woman wearing an exquisite evening gown, with a cold sore on her lips, the blemish would mean nothing but a minor affliction, and one would ignore it. But a painting of such a woman would be a corrupt, obscenely vicious attack on man, on beauty, on all values—and one would experience a feeling of immense disgust and indignation at the artist. . . . The emotional response to that painting would be instantaneous, much faster than the viewer's mind could identify all the reasons involved. The psychological mechanism which produces that response (and which produced the painting) is a man's sense of life."[16] A sense of life, then, is not the same as a philosophy; nothing that explicit may even have been consciously held by the artist, nor can it be expressed in some kinds of art, such as music. It is not manifest in statements, even when the work contains them: Victor Hugo's sense of life—positive, confident, in full control of his powers and faculties, so that to read his work is like Voltaire's comment on Homer's *Iliad*, "It makes me feel twenty feet tall"—is often at odds with the explicit moral and philosophical tenets which he regards with approval; the sense of life comes through in spite of the officially held

---

[13] Ayn Rand, *The Romantic Manifesto* (New York: New American Library, 1971), p. 34–35.
[14] *Ibid.,* pp. 34, 35.
[15] *Ibid.,* pp. 36–37.
[16] *Ibid.,* p. 34.

moral views in which he was simply a child of his time, which his own sense of life far transcended.

## 4. IMPLIED TRUTHS

Unlike a painter, sculptor, or composer, an author, since his medium is words, can make statements *in* his artistic medium. And regardless of whether he is asserting or saying, regardless of whether it is his own views or those of an unnamed speaker, some of the statements he makes—about the world, about life, about people, about history, and so on—may be *true*. Such statements do often occur in works of literature, and they offer us no particular problems. If a statement is made, it is either true or false; and if a statement is made in a work of literature—whether uttered or asserted, whether the author's view or not—it too is either true or false.

The *theme* of a work of literature is its underlying idea: a literary work may have as its theme the greatness of life, the waste of life, the futility of life, the ruination of life through fortuitous circumstances, and so on. The *thesis* of a work of literature is always something true or false: it is *that* something or other is or is not the case: for example, *that* all men are evil, *that* love is blind, and so on. An *explicit* thesis in a work of literature is one that is stated in the text; an *implicit* thesis is one that is not stated outright, but is implicit, or implied.

Many works of literature contain no thesis at all; a work of fiction may just be a good story and nothing else. But very often the story illustrates some general point that is nowhere stated in the text. Implicit theses occur quite often in works of literature: nowhere in the novel or drama is it said explicitly that a certain thesis is true, yet the entire work may be an illustration of it, and it may be the centerpin of the work.

Consider a simple case, Aesop's fables. "The mouse said to the lioness, 'Why is it that I have many children in a year, and in two years you have only one?' And the lioness replied, 'Though he is but one, yet he is a lion.'" Surely the implicit thesis of this tale is that quality is more important than quantity. Similarly, the famous tale of the shepherd-boy who cried "wolf" too often is that the liar is not believed, even when he tells the truth. These theses are implicit, since they are not stated, but they are pretty close to the surface.

It is easy to know what an explicit thesis is, since it is stated outright. But how can we know what the implicit thesis, if any, is?

1. One could say that the thesis of a work of literature is whatever the author meant or *intended* it to be. But we have already considered the problems in such a solution. (a) We have no idea most of the time what the author intended, other than from examining the work itself. We have no idea, for example, what was in Aesop's mind; we know only what he wrote. (b) Intention

may misfire: an author may intend to do A, and think he has done A, but he has not achieved A, but something else instead, B, which is quite different.

2. One could say that the implicit thesis of a work of literature is whatever you or I or most people *get out of it*. But this won't do either: an audience may be insensitive, or not see what's there, or see things that aren't there. You may, I may, most people may. And then the implicit thesis would vary from case to case, depending on who was doing the reading.

3. Perhaps then we can say simply that a work of literature may *imply* some thesis. But the ordinary sense of "imply" discussed in logic textbooks will not do here. The Aesop fable does not *logically* imply the moral we draw from the tale, since one cannot logically deduce "Quality is more important than quantity" from any sentence in the tale, nor from the whole of it. Yet we are quite sure that the moral is "there."

We do talk about implication in ways other than strict logical implication. For example, consider the famous example given by the philosopher G. E. Moore: when I say I went to the movies last Tuesday, I thereby imply that I *believe* I went, although I nowhere *say* that I believe I went. If I said it in an ironic tone of voice, or with gestures and facial expessions that would indicate that I am joking, this is a clue that I do not believe what I said and that you are not to believe it either. But if I say it in an ordinary straightforward tone of voice, with no counterindications, you are *entitled to conclude* that I believe what I said. If I was lying, and thus did not believe what I said, I was deceiving you: you were entitled to conclude it, yet I, the speaker, knew that what you concluded was not true. Or if I later say that I didn't mean it and was only exercising my vocal cords, you would not excuse me: you would say, "But you implied it by what you said and the way you said it."

The clue to the idea of implicit theses is plausibly found in the concept of *suggestion*. I may suggest what I do not say, and often the suggestion is just as clear as if I had said it. In oral discourse, I may suggest by my tone of voice and gestures what is not suggested by my words. But in written discourse, the audience has only my words to go by. Yet the words—the choice of words used, the order in which they are presented, which ones are reiterated or emphasized, the general tone that results—all these may suggest a great deal that is not said explicitly. For example, the writer of a letter may *suggest* that I am to blame for something, even though he nowhere says it—but the tone of his letter bristles with moral indignation, and he refers to me in ways that he would not do if he were not indignant. It is an *angry* letter. We are not talking now about *inferring* from his words that *he* is angry; we are saying that his words and sentences *suggest* things about me that they do not say, regardless of what the feelings of the author of the letter may be. (I can infer from his letter that he is crude, but there may be no suggested (implicit) thesis in his letter at all.)

We are all familiar with the suggestive power of language in contexts other than works of literature. When a man says, "Of course the man died, I wasn't his physician," he isn't *saying* that if he had been the patient's physician the patient would not have died, but he is surely, by the juxtaposition of the two clauses, suggesting that there is a causal connection. When someone says, "They had children and got married," he is suggesting, that they had the children first, though not saying it (you couldn't accuse him of saying it in a court of law). Ordinarily, unless there are indications of the contrary, the order of events is taken to be the order of the telling, and hence the suggestion in this sentence that the children came before the marriage. "No, I would not say he was a person of sanitary personal habits" certainly suggests that his habits were unsanitary, though the speaker doesn't say so—the statement would be true even if he didn't know the person at all and hence didn't know whether his habits were sanitary or unsanitary. We pick up such suggestions when we learn the meanings of words and sentences in a language.

There is a much wider popular sense of the word "suggest" according to which A suggests B whenever A becomes associated in one's mind with B. In this sense, anything can suggest anything else, just as the utterance of a word can suggest almost anything, depending on the individual's mental associations with the term. Seeing a black cat may suggest to one person bad luck; to another, the safety of one's own cat; to another, night and darkness; to another, evil; to another, fond memories of one's last cat; to another, the midnight sky as one experienced it long ago one romantic night; and so on. There is virtually no limit to what can be suggested in this sense. What is suggested in this sense is highly variable and "subjective." It is clearly not this that is now under discussion. What we are now discussing is (a) a suggested *thesis* (something that is true or false) and (b) suggestion in some more "objective" sense, one in which what a sentence suggests is about as clearly marked out as the meaning of a word in a language with which one is familiar. The word "cat" may be associated with practically anything in one's mind on a given occasion, but the word "cat" *means* a certain specific type of quadruped; that is the meaning of the word as one has learned it, and by means of which one communicates with other people who speak the same language. In the same way, saying "They had children and got married" suggests, to anyone who knows English, that they had the children first, and if one does not know this one has not yet mastered the idiom of one's language.

Sometimes the suggestion is obvious, sometimes more subtle. Jonathan Swift, in *A Modest Proposal, says* that the Irish could solve their malnutrition problem by eating their own children; what he *suggests* (not very subtly) is that the English are mistreating the Irish and that they should stop doing so. He does this in a more dramatic way than he could have done by direct statement, for example, writing a tract. In this case, he does it through *irony.* (One could define irony intentionalistically, as *saying* the opposite of what you *mean;* but we can now define it more satisfactorily, without the reference to intention, as *suggesting* the opposite of what you *say.*)

One and the same work of literature may often suggest incompatible theses. Throughout Milton's *Paradise Lost* is the suggestion (as well as the explicit statement by some of the characters) that the Fall of Man was a dire catastrophe, brought about by man's free will; there is also the suggestion that the whole series of events was foreordained by God and, in view of divine benevolence, not really a catastrophe; and still other evidence that man's state after the Fall is much better, in the sense that he has freedom to choose more widely than before ("a paradise within thee, happier farr"). Our question now is not "What did Milton believe?" or "What did Milton intend?" but, rather, regardless of what he believed or intended, "What beliefs got embodied in the poem? which ones are stated, and what further ones are suggested?" To exhaust all the suggested theses is, of course, a matter requiring detailed acquaintance with the text of the poem—but not with Milton's biography. (Knowledge of his biography is needed for inferring what his *beliefs* were.)

The novels of Thomas Hardy suggest, though occasionally they also state, that the basic factors on which human happiness depends is largely the result of chance—of inheritance, temperamental features formed early in life, and most of all of who one happens to meet at certain times—meeting person X might have led to happiness at time $t_{-1}$ but led only to misery since it occurred at time $t_{-2}$. How do we know, aside from explicit statements by the author, that such a general belief is suggested? Because, in one novel after another, this is always the way things happen: one person meets another at a certain time on Egdon Heath, and the end-result, through a complex causal chain, is catastrophic, and it always turns out that way, so it is as if human lives are dominated and their course determined by a malevolent fate. One *could* argue that this holds only for the characters in the novel and not for humankind in general; yet the overwhelming impression, to most readers of Hardy's novels, is that the situations depicted are to be taken as typical in human life, not exceptional cases. This is, however, a matter for controversy.

There is, indeed, a tendency to "overgeneralize" the implicit theses. In Arthur Miller's play *All My Sons,* a plane manufacturer knowingly produces planes with defective parts and before the play is over his own son, a pilot, is killed in one of these defective planes. Many people have taken Miller's play to suggest that *all* armament manufacturers are dishonest; some have taken the play to be communist propaganda. Miller replied to these charges by saying that the play contained no such suggestions—that he in no way said or implied that the case treated in the play was typical (or even that it had actually occurred, even once); that if it had been typical, it would not have been so noteworthy; and that he was treating an exceptional case, and therefore that he was *attacking* the thesis that all armament manufacturers are dishonest. There can, then, be disagreement about what the play suggests, but each opinion will have to be confirmed by reference to the text of the play—and in this case the play does not seem to confirm any of them; only one case is treated, with no implication that this case is typical, or on the other hand that it is not.

A book exposes the practices of a businessman, and people conclude that the "message" is that all businessmen are crooks. This may possibly be what the author *intended,* but it is likely that nothing of the kind is to be inferred from the book itself: in the book there is no attempt to generalize from "one" to "all," nor is it even said or implied that the case presented is a typical one. One might go even farther and say that, since the characters are fictitious, "any resemblance to actual persons living or dead is strictly coincidental" and that there is not even a thesis about even *one* actual living person.

Many viewers objected to the film *The Deer Hunter* because it showed white American draftees captured and tortured in Vietnam by the Viet Cong. They admit that there were occasions when this sort of thing occurred; what they object to is that the film did not show anything of an opposite nature, Vietnamese being killed or mistreated by American soldiers. But it is probable that they are overgeneralizing any thesis the film may have: nowhere is it stated or implied in the film that American soldiers were never guilty of atrocities in Vietnam. Indeed, another film, *Apocalypse Now,* shows precisely this happening. But *The Deer Hunter* simply does not deal with that particular subject-matter; every book or film has to select some subject or other out of the infinite number possible, and the producers of this film elected to show a group of rather typical small-town Americans who suddenly find themselves in an entirely alien environment and the subsequent psychological effects on them and their community when they return to their homes in America. It exposes the horrors of the Vietnam war, just as much as does *Apocalypse Now;* only the selection of the specific subject-matter to illustrate these horrors is different. The criticism by those who spell "America" with a "k," that it is a "fascist film," is the result of grossly overgeneralizing a thesis. If they take the thesis to be that "*all* American soldiers were innocent victims," this thesis is of course false; but nothing is said or implied about all American soldiers. At most it deals with *three* American soldiers. By the same criterion one would have to say that a film about a wounded bird implies that all birds are wounded.

Besides all this, the characters themselves are fictitious; but the setting is not: since the setting of the film is a real place, Vietnam, and this fact is explicitly indicated in the film, the film makers could not "get themselves off the hook" (not that they would want to) by saying that the film takes place in an imaginary locale somewhere. But they would have every reason to resist overgeneralization by viewers on the thesis of the film, and indeed they might well allege that the film, while having war and the effects of war as its subject-matter, really has no thesis at all.

Yet, difficult as it is often to pin down exactly what is suggested and how broadly it is to be construed, many works of literature seem to illustrate some general thesis, which is never stated but which nevertheless seems to be the main point (or one of the main points) of the entire work. At first, as one reads the seven-volume saga *Remembrance of Things Past* by Marcel Proust, it is just a fascinating story; but themes begin to recur, and events regularly issue in a certain way, and one begins to suspect that there is some general thesis behind the narrative—that it isn't *just* a narrative but that a general statement is being made. According to André Maurois in his *The Quest for Proust,* a whole philosophy of love is implicit in the novels. According to him, love

> begins in unattached desire and anguish which spur us on to make choices. But every attachment springs from the subjective temperament, not from any objective evaluation. "What we are really doing [in loving a woman] is to project in her a state of *ourselves.*" The lover and the beloved are consequently involved in a double misconception in that each person expects of the other what each has only imagined exists in the other but does not really. And this is why "in love we cannot but choose badly." The discrepancy between the person we have imagined and the person we have gotten becomes more and more obvious, giving rise to a basic disillusionment even in the state of actual possession. It is here that love is aided by another element in the cycle—doubt. "Love can survive possession, can even grow, so long as it contains an element of doubt." We seek happiness, inevitably we get suffering. Thus, our nature drives us to love with all its illusions, for which the only rewards are continuing misery. . . . "The beloved has no real existence outside the imagination of the lover."[17]

Is all this really suggested in Proust's saga? It is for literary critics to try to resolve this question by close examination of the text. Even if it is all suggested, a still different question is whether the suggested theses are *true:* is it true that all human love relationships are like this? To appreciate the work, one need not agree that the explicit or implicit theses are *true;* one must, however, try to *understand* what they are, if one is to be sensitive to "what is going on" in the novel. However, one must be cautious: if it is undesirable not to be aware of theses that are there, it is also undesirable to read into the text theses that are not there, thus misperceiving what the novel is all about.

Works of literature can and sometimes do suggest *hypotheses* about life, about the world, about human nature, about human relations, that are nowhere else so clearly brought out—sometimes new hypotheses that have never before been suggested. This is one of the values we find in a work of literature. Even if the hypothesis suggested is false, it may be fruitful to think about and evaluate, and also rouse us from our dogmatic slumbers.

Does it matter whether the thesis of a work of literature—be it implicit or explicit—is *true?*

One view is that one must understand the thesis, one need not agree with it. The truth of the implicit or explicit thesis is irrelevant to one's appreciation of

---

[17] Morris Weitz, "Truth in Literature," *Revue Internationale de Philosophie,* Vol. 9, 1955. Reprinted in John Hospers, ed., *Introductory Readings in Aesthetics* (New York: Free Press, 1969); passage quoted is on p. 218.

it as a work of art. Artistic value is one thing, truth is another; they should not be confused with each other. If one can appreciate only those works of literature with whose theses one agrees, this is a suspicious sign that one is not appreciating it as a work of art but that one is only giving approval to those views with which one already agrees. The work of art says merely, "Look, feel, appreciate." It does not say, "Agree with me." We should be able to appreciate a work of art whose thesis we find to be false, just as much as with one whose thesis we find to be true. Certainly we may "feel closer" to the work of art with whose thesis we agree, but we should not let this disturb our judgment: the one with whose thesis we disagree may be just as fine a work of art, and we should appreciate it none the less for all that. We should not allow our cognitive judgments to get in the way of our artistic evaluations.

Perhaps that is the end of the matter. Still, one may have lingering doubts. There are many readers

> whose appreciation is greater than it would otherwise be when they feel that a specific work does contain an important or novel truth. . . . There are plenty of readers of Proust who agree with Maurois that the greatness of *Remembrance* is based in part upon some of the truths that it contains. I cannot see that there is anything in this that is aesthetically at fault; the novel has not been converted into science or history. It remains a work of art which is to be responded to, as it is sometimes said, "in and through itself," *i.e.,* as a totality of elements in relation to each other. Those of us who do not accept the claims of Proust can recognize the quality of this assessment. For these readers, Proust is simply their kind of art; and for them, that ends the matter. Of course, in return, we demand a similar tolerance for our choices. And, at least in my own case, I cannot but think that there is that added moment of greatness in *The Brothers Karamazov* or *Anna Karenina* precisely because Dostoyevsky and Tolstoy, in those novels, see something which is true about our world that neither Eliot nor Proust nor many others ever do.[18]

There is an interesting kind of case in which a stated or implied thesis must be perceived as true if the work is to have its desired effect, and that is *humor*. There are jokes and verses which are found to be extremely funny in totalitarian nations which would lack any point in freer nations. Consider this "underground" joke in the Soviet Union on the difference between an optimist and a pessimist: "An optimist is a person who expects to be deported to Siberia; a pessimist is a person who expects that they will make him walk all the way." To us who do not live in the constant shadow of midnight knocks on the door, sudden and permanent disappearances, and exile to death camps, the joke seems fairly pointless (unless, of course, we know of the conditions in which they live and empathize with them); it is not funny unless the background conditions in which the joke occurs really exists, that is, the conditions explicitly or implicitly referred to, are *true*. Or consider:

[18] *Ibid.,* pp. 223–224.

In the 21st century, the Russians had at last achieved Communism.
A child reads an historical novel.
"Mummy, what does *queue for meat* mean?"
"Well dear, a *queue* is an expression from the bad old times. It means a long line of people waiting to buy goods."
"Yes, mummy," said the child. "But what does *meat* mean?"[19]

Had there been no queues and no constant shortages, the story would not be funny. That the conditions described or implied exist must be true.

### Implied Truths in the Non-literary Arts

Can non-literary works of art suggest statements, true or false?

It depends on what sense of "suggest" is being used. In the popular sense, anything can suggest anything else, to the mind of someone or other. A painting of Madame de Staël may suggest all sorts of things connected with my mother, whom she may resemble, or for some other reason remind me of her. But our question is more specific: can the non-literary work suggest *theses,* true or false statements? Again, in the popular sense, surely it can: a painting of the Madonna and Child may suggest to some that Catholicism is the only true religious faith. It can't prove it, of course, but it may suggest it to some minds.

But when we discussed suggestion in works of literature, we meant something much more fixed in meaning than that: when we said that "They had children and got married" suggests that they had the children first, we observed that a person learns to "pick up" this suggestion along with learning the language itself. Is there anything analogous to this in nonliterary arts?

In a mural done by Orozco for the New School for Social Research, Stalin is shown "in a stiff row with five Soviet soldiers of different races, all armed with hammers and all looking very glum."[20] The mural was kept behind a curtain, and the president of the university explained that the painting "does not express the philosophy of the faculty." But though a painting may *grow out of* a philosophy, and would not have been created without the background of that philosophy, is it true that a painting may *imply* that philosophy or contain it as an implicit thesis? Could you know what the philosophy was just by looking at the mural? What if someone said it was just five glum-looking men? What if someone recognized them as Soviet but said that the painting contains or implies no philosophical thesis, or any other proposition? What exactly are the propositions which the painting is supposed to suggest? If one person says it implies one proposition and another says it's a different proposition, how do we find whose allegation is true? In sentences, such as "Jones

---

[19] These two jokes are contained (among many others) in Petr Beckmann, *Hammer and Tickle* (Boulder, Colo.: The Golem Press, 1980), pp. 10, 76.

[20] Monroe C. Beardsley, *Aesthetics* (New York: Harcourt Brace, 1958), p. 370.

is fat," we have an indexical part, "Jones," and a characterizing part "is fat"; where in the painting do we find these two aspects? and don't we need them both? doesn't a declarative say something about something (or someone)? where is this to be found in painting?

If we want the best possible examples of nonliterary creations suggesting a thesis, we shall probably find it in cartoons—and they must be cartoons without captions, for the caption often tells us what the suggested thesis of the cartoon is, but the caption is not a part of the visual creation itself. One cartoon, for example, is clearly a portrayal of President Carter—it has some of his distinctive facial configurations—but it also shows him as an engineer on a wrecked train. It seems quite clear in this case that the cartoon is suggesting (but not stating, since there are no words) that the way in which the engineer has handled the train is like the way in which the president has handled the nation.

If all one gets out of the cartoon is that an engineer is sitting in a wrecked train, one has not seen the point of the cartoon; the cartoon has an implied *thesis*. But such a suggestion is present only *in a certain context:* we cannot grasp the import of cartoons of political figures a hundred years ago unless we know what the issues and controversies were at that time; without that background knowledge, cartoons appear to us as peculiar representations whose implied thesis, if any, is unclear.

With the aid of a specific context, then, cartoons *can* suggest theses, even without captions. Political cartoons are specifically designed to suggest theses, and ordinarily we look for such theses at once. Paintings and sculptures are ordinarily valued quite apart from their having an implicit thesis, and usually they have none at all. Still, some paintings may be said to suggest a thesis, though we must be very careful in deciding what that thesis is. The series of paintings by Goya, *Disasters of War,* may be said to have a thesis, but what is it? "War is terrible" might be one answer, but this general thesis is one of which we probably do not need to be reminded—if the paintings existed simply to illustrate that thesis, they would have little value for us. There are many paintings whose subject-matter is war, and the fact (if it is a fact) that they all have a thesis about war isn't what makes them better or worse than other paintings. One can appreciate the paintings, unlike the cartoons, without coming to any conclusions about what, if anything, the thesis is. Picasso's *Guernica* shows one aspect of the horror of war, but does it have a thesis? Is it saying (suggesting) that war is horrible? that the Spanish War specifically is? or that the atrocities were committed only by the other side? Is its thesis specifically anti-Franco? If so, we need not only the painting but the historical context to conclude what the thesis is.

The trouble with such speculations about the thesis of works of visual art—music would be even a worse case, since in visual arts at least persons and objects are represented—is that we do not have the kind of *anchor* to ground our speculations that we have in literary arts. In literature, words have definite meanings, and they also have, contain, in combination, definite suggestions, which people who understand the language already understand. Paintings and sculptures can *show* people engaged in certain activities, but they cannot *say* anything; and to infer what is being *said* (even less, what is asserted) from what is merely *shown* is, to put it mildly, an extremely risky business.

## 4. ART, REVELATION, AND KNOWLEDGE

Some may agree that some arts—literature at least—can make true statements, can suggest others, and can be in some sense true to human nature. But, they will add, the story does not end there. The arts also afford us (here the terms vary) "immediate knowledge," "insight into the nature of things," "revelation of reality." All the terms involved here are very slippery ones, and we shall have to tread carefully.

Do the arts give us *knowledge?* We usually distinguish knowing *how* from knowing *that.* We learn how to drive a car, to swim, to play golf, and so on, partly by being taught, partly by practicing and doing it. We also learn *that* so-and-so is the case—this is the "propositional" sense of knowledge; whenever we learn some fact about ourselves or the world, we have acquired another bit of knowledge—that. We may indeed come to know certain facts from a work of music, such as that many horns and drums are used; indeed we acquire some knowledge from all experiences. Acquiring knowledge is central in all the sciences, and indeed in learning about the lives of artists and the historical facts about the period in which they lived, but the *appreciation* of art is not primarily a matter of acquiring new knowledge. We may learn quite a bit about life in England in the eighteenth century by reading eighteenth-century English novels, but most readers would consider this a fringe benefit: if we wanted straight history, we would read history books; what we learn about history from novels is usually quite incidental. A person who wanted only historical knowledge from novels might acquire more of it from a tenth-rate novel than from great novels like *Tom Jones* and *Middlemarch.*

It is a third "kind" of knowledge, however, that the arts are often alleged to provide us: not knowledge *that* so-and-so is true (*Wissenschaft*), not even facts of psychology, but some kind of *immediate* (unmediated) awareness (*Erlebnis*). The fact to be faced, however, is that there is a clear distinction between immediate *experience,* however intense, and anything we could call *knowledge.* Hearing the Bach *B Minor Mass* may put us in a state of "high exaltation" more intense than any experience outside of the arts; but the question is, what exactly does listening to the *Mass* enable us to *know* that we did not know before? Knowledge is one thing, richness of experience is another; why confuse them? We have a perfectly familiar way to distinguish the two—by speaking of *knowledge* as opposed to *acquaintance.* When I read facts about the governor's life, I acquire knowledge about him; when I see him personally, I become acquainted with him. If I am blind from birth, I may study physics books and learn many facts about green, blue, red, and other colors, but never see them; but without reading any books, if I am not blind, and I *see* green, I am *acquainted* with the color, although I may know nothing *about* the color, for example, the light waves that cause my perception of it. Once the issue has been put this way, we may ask of the arts the following: granted that the arts give us *experiences* unlike any we ever had before, what do they provide us with that can plausibly be called *knowledge*?

One answer is, "Works of art *reveal* things to us that we had never been aware of before." It is the word "reveal" that causes trouble here. (1) If the sentence means simply that works of art evoke experiences of depth and intensity in us the like of which we never had before, nor ever could have outside of art, this is surely true. But this is not the same as "revealing reality." (2) If it means that aspects of the artist's personality are made known to us through the work of art, just as a baby's rage is revealed to us by his crying and stamping (remember Dewey on this, p. 193), then again it may be true, though again we must be careful about drawing conclusions about artists from their works (p. 255). (3) Often, however, what is meant is that some truth about reality—not about the artist, but about the universe—is made known —"revealed"—to us through the work of art. This is the important assertion, but it is also the one most open to question.

When a scientist claims to have revealed to us the danger of certain drugs, he has not only presented us with a claim, but he has *provided evidence* for that claim. If he had made a claim and left it unsubstantiated, no one would say that he had "revealed to us the dangers of ingesting drugs." We would simply say he had asserted it and left his assertion unproved; hence no truth was "revealed" to us. The artist, even the literary artist who states or suggests some truth claim, does not ordinarily provide much in the way of *evidence* that his claim is true: novelists like Proust are exciting partly because they *suggest* hypotheses about human nature, but the only *evidence* they supply is the particular individuals described in the novel (who are usually fictitious); the most they supply by way of evidence is that *one* person or group of people behaved in accordance with the hypothesis.

Many would allege that some truths, including those to be found in the arts, do not *require* evidence: they are not the sort of truths that require evidence, they are known through *intuition*. Now, "intuition" is a harmless term when it is not used to make some knowledge claim: in discussing Croce we described the artist's artistic process as the coming-into-being and the development in the artist's mind of various intuitions or artistic ideas. But when one claims to know the *truth of a proposition* through intuition, he must face a severe problem: one person may claim that he knows through intuition that a proposition, *p,* is true, and a second person may claim that he knows through intuition that that same proposition is false or that some contradictory one is true. As a way of knowing truths, intuition is at an impasse when faced by this problem. On this rock, it would seem, all theories of intuition as a method of acquiring knowledge break—including "intuitive knowledge" alleged to be revealed to us in the arts.

Still, the writers who have defended revelation of intuition in art were trying to get at something, and we cannot dismiss it with a few deft remarks. Let us try a few cases:

1. Albert C. Barnes writes, "The artist illuminates the objective world for us, exactly as does the scientist. . . . The artist is primarily the discoverer, just as the scientist is; the scientist discovers abstract symbols which may be used for purposes of calculation and prediction; the artist, the qualities of things which heighten their human significance."[21]

As we have already observed in discussing representation, the painter depicts features of the world which had previously escaped us and which we can be brought to see after we have carefully looked at his paintings. More frequently, we can be brought to see the world in a certain way which is not our ordinary way—we can see a landscape through the eyes of Cézanne, and so on. The artist is surely not simply exercising his subjective whim or fancy: if that is what the claim is, it is surely true. The painter intensifies our awareness of and receptivity to the felt qualities of things in the world.

Are these "verifiable truths" as are the discoveries of the sciences? This depends on what meaning we attach to "verify": "we can verify these artistic revelations, such as Cézanne's way of viewing the world, in our experience," one might say, and if this means that as Cézanne saw it we too can see it, it is true. But if it means that we verify it as a scientist does, that a proposition is presented for which evidence is then amassed, this is not so: science is strictly concerned with the expansion of our knowledge of the world, and the painter is usually more interested in the expansion of our *perception*.

2. J. W. N. Sullivan, speaking of "the colossal and mastered experience which seems to be reflected in the Heilgesang of Beethoven's A minor quartet [Op. 130]," writes, "The perceptions which made that experience possible were in no sense illusory; they were perceptions of the nature of reality, even though they have no place in the scientific scheme."[22]

Let us admit that the experience of listening to the last quartets of Beethoven (Op. 127-135) is unique in music: we seem to be in a different world here, a world of intense and exalted spirituality, much different from the equally exalted but more extroverted spirituality of Bach in his masses and cantatas, more inward-turning, poignant, and mystical. Had Beethoven never written these last quartets, there is a whole range of experience which we as listeners would never have had. But having said this, we must be careful to

---

[21] Albert C. Barnes, *The Art in Painting* (New York: Harcourt Brace, 1937), pp. 7, 13.

[22] J. W. N. Sullivan, *Beethoven: His Spiritual Development* (New York: Knopf, 1927), p. 23.

keep separate the *experience itself,* however valuable and induplicable, from the *claims* one is inclined to make about it, especially while under the influence of that experience.

What would these claims be? What are the truths which are "revealed" by the late quartets? Some people say that they "tune us in" on a religious, even a mystical, reality; others deny that these quartets are religious at all, but simply present us with unique expressive qualities, for example, peace and tranquility alternating with a unique kind of agitation—perhaps the qualities of a highly sensitive man who has become deaf and is tragically unable to hear the music he himself composed. What shall we say? Until we have before us, stated explicitly for our examination, some of the "spiritual truths" which the quartets are claimed to reveal, and some way of validating the claims once they are made (and people disagree on what these "truths" are, and even whether there are any), there is no point in trying to discuss them further. Meanwhile we can value the experience of hearing the quartets just as much as ever.

Sullivan himself says, "Beethoven does not communicate to us his perceptions or his experiences. He communicates to us the *attitude based on them.* We may share with him that unearthly state where the struggle ends and pain dissolves away, although we know but little of his struggle and have not experienced his pain." He continues, "Music can no more express philosophical ideas than it can express scientific ideas. And nothing that Beethoven wanted to express can be called a philosophy. . . . Belief in a Heavenly Father cannot be expressed in music; what can be expressed, and with unexampled power, is the state of soul that such a belief, sincerely held, may arouse."[23]

A careful reader should be able to clarify this account considerably. For example, we have already seen problems with the term "communicate" (p. 207); it would have been clearer had he said that what can be *evoked* in the listener is an experience in which the struggle ends, for example. Hearing his music can evoke in us an attitude; but does it "communicate" *Beethoven's* attitude—and how do we know what that was? It may be that our experience of his quartets is very different from his own; and if so, does this matter, if we can come to treasure the quartets in our own way and find ourselves enriched for the experience?

3. It is the unique ability of works of art to take an entire range of human experience and suddenly put it in sharp focus—much as the concave lens, catching and concentrating the rays of the sun, is able to ignite dead leaves. Various strands of human experience, some not previously perceived as related, are brought together and are integrated into a new and unique whole, giving the presentation a sudden and overpowering impact, striking us almost like a lightning bolt with a dizzying "feeling of revelation." What description of conditions in Nazi prisons, even under conditions more horrible than those

---

[23] *Ibid.,* pp. 24, 120.

Zweig describes, can communicate to us the terror of uncertainty in "Part 2" of "The Royal Game"?

Solzhenitsyn's three-volume work, *The Gulag Archipelago,* gives us a non-fictional account of conditions in the Soviet Union from the 1917 revolution to 1966: of sudden arrests in the night, of interrogation and torture, of malnutrition and cold and starvation from overwork in Siberian labor camps. Informative and moving as these accounts are, they do not match the devastating impact of his works of fiction on the same themes, such as *The First Circle.* There is a particularly evocative scene in *Cancer Ward* in which a charwoman in the hospital has a conversation with one of the patients. Her husband is in a labor camp somewhere in Siberia—she has not heard from him for several years now; he was taken away by the secret police one night, for having spoken a few words against the regime when he was drunk, and someone had reported him. She is trying to bring up her small son, trying to eke out a living in a miserable hovel on her hospital wages. "In her youth," writes Solzhenitsyn, "she might have been called Lily. There could have been no hint then of the spectacle marks on the bridge of her nose. As a girl she had made eyes, laughed and giggled. There had been lilac and lace in her life, and the poetry of the symbolists. And no gypsy had ever foretold that she would end her life as a cleaning woman somewhere in Asia."[24]

> "These literary tragedies are just laughable compared with the ones we live through," Elizaveta Anatolyevna insisted. "Aïda was allowed to join her loved one in the tomb and to die with him. But we aren't even allowed to know what's happening to them. . . . Children write essays in school about the unhappy, tragic, doomed life of Anna Karenina. But was Anna really unhappy? She chose passion and she paid for her passion—that's happiness! She was a free, proud human being. But what if during peacetime a lot of greatcoats and peaked caps burst into the house where you were born and live, and order the whole family to leave the house and town in twenty-four hours, with only what your feeble hands can carry? . . . With a ribbon in her hair, your daughter sits down at the piano for the last time to play Mozart. But she bursts into tears and runs away. So why should I read *Anna Karenina* again? Maybe it's enough—what I've experienced. When can people read about us? *Us?* Only in a hundred years?"[25]

In nonfictional accounts of Soviet history, such references to *Aïda* and *Anna Karenina* would not of course have been included. But these are the very features which "work the miracle" in fiction; no recital of historical facts could so tellingly strike the emotional jugular. Through the selection of a few details, not strikingly significant by themselves but related by analogies to other areas of life, the author within a small compass brings into focus an enormous range of human experience, like the sunlight igniting the leaves.

---

[24] Aleksandr Solzhenitsyn, *Cancer Ward* (New York: Farrar, Straus, & Giroux, 1969), Bantam Books ed., pp. 478–479.

[25] *Ibid.,* p. 479.

And in doing so his work carries more tellingly than anything outside art the powerful ring of truth.

## EXERCISES

1. T. S. Eliot wrote, "In truth, neither Shakespeare nor Dante did any real thinking—that was not their job." (*The Intent of the Critic,* ed. Donald Stauffer, p. 76.) Discuss.

2. If a musical composition can contain no ideas, what can possibly be meant by saying that a work of music is *profound?*

3. a. Is a work such as Truman Capote's *In Cold Blood* fiction or nonfiction? Is there an implicit claim to historicity? in all the events described? How would you decide this question?

   b. Compare Solzhenitsyn's three-volume nonfiction work, *The Gulag Archipelago,* with one of his fictional accounts of Gulag such as *The First Circle.* What are the differences in treatment? in implicit claim to truth?

4. "The reason characters do certain things and not others, and certain things happen to them and not others, has much more to do with the type of work it is than with anything like truth to human nature. In comedies, people don't suddenly get bludgeoned and killed; in Westerns, monsters don't appear; in historical dramas, well-known facts of history as not usually falsified. To do such things would be a violation of the 'rules of the game' set up when you know it's a comedy or historical film you're going to see—like the violation of a contract." Discuss.

5. When Napoleon III sent Maximilian to be emperor of Mexico, a "Mexico for Mexicans" movement had already taken shape under the man who later became Mexico's first president, Benito Juarez. Maximilian, had not Napoleon removed his the French forces from Mexico and left Maximilian "holding the bag," would have been a "benevolent despot" and (so far as we can tell) a wise ruler; but his theory of government, that a king, having everything, needs nothing, and is above all political party strife, was utterly opposed to Juarez's democratic views. In real life Juarez and Maximilian never met, not even when Maximilian was captured and shot by Juarez's forces. The makers of the film *Juarez* decided to follow history, thus preventing them from inventing a confrontation scene between the two leaders, which could have dramatized powerfully their opposing political philosophies, the way Schiller did between Queen Elizabeth and Mary Stuart in his play *Mary Stuart.* Was it incumbent on the film makers to follow history? or should they have devised a confrontation scene which would have added power to the movie and provided a fitting climax to the film?

6. In Schiller's play *Jungfrau von Orleans,* Joan of Arc is portrayed as dying on the battlefield rather than at the stake, an historical inaccuracy which is also followed in Verdi's early opera *Giovanna d'Arco.* Do these historical inaccuracies, in your view, lessen the value of the works of art in which these inaccurate portrayals occur? If they disturb you, in what way do they disturb you?

7. "Biographical facts certainly *are* relevant. If I happen to know that a certain playwright is homosexual, I shall no longer put any trust in his characteriza-

tions of people of the opposite sex—I'll know that he doesn't know the opposite sex well enough to make his characterizations true to human nature.'' Discuss.

8. Discuss the role of *chance* events in works of literature. Should these never occur, because they bring in extraneous causal chains which compromise the unity of the work? or is there a place for them in literature? (Hardy's novels, for example, are full of chance events which determine the fate of the characters.)

9. History is more restrictive than fiction in that it cannot invent incidents but must faithfully record what happened (though not necessarily all that happened). But in what ways is fiction more restrictive than history?

10. What is a metaphor, and what connection has metaphor with truth? (See Max Black, ''Metaphor,'' in *Proceedings of the Aristotelian Society,* 1954–1955; Monroe Beardsley, *Aesthetics,* pp. 134–144; Arnold Isenberg, *Essays in Aesthetics and Philosophy of Criticism,* the chapter on metaphor.)

11. Comment on the following passage (from J. W. N. Sullivan's book *Beethoven*) sentence by sentence:

We cannot say that art communicates knowledge, as science does, for we should be open to the objection made to the Revelation Theory of Art that we cannot say what the revelation is *of.* But what art does do is to communicate to us an *attitude,* an attitude taken up by the artist consequent upon his perceptions, which perceptions may be perceptions of factors in reality.

Beethoven does not communicate to us his perceptions or his experiences. He communicates to us the attitude based on them. We may share with him that unearthly state where the struggle ends and pain dissolves away, although we know but little of his struggle and have not experienced his pain.

Music can no more express philosophic ideas than it can express scientific ideas. And nothing that Beethoven wanted to express can be called a philosophy. The states of consciousness he expresses, his reactions to perceptions and experiences, are not ideas. Belief in a Heavenly Father cannot be expressed in music; what can be expressed, and with unexampled power, is the *state of soul* that such a belief may arouse. The Credo of Beethoven's Mass in D is not the musical interpretation of certain Latin propositions; the Latin propositions express beliefs—the music expresses states of the soul that may be aroused by those beliefs. (pp. 23, 24, 120–121)

12. According to Albert C. Barnes, *The Art in Painting,* p. 7, ''The painter illuminates the *objective world* for us, exactly as does the scientist, different as the terms are in which he envisages it: art is a little plaything, a matter of caprice or uncontrolled subjectivity, as is physics or chemistry. What has made the study of science valuable and fruitful is method, and without a corresponding method of learning to see the study of art can lead only to futility. We must understand, in other words, what the distinctive *aspects of reality* are in which the artist is interested, how he organized his work to reveal and organize those aspects.'' Discuss.

13. According to the nineteenth-century German philosopher Arthur Schopenhauer (1788–1860), the entire universe—mankind included—is a reflection of a Cosmic Will, which is eternally striving and struggling, yet never ar-

riving at its sought-for goals. Music has a special place among the arts because it puts us directly in tune with the striving Cosmic Will: "We must attribute to music a far more serious and deep significance, connected with the inmost nature of the world and our own self, and in reference to which the arithmetical proportions to which it [music] may be reduced, are related, not as the thing signified, but merely as the sign. . . . Its representative relation to the world must be very deep, absolutely true, and strikingly accurate, because it is instantly understood by everyone, and has the appearance of a certain infallibility, because its form may be reduced to perfectly definite rules expressed in numbers, from which it cannot free itself without entirely ceasing to be music, yet the point or comparison between music and the world, the respect in which it stands to the world in the relation of a copy or repetition, is very obscure. Men have practised music in all ages without being able to account for this; content to understand it directly, they renounce all claim to an abstract conception of this direct understanding itself.

"Music is as *direct* an objectification and copy of the whole *will* as the world itself, nay, even as the Ideas, whose multipled manifestation constitutes the world of individual things. Music is thus by no means like the other arts, the copy of the Ideas, but the *copy of the will itself*. . . . This is why the effect of music is so much more powerful and penetrating than that of the other arts, for they speak only of shadows, but it speaks of the thing itself. . . . The composer reveals the inner nature of the world, and expresses the deepest wisdom in a language which his reason does not understand, as a person under the influence of mesmerism tells things of which he has no conception when he awakes." (Arthur Schopenhauer, *The World as Will and Idea,* Section 52.)

Thus, according to Schopenhauer, music is (a) a representational art, (b) the ultimate in expression, and (c) a "revelation of the true nature of reality." Read the entire work from which this quotation is taken and analyze or assess this view.

14. Is the truth of a belief ever relevant to the artistic value of a work of art? Assume that humor is such a value: the following underground jokes in the Soviet Union are considered funny in the situation in which the residents of a totalitarian nation find themselves. In freer nations they would have little point. Are they funny in the Soviet Union because they express a truth? (Examples taken from *Hammer and Tickle,* edited by Petr Beckmann, The Golem Press, Boulder, Colorado, 1980.)

   a. Gottwald has lost his pipe and phones the Minister of the Interior (in charge of the secret police). But half an hour later she brings it to him; it had slipped under the couch. He phones to rescind his previous orders.
      "Too bad," says the minister. "The boys have arrested 150 suspects, and 120 of them had already confessed. . . "

   b. Long before anybody seriously anticipated a Soviet-Chinese rift, the Czechoslovak minister of information, responsible for indoctrinating Czechoslovakia's 14 million inhabitants, visited China.
      "How many Chinese, do you suppose," he asked Mao Tse Tung, "are opposed to your regime?"
      "Very few," says Mao. "Not more than about 14 million, I would think. And in Czechoslovakia?"
      "Not more than that, either."

# SELECTED READINGS

AIKEN, HENRY D. "The Aesthetic Relevance of Belief," *Journal of Aesthetics and Art Criticism,* 9 (1951).

AIKEN, HENRY D. "Some Notes Concerning the Aesthetic and the Cognitive," *Journal of Aesthetics and Art Criticism,* 13 (1955).

ARISTOTLE, *Poetics.* (Many editions).

BEARDSLEY, MONROE C. *Aesthetics.* New York: Harcourt Brace, 1958. Chapters 8 and 9.

BUTCHER, S. H. *Aristotle's Theory of Poetry and Fine Art.* London: Oxford Univ. Press. 1923.

EASTMAN, MAX. *The Literary Mind: Its Place in an Age of Science.* New York: Scribners, 1933.

FORSTER, E. M. *Aspects of the Novel.* New York: Harcourt Brace, 1937.

GREENE, THEODORE M. *"Beauty and the Cognitive Significance of Art." Journal of Philosophy,* 37 (1940).

HEYL, BERNARD C. "Artistic Truth Reconsidered." *Journal of Aesthetics and Art Criticism,* 8 (1950).

HOFSTADTER, ALBERT. *Truth and Art.* New York: Columbia Univ. Press, 1965.

HOSPERS, JOHN. "Implied Truths in Literature." *Journal of Aesthetics and Art Criticism,* 19 (1960).

HOSPERS, JOHN. "Literature and Human Nature." *Journal of Aesthetics and Art Criticism,* 17 (1958).

HOSPERS, JOHN. *Meaning and Truth in the Arts.* University of N.C. Press, 1946, Ch. 5-8.

HOSPERS, JOHN. "Truth and Fictional Characters." *Journal of Aesthetic Education,* 1980.

ISENBERG, ARNOLD. "Music and Ideas." In his *Aesthetics and the Theory and Criticism.* University of Chicago Press, 1973, pp. 3-21.

ISENBERG, ARNOLD. "The Problem of Belief." *Journal of Aesthetics and Art Criticism,* 13 (1955).

JAMES, D. G. *Scepticism and Poetry.* London: Allen and Unwin, 1937.

KUHNS, RICHARD. *Structures of Experience.* New York: Harper, 1970. Chapter 1.

MACDONALD, MARGARET, AND MICHAEL SCRIVEN. "The Language of Fiction." *Proceedings of the Aristotelian Society,* Suppl. Vol. 27 (1954).

MEW, PETER. "Metaphor and Truth." *British Journal of Aesthetics,* 11 (1971).

MEYER, LEONARD B. *Music, the Arts, and Ideas.* Univ. of Chicago Press, 1967.

MORGAN, DOUGLAS N. "Must Art Tell the Truth?" *Journal of Aesthetics and Art Criticism,* 26 (fall 1967). Reprinted in Hospers.

PRICE, KINGLEY. "Is There Artistic Truth?" *Journal of Philosophy,* 46 (1949).

RALEIGH, HENRY P. "Art as Communicable Knowledge." *Journal of Aesthetic Education,* 5 (1971).

REID, LOUIS A. *Meaning in the Arts. London: Allen and Unwin, 1969.*

RICHARDS, IVOR A. *Science and Poetry.* London: Kegan Paul, 1926.

SANTAYANA, GEORGE. *Interpretations of Poetry and Religion.* New York: Scribners, 1960.

SESONSKE, ALEXANDER. "Truth in Art." *Journal of Philosophy,* 53 (1956).

SIRRIDGE, MARY. "Truth from Fiction?" *Philosophy and Phenomenological Research,* 35 (1975).

SPARSHOTT, FRANCISE. "Truth in Fiction." *Journal of Aesthetics and Art Criticism,* 26 (fall 1967).

WALSH, DOROTHY. "The Cognitive Content of Art." *Philosophical Review,* 52 (1943).

WEITZ, MORRIS. "Truth in Literature." *Revue Internationale de Philosophie,* 9 (1955). Reprinted in Hospers.

WOLLHEIM, RICHARD. *On Art and the Mind.* Cambridge: Harvard Univ. Press, 1974. Ch. 1, 13, 14.

YANAL, ROBERT J. "Denotation and the Aesthetic Appreciation of Literature." *Journal of Aesthetics and Art Criticism,* 36 (1978), pp. 471–478.

ZINK, SIDNEY. "Poetry and Truth." *Philosophical Review,* 54 (1945).

# 6

# Art and Morality

One of the most tragic passages in the biographies of artists occurs in Hector Berlioz's *Memoirs* when he tells his readers about a work of music that might have been created but was not:

> I dreamt that I was composing a symphony. On awaking next morning I recollected nearly the whole of the first movement, which I can still remember was an allegro in 2 time, in the key of A minor.
>
> I had gone to my table to begin writing it down when I suddenly reflected: "If I write this part I shall let myself be carried on to write the rest. The natural tendency of my mind to expand the material is sure to make it very long. I may perhaps spend three or four months exclusively upon it (I took seven to write *Romeo and Juliet*); meantime I shall do no feuilletons, or next to none, and my income will suffer. When the symphony is finished I shall be weak enough to allow my copyist to copy it out, and thus immediately incur a debt of one thousand or twelve hundred francs. Once the parts are copied I shall be harassed by the temptation to have the work performed; I shall give a concert, in which, as is sure to be the case in these days, the receipts will barely cover half the expenses; I shall lose what I have not got; I shall want the necessaries of life for my poor invalid [wife], and shall have no money either for myself or for my son's keep on board ship!" These thoughts made me shudder. I threw down my pen, saying, "Bah! I shall have forgotten the symphony tomorrow." But the following night the obstinate symphony again presented itself, and I distinctly heard the allegro in A minor, and, what was more, saw it written down. I awoke in a state of feverish agitation, and hummed the theme. The form and character of it pleased me extremely; I was about to rise . . . but the reflections of the preceding night

again restrained me. I hardened myself against temptation. I clung to the hope of forgetting. At last I fell asleep again, and when I awoke next day all recollection had vanished for ever.[1]

That art is, or should be, of great importance in the life of man will hardly be questioned by those who enroll for courses in the arts, not to mention courses in philosophy of the arts. Artists themselves have to contrive to keep body and soul together before they can create. But the importance they attach to artistic creation, often so great that they will willingly want for almost everything in order to continue it, is so great as to transcend almost everything else. Snipings from those who do not revere the arts as they do are likely to leave them angry, frustrated, and impatient. Criticisms of their work on moral grounds are no more likely to deter them. They will be inclined to place such great value on the creation of art that nothing else should stand in its way.

But can works of art, even great works of art, command such exclusive importance? According to the view called *aestheticism,* they should: whenever there is a conflict between artistic values and others (such as moral), it is the others that must give way.

> What is the good of life itself, except to be as fully alive as we can become—to burn with a hard gemlike flame, to choose one crowded hour of glorious life, to seize experience at its greatest magnitude? And this is precisely our experience of art; it is living in the best way we know how. Far from being a handmaiden to other goals, art gives us immediately, and richly, the best there is in life, intense awareness; it gives us what life itself aims at becoming, but seldom achieves outside of art. . . . If this is true, then the undesirable side effects of art cannot really matter. They are inconveniences we have to put up with for the sake of the best, but, no matter how regrettable, they can never outweigh . . . aesthetic value.[2]

> What care I that some millions of wretched Israelites died under Pharaoh's lash or Egypt's sun? It was well that they died that I might have the pyramids to look on, or to fill a musing hour with wonderment. Is there one among us who would exchange them for the lives of the ignominious slaves that died? What care I that the virtue of some sixteen-year-old maid was the price paid for Ingres's *La Source?* That the model died of drink and disease in the hospital is nothing when compared with the essential that I should have *La Source,* that exquisite dream of innocence.[3]

From such extremes of aestheticism most people will shrink in revulsion, only to retreat into its opposite, *moralism.* Moralism is the view that, whenever there is a conflict between art and morality, it is morality that comes first and art that should give way, that art may be tolerated as a kind of lux-

---

[1] Hector Berlioz, *Memoirs* (New York: Knopf, 1932), pp. 477–478.

[2] Monroe C. Beardsley, *Aesthetics* (New York: Harcourt Brace, 1958), p. 563.

[3] George Moore, *Confessions of a Young Man* (New York: Brentano's 1917), pp. 144–145.

ury, but that it is moral values that are of primary importance. Indeed, the moralist often holds that all art should be no more than a handmaiden to morality.

## 1. ART AS AN IMMORAL INFLUENCE

According to the moralistic view of art, the arts are at best a harmless interlude in the serious business of life and, at worst, a menace to morality and to society itself. Art gives people strange new ideas, those not accepted by the general public; it disturbs beliefs which most people would rather have left alone; it emphasizes individuality rather than conformity; it may even undermine beliefs on which, it is believed, the social fabric rests. Art is a kind of gadfly stinging at the body of established beliefs, often at precisely those places where custom and tradition do not wish to be disturbed. Art is always at work, breeding discontent, rebellion, nonconformity—and it seems to many people that art is always being directed against the established order, never in its favor. Because of all this, art is viewed with suspicion by the guardians of custom. When art does not affect people very much, it is considered a harmless pleasure, a means of escape, but always a luxury rather than a necessity—often as something not to be enjoyed but to be at best tolerated because some people seem to want it, but always skirting on the edge of becoming insidious and dangerous, gnawing at the established order, including people's most cherished beliefs and attitudes.

In classical Greece Plato was the most famous representative of this view of art, which is all the more remarkable because Plato was himself a great literary artist. In some of his dialogues, such as the *Ion, Symposium,* and *Phaedrus,* artists were extolled, and the view was developed that they were inspired with a kind of divine madness. But in his most renowned work, *The Republic,* Plato was concerned with the principles on which an ideal state should be established, and here his view on art became quite moralistic. The well-being of the entire society depends on the kind of rulers that are at the helm of the ship of state, and with the survival of the entire society at stake, nothing, not even art, must get in the way. Plato spends many pages describing in detail the training of these rulers-to-be. If their morality is to be pure, they must be removed from all influences which would tempt them away from the nobility of character which as rulers they must possess. They must not be permitted to witness dramas in which wickedness prospers—and since one never knows at the time of their childhood or adolescence who these rulers are going to be, such dramas should never be permitted to be performed. They must not be told stories of the gods in which the gods are criticized or described as ignoble or as committing immoral acts—even the incidents in Homer, who to the Greeks was almost what the Bible is to the Christian tradition, were to be excised. Plato even considered it dangerous for his rulers-to-be to listen to sensuous music; it would loosen the moral fiber of the impressionable youth and might cause him to swerve from the path of personal austerity which he must tread it he was to remain uncorrupted and incorruptible in his future office.

All these strictures may strike one as extremely dubious: granted that rulers of state should be incorruptible, one could plausibly contend that the only way to combat evil is to know something about it—if not in one's own life, then at least that it exists and how it works, in great detail. And if a person can't even withstand the effects of sensuous music, he must be a hot-house plant indeed, too weak a reed to take his place in the real world, and this might well *disqualify* him for public office. A person who knows nothing of the evils of the real world may be so naîve and unsuspecting that he will unintentionally be the first to fall into evil's trap.

At any rate, Plato imposed all these strictures on art, not because he was insensitive to art, but because he was convinced that the welfare of the entire society was more important than the delights of art, so that even the price of censorship of the arts was not too high a price to pay. The delights of art are sacrificed, reluctantly but firmly, not because Plato had no respect or love for art, but because he was convinced that the most important thing of all was the moral well-being of the entire society. Where the welfare of the society was involved, even so great a price as that of art was not too great a one to pay. For no lesser reason would so great a thing be sacrificed.

Tolstoy's condemnation of art was more sweeping. After he had written *War and Peace, Anna Karenina,* and almost all of his great fiction, he underwent a religious conversion which led him, in his book *What Is Art?* (1895), to condemn all art except that which, as he put it, "tends to deepen the religious perceptions of the people." Art which did not have a religious theme was still acceptable as long as it tended to unite mankind into one great Christian community. But art which concerned itself with the political squabbles of a particular time or place, or sexual conflicts and disturbances, or with the life of the upper classes and its triviality and boredom, all this Tolstoy condemned without further ado. Even more sweeping, all art which was not simple enough to be understood and enjoyed at once by all people, even the simplest peasant, was given the axe. Thus Shakespeare, Milton, Beethoven, Wagner, and countless others, almost the entire corpus of nineteenth-century literature including Tolstoy's own great novels, were all, at one stroke, thrown into the trash heap.

One cannot accuse Tolstoy of inconsistency or of shrinking from the task of applying his own principles. One can, however, question the principles that implied such a wholesale condemnation as this. But to do so here would require a detailed critique of that form of early and rather primitive Christianity which Tolstoy embraced at this period of his life; and that is far removed from our subject. Tolstoy, like Plato, condemned art for reasons of morality, being convinced that, when it comes to a conflict between them, it is art that must go. For Tolstoy, art is not merely the harmless pleasure of an idle moment—art (most art, at any rate) is a disturber and uprooter of the True Morality. Art, in order to be permitted at all, must be used completely and utterly in the service of morality, and only art which does this should be condoned, even though much art of aesthetic, rather than moral, merit would thereby be excluded.

Not all of us would go along with the special twists given the moralistic theory by Plato and Tolstoy, but many people, including perhaps the majority of Americans, tend to accept the general position of Moralism. They may not think that art and morality conflict as readily or as often as Plato and Tolstoy believed but they tend to believe that art is a servant of morality, and that in cases of conflict between art and morality it should always be morality that wins.

The moralistic theory is premised on the view that works of art can have great moral (especially immoral) effects, that as a direct *consequence* of reading, seeing, and listening to works of art people can be led to commit immoral acts, presumably acts which they would not have committed without having been exposed to those works of art. And this is a premise which is extremely difficult to establish. The fact that a person read a certain book or saw a certain film and then, some time later, committed some crime, does not prove that the person committed the crime *because* he had seen the film; it is possible that he might have committed it anyway. Does reading books and seeing plays and films and television programs really affect one's subsequent behavior in this way?

In his book *The Principles of Art,* R. G. Collingwood makes an interesting distinction between works of art whose influence spills over into our practical lives and works of art which do not. The first he calls *magic,* the second he calls *amusement.* The censors, and the "guardians of custom," tend to assume that all art is magic—that whatever we read about, or see on films or television, will influence our subsequent behavior: for example, if we see a robbery on television, we will be more apt to commit a similar robbery ourselves. But if it is only "amusement," then there will be no such influence: if we did have a tendency to commit robbery, such aggressive tendencies will be worked off through seeing the television show via *substitute gratification,* and the substitute gratification will make us *less* likely to do the real thing. If a movie shows a rape, if it is "magic" the observers will be more likely to commit rape themselves—they will tend to imitate what they have seen; but on the other hand, if the movie is taken as "amusement," then if they had an impulse to rape, the impulse will have been drawn off through the substitute gratification of seeing the film. Like Aristotle's account of catharsis, in which pity and fear are "siphoned off" by seeing a tragedy and so will no longer be around to bother us, the sexual or aggressive impulses will be drawn off through the experience of seeing the film: seeing it will act as a kind of safety valve for our "socially unacceptable" impulses.

What, then, are we to say of books, films, and other works of art (good or bad) that have come under fire from those who would ban them on moral grounds? Are they magic, in which case the indictment of them would be justified, or are they amusement, in which case they should be tolerated if not positively encouraged?

Since there are so many kinds of works of art, and so many different kinds of people who are consumers of them, there is probably no single clear answer to this question. But let us take a few examples:

1. For many years James Joyce's *Ulysses* was banned in the United States, until, in a famous 1924 court decision, Judge Wolsey permitted the book to be published in the United States, saying that in spite of certain passages the "dominant intent" was in no way immoral and that in view of its limited audience the book in any case would work no ill effects. For the same reason the unexpurgated edition of D. H. Lawrence's *Lady Chatterley's Lover* was prohibited in the United States, but is now admitted—in fact it seems quite tame today compared with thousands of books now available in American bookshops. There is no evidence that the admission of these two books caused any increased incidence of crime in America or that it caused any "moral pollution" in the population. Those not already uttering four-letter words or inclined toward adultery were hardly likely to change their inclinations as a result of reading them. It would be an unusually "protected" person who would encounter these things for the first time on reading the novels.

2. Consider the reading of murder mysteries and novels that deal with crime and crime detection. There are millions of avid readers of these novels, from Wilkie Collins and Sir Arthur Conan Doyle to the present, and for the most part they are law-abiding citizens, not inclined in the least to commit murder themselves. Reading such stories is like a chess game: it presents a challenge, "Can I figure out who the killer was?" as well as suspense, and something akin to emotional catharsis. There is no evidence that reading about murder makes them more inclined to commit murder.

3. What of the effects of X-rated films? The censors' view is that these are magic: that if people see sex acts occurring on the screen they will be led thereby to commit such acts themselves. One might ask, "What's so bad about that? Don't most of them engage in sex anyway?" but in the case of rape at least this would be an issue. But considering how deep seated are the causes of the various manifestations of sexual behavior, it would be unusual indeed (some would say impossible) for a person who had no previous attraction to rape to suddenly turn into a rapist from seeing an X-rated movie, or for a person with no previous homosexual tendencies to suddenly change his or her entire sexual orientation as a result of seeing a film in which homosexual acts are depicted. Most nonhomosexual persons are "turned off" by the

idea of homosexuality and would be equally turned off by seeing it depicted on the screen—indeed they would be extremely unlikely to go to see such a film in the first place.

For the vast majority of viewers, seeing sex on the screen is not magic but simply amusement. Instead of causing people to go and do these things, the films provide a *substitute gratification.* Instead of inciting crimes, they are more probably a kind of behavioral safety valve; the viewer has his substitute gratification in the theater rather than getting the real gratification in life outside the theater. He has fulfilled his desires in fantasy rather than in reality.

4. The same is probably true of most adults that watch violence on television—but there are occasionally cases in which children or particularly impressionable teenagers have committed some crime and point to a television program as their "inspiration" for having committed it. (a) But if one person out of a million commits a crime as a result of seeing a television program, is the entire remainder to be denied seeing the program because of that one person? (b) And what is the evidence that seeing the program *caused* that one person to commit the crime? He was probably prone in that direction already and only committed the crime *in this specific manner* because of the program. There is even some evidence the other way:

> Children are pretty sensible about TV. Even the youngest children in the study, the 4-year-olds, understood that cartoons and shows like *Bewitched* were just make-believe. They all knew, for example, that when the Roadrunner is flattened by a boulder it's not really happening. They accepted what they were watching for what it was—fantasy. But their reactions were entirely different when they considered a show to be real. In those cases, violence really sickened them and they didn't want to watch it.[4]

5. Still, one must admit that *some* films act on *some* people as magic rather than amusement.

> Who can say that Charles Manson, who saw himself as the child of the devil, was not influenced in his speculations by *Rosemary's Baby?* And isn't there even more evidence to support the speculation that David "Son of Sam" Berkowitz was influenced by *The Exorcist?* Did he come up with the notion that he was possessed by a 6,000-year-old demon all by himself, or was the seed of his madness planted and nurtured by possession pictures like *The Exorcist?* What else but the popularity of such films and the pervasiveness of the notion of possession could have convinced him against all reason that the mass of Americans would *understand* his plea of involuntary possession and therefore absolve him of having to account for his actions? All he ever wanted was to be exorcised, he would tell psychiatrists in prison.[5]

[4] *Channel One.* October 19, 1976, p. 15.
[5] Ron Rosenbaum, "Gooseflesh," *Harpers,* September 1979, p. 92.

We cannot hope here to decide every individual case, but several general comments are in order:

1. A work of art of any lasting value is a thing of considerable complexity, not likely to be appreciated by the vast majority of people at any one time or place. If what one wants is to engage in sexual fantasizing or to satisfy one's appetite for blood and gore, there are thousands of pulp novels on dime-store shelves that will satisfy such desires much more easily than the masterpieces of literature. Who has ever been turned into a lecher by reading Chaucer's *Canterbury Tales*? For this reason, when a charge of immorality is hurled at an acknowledged masterpiece, such as W. K. Wimsatt does against Skakespeare's *Antony and Cleopatra,* it seems almost beside the point:

> What is celebrated in *Antony and Cleopatra* is the passionate surrender of an illicit love, the victory of this love over practical, political, and moral concerns, and the final superiority of the suicide lovers over circumstances. . . . There is no escaping the fact that the poetic splendor of this play, and in particular of its concluding scenes, is something which exists in closest juncture with the acts of suicide and with the whole glorified story of passion. The poetic values are strictly dependent, if not upon the immorality as such, yet upon the immoral acts. Even though, or rather because, the play pleads for certain evil choices, it presents these choices in all their mature interest and capacity to arouse human sympathy.[6]

Assuming for the sake of argument that the play depicts immoral acts, even that it "celebrates" them, one still would hardly find it to be "magic": it vividly depicts Cleopatra's situation and feelings, but it is doubtful that a single reader of the play since its first production has been turned into a wanton slut by reading it. Indeed, as we shall see, the shoe may be on the other foot: the play may have positive moral value for some readers who have never imagined in detail the passions of anyone in Cleopatra's situation.

If there is a moral problem, it lies not with the masterpieces but with the trash. Trashy books, films, and television programs abound, and the effect of these on people who are addicted to them must be deleterious indeed. Their effect on the mind can be compared with the effect of junk foods on the body. For one thing, there is the enormous waste of one's time, taken from more constructive activities such as (in the case of adults) getting one's day's work done and (in the case of children) learning to read and write. For another, there is the oversimplified picture of life that emerges: that people are divided into two groups, the goodies and the baddies and that it takes only a few minutes to discover which is which; that things always turn out all right in the end (if you're one of the goodies), rather quickly, it is hoped, like at the end of an hour television segment; that people who engage in constructive but unimaginative labor, such as keeps a nation's economy going, are stupid or

[6] W. K. Wimsatt, "Poetry and Morality," in *Thought,* pp. 281–299; reprinted in Eliseo Vivas and Murray Krieger, eds., *The Problems of Aesthetics* (New York: Rinehart, 1953), pp. 541–542.

uninteresting and that, to be worthy, one's life must be an unending melodrama, with emotionally charged scenes being a desirable par for the course in human relations.

To counteract these effects, some training in the creation, performance, appreciation, or history of one of the arts could well be a helpful corrective. Such activity in one or more of the arts imposes upon the person who engages in it at least one cardinal virtue, the very high degree of self-discipline required to be even a competent pianist or sculptor, a self-discipline that can then stand one in good stead in other areas of life. Some creative artists, such as Richard Wagner, may have been unscrupulous in their dealings with others in their private lives, but the high degree of concentration and self-discipline required to create the works they did may well outweigh all these personal character defects: those to whom Wagner broke promises are gone and virtually forgotten, but the music he created remains for posterity and undiminished source of appreciation. Even to be in occasional contact with such works must rate as a moral plus: the father who said, "Study the violin, my son, it will be good for your morality," was not giving pointless advice, both because of the self-discipline required to pursue such a difficult art and because of the "heightened tone" that is lent to the student's life from spending a portion of his life in the company of masterworks in a long artistic tradition.

2. Books and films that may incite one person to crime may be simply idle amusement for a million others. A work which strikes one person as immoral may seem quite moral to another and a crashing bore to a third. In view of this enormous diversity of personalities and of interests, an acute problem arises about censorship. When the government of a nation, state, or city bans a film or a play, it may possibly be removing a source of moral pitfall to some, but by the same act it withholds from many other persons something that may be for them a source of profit or wisdom or amusement. Is everyone to be prevented from seeing something they desire to see because others might in some way be "led astray" by it?

It is one thing to believe that the moral influence of a certain work is undesirable on some persons and even to advise or remonstrate against their being exposed to it; to *forcibly prevent* (as a censor does) their being able to see it for themselves is to play God with their lives. Except perhaps in the case of children, shouldn't they be free to make up their own minds whether to see it or not? How can a person develop in character and judgment, as well as morality, if he is not permitted to make his own decisions, for the better or for worse, but must have them made *by others* while yet they affect his life? If a film is banned before I get to see it, I do not know from personal experience what it is that I am not permitted to see; I only know that a group of other people has by their action prevented me from making the choice myself—and I do not even know whether their choice was a good one. I am supposed passively to take their word for it that what they say would not be good for me would really not be good for me. The assumption is that I am too weak or too unstable to make the decision for myself. It is assumed that the censor is better able to make the decision *for me* than I am; and how do either the censor or I know that this assumption is justified? When censorship occurs, one body of human beings is sitting in judgment upon another body of human beings, telling them what they may and may not read or see. What assurance is there that they are worthy to do this? And even if they are, is not every such act of censorship an invasion of my own freedom to act in accordance with my own choices? Speaking of morality, that may well be the most immoral act of all.

## 2.  ART  AS  A  MORAL  INFLUENCE

If censors construe art to be magic, in Collingwood's terminology, they might have a better case if they held that art, at least those works that have withstood the test of time, have positive (desirable) moral effects rather than negative (undesirable) ones. Censors and other guardians of the *status quo* are interested only in the effects they consider undesirable. If they looked instead for desirable effects on a person's life or character, they might well find an array of possibilities which are more promising than the negative ones that they emphasize.

The English poet Percy Shelley wrote, in his classic essay *A Defense of Poetry* (1821), that the positive moral effect of art (at least of literature—he did not speak of the other arts) is enormous and is so important that art is itself indispensable for sustaining any morality worthy of the name:

> The exertions of Locke, Hume, Gibbon, Voltaire, Rousseau, and their disciples, in favor of oppressed and deluded humanity, are entitled to the gratitude of mankind. Yet it is easy to calculate the degree of moral and intellectual improvement which the world would have exhibited, had they never lived. A little more nonsense would have been talked for a century or two; and perhaps a few more men, women, and children, burnt as heretics. We might not at this moment have been congratulating each other on the abolition of the Inquisition in Spain. But it exceeds all imagination to conceive what would have been the moral condition of the world if neither Dante, Petrarch, Boccaccio, Chaucer, Shakespeare, Calderon, Lord Bacon, nor Milton, had ever existed; if Raphael and Michel Angelo had never been born; if the Hebrew poetry had never been translated; if a revival of the study of Greek literature had never taken place; if no monuments of ancient sculpture had been handed down to us; and if the poetry of the religion of the ancient world had been extinguished together with its belief.[7]

1. *Didactic art.* Sometimes a work of art is related to morality in a very obvious way: it presents us with a philosophical system, of which a system of morality is a part. And it endeavors to defend such a system against its at-

[7] Percy Bysshe Shelley, *A Defense of Poetry.* 1821. (Many additions.)

tackers. Art which defends one view against others is called *didactic* art. There are many works of literature which defend one side of an issue, and many more which adopt one side without defending it; yet they are not found deficient as literature on this account. What *is* considered to be a defect in literature is not didacticism but *propaganda*. The difference is one of degree, yet it can be very great. In propaganda, as in a political or religious tract, one feels that "the dice are loaded"—if something is said on one side of a question and something else can be said on the other side, the latter is ignored, distorted, or oversimplified to give the author's views an unfair advantage. When this occurs, the reader comes to doubt the integrity of the author: it is as if the author had placed "emotional blinders" on himself, to keep him from seeing the other side of the issue. When the work is fictional, the story line is "rigged" so that events always turn out in such a way as to underwrite the author's ideas, and the characters, if they are not empty stereotypes to begin with, are made to perform actions which are out of character so as to fall into line with the author's pet thesis. The majority of stories and novels written in the Soviet Union, churned out by hacks to remain in the employ of the Soviet government, fall into this category: boy meets girl; boy is separated from girl because they are needed in places geographically distant from each other; but after many vicissitudes and much heroism, boy is reunited with girl; and as a reward to both they are each given a medal and membership in the Komsomol (Communist Youth Organization).

Didactic works may succeed as literature; but there is always the danger that didacticism will degenerate into propaganda. Many of George Bernard Shaw's plays, in which the characters are chiefly mouthpieces for ideas, have been accused of this and are only rescued from it (if at all) by the breadth of the author's vision, which is inclusive enough to include other points of view (though often as foils) presented with vigor and imagination. Shelley offers the following counsel:

> A poet therefore would do ill to embody his own conceptions of right and wrong, which are usually those of his place and time, in his poetical creations, which participate in neither. By this assumption of the inferior office of interpreting the effect, in which perhaps after all he might acquit himself but imperfectly, he would resign a glory in a participate in the cause. There was little danger that Homer, or any of the eternal poets, should have so far misunderstood themselves as to have abdicated this throne of their wildest dominion. Those in whom the poetical faculty, though great, is less intense, as Euripides, Lucan, Tasso, Spenser, have frequently affected a moral aim, and the effect of their poetry is diminished in exact proportion to the degree in which they compel us to advert to this purpose.[8]

Yet, it is possible for a literary masterpiece to be didactic. Lucretius' *De Rerum Natura* is a long series of arguments in favor of Democritean materialism and the ethical system which is a part of it. But the lines glow with

---
[8] *Ibid.*

passion, the poetry rises to incandescence, and we are carried away by it, whether or not we agree with the idée fixé which dominates it. As Lascelles Abercrombie remarked in his book *A Theory of Poetry,* even the attempt to prove the forty-seventh proposition of Euclid's geometry could become great poetry, if the poem led us to experience the creative ecstasy of discovering the truth of that proposition. One might say that Dante's *Divine Comedy* is a tract for a Roman Catholic world-view; but Dante does not so much argue for the view as to steep us in it through his characters and his poetic imagery. Most readers treasure the poetry whether or not they accept the message.

> The Franciscan faith is present in Giotto, who expresses while he dominates it. As an atheist, I shall seek in it not reasons for believing, but the flavor of a particular state of mind. And so, for the space of a second, I, the unbeliever, must become like the man whose faith persuaded the beasts of the field, yet without ceasing to be the stranger who looks on, as Giotto doubtless never ceased, in the presence of the saint he loved, to be the stranger who looks on and paints.[9]

2. *Fictional situations as vehicles for moral reflection.* Most works of art are not didactic. If they teach us, it is not by explicit preachment. "Art teaches as friends and life teach—by *being,* not by express intent."[10] But how do they "teach simply by being"? By presenting us characters in situation of conflict and crisis, the work becomes for us a *vehicle for moral reflection.* Whether it is the characters in George Eliot's *Middlemarch,* or Dostoyevsky's *The Brothers Karamazov,* or Tolstoy's *Anna Karenina,* or in any of Shakespeare's tragedies and historical plays, we see a variety of vividly drawn characters in action, in which they must make life-or-death decisions, for themselves and for those around them. We are made to see the full consequences of these decisions on the protagonists themselves. We are not spared any of the cause-and-effect relations, as we often are in life, when reality interrupts the chain of events with irrelevancies which blunt or obscure the effects of human action. In life, Macbeth could plausibly have slipped on a wet board and have broken his neck; but in Shakespeare's drama, the final effect of his and Lady Macbeth's power-lust is forcibly brought home to us. The work of literature does not itself preach any moral, but it provides enormous stimulus for moral reflection by us, in the reading of it.

3. *Imaginative identification with characters.* It can do this, of course, only if the characterization is vivid and "true" enough to enable us to *imaginatively identify* ourselves with the characters. We may not approve of Anna Karenina's actions, but we can put ourselves into her frame of reference and understand why she did what she did; and we see it, so to speak, "from the inside," from knowing her thoughts and feelings at every turn, as only a literary artist can present it. To be able in imagination to put ourselves in the place of another person, to see his situation as he sees it ("what would *I* have

---

[9] Charles Mauron, *Aesthetics and Psychology* (London: The Hogarth Press, 1935), pp. 66–67.

[10] John Dewey, *Art as Experience* (New York: Minton, Balch & Co., 1934), pp. 346–347.

done in this situation and why?''), is a major moral achievement, and literature provides it better, probably, than anything else in the world. By doing this, the reader learns (though this was usually not his purpose in reading) an important moral lesson, that of *tolerance* for persons unlike himself. He has now seen their situations and problems in the most intimate possible way, which cannot easily be shrugged off or forgotten.

Most persons are inclined to think of other persons, especially those unfamiliar to them or removed from them in time or space, in stereotypes, as foreigners, wastrels, Russians, blacks, peasants, countesses, bankers, espionage agents, and so on. After reading many works of great literature this "thinking in stereotypes" is progressively dissolved: we now see each person as an individual and judge him or her as an individual, not simply as a member of a class. In this way the hasty judgments, and the injustices that result from thinking of other people in stereotypes rather than in terms of their individualizing features, tend to disappear through the reading of literature. Surely this also must be counted as a major moral achievement.

4. *The moral potency of the imagination.* Literature has moral effects, and in turn impregnates morality with fresh ideas, by acting on what Shelley calls "the greatest instrument of moral good," the *imagination.* Art (and not merely literature, of which Shelley was speaking) has a *leavening* influence on morality. It loosens us from the bonds of our local position in space and time; it releases us from exclusive involvement with our struggles from day to day; it enables us to see our own problems, in Spinoza's phrase, *sub specie aeternitatis* (under the aspect of eternity); we can even view ourselves as if from far off, or from an enormous height. It does this through the continuous exercise of our imaginative faculties. On this point Shelley spoke eloquently:

> The whole objection . . . of the immorality of poetry rests upon a misconception of the manner in which poetry acts to produce the moral improvement of man. Ethical science arranges the elements which poetry has created, and propounds schemes and proposes examples of civil and domestic life: nor is it for want of admirable doctrines that men hate, and despise, and censure, and deceive, and subjugate one another. But poetry acts in another and diviner manner. It awakens and enlarges the mind itself by rendering it the receptacle of a thousand unapprehended combinations of thought. . . . A man, to be greatly good, must imagine intensely and comprehensively: he must put himself in the place of another and of many others; the pains and pleasures of his species must become his own. *The great instrument of moral good is the imagination; and poetry administers to the effect by acting upon the cause.* Poetry enlarges the circumference of the imagination by replenishing it with thoughts of ever new delight, which have the power of attracting and assimilating to their own nature all other thoughts, and which form new intervals and interstices whose void for ever craves fresh food. *Poetry strengthens the faculty which is the organ of the moral nature of man, in the same manner as exercise strengthens a limb.*
> The drama at Athens, or wheresoever else it may have approached to its perfection, ever co-existed with the moral and intellectual greatness of the age. . . The imagination is enlarged by a sympathy with pains and passions so mighty, that they distend in their conception the capacity of that by which they

are conceived. . . [The drama] is as a prismatic and many-sided mirror, which collects the brightest rays of human nature and divides and reproduces them from the simplicity of these elementary forms, and touches them with majesty and beauty, and multiplies all that it reflects, and endows it with the power of propagating its like wherever it may fall.[11]

If at first this seems to be an overstatement, let us consider what a morality is usually like when those who pledge allegiance to it do so *without* the exercise of the imagination, which works of art more than anything else can provide. Consider the average morality of a small community, relatively isolated from centers of culture and unexposed to any artistic tradition. Their morality tends to be rigid and circumscribed, intolerant of opposition, blind to anything but obedience to a set of exceptionless rules. People who deviate from the community's norms, especially those of a different race or religion or culture, are looked upon with suspicion as outsiders, and often condemned or ostracized. Their morality is cramped and arid, in large measure because they have not know the leavening influence of art, which more than anything else could enrich their moral reflections. Art can do this even more than travel; many people can tour the world several times over and come back with the same stereotypes and the same prejudices with which they left their own living rooms. But one cannot be a frequent and reflective reader of the world's literature and yet remain indifferent to, or intolerant of, the situations, problems, and moral dilemmas of persons in situations other than one's own. Even the study of philosophy is not as potent a moral force as is art: for philosophy typically reveals to us what various people *thought,* while art shows us (among other things) how they *felt,* what their fundamental drives and attitudes were, how they "came at" the world, and how they responded to it. To reveal to us how the ancient Greeks felt about man and the universe, Greek art is for most people a more powerful force even than Greek philosophy; and the perception of it can "heighten the tone" of one's life.

What is it about other times and other places that we most remember today? It is not their political turmoils, their wars, their economic upheavals—these are known in detail only to historians, but even then they do not usually make the *dent* on our personal lives that art does. What is alive today about ancient Egypt is its sculpture and its pyramids; what is alive today about the Elizabethan period, even more than the defeat of the Spanish Armada and the reign of Queen Elizabeth, is its poetic drama, with its vivid characterizations and boundless energy. Other civilizations and other cultures may be sources of facts and theories which may fill our heads; but what makes us feel "at one with them" is not their politics, not even their religion, but their art. The advance of science is cumulative, and the science textbooks of even ten years ago are now out of date; we study of the science of the Greeks and the Elizabethans only as historical curiosities. But their art is not dated; it

[11] Shelley, *op. cit.* Emphasis added.

can still present to us its full impact, undiminished by time. Shakespeare will never be out of date as long as human beings continue to feel love, jealousy, and conflict. The artists whose works we now revere may have died unsung, and most of them even if appreciated in their lifetime, were considered far less important than the latest naval victories or the accession of the current king; and yet today these things have all passed into history, but their art survives and continues to be a force in our lives. The art of the past molds in countless ways the attitudes, responses, dispositions of our daily lives, including our moral ones. We could paraphrase a Biblical statement and say, of nations and civilizations, "By their arts shall ye know them." And from their arts much of what is worth preserving in our own moral outlook draws its inspiration and sustenance.

What shall we say, then, of the moralistic theory of art? Art is no more the handmaiden of morality than morality is a handmaiden of art. If it is true that some works of art are sometimes best withheld from some people (such as children), it is equally true that morality becomes poverty stricken without the leavening influence of art; by its unique ability to work on the imagination and stimulate our powers of reflection, art is itself a tremendously potent moral influence. The relation between art and morality is a two-way one: if we want a name for this view, to contrast it with aestheticism and moralism, we can call it *interactionism*.

## EXERCISES

1. Take one of the following classic works of literature and examine it for its (implicit or explicit) study of art and morality. Are the moral problems brought out more clearly in the work of literature than they would have been in an essay? Explain.

      a. Schiller, *Maria Stuart*

      b. Tolstoy, *Anna Karenina*

      c. Dostoyevsky, *Crime and Punishment*

      d. Dostoyevsky, *The Possessed* (*The Devils*)

      e. Dostoyevsky, *The Brothers Karamazov*

      f. Fielding, *Joseph Andrews*

      g. Sophocles, *Antigone*

      h. Goethe, *Faust*

      i. George Eliot, *Middlemarch*

      j. Flaubert, *Madame Bovary*

      k. Theodore Dreiser, *Sister Carrie*

      l. Nathaniel Hawthorne, *The Scarlet Letter*

2. A man who had escaped from Auschwitz said of Rolf Hochmuth's play *The Deputy*, "*The Deputy* should not be considered as a historical work or even as a work of art, but as a moral lesson." (The *New York Times*, May 4, 1966.) Since something can be a work of art and also give a moral lesson, how do you construe such a statement?

3. Why didn't Tolstoy want literature with lots of sex in it? If there's anything that all people have in common and that would tend to unite them because they understand it, it would seem to be sexual urges and sexual conflicts. How do you suppose Tolstoy might have responded to this?

4. It is often said that an author should not preach to us directly: he can convey his message through the words and actions of his characters, but never in his own name, as author. Should the following passages be condemned for violating this rule, or should the rule itself be condemned?

   a. In *Tom Jones*, Henry Fielding is describing the behavior of the village spinster, Bridget Allworthy, who "very rightly conceived the charms of a person in a woman to be no better than snares for her as well as for others; and yet so discreet was she in her conduct, that her prudence was as much on the guard as if she had all the snares to apprehend which were ever laid for her whole sex. Indeed, I have observed, though it may seem unaccountable to the reader, that this guard of prudence, like the Trained Bands, is always readiest to go on duty where there is the least danger. It often basely and cowardly deserts those paragons for whom the men are all wishing, sighing, dying, and spreading every net in their power; and constantly attends at the heels of that higher order of women for whom the other sex have a more distant and awful respect, and whom (from despair, I suppose, of success) they never venture to attack." (Henry Fielding, *Tom Jones*, Modern Library ed., pp. 4–5.)

   b. After depicting numerous situations in which indiscretion goes unpunished, Fielding remarks, "There are a set of religious, or rather moral writers, who teach that virtue is the certain road to happiness, and vice to misery, in this world. A very wholesome and comfortable doctrine, and to which we have but one objection, namely, that it is not true." (p. 672)

   c. Having described the behavior of the philosopher Square, Fielding remarks, "Philosophers are composed of flesh and blood as well as other human creatures; and however sublimated and refined the theory of these may be, a little practical frailty is as incident to them as to other mortals. It is, indeed in theory only, and not in practice, as we have before hinted, that consists the difference: for though such great beings think much better and more wisely, they always act exactly like other men. They know very well how to subdue all appetites and passions, and to despise both pain and pleasure; and this knowledge affords much delightful contemplation, and is easily acquired; but the practice would be vexatious and troublesome; and, therefore, the same wisdom which teaches them to know this, teaches them to avoid carrying it into execution." (p. 173)

   d. Best of all are Fielding's remarks on *deus ex machina* and tragic denouement in relation to actual human life, pp. 758–759.

5. Consider the following theories of tragedy and evaluate each. (Quotations in a–d are from DeWitt Parker, *The Principles of Aesthetics*, pp. 110–113.)

   a. "It is often assumed that a tragedy should represent the good as ultimately triumphing, despite suffering and failure. But how can the good triumph when the hero fails and dies? Only, it is answered, if the hero represents a cause which may win despite or even because of his individual doom; and it is with this cause, and not with him, that we chiefly sympathize. This was Hegel's view, who demanded that the tragic hero represent some universal interest which, when purged of the one-sidedness and uncompromising insistence of the hero's championing, may nevertheless endure and triumph in its genuine worth.''

b. The Protestant theological theory of tragedy, "by assuming that there is no genuine loss in the world, that every evil is compensated for in the future lives of the heroes,. . . takes away the sting from their sacrifice and so deprives them of their crown of glory. It makes every adventure a calculation of prudence and every despair a farce. It is remote from the reality of experience where men stake all on a chance and, instead of receiving the good by an act of grace, wring it by blood and tears from evil.''

c. On the retributive "tragic flaw" theory, "the moralistic theory which requires that the misfortunes of the hero should be the penalty for some fault or weakness. This view, which has the authority of Aristotle, is also based on the doctrine of the justice of the world-order. . . . It must be admitted . . . that this idea, so deeply rooted in the popular mind, has exerted a profound influence on the drama; yet it cannot be applied universally without sophistry. To be sure, in *Romeo and Juliet,* the young people were disobedient and headstrong; in *Lear,* the old father was foolishly trustful of his wicked daughters; these frailties brought about their ruin. But did they deserve so hard a fate as theirs? Did not Lear suffer as much for his folly as his daughters for their wickedness? This is always true in life, and Shakespeare holds the mirror up to nature—but is it consistent with the theory of retributive justice?''

d. All such theories, says Parker, take the tragedy out of tragedy: They justify the tragic outcome, making it no longer tragic. In tragedy, on the contrary, the "cosmic disharmony" remains. "It ceases to be chargeable to an external fate or God, to the environment or convention, which might perhaps be mastered and remolded; and is seen pervading the nature of reality itself, no accidental circumstance, but essential evil, ineradicable. The greatest tragic poets see it thus. And then blame turns to understanding and resentment into pity.''

e. According to A. C. Bradley, the central feeling of tragedy is the impression of *waste.* "The pity and fear which are stirred by the tragic story seem to unite with, and even to merge in, a profound sense of sadness and mystery, which is due to this impression of waste. 'What a piece of work is man,' we cry; 'so much more beautiful and so much more terrible than we knew! Why should he be so if this beauty and greatness only tortures itself and throws itself away?' We seem to have before us a type of the mystery of the whole world, the tragic fact which extends far beyond the limits of tragedy. Everywhere, from the crushed rocks beneath our feet to the soul of man, we see power, intelligence, life and glory, which astound us and seem to call for our worship. And everywhere we see them perishing, devouring one another and destroying themselves, often with dreadful pain, as though they came into being for no other end. Tragedy is the typical form of this mystery, because that greatness of soul which it exhibits oppressed, conflicting and destroyed, is the highest existence in our view. It forces the mystery upon us, and it makes us realize so vividly the worth of that which is wasted that we cannot possibly seek comfort in the reflection that all is vanity.'' (A. C. Bradley, *Shakespearean Tragedy,* p. 23. See also Prosser H. Frye, ''The Idea of Greek Tragedy,'' in his *Romance and Tragedy,* reprinted in *American Criticism,* ed. Norman Foerster.)

# SELECTED READINGS

ALEXANDER, SAMUEL. *Beauty and Other Forms of Value.* London: Macmillan, 1933. Part 2.

BEARDSLEY, MONROE C. *Aesthetics.* New York: Harcourt Brace, 1958. Chapter 12.

DANIELS, C. "Tolstoy and Corrupt Art." *Journal of Aesthetic Education,* 33 (1975).

DEWEY, JOHN. *Art as Experience.* New York: Minton Balch & Co., 1934. Chapter 14.

FRANK, JEROME. "Obscenity and the Law." In Marvin Levich (ed.), *Aesthetics and the Philosophy of Criticism.* New York: Random House, 1962.

GROSSMAN, MORRIS. "Art and Morality." *Journal of Aesthetics and Art Criticism,* 31 (1973).

HOSPERS, JOHN. "Art and Morality." *Journal of Comparative Aesthetics,* 1, 1978.

HYMAN, LAWRENCE W. "Literature and Morality in Contemporary Criticism." *Journal of Aesthetics and Art Criticism,* 29 (1971).

KAPLAN, ABRAHAM. "Obscenity as an Aesthetic Category." In Sidney Hook, ed., *American Philosophers at Work.* New York: New York Univ. Press, 1956

KRISTOL, IRVING. "Pornography, Obscenity, and the Case for Censorship." *New York Times Magazine,* March 28, 1971.

KUHNS, RICHARD. *Structures of Experience.* New York: Harper, 1970. Chapter 4.

MORAWSKI, STEFAN. "Art and Obscenity," in *Inquiries into the Fundamentals of Aesthetics.* Cambridge: M.I.T. Press, 1974.

MURDOCH, IRIS. *The Fire and the Sun: Why Plato Banished the Artists.* New York: Oxford Univ. Press, 1977.

PLATO, *Republic.* Many editions.

POLE, DAVID. "Morality and the Assessment of Literature." *Philosophy,* 30 (1955).

PORTNOY, JULIUS. *Music in the Life of Man.* New York: Holt, Rinehart, & Winston, 1963.

SANTAYANA, GEORGE. *Three Philosophical Poets: Lucretius, Dante, Goethe.* New York: Scribners, 1910.

SHELLEY, PERCY B. *A Defense of Poetry.* 1821.

TOLSTOY, LEO. *What is Art?* Translation by Aylmer Maude. Oxford Univ. Press, 1928. (1895.)

WIMSATT, W.K. "Poetry and Morals: A Relation Reargued." *Thought,* XXIII (1948), 281–299.

ZINK, SIDNEY. "The Moral Effect of Art." *Ethics,* LX (1950), 261–274.

# 7

# Artistic Criticism

When you read a critical review of a poem, play, novel, or symphony, you will find many different kinds of comments. Not all of them deal directly with the work of art; yet in one way or another they are all assumed to have some relation to it, else there would be no excuse for mentioning them in a review of the work. Here, for example, is a review of the acclaimed Japanese film, *Dersu Uzala, the Hunter:*[1]

South of the frozen tundra of the Siberian Arctic, there lies a huge belt of land, larger than the entire United States, called the taiga—endless forests of birch and larch, swamps and lakes and clear rushing rivers, and bands of native tribesmen who make their living from hunting and fishing and who even today have not been Sovietized. To my knowledge this vast expanse has never been photographed in detail for the Western world to see. One can read about it in George St. George's book *Siberia* and Farley Mowat's *The Siberians*, but almost all of it is out of bounds to foreigners. It is therefore a matter of considerable interest to have a two-and-a-half-hour motion picture filmed entirely in this seemingly endless land of wild and primitive beauty. One has to go back to *Lawrence of Arabia* to find such breath-taking natural splendor on film.

If this were all, we would have an interesting documentary of the *National Geographic* type. But *Dersu Uzala* is much more than this. It is a story, set in 1902–5, whose plot-line is simple but whose every moment pulses with drama and elemental power. The film opens as a party of Czarist soldiers on a surveying mis-

[1] From the monthly column of film reviews by John Hospers in *Reason*, 10, no. 1 (May 1978), p. 65.

sion in this uncharted land encounter in the wilderness an old Ussuri tribesman who has spent his life hunting and trapping in the area bounded by Khabarovsk on the south and the Arctic Circle on the north. The story is about their subsequent adventures and the interactions between the men of the Czar's military forces and the ethos of the native tribesman, Uzala.

Now add to these two a third ingredient, the genius of the Japanese filmmaker Akiro Kurosawa, whom many believe to be the world's greatest living film director (*Rashomon, The Seven Samurai, The Lower Depths, Throne of Blood, The Hidden Fortress,* etc.). Perhaps no one but Kurosawa could have presented so tellingly, against this rich natural background, such a quietly moving and powerful story of the encounter of the native with civilization. One by one the character-traits of the hunter unfold, so that by the time the film is ended we have had laid before us one of the finest characterizations in modern times. Kurosawa adapted the film from the memoirs of the Russian army captain who encountered Uzala in the Ussuri taiga in 1902. But the film is no mere documentary—Kurosawa has leavened the material of history and transformed it into a thing of artistic incandescence.

There have been complaints that the film "drags." To those who are accustomed to rapid-fire action as a requirement for all film fare, with at least one character raped or shot every two minutes on schedule, this may be the case. But Kurosawa, who has no truck with such conventions, proceeds at his own pace, enabling us to savor the wild beauty of the landscape and the slowly evolving interaction among the characters, through incidents both comic and heroic, until a drama of great power and beauty is born. There are segments of the film in which little external action occurs, yet only a Kurosawa could keep it alive and building through every moment, filled with high drama even when there is only a smile or a sunset. Only in a rare film such as this would missing a minute of it be a jarring interruption of an exquisitely rendered flow of continuous ongoing life.

The adjectives one is left with in retrospect are: sublime, universal, magnificent, dignified, noble, well-rounded, stately, controlled, perfectly etched. One is left also with a deep impression of the central character, the illiterate hunter with more civilization than the civilized, a humble figure of heroic proportions. Perhaps most of all, one is left with images of abiding beauty: the endless taiga seen from a hilltop in summer, the primeval power of the Ussuri River as one tries to cross it, the sun setting on a frozen ice-cap as a storm begins to rage—and countless other visually compelling images from this vast realm of unconquered nature. And when Uzala is himself finally conquered, not by nature but by the treachery of man, the only words that the grief-stricken captain can pronounce on his grave are the words of his name.

Many of the remarks in this bit of film criticism do not deal directly with the film itself. This is typical of criticism throughout the arts: we are told about the director and his other films; sometimes about his intentions with regard to the project; sometimes a comparison and contrast with other films, especially of the same kind. In the present case, some remarks deal with the topography of Siberia. One could question whether remarks of this kind are necessary for appreciating the films: surely one could go into the theater ignorant of such facts and still appreciate the film. Still, one could contend that (1) many of these things, not presented in the film itself, provide a "background of appreciation" which makes the appreciation richer than it would otherwise have been; that (2) some of them may, in fact, be necessary conditions for appreciation—knowledge of some things is just presupposed when one sees the film, and facts that Asiatic viewers are acquainted with may not be known to American viewers, just as many important facts about Napoleon's campaign of 1812 are not delineated in Tolstoy's *War and Peace* because Tolstoy assumed that his readers were already acquainted with them—and that (3) there are many things that are simply "interesting to know," whether or not they illuminate the work of art which is being discussed.

But assuming that the critic is discussing the work of art itself, what sorts of things does he do?

## 1. CRITICISM: DESCRIPTIVE AND INTERPRETATIVE

One may appreciate a work of art in total silence; but if one embarks on criticism, one must say something. "Criticism"does not mean here what it does in the popular sense, of making nasty remarks about whatever or whomever it is you are talking. Criticism in the arts is the enterprise of *describing, interpreting,* and *evaluating* works of art. Sometimes it is not a single work of art that the critic discusses but an entire group of them, for example, all the works by a certain artist, or works in a certain style, or works in a certain historical period.

As a rule, art criticism is simply a means to an end: the end is increased understanding or appreciation of the work of art (or style, period, etc.), and the means employed is the written work of criticism. Criticism is occasionally read, as works of art usually are, because it is enjoyable or entertaining or challenging; but usually its main function is to cast some light upon the work of art which the critic is discussing—to make the work intelligible to us, to illuminate it for us, to help us to see things in it we failed to see before, or to put the things we did see into a new pattern or perspective.

If we don't understand some of the things going on in *Hamlet,* we may read Goethe or Coleridge on the subject, or A. C. Bradley's *Shakespearean Tragedy,* or G. Wilson Knight's *The Wheel of Fire,* or any of a number of other books and essays which address themselves to "the interpretation of *Hamlet,*" and then, if the works of criticism have been successful with us, we should see many qualities and relations in the play that we had not seen before. Perhaps we could have got them from repeated readings, but criticism provides a kind of shortcut to appreciation: we can see quickly many things in a work of art that we were too dull, or our attention too fleeting or superficial, to discern on our own.

Some works, such as the novels of Walter Scott or Robert Louis Stevenson, don't usually require critical reading: the narrative is fairly simple and straightforward, there are no hidden meanings or obscure symbolism, and whatever apparatus we need to understand or appreciate these works we can easily provide ourselves as we read. (But let's not be too confident: even here, works of criticism can be extremely illuminating, particularly if we don't know the periods.) When, however, a work of art is difficult or obscure and "doesn't bear its meaning on its face," then criticism is most helpful. However much we may think we understand some of T. S. Eliot's poems, we are likely to profit by a work such as F. O. Matthiesen's *The Achievement of T. S. Eliot.*

Some works of criticism are purely *descriptive*. Some describe aspects of the historical background which may be necessary or helpful for appreciating the work of art; we have to know something about life in medieval England to appreciate Chaucer's *Canterbury Tales*, and we would lose a great deal of it if we came to it "cold." Some works of criticism emphasize the cultural background, the tenor of the times, the technical innovations in architecture or musical instruments which help us to understand why certain buildings were constructed as they were or why the instrumentation was as it was. Other works of criticism describe the work of art itself: if there are obscure passages, or references with which we are probably not familiar, the critic *explicates* their meanings—this has to be done constantly if we are reading Chaucer in middle English. Meanings which are obscure or unintelligible are "unpacked" by the critic. When a painting contains symbolism, the historical critic explains what the various represented objects symbolized at the time. When a passage explains some possible meaning, such as Hamlet's opening line "Not so, my lord; I am too much in the sun" (which could also be read "son"), the critic sets this forth and explores it.

But already this last example seems to take us from pure description into *interpretation:* one critic may point to a possible double meaning and another will deny it, and now it is "a matter of interpretation." The line between describing and interpreting is not a very sharp one. Clear cases of description occur when one says that a composition is in the key of F major, in 4:4 time, and contains four movements. This is something that anyone with eyes, ears, and reasonable intelligence can verify for himself if he wants to. But there are many things said of a work of art which go far beyond this: an interpretation may be made "plausible" or "reasonable" on the basis of evidence cited by the critic, but it is still interpretation rather than description.

How difficult it is to draw the line is best seen if we consider what is sometimes called *elucidation*. Elucidation "tells us what's going on in a work of art"; if a reader doesn't know why Dr. B agreed to take on Czentovic in a chess match, he may cite passages to provide the motivation. But the reader may doubt whether Dr. B's statement of his own motive isn't the real motive and may even find passages in the text which he says bear out his claim. What one usually does in this situation is to make a *causal inference:* the author doesn't tell you that A did B because of C, but since people in the real world often do B because of C (e.g., engage in acts of revenge out of jealousy), we (reader or critic) infer that A did so also. In this the critic may claim to "lay bare" what is really implicit in the work of art—"it's really there," and the critic is just describing to us what is going on in the work, or what one must conclude is going on to make sense of the work.

But now problems begin to arise. Since the author nowhere *says* that A did B from motive C, the critic *infers* it (he doesn't find it in the text itself); a different critic might infer something else, so don't we have already a difference in interpretation? Consider again the case of Henry James's *The Turn of the Screw*. Are the apparitions real, and really seen by the governess, or do they occur in her mind? Are the children innocent victims of the governess's projections (due to deep-seated unconscious conflicts), or are the children malevolent agents with the governess as the innocent victim? There are passages in the story to support both these views, and the author leaves the issue unresolved at the end: even then we can take it either way. Surely this is a difference in *interpretations* of the story. Others could contend, however, that, when you have shown how the text of the story will support either interpretation (which we are sure must have been deliberate), you have only elucidated the story, only in this case the elucidation contains a (deliberate) ambiguity.

What, again, of the Hamlet case? Most people would certainly call Freud's view of it an interpretation, even though a Freudian critic might say that it is simply an elucidation: he's giving us "the most plausible account" of "what's going on in the play," and inference that accounts for all the events in the play. But even if it does, it would seem that Freud and Ernest Jones go beyond description, and are giving an interpretation, and a highly controversial one at that.

> I can recall . . . attempting to retail a very ingenious interpretation of Tennessee Williams' *A Streetcar Named Desire* . . . to the effect that the play involved an inversion of Plato's "Myth of the Cave." The streetcar's name, the locale (a district called Elysian Fields), the divisions of Stella Kowalski's apartment—particularly the interior bath, the outer room and the colored light of the interior room, the presence of a second story that only Stella ascends to, the remembered plantation Belle Rêve, a blind woman's selling artificial flowers for the dead, the emphasis on make-believe, and a thousand other such details all fall into place convincingly with this superstructure provided.[2]

Is this interpretation, or is it elucidation? If we are inclined to call it an interpretation, it is probably because we feel that this is clearly a case of "reading into the play" (perhaps not unfruitfully, but still reading in). (If we learned that Williams had no knowledge of Plato, this would not necessarily invalidate the interpretation: the work might be fruitfully *seen* in this light,

[2] Joseph Margolis, *The Language of Art and Art Criticism* (Detroit: Wayne State Univ. Press, 1965), p. 95.

and might fall into place when this interpretation was given, even though it may never have occurred to the author.) This would count as an interpretation —a far-out one perhaps, but an interpretation nonetheless; or might someone still say that he was simply giving us an elucidation of what was "really in" the play?

The difference seems to be similar to the difference between laws and theories in science: we discover laws, we invent theories. Yet the difference is not as simple as this, and some of the things that are called laws by some (such as the structure of the atom) are called theories by others. Description is "uncovering what's there," while interpretation is "reading into the script." But saying that Dr. B took on Czentovic in a chess match *in order to* prove to himself that the public game was the same as the private one he had played in his cell—is that describing why he did it or giving an interpretation of his doing it? Hamlet's actions are set forth in the text, his motivations aren't; but are even the simplest and most obvious feelings and motives that aren't described in the text, for example, that he was angry with his mother in the bedroom scene, therefore to be called interpretation?

Thus far we have examined only cases of interpretation in which the critic *tells* us how a work of art should be interpreted. But in the performing arts, a performer can interpret a work of art not by telling us how it should be done, but by *doing* it. Thus, an actor performing *Hamlet* may perform the title role as if the Freudian interpretation were the right one: the innuendos, emphasis given certain lines, looks directed at his mother, and so on. And two pianists may interpret the same musical composition in different ways. Schnabel's interpretation of Beethoven was very different from Ghiseking's as Serkin's is from Rubenstein's. There are supposed to be four different ways for conductors to interpret Bruckner symphonies: exhibitionistic ("sock it to 'em"), no-nonsense ("keep it moving"), straightforward ("let the music play itself"), and expressive ("feel it from the heart"), though every one of them may be faithful to every note in the score.

When we are talking about interpretations of musical compositions, dances, and dramatic performances, it is difficult to call one interpretation "true" and another one "false"; we can speak of one as more appealing than another, or as more rewarding in the long run: and an interpretation one listener finds rewarding will not necessarily be found to be so by another. But what about the case of a literary work, where there is a text? Can't we speak of true or false interpretations here? That depends: it depends largely on whether an interpretation is *imposed* on a poem (from the outside, as it were), through an ideological bias which the reader brings with him to whatever he reads, or whether he is willing to *find* clues in the poem as to how it is to be interpreted.

Sometimes the first happens. A poem *can* be treated like a Rorschach test—you can see all kinds of figureheads, animals and birds, in the shapes, but there is no *correct* reading of the shapes (that's the way they are designed). This can also be true of literary works:

> The story of "Jack and the Beanstalk," for example, can no doubt be taken as Freudian symbolism, as a Marxist fable, or as Christian allegory. I emphasize the phrase "can be taken as." It is true that "readings" such as these need not exclude each other. But the reason is surely that they do not bring out of the work something that lies momentarily hidden in it; they are rather ways of *using* the work to illustrate a pre-existent system of thought. Though they are sometimes called "interpretations" (since this word is extremely obliging), they merit a distinct label, like *superimpositions.*[3]

On the other hand, if an interpretation is "reasonable," then reasons can be given to show how it is superior to some alternatives; and how could the reasons count unless there are reasons for believing it to be true? And if it is a *plausible* interpretation, isn't it possible that it is also true? "Plausibility is at least an appearance of truth based upon some relevant evidence, and any statement that is plausible must be *in principle* capable of being shown to be true or false.[4] If two proposed interpretations are logically incompatible with each other, must not at least one of them be rejected?

For example, in Wordsworth's poem "Lucy," one critic believes that Lucy in her grave was assimilated to inorganic things—"rocks, stones, and trees." But trees at least are not inorganic things; perhaps it is being suggested that rocks and stones (and the dead Lucy) are like trees, "having an inner life of their own." Various references in the poem tend to confirm this interpretation.

> She is "rolled round in earth's diurnal course." The question is, how much can we legitimately find in the meaning of "rolled" here? The available repertoire of connotations for the work "rolled" is certainly quite rich. We can open some of them by thinking of kinds of motion that we would strictly describe as "rolling"—that of the billiard ball, the snowball on the hill, the hoop propelled by a child. By exploring these familiar contexts for the term in its literal standard uses, we remind ourselves of the various forms of motion that can be classified as rolling. And by contrasting these forms of motion, we inventory the potential connotations of the term. There are steady boring motions, ungainly decelerating motions (the wagon rolling to a stop), scary accelerating motions (the car rolling downhill), etc. But what about the present context? Here what must strike us forcibly is the way the other words in this line qualify and specify the motion that Lucy has: it is a regular motion, with a constant rate; it is a comparatively slow and gentle motion, since one revolution takes 24 hours; it is an orderly motion,

[3] Monroe C. Beardsley, "The Testability of an Interpretation, "in *The Possibility of Criticism* (Detroit: Wayne State Univ. Press, 1970); reprinted in *Philosophy Looks at the Arts,* 2nd ed., ed. Joseph Margolis (Philadelphia: Temple Univ. Press, 1978), pp. 370–386; passage quoted is on p. 373.

[4] *Ibid.,* p. 373.

since it follows a simple circular path. In none of these respects is it terrifying or demeaning; if anything, it is comforting and elevating. If we accept these connotations, the poem contains a hint of pantheism or at least animism.[5]

And thus an interpretation of the poem is generated which is pantheistic (quite apart from the fact, known from external sources, that Wordsworth espoused pantheism). By subjecting the poem to analysis, we find considerable internal evidence that the poem is pantheistic rather than materialistic in its point of view. "Interpreting a poem is not like arranging a sack of children's blocks in a deliberately selected and imposed order. . . . It is more like putting a jigsaw puzzle together, or tracing out contours on a badly stained old parchment map. But it can be done better or worse; and the results can be judged by reason."[6]

## 2. EVALUATIVE CRITICISM

Finally, there is *evaluative* criticism, which renders *verdicts* on works of art, usually on one work in relation to others. This is good, this is excellent, this is poor stuff, this is better than that.

But for all this the critic has *reasons*. Without reasons to support them, such judgments are unlikely to have much influence on an intelligent reader; they remain simply the unsupported opinions of the person uttering the judgment. In fact, some critics eschew making such judgments entirely: they tell you what's going on in the work, they elucidate it as best they can, and then they leave it to you how to evaluate the work in the light of their remarks.

"What is the point of trying to do it at all?" one might ask. "All the critic's verdict on a work of art amounts to is that he is revealing to the reader what his own tastes in works of art are like. And, as the old saying goes, *De gustibus non est disputandum* (concerning taste there is no disputing)."

But such a conclusion would be quite premature. Suppose a person says that this seascape is a good one because it reminds him of his childhood in Hawaii; or that the novel is a good one because it keeps him absorbed or entertained. All the person has done so far is to tell us why he *likes* the work; and liking it and giving it a high mark as a work of art are not the same thing. Reminding him of his childhood in Hawaii may tell us why he *likes* it, and might explain why he enjoys having it hang in his living room (to trigger nostalgic recollections), but it hardly gives an account of why he considers the painting a good one, if he does.

In some situations we all admit the difference: a person may say, "I like this, but I know it's a piece of trash" or "I grant that is a great work of art, but I can't say I *like* it or would want to see/hear it again." A person may like

---

[5] *Ibid.,* p. 375.
[6] *Ibid.,* p. 383.

the novels of Mickey Spillane although not holding them up as works of art, and he may grant Picasso the title of original and imaginative painter while not liking Picasso's works or caring to see any more of them.

There are, of course, differences in taste, or personal *preferences*. "I like this work of art because . . ." is not an attempt to justify the verdict that this is a worthy work of art, but only gives a reason (or cause) why the person likes it. If I prefer Wagner to Verdi and you prefer Verdi to Wagner, the statements "I prefer Wagner to Verdi" and "You prefer Verdi to Wagner" are both true; there is *no statement* which is in dispute. There would be dispute only if one person thought the other was lying or possibly deceiving himself: "Come now, you don't *really* prefer Wagner, do you?" If I say, "I prefer crab to lobster" and you say "I prefer lobster to crab," so far there is no dispute, no disagreement, no statement which the one person thinks is true and the other thinks is false. Since each person is usually conceded to be the final authority on what he likes, neither party usually contests the other's statement of preference. If the statements are about one's own personal preferences, which may have nothing to do with the qualities of the work of art, it is true but rather trivial that "there's no disputing about it."

But while we don't disagree about one another's statements of *preference,* we do often disagree with one another's *evaluations*. You may say that this is a good car, or a good road, or a good college, or a good student, or a good racehorse, or a good work of art, and I may deny it, and then we do dispute about the matter—we disagree in the fundamental sense of that term: each person says something that the other believes to be false. When we express different preferences for Verdi and Wagner, we thereby reveal our tastes to one another, but we do not yet disagree on anything (A does not doubt that B dislikes the work); but when I say "Taken as a whole, the works of Wagner are greater (better, more worthy of admiration, represent a greater achievement, etc.) than those of Verdi," I am making a judgment concerning which you may well disagree. And when we disagree, we then usually go on to present *reasons* for our comparative evaluation.

Sometimes, of course, we do not go so far; we each express our preferences and let it go at that. This is what we ordinarily do with foods or drinks: I am not likely to say to you that crab is "inherently superior" to lobster—doubtlessly because I would find such a judgment very hard to defend. If I could show you that it had superior nutritive properties or that lobster contains some danger to health, then I would be making a true empirical judgment about its effects on those who eat it; but if I were saying only that there is something superior about its flavor, you need only reply that you prefer the flavor of lobster and that is that. Nutritional qualities aside, why should you eat it if you don't like it?

Still, we do sometimes dispute even about food and drink. A child, let us say, begins by liking Velveeta cheese; then later he comes to like Münster or Monterrey Jack; and only much later will he cultivate a taste for Roquefort.

But once he has done this, he will seldom go back to Velveeta—he has left this far behind. If someone now said to you, "I prefer Velveeta to all other cheeses," you might well dispute him—you wouldn't deny that he prefers Velveeta, but you might feel sorry for him, you would think how much he was missing by not cultivating a taste for other cheeses, and—whether you could give him arguments or not—you might not be content with the mutual expression of preferences, you would try to get him to cultivate a taste for other cheeses. In the same way, if someone said "I prefer Ogden Nash to Shakespeare," you might realize how much he was missing and try to go over some Shakespeare with him to try to get him to *change* his preference, and you would do so by pointing out some of the qualities of Shakespeare's poetry that are not qualities of the poems of Ogden Nash. You don't dispute his present statement of preference, but you hope, through showing him some of the qualities of Shakespeare, to get him to change that preference, and even in time to admit that Shakespeare is better.

## 3. CRITICAL REASONS

Whether we arrive at a favorable or unfavorable judgment on a work of art will usually depend on a number of factors. "It is a worthy work in that it has quality Q; but on the other hand, it is made less good because of having other qualities, R and S." We then try to decide whether Q counts in favor or the work more than R and S count against it. Since there are so many features in any work of art, the final judgment on it will be an "on balance" judgment— just as the decision between one car and another will usually be: this car is softer and more comfortable to sit in than that one; but, on the other hand, the first one has a higher back, and is composed of more durable materials; but the first one is more expensive . . . and so on.

But what *are* the factors which have to be weighed against one another in evaluating a work of art? Are there any general factors—features of a work of art that tend to make it good (or better than it would have been otherwise) whenever and wherever they are present? If so, what are they, and how do we defend the view that they *are* factors to be considered? What, if any, *are* the "good reasons" that follow the word "because" in such sentences as "This is a good work of art, because . . ." and "This is a better work of art than that, because . . ."?

Once we have reached this point, we seem to be confronted by an endless multiplicity of reasons. One critic thinks ill of a play because it has a "depressing subject-matter"; another admits that the subject-matter is depressing but praises the "expert treatment of the theme." One critic thinks ill of a film because it departs too much from the novel on which it is based; another considers this a virtue, because the novel "has been translated into cinematic terms." One thinks well of a novel because it contains a powerful characterization which emblazons itself on his memory long after he has forgotten most of the plot; another dismisses the novel as "little more than a character portrait," instead of what novels "ought to consist of," action and movement. One deplores a poem for "the paucity and unoriginality of its ideas," whereas another, admitting the unoriginality, praises the "richness of the metaphors." Some consider a work of literature superior because it contains "a true vision of reality," whereas others consider the matter of truth to be irrelevant. Some think a portrait is a good one because it is an accurate representation of the sitter; others find this irrelevant but praise it because it is well drawn. And so on, in seemingly endless profusion. Are there any limits to the kinds of reasons that can be given, and is there any way to dismiss some of them as irrelevant?

There are some kinds of reasons (or statements purporting to be reasons) which, once we have isolated them, we may be able to dismiss as irrelevant at the start. First among them are statements having to do with the coming-into-being, or genesis of a work of art; these are often called *genetic* reasons.[7] Sometimes people value a work of art more highly because the creation of it was particularly difficult or it took an extremely large amount of time, effort, or concentration. But this, it would seem, is grounds for praise of the *artist*, for having qualities of courage or tenacity, but not for giving high marks to the work of art itself. If Mozart created his music with unbelievable rapidity and Brahms created his only after much weeping and gnashing of teeth, does this make Brahms's music better? One might praise him more for going ahead with it at all, but this is not praise of the music but the composer. Many people put forth great effort and have little to show for it in the end; one cannot judge the quality of the product by the nature of the process that led to it.

Or suppose that the artist had a certain fixed intention with regard to his work and followed it through unswervingly to the end. One may praise him for realizing his intention, but nothing yet is said that is a basis for judging the quality of the work; perhaps he intended to write a potboiler and succeeded completely. Or suppose that in creating his work he had profound emotions to express, and expressed them to the full in the creation of the work. This is indeed of interest to his biographer and his psychoanalyst, but not to the person who wants to arrive at an evaluation of the work itself: his great fulfillment experience in creating the work may not be matched by any corresponding qualities of the work. "In creating this work I expressed myself completely," the artist may say, to which one might reply, "In that case there wasn't much of a self to express"; or if he says "It was for me an experience of total realization," one may retort that it is doubtful whether in that case there was much there to realize.

Second, there are statements which are not about the work of art itself but,

---

[7] Monroe C. Beardsley, *Aesthetics,* pp. 457-460.

rather, about how it affects the consumer; these are sometimes called *affective* reasons.[8] "It made my heart pound"; "It moved me deeply"; "It buoyed up my spirits so that I could get through the day"; "It relaxed me"; "It converted me to its point of view": "It made me see how much I'd been missing by not living life more fully"; "Seeing that film made me fearful of being the next crime victim"; and so on, endlessly, describing what effects the work had on the viewer, reader, or listener. The effect on one consumer of art is not the same as the effect on another, so the fact that it affected one person in a certain way can hardly count as a reason for attributing merit to the work of art: at most it ascribes a *cause* to the fact that *this* individual likes or dislikes it. In fact the same work of art may affect the same individual in very different ways at different times, depending on the individual's mood or state of mind at the time.

"But if the work [for example] moved you deeply, isn't that a reason for *you* not only to like it, but to evaluate it favorably?" Not by itself: it might have moved you deeply because it reminded you of someone now dead with whom you sometimes enjoyed that work of art in the past, or for any of a multitude of such personal reasons. What we as evaluators of the work of art want to know is not how it affected a certain person at a certain time, but what there was in the work of art itself to evoke the effect in question. It's not that the effects of a work of art on consumers don't matter—far from it—but that critical evaluation must be grounded in the work of art itself, and instead of asking what the effect was without inquiring why, we must inquire what qualities the work of art had that enabled it to produce these effects. Even if a work of art *regularly* has a certain kind of effect on virtually all consumers, we want to know what it is about the work of art that gives it these powers. If it is the work of art and not its effects that we are evaluating, shouldn't the grounds for such praise lie in its qualities, and not those of the consumer?

And thus we are led to concentrate on the *work of art itself,* as the basis for critical evaluation. It is *its* qualities that make a work of art good or bad, better or worse than another work. The fact that a certain listener enjoys hearing a certain musical composition may be a good reason for *that* listener to hear the composition again, but it cannot be a general reason for a favorable verdict on the work of art. We turn, then, to a third group of reasons, *objective* reasons.

But a work of art has a huge array of qualities. Even if we confine our attention to the qualities of works of art and not those of creative artists or consumers of art, which qualities of a work of art relevant to a favorable or unfavorable judgment on it as a work of art? Even among objective reasons, are not some clearly irrelevant? Perhaps so, but even among critics there is no universal agreement on this matter. Let us examine the principal groups of objective reasons, cognitive, moral, and aesthetic:

[8] *Ibid.,* pp. 460-461.

1. *Cognitive reasons.* A statement or set of statements in a work of literature may be true; and when it is, the work has to that extent cognitive value. Or a work of art may contain a view of life or the universe which the reader finds true or acceptable to him and will value the work of art more highly (not merely like it better) on that account. Most critics will probably reject such cognitive reasons as irrelevant, claiming that whether it is a good work of art is one thing, and whether it contains a true view is quite another, and that it is folly to confuse them or even to subsume the one under the under: perhaps the reader is failing to distinguish different kinds of reasons in his own mind, and in that case some sorting out of reasons is called for:

> Suppose he is interested in the philosophy of a literary work—say, Tolstoy's philosophy of history, in *War and Peace.* Then we may want to suggest a distinction: if what interests him is the truth of that philosophy or its logical consistency or its historical antecedents and influence, then his interest in the novel is not aesthetic; but if what interests him is the character of that philosophy (its bold sweep, say) or its organic relationship to the structure and recurrent themes of the novel, then his interest *is* aesthetic.[9]

But other philosophers of art do not share this view. For example, Lionel Trilling writes concerning the recent American novel, "It is questionable whether any American novel since *Babbitt* has told us a new thing about our social life. In psychology the novel relies either on a mechanical or classical use of psychiatry or on the insights that were established by the novelists of fifty years ago."[10] And Professor Marshall Cohen comments on this that we here seem to have a case of a scientific criterion employed in making a judgment on a work of art, for in this passage "Trilling means to condemn the recent American novel *as an artistic achievement.*"[11]

2. *Moral reasons.* The same divergence of opinion is found in the assessment of moral reasons. A work of art may present a moral ideal as well as a true picture of some aspect of the world; and if moral ideals are counted as true or false, as of course not everyone would agree, then moral reasons become a species of cognitive reasons. A novel may present moral characters (which may inspire us) or be imbued with a certain moral tone, or present characters (and views held by them) and situations which will be regarded with moral approval or disapproval. Again, it will seem obvious to many critics that moral reasons are one thing and aesthetic reasons another, that to praise a work on aesthetic grounds is very different from doing so on moral grounds, and that, however much one may be repelled by the morality set forth or implied in a novel, one must not let one's moral disapproval stand in the way of

---

[9] Monroe C. Beardsley, "The Philosophy of Literature," in *Aesthetics,* eds. George Dickie and Richard Sclafani (New York: St. Martin's Press, 1977), p. 328.

[10] Lionel Trilling, *The Liberal Imagination* (New York: Viking Press, 1950), p. 263.

[11] Marshall Cohen, "Aesthetic Essence," in *Philosophy in America,* ed. Max Black (London, 1962); reprinted in Dickie and Sclafani, *Aesthetics;* passage quoted is on p. 497. (Emphasis added.)

a (possibly favorable) aesthetic judgment ("I have to admit it's a worthy film, but its morality stinks").

The distinction is neat and plausible, yet many will not go along with it. Some say, for example, that to criticize a novel for "lack of moral maturity" is a perfectly proper reason for rejecting it as a satisfactory work of art—that it would be a *better novel* if in its moral dimension it were "more mature."

One might suggest a way around this by saying that the critic is not really criticizing lack of maturity as such but is confusing maturity, which is a moral quality, with complexity, which is an aesthetic quality, and that the real basis of the criticism is that, with the characters' moral outlook lacking maturity (as often happens in young and inexperienced authors), there is an important dimension of complexity that is consequently missing. Thus interpreted,

> the psychological criterion of maturity is to be understood as a demand for complexity, and they find that the epistemological criterion of truth to experience "registers itself in aesthetic terms of vividness, intensity, patterned contrast, width or depth, static or kinetic." This will not do. Obviously, many works regarded as mature . . . are not remarkable for their complexity. The maturity of *Oedipus at Colonus, the Tempest,* and *When We Dead Awaken* is evidenced by the authority of their relative simplicity, and they are less complex than *Oedipus Rex, Troilus and Cressida,* and *Peer Gynt.* And surely, the truth to experience Eliot has in mind displays itself in the calm of Dante (as narrator, not pilgrim) rather than in the intensity of Shelley, in the muted measure of *Four Quartets* rather than in the vividness of "The Hippopotamus" or "Mr. Appollinax." It simply does not seem possible to reduce the criterion of maturity to that of complexity. And more importantly, it does not seem possible to reduce the criterion of truth . . . to an aesthetic criterion. If that is so, it would appear to be the case that scientific—and, as it would be still simpler to show, moral—criteria are relevant to the making of aesthetic judgments. [The] assumption that the sub-set of such criteria will exclude moral, intellectual, and other criteria, is false. And the hope of discovering some property common to the criteria relevant to aesthetic judgement . . . will lose its plausibility.[12]

If we still say, as most critics probably would, that moral reasons are one thing and aesthetic reasons another, what shall we say in reply to such charges as Cohen's? Are they simply to be left by the wayside, unrefuted? Or do we just agree to disagree? There is one suggestion that may be helpful in trying to resolve this issue. The fact that the presence of a certain quality Q would make something a better *work of art* does not imply that the presence of Q would guarantee a higher aesthetic judgment on it. Works of art contain many qualities that are not aesthetic qualities, and a work of art may be better *as a work of art* for having them, even though the qualities are not aesthetic qualities. For example, that a characterization in a novel "rings true," "is convincing," "is true to human nature" (these expressions are not synonymous) is a feature that, one might suggest, makes it a better novel, bet-

[12] *Ibid.,* pp. 497-498.

ter *as a novel*, than it would be if the characters did not "ring true"; but it hardly seems that truth to human nature is an aesthetic quality (more of this in Chapters 8 and 9), and the presence of this feature does not make the novel aesthetically better. (Of course, truth to human nature may, and usually will, enhance unity or complexity or some other aesthetic quality, but then a novel is aesthetically better because of the aesthetic quality, not because of the truth *per se*.)

If we keep this distinction in mind, it may help to solve a perennial puzzle. Aesthetically Jane Austen's novels are better (at least most critics would say so) than are those of Dostoyevsky, but Dostoyevsky's novels are better (on the whole, on balance) than are those of Austen, *as novels*—and as examples of total works of art, of which novels are one species—although *not* as embodiments of aesthetic qualities. We evaluate novels aesthetically, but not *only* aesthetically. What aesthetic qualities the rich and insightful characterization of the three brothers Karamazov adds to the novel (and it does add some) could be disputed at length; but what is not disputable, at any rate ever so much less disputable, is that these characterizations make of the book a much greater *novel*. Aesthetically it may be that, as Pater said, all art aspires to the condition of music; but *artistically* (as works of art), works of literature, though on the whole possessing fewer and less pronounced aesthetic qualities, do not have to take second or third place among the arts, for our reasons for praising something *as a work of art* are more inclusive than are our reasons for praising something *aesthetically*. We expect "true" characterizations of works of literature; indeed this is one of the things we go to literature for—and this would not be so if our interest in literature were purely aesthetic. Our response to Mondrian may be mostly or wholly aesthetic, but with a work of literature this is seldom or never the case: literature has other fish to fry and only catches some aesthetic fish in its net along the way.

3. *Aesthetic reasons.* Finally, there is a class of reasons called "aesthetic." We have not yet examined what is involved in the use of this term, and it is possible that, after you have read about it (in the next two chapters), you will be more confused about it than ever. At any rate, there are reasons constantly given for praising works of art which are called "aesthetic reasons" by those who give them. Some of them have already been indicated, in contrast to cognitive and moral reasons. The problem is, again, that there appear to be so many of them that we may have on our hands the same problem as we had before sloughing off subjective reasons (genetic and affective) and some objective reasons (cognitive and moral) from the total array of reasons to be considered—the problem of finding some assignable limit to the kinds and numbers of reasons to be found.

Although many writers talk about the nature of reasons, including aesthetic reasons, and constantly employ numerous criteria for judging works of art, very few are willing to go out on a limb to present any specific list of criteria which are separately necessary and jointly sufficient for the evaluation of a work of art. A rare exception to this rule is Monroe Beardsley, who has actually presented and defended such a list, in his book, *Aesthetics* (1958), and again ten years later in his article, "The Classification of Critical Reasons":

> In my view, there are exactly *three basic criteria* that are appealed to in relevant critical reasons, and all of the other features of works of art that are appealed to in such reasons are subordinate to these, or can be subsumed under them. There is *unity*. . . . There is *complexity*. . . . And there is *intensity* of regional quality.[13]

Many pages in this book have already been devoted to the concept of unity in works of art. A work is unified if it "hangs together," and the two principal aspects of unity are *completeness* (nothing is required that isn't there) and *coherence* (everything that is required is there). Other things being equal (which they seldom or never are), the higher the degree of unity, the better the work of art. A work of art may be an excellent one in spite of the fact that it lacks a high degree of unity (it may fulfill other criteria to a high degree to make up for the comparative lack of unity), but it is never a better work than it would otherwise have been *because* of lack of unity. For example, when a reviewer says of George Gershwin's *Rhapsody in Blue,* "The humor, gusto, and sentiment are all there; the work is not tightly organized by symphonic standards, but its very looseness of design adds to its charm," Beardsley says, "I think this has to mean, not that it is better precisely because it is loosely organized, but that its peculiar qualities, its 'humor, gusto and sentiment,' would perhaps be weakened by a more highly organized form."[14]

But works of art in the various media differ enormously from one another, partly because of the difference in media. Do we mean the same thing by "unity" in paintings, for example, as we do in dramas and symphonies?

> We can surely find examples of pairs of paintings or prints where it is perfectly evident that one is more unified than the other. And even though what tends to unify a painting is, of course, not identical to what tends to unify a poem or a musical composition, as far as I can tell I mean the same thing when I say that one poem is more unified than another as when I say that one painting is more unified than another.[15]

But how do we know what a judgment such as "This painting is highly unified" (or isn't) is justified?

[13] Monroe C. Beardsley, "The Classification of Critical Reasons," *Journal of Aesthetic Education,* Vol. 2 (1968); reprinted in Melvin M. Rader (ed.), *A Modern Book of Aesthetics,* 5th edition, (New York: Holt, 1979), pp. 388-394; passage quoted is on p. 390.

[14] Monroe C. Beardsley, *Aesthetics* (New York: Harcourt Brace, 1958), p. 462. Reprinted in John Hospers, ed., *Introductory Readings in Aesthetics,* p. 246.

[15] Monroe C. Beardsley, "The Classification of Critical Reasons," p. 390-391.

When we look at a painting and it fails to hang together, that may be because we are tired, or our perceptions are dulled by an adverse mood, or we are not attending closely enough, or we have had too little acquaintance with works of that sort. A negative conclusion must usually be somewhat tentative and rebuttable; for it may well be that if later we come to the painting again, in a more serene mood, with sharper faculties, and with greater willingness to give in to whatever the painting wishes to do to us, we may find that in fact it has a tight though subtle unity that is perfectly apparent to the prepared eye. But if we return again and again, under what we take to be the most favorable conditions, and it still looks incoherent, we have reasonable grounds for concluding that probably the painting cannot be seen as unified.

Even a positive conclusion may not be final. The painting may on occasion fleetingly appear to us as unified. But suppose that unity turns out not to be a stable property—that it is hard to capture and to hold. Then we may decide that we were the victim of an illusion. The judgment of unity ultimately has to be based on a *gestalt* perception—on taking in the regional qualities and dominant patterns of the whole. But such perceptions can always be checked by analysis—by which I mean simply the minute examination of the parts of the work and their relationships with one another. A prima facie description of the work as having unity or disunity to some degree does have this kind of check: that it should hold up under analysis. For the perception that occurs after analysis may correct the earlier one: it may turn out that we have overlooked some parts or some internal relationships that, when taken into account in perception, make the work more unified—or less unified—than it as first appeared.[16]

The second criterion, complexity, is also familiar to us from previous chapters: indeed, the two are often combined as variety-in-unity or unity-in-variety. Unity is no great achievement when a work lacks a variety of elements; they must be "held in suspension" by an overall unity, and the more complex a work is, the more difficult this is to achieve, and the more valuable the work is once it is achieved.

Should one say, however, that (other things being equal) the more complex a work is the better? Is there no limit to the complexity that is found desirable or rewarding? Yes, one might say, there is a limit, because beyond a certain degree of complexity, the more complex a work is the less it can be perceived as a unity, and thus unity is compromised because of the great complexity.

"But an enormously complex work could still *be* unified—it's just that it would no longer be possible to *perceive* its unity, after you get past a certain point in complexity (that point varying, of course, from one consumer to another)." One may grant this point; but it is *perceivable* or *discernible* unity that counts: if one could prove to you that a work was unified but was so complex that you couldn't be aware of the unity, presumably such a (theoretical) unity would not be an aesthetic virtue: if it's inaccessible it might as well not be there. The complexity, then, must not be so unmanageably great as to inhibit the consumer's gestalt *perception* of unity.

[16] *Ibid.*, p. 391.

Sometimes, however, a work of art, or some portion or aspect of it, is praised not for its complexity but for its very *simplicity*. Compositions by Bach and Handel possess great structural and textural complexity, but the *melodies* typically differ in that Handel's are ever so much simpler, consisting of just a few tones, with no "long way round" getting to the conclusion as so often happens in Bach, but by the most "simple and direct" route possible: consider, for example, the stunning simplicity of such melodies as "He was despised" from the *Messiah,* the "Death March" from *Saul,* the children's chorus from *Israel in Egypt,* or the hauntingly lovely theme of the slow movement of the Concerto Grosso No. 6 of Op. 6. Surely it is not unreasonable to praise them for their very simplicity? George Bernard Shaw wrote of the arias ("Queen of the Night," "O Isis and Osiris," and others) from Mozart's *The Magic Flute* that they were the only melodies ever written that could proceed from the mouth of God without embarrassment: they are exquisitely simple, composed usually of only a few tones close to one another on the scale; it is amazing, even mysterious, how such simple melodies can be heard again and again year after year with no diminution in their effect, when most simple melodies (such as most of those one hears on the jukebox) become tiresome after a few hearings and are soon replaced by other (equally tiresome) ones. In whatever ways these differ from Mozart's, one might say, it is not with regard to simplicity. (The entire opera, of course, is quite complex, but it is only the arias we are now considering.)

"The sleeper of the year," wrote film critic Ernest Schier, "is a bone-bare, simple, and convincingly honest treatment of the life of Jesus, *The Gospel According to St. Matthew* (directed by Pasolini)." Beardsley writes of this, "Insofar as the simplicity of Pasolini's film is regarded as a positive merit, I take it not as a low degree of complexity but as absence of 'excessive detail and over-decoration.' "[17]

It is true that both the film and the arias already discussed are distinguished by "absence of excessive detail and over-decoration" (the very prefix "over" already implies "too much"). But is that why we want to hear them over and over again, for years on end? Many equally simple works, also distinguished by "lack of excessive detail and over-decoration," are simply banal and boring. What is the difference? It does not appear to be lack of simplicity in the Mozart–Handel cases; this doesn't seem to get a handle on the difference between them at all. One is reminded here of Gurney's criticism of expressiveness ("This melody is sad"), that it gives about as much of an explanation of the difference between a good melody and a bad one as a heap of scattered clothes on the floor gives a clue to "the living beauty of face and form." One is reminded also of Clive Bell's remark that in a good melody tones are "combined according to the laws of a mysterious necessity"—a remark which, to be sure, doesn't give a single specific clue as to what makes

[17] *Ibid.,* p. 390.

one melody memorable and another banal: but while it leaves it a mystery why one melody can move us deeply while an almost identical one is simply boring or irritating (and *isn't* it a mystery? has anyone ever given even the *beginnings* of an answer to that question?), at least it doesn't lead us up a blind alley by giving us an erroneous or mistaken reason.

One might argue, in opposition to this, that the Mozart and Handel melodies are *not* after all simple, but only seem to be so: that (for example) although the melodies have only a few tones with very simple harmonic relations to each other, there are *implicit* complexities: that unlike Mancini's song *Days of Wine and Roses,* "The Mancini piece uses only primary chords, chords which are directly related to the F major tonic. In contrast, the Mozart contains many secondary chords, chords which are directly related to the primary chords of the key D minor. . . . The harmonic palette uses a wider variety of colors than the Mancini . . .".[18] The data submitted are true enough, but whether they support the general conclusion that the memorable melodies are "really not simple" and nonmemorable ones are, is disputable, and would take detailed analysis of many cases, in the professional language of musicologists, to argue pro or con.

On the other hand, one could take Beardsley's line that a work of art (or portion thereof) may be worthwhile *and* simple but never worthwhile *because* it is simple—the simplicity must be countered by a high degree of other qualities:

> It seems to me that whenever simplicity is held up as a desirable feature, either it is not strictly simplicity (the opposite of complexity) that is referred to, but some sort of unity, or it is not the simplicity that is admired but the intensity of some regional quality that happens to be obtainable in this case only by accepting simplicity.[19]

And thus we come to the last of the three suggested criteria, *intensity.* This one is harder to grasp quickly, and it is not a formal quality of the work of art, but a pervasive "regional quality" either of the work of art as a whole or some part or aspect of it.

Ordinarily when we talk about intensity we have in mind intensity of *experience:* "Listening to the Verdi *Requiem* is a very intense experience." There is, to be sure, a connection between intensity as a quality attributed to a work of art and the intensity of the experience one thereby gleans from it; but, again, one could have intense feelings for a variety of irrelevant reasons, or one could read or listen to an intense work of art without any feelings at all, depending on one's mood. Beardsley uses as examples of intensity "the 'overall spirit of joy' in Haydn; the 'cry of terror' in Edvard Munch." The central idea in the concept of intensity seems to be that a work of art must

[18] Jane Harty, "Simplicity and Aesthetic Durability." Not yet published.
[19] Monroe C. Beardsley, "The Classification of Critical Reasons," pp. 391-392.

have *some marked affective quality* or series of such qualities: it may be exuberance and vivacity, as in the opening movement of Vivaldi's *Concerto for Diverse Instruments;* it may be anguish, as in the last movement of Tschaikovsky's *Pathètique* Symphony (No. 6) or much of Mahler's Symphony No. 6; it may be calm and peace, as in Tintoretto's painting *Christ Walking on the Water*; It may be quiet exaltation, as in the concluding movement of Bach's *St. Matthew Passion,* or world-weariness and resignation, as in many Mahler adagios. Or it may be a quality for which we have no words at all that even approximate it. In either case, what is involved in intensity is the presence of some embodied *expressive quality* (named or unnamed), which was discussed in Chapter 4.

What intensity is may be best illustrated by trying to exhibit its presence in passages of Shakespeare's poetry. If one is going to talk about intensity at all, its presence to a high degree in Shakespeare is almost beyond question, in numerous passages that "bowl you over" and almost "blow you away" with their intensity. Consider for example the curse that King Lear invokes on his eldest daughter Goneril:

> Hear, nature, hear; dear goddess, hear!
> Suspend thy purpose, if thou didst intend
> To make this creature fruitful!
> Into her womb convey sterility!
> Dry up in her the organs of increase;
> And from her derogate body never spring
> A babe to honour her! If she must teem,
> Create her child of spleen; that it may live,
> And be a thwart disnatured torment to her!
> Let it stamp wrinkles in her brow of youth;
> With cadent tears fret channels in her cheeks;
> Turn all her mother's pains and benefits
> To laughter and contempt; that she may feel
> How sharper than a serpent's tooth it is
> To have a thankless child!

(Act 1, scene 4)

The following passage from *Antony and Cleopatra* is intense with nostalgic recollection. Antony is dead, his glory gone, and Cleopatra's lament tells us how she remembers him:

> His face was as the heavens; and therein stuck
> A sun and moon, which kept their course and lighted
> The little O, the earth . . .
> His legs bestrid the ocean; his rear'd arm
> Crested the world: his voice was propertied
> As all the tuned spheres, and that to friends;
> But when he meant to quail and shake the orb,
> He was as rattling thunder. For his bounty,

There was no winter in 't; an autumn 'twas
That grew the more by reaping; his delights
Were dolphin-like; they show'd his back above
The element they lived in; in his livery
Walk'd crowns and crownets; realms and islands were
As plates dropp'd from his pocket.

(Act 5, scene 2)

But lest we think that intensity must be of some aggressive or violent quality, consider Prospero's parting speech at the end of *The Tempest,* full of intensity also, but now an intensity of calm and resignation:

Our revels now are ended. These our actors,
As I foretold you, were all spirits and
Are melted into air, into thin air:
And, like the baseless fabric of this vision,
The cloud-capp'd towers, the gorgeous palaces,
The solemn temples, the great globe itself,
Yea, all which it inherit, shall dissolve
And, like this insubstantial pageant faded,
Leave not a rack behind. We are such stuff
As dreams are made on, and our little life
Is rounded with a sleep.

(Act 4, scene 1)

In Shakespeare's *Measure for Measure,* Angelo, who has been condemned to die the following morning, utters the following lines about the fate that awaits him:

Ay, but to die, and go we know not where;
To lie in cold obstruction and to rot;
This sensible warm motion to become
A kneaded clod; and the delighted spirit
To bathe in fiery floods, or to reside
In thrilling region of thick-ribbed ice;
To be imprisoned in the viewless winds,
And blown with restless violence round about
The pendant world; or to be worse than worst
Of those that lawless and incertain thoughts
Imagine howling; 'tis too horrible!
The weariest and most loathed worldly life
That age, ache, penury, and imprisonment
Can lay on nature is a paradise
To what we fear of death.

(Act 3, scene 1)

The metaphors tumble over one another in an endless flow, each image adding to the intensity of what has preceded. There is a staccato finality (like death itself) in such expressions as "cold obstruction"and "rot," replaced by a series of m's in the next line as the mood temporarily changes, then taking off to dizzying heights with a flow of metaphors ("thick-ribbed ice," "viewless winds,"and so on), each reinforcing the other. The very ambiguity of "viewless winds" (taken from Dante's *Inferno*) enhances the effect: viewless in the sense of blind? Winds *from* which there is no view? Winds *of* which there is no view because they are invisible? No matter which interpretation is chosen, all fit the context. Or consider "pendant[hanging] world": what if it had read "earth" instead? There is a fullness, a roundness about "world," whereas "earth" is flat; with the word "world" we get the image of a round ball, hanging in space—the context is astronomical, whereas the earth is that which is beneath one's feet. The cumulative effect of these images is tremendously powerful, almost shattering; a poem could not long remain at that peak of intensity.

But doesn't every work have some quality or other, whether easily describable in words or not, and thus doesn't every work have intensity? On the contrary. Many works may be impeccable in unity as well as in complexity but have no distinctive regional qualities at all—they are just "blah" (which is as good a word as can be found for the opposite of intensity). And isn't this, one may ask, why certain works, which may be well put together (such as many student compositions), nicely unified and so on, still seem to us quite trivial, or at any rate totally unmemorable? At a time when "formal correctness" was the main criterion, Ludwig Spohr was almost as famous a composer as Beethoven, yet today he is not only unremembered but his works when performed seem to us not to be in any way memorable: they "have no vitality," they embody no strong affective qualities of any kind, they seem "smooth but inane," as opposed to the vigor, passion, and pride (if that is the word) that characterize virtually every measure of Beethoven's music.

Does intensity of just *any* expressive quality count toward a favorable evaluation of the work of art? There are scenes in Hitchcock's film *Psycho* which contain as their principal quality sheer terror; but not everyone considers terror embodied in a work of art to be a desirable quality. Some veiwers vomit, others leave the theater because they can't "take" such a high degree of this quality, just as in the opening scene of Bunel's short film *The Andalusian Dog* which shows a close-up of a human eye and then a razor slicing the eye in two. Are there no limits to the kinds of qualities that works of art may embody, however intensely?

The usual answer to this is to say that "if you can't take it, don't try, but you really have missed something. I understand why you may not be able to assimilate some intense regional qualities, such as terror at being stalked by a madman (especially if this has happened to you), but then, however understandably, you have a blind spot as far as appreciation is concerned. But that's just what it is, a blind spot, and don't pretend you aren't missing something that you would find rewarding if you did not have the blind spot."

Certainly this is a highly plausible response. Yet there are embodied qualities which some people take objection to, and not simply because of some incident in their own personal lives. Some viewers object to the depiction of highly erotic scenes, such as mass orgies—but this may be for moral rather than for aesthetic reasons. Others object to scenes depicting human dismemberment or prolonged torture; here the reason given, "I can't stand seeing that sort of thing," is not so obviously based on moral grounds; isn't it more aesthetic than moral revulsion? Immanuel Kant thought that any kind of embodied quality was acceptable except the *disgusting* (realizing, of course, that what is disgusting to one person may not be to another). If something disgusts you, it hits you in the aesthetic jugular in such a way that, however worthy the work may be otherwise, you cannot enjoy it, or even (probably) give due attention to its other qualities.

Still, one could make the same reply as before: "If something disgusts you, you are not likely to enjoy it; but it may have many qualities that you *could* appreciate if you could just overcome the disgust, and I believe you should try; at any rate, the inability to appreciate such a work is *your* failing, and it is you who are missing something by not being able to 'assimilate' works which possess this quality. Granted that (for example) most sexually explicit films are crude and badly done (they cater to audiences that don't care about artistic merit), there are a few that possess valuable qualities, and it's a pity that your inability to overcome your revulsion toward things having the quality you object to (however understandable) prevents you from appreciating the other qualities the work possesses. You are, I'm afraid, throwing the baby out with the bath-water."

Other General Criteria

Are there any other interart criteria that could be suggested—criteria for judging works of art in all of the various media? Let us consider a few, and see whether they can be subsumed under the three already considered.

1. *Technical mastery of the medium.* When a work of art displays mastery of the medium, this is regularly an occasion for admiration, even when we care little for the work in other respects. A sculptor may not have many creative ideas, but if he can "bend a recalcitrant material to his will," whether stone or glass or wood or metal, he is revered (and his work more highly regarded) because of this, even though his productions may not strike the viewer as particularly noteworthy otherwise. A play may be sloppy in dramatic construction or uninvolving in content, but if its production is smooth and coordinated, the timing perfect through countless careful rehearsals, and everything happens on cue with no slip-ups, at least (we say) it may be worth seeing for that. The admiration for technique applies to both the primary and the secondary artist: to the painter or sculptor in whose arts there

is no secondary artist and to the performer in any of the arts of performance. "Horowitz has a fabulous technique," people say on emerging from the concert hall, whether or not they think highly of Horowitz's interpretation of the particular compositions played.

Is technical mastery a criterion independent of the three already discussed? The presumption is in favor of a "yes" answer, unless the criterion can be totally assimilated into one or more of the others. Does technical mastery always add to unity, complexity, and intensity? A sloppily played composition will doubtless give less of an impression of unity than an expertly played one, even if the notes are the same; and if some notes are unplayed, there is of course less complexity. A composition played with "fabulous technique" (perhaps almost impossible combinations of notes, with all ten fingers at once) may yet lack intensity if the pianist "puts no feeling into the work"—it may be technically admirable but cold, uninvolving, "blah." It is indeed a matter for controversy how much technical mastery contributes to the fulfillment of the other criteria. But it seems doubtful that it is nothing more than a special case of the other three.

2. *Suitability to the medium.* Some scenes and subjects are perfect for watercolors but not for oils, and some the other way round. Some figures are best done in stone, which gives a weighty massive quality to its subject-matter; others are better done in wood, an organic substance which better conveys the feeling of aliveness and motion. When organ toccatas by Bach were orchestrated by Stokowski, and instead of every tone in the complex whole being sharp and distinct we hear instead a syrupy mélange of melting strings, blurring the complex structural and textural details of the piece, we conclude that organ works (at any rate those composed for baroque organ, such as Bach's) are simply not suited to adaptation for strings. On the other hand, Bach might well have enjoyed the adaptation of some of his organ works for the Moog synthesizer, for here no matter how numerous the tones simultaneously played or how fast they succeed one another, every tone stands out naked and distinct. But when his sonatas for harpsichord are played on the piano, although the succession of tones is the same (and the unity and complexity the same), the peculiarly "pungent" ("pingy and twangy") quality of the harpsichord is lost in its performance on the more "vanilla-flavored" piano, even if the succession of tones is not blurred by the use of the damper pedal. (Translation of a poem into another language, as we saw in Chapter 1, is not exactly adaptation to another medium, but a different poem created in the other language.)

That a misadaptation of the material to the artistic medium can result in a loss of intensity seems beyond dispute, as well as a diminution of the other two factors if (for example) some of the structural details are blurred. But this does not by itself make suitability to the medium *reducible* to one or more of the three criteria. Could not one plausibly say that his appreciation of the "fitness" of the material to the medium (such as the "pianistic" quality of

Chopin's études and nocturnes, their suitability to the piano and no other instrument) is a source of admiration, and of high ratings, distinguishable from and not reducible to any of the other three, or to all three in combination?

3. *Originality.* Works of art are often praised for being original. But originality is a peculiar kind of property: by examining a work in isolation from other works, you couldn't tell whether it was original or not. Originality is not intentionalistic—you don't have to know whether the artist intended to do something unlike anything ever done before—but it *is* contextual, not with respect to the history of *culture* but with respect to the history of *art,* especially the art-medium in which the work exists. To know whether a given work is original, you have to examine the historically preceding works in the same genre. Originality, then, is not an intrinsic quality of a work of art, but a *relation* between a work of art and its predecessors.

One might contend that an artist's work is original if he *thought* when he created it that no one had done anything like it before. If somewhere in Japan someone had been painting very Cézanne-like paintings, but had never seen or heard of Cézanne's, then, one might say, his work was as original as Cézanne's even if they were created somewhat later in the history of art, because he worked out the style quite independently of Cézanne. Others would say that, just as the first man to make application to the Patent Office is officially the inventor of the new machine, so the first person to do a certain thing in the history of art is the original one, and the other person was not original even if he thought he was.

Every work of art, since it is unlike all previous works in some respects, necessarily has a degree of originality. But such epithets as "highly original" are usually reserved for works, or the invention of new genres or styles, which display an unusually high degree of novelty or departure from tradition. And the originators are not necessarily the greatest users of what they have originated: they may be more important *historically* than they are artistically. Erik Satie was a pioneer of impressionistic music, and as such his compositions are much more original (radical departures from tradition) than are those of Debussy. But Satie's output was very small, and Debussy's work, considering the whole body of it, is probably of greater value than that of Satie (whose compositions would you rather do without?), though taking much of their inspiration from Satie. Picasso was highly original and initiated a number of painterly styles, but many observers would allege that the originality didn't always pay off, and they believe that he would have done better to have stuck to and have developed some of his earlier styles.

Originality by itself, then, is not necessarily a virtue: it all depends on *what* you are original in doing. If I place a yellow crescent moon in the lower left-hand corner of every painting I paint, this feature may be original in the sense that nobody ever did it before, but it is hardly an originality worthy of artistic immortality. The radical innovators in the history of art are those whose originality has been in creating something that posterity has found worth originating and sustaining. As a rule, but not always, the originality that is most respected is that which has turned out to be *fruitful* or productive throughout an entire artistic tradition: not merely a dead end, ending with the artist's own work, but something that offered a potential for future artistic development in directions not even envisaged by the artist who first conceived the innovation.

Since originality is not a quality of a work of art, but a relation of a work of art to its predecessors, it cannot be judged "on all fours" with the other criteria. We would have to say, "Show me the work, and I'll try to give it a rating with respect to its qualities. In doing so, I have no idea to what degree this work was original. If now you show me other works that prove to me how very original this one was, I shall still have to reserve judgment on the work until I estimate *in respect of what qualities* in the work it was original. Some innovations may be worthwhile, other ones not worth the trouble. At that point, I may decide that the qualities with respect to which the work exhibits originality are qualities that enhance unity, complexity, and intensity, and thus make them better works. Or on the other hand, I may believe that these three criteria be inadequate or incomplete, and in that case I may judge the work of art differently, but still with respect to *its* qualities, not with respect to whether preceding works of art also possessed those qualities."

## Specific Criteria

In addition to the three general criteria (applicable to all the arts), Beardsley also suggests some *specific* criteria, criteria applicable to one art but not to others, though no determinate number of these is suggested. The use of various figures of speech by a poet is something for which his work is praised (or dispraised). A poem is praised for the kinds of metaphor and other figures of speech employed in it: but such grounds for praise are applicable only to those arts which employ language—literature and those mixed arts that have literature as a component. A painter is praised for being imaginative in his use of color, but such praise would not be applicable to music or literature. A work of sculpture or architecture is praised for the kinds and combinations of physical materials used, again something which is not applicable to most other arts. A composer is praised for his "feeling for" various instruments of the orchestra to which he assigns parts of the score, but such considerations do not apply to arts that do not use musical instruments.

All these are criteria used in one art-medium but not in others. But we can go further: there are others which are applicable to some genres of art within a given medium but not to other genres. We do not use the identical criteria in evaluating dramas that we do in evaluating novels and poems. Further still, we do not use identical criteria in evaluating some dramas (such as tragedies) that we do in evaluating other dramas (such as comedies). And we can get still more specific: we do not evaluate Greek tragedies in precisely the ways we evaluate Elizabethan tragedies. And perhaps we do not evaluate even one Shakespeare tragedy by criteria identical with those by which we evaluate another: is it certain that we judge *Hamlet,* much of whose drama is internal, by exactly the same criteria we use in judging *Julius Caesar?*

Are all the special criteria we use, those for evaluating comedies as well as tragedies, those for evaluating sophisticated comedies as well as slapstick comedies, classical as well as Eugene O'Neill–Arthur Miller tragedies, all *just special applications* of the three general criteria, or a slightly expanded list of five or six? Are they all subsumable under the three or more criteria, in the way that cats and weasels and wolves are subsumable under (are species of) mammals? Some would say yes; others would say that the kinds of experience generated by these many different art-forms are so multitudinous and so various that it would be surprising if they all turned out to be reducible to three, or even some small number, of basic criteria.

At any rate, let us take a few actual cases and see what happens. Here are two poems. What are the qualities that might make one think well of the poem *Eight O'Clock* by A. E. Housman?

> He stood, and heard the steeple
> Sprinkle the quarters on the morning town,
> One, two, three, four, to market-place and people
> It tossed them down.
>
> Strapped, noosed, nighing his hour,
> He stood and counted them and cursed his luck;
> And then the clock collected in the tower
> Its strength, and struck.

If one is inclined to praise it, it would seem to be for qualities not shared by most other poems. Rhyme and rhythm are unusually important in this one, unlike many other poems. The peculiar staccato rhythm generated by the piece, like that of the clock itself, is unusual and arresting. One might praise it also for the *spareness* with which the effect is achieved: not a wasted syllable, its sparseness and understatement, leaving the reader to make the proper inferences. The first stanza is about only the clock; only in the second stanza does the event appear, a prisoner about to be hanged as the clock strikes eight—then, like the inanimate mechanical object who knows not whose fate it portends, inexorable fate has its way and the prisoner hangs.

How different would be our comments in praise of Randall Jarrell's poem, *The Death of the Ball Turret Gunner:*

> From my mother's sleep I fell into the State
> And I hunched in its belly till my wet fur froze.
> Six miles from earth, loosed from its dream of life,
> I woke to black flak and the nightmare of fighters.
> When I died they washed me out of the turret with a hose.

Here the rhythm is irregular, the rhyme almost nonexistent; the main source of its power lies in the pregnancy of its metaphors, a feature almost entirely absent from the Housman poem. The mixture of ordinary vernacular with far-out metaphors is striking. And so on. But are there any qualities *common to both poems* which would constitute grounds for praise (or adverse criticism)? And if there were, would the common features be as important as those which distinguish the poems from each other? And if we cannot say that poems are good because of certain features, A, B, C, which they possess in common, how much more hopeless would be the attempt to say that all *works of art,* whatever their medium, are good or worthwhile because they possess in common the *same set* of "good-making" features!

> One picture is good for one sort of thing, and another for something quite different. We may praise a water color for its translucency and an oil for the thickness and richness of its impasto. We praise the brightness and clarity of an Impressionist painting, but do not condemn a Rembrandt for lacking these qualities. It is clear that we look for something different in each case. We praise a Botticelli for the poetry of its theme and a Degas for its realism. And how do we praise a realistic picture? We say that the artist has caught the exact pose, the kind of thing one might see at any moment. And the very banality of that pose (in the case of Degas) is a merit. But we do not condemn Botticelli because we fail to meet his goddesses and nymphs as we walk through the street. On the contrary, we praise him for his flowing rhythm, but do not condemn Byzantine art for being rigid, nor Cézanne for being ponderous. Suppose we are considering the work of a colorist, a member, let us say, of the Venetian school. We praise it for subtle nuances of color and for atmospheric unity, the kind that obscures the contour of things. We praise it for the richness of paint, for richness and vitality of effect. And if it fails in these respects we condemn it. But of course we do not condemn a fresco painting of the fifteenth century because it has none of these qualities. In this kind of painting we look for something quite different, for perfection in each part, for unity achieved by the balance of independent wholes, for simplicity in color and thinness of paint, for its simple and dignified effect.[20]

The problems here are multiple:

1. There is a problem about the *number* of criteria to be used. When we get to actual works of art, the reasons given for praising or dispraising them seem to multiply as we probe more deeply. It seems impossible to set a limit to the number of criteria that can be used—and not only *can* be used, but should be used. Every time we think we have them pinned down, we come across new ones. And then the disturbing thought arises that there may be *no limit* to the number of possible criteria.

2. There is not only a problem about how many criteria are to be used, but about their *vagueness.* Different people can agree that unity is a criterion, and

[20] Helen Knight, "The Use of 'Good' in Aesthetic Judgments," *Proceedings of the Aristotelian Society,* 36 (1935-1936); reprinted in *Art and Philosophy,* ed. W. E. Kennick, 1st ed; quoted on p. 593.

yet disagree about whether a specific work of art is unified. Not only do they do this at a superficial level, before they've really analyzed the work of art in detail; they may still do so after thorough investigation.

Consider the remark, "This work of art has a marvelous *freshness* about it." Even if we all agree about the desirability of freshness in a work of art, it's very difficult to pin down, and a work of art that seems fresh to one observer will not necessarily seem so to another. And a quality that was fresh at one time could become a cliché at a later time if often repeated.

3. There is also a problem about the *weight* which is to be attached to different criteria. Suppose that we were all to agree on certain criteria, A through G. Suppose also that we were clear about their meaning. It could still be the case that one person would give great emphasis to one and comparatively little emphasis to another, whereas another person would reverse this emphasis. One person might place great weight on unity as a quality in works of art, whereas another wouldn't care whether it was highly unified as long as it contained imaginative or expressive qualities.

## 4. CONTEXT-DEPENDENCE

What shall we conclude from this frustrating attempt to discover general criteria for the evaluation of works of art, even criteria for the individual arts? One conclusion that has been drawn by some philosophers of art is that there are no general criteria at all and that the search for them is at best idle and at worst pernicious: each work of art is a unique entity, and if we are to appreciate each work of art in all its uniqueness and individuality, we shall only be led away from this attempt by trying to find general criteria to apply to them all—to look for general criteria is to try to discover not what makes works of art unique but what properties that they have in common, in other words, to lump various works of art together under the same mantle, and thus to lead us in the very opposite direction from uniqueness and individuality.

Take any quality, Q, of a work of art (unity, for example). According to traditional reasoning on the matter, the critical argument should go like this:

N: Any work of art which has quality Q is *pro tanto* (to that extent) good. *(Norm)*
R: This work of art has quality Q. *(Reason)*
V: Therefore, this work of art is *pro tanto* good (better than if it lacked Q). *(Verdict)*

But all this is mistaken, says (among others) Arnold Isenberg. The fault lies in the major premise, the first sentence in the argument: there simply are no general norms or standards for the evaluation of works of art. When asked to defend our verdict on a work of art, we give such a bewildering variety of reasons that it almost boggles the mind to try to classify them, let alone reduce them to three or four. One reason this play is good, some people say, is that it is so *exciting;* but the Tintoretto painting is good because it is so *calm* and *peaceful;* the music has such a *rhythmic beat;* the story is so *involving;* the lines in the painting are *graceful;* Handel's music is great because it is *stately* and *dignified;* other music, however, is good because it is *colorful,* and still other works (in both musical and dramatic art) because they have such *tension.* Barber's *Adagio for Strings* is great because of its "utter simplicity," yet other works are admired for the opposite reason, eschewing "mere simplicity." A certain metaphor is "just right" in one poem but totally inappropriate in another poem. A certain work is admired for its intensity of feeling, yet another work will be praised for its low-keyed relaxed quality. In fact, says Isenberg,

> There is not in all the world's criticism a single purely descriptive statement concerning which one is prepared to say beforehand, "If it is true, I shall like that work so much the better." . . . *The truth of R never adds the slightest weight to V,* because R does not designate any quality the perception of which might induce us to assent to V. But if it is not R, or what it designates, that makes V acceptable, then R cannot possibly require the support of N.[21]

In other areas we may argue in this syllogistic manner—"All whales are mammals; so if this is a whale, then this is a mammal"—but in art-criticism the method is fruitless and sterile.

Is art-criticism then a pointless endeavor? Not at all. If the critic attempts to elicit general criteria for all art, or even for different types of art, then it is, for no such general criteria are to be found. But the critic's job lies elsewhere, as Isenberg now proceeds to explain.

Ludwig Goldscheider, on El Greco's painting *The Burial of Count Orgaz,* says:

> Like the counter of a violently rising and falling wave is the outline of the four illuminated figures in the foreground: steeply upwards and the downwards about the grey monk on the left, in mutually inclined curves about the yellow of the two saints, and again steeply upwards and downwards about . . . the priest on the right. The depth of the wave indicates the optical center; the double curve of the saints' yellow garments is carried by the greyish white of the shroud down still farther; in this lowest depth rests the bluish-grey armor of the knight.[22]

The passage appears to be written in support of a favorable judgment of the painting. And the reason for the favorable judgment lies in qualities like the "steeply rising and falling curve." But, says Isenberg, "the same quality

---

[21] Arnold Isenberg, "Critical Communication," *Philosophical Review,* 58 (July 1949), 330-344; reprinted in *Introductory Readings in Aesthetics,* ed. John Hospers, pp. 254-267; passage quoted on p. 261.

[22] *Ibid.,* p. 259.

("a steeply rising and falling curve," etc.) would be found in any of a hundred lines one could draw on the board in three minutes. It could not be the critic's purpose to inform us of the presence of a quality as banal and obvious as this."

And yet it seems from the critic's language that it is indeed the presence of the curve that helps to make the painting a good one; he mentions the curve as if its presence was a basis for praise. What are we to make of this?

> It seems reasonable to suppose that the critic is thinking of *another* quality, no idea of which is transmitted to us by his language, which he sees and which by his use of language he gets *us* to see. This quality is, of course, a wavelike contour; but it is not the quality designed by the expression "wavelike contour." Any object which has this quality will have a wavelike contour; but it is not true that any object which has a wavelike contour will have this quality. At the same time, the expression "wavelike contour" *excludes* a great many things; if anything is a wavelike contour, it is not a color, it is not a straight line. Now the critic, besides imparting to us the idea of a wavelike contour, gives us directions for perceiving, and does this *by means* of the idea he imparts to us, which narrows down the field of possible visual orientations and guides us in the discrimination of details, the organization of parts, the grouping of discrete objects into patterns. It is as if we found both an oyster and a pearl when we had been looking for a seashell because we had been told it was valuable. It *is* valuable, but not because it is a seashell.[23]

The quality he describes or points to, A (the rising curve), may lead us—often not immediately—to discern *another* quality, A', which is so subtle or complex that it is incapable of description in words. But once we discern it, we see that it is A' and not A that is the valuable quality: the only point in showing us A is that it acts as a pointer or indicator to lead us toward the perception of A'. A is a curve of a kind that is by itself not noteworthy; but if we look carefully at the curve, we can see another feature (of features) of the painting, A', which we may come to value enormously, but which without the indicator A we might never have been led to see. Compare this: "The expression on her face was delightful." What was delightful about it?" "Didn't you see that smile?" The smile (A) he can point to—the precise configuration of her mouth that made it delightful (when not all smiles are) he will have to discern for himself. "The speaker does not mean that there is something delightful about smiles as such," says Isenberg; but by mentioning the smile he may be able to focus our attention on the precise quality of *that* smile—and that is what art-criticism is all about: to *show* us qualities of works of art which we might otherwise have missed.

A is the signpost, A' is what it leads us to examine. Sometimes the signpost is not necessary—the listener or viewer comes to discern the desirable features for himself, without assistance; but when having a signpost makes our path easier, when it illuminates for us a quality we might otherwise have missed,

---

[23] *Ibid.,* p. 259.

then art-criticism has justified its existence; it does this by making us aware of features of works of art which lead us to treasure them, but *not* by pointing out features that this work of art has in common with all others.

But if there are no general criteria for evaluating works of art, are we to conclude that there is no reason for preferring this work to that one? No such conclusion follows. One work of art may indeed be greatly preferable to another (this will be discussed in detail in Chapter 9), but no *general reasons* can be given for saying so. The moment we try to give them, we find qualities whose presence (we believe) makes for excellence in one work of art *but not in another.* The reason for this is that one can't pick the qualities (A') out as one picks plums from a plum cake—they are so deeply embedded in the specific *context* in which they occur in the particular work of art that one can no more pluck it from its context and still have a thing of value than one could dissect an animal and still have a living breathing thing. Just as an organ in a body must function in the context of all the rest of the organism, so the valuable qualities in a work of art (the A's) are sources of excellence only *in* the context of the work of art in which they are embedded. The sources of excellence are there, but they are *context dependent.*

Two compositions—say, two quintets by Mozart, the two trios by Schubert—may constitute almost identical workings out of the sonata form, and analytical diagrams of each pair would be almost identical. If we find the one to be more memorable than the other, it is because of very specific features such as that starting on a low B flat, it ascends gradually then more rapidly, not to the B flat octave which we expect, but to the C above it, then rests on the B flat and lingers there. *That* is the difference that makes the difference: that a certain indescribable quality is rendered by this musical pattern. Let us call its description just given A and the quality we cannot describe which occurs when the description is satisfied A'. Yet not every musical pattern that fulfills this description produces the A' which we value. That depends on the total context in which it occurs.

To be sure, if two works were identical in *all* respects, then whatever criteria are used in evaluating the one are those used in evaluating the other. This is true and utterly trivial. But suppose the two differ ever so slightly—just that touch of cerulean blue on the lower right; that slight difference changes everything. One could not say in general "A touch of cerulean blue can always be relied on to help a painting"; in another painting it could be catastrophic. Not only would it not be applicable to all paintings, it would not be applicable to all landscape paintings, or to all landscape paintings by Vlaminck, or indeed (perhaps) to any painting besides this one before us. That touch of blue at that spot makes it "just right"; but that bit of blue at that spot might not make any other painting in the world "just right." It all depends on the specific context in which that touch of blue is placed.

The most difficult grounds for praise to describe have not to do with structure but with texture—for example, the combination of tones of which a particular melody is constituted. Most suggested criteria are silent about texture. And what general criteria about texture can possibly be given? To say that an A flat should always be followed by a C would be as ridiculous as saying that the word "ago" should always be preceded by the word "long": sometimes yes, sometimes no, depending on the tones or words in their specific context.

Toward the end of the "Offertory" movement of Berlioz's *Requiem,* the music, now quiet and stately after the turbulence that has gone before, remains somberly in the minor key, then seems once or twice as if it were about to modulate into the major, but after a brief tendency in that direction, hovering on the brink, settles back into the minor ("sanctum, quam olim Abrahae promisisti et semini eius"); then for a few moments everything hangs on a single note (B flat) in the strings as if hesitant as to where to go, and then from the bass strings we get an E flat and G that quietly but firmly turn the chord into the major key ("Domine, Jesu Christe, Amen"). At this moment there pervades the music an unearthly peaceful splendor; but just when we think the movement is concluding in this state of quiescence, the melody in the treble ascends step by step while the one in the bass simultaneously descends, down to E flat in the bass, and the effect is as if the heavens are opening, and we feel almost as if we ourselves are being levitated off the earth. This double magic, first the transition from minor to major (first halting, then firm and secure) followed by the ascent of the high tones while the low ones descend farther, seldom fails in my experience to move listeners to a kind of awed and silent rapture. Only students of music can say by exactly what musical means this magic has been wrought, but the experience itself they find incapable of description in words—yet it occurs with remarkable regularity. Long after repeatedly experiencing this passage I read that when Franz Liszt heard it he exclaimed, "This surpasses all."

Yet if one were to describe all the harmonic and contrapuntal devices used by Berlioz in this minute or two of music, one could not say, for example, that "Make the minor chords tremble on the verge of turning into major chords once or twice before you actually do it" is a good general rule for producing great music (it wouldn't apply to the other arts at all, of course). Any student in a course in harmony and counterpoint could compose such a passage, and the result in most cases would be disastrous. But in *this* passage of music, which has been prepared for in just the way Berlioz did it in the preceding measures of this movement, it produces the unique and indescribable quality we value. At the beginning of the movement it wouldn't have worked at all, with nothing leading up to it; in a different movement, such as the "Deus Irae," it would have been ridiculously out of place. It is only here, in this specific context, that it rises to greatness. Take away the context and the magic disappears. It is not that there are no qualities that help to make works of art great, but that these qualities are so context dependent that they cannot be ripped from that context and then singled out as qualities that help produce greatness wherever they occur, that is, independently of that context.

The climactic quality of the last few pages of "The Royal Game," the feeling of all the pieces now fitting together and being propelled headlong toward a climax, is shared by many other works of fiction as well as music, but not in quite the same way as it happened in "The Royal Game"; and such passages would be inappropriate in the first pages in which the author was setting the stage and initiating the action. The "placid benevolent sweetness" of a Giorgione would be out of place among the sharply delineated architectural shapes of a Canaletto or the *Disasters of War* paintings of Goya. The "twilight hush" that concludes the Brahms Third Symphony would be quite out of place in the climactic passages of Beethoven symphonies and overtures, which often conclude with a series of loud staccato chords in the tonic.

When Shakespeare's tragedy *King Lear* is about to end, and Lear is dying near the dead body of his one faithful daughter Cordelia, his last words are

> . . . No, no, no life!
> Why should a dog, a horse, a rat, have life,
> And thou no breath at all? Thou'lt come no more,
> Never, never, never, never, never!
> Pray you, undo this button: thank you, sir.
> Do you see this? Look on her, look, her lips,
> Look there, look there!

(Act 5, scene 3)

By most "canons of criticism" it would be quite impermissible, even outrageous, to have a line of poetry consisting of "never" repeated five times, followed by a one-line change of subject just before the passage is supposed to end on a note of exaltation; yet in this context, in which "the simplest and most unanswerable cry of anguish rise note by note," it achieves incandescence.

> To make a verse out of this one word ("never") required the boldness as well as the inspiration which came infallibly to Shakespeare at his greatest moments. But the familiarity, boldness and inspiration are surpassed (if that can be) by the next line, which shows the bodily oppression asking for bodily belief. The imagination that produced Lear's curse or his defiance of the storm may be paralleled in its kind, but where else are we to seek the imagination that could venture to follow that cry of "never" with such a phrase as "undo this button," and yet could leave us on the topmost peaks of poetry?[24]

Shakespeare could break every rule in the book and come out with great poetry; most other poets cannot. Had he followed a list of "general rules to be followed in writing poetry," he would not have the poetry that we have from

---

[24] A. C. Bradley, "King Lear," in *Shakespearean Tragedy* (London: Macmillan, 1904), p. 293.

his pen, and if a freshman student in a literary composition course came up with such lines as these, he would probably be put down by his teacher for having switched subjects (perhaps even"compromised the unity") so rapidly as to lapse into incoherence. Yet in the case of the Shakespeare passage one can hardly resist saying that the passage is a great one partly *because* of (certainly not in spite of) these abrupt changes. One would shudder to try to state a criterion which would be appropriate to this example, but whatever criterion one could come up with would probably be *specific to this context* and could in no way be generalized to suit other, and different, contexts. That is why one hesitates to set any limit to the variety of reasons that can be given to support one's judgments of artistic merit.

It may be that there is a bottom line to all this that is disarmingly simple: that all the features of works of arts, so peculiar to the individual work and dependent on the specific context, are just different ways of bringing about greater *intensity*. Perhaps. But if this is so, one can at least remark that even if intensity is achieved by all the devices described, one cannot refrain from being interested in *how* it is achieved, and in the fact that there are no general rules for its achievement, but that they vary so much from case to case that no rule can be devised that tells us anything beyond that one case. And this conclusion, if true, is certainly of interest: it would be like the situation in ethics if there were an infinite multiplicity of moral rules because when the situation changes ever so slightly a different rule would become applicable; and thus a certain rule might have an application in one specific situation, but never in the whole history of the world another.

## EXERCISES

1. "What's so great about the second movement of Brahm's Piano Concerto No. 2? It's that place in the middle of the movement when the rhythm changes suddenly, like water being sucked into a vortex and emerging transformed, or like a car going from forward into reverse, setting up a whole new musical situation in midcourse. Seldom in a work of music does this feature occur, and seldom would it be successful; but in this one it works, and never ceases to be exhilarating." Is this reason subsumable under one of the others discussed in this chapter?

2. Can something be a reason for me to like a work of art but not for you to like it? Can something be a reason for me to consider it a good work of art but not for you so to consider it?

3. We often speak of technique in relation to a secondary artist (the violinist's technique, the pianist's technique, the actor's technique). But we also speak of technique in the case of the primary artist—not merely the painter and sculptor who handles physical materials and shapes them, but the composer, whose only physical activity is writing the score, and the poet, whose physical

activity consists in writing the words down. What then is meant by the technique of writing fiction? the technique of musical composition? (Is "Brahms does more imaginative things with the piano in his concertos than Beethoven does" a technique statement?)

4. Can some feature of a work of art be a good-making feature at one time or place and a bad-making one at another? Can a metaphor be good in one poem and bad in another, written at a later time when the metaphor has grown stale?

5. If someone says, "I admit that the Brahms quartets and quintets are highly unified and complex and contain intense regional qualities, but I can't *stand* those particular Brahmsian regional qualities—there's something about the way he arranges tones that I find intolerable." Does this kind of comment tend to cast doubt on the acceptability of the three criteria, or their exclusiveness?

6. "The same features which in one work of art contribute to delicacy will make for flabbiness in another work of art, and what is powerful realism in one work of art will be crude vulgarity in another." (Eugene Blocker, *Philosophy of Art,* p. 264.) Can the same feature which is a merit in one work be a defect in another? Discuss.

7. Do you think a work of art can ever be praised or condemned on the grounds that it contains a certain kind of subject-matter? Why? (Example: The film *Murmur of the Heart* was condemned in some quarters because it dealt with the subject of incest.)

8. Edward Fitzgerald's *The Rubaiyat of Omar Khayam* contains the following stanza:

> The moving finger writes; and having writ,
> Moves on; nor all your piety nor wit
>     Shall lure it back to cancel half a line,
> Nor all thy tears wash out a word of it.

The poet was writing about "the moving finger of Fate"; but a secretary reading it thought he was talking about electric typewriters. Is there any way to refute this interpretation?

9. Do you consider the following to be relevant to an evaluation of works of art? Why?

    a. It contains true views of astronomy and geology.

    b. It shows what's wrong with our society.

    c. It accurately depicts rural life in England in the eighteenth century.

    d. It made me cry when I read it.

    e. It is morally profound.

    f. It is full of insights into human nature.

    g. This kind of work is very much needed in our day.

    h. In an iconoclastic age, it upholds great moral ideals.

    i. It is a highly original work.

    j. The artist is obviously a master of his medium.

    k. It presents both sides of the issue fairly.

l. It's full of emotion, but only on one side of the issue.

m. It must have been difficult to get those shots—they must have taken them from a helicopter.

n. The movie was memorable for those beautiful panoramas of the Mediterranean coast.

10. Of Carl Dreyer's films (*Day of Wrath, Passion of Joan of Arc, Ordet,* etc.) one could say, "The thing that distinguishes them so notably is perhaps best called *atmosphere.* No matter at what point you come into the theater, after two minutes you could cut the atmosphere with a knife: it is absolutely compelling, totaling absorbing. Even if, externally, nothing much is going on, the same effect occurs. His films are so clear and clean that compared with them every other film maker's work is like a smudged carbon copy compared with an original." Under what category would you place this kind of praise? Is it a separate criterion by itself, or does it fall without remainder under one or more of the others already considered?

11. A film has unrelenting tension to the end. A critic says, "The film allows no relaxation. It should have let down from time to time, to give the viewer a chance to breathe or catch his breath. ("This film strikes and maintains such a relentlessly shrill, bombastic note that it becomes abusive of the viewer." (Review of Marjoe Gortner's film *When You Comin'g Back, Red Ryder?"* in *Los Angeles Times,* 2 February 16, 1979, p. 23.)

Now suppose it had had that occasional relaxation. Then the reviewer might have said, "This film is inconsistent in its tone. It should have kept up its relentless tempo throughout, but it varies it so that the viewer once he has become accustomed to one rhythm is then confronted by another, and the result is confusion."

Of course, it may be possible that it should be totally tense for one kind of movie *(Psycho)* and "let go" for another *(Agatha)* and that one can't generalize. But at any rate one shouldn't say "It's bad *because* it has no release from tension" because others are good for that very reason. Or could one, perhaps when conjoined with other reasons?

12. A review of Robert Altman's film *Quintet (Los Angeles Weekly,* February 15, 1979) reads in part, "The film proceeds with a deliberate, infuriating slowness. Its rhythm is the rhythm of its people, half-frozen and at the same time half-crazed. *Altman doesn't let us perceive anything faster than we would if we were always cold, always hungry.* He keeps what we perceive at a bare, glazed minimum. We see the city as though we're walking with our heads down, depressed, only occasionally looking about us." These remarks are used as the basis for an unfavorable verdict on the film. Yet almost identical remarks were made by other critics as the basis for a favorable verdict on the same film. Which should it be, and why? or could it be both? Discuss.

13. Which of the following poems (or excerpts from poems) about death do you consider the best? Rate them in descending order of evaluation. Then try to state the criteria you employed in giving them the rating you did.

a. So live, that when thy summons comes to join
    The innumerable caravan, which moves
    To that mysterious realm, where each shall take
    His chamber in the silent halls of death,
    Thou go not, like the quarry-slave at night,

Scourged to his dungeon, but sustained and soothed
By an unfaltering trust, approach thy grave
Like one who wraps the drapery of his couch
About him, and lies down to pleasant dreams.

(From William Cullen Bryant, *Thanatopsis*)

b. Life is real! Life is earnest!
    And the grave is not its goal;
Dust thou art, to dust returnest,
    Was not spoken of the soul. . . .

Let us, then, be up and doing,
    With a heart for any fate;
Still achieving, still pursuing,
    Learn to labor and to wait.

(From Henry W. Longfellow, *A Psalm of Life*)

c. Death, be not proud, though some have called thee
Mighty and dreadful, for thou art not so;
For those whom thou think'st thou dost overthrow
Die not, poor Death; nor yet canst thou kill me.
From rest and sleep, which but thy picture be,
Much pleasure, then from thee much more must flow;
And soonest our best men with thee do go—
Rest of their bones and soul's delivery!
Thou'rt slave of Fate, chance, kings, and desperate men,
And dost with poison, war, and sickness dwell,
And poppy or charms can make us sleep as well,
And better than thy stroke; why swell'st thou then?
One short sleep past, we wake eternally,
And death shall be no more: Death, thou shalt die!

(John Donne, sonnet, "Death Be Not Proud . . .")

d. I was ever a fighter, so—one fight more,
    The best and the last!
I would hate that death bandaged my eyes, and forbore,
    And bade me creep past.
No! let me taste the whole of it, fare like my peers
    The heroes of old,
Bear the brunt, in a minute pay glad life's arrears
    Of pain, darkness, and cold.
For sudden the worst turns the best to the brave,
    The black minute's at end,
And the elements' rage, the fiend-voices that rave,
    Shall dwindle, shall blend,
Shall change, shall become first a peace out of pain,
    Then a light, then my breast,
O thou soul of my soul! I shall clasp thee again,
    And with God be the rest!

(From Robert Browning, *Prospice*)

# SELECTED READINGS

BATTIN, M. P. "On the Generality of Critical Reasons." *Journal of Philosophy,* 59 (1962).

BEARDSLEY, MONROE C. *Aesthetics.* New York: Harcourt Brace, 1958, Chapter 10.

BEARDSLEY, MONROE C. "The Limits of Critical Interpretation." In Sidney Hook, ed., *Art and Philosophy.* New York: NYU Press, 1966, pp. 61–87.

BEARDSLEY, MONROE C. *The Possibility of Criticism.* Detroit: Wayne Univ. Press. 1970.

BRUNIUS, TEDDY. *David Hume on Criticism.* Stockholm, 1952.

GREENE, THEODORE M. *The Arts and the Art of Criticism.* Princeton: Princeton Univ. Press, 1940.

HAMPSHIRE, STUART. "Logic and Appreciation." *World Review,* Oct. 1952. Reprinted in Kennick and Weitz.

HARRISON BERNARD. "Some Uses of 'Good' in Criticism." *Mind,* 69 (1960).

ISENBERG, ARNOLD. "Critical Communication." *Philosophical Review,* 58 (1949). Reprinted in Margolis, Kennick, Hospers Weitz.

JARVIE, I. C. "The Objectivity of Criticism in the Arts." *Ratio,* 9 (1967).

KNIGHT, HELEN. "The Use of 'Good' in Aesthetic Judgments." *Proceedings of the Aristotelian Society,* 36 (1935-6).

KUHNS, RICHARD. "Criticism and the Problem of Intention." *Journal of Philosophy,* 57 (1960).

LYCAN, WILLIAM, and PETER MACHAMER. "A Theory of Critical Reasons." In Tilgman, *Philosophy of Art and Aesthetics.* Reprinted in Kennick.

MACDONALD, MARGARET. "Some Distinctive Features of Arguments Used In Criticism of the Arts." *Proceedings of the Aristotelian Society,* Supplementary Vol. 23. Reprinted in Weitz.

MARGOLIS, JOSEPH. *Art and Philosophy.* Atlantic Highlands, N.J.: Humanities Press, 1979. Part II.

MARGOLIS, JOSEPH. *The Language of Art and Art Criticism.* Detroit: Wayne Univ. Press. 1965.

MEYER, LEONARD B. "Greatness in Music." *Journal of Aesthetics and Art Criticism,* Vol. 17 (1958).

MORRIS, BERTRAM. "The Philosophy of Criticism." *Philosophical Review,* 55 (1946).

MORRIS-JONES, H. "The Logic of Criticism." *Monist,* 50 (1966).

OSBORNE, HAROLD. *Aesthetics and Criticism.* London: Routledge & Kegan Paul, 1952.

OSBORNE, HAROLD. "Reasons and Description in Criticism." *Monist,* 50 (1966).

PEPPER, STEPHEN. *The Basis of Criticism in the Arts.* Cambridge: Harvard University Press, 1949.

SIEGLER, "On Isenberg's 'Critical Communication.' " *British Journal of Aesthetics,* 8 (1968).

SILVERS, ANITA. "Aesthetic Akrasia: On Disliking Good Art." *Journal of Aesthetics and Art Criticism,* 31 (1972).

SLOTE, MICHAEL A. "The Rationality of Aesthetic Value Judgments." *Journal of Philosophy,* 68 (1971).

STERNE, LAURENT. "On Interpreting." Journal of Aesthetics and Art Criticism, 39 (1980), 119–130.

STEVENSON, CHARLES L. "Interpretation and Evaluation in Aesthetics." In Max Black (ed.), *Philosophical Analysis.* Cornell Univ. Press, 1950. Reprinted in Weitz.

STRAWSON, P. F. "Aesthetic Appraisal and Works of Art," in *Freedom and Resentment and Other Essays.* London: Methuen, 1974.

VERMAZEN, BRUCE. "Comparing Evaluations of Works of Art." *Journal of Aesthetics and Art Criticism,* 34 (1975). Reprinted in Kennick.

WALSH, DOROTHY. "Critical Reasons." *Philosophical Review,* 69 (1960).

WEITZ, MORRIS. "Reasons in Criticism." *Journal of Aesthetics and Art Criticism,* 20 (1961).

ZIFF, PAUL. "Reasons in Art Criticism." In Israel Scheffler (ed.), *Philosophy and Education:* Boston, Little Brown. Reprinted in Kennick.

# 8

# Aesthetic Attitude and Aesthetic Experience

## 1. THE AESTHETIC ATTITUDE

For at least two centuries it has been a dominant view in aesthetic theory that, when we appreciate objects in nature and works of art, we are in some special frame of mind, or in some "mental set" or attitude, and that if we are not, we cannot appreciate whatever beauties may lie waiting for us in the world of nature or of art. Our first task will be to present several accounts that have been given of the nature of this special "way of coming at" the world, this frequency to which we must be tuned in if we are to respond, in a way that is called aesthetic, to the world around us.

1. *Aesthetic versus practical.* In the vast majority of our interactions with the world around us, the needs of our daily lives are constantly pressing. We must get to class by a certain time; we must have lunch; we must get to work by 3 P.M.; and so on. We are constantly pursuing goals, sometimes long-range ones like preparing for a job or profession, but most frequently short-range ones like getting a snack from the kitchen, setting the alarm clock so as to wake up on time, and so on. In all this, there is nothing in our experience that could be described as aesthetic. Aesthetic response comes when we stop, even briefly, to look, to listen, so *savor* the qualities of experience beyond what is required for fulfilling our practical needs. Roger Fry put it this way:

The needs of our actual life are so imperative that the sense of vision becomes highly specialized in their service. With an admirable economy we learn to see only so much as is needful for our purposes; but this is in fact very little, just enough to recognize and identify each object or person: that done, they go into an entry in our mental catalogue and are no more really seen. Almost all things which are useful in any way put on more or less this cap of invisibility. It is only when an object exists in our lives for no other purpose than to be seen that we really look at it, as for instance at a China ornament or a precious stone, and towards such even the most normal person adopts to some extent the artistic attitude of pure vision abstracted from necessity.[1]

On this view, the term "aesthetic" describes a *way of coming at* things, which is not the normal or usual way, but which does occur when we stop to look, to listen, to feel intensely. Most of the time we cannot afford to do this: if we are rushing to class we cannot stop to admire the cloud formations; the snake may be beautifully marked, but if it is poisonous and poised to strike, that is no time to admire its beauty. Our aesthetic sense, or sense of beauty, comes into play when our goal-oriented interests are suspended and we stop to dwell on the sight, the feel, the sounds of the world around us. It is rather amazing, when one thinks of it, that human beings are able to do this at all: if, as Darwin believed, only those capacities that are biologically useful continue to exist, one cannot help wonder how the capacity to perceive beauty, which no other animal appears to have, ever arose or survived in the human race.

Not only is it possessed by gifted artists, it seems to be present in almost everyone to some degree: certain styles and arrangements of furniture are rejected by the housewife, not because they are not practical or useful, but because she finds them aesthetically displeasing; more cars are probably bought on the basis of their appearance—their colors and lines and contours—than on the basis of their mechanical functioning. Only occasionally, as in listening to a moving piece of music, is our attention one of total absorption; but on the other hand, it is seldom entirely absent either: even in the midst of fulfilling an urgent practical need, such as an important appointment, a certain building along the way may suddenly strike us as beautiful or ugly. Even in a situation of practical danger we may come to look at something aesthetically:

A fog at sea can be a source of intense relish and enjoyment. Abstract from the experience of the sea fog, for the moment, its danger and practical unpleasantness, just as everyone in the enjoyment of a mountain-climb disregards its physical labor and danger . . .; direct the attention to the features "objectively" constituting the phenomenon—the outline of things and distorting their shapes into weird grotesqueness; observe the carrying-power of the air, producing the impression as if you could touch some far-off siren by merely putting out your hand and letting it lose itself behind that white wall; note the curious creamy smoothness of the water, hypocritically denying as it were any suggestion

[1] Roger Fry, *Vision and Design* (London: Chatto and Windus, 1926), pp. 24–25.

of danger; and, above all, the strange solitude and remoteness from the world, as it can be found only on the highest mountain tops; and the experience may acquire, in its uncanny mingling of repose and terror, a flavor of such concentrated poignancy and delight as to contrast sharply with the blind and distempered anxiety of its other aspects. This contrast, often emerging with startling suddenness, is like a momentary switching on of some new current, or the passing ray of a brighter light, illuminating the outlook upon perhaps the most ordinary and familiar objects—an impression which we experience sometimes in instants of direct extremity, when our practical interest snaps like a wire from sheer overtension, and we watch the consummation of some impending catastrophe with the marveling unconcern of a mere spectator.[2]

The aesthetic attitude, then, is contrasted to the "practical" attitude toward things. But the word "practical" is somewhat vague. Suppose you read poems not for enjoyment but to pass a test on them the next day: is this a practical activity, and is one's attitude toward them therefore not aesthetic? Is reading to expand one's knowledge practical? They certainly need not be practical in the sense of adding to our income or improving the economic quality of our lives; but if improving the general character of our lives—making us better persons, or more appreciative of life and the world—is called practical too, then countless additional activities are practical that are not in the narrower sense. In the broad sense, listening to a recording of enjoyable music at the end of a long day, when one is tense or tired and one's nerves are about to snap, could itself be called an eminently "practical" activity—"the most practical thing to do under the circumstances."

2. *End in itself versus means to an end.* Often what the person has in mind is not so much whether the activity is practical as that it is undertaken as a means to an end. And this consideration opens up another way of distinguishing the aesthetic attitude: when the activity is undertaken as a means to an end, one's frame of mind is nonaesthetic, but when one undertakes it "for its own sake," "without ulterior purpose," then it is aesthetic. The person who reads the poems for enjoyment is coming to them aesthetically; the person who reads them to pass a test is not.

However, the phrase "for its own sake" needs explaining. One might object that everything that one does is done for *some* purpose or other, even if that purpose is just to enjoy oneself. "If you have the painting hanging on the wall not to impress the neighbors (clearly a means to an end) but because you enjoy looking at it, it 'teases the eye' and you turn back to it again and again, that's an aesthetic interest all right, but it isn't viewing the painting for its own sake—it's viewing it for the sake of (that is, in order to get) enjoyment or satisfaction. You're still using the painting as a means to an end!"

But there is a difference. In daily life, when we say that we do something for its own sake, what we usually mean by this is that we do it for the enjoy-

[2] Edward Bullough, "Psychical Distance as a Factor in Art and Aesthetic Principle," *British Journal of Psychology,* 5 (1912), 88.

ment or satisfaction we get out of doing it—we find the activity *itself* enjoyable, and we do not engage in it because it leads to something else which we hope to get from it. Some people engage in daily exercise for its own sake (they enjoy swimming or tennis and do it because they enjoy it); others don't like it but do it to improve their health or appearance (that is, as a means to an end). In the same way people look at paintings or listen to music just for the pleasure they have in doing it, and without any end-in-view beyond that, and when this happens their attitude is described as aesthetic.

These examples show us, however, that "doing something for its own sake" is not limited to the aesthetic: when we play games, not for money but for fun, we are doing it "for its own sake," that is, because we enjoy playing; does that mean that we are coming at the game with an aesthetic attitude? People have sex not only to have children but also because they enjoy it; does this make one's attitude in having sex aesthetic? When a person robs a store or mugs someone on the street, not for money, but just "for the hell of it" (because he likes doing it), is his attitude aesthetic? There are countless activities which we engage in for their own sake which one would be likely to call aesthetic. Thus the class of activities we engage in for their own sake is far broader than the class of activities we engage in with an aesthetic attitude.

3. *The aesthetic versus the personal.* One dominant strand in the concept of the aesthetic attitude is the opposition of the aesthetic attitude to that of personal involvement in a situation. If you are involved in a shipwreck, your attention is likely to be totally absorbed in trying to save your life and the lives of those around you; but if you see a newsreel of a shipwreck, or a painting of one, or film involving one, you are in a different frame of mind than you are when you are yourself involved in the situation. In the real-life situation you are participant, an actor; in the other, a spectator. Personal involvement in a situation forecloses the aesthetic attitude toward it.

Consider these cases:

(a) A yokel in the gallery of a theater sees the villain on the stage about to kidnap the heroine, and following his frontier instincts, takes out a pistol and shoots the villain from the gallery.

(b) A man goes to a performance of Shakespeare's *Othello,* but can't get much out of the play because it constantly reminds him of his own domestic situation with his wife, which is extremely similar to the one depicted in Shakespeare's play.

(c) A person can't enjoy a painting because it's a portrait of someone who greatly resembles his father, whom he detests.

(d) A person enjoys hearing a certain symphony when it is played before guests in his own home on his own superb hi-fi set, but doesn't enjoy it at all when it is the same performance of the same symphony played on an identical set in someone else's home.

(e) A man goes to see a play on opening night and enjoys the occasion thoroughly because there is a full house and he is the financial backer of the production.

(f) A critic goes to see the play because he has been assigned to write a review of it for the next morning's edition of the daily newspaper.

(g) A male student, a freshman in art class, hears his instructor deliver a lecture on the virtues of one of Botticelli's paintings (a slide of which is shown in class), but he is so turned on by the female nudes in the painting that he can't pay attention to the lecture.

What has gone wrong in these cases? According to the present version of the aesthetic attitude theory, the person has become *personally involved* in some way in the situation, though not always in the same way. The yokel mistook the stage-situation for a real-life situation and did what he would have done to a person in real life who was about to make off with a damsel in distress. He was oblivious to the fact that it's a make-believe world on the other side of the proscenium arch. The man watching *Othello* didn't interfere with the action on the stage; he was trying hard to respond to the details of the play, but he failed because the nature of the plot kept reminding him of his own real-life situation with his wife. The person who couldn't bear to look at the painting because it reminded him of his father was responding primarily to his father, not to the painting (though he had to look at it briefly to notice the resemblance). The person who could enjoy recordings only on his own stereo set was apparently so filled with pride of possession that he reveled in that rather than in the music, since he was unable to enjoy the same music on someone else's (equally good) set. The fact of personal possession got in the way of his appreciation. In all cases it's some aspect of his own personal relation to the work of art, or something in it or the circumstances surrounding it, that he responds to, not the work of art itself.

Examples such as these are often used to show that the person's attitude "is not aesthetic" because of some personal relation between himself and the work. In the case of the impresario, it is not because the play is excellent that he feels good, but because the play is popular and he stands to profit from this fact. It's not his enjoyment that is considered objectionable, but what the enjoyment is *of*: he is enjoying the full house (with all that this implies for him) rather than the qualities of the play itself. (Of course, he may enjoy the play too, with part of his attention, and to this extent his attitude could be aesthetic.)

The case of the critic is more problematic. He is, indeed, attending the play at least primarily as a means to an end: writing a column and getting paid for it. But is he "personally involved"? Surely not in the way that the Othello-watcher is. He has personal reasons for going to the play, but it does not appear that he is personally involved in the *action* of the play. And how does he lack the aesthetic attitude just because he's going to write a review of it? While watching it he may enjoy it as much as anyone else—paying even more attention to its details than most of the audience because he has to write a review of it; he may not even think of his forthcoming column until after the play is over. Yet this very example of the critic has been used to allege that the critic cannot be in an "aesthetic attitude" because (a) he is using the play as a means to an end, (b) his motivation in going to see it is a "practical" one, and (c) his function as critic makes him "personally involved." And if the critic, because of his function, can't be in "the aesthetic attitude," what about the author? Is he necessarily "too personally involved" to appreciate his own play?

The student is indeed in a pleasurable state; he enjoys looking at the painting. Not only this, it is some aspect of the painting that he is enjoying the nude females in it; it is not as if, like the Othello-watcher, he was attending to something outside the painting. What then is supposed to have gone wrong? Is it that he is attending to only *some* aspects of the painting but not the rest—for example, those that his art teacher emphasizes? But this would indicate only limited appreciation rather than no appreciation at all—and whose appreciation is not limited in some way? Who is there who is sensitive to *all* aspects of the painting? He enjoys the female nudes and nothing else; but someone else might enjoy the harmony of color and line and nothing else, and yet the same kind of objection would not be presented in the latter case. No, if his attitude is objected to as nonaesthetic, it is because it is that not of pure contemplation but of sexual involvement (via his imagination). It is not that he turns from the painting to his own sexual frustrations (for in the example he doesn't), but that viewing the painting "turns him on" and this makes, or is supposed to make, his attitude toward the painting nonaesthetic.

It may be said that he is using the painting as a means to an end, his sexual gratification (via the imagination). But it is far from clear that he is *using* the painting *in order to* gain this gratification. If one says he's using the painting as a means to an end, his own vicarious sexual enjoyment, then why can't one say that another student who views the painting in accordance with the art teacher's suggestions is viewing it as a means toward his aesthetic enjoyment? As we have already seen, "doing it for enjoyment" *is what we mean* when we speak of doing it "for its own sake"; perhaps it is a different sort of enjoyment in the two cases, but as long as he views it for his own enjoyment can one really say that he is using it as a means toward an end?

"But he isn't enjoying it for its *aesthetic qualities*." If this is the objection, it is irrelevant to any discussion of his attitude: it shifts the controversy from his attitude to the thing (and its qualities) which is enjoyed. Nor can you say he isn't paying attention to the work, for he is paying very close attention to the curves of the female bodies (though to nothing else). True, the painting induces in him a strong physiological response; but so does the listener to the climax of a Brahms symphony whose blood pulses and whose heart beats faster as the performance reaches its exciting conclusion.

"But his attitude isn't sufficiently distanced," one might say—and this brings up yet another concept of the aesthetic attitude:

4. *Aesthetic distance.* According to Edward Bullough in his famous essay "Psychical Distance," the aesthetic attitude consists of *distancing* oneself from the object or scene before one. This doesn't mean physical distance, put-

ting it seven feet away from you; it means psychologically distancing it—detaching yourself from it. "Distance" here is a metaphor, and so is "detachment," since you don't literally detach yourself from contact with the work of art. What it means is best seen in some of the examples Bullough cites, which repeat some of those already given, as indeed the concept of distance itself overlaps most of the criteria already discussed.

In the case of the fog at sea, which is Bullough's example, you lose interest in practical concerns, even your own danger, and view the scene as you would a hugh mural spread out before you. You watch the play of colors and shapes with no reference at all to your relation to the whole scene.

In the Othello case, also his example, the man's attitude is *underdistanced:* he cannot "preserve the distance" between himself and the play; he gets personally involved in it, his thoughts turn to himself and his problems. He cannot watch the action of the play except in regard to how it affects him personally.

In the yokel example, which is also his, the man's attitude is again underdistanced. Instead of being a spectator of the action, he involves himself *in* the action, unaware that what's represented on the stage isn't happening in real life. He's supposed to watch it, not change it. This is a somewhat different kind of underdistancing than in the Othello case, where the man is not trying to change it, but still can't retain psychological distance required for appreciating the performance.

When we look at Greek sculpture, says Bullough, our attitude is less "distanced" than when we look at Egyptian sculpture, since the Greek gods are represented as (somewhat glorified) human beings whereas the Egyptian gods are represented as huge, savage, forbidding, and no one would say they look like actual persons. Again, he says, works of great formal complexity evoke an attitude of greater psychological distance, since it takes longer to come to know them intimately and feel at home with them. The high degree of distance occurring when one first becomes acquainted with complex works of art tends to diminish with increased familiarity.

These last examples raise a host of questions which we cannot pursue here, other than to say that the term "distance" is used ambiguously. In the early examples, lack of distance had to do with something interfering with one's contemplation of the work of art; distance in the last two examples has to do with the degree of "feeling-tone" one attributes to the work of art, a degree which normally increases with greater familiarity. Decrease of distance in the first sense is a very different thing from decrease of distance in the second sense, and they seem to be not at all correlated.

Sticking to the first meaning, problems arise similar to those already touched on in discussing other criteria. The art student, for example, would be considered "insufficiently distanced" or "not sufficiently detached." But the application of these terms is far from clear. What exactly does "detached" mean here, and how far should one be "detached" in one's experience of a work of art? Admitting that one shouldn't be as "involved" (which presumably is the opposite of "detached") as the Othello-watcher is, shouldn't one nevertheless be personally involved in the sense that he *identifies imaginatively* with the characters in the play or novel and cares what happens to them? Doesn't this caring keep one reading page after page, with mounting tension to see how the characters fare? This surely would not be called "detachment"—and it does seem to be a *sort* of "personal involvement" with the characters. Is "detachment" really the proper attitude with which to approach a work of art?

When one witnesses a tragedy, one may think, "I could have been that man" or "There but for the grace of God and a favorable early environment go I." But even to think this is not to concentrate on the play itself but to relate it to one's *own* life and fate—perhaps not as crudely as the Othello-watcher, but to relate it just the same. Does doing this make one's attitude nonaesthetic? Surely we are not to respond to works of art with emotionlessness? Aristotle, writing about tragedy, considered the proper response to it to be an emotional catharsis, a purging away of pity and fear—hardly a state of "distance" or "detachment." Although we need not be like the Othello-watcher, surely a response of strong emotionality to some works of art is legitimate and even desirable? Perhaps people who go to melodramatic movies to vent tears are not paragons of aesthetic appreciation, but then neither, would it seem, are people whose response is cold or analytical. "At least she feels *something*"—and as far as it goes, isn't this a plus? One's degree of appreciation need not be in proportion to one's intensity of emotional response, yet can a "proper" appreciation consist in the *absence* of such response? If that kind of state—detachment—is characterized as aesthetic, then one begins to wonder how desirable such a state of mind is when one confronts a work of art.

There is a famous scene in the film made from Steinbeck's novel *East of Eden* in which the son (James Dean), to gain the love of his father, gives him his entire income from his truck garden as a birthday present, and the father moralistically rejects it. This scene is, for most viewers, enormously emotionally involving. A large part of the strong emotional impact of this scene depends on the viewer's *identifying* with the son's conflict in his relation to the father, and if a person has been a son himself, with a similar father, will he not be that much more moved by it? Isn't the ability to be moved at all by it dependent on some degree of imaginative identification with one or both of the characters? But this is prohibited by the requirement that one not consider the relation of the scene to oneself but just the scene itself in isolation to one's own particular background or emotional "bias." Only this is really "distanced." But such a reaction would be a "cold" one, like that of a person who never had parents or parent-surrogates whose love he sought or whose environment was so entirely different from that of most people that he couldn't identify with, or be moved by, the depiction in the book and the film.

And would this be a desirable response to the scene? Surely such a scene, along with countless others in film, drama, and novels, can elicit a strong response only if one imaginatively identifies with the characters and responds to them against a background of sufficiently similar experiences in one's own life. But perceiving a relation between the scene depicted and one's own early experiences would seem to be ruled out as "underdistanced", "not sufficiently distanced," just as in the Othello case. In both cases one is attending to the work of art in relation to, or against the background of, one's experience of life.

Why is such "personal involvement" held to be "insufficiently distanced" and "not sufficiently detached"? One answer that has been given is that it is not sufficiently *disinterested*. And this brings up the best known, historically, of all the criteria that have been suggested for distinguishing the aesthetic from the nonaesthetic.

5. *Interestedness versus disinterestedness.* The term "disinterested" has its home base in moral and legal discussions: a judge is said to be disinterested if he is impartial, unbiased, unprejudiced. A judge in court is supposed to be a "disinterested party" in the dispute which he is to adjudicate—not an *un*interested party, for he may be extremely interested in the case, it may fascinate him utterly, and this does not disqualify him from judging it: rather, he must be *dis*interested, impartial, in the handling of it. He is "an interested party" if he is, for example, a friend or a relative of the defendant, or if he is known to have views which would make it impossible for him to judge the case fairly—for example, if he was a white racist and the defendant was black. In such an event he is supposed to "step down from the bench" in judging that case.

This central idea of the absence of bias carries over into the idea of aesthetic disinterestedness also. Yet aesthetic disinterestedness is not the same; it has nothing to do with justice as between conflicting or contending parties. When one is talking about aesthetic attitudes or responses, it is much more difficult to pin down the meaning of the term "disinterested." Whatever it is, the aesthetic attitude is supposed to be one of disinterestedness, and becoming "an interested party" involves an abandonment of the aesthetic attitude.

The notion of "aesthetic disinterestedness" was first developed in seventeenth century British thought. Disinterested attention, according to Lord Shaftesbury (1621-1683), means "not motivated by self-concern."[3] Regarding a beautiful object is like loving God disinterestedly, "simply for His own sake" (2, 55). When we perceive the beauty of mathematical objects, this "relates not in the least to any private interest of the creature, nor has for its object any self-good or advantage" (1, 296). "The admiration, joy, or love turns wholly upon what is exterior and foreign to ourselves." He then opposes

[3] Anthony Ashley Cooper, Third Earl of Shaftesbury, *Characteristics of Men, Manner, Opinions, Times,* 3 volumes (London, 1711). London, 1900, I, p. 69.

disinterestedness to the desire to possess the object, or to use it. The desire to possess something is "very different from that which should naturally follow from the contemplation of (its) beauty" (2, 127).

A dangerous object, said Edmund Burke (1729–1797), can arouse delight only "if it can be regarded disinterestedly."[4] "The distinction between the sublime and the simply terrible is that, in the case of the former, the interest in perceiving it is not usurped by the practical interest in preserving oneself."[5] Archibald Alison commented that "that state of mind . . . is most favorable to the emotions of taste . . . in which the attention is so little occupied by any private or particular object of thought, as to leave us open to all the impressions, which the objects that are before us can produce."[6] To be disinterested in one's attention is not to be self-centered but, rather, to be *object* centered.

What range of cases is the concept of "aesthetic disinterestedness" designed to cover? It seems that "aesthetic disinterestedness" is opposed to many things: it is opposed to cases in which our attention is distracted from the object back to ourselves; it covers cases in which we wish to possess the object, or use it in some way, rather than contemplate it. Indeed, it seems to cover *all* the cases we have considered so far and to incorporate within itself all the criteria we have discussed. And in doing so it inherits all the same problems. The Othello-watcher is not contemplating the play disinterestedly; but is the person who compares the tragic drama he is witnessing to the "stage of life" as a whole also failing in disinterestedness? Is disinterestedness incompatible with being moved by a scene, when one could not be moved except by comparing it with one's own environment of early childhood? "Disinterestedness" has as its synonym *impartiality;* but *when is one being aesthetically impartial?* Should one be moved to awe, but not to tears? How much imaginative identification is permitted? how much, if any, required?

This problem haunts not only the idea of aesthetic disinterestedness, but of moral and legal disinterestedness as well (from which it is taken). How much imaginative identification is required of, or precluded by, the impartial (disinterested) judge? In divorce court, he should sympathize with the husband, but not so much as to exclude the interests of the wife, and vice versa; and neither so much as to exclude the children. But how much emphasis is to be attached to each? And if he sympathizes with the husband because he too is a husband, or with the wife because she has experienced hardships as the mother of children, are these sympathies incompatible with disinterestedness? Even in legal contexts, the term "impartiality" seems to contain a great deal

[4] Samuel Monk, *The Sublime* (New York: Modern Language Assn., 1935), p. 207. See also Edmund Burke, *An Essay on the Sublime and Beautiful* (1756).

[5] Jerome Stolnitz, "The Origins of 'Aesthetic Disinterestedness,'" *Journal of Aesthetics and Art Criticism,* Vol. 20 (Winter 1961); reprinted in *Aesthetics,* ed. George Dickie and Richard Sclafani, pp. 607–625; passage quoted is on p. 615.

[6] Archibald Alison, *Essays on the Nature and Principles of Taste,* 4th ed., Edinburgh 1815, Vol. 1, Essay 1, Chapter 1, Section 2.

of vagueness; two judges, neither of them "personally involved" in the case, might agree on the same facts of the case and yet arrive at different decisions. Even where the concept is most at home, it is difficult to know how to apply correctly in individual cases.

If this is so in legal contexts, it is much more so in aesthetic ones. If one asks exactly what "aesthetic disinterestedness" means, one is led to answer that it is a kind of catchall term: it applies when there is no factor standing in the way. Standing in the way of what? Of aesthetic appreciation. Appreciation of what? Of aesthetic qualities. But to say this is to place the focus of the discussion, once again, not on the way in which one comes at a work of art but on the qualities of the work of art itself. One is no longer talking about one's attitude or even one's response to the object, but to the nature of the object. And perhaps in the end that is what one has to do, but to do it now is to give up on the present project, that of trying to find some criterion that distinguishes an aesthetic way of "coming at" objects from a nonaesthetic one.

By this time, if not long before, someone may well object, "Let's stop pussyfooting around. The issue is really simple: it is whether we pay attention to the object and *its* qualities ("internal relations"), in which case our attitude may be called aesthetic, or whether we pay attention to what is not a part or aspect of the object before us but something that is external to the object ("external relations"), such as our own life-situation, our personal reactions to people or things or theories or theologies, which may all be evoked by attending to the work of art or some aspect of it, but are not, when they occur, responses to the work of art itself." We are thus led to yet another way of distinguishing aesthetic from nonaesthetic attitudes toward the objects around us.

6. *Concentration on the object.* On this view, there is no special kind of attitude one has toward the object, other than total concentration upon *it,* and not on anything else. The art critic Erwin Panofsky writes,

> It is possible to experience every object, natural or man-made, aesthetically. We do this, to express it as simply as possible, when we just look at it (or listen to it) without relating it, intellectually or emotionally, to anything outside of itself. When a man looks at a tree from the point of view of a carpenter, he will associate it with the various uses to which he might put the wood; and when he looks at it from the point of view of an ornithologist he will associate it with the birds that might nest in it. When a man at a horse race watches the animal on which he has put his money, he will associate its performance with his desire that it may win. Only he who simply and wholly abandons himself to the object of his perception will experience it aesthetically.[7]

This is as "pure" a view of looking or listening as any isolationist could

[7] Erwin Panofsky, "The History of Art as a Humanistic Discipline," in *Meaning in the Visual Arts* (Garden City, N.Y.: Doubleday, 1955).

wish. But there are two major difficulties with it: (a) aesthetic attention may include more than the object, and (b) concentration on the object may include kinds of attention that are not aesthetic.

a. We have already considered some problems in connection with the first difficulty. If this view were accepted, any comparison of our own lives to that of the tragic protagonist, any inclination to wonder about the state of man in the universe, would be a nonaesthetic response, since it is not a concentration on the tragedy alone but of its implications for human life in general or our own lives in particular. Doesn't this make the field of aesthetic attention unduly narrow?

Consider also the *setting* in which works of art may be placed. Paintings by Turner placed on a red wall seem much more dramatic and exciting than when one sees them against a gray wall. Should one's attention be to the painting only, not at all to its visual background? Should one attend *only* to the Temple of Poseidon to appreciate it? Isn't part of the charm of this ancient Greek temple the fact that it is built on a promontory, and that no matter from what angle one sees it (almost) one sees through the columns the deep blue of the Aegean Sea? Shouldn't one at least concentrate on the temple *in* its natural setting? The temple was after all designed and built to be at this spot; should one ignore this fact by viewing the temple in isolation from this natural setting?

There is not only the natural setting but the *historical context* of the work of art. Sometimes knowledge of historical facts is only a *necessary condition* for the appreciation of a work of art—a knowledge of the meanings of words in Middle English as well as some knowledge of the historical period are both required to appreciate Chaucer's *Canterbury Tales*. Here one could say that, while we can't appreciate the work without this prior knowledge, once we have it, the appreciation is of the work itself. (Panofsky himself is one of the most historically oriented of art critics in this respect.) But may it not be plausible to go further and say that historical knowledge may not be only a necessary condition for appreciation, but part of *that which is appreciated*—that what one appreciates is the work of art *in* its historical setting? Consider for example a Constable landscape

which looks to us as ordinary as a picture postcard. Yet critics at the time found it unacceptable and monstrous. "Too green," they said. As it turns out, previous landscapes had depended on a color gradation of brown in the foreground to blue in the background which Constable had not used. The point is this: although we *may* directly perceive the colors in a Constable or pre-Constable landscape, we do not directly perceive the significance of the difference in colors. *That* requires familiarity with the expressive potential of the different color-ranges Constable and his predecessors took themselves to be working within. To approach an art object without preconceptions is not to approach an art object.

If someone says of a painting, "I don't care when it was done or who painted it, it's just a dull painting," one is prompted to reply, "You're just not in a position to tell."[8]

Without such historical knowledge, it is often impossible to appreciate the technical problems an artist has overcome to create the work of art at all. Suppose one wonders how Gothic cathedrals could be built to such a height, stone on stone, without steel girders; is attention to this problem nonaesthetic? Many would say that it is. Remember the example of the Gibbs façade (p. 83).

When you see a film, you may speculate about many things:

1. How much money did it take to produce it?
2. How long did it take to shoot the film?
3. What are those portions of the film like that got edited out and ended up on the cutting-room floor?
4. Was the film adapted from a stage play?
5. Is the house in the background a real one or only a façade?
6. What was going on just outside camera range as this scene was being shot?
7. How much wattage was needed to make this scene visible, since it was apparently shot indoors?
8. What materials and what lighting were used to achieve this peculiar effect of incandescence?
9. Are the birds in Hitchcock's *The Birds* real or mechanical?
10. What kind of film was used to achieve the color effects?
11. What technical means were used to achieve the special effects (as in *Star Wars*)?
12. Did some of the events depicted reflect incidents in the actress's own life?
13. Who was the director? His work is worth watching in the future.

As you watch a film, it's difficult to avoid asking at least some of these questions. Yet all of them are extraneous to the film itself; they are not really concerned with *what you see* on the screen—and this, together with the sound track (both music and spoken words), is what constitutes the film, isn't it? But all these questions are concerned with some relation or other to what's outside the film: the life of the actress, the technical means by which what you see *came to exist*. You are supposed to be concerned with what you see and hear only, not with what devices may have been used to enable you to see and hear what you do; these are problems for film makers, not for film viewers. Many film viewers do indeed ask them; and when they do, their concentration is not wholly on the sights and sounds before them in the theater, and so, according to the criterion we are now considering, attention to such matters is

[8] Robert Schultz, "Does Aesthetics Have Anything to Do with Art?" *Journal of Aesthetics and Art Criticism,* Vol. 36 (summer 1978), p. 435.

nonaesthetic. But is it really that clear that attention to technical matters, which were solved in creating a work of art, is nonaesthetic? They aren't what you see, but perhaps they are necessary, at least sometimes, to appreciate fully what you do see? Should they all be called "aesthetically irrelevant"?

In J. M. Barrie's play *Peter Pan,* the actress playing the central role appears to fly about on the stage. She doesn't really, since she is manipulated by wires (normally invisible to the audience) from far above the stage. The wires are not a part of what the playgoer sees. Yet it makes a considerable difference to an evaluation of her performance whether she is held by invisible wires or not at all. In the latter case, if she was *really* flying about unaided, her performance would be ever so much more remarkable![9]

b. Even if our attention is concentrated wholly on the work of art before us, it would seem that *not all kinds of concentration* on the object should be counted as aesthetic. Continuing our list of examples,

(h) A student turns on the radio to music as soon as he comes into his apartment and doesn't turn it off again until he leaves, perhaps the next day. The music is background for him, he doesn't really listen to it, and he could never tell you what pieces he's heard or even what sort of music it was, but he can't stand the silence if he doesn't have it turned on.

(i) A tour guide in the Greek islands (p. 78) knows every bit of architecture in the area, can identify every ruined temple, can discourse on styles and periods of Hellenic art, and can answer every question on Greek sculpture and architecture that is posed by the tourists. But he doesn't appreciate any of them: he doesn't enjoy any of the art-objects whose history he explains. For him it's just a job, not particularly different from reeling off statistics on the birth rate in Pakistan.

(j) A person pays attention to various aspects of works of art, but the only thing he really likes and admires is the solution by the artist of some technical problem, such as how the painter got that appearance of phosphorescence to pervade the painting, or how the special effects department in a film generated the illusion of spaceships shattering the earth, or how the illusion of a conflagration was generated onstage in a performance of Wagner's opera *Götterdämmerung.* He doesn't really care about the objects before him (works of art and performances thereof) at all, only the technical problems that were solved in order to produce it.

(k) A student reads Lucretius, Dante, Goethe, Shakespeare, and other authors of works of literature, not because he cares about unity or intensity or climax or expressive qualities but because he is interested solely in the philosophical views, explicit and implicit, contained in these works.

The cases are of course not all alike. The radio addict is not like the Othello-watcher: his attention is not deflected from hearing the music by in-

[9] This example is used by George Dickie, *Art and the Aesthetic* (Ithaca: Cornell University Press, 1974), Chapter 4.

trusions from his personal life or by projections from his personal life into the music. Nor is there any desire for possession or use, no diversion from the work of art back to his own biography. His appreciation of what he hears, if we may call it that, is (we would be inclined to say) too *superficial:* he takes in very little of the music, although the soundwaves strike his ears and are conveyed to his brain. His reception of the work is too *passive:* we could say that he is hearing but not listening. Listening is active and hearing is passive, just as looking is active and seeing is passive; you can decide whether or not to look in a certain direction, but when you do you can't help what you see. His was not a case of personal involvement or lack of "distance" but, rather, of superficial attention or even inattention. Nor does this case come in any clear way under the heading of "lack of disinterestedness"; is he really failing to be disinterested? We can call it that only if we *stipulate* that among the things that are to count as failure of disinterestedness, superficial attention is one of them. We can do this, of course; we can say that aesthetic attention is active, not passive, and that the opposite of "aesthetic" should be "anesthetic." Still, it seems to be stretching things to say that his hearing "fails to be disinterested": whatever exactly "aesthetic disinterestedness" is (and we have already considered some problems about this), *that* doesn't seem to be the problem in this case. And if the problem is a failure to pay attention to the object (the music), this really isn't because he's paying attention to something else: he may be concentrating on nothing at all, and he is probably even less aware of the historical or artistic context of the music than he is of the music itself. The case doesn't appear to fall under any of the criteria we have already considered.

Unlike the inattentive student, the tour guide, the technical expert, and the philosophical student do not suffer at all from inattention or lack of concentration. Nor is their attention diverted away from the works in question; on the contrary, all three persons concentrate on the works of art to which they are attending. Yet there is something about their concentration on the object, however intense, that leads many people to refuse to describe as "aesthetic" their manner of attending to it.

The literature student does not find his interest deflected from the novels and poems he reads; he concentrates on them; his attention is far from superficial; he doesn't read to pass an exam or to impress other people; and he is not only totally absorbed in what he reads, he greatly enjoys it. And if one objects, "But he does it as a means to an end, gaining *knowledge*," one could reply, "No more than the appreciator reads as a means to an end, gaining his peculiar kind of enjoyment." They each turn to the work, but for different reasons; or, one might say, they each turn to the work, but they seek from it different qualities.

"But the people in cases i–k aren't concentrating on the works *aesthetically*." Perhaps; but if this is so, aesthetic attention isn't just close attention to the work, for all these *are* attending to it closely and yet apparently "missing the boat" aesthetically. Their interest, one might say, is not aesthetic but *cognitive;* not in appreciation, but knowledge.

7. *Aesthetic versus cognitive.* Cognitive interest in works of art has been contrasted to the aesthetic since the eighteenth century. In 1815 Archibald Alison wrote of classic Greek statues that someone "may observe their dimensions, he may attend to the particular state of their preservation, the history of their discovery, or even the nature of the marble of which they are made," without appreciating "their majesty and grace."[10] Sir Francis Hutcheson excluded from the aesthetic any concern for knowledge about the object. "Such knowledge may be welcomed 'from prospects of advantage' and it may arouse intellectual or cognitive pleasure. Yet it is wholly different from the enjoyment of beauty and can have no effect on this experience."

There certainly seems to be a difference between attending to works of art with cognitive interest and attending to them with an interest in form, line, color, harmony, and so on. Both fulfill the requirement that one concentrate on the object. But how are the two different? Shall we say that they are concentrating on different *qualities*—in which case, again, the difference lies in the qualities attended to, not the type of attention given? Or shall we say that they come to the work of art with different *motives?* or that they are *perceiving* the work of art differently? or what?

The whole idea of a specifically aesthetic attitude, which seemed intuitively so obvious, has turned out to be so elusive, so chameleon-like, that some writers have been led to deny that there is any such thing as a special attitude taken toward works of art or nature that should be called *"aesthetic."* Chief among these critics is George Dickie. His main contentions can be summarized under two headings:

1. *Attention versus inattention.* Dickie rejects the whole battery of distinctions—distanced versus underdistanced, involved versus uninvolved, interested versus disinterested, and the rest—by which various writers have attempted to distinguish aesthetic from nonaesthetic attitudes. The whole idea of an aesthetic attitude, he contends, is a confusion. Much of the terminological baggage which attitude-theorists have accumulated could be eliminated by making one simple distinction, between concentrating on the work and not doing so.

The trouble with the Othello-watcher, for example, is simply that he is not attending to the play; he is paying attention instead to his own problems and conflicts, awareness of which are reevoked by attending the performance. This is not attention to the play, it is inattention; and inattention is not a special kind of attention. But isn't he "underdistancing"? You can use the term if you like, but it is entirely unnecessary: it is enough to say that his attention is not focused on the play. "If 'to distance' and 'being distanced'

[10] Archibald Alison, *Essays on the Nature and Principles of Taste,* 4th ed. (Edinburgh, 1815), Vol. 1, p. 98.

simply mean that one's attention is focused, what is the point of introducing new technical terms and speaking as if these terms refer to special kinds of acts and states of consciousness?''

But surely you put the play ''out of gear'' with your practical interests? ''This question seems to me to be a very odd way of asking (by employing the technical metaphor 'out of gear') if I attended to the play rather than thought about my wife or wondered how they managed to move the scenery about. Why not ask me straight out if I paid attention? . . . To introduce the technical terms 'distance,' 'under-distanced', and 'over-distanced' does nothing but send us chasing after phantom acts and states of consciousness.''[11]

What then of ''aesthetic disinterestedness''? There is no such thing, says Dickie, as ''disinterested attention'' to the object. According to the view, a ''noninterested'' viewer can watch the play aesthetically, but the critic can't because he has an ulterior purpose in going, namely, to review the play. But this won't wash. The one may be as intensely absorbed in the play as the other; the critic, because he is going to write a review, will probably notice more details than the ordinary viewer—and they will be details of the play (not of himself, as in the Othello case), its plot, character, motivation, internal structure, style. There is no reason why the one should be called aesthetic any less than the other.

2. *Motivation.* There is, however, a difference in their *motivation.* ''The one is going for the sake of enjoying the play (what is called ''for its own sake''), whereas the critic is going as a means to an end: he's being paid to write a review.'' But all that this shows is that the two have different motives in going to see the play—it doesn't tend in the slightest degree to show that they notice different qualities or perceive the play differently.

What initially appears to be a perceptual distinction—listening in a certain way (interestedly or disinterestedly)—turns out to be a motivational or an intentional distinction—listening with a certain purpose. Suppose that Jones listens to a piece of music with the purpose of being able to analyze and describe it on an examination the next day and that Smith listens to the same music with no such ulterior purpose. There is certainly a difference between the motives and intentions of the two: Jones has an ulterior purpose and Smith does not. ''But this does not mean that Jones's *listening* differs from Smith's. . . . There is only one way to *listen* to (attend to) music, although the listening may be more or less attentive, and there may be a variety of motives, intentions, and reasons for doing so and a variety of ways of being distracted from the music.[12]

Nor is there a case for ''aesthetic disinterestedness.'' There is a distinction

---

[11] George Dickie, ''The Myth of the Aesthetic Attitude,'' in *Introductory Readings in Aesthetics,* ed. John Hospers, p. 30.

[12] *Ibid.,* p. 32.

between "being an interested party" and not being one, but it is not a distinction that has anything to do with the kind of attention being exhibited. Consider the case of the man whose delight is solely the result of the fact that there is a full house, and he is the financial backer of the production. He has indeed economic satisfaction, taken in the money he will make rather than in the internal qualities of the play. "The impressario is certainly an interested party in the fullest sense of the word, but is his behavior an instance of interested attention as distinct from the supposed disinterested attention of the average citizen who sits beside him?"[13] If his sole concern is with the till, his attention is directed at the size of the house, not to the details of the play. And the same with the spectator whose daughter is in the play, if his attention is solely on the effects on the audience of her performance; or the person who is concerned only with the effects of the play on the viewers' subsequent conduct. "All three of these candidates which the attitude-theorists would propose as cases of interested attention turn out to be just *different ways of being distracted* from the play." They may not, of course, be *entirely* distracted from the play; and in that case they are not entirely, or all the time, "interested parties." Consider the case of a man who attends closely to the play *with* an ulterior motive, the need to rewrite part of the script.[14] Perhaps he doesn't "appreciate" the play because he is too busy taking notes or focusing on one of the characters whose part needs reworking; but this doesn't show that his attention to the play is different in kind from that of a "noninterested" spectator. Indeed, he might well be able to appreciate the performance *with* his "ulterior motives" animating him all the time, noticing various things he believes need changing, and making him more, not less, sensitive to the plot, structure, and characterization than the ordinary viewer would be. That his *motivation* is different doesn't show that his *type of attention* is different ("nonaesthetic" as opposed to "aesthetic"). To the extent that one attends to the play, the type of kind of attention is the same.

It is not clear, however, what Dickie would say about the last series of cases (h-k) discussed. There is *some* difference between the student who studies literature only for its philosophy and the one who does so in order to savor fully the author's style, characterization, development and climax, and so on.

Consider someone who likes (or buys, or keeps, or looks at) a vase because of its delicate colors and graceful shape: no one (I suppose) will be unwilling to call his interest in the vase aesthetic. And if he is interested in the shape of a novel's plot—in the neat way the complications are developed and worked out to dramatic climax, with a final tying up of all the threads (as in *Tom Jones*)—that interest, too, is evidently aesthetic. This is fairly easy to agree on, and we may even risk the generalization that any interest in form or quality for its own sake is an aesthetic interest. . . . Now suppose he is interested in the philosophy of a literary work—say, Tolstoy's philosophy of history in *War and Peace*. Then we

[13] *Ibid.*, p. 33.
[14] George Dickie, *Art and the Aesthetic*, p. 120.

may want to suggest a distinction: if what interests him is the truth of that philosophy or its logical consistency or its historical antecedents and influence, then his interest in the novel is not aesthetic; but if what interests him is the character of that philosophy (its bold sweep, say) or its organic relationship to the structure and recurrent themes of the novel, then his interest *is* aesthetic—indeed, it is an interest in form and quality.[15]

The distinction made here seems clear enough. The question is whether the term "aesthetic" should be reserved for the kind of *interest* he takes in the novel, in which case it remains to be clarified, or whether it characterizes only the different *qualities* present in the novel itself, in which case the only difference is "interest" or "attitude" lies not in the psychological state of the reader but in the qualities on which the reader concentrates his attention. In the second case, there will be no such thing as the "aesthetic attitude" toward the object on which one directs his attention, but only a difference in the kinds of qualities to which this attention is directed.

## 2. AESTHETIC EXPERIENCE

The aesthetic attitude, which seemed so promising at the outset, has turned out to be, at best, a welter of overlapping ideas and, at worst, a phantom no longer worth chasing.

But there is still hope. Many who would never speak of having, or being in, or possessing, an "aesthetic attitude" would still assert that they have aesthetic *experiences*. This, of course, doesn't help unless we know what kind of experiences aesthetic experiences are. And on this point subject seems to be almost as much diversity as on the aesthetic attitude.

"The aesthetic experience," writes Jerome Stolnitz, "is the experience one has when the aesthetic attitude is sustained." This definition makes the experience depend on first having the attitude; and it has the unfortunate consequence that, if it turns out that there isn't after all an aesthetic attitude, then there can be no aesthetic experience either, since the experience is defined in terms of the attitude.

There is another problem also: what if we were in the proper attitude (whatever that might be) for enjoying a work of art, and the work did not repay the taking of the attitude? What if one was all "hyped up" to enjoy a new work of music, but it turned out to be written by a C student in sophomore composition class or even a work by a recognized composer who this time turned out a piece of rubbish? It would be as if one were all prepared to watch a good ball game, but it turned out to be a lousy game. One might be in the proper attitude, but one would not have an enjoyable experience. Con-

---

[15] Monroe C. Beardsley, "The Philosophy of Literature," in George Dickie and Richard Sclafani, *Aesthetics,* p. 328.

trariwise, might not one have the experience unexpectedly, as a sudden surprise, without being in any special frame of mind at all to receive it? It would seem, then, that the two are separable.

What kind of experience is the aesthetic experience supposed to be? One might take as a necessary condition, but hardly sufficient, that it must be a *pleasurable* experience, an experience one enjoys. Can't everyone at least agree on this condition? Possibly, if one is talking about "positive" aesthetic experiences (in which one finds the object beautiful or satisfying) rather than "negative" aesthetic experiences (in which one finds the object ugly or unsatisfying). But even here there is a problem: often, if we wish to describe our experience of those works of art we value the most, we would not use the term "pleasure" or "pleasant." If someone asked you your reaction to Beethoven's late quartets, would you say "I found them pleasing"? If you did, the person might suspect, with reason, that you hadn't really appreciated them. Would you say you found Picasso's *Guernica* "pleasant"? Works of art can do more than please you: they can move you, shock you, startle you into a new awareness, channel your mind into new modes of perceiving, the experience of which (especially at the outset) you would hardly describe as pleasant. One could, of course, cut off the whole controversy at the beginning by saying that then it's some other kind of experience one is having and not an aesthetic experience; or that one finds it pleasant *in addition* to having the other qualities, or that if the experience weren't pleasant, then (by definition) it wouldn't be an aesthetic experience, no matter what other qualities it had. Still, to impose such a limit on the definition seems a bit arbitrary: it would seem strange to say of a simple linoleum pattern that it was pleasing and our experience of it aesthetic, while the experience of some great and enduring work of art is not, simply because "pleasant" is not a word that really describes the latter experience.

One must be careful, however. A picture of an ugly object need not be an ugly picture—it could be an ugly object beautifully painted or painted in such a way as to bring out some new insight, and the experience of these things is really pleasant. And so perhaps it is. Still, one does not value works of art in proportion to the pleasure they give one: here is a combination of lines or tones which one finds utterly pleasing; there is a work of art that one would call great but it is disturbing, perplexing, or shocking. (Does one really get more *pleasure* from *The Deer Hunter* than from the latest screwball comedy?)

But even if all aesthetic experiences are pleasant, this is not enough to distinguish them from other kinds of experiences. Sexual experiences are pleasant; are they aesthetic experiences? The experience of breaking a roomful of crockery is pleasant to those who want to work off some tension; that of beating up old ladies is pleasant to hoodlums. These can hardly be called aesthetic. The experience of playing games is or can be pleasant; is it therefore aesthetic? To call all pleasant experiences aesthetic will be to cast our net much too wide.

"What makes a pleasure aesthetic," wrote Curt J. Ducasse, "is not some peculiarity intrinsic to it, but only the fact that the pleasure is one being obtained through *the mere contemplation* of the object that is the source of it.''[16] This would eliminate most kinds of pleasures. One does not contemplate a game, one plays it; one does not merely contemplate sex partners, one interacts with them.

Still, is this enough? Is the mystic who contemplates his oneness with God (or the Infinite, or the Alone, etc.) having an aesthetic experience? Some might say he is; but others would say that he is having a deep religious experience, but not an aesthetic experience, and that aesthetic experiences have some similarity or analogy to religious experiences but aren't the same things (for example, religious experiences involve an attitude of worship or reverence to a higher being which aesthetic objects don't). Or, to take a mundane example, one may contemplate the various dancers in a ballet and note that A dances with B but not with C, and numerous things of that sort, and all this does seem to be contemplation of the dancers and of the dance, but is the experience of all this necessarily aesthetic? (Or one might be, in a somewhat different sense of "contemplate," lost in contemplation and not really observe anything, but just be wool-gathering. And would one call such an experience aesthetic?) Also, is it enough to specify *that* one is contemplating something, without further specifying for what *purpose* one is doing this, or if it is done for a purpose at all? One can contemplate the details of the yard in order to estimate its dimensions or to decide whether it's worth spading or planting vegetables in. Is such an experience aesthetic, or is it aesthetic only when it's done not for a purpose but "for its own sake"? Here it is easiest just to say "It must be for its own sake"; but then is wool-gathering, which is surely a purposeless activity and "done for its own sake" if anything is, to be construed as aesthetic?

One could try to be more specific: The aesthetic experience must not only be pleasurable, and it must not only be contemplation (for its own sake); it must fulfill another condition. "The aesthetic experience is a pleasurable absorption in the *perceptual aspects* of phenomena."[17]

Here the term "perceptual" is being opposed primarily to "conceptual." To identify something as an aardvark is a conceptual achievement, and so is understanding an argument in logic or mathematics; these are conceptual, not perceptual, enterprises. By contrast, in aesthetic experience we are concerned with *percepts,* not *concepts:* we appreciate sounds and patterns of sound, shapes and colors, and patterns of them—sights and sounds (and perhaps other sensory data) and the organization of these. What is defining of the aesthetic experience is its *perceptual* character.

The pleasure of recognition or identification is not in itself aesthetic, although probably no experience is more frequently considered such. Looking at a picture

[16] Curt J. Ducasse, *Art, the Critics, and You* (New York: Liberal Arts Press, 1944), p. 92.

[17] Hunter Mead, *Aesthetics* (New York: Ronald Press, 1950), p. 29.

and picking out certain objects we can identify as "tree," "river," "old mill," "horse," or "sunset" has little to do with the aesthetic experience. Admittedly this is often a pleasurable (and certainly a harmless) pastime, particularly enjoyable to children and to those adult minds that remain perpetually amazed and intrigued by the artist's ability to represent natural objects. However, the innocent pleasure which this identification activity yields is a simple form of *intellectual* (i.e., conceptual) satisfaction. For it is essentially a process of putting things in their pigeonholes: it involves matching the present "tree" or "river" with our idea or concept of these things. . . . The satisfaction arises from a utilization of [the perceptual] for a conceptual purpose, and not from any delight in perceptual experience as such.[18]

To consider this pleasure of identification and classification aesthetic is the main mistake that the "uncultured" layman makes when he turns to the arts at all. But the "cultured" student of the arts often makes a mistake equally serious: he seeks names, dates, schools, epochs, movements, influences. The genuine aesthetic appreciator finds pleasure in the perceptual relationships to be found in works of art.[19]

Not only are such intellectual responses nonaesthetic, most emotional responses are too. The aesthetic experience can be pleasant, yet, but pleasure is not an emotion (psychologists classify it as a sensory, not an emotional, state). But what makes it aesthetic is not its emotionality but its sensory character.

Yet to limit aesthetic experiences to the pleasurable apprehension of visual, auditory, and other sensory patterns would seem to many persons to be unduly narrow. When you appreciate the neatness, economy, and elegance of a mathematical proof, would we not call the experience of this aesthetic? The motivation of many students of pure mathematics (not applied mathematics, such as engineering) is primarily aesthetic—that is, the apprehension of the mathematical relations is for them an aesthetic experience. Yet that which they are appreciating is not perceptual at all. It isn't the chaotic-looking melange of chalk marks on the blackboard that one is appreciating—visually one wouldn't find *that* beautiful at all. It is the mathematical *relations* themselves that we appreciate, and these are not perceptual, but abstract entities, which are only represented by the numerical and other mathematical signs one sees on the paper or blackboard. Yet nothing is more familiar or understood than a remark like "My interest in mathematics is aesthetic." The appreciation of mathematical relations seems to be about as aesthetic as anything could be, yet it is not the appreciation of any pattern of colors or shapes or sounds or smells.

But we need not go even so far as mathematics: one of the major arts, literature, presents the greatest stumbling block to this conception of aesthetic experience. Can we not have aesthetic experiences of literature? Yet it is not the sights (printed words on a page) that we appreciate, or even the sounds

[18] *Ibid.*, p. 43.
[19] *Ibid.*, p. 48.

(words spoken aloud), when we appreciate a work of literature (see pp. 49–50). What we appreciate is not a sensory order of any kind. One could say, as Roger Fry does, that the appreciation of literature is not really aesthetic, or only minimally aesthetic (confined to a few things like the sound patterns in poems); but literature is a major art, not to be summarily swept under the rug, and many persons would contend that the appreciation of literature is no less aesthetic than that of the other arts, but that it is markedly *different* from them and that any definition of aesthetic experience should be accommodating that difference rather than throwing literature out because it does not fulfill some unduly narrow requirement, such as being perceptual.

One could say, and many have said, that literature gives us a sensory order after all, but an *imagined* one which we as readers must create in our minds rather than one presented directly to the eyes and ears like visual arts and music. The author, it is said, creates through the words in his novel an imaginary world containing persons and situations, and the sights and sounds and smells of that world are vividly imagined by us, the readers.

But it does not appear that this suggestion is all that plausible. (1) When you appreciate a work of literature, is it always the world the author has created (or which you create in your mind, acting on the verbal cues he gives you) that we appreciate? It might be, and often is, a very ugly world—and yet the literary work may be beautiful (through the author's style, for example) although the world he creates for us is hideous or depressing. (2) Isn't appreciation of the author's word choices or style also aesthetic? But this is not part of the world which he creates for us through the words. (3) In lyric poems there is usually no plot and no characters; no imaginary world is created at all in a love sonnet, we just hear the poet (or speaker) complaining about his lost love, without even knowing who the speaker is or what he or she looks like. If what one appreciates aesthetically is always a combination of percepts (imagined characters and scenes), what is one appreciating in the case of the love sonnet? (4) The appreciation of literature involves first and foremost the apprehension of *meanings,* which are abstract entities like those of mathematics and not sensory items at all. When the appreciation of a poem turns on the double meaning of a word, for example, one cannot really say that one is appreciating a perceptual item. Meanings are understood, not perceived with the senses. But most of the appreciation of literature is not of sound or sight qualities but of primary and secondary meanings which we as readers apprehend.

In view of all this, (1) one could insist that the appreciation of literature is not aesthetic, or (2) one could say that it is, and therefore that the definition of "aesthetic" in terms of sensory order is inadequate.

Let us turn, then, to another definition of "aesthetic experience." "A person is having an aesthetic experience during a particular stretch of time if and only if the greater part of his mental activity during that time is united and made pleasurable by being tied to the form and qualities of a sensuously presented or imaginatively intended object on which his primary attention is concentrated."[20]

The inclusion of the term "pleasurable" has already been discussed. What the pleasurable experience is *of* is broader than in the previous definition: it is of the "form and qualities" of a "sensuously presented or imaginatively intended object." "Imaginatively intended object" is doubtless added so as to include literature; but whether this ploy succeeds is also a point that has already been discussed. But now a more specific characterization of aesthetic experience follows, in terms of four characteristics:

1. In aesthetic experience, one's attention is firmly fixed on the interrelated components of a *"phenomenally objective field*—visual or auditory patterns, or the characters and events in literature." "The eye is kept on the object, and the object controls the experience."[21]

2. It is an experience of some *intensity*. It need not be an intense *emotion,* for many experiences of works of art, such as most paintings and sculptures, are not really emotional: they are "cool" experiences, such as satisfaction taken in a line or curve or color combination and not the "warm" heart-thumping response one has to the Bach *Magnificat* or the finale of Brahms' First Symphony. The experience of a Mondrian is *sensuously* intense without evoking any emotions at all, only an overall pleasurable affect.

    The pleasure is not often comparable in intensity to the pleasures of satisfying the ordinary appetites. But the concentration of the experience can shut out all negative responses—the trivial distracting noises, organic disturbances, thoughts of unpaid bills and unwritten letters and unpurged embarrassments—that so often clutter up our pleasures. It does what whisky does, only not by dulling our sensitivity and clouding the awareness, but by marshalling the attention for a time into free and unobstructed channels of experience.[22]

3. The experience *hangs together, is coherent,* to an unusually high degree.

    One thing leads to another; continuity of development, without gaps or dead spaces, a sense of an overall providential pattern of guidance, an orderly cumulation of energy toward a climax, are present to an unusual degree. Even when the experience is temporarily broken off, as when we lay down the novel to water the lawn or eat dinner, it can retain a remarkable degree of coherence. Pick up the novel and you are immediately back in the world of the work, almost as if there had been no interruption.[23]

4. The experience is unusually complete in itself:

---

[20] Monroe C. Beardsley, "Aesthetic Experience Regained," *Journal of Aesthetics and Art Criticism,* 28 (1969), pp. 3–11; passage quoted is on p. 5.

[21] Monroe C. Beardsley, *Aesthetics* (New York: Harcourt Brace, 1958), p. 527.

[22] *Ibid.,* p. 528.

[23] *Ibid.,* p. 528.

The impulse and expectations aroused by elements within the experience are felt to be counterbalanced or resolved by other elements within the experience, so that some degree of equilibrium or finality is achieved and enjoyed. The experience detaches itself, and even insulates itself, from the intrusion of alien elements.[24]

This is as systematic an account of the experience of a person concentrating on a work of art as one is likely to get. But it is more descriptive of some of the experiences one has in enjoying the arts than of others. The third condition, for example, applies in an obvious way to temporal arts such as literature and music, but not as clearly to spatial arts such as painting and sculpture.

Some of the features listed as belonging to aesthetic experience are also features of works of art themselves. It is only to be expected, one may suggest, that recurring features of works of art should also enter into the description of our experience of them.

A more worrisome point may be that some, or perhaps even all, of the features mentioned in the description also characterize *other* kinds of experience that no one would be likely to call aesthetic. Don't at least some of the features described as characterizing aesthetic experience also characterize, for example, a sexual experience or an absorbing chess match? If two kinds of thing produce (more or less) the same kind of experience, then it is not the kind of experience produced that distinguishes the two things from each other, but the nature or qualities of the objects themselves. And in that case our attention, once again, turns from the qualities of the experience produced to the qualities of the object that produces it, and our attention must turn to an attempt to distinguish aesthetic *qualities* rather than to describe the *experiences*.

The experiences that are generated by works of art, as well as natural objects, are extremely various, and the question is whether they can all be incorporated under one description, even a careful one such as Beardsley's, in such a way as to distinguish them from all other experiences. We don't usually speak, for example, of "scientific experiences." The experiences of scientific research and discovery differ vastly from case to case. We know what scientific endeavors are, how the sciences themselves (the objects studied) are to be distinguished from one another; but is there one kind of *experience* which they generate, which is sufficiently distinctive to be separated from all other kinds of experience? Similarly, is there any one "artistic experience," a class of experience that all artists have? If we read the biographies of artists, their creative processes, their motivations, their experiences while creating, are widely different from each other. One is tempted to suggest that the same may be true of the experience of works of art from the consumer's end—what is called an "aesthetic experience." Is the experience you have reading a

[24] *Ibid.*, p. 528–529.

Dostoyevsky novel really very similar to the experience you have looking at a Matisse still life or listening to a Monteverdi madrigal?

Consider the following conversation:

A: What kind of experience was it when you heard Bach's *B Minor Mass*?

B: It was an experience of great splendor and exaltation. But not like going to church, because the experience wasn't accompanied by any specific belief.

C: It absolutely wore me out. It was emotionally draining.

A: Digging ditches all day would wear you out too.

C: Yes, but not in the same way. I felt exhausted, yet elevated to great heights at the same time . . .

D: It *was* emotionally draining, though.

A: You mean like a lovers' quarrel?

D: No, not like that at all. It took everything out of me, but I felt on top of the world at the same time . . .

E: That's right. It set me on top of the world. A terrific "high."

A: You mean like good sex? or a potent drug?

E: Of course not—not like that at all . . . You don't see it at all . . .

Is it merely that words fail us? or are the experiences so diverse as not to be includable under any general umbrella such as "aesthetic experience"?

Consider, for example, the case of humor, which is not the kind of thing we usually think about when we set out to consider the distinguishing marks of aesthetic experience. Is the appreciation of humor aesthetic? If tragedy, why not comedy? If *Oedipus,* why not *The Frogs?* If *Rashomon,* why not the comedies of Chaplin and Keaton? Yet our experience of comedy is quite different from that of other genres. The experience of suddenly seeing the point of a rather subtle joke or pun is qualitatively a very different one from that of reading a serious story. But if the experience is not to be classified as aesthetic, why not? Yet the descriptions of "aesthetic experience" do not seem to include comedy in any clear way.

That is, indeed, the main problem involved in trying to classify experiences into kinds or categories, including the category labeled "aesthetic experience": the felt qualities of the experiences of various persons, even those thoroughly steeped in the arts, are extremely various. This is all the more so when we consider not only the variety of persons doing the experiencing, their diverse backgrounds and temperaments, but also the great differences in the artistic media, and the various genres of art within each medium, not to mention the even greater differences between our responses to art and our response to nature. If we take all these experiences together considering both the variations in the persons who have them and the variations in the kinds of object which caused them, it may well be that the variety of experience is too great to be included under any category label, such as "aesthetic experience."

# EXERCISES

1. Discuss the following examples in reference to "the aesthetic attitude":

   a. In Galsworthy's *The Forsyte Saga,* Soames Forsyte is an avid collector of paintings and takes obvious pride in them whenever he shows them to friends. To all appearances his main interest in them derives from the fact of his ownership of them and the pride he takes in this ownership. Is this incompatible with viewing them aesthetically? Does it show that he is not a discriminating collector and sensitive appreciator of paintings?

   b. Someone is reacting against a strong religious unbringing and can't stand religious paintings, but he studies them thoroughly along with the rest of the class in art history and gets an A in the course.

   c. A painter takes special pride in the canvases which he himself has painted. Is there something wrong with this attitude? does it display lack of aesthetic sensitivity?

   d. A student studies St. Augustine's work very closely, ignoring his style and construction, concentrating only on fine points of theology.

2. According to Jerome Stolnitz, "The aesthetic attitude is one of disinterested and sympathetic attention to, and contemplation of, any object of awareness whatever, for its own sake alone." (a) Analyze the meanings of the key terms in this sentence, and (b) show why an antiaesthetic view such as Dickie's would find it objectionable.

3. "Suppose someone reads one book of the *Iliad* each week at a single sitting until he has finished the poem. Has he had twenty-four aesthetic experiences or just one?" (W. E. Kennick, in *Art and Philosophy,* p. 474.) Discuss.

4. "An aesthetic experience is an experience of rapt attention which involves the intransitive apprehension of an object's immanent meanings in their full presentational immediacy." (Eliseo Vivas, "A Definition of Aesthetic Experience," *Journal of Philosophy,* 34 (1937), 628–634.) Discuss.

5. Which of the following two responses is, in your view, "more aesthetic"? Has the first too little "aesthetic distance" and the second too much? How would you describe and/or evaluate the difference? (Both examples are quoted in Müller-Frienfels, *Psychology of Art,* Vol. 1, pp. 66–67 of English translation.)

   a. "I completely forget that I am in the theater. I forget my personal existence. I only experience the feelings of the characters. Now I rave with Othello, now I tremble with Desdemona. Now too I would wish to intervene and save them. I pass so quickly from one state to another that I cannot control myself, above all in the modern plays. Yet, in *King Lear,* I have noticed that, by the end of the play, out of terror I have latched onto a friend."

   b. "I am seated in front of the scene as one seated before a picture. I am continually aware that this is not reality. I do not forget for a moment that I am seated in the orchestra. Granted that I feel the emotions or the passions of the characters, but they are only material for my own aesthetic feeling. I do not feel the emotions represented but rather feel beyond them. My judgment remains awake and clear. My emotions are always conscious. There is no involvement, or if there should be, I would find it discomfiting. Art begins when one forgets the *what* and interests himself only in the *how*.''

6. ''A man who habitually flies off into emotional ecstasy in the presence of a work of art is likely to lack depth of appreciation, even if the emotion is relevant. But it is better to do this than drift into the opposite habit of considering a work of art only in a cold, analytical way. This hard-boiled attitude is very disconcerting to a novice who is eager to appreciate, and full of potential enthusiasm. The calm technical judgments of a connoisseur, especially when flavored with sarcastic innuendos about callow ebullitions, is stifling to emotion and the young man becomes afraid to enter into the work he wants to appreciate. He begins insincerely to emulate the manner of the expert, and to imitate his witticisms. Actually, if he but knew it, his natural effusions, thin as they may be, are closer to a realization of the work, than the erudite comments of such an expert.'' (Stephen Pepper, *Aesthetic Quality*.) Discuss.

7. Which of these various responses to Orson Welles's film *Citizen Kane* would you call aesthetic, and why?

   a. An historian focuses his attention predominantly on the historical accuracy of the film's portrayal of American life in the first half of the twentieth century.

   b. A personal friend of William Randolph Hearst, the famous newspaper publisher, takes the film to be a parody on the life of his friend. He took and now takes the film to be an intentional slur on Hearst. Every time he has seen the film since its first appearance, he has found himself unable to focus attention on much other than the relation between the film and his friend.

   c. A film maker focuses his attention on still another set of features . . . the relations of the visual and auditory qualities of the film to film craft. He attends to the framing of the scenes, to camera movement, to editing, to the kind of color patterns . . . and compares them with their occurrence in films of similar structure and subject-matter.

   d. A woman recently deserted seizes upon the similarity between her own marital situation and that of Kane's first wife, Emily. From that scene on, she becomes absorbed in thoughts about the breakdown of her marriage. For her, the film becomes a stimulus for a series of remembrances.

   e. A fifth observer focuses on a combination of internal and external relations of the film to roughly comparable extents. Much of the time he focuses on the relations of the film to the historical situation which it portrays, the implied truths about the human condition which it contains, the similarities and dissimilarities between Charles Foster Kane of the film and William Randolph Hearst, and the relations between Welles's use of visual and auditory qualities for creative effect and other film makers' use of similar qualities in their films. However, to roughly the same extent, he focuses on internal qualities and internal relations of the film: he attends to such visual and auditory qualities as the framing of scenes so as to keep the dominant character, Kane, in sight, thereby emphasizing his importance to the social and professional circles in which he moved and worked; the identity of snow with naturalness; the mystery of Rosebud; the two-sided character of Kane, alternatively as the man of action and power and the man who is incapable of keeping what he really values most. (From Allan Casebier, "The Concept of Aesthetic Distance," *The Personalist,* Vol. 52 (Winter 1971), 70–91.)

8. A certain novel or film is based on a true story of someone's life. This surely makes a difference to the way we respond to it. Could the difference be labeled "aesthetic" if we view it as imaginary, and "nonaesthetic" if we view it as a historical life story, for example? Is a person who enjoys reading stories or seeing films only if the stories are true approaching them unaesthetically?

9. "I didn't even get to touch her. Just seeing her, all that dazzling beauty, did things for me. It gave me a lift for the rest of the week. It was a great aesthetic experience." Is this properly labeled an aesthetic experience? or was it nonaesthetic because it involved personal desire? or was it a kind of "first cousin" to an aesthetic experience?

10. Someone is enjoying the tunes of Weber's *Invitation to the Waltz,* whistling the tunes. A musician then explains to him, "This isn't merely a string of waltzes. It is a rondo in which one of the waltzes recurs, setting up a pattern of repetition," and so on. The listener absorbs this information, and now perceives the composition as "hanging together" as a coherent whole in a way that he did not before. "But now a problem arises. We would all agree that before the musician came along to instruct him, our listener was not having a particularly deep or rich experience; but he was having an *aesthetic* experience, albeit a shallow and undistinguished one. Yet the work was not seen by him to 'hang together,' nor did he see its emotional and human significance. It would certainly be odd to insist that his experience of *Invitation to the Dance* was, prior to instruction, not an aesthetic experience. If that wasn't an aesthetic experience, what was it? Nevertheless, it was an experience, in which what was being perceived was *not* perceived as 'hanging together,' was *not* perceived as emotionally and humanly significant." (Peter Kivy, "Aesthetic Perception," in his *Speaking of Art.*) Does this show that those who speak of aesthetic experience as being of (for example) "experiencing something as a coherent whole" are mistaken? or what?

11. "Consider a surgeon performing a successful appendectomy, or an eager student listening to a brilliant lecture on medieval cosmology, or a suitably excitable person watching the sleaziest of pornographic movies. . . . The experience of the pornography consumer [to quote Mark Sagoff] 'could certainly beat in intensity, duration, certainty, propinquity, fecundity, purity, and extent the pleasure anyone gets from looking at a painting' such as Picasso's *Guernica.*" (W. E. Kennick, in *Art and Philosophy,* p. 474.) Do you agree? If so, is it fatal to the concept of aesthetic experience, or any particular formulation of it?

# SELECTED READINGS

ALDRICH, VIRGIL. *The Philosophy of Art.* Englewood Cliffs, N.J.: Prentice-Hall, 1963.

BERLEANT, ARNOLD. *The Aesthetic Field.* Springfield, Ill.: Charles Thomas, 1971.

BINKLEY, TIMOTHY. "Contra Aesthetics." *Journal of Aesthetics and Art Criticism,* 35 (1977).

BUERMEYER, LAURENCE. *The Aesthetic Experience.* Merion, Pa.: Barnes Foundation Press, 1924.

BULLOUGH, EDWARD. "Psychical Distance as a Factor in Art and an Aesthetic Principle." *British Journal of Psychology,* V (1912).

COHEN, MARSHALL. "Appearance and the Aesthetic Attitude." *Journal of Philosophy,* 56 (1959).

COLEMAN, FRANCIS X. J. "A Phenomenology of Aesthetic Reasoning." *Journal of Aesthetics and Art Criticism,* 25 (1966).

DEWEY, JOHN. "Having an Experience," Chapter 3 of *Art as Experience.* New York: Minton, Balch & Co., 1934.

DICKIE, GEORGE. *Art and the Aesthetic.* Ithaca, N.Y.: Cornell Univ. Press, 1974.

DICKIE, GEORGE. "Beardsley's Theory of Aesthetic Experience." *Journal of Aesthetics Education,* 8 (1974).

DICKIE, GEORGE. "Beardsley's Phantom Aesthetic Experience." *Journal of Philosophy,* 62 (1965).

DICKIE, GEORGE. "Bullough and Casebier: Disappearing in the Distance." *The Personalist,* 53 (1972).

DICKIE, GEORGE. "The Myth of the Aesthetic Attitude." *American Philosophical Quarterly,* 1 (1964). Reprinted in Hospers.

DICKIE, GEORGE. "Psychical Distance: In a Fog at Sea." *British Journal of Aesthetics,* 13 (1973).

DICKIE, GEORGE. "Taste and Attitude: The Origin of the Aesthetic." *Theoria,* 37 (1973).

DUCASSE, CURT J. *Art, the Critics, and You.* New York: Liberal Arts Press, 1944.

DUCASSE, CURT J. *The Philosophy of Art.* New York: Dial Press, 1929. 134–147, 189–201.

EICHNER, HANS. "The Meaning of 'Good' in Aesthetic Judgments." *British Journal of Aesthetics,* 3 (1963).

GOODMAN, NELSON. *The Languages of Art.* Indianapolis: Bobbs Merrill, 1968. Ch. 6.

HENZE, DONALD F. "The Work of Art as a Rule." *Ratio,* 11 (1969).

HEVNER, KATE. "Aesthetic Experience: A Psychological Description." *Philosophical Review,* 44 (1937).

KORSMEYER, CAROLINE. "On the 'Aesthetic Senses' and the Development of the Fine Arts." *Journal of Aesthetics and Art Criticsm* 34 (1975).

LANGFELD, H. S. *The Aesthetic Attitude.* New York: Harcourt Brace, 1920.

LIND, RICHARD. "Attention and the Aesthetic Object." *Journal of Aesthetics and Art Criticism,* Vol. 39 No. 2 (Winter 1980), pp. 131–142.

MARGOLIS, JOSEPH. "Aesthetic Perception." *Journal of Aesthetics and Art Criticism,* 19 (1960).

MARGOLIS, JOSEPH. "Proposals on the Logic of Aesthetic Judgment." *Philosophical Quarterly,* 9 (1959).

McGREGOR, ROBERT. "Art and the Aesthetic." *Journal of Aesthetics and Art Criticism,* 32 (1974).

MEAGER, RUBY. "The Uniqueness of a Work of Art." *Proceedings of the Aristotelian Society,* 59 (1959).

MEYNELL, HUGO. "Remarks of the Foundations of Aesthetics." *British Journal of Aesthetics,* 8 (1968).

MICHELIS, P. A. "Aesthetic Distance and the Charm of Contemporary Art." *Journal of Aesthetics and Art Criticism,* 18 (1959).

NEVILLE, M. R. "Kant's Characterization of Aesthetic Experience." *Journal of Aesthetics and Art Criticism,* 33 (1974).

POLE, DAVID. "Varieties of Aesthetic Experience." *Philosophy,* 30 (1955).

PRICE, KINGSLEY, "The Truth About Psychical Distance." *Journal of Aesthetics and Art Criticism,* 35 (Summer, 1977).

RICHARDS, I. A. *Principles of Literary Criticism.* New York: Harcourt Brace, 1928. 107–113, 242–252.

SCHULTZ, ROBERT A. "Does Aesthetics Have Anything to Do with Art?" *Journal of Aesthetics and Art Criticism,* 36 (1978).

SIBLEY, FRANK. "Aesthetics and the Looks of Things." *Journal of Philosophy,* 56 (1959).

SILVERS, ANITA. "Aesthetic Akrasia: on Disliking Good Art." *Journal of Aesthetics and Art Criticism,* 31 (1972).

SNOEYENOBS, MILTON. "Attitudes and Aesthetic Theory." *The Personalist,* 60 (April 1979), pp. 139–150.

STOLNITZ, JEROME. *Aesthetics and the Philosophy of Art Criticism.* Boston: Houghton Mifflin, 1960. Chapter 1 reprinted in Hospers.

STOLNITZ, JEROME. "On the Origins of 'Aesthetic Disinterestedness.'" *Journal of Aesthetics and Art Criticism,* 20 (1961). Reprinted in Dickie and Sclafani.

STOLNITZ, JEROME. "On the Significance of Lord Shafesbury in Modern Aesthetic Theory." *Philosophical Quarterly,* 11 (1961).

STOLNITZ, JEROME. "Some Questions concerning Aesthetic Perception." *Philosophy and Phenomenological Research,* 22 (1961).

TOMAS, VINCENT. "Aesthetic Vision." *Philosophical Review,* 68 (1959).

UPHAUS, ROBERT W. "Shaftesbury on Art: the Rhapsodic Aesthetic." *Journal of Aesthetics and Art Criticism,* 27 (1969).

URMSON, J. O. "What Makes a Situation Aesthetic?" *Proceedings of the Aristotelian Society,* 31 (1957–8). Reprinted in Dickie and Sclafani.

VIVAS, ELISEO. "A Definition of the Aesthetic Experience." *Journal of Philosophy,* 34 (1937). Reprinted in Vivas and Krieger.

WEITZ, MORRIS. "Professor Goodman on the Aesthetic." *Journal of Aesthetics and Art Criticism,* 29 (1971).

# 9

# Aesthetic Qualities, Beauty, and Aesthetic Value

## 1. AESTHETIC QUALITIES

Perhaps there is no such thing as an aesthetic attitude. Perhaps—let's admit for the sake of argument—there isn't even such a thing as aesthetic experience. But (one might allege) what does it matter as long as there are objects with aesthetic *qualities* which we can enjoy or appreciate? And if there *are* aesthetic experiences, what are they experiences of? Among other things, works of art—but not *all* aspects or qualities of works of art. A painting is a huge conglomeration of atoms and electrons, yet we don't appreciate these. That's because we can't see the atoms, one may say; but one does see that the painting is rectangular, and yet that would not seem to be a quality one appreciates aesthetically. What qualities, then, *could* one plausibly describe as aesthetic qualities?

First, what qualities can be *excluded*? Are there kinds of qualities that cannot qualify as aesthetic, and why? Let us examine several suggestions along this line.

1. *Physical vs. perceptual.* A painting is a physical object, possessing many qualities (or properties). It is a hurly-burly of atoms and electrons. It has many features which can be discerned only through powerful microscopes, and some not even then. There are light waves emanating from it to the eye of the observer, whose wavelength partially determines which colors the observer

366

will see. But electrons and light waves are not *what* we see; the existence and nature of these things was discovered only with the rise of modern science. They are a part of the subject-matter of physics, not of aesthetics. The aesthetician is concerned only with the qualities that can be perceived.

The same considerations apply in music. Sound waves are one thing, the sounds we hear are another. And even if the word "sound" is used in both a book on music and a book on physics, the word has quite different meanings in the two contexts.

> When you speak of the tone-color of an orchestral composition by Debussy, or the sensitivity of phrasing in a performance of a Schumann piano composition, or the harshness of certain passages in Bartok's Third String Quartet, you are talking about something you can *hear*. The number of vibrations per second produced by the Middle C key of the piano, the mechanical action of the harpsichord, the width of the grooves in a longplaying record, are not things you can hear, however much you can study them as a physicist and describe their behavior in rigorous mathematical terms; they are therefore not part of the music they produce.[1]

When you talk about the way in which paints have to be mixed to get a certain vivid color, you are talking about the *physical* object; when you talk about the vivid color itself (no matter how it got there), you are talking about the *perceptual* object, the object as perceived. It is only the second that is of *aesthetic* interest; the first may tell the painter what he has to do to produce certain experienced qualities, but when you are talking about aesthetics you are talking about the experienced qualities themselves, not what has to be done to get them there.

> When a critic says that Titian's later paintings have a strong atmospheric quality and vividness of color, he is talking about aesthetic objects. But when he says that Titian used a dark reddish underpainting over the whole canvas, and added transparent glazes to the painting after he laid down the pigment, he is talking about physical objects. . . . To describe the perceptual painting as such is to say nothing about how its physical basis was produced—whether the colors were painted on, dripped on, spashed on, blown on, thrown on, photographed, engraved, drawn, or merely spilled. What matters is the visible result.[2]

But to appreciate painting, don't you have to know something about the physical processes that the artist used to produce the experienced qualities? That depends on how broadly we use the term "appreciate." To perceive an aesthetic quality, for example, a certain color contrast, it is not necessary to know how the artist put it there. But it may be that there is a further kind of appreciation, of how the artist mastered his materials so as to achieve a cer-

[1] Monroe C. Beardsley, *Aesthetics* (New York: Harcourt Brace, 1958), pp. 30-31.
[2] *Ibid.,* pp. 33-34.

tain result. Is part of the appreciation of sculpture an appreciation of the difficulty of doing exacting work in stone? When you see a jade carving, and realize that one misstep of the chisel in the sculptor's fingers would have meant an end to years of work, some would say you are appreciating the work of art, though others would say you are admiring the artist for doing a difficult or exacting job. At any rate, there is a kind of appreciation that comes from acquaintance with the kind of materials the artist worked with, and which is lost on us if we have no knowledge of this.

There is, as usual, a problem about literature. What is the perceptual object there? What we hear when it is read aloud is a collection of sounds, some of which we may describe as beautiful, but most of which as sounds are not of much interest—we work through the sounds to what they mean. Similarly, what we see on the printed page is a bunch of strange looking ink marks, which is that we strictly perceive. Those who see the ink marks clearly but can't read the language have no conception of the work of literature. Unlike the sights of visual art and the sounds of music, the literary work is not a perceptual object at all. Thus, if aesthetic qualities have to be perceptual qualities, and literature lacks these aesthetic qualities, a work of literature is not an aesthetic object (a thing with aesthetic qualities). This is a very drastic consequence if one wants to cover all the arts under the rubric of the aesthetic. On the other hand, one could follow Roger Fry and say that, in the way in which the qualities of music and painting are aesthetic, literature lacks aesthetic qualities.

2. *Appearance versus reality.* There is another stricture that has sometimes been suggested for the aesthetic, which is not the same as the one just discussed, although it at first sounds similar. Aesthetic qualities, it is suggested, are qualities only of the *appearance* of things, and when we take an aesthetic interest in something we are not at all concerned with what qualities it actually has, or even whether it actually exists, but—in appearances only—in what qualities it appears to have. Appearances, not reality, are what count.

(a) Suppose that you have a reproduction of a painting that was so perfect that neither you nor anyone else can detect the difference between the original and the copy (at least without a microscope), or between the original and a forgery. Then, the contention is that *aesthetically* it makes no difference which you have hanging on your wall. As far as economic value is concerned, there is a big difference between them; if you try to sell the original you will be offered much more for it than for the copy. But if it is really true (which isn't likely) that they cannot be distinguished from each other by your senses, then *aesthetically* it makes no difference which one you look at. Why does it make no difference? Because in aesthetics we are concerned with how things look, not how they really are. If you couldn't tell the Vermeer apart from the Van Meergren (who passed off his paintings as Vermeers for years and even experts couldn't tell the difference), then as far as the rewards of your looking are concerned—and this is what you are interested in aesthetically—they are exactly the same.

(b) Suppose a perfect imitation of a bronze statue is carved from cheese, so that you can't see any difference. One could say that they will *feel* different to the touch and that sculpture is not a visual art but a visuotactual art, so the touch difference does count. But now suppose (again unlikely) that you couldn't tell the difference between them by means of sight or touch—then they would be aesthetically identical.

> I propose to count as characteristics of an aesthetic object *no* characteristics. . . that depend on knowledge of their causal conditions, whether physical or psychological.[3]

(c) A modern Gothic building is agreed to look sturdy and graceful and so on, but unlike traditional Gothic cathedrals, it is not supported by the weight of its own stone; this building was secretly built around a stone framework. It looks as if the stone is holding it up, but really the steel is. To a person who knows this, the building may be considered "phony." Yet, going by the criterion[4] we are discussing, it shouldn't: if it "appears phony" this is because you are importing knowledge of its causal conditions. You couldn't tell the difference between two otherwise identical cathedrals, the one supported by stone and the other by steel, just by *looking* at them; and aesthetic qualities are those you can *perceive*. (It's true that you could perceive the difference if you demolished the cathedral; but cathedrals presumably are supposed to be visually enjoyed when whole, not when in ruins.) "If a thing looks to have a characteristic . . . its looking so is a proper ground of aesthetic appreciation. What makes the appreciation aesthetic is that it is concerned with a thing's looking somehow without concern for whether it really is like that; beauty, we may say, to emphasize the point, is not even skin-deep."[5]

(d) Most people do not concentrate very much on how things look. "The commuter has been reading the *New York Times,* for a half hour five mornings each week for five years. Yet if you asked him whether, in the *Times,* a 't' appears short and squat or long and slender, or whether an 'O' has a fat and jolly look or a lean and hungry look, he would not know what to say. He never noticed how the letters looked."[6] When we view the page with a view to

[3] *Ibid.,* p. 52.
[4] *Ibid.,* p. 50.
[5] J. O. Urmson, "What Makes a Situation Aesthetic?" *Proceedings of the Aristotelian Society,* Supplementary Vol. 31 (1957); reprinted in *Art and Philosophy,* ed. W. E. Kennick, pp. 398–410; passage quoted is on p. 408.
[6] Vincent Tomas, "Aesthetic Vision," *Philosophical Review,* Vol. 68 (1959); reprinted in *Aesthetics and the Philosophy of Criticism,* ed. Marvin Levich (New York: Random House, 1963), pp. 255-269; passage quoted is on p. 256.

aesthetic qualities we are concerned with how the letters look, not with what they signify.

But now the problems start to come upon us. Consider the last example. The person was asked to notice whether the t is fat and squat or tall and slender—not whether it *appears* that way, but whether it *is* that way. Some t's are taller than others, depending on the type style; and isn't what we are being asked to notice—not just how they look but what shapes they really have?

Noticing not only how something appears but how it really is often seems to be of some importance, even aesthetically. Sir Joshua Reynolds (1723–1792) writes in his fourteenth of his *Discourses*,

> it is certain that all those odd scratches and marks, which, on close examination, are so observable in Gainsborough's pictures and which even to experienced painters appear rather the effect of accident than design; this chaos, this uncouth and shapeless appearance, by a kind of magic, at a certain distance assumes form, and all the parts seem to drop into their proper places, so that we can hardly refuse acknowledging the full effect of diligence, under the appearance of chance and hasty negligence. That Gainsborough himself considered this peculiarity in this manner, and the power it possesses of exciting surprise, as a beauty in his works, I think may be inferred from the eager desire which we know he always expressed, that his pictures, at Exhibition, should be seen near, as well as at a distance.[7]

Thus far we have spoken only of visual appearance versus reality. Things become much more murky when we turn from sight to sound. Do we only care what sound qualities the orchestral instruments *appear* to have, not what sound qualities they *really* have? "In what sense am I attending to an 'appearance' when listening to a symphony and a 'stimulus object' when a fire engine goes by? Whatever I hear, it is the same kind of thing in both cases, and I am at a loss really whether to call it 'appearance' or 'stimulus object.' But I certainly know how to describe what I hear: a siren, concert A, the screech of tires, an oboe, a bell, a diminished seventh. Which is the 'appearance' and which the 'stimulus object'?"[8]

Sometimes, at least, the effect of a work of music depends on whether we perceive the music as being "really like that" rather than just "sounding like that" and not being sure whether it really is like that or not. For example, "Haydn needed *three* upbeats to write the finale with the most outrageous rhythmic effects, that of the Quartet in E flat major, Op. 76 No. 6, which surpasses even the duplicity of the minuet of the Oxford Symphony in fooling the listener as to the place of the downbeat. The opening, indeed, sounds clearly

---

[7] Sir Joshua Reynolds, *Discourses* (London: Kegan Paul, 1883), p. 263. Quoted in Peter Kivy, *Speaking of Art* (The Hague: Martinus Nijhoff, 1973), p. 79.

[8] Peter Kivy, *Speaking of Art,* p. 73.

not like three upbeats, but like *five*."[9] Concerning this W. E. Kennick writes, "Is what *makes* a listener's reaction aesthetic in this case the fact that it is concerned with the opening's sounding like five upbeats without concern for whether it really is like that? Does not appreciation of the duplicity in question require that one know that there are only three upbeats, albeit it sounds like five?"[10]

If we have doubts with regard to music, what happens when we turn to literature? In literature we are not presented with a sensory field at all; or, rather, the sensory field we have—the printed page—is not the work of literature. Whether the letter "t" is printed in a typeface that is tall may be of concern to the typesetter but not to the poet or novelist. It may concern the reader (we find some typefaces pleasing and some annoying), but criticism of the typeface is not criticism of the work of literature. In what possible way, then, can the remarks about being concerned with appearance and not reality be applied to literature at all?

One may say that, just as one is not concerned with whether there was a historical Napoleon when one sees a painting of Napoleon—it doesn't matter aesthetically whether the figure on the canvas corresponds to any real man—so one does not care in reading "The Royal Game" whether Czentovic or Dr. B. really existed, one only cares about them as characters *in* the story. If *that* is all that is meant by saying one is concerned with "appearance" rather than with "reality," the point may be granted. Still, as we have seen, the actions and motives of characters must be like those of real people, at least enough so we can understand them; and we *imagine* the characters as inhabiting the real world, for example, the Nazi hotel room-prison and the boat en route to South America. Without reference to the real world and our experience of it, we could not understand the story.

And as far as the story's relation to our daily life is concerned, must we not be assured at least that it is *not* happening now and preventable by us? "Hobbes would obviously be right in ascribing our pleasure in tragedy to sadism, if it were not perfectly clear that the tragic events did not transpire."[11] And "it would be absurd to admire the brilliant craftmanship, the stylistic originality, the relationship to the tradition of an image which might turn out to be a real live man." Even supposing that this doesn't matter, we are still not dealing in literature with "mere appearance": "The comment that two people are perfectly suited, each setting off the other, might be an aesthetic one; but it concerns their characters, temperaments, or interests, not their ap-

---

[9] Charles Rosen, *The Classical Style* (New York, 1972), p. 339; quoted in W. E. Kennick, *Art and Philosophy*, p. 471.

[10] W. E. Kennick, *Art and Philosophy*, p. 471.

[11] Marshall Cohen, "Appearance and the Aesthetic Attitude," *Journal of Philosophy*, Vol. 56 No. 10, pp. 915-926; reprinted in *Aesthetics and the Philosophy of Criticism*, ed. Marvin Levich (New York: Random House, 1963), pp. 282-294; passage quoted is on p. 289.

pearances only.''[12] In fact the whole distinction between ''the way things are'' and ''the way they appear'' doesn't apply in the same way to literature as to visual art. We don't care about the printed page, either the way it appears or the way it is, except as a *vehicle* for grasping the meanings of the words and sentences; via the sentences the scenes and characters come to life in our imagination.

The whole ''appearance versus reality'' way of talking is in fact extremely ambiguous, and varies with the context. ''When we describe a person's appearance we describe the person. Even when we speak of the way things appear from unusual angles we are describing the way *they* appear.''[13] Sometimes, when I talk about an appearance (what is *merely* appearance, not reality), as when Macbeth asks if it is a dagger which he sees before him, then I am talking about *my own visual experiences,* and if others do not have them then I am having a hallucination. But much more often, when I talk about an appearance, I am talking about something real: looking at a photograph I say, ''Yes, the river does appear like that from that hilltop,'' that is, it will look that way to others also, as well as to the camera. One might even say that this is the way the scene *''really''* looks; or for that matter ''really *is*, when seen *from* that spot.'' It is this ''public'' kind of appearance which usually is of importance in discussing works of art. ''The angel on the chancel screen is properly foreshortened only from below. . . . Only in a certain light will the sculpture have the proper eye-shadowing. These are not 'subjective' appearances, certainly, and if they are public appearances obtained from the right spot under the proper conditions they are, far from being mere appearances, the way the things actually look.''[14]

We could go still further and say with Eddington that the hurly-burly of atoms and electrons is the ''real'' table and that what we see even from a good angle in a good light and so on is never the real table but only the appearance. We can go even further than that and say with Kant that even the atoms and electrons are not real, but belong to the ''phenomenal world'' or world of appearance, whereas only the ''noumenal'' world, to which our human senses never have access, is real. If you make your definition of ''real'' far-out enough, nothing you will ever encounter will be real and everything will be ''appearance only.'' But now the distinction no longer has any value for aesthetics.

What qualities or combinations of them, then, do qualify as aesthetic qualities?

1. There are the outright *sensory* qualities, whose role is hardly in dispute.

---

[12] Frank Sibley, ''Aesthetics and the Looks of Things,'' *Journal of Philosophy,* Vol. 56 No. 10 (1959), pp. 905-915; reprinted in *Aesthetics and the Philosophy of Criticism,* ed. Marvin Levich (New York: Random House, 1963), pp. 270-281; passage quoted is on p. 275.

[13] Marshall Cohen, *op. cit.,* p. 287.

[14] *Ibid.,* p. 285.

We like the sky (think it beautiful) for its vivid shade of blue or the landscape for its lush green. We often praise a painting because the colors are vivid or subtly blended or contrasted. This doesn't mean, of course, that every color and every color combination give the painting *desirable* aesthetic qualities but only that such qualities are aesthetically relevant—in the realm of the aesthetic, in the aesthetic ballpark.

The same is true of sounds: lush sounds, quiet sounds, rubato, pizzicato. . . . It is seldom that we respond to a single sound, such as middle C, the way we do to single colors, for example, crimson; most people cannot even identify single sounds when they hear them. All the same, sounds make an aesthetic difference: not only the timbre of the instrument that emits the sound (clarinet versus an English horn playing the melody), but also the pitch and loudness of the sound (B flat rather than B). "I may value a rose bush because it is hardy, prolific, disease-resistant, and the like, but if I value a rose aesthetically, the most obvious relevant grounds will be the way it *looks*, both in color and in shape, and the way it smells; and the same grounds may be a basis for aesthetic dislike."[15] Even literature, especially poetry, can be esteemed higher or lower aesthetically because of its sound patterns.

2. Some qualities are not exactly perceptual qualities: we do need to perceive something, but we also need some underlying idea behind the percept. "We admire a building not only for its color and shape but because it looks strong or spacious, or admire a horse because it looks swift as well as for its gleaming coat."[16] We are not here enjoying only a pleasing interplay of forms, but we have some idea of the purpose which we want the object to serve. As Kant put it, "There are two kinds of beauty: free beauty and merely dependent beauty. The first presupposes no concept of what the object ought to be; the second does presuppose such a concept and the perfection of the object in accordance therewith."[17]

3. Another kind of quality which is of obvious aesthetic relevance has to do with form—the arrangement of the elements in a complex. We admire the sweep of the branches of a tree and the intricate tracery of the leaves; the shape of a leaf may be much more pleasing to us than its color, and we find the leaves of some plants (such as the Australian tree fern) extremely pleasing even if their color is not particularly distinguished. Again, there are certain postcard picture views of a famous scene—the mountain in the background, lake in the foreground, trees on the sides, in Glacier National Park—which are recurrently found pleasing in their combination of forms much more because of the arrangement of their parts than because of the sensory ingre-

[15] J. O. Urmson, *op. cit.,* p. 560.
[16] *Ibid.,* p. 561.
[17] Immanuel Kant, *The Critique of Judgment:* I, The Analysis of Beauty: Third movement, "Purposiveness without Purpose."

dients themselves. (It is almost always from that one angle that the pictures are taken; from a bit to the right or the left, the scene becomes unbalanced.)

Examples of form in works of art are usually more complex than in nature, having been created (at least in part) to satisfy a developed sense of form. If a complex painting or symphony "hangs together," and all the strands are unified, we feel a peculiar satisfaction in the interplay of forms.

Not all formal satisfaction, however, arises from regarding the components of a sensory field. Painting and sculpture do (visual presentations), and music does (auditory presentations extended through time), but literature does not. Yet literature does provide great formal satisfaction: we feel in "The Royal Game" the various elements gradually melding together, the story being propelled toward forward toward a climax which draws all the previously presented elements forward with it. This formal unity is not of a sensory field, but it is no less powerful for all that. Indeed, we grasp the unity in a musical or visual complex, but do we really *see* or *hear* it? Animals see and hear better than we do and they have no idea of it. Is it not, like literature, grasped by the intellect?

A formalist would stop at this point in his list of aesthetic qualities. Most students of the arts, however, would go farther and say that other qualities can count as aesthetic when embodied in works of art: for example being graceful or delicate as well as the array of feeling-states discussed under expressiveness, such as joy and sadness, tension and release, turbulence and quiescence, and so on.

Are there any other qualities that should be added? There is quite an array of qualities that might be suggested. Some would say that, if a characterization in a work of art is true to human nature, this is an aesthetic quality which gives the work an aesthetic plus. Others would say the same for truth, both explicit and implicit. Some would say the same for moral qualites. Still others would deny all this just as vehemently, saying that it is just mixing up the aesthetic with the cognitive and the aesthetic with the moral. We should also keep in mind the point made on pages 308–309 that valuing something *aesthetically* is not the same as valuing it *as a work of art.*

Walter Pater said that all arts aspire to the condition of music. This may well be true, if we are talking about aesthetic qualities, unmixed with others. Literature of all the arts has a larger number of qualities that make it worthwhile as literature which are not aesthetic qualities at all. Perhaps Fry was right in saying that literature is the "least aesthetic" of the arts; literature is more deeply embedded in the life around us, and it reflects that life with a completeness that the other arts never do. Our response to a Mondrian is primarily an aesthetic response to form and color, but our response to "The Royal Game," though partly a response to formal qualities such as unity and development, is also in great measure a response to a description of man and his condition.

Aesthetic Qualities and Taste

We have been considering the kinds of qualities that could be considered *relevant* to making aesthetic judgments. But the presence of such qualities will not, at least not in every case, certify the truth of a judgment of aesthetic value. Purple is a color, and color is a sensory quality, and sensory qualities are (among others) aesthetic qualities, qualities relevant to making aesthetic judgments. When we have pointed out the presence of this quality (purple) in a certain painting, we have by no means ensured that an aesthetic judgment on the painting will be favorable or even more favorable than it would have been without the purple. Calling attention to the sensory quality has placed it in the right ballpark, but it doesn't ensure that its presence will win the game.

According to one current view, aesthetic qualities, though they presuppose the presence of sensory qualities, are not themselves sensory qualities. On this view, there are two broad groups of statements made in describing works of art:

> We say that a novel has a great number of characters and deals with life in a manufacturing town; that a painting uses pale colors, predominantly blues and greens, and has kneeling figures in the foreground; that the theme in a fugue is inverted at such a point and that there is a stretto at the close; that the action of a play takes place in the span of one day and that there is a reconciliation scene in the fifth act. Such remarks may be made by, and such features pointed out to, anyone with normal eyes, ears, and intelligence.
>
> On the other hand, we also say that a poem is tightly-knit or deeply moving; that a picture lacks balance, or has a certain serenity and repose, or that the grouping of the figures sets up an exciting tension; that the characters in a novel never really come to life, or that a certain episode strikes a false note. It would be natural enough to say that the making of judgments such as these requires the exercise of *taste, perceptiveness, or sensitivity, of aesthetic discrimination or appreciation;* one would not say this of the first group. Accordingly, when a word or expression is such that taste or perceptiveness is required in order to apply it, I shall call it an *aesthetic* term or expression, and I shall, correspondingly, speak of *aesthetic* concepts or *taste* concepts.[18]

There are many such terms, for example, "unified," "balanced," "integrated," "lifeless," "serene," "somber," "dynamic," "powerful," "vivid," "delicate," "moving," "trite," "sentimental," "tragic," "telling contrast," "sets up a tension," "conveys a sense of," "holds it together."

What is the difference between detecting these qualities and detecting the presence of the qualities in the first group? To detect the presence of the qualities in the first group, you need only normal eyes, ears, and intelligence; you could be bored by the work, or be an aesthetically insensitive clod who

---

[18] Frank Sibley, "Aesthetic Concepts," *Philosophical Review,* 58 (1959), 421-460. Passage quoted is from p. 421. Reprinted in Kennick and in Dickie & Sclafani. (Some emphasis added.)

cares nothing for any of the arts, and still be able to see that the painting is primarily whites and blues, or that there are two matching curves on the left, or that the theme of the first movement of the concerto is repeated twice. But to detect the presence of the qualities on the second list is a mark of ability to *appreciate*, not merely to perceive. The second list comprises the distinctively aesthetic qualities.

What is the relation between the outright perceptual qualities and the distinctively aesthetic qualities? No description of the nonaesthetic qualities will ever entail (logically imply) the presence of any of the aesthetic ones. "On *seeing* the picture one might say, and rightly, that it is delicate or serene or restful or sickly or insipid, no *description* in nonaesthetic terms permits us to claim that these or any other aesthetic terms must undeniably apply to it." In this respect, aesthetic terms are unlike other vague terms we constantly use, such as "intelligent" and "lazy." Although there are many actions of a person that would make us say, rightly, that he is intelligent or lazy, there is no definite set of conditions that have to be fulfilled (necessary conditions) in order for us to say this rightly; and often one feature alone will be a *sufficient* condition. If a person can pass an I. Q. test with a score of 150, we cannot deny that he is intelligent; if he is so disinclined to work that though able to do it he refuses even if he has no resources and refusing to work means missing his next meal, we can definitely say he is lazy. "But we cannot make any general statement of the form 'If the vase is pale pink, somewhat curving, lightly mottled, and so forth, it will be delicate, *cannot but be* delicate. . . '. Things may be described to us in nonaesthetic terms as fully as we please, but we are not thereby put in the position of having to admit (or being unable to deny) that they are delicate or graceful or garish or exquisitively balanced." In other words, no group of nonaesthetic qualities is ever sufficient to establish beyond doubt the presence of an aesthetic quality. In fact, "an object described very fully, but exclusively in terms of qualities characteristic of delicacy, may turn out on inspection to be not delicate at all, but anemic or insipid. The failure of novices and the artistically inept prove that quite close similarly in line, color, or technique gives no assurance or gracefulness or delicacy."

Thus, "This is red" is never an aesthetic judgment, but "This spot of red at this place gives it just the touch that keeps it from being anemic" is. The first judgment requires only normal perception; the second requires an additional faculty, the exercise of *taste*—which, of course, many people who are not color-blind or tone-deaf entirely lack, yet it is just this ability which is required to detect (and describe) the distinctively aesthetic features of the object.

We often speak of a person as having taste or lacking taste, and having it has something to do with the *ability to discriminate qualities,* especially subtle ones that many or most people are unable to distinguish. We are all acquainted with hostesses who prepare a dish according to a recipe and proudly invite their guests to partake of it, when it seems to many of the guests to be flat or lacking some necessary ingredient or having a bit too much of some spice; but the hostess is apparently unable to distinguish these more subtle qualities and eats it as happily as if she had prepared a gourmet feast—which, indeed, she may believe she has done. She can't tell the difference, but many of her guests can, since they can distinguish the presence or absence of even small amounts of ingredients to which she is quite oblivious. They say she is "lacking in taste"—although it is possible that by arduous cultivation she may come in time to make the same discriminations they do. This happens when someone who can't tell the difference between cheap hamburgers and expensive steaks is exposed to the expensive ones for a while and then gradually discovers what he has been missing.

Some problems occur, however, when one introduces the concept of taste to distinguish aesthetic from nonaesthetic qualities. Here are a few:[19]

1. What about bad taste? What if you *falsely* attribute gracefulness or delicacy to some object? Does that require taste too? It would seem that if $p$ is a judgment that requires the exercise of taste, *not p* is too. If to assert $p$ requires a certain faculty or ability is not the same true of *not p*? But it does seem strange to say that a person with such "bad taste" as to regularly attribute delicacy to ungainly objects is exercising taste, or is engaged in an activity that requires a special faculty.

2. If there is good taste and bad taste, how do you know if you have *good* taste? At the time we utter them we consider our taste judgments to be correct. How do we discover that some of them are not?

3. Indeed, how do you show that this faculty exists at all? When you have it, is your judgment supposed to be infallible, like an intuition? And when the use of the faculty results in true statements, how do we know they are true? How does it help us in a dispute between two people, one of whom says the vase is delicate and the other says it isn't?

4. In any event, there seems to be no reason to say that such judgments (requiring taste) occur in the aesthetic realm only. "What that painting requires is a spot of deep red, right there, to make the whole composition come together." If that aesthetic judgment requires taste, how about this moral judgment: "He's a good man but not great—it would require just a touch in a certain place in his temperament or dispositions to make him a saint"?

The most systematic questioning of the whole distinction between qualities whose presence must be discerned by a special faculty of taste and those that don't has come from Ted Cohen: there seems to me no sensible and important way of dividing terms according to whether taste or only normality is needed to apply them.[20]

[19] These are comments about the concept of taste in general, not specifically about Sibley's account of them, which is not open to some of these objections.

[20] Ted Cohen, "A Critique of Sibley's Position," *Theoria,* 39, 1973, 113-152. Reprinted in *Art and Philosophy,* ed. William Kennick, and in *Aesthetics,* ed. Dickie and Sclafani.

Here are three lines: one is straight, the second is jagged, the third is gently curved. Which is the graceful one, or the least ungraceful? The first two are eliminated at once, so it must be the third one. Did you need the faculty of taste to make this judgment? "Is it always the case with 'graceful' that taste is needed to apply it? I say no."

It is true that many terms require either more than normal intelligence or more than normal perceptiveness to apply properly. There are people who "can tell on sight, by attending to people's size, shape, posture, gesture, gait, etc., Jews, Northern Europeans, homosexuals, New Yorkers, etc. . . . Some . . . amateurs with good ears can identify East Texans, Canadians, Native Bavarians, etc., by hearing them speak English." Handwriting experts can identify signatures more accurately than other people though they have no more intelligence and no better eyes. They have apparently an unusual *ability to "notice" syndromes.* Some doctors, even prior to laboratory tests, can identify cases of diabetes and hypoglycemia, and later results bear them out. We're not sure how they do this, but should one describe such more than normal abilities as the exercise of taste?

> If there are any aesthetic terms, they are terms whose (successful) application invariably requires an *"ability to notice"* which is something more than the abilities that go with normal intelligence and sense organs. . . . I think there are no such terms . . . I seem to be able to find, for any given term . . . an application of it which could be managed by any normal man. "Graceful" has already been considered. "Can't you imagine situations in which it would be natural, easy, and obvious to say 'It's a lovely day today,' 'this glove is too big, you have a rather dainty hand,' 'He's an elegant old gentleman,' 'The sun has finally broken through and now the sky is pretty,' 'I couldn't see the vessels clearly on the last one, but this earthworm is a beautiful specimen.'? Do you insist that taste is required to make these judgments? . . . The only question is whether *taste* has been exercised, and it needn't have been if normal intelligence and senses are enough. I don't see why they should not be enough.[21]

What is the upshot of all this? According to Cohen, we were on the wrong track in trying to distinguish aesthetic qualities from nonaesthetic by means of the concept of taste. Suppose, he says, that a person is given two sheets of paper, headed *aesthetic* and *nonaesthetic,* each containing the first few entries in a list. Under "aesthetic" are "lovely," "pretty," "beautiful," "dainty," etc.; under "nonaesthetic" are "red," "noisy," "brackish," etc. We give the person instructions: "Go on making these two lists."

What will happen? I submit he says, "that the subject will have no idea how to proceed. What if "noisy" were not on either initial list and when he came to "noisy" he happened to think not of pneumatic drills but of a section of some Mahler symphony? or what if he came to "flat" and thought of a Mondrian?"[22]

---

[21] Ted Cohen, *op. cit.,* pp. 850-851 in Dickie and Sclafani.
[22] *Ibid.,* p. 856.

Or how about terms like the following: baroque; colorful; classical; derivative; dissonant; funny; impressionistic; Kafkaesque; lyrical; metaphysical; muted; poetic; pompous; powerful; pretentious; realistic; religious; romantic; sad; sentimental; youthful? Consider "in the style of Beethoven"; is this an aesthetic expression or not?

> Not everything by Beethoven is Beethovenian, nor is everything in the style of Beethoven by Beethoven. What is required to apply "in the style of Beethoven" to various works of Liszt and Brahms? Obviously some training or informed experience is needed. But what is that: the development of taste or the directed training of one's normal faculties?[23]

If we cannot classify these qualities clearly in one or the other of the two columns, what are we left with? A radical and upsetting conclusion follows, that the entire aesthetic-nonaesthetic distinction goes down the tubes. This is indeed what Cohen suggests. Following Quine's attack on the analytic-synthetic distinction which was long held sacred, he has turned his intellectual microscope on the aesthetic-nonaesthetic distinction and found it similarly wanting. Since the distinction is impossible to apply (at worst) or a subject of endless disagreement as to when it is applicable (at best), we should simply try to get along without it.

But the case may not be as hopeless as this. Some of the terms used are ambiguously or at least used differently in different contexts: "flat" has an ordinary meaning ("The roof is flat") and a somewhat different one when speaking of works of art ("that passage is utterly lacking in energy, quite flat"). "Let's make the test more interesting: each time the subject adds a term to either list we ask him to give an example of its use in some context. This will allow the same term, for example, 'noisy' or 'flat,' to appear in both lists. But is it now clear that 'taste' will not be required for the uses specified under the heading *aesthetic*?"[24]

The word "taste," as Cohen reminds us, is itself ambiguous. Does it include just an ability to *notice*, or also an ability to *enjoy*? In our cookery example, is taste the ability to make fine taste discriminations or the ability to *enjoy* the gourmet dishes? If some could make very fine discriminations but enjoyed no dishes whatever, would such a person be a person of taste? "If you, having more delicate taste, respond to a work to which I am indifferent, must it be that you *notice* something which escapes me, or could it be that everything to be noticed is seen by us both, while only you also feel *pleasure*?"[25]

If aesthetic qualities are those that require a special degree of noticing (not

---

[23] *Ibid.,* p. 857.
[24] W. E. Kennick, *Art and Philosophy,* p. 639.
[25] Ted Cohen, *op. cit.,* p. 864.

an additional faculty called "taste"), then, if Cohen is right, they are no different from many other kinds of qualities. Perhaps then they are qualities or combinations of qualities that make us feel pleasure. But what kind of pleasure? A rapist may take pleasure in certain qualities of his victim, but is that what is required here? No, we are inclined to say, it's *aesthetic* pleasure and not just any kind of pleasure that we mean. But what kind of pleasure then is aesthetic pleasure? "Pleasure in the mere contemplation . . ." and so on—and here we return to descriptions or definitions of aesthetic *experience*. But this directs the argument away from aesthetic qualities and back to aesthetic experience, which we considered in Chapter 8.

Whichever noun we start with to follow upon the adjective "aesthetic"— attitude, experience, qualities—we seem to get into trouble, and to get ourselves out of it we turn to one of the other nouns, which then gets us into trouble all over again.

Still, to throw out the term "aesthetic" entirely because of difficulties in its application, at least in certain instances, is surely the counsel of despair. The term "aesthetic" has arisen in our language for a reason, and like other terms it seems to mark off, however vaguely, some territory occupied by nothing else—hence the need for the term. To be told suddenly, after several hundred years of using the term, that after all it has no application, would be almost as surprising as if, having used the term "callous" for years, we were to be told that the term has no application and that no callous people exist. Indeed, even if a term has no application it may still have a meaning: no unicorns exist, and yet we know what "unicorn" means—a horse with a horn protruding from its forehead—and we could recognize one if we ever came across one.

One may have trouble pinpointing the boundary between aesthetic and nonaesthetic. But this in no way shows that there is no distinction. Even the line between yellow and orange is hard to draw, and if shown certain shades people would disagree on whether they are yellow or orange, and yet there are clear cases of yellow and clear cases of orange. Similarly, aren't there clear cases of being aesthetic? Consider the mathematics student who is not preparing for engineering but revels in the abstract play of numbers and proofs, their elegance and neatness and the way in which they fit into place. "No, I didn't go into math for any practical reasons," the student says, "and I don't care whether I ever make any money from it—I am attracted to mathematics for *aesthetic* reasons." Don't we understand, at least approximately, at least as well as with many words we use, what the student is saying? Or suppose someone asks, "Why do you keep looking at that vacant lot? Are you planning on buying it?" and you reply, "No, I'm looking at the gentle curve of the hills in the background and the tracery of the branches of the trees against the vivid blue sky—I'm enjoying it aesthetically." Would it be appropriate in this context to reply, "Your statement is unintelligible, because there is no distinction between aesthetic and nonaesthetic"? In this and many other contexts, the term "aesthetic" has a use, which speakers can employ and hearers can understand.

In any case, we have not yet examined the term "aesthetic" in all its contexts. We have discussed aesthetic attitude, aesthetic experience, aesthetic qualities; we turn now to aesthetic evaluation.

## 2. BEAUTY AND AESTHETIC VALUE

When people compare preferences with one another, they are not surprised if one of them likes or enjoys works A, B, C, while another person dislikes these but likes D, E, F. When it comes to judgments of beauty, however, people do not as a rule believe that they are just comparing notes. When one of them believes that a certain painting by Titian is beautiful, and another does not, the first person is quite inclined to think that there is some reforming to be done. He believes that (unlike the case of disparate tastes) they are *disagreeing* about something: that if the judgment "X is beautiful" is true, then the judgment "X is not beautiful" must be false, and that if one of them says the painting is beautiful and the other says it is not, one of them must be mistaken. Immanuel Kant wrote in 1790 in his *Critique of Judgment* that

> As regards the *agreeable* everyone concedes that his judgment, which he bases on private feeling, and in which he declares that an object pleases him, is restricted merely to himself personally. Thus he does not take it amiss if, when he says that Canary wine is agreeable, another corrects the expression and reminds him that he ought to say: it is agreeable *to me*. This applies not only to the taste of the tongue, the palate, and the throat, but to what may with any one be agreeable to eye or ear. A violet color is to one soft and lovely, to another dull and faded.
>
> The beautiful stands on quite a different footing. It would, on the contrary, be ridiculous if anyone who plumed himself on his taste were to think of justifying himself by saying: This object (the building we see, the dress that person has on, the concert we hear, the poem submitted to our criticism) is beautiful *for me*. For it merely pleases *him*, he must not call it *beautiful*. Many things may for him possess charm and agreeableness—no one cares about that; but when he puts a thing on a pedestal and calls it beautiful, he demands the same delight from others. He judges not merely for himself, but for all men, and then speaks of beauty as if it were a property of things. Thus he says the *thing* is beautiful; and it is not as if he counted on others agreeing in his judgment of liking owing to his having found them in such agreement on a number of occasions, but he *demands* this agreement of them, He blames them if they judge differently, and denies them taste, which he still requires of them as something they ought to have.[26]

[26] Immanuel Kant, *Critique of Judgment*, Book I, Section VII.

But why should everyone agree, if the quality of beauty were not a quality of the objects to which we ascribe beauty?

## A. Beauty as objective

The most "natural" view to adopt is that there is a quality that some things have and others do not, a quality which may be present in varying degrees in different things and absent from others, a quality which is called "their beauty." When we say that the table top is rectangular, we mean that it, the table top itself, not merely our perception of it, is rectangular and that anyone who says it's round is not merely differing from us but is mistaken. When we say that this leaf is green, we mean that there is a quality of greenness (or being green) which is possessed by the leaf and that anyone who says the leaf is blue or purple or pink is mistaken. Similarly, when we say that an object is beautiful, we are attributing to that object a quality, namely, beauty, and if we correctly attribute this quality to a certain object, anyone who says it isn't beautiful is mistaken. In other words, beauty is an objective quality of things, just like rectangularity and greenness.

> When I attribute beauty to an object, the tribute seems to be wrung from me by the object; and if on reflection I conclude that I have misapprehended the object, I am unable to retain the attribution . . . I cannot at pleasure give it, withhold it, or change it. Under the influence of a mood beauty may lose its savor, but not its beauty; in a reflective person the judgment remains the same so long as the object does.[27]

Thus, beauty is not necessarily connected with liking or even with enjoying. I may see a painting so often that I am tired of it and no longer enjoy it, but I would still believe that it's beautiful (it didn't lose its beauty just because I became overexposed to it or because I am in a sour mood on a certain day). The judgment that it is beautiful is "wrung from me by the object," and it is from an experience of the object that I make the judgment. I may at times cease to appreciate an object's beauty, but "that's my problem": these details of my autobiography do not change the nature of the object, and beauty is a part of the nature of the object itself.

> I do meet objects with the judgment that they are beautiful, and all that is theoretically required of judgment is that it shall be true; the emotion that accompanies it is logically irrelevant, irrelevant because it is bound up with an individual set of mental and bodily conditions. . . . It [the judgment] is not about me but about the object. Nor is it a blank assertion of the object's potency over me, but about some feature in it that wields that potency. And the potency it primarily wields is not over my feelings, but over my powers of judgment. The

[27] T. E. Jessop, "The Definition of Beauty," *Proceedings of the Aristotelian Society,* 33 (1932-3); reprinted in *Introductory Readings in Aesthetics,* ed. John Hospers, pp. 271-281. Passage quoted is on p. 274.

minimum and distinctive quality of beauty is that it wins for itself admission; whatever else it wins is largely a matter of accident, the accident of association, of mood, and of taste.[28]

Just as all that is required of a judgment about how many chairs there are in this room is that the judgment be true (there must really be exactly as many chairs in the room as one claims), so all that is strictly required of a judgment of beauty is that it be true. If I enjoy the object or become ecstatic when I regard it, so much the better, but whether or not I like it does not affect its truth. If beauty were not an objective quality of things, then

> Even the most discerning piece of art-criticism would be no more than a personal confession, to be read, if read at all, only in order to know what the critic feels about his object, not whether he has detected in this some aspect or relation which I may have overlooked. I must accept his judgment as final for himself and irrelevant for me. On this view the aesthetic judgment disappears, becomes a synonym for a judgment of introspection, being reducible without any loss of meaning to "I feel in such and such a way towards this object."[29]

There is, then, an objective quality of things, as much present in them as their redness or roundness, whose presence we recognize intellectually and hopefully respond to emotionally.

In popular parlance, however, the word "beauty" is often used so loosely as to be quite confusing. (1) Sometimes when we say "It's beautiful" we are not really attributing a quality to the object: If I see the skies clear after two weeks of rain, I may say "It's beautiful" when all I mean is that it pleases me, or that it's a relief after what's gone before, or that it makes me feel good once again, or any of a number of similar things. (2) When a man says of a woman "She's beautiful," he may (but need not) mean merely that she attracts him sexually. Clive Bell wrote, "With the man in the street, 'beautiful' is more often than not synonymous with 'desirable'; the word does not necessarily connote any aesthetic reaction whatever, and I am tempted to believe that in the minds of many the sexual flavor of the word is stronger than the aesthetic. . . . A beautiful picture is a photograph of a pretty girl; beautiful music, the music that provides emotions similar to those provoked by young ladies in musical farces; and beautiful poetry, the poetry that recalls the same emotions felt, twenty years earlier, for the rector's daughter." (Because of this, Clive Bell eschewed the use of the word "beauty" entirely, believing that the word had been so constantly misused as to be past redemption.) (3) When people say, "Peace, it's beautiful," they are not reporting any state-of-affairs to which they respond aesthetically at all but only one which they favor. (4) Even when one does respond aesthetically, it is often the case that a person says "It's beautiful," not meaning to attribute a quality to the object, but simply to *express* pleasure or delight: in other words, "beautiful"

[28] *Ibid.,* pp. 275-276.
[29] *Ibid.,* p. 274.

is used as a "gush word" (the opposite of a "snarl word") rather than to attribute a quality, beauty, to an object.

Once we have sloughed off these popular but irrelevant ways of using the term "beauty," some questions present themselves concerning the view that beauty is an objective quality. What kind of quality is it? How are we to detect its presence? How are we to resolve disagreements about whether or not it is present?

1. *Is beauty one quality?* Is there one quality, beauty, which is the same in all its manifestations?

It can be present in greater or lesser degree, but according to the beauty theory it is the very same quality which is present in those varying degrees—just as redness is the same quality wherever it occurs: although it may occur pure (in primary red) or mixed with other colors (as in vermilion, mauve, violet, orange, pink), it is the same quality, redness, that occurs, either pure or in these combinations.

The case seems clear enough with red, but how does it stand with beauty? Is it the same quality we perceive when we say a poem is beautiful, that a sonata is beautiful, that a landscape painting is beautiful? Is it the very same feature throughout, varying perhaps only in degrees? Let us also remember that we speak not only of works of art but also of objects in nature as beautiful: of the starry sky, of a sunset, of clear lakes, of rushing rivers, of high mountains, of the desert landscape at sunset, and so on. When we say that something in nature is beautiful, such as a mountain seen reflected in a lake in Glacier Park, is it the same quality we discern as we do when we say that Beethoven's *Archduke Trio* (Op. 97) is singularly beautiful?

To complicate things further, we should keep in mind that to call something beautiful is not the same as to call it great art. We may speak of the poetry of Dante or the chamber music of Fauré as beautiful, but we do not customarily characterize Dostoyevsky's *The Brothers Karamazov* as beautiful, even though we may classify it among the greatest works of art.

As we saw in Chapter 7, art, has other values to offer than aesthetic ones, and *The Brothers Karamazov* has so much to say about life and human nature that one values it for that more than for beauty. Art, especially literature, as we saw, has other fish to fry and only picks up some aesthetic fish along the way. Only the aesthetic fish should be called beautiful, no matter how much (in other ways) we may value the other ones.

There is a further complication still: even in its "careful" sense—excluding its uses as a "purr word"—the word "beauty" is used ambiguously:

[There are] two distinct uses of the word "beauty," one for that which has *sensuous charm,* and one for the aesthetic approval of works of *imaginative art* where the objects presented to us are often of extreme ugliness. Beauty in the former sense belongs to works of art where only the *perceptual* aspect of the imaginative life is exercised; beauty in the second sense becomes as it were *supersensual,* and is concerned with the *appropriateness and intensity of the emotions aroused.* When these emotions are aroused in a way that satisfies fully the needs of the imaginative life, we approve and delight in the sensations through which we enjoy that heightened experience, because they possess purposeful order and variety in relation to those emotions.[30]

We sometimes distinguish experiences of "cool beauty" from those of "warm beauty." In the "cool" sense, the beauty of something has to do with its being *pleasing to the senses*: the Mondrian rectangles tease and delight the eye, the Mozart concerto for glass harmonica teases and delights the ear, and we may call them both beautiful. But when we have finished hearing a Bach mass, or watching a performance of Schiller's *Maria Stuart,* or Martha Graham's dance *Clytemnestra,* it's not so much that our eyes or ears have been titillated as that we have been deeply and profoundly moved; still deeply affected emotionally by the experience, we may murmur, still under the spell the work has cast on us, "It's beautiful."

### Kant's theory of beauty

Kant confined the use of the word "beauty" to the first of these two: To Kant, beauty had to do with what was pleasing to the senses, but Kant believed that what was universally pleasing to the senses, once shorn of association with real objects, was always certain formal combinations of elements: Kant was a formalist much in the manner of Clive Bell. Yet he did not believe that any principle could be stated about what kinds of forms made something beautiful:

> There can be no objective rule of taste by which what is beautiful may be defined by means of concepts. For every judgment from that source is aesthetic, i.e., its determining ground is the feeling of the subject, and not any concept of an object. It is only throwing away labor to look for a principle of taste that affords a universal criterion of the beautiful by definite concepts; because what is sought is a thing impossible.[31]

What one *could* do, Kant thought, was to distinguish "pure beauty" from extraneous concepts with which it could easily be confused. Thus, whether we regard something as beautiful should have nothing to do with our own personal associations: if we like a tune because it is the anthem of the nation we inhabit and toward which we feel patriotism, this is irrelevant to any judgment of its beauty. Second, the judgment of beauty should have nothing to do with what kind of represented object there is in the work: our judgment of whether what is represented by the round shape is a melon, balloon, or a globe representing the world. Third and most important for Kant, the judgment of beauty should have nothing to do with the purpose or function of an object,

---

[30] Roger Fry, "An Essay in Aesthetics," in *Vision and Design* (London: Chatto and Windus, (1924), Penguin Classics edition, p. 34. (Emphasis added.)

[31] Immanuel Kant, *Critique of Judgment,* Part I, Section XV.

either real or imputed. People may call a horse beautiful because it runs swiftly; this is a quality which (in real life) people expect of horses, since horses are used for running; but this has nothing to do with whether the shape of a horse, quite apart from this function, is beautiful or not. Judgments of beauty should be separated from judgments of the degree to which a natural object attains perfection ("a perfect horse") in fulfilling a certain function.

> Hardly anyone but a botanist knows the true nature of a flower, and even he, while recognizing in the flower the reproductive organ of the plant, pays no attention to this natural end when using his taste to judge of its beauty. Hence no perfection of any kind—no internal finality, as something to which the arrangement of the manifold is related—underlines this judgment. Many birds (the parrot, the hummingbird, the bird of paradise), and a number of crustacea, are self-subsisting beauties which are not appurtenant to any object defined with respect to its end, but please freely and on their own account. So designs *à la grecque,* foliage for framework or on wall-papers, etc., have no intrinsic meaning; they represent nothing . . . and are free beauties. We may also rank in the same class what in music are called fantasias (without a theme), and, indeed, all music that is not set to words.
>
> But the beauty of man (including under this head that of a man, woman, or child), the beauty of a horse, or of a building . . . presupposes a concept of the end that defines what the thing has to be, and consequently a concept of its perfection.[32]

Once these irrelevancies are sorted out and excised from our judgments of beauty, such judgments should, Kant thought, be universal—that is, should command everyone's assent—although no principle can be stated as to which formal arrangements are beautiful and which are not. Apparently Clive Bell agreed with Kant on this, for he too, though eschewing the work "beauty" in favor of his own term "significant form," never stated any general principle by means of which genuine instances of "significant form" could be detected, although he believed in the objective existence of the quality of beauty as strongly as Kant did.

Still, the fact remains that many people find many things beautiful other than strictly formal qualities. We may call the sky beautiful on a day when its color is an intensely vivid blue, and this beauty seems to be of a color, not of a form. The light clashes of cymbals in the "Sanctus" of the Berlioz *Requiem* are experienced by countless listeners as supremely beautiful, but one can find little formal reason for this: it has rather to do with the tonal quality of that instrument at just that juncture in the work (the same clashes of cymbals in isolation would admittedly not be experienced as beautiful). Cannot beauty depend, not only on formal qualities, but on sensuous qualities on the one hand, and on expressive qualities on the other? And if not, why not? The variety of things and qualities we call beautiful in both nature and art, and in

---

[32] *Ibid.,* Part I, Section XVI.

both the "cool" and the "warm" senses (and why exclude one or the other?), is so vast that we cannot help wondering what quality they all have in common to which we can assign the traditional term "beauty."

## Schopenhauer's theory of beauty

An entirely different view from Kant's is that of Arthur Schopenhauer, who distinguishes works of art characterized by what he calls *beauty* from others characterized by what he calls *interest:* "The beauty of a work of art consists in the fact that it holds up a clear mirror to certain *ideas* inherent in the world in general; the beauty of a work of poetic art in particular is that it renders the ideas inherent in mankind, and thereby leads it to a knowledge of these ideas. The means which poetry uses for this end are the exhibition of significant characters and the invention of circumstances which will bring about significant situations, giving occasion to the characters to unfold their peculiarities and show what is in them; so that by some such representation a clearer and fuller knowledge of the many-sided idea of humanity may be attained."[33] Beauty is always "an affair of *knowledge,* and . . . appeals to the *knowing subject,* and not to the will; nay, it is a fact that the apprehension of beauty on the part of the subject involves a complete suppression of the will."

Quite opposed to this are dramas or descriptive poetry that depict

> actions of a kind which necessarily arouse concern or sympathy, like that which we feel in real events involving our own person. The fate of the person represented in them is felt in just the same fashion as our own; we await the development of events with anxiety; we eagerly follow their course; our hearts quicken when the hero is threatened; our pulse falters as the danger reaches its acme, and throbs again when he is suddenly rescued. Until we reach the end of the story we cannot put the book aside; we lie awake far into the night sympathizing with our hero's troubles as though they were our own. . . . What is affected by poetry of this character is our *will,* and not merely our intellectual powers pure and simple. The word *interest* means, therefore, that which arouses the concern of the individual's will . . . and here it is that beauty is clearly distinguished from interest. The one is an affair of the intellect . . . the other works upon the will.[34]

In works of art in which only interest is aroused, we read on anxiously to see what happens next; but if this is all that keeps us going, we shall not care to read the work (or watch the film) a second time, for we already know how things turned out. "Dramatic representations which depend for their value on their interest lose by repetition, because they are no longer able to arouse

---

[33] Arthur Schopenhauer, *Complete Essays of Schopenhauer* (New York: Crown Publishers, n.d.), Part 6 ("The Art of Controversy"), essay "On the Comparative Place of Interest and Beauty in Works of Art," p. 43.

[34] *Ibid.,* p. 44.

curiosity as to their course, since it is already known. To see them often makes them stale and tedious. On the other hand, works of which the value lies in their beauty gain by repetition, as they are then more and more understood. . . . Beauty is the true end of every art."[35]

Why then are we able to witness certain dramas over and over again without diminution of attention? Why would we react unfavorably to a remark by a person we had invited to see a peformance of *Hamlet*, "I've seen it once, and I already know how it turns out"? Because great dramas do not appeal primarily to interest.

> Significant characters may be represented, that open up the depths of human nature, and it may all be expressed in actions and sufferings of an exceptional kind, so that the real nature of humanity and the world may stand forth in the picture in the clearest and most forcible lines; and yet no high degree of interest may be excited in the course of events by the continued progress of the action, or by the complexity and unexpected solution of the plot. The immortal masterpieces of Shakespeare contain little that excites interest.
>
> Homer lays the world of humanity before us in its true nature, but he takes no trouble to attract our sympathy by a complexity of circumstance, or to surprise us by unexpected entanglements. His pace is lingering; he stops at every scene; he puts one picture after another tranquilly before us, elaborating it with care. We experience no passionate emotion in reading him; our demeanor is one of pure perceptive intelligence; he does not arouse our will, but sings it to rest; and it costs us no effort to break off in our reading, for we are not in condition of eager curiosity. This is all still more true of Dante, whose work is not, in the proper sense of the word, an epic, but a descriptive poem.[36]

Nevertheless, a considerable degree of interest is to be found in some acknowledged masterpieces of literature. "We have it in Schiller's dramas in an appreciable degree, and consequently they are popular; also in the *Oedipus Rex* of Sophocles. Amongst masterpieces of description, we find it in Aristo's *Orlando Furioso;* nay, an example of a high degree of interest, bound up with the beautiful, is afforded in an excellent novel by Walter Scott, *The Heart of Midlothian*."[37]

Interest may be useful in much the way representation may be useful in visual art according to Clive Bell:

> With dramatic and descriptive literature an admixture of interest is necessary, just as a volatile and gaseous substance requires a material basis if it is to be preserved and transferred. The admixture is necessary, partly, indeed, because interest is itself created by the events which have to be devised in order to set the characters in motion; partly because our minds would be weary of watching scene after scene if they had no concern for us, or of passing from one significant picture to another if we were not drawn on by some secret thread. It is this that we call interest; it is the sympathy which the event in itself forces us to feel, and

---

[35] *Ibid.,* pp. 48-49.
[36] *Ibid.,* pp. 50-51.
[37] *Ibid.,* pp. 51-52.

which, by riveting our attention, makes the mind obedient to the poet, and able to follow him into all the parts of his story.

If the interest of a work of art is sufficient to achieve this result, it does all that can be required of it; for its only service is to connect the pictures by which the poet desires to communicate a knowledge of the idea, as if they were pearls, and interest were the thread that holds them together, and makes an ornament out of the whole. But interest is prejudicial to beauty as soon as it oversteps this limit; and this is the case if we are so led away by the interest of a work that whenever we come to any detailed description in a novel, or in a drama, we grow impatient and want to put spurs to our author, so that we may follow the development of events with greater speed. Epic and dramatic writings, where beauty and interest are both present in a high degree, may be compared to the working of a watch, where interest is the spring which keeps all the wheels in motion. If it worked unhindered, the watch would run down in a few minutes. Beauty, holding us in the spell of description and reflection, is like the barrel which checks its movement.[38]

We see from Schopenhauer's account how closely his conception of beauty approximates that of what we called "cool beauty." When we view a painting or a sculpture, we coolly contemplate the relations of forms and the representations of people and things. We do the same in those works of literature he calls great, such as Homer and Shakespeare, in which human nature and action are set before us for our contemplation, exhibiting various truths about human character and motivation. But when we become interested in "what happens next," it is not the contemplating mind but the active will that becomes involved, and we read on faster, wanting no interruptions. The same thing happens when we listen to music—as it approaches its climax we cannot bear to have it interrupted—and indeed Schopenhauer's view of music (see pp. 272–73) is that music is a manifestation of the primordial will itself, with its patterns of frustration and fulfillment, rising and falling, climbing from the depths and descending again, endlessly striving toward a goal and, on reaching it, endlessly leaving it to strive again. Music is not an art of "cool" contemplation but of heart-pounding involvement. Since music, according to Schopenhauer, is the most emotionally involving of the arts, its rhythms matching those of human conation and striving (evoking maximum "interest," in his terminology), it would be the art furthest removed from Schopenhauer's conception of beauty.

One might question, of course, whether all music is like this: doesn't some music exhibit "cool beauty" too—not the Romantic music Schopenhauer had in mind (Beethoven, Brahms, Wagner), but the formally pleasing patterns of tones one hears for example in Scarlatti sonatas and Haydn trios? In the House of Beauty aren't there many mansions, each suited to different impulses, moods, and temperaments? Why select one kind only and limit beauty to that? At any rate, Schopenhauer's view provides another example of the variety of ways in which beauty is conceived, or perhaps we should say, in

[38] *Ibid.,* pp. 52-53.

which the word "beauty" is used. Thus far, the views we have examined have all been objectivist theories, identifying beauty as some quality (but not always the same quality) of the object contemplated.


Problems concerning objectivist theories

2. *Is beauty an intrinsic quality of things?* Is the quality intrinsic or relational?

A quality is intrinsic to an object if the object would have the quality quite independently of its relations to other things, including observers. Thus, a rubber ball is spherical and made of rubber: these are intrinsic properties of the ball, and the ball would have them even if all other objects were somehow to disappear. But if one ball is placed to the north of another ball, "being to the north of" is a *relation* in which that the one ball stands to another; being north of the second ball is not an intrinsic property of it. Sometimes the relation is between objects and perceivers of the object: if object O is red, it is plausible in the light of modern physical theory to say that redness is not intrinsic to it: the object emanates light of certain wavelengths, and when these impinge on the retina of the human eye and are transmitted along the optic nerve to the brain, only then does the experience of that particular color quality, red, arise. Redness, then, is a relational quality, a relation the object has to human perceivers, at least those who are not blind or color-blind. The object does not have this relation to many nonhuman beings, animals who can't see colors at all. Why then do we say that an object is simply "red," as if it were an intrinsic quality rather than "red for man" but not "red for flies"? Undoubtedly this is because our language is adapted to *human* experiences, and in human experience certain things regularly look red.

It would be not only daring but implausible to suggest that beauty is an intrinsic characteristic of things. What people perceive as beautiful, animals apparently do not; and how Martians or Venusians would respond to the things we call beautiful is completely unknown. If beauty is a quality of things, it must clearly be a relational quality—a quality possessed in relation to the nature of the human organism, with human perceptions and human affective life. "Beautiful" must then mean, at most, "beautiful for human beings," but the phrase is not added for the same reason that we don't say "red for human beings," because the implied context is that of human life, and if any question arises about the contrast between human beings and other organisms, we can then add "beautiful for human beings" just as we added "red for human beings." In any case, relational qualities are still objective: it is objectively the case that this rose is red, not blue or black; and according to the beauty theory, the same is true of beauty.

Of course, beauty may not even be a quality that things possess in relation to *all* human beings. We may have to go farther and say "beautiful for

Cretans but not beautiful for Phoenicians,'' or ''beautiful for you but not beautiful for me.'' But this would land us in subjectivistic theories of beauty, which we shall consider in the next section. The point here is that, if beauty is to be considered a property of things at all, it must be a relational one, and as long as the relation is to mankind in general rather than to particular human beings, one can go on speaking *as if* it were intrinsic, while yet keeping in mind that just as art is *by* human beings and *for* human beings, so too beauty is something appreciated by human beings and created (in art at least) for human beings—not for Martians, of whose possible sensory equipment and responses to objects we can say nothing.

3. *Is beauty a simple quality?* Is beauty a *simple quality* or a complex one? Considering all the controversy that has raged in ethics concerning whether the word ''good'' is the name of a simple quality, it is surprising how little controversy there has been about the analogous issue in aesthetics. ''Simple'' here does not mean the opposite of difficult; a simple quality is one that cannot be conceptually analyzed or broken down into components. ''Red'' is the name of such a simple quality—as are the names of other colors, as well as tastes, smells, ''feels'' (touches), feelings, emotions, moods. If you have been aware of them in your own experience you know what (relational) qualities the words ''red'' (color), ''pungent'' (smell), ''rough'' (tactile sensation), ''sour'' (taste), and so on refer to, but if you have not, no amount of verbal description can give it to you. A person who was born blind could never know what red looked like and hence could never know what kind of experience people were talking about when they used the word ''red.'' And no set of verbal instructions could help to produce in him the experience, or even enable him to imagine it. (''Red is like the sound of a trumpet,'' someone might tell him; but then when he heard the word ''red'' he would imagine the sound of a trumpet, which as we well know is not the color red, nor does it help us to imagine what red looks like.) The blind person could, of course, learn from books what frequency of light waves produces the experience in the normal human eye that people call red, but that still wouldn't tell him what the color with which those waves are correlated looks like to those who can perceive it.

By contrast, the concept of a square is complex. If one has never seen a square, one can imagine one or draw one according to instructions; a square consists of (1) four straight lines, (2) of equal length, (3) intersecting each other at right angles, (4) so as to form a closed figure. Similarily none of us has seen a unicorn (only pictures of unicorns); but even if we have not seen one we can easily imagine a creature which (1) resembles a horse but (2) has a horn protruding from the middle of its forehead. (The idea of a horse is also a complex idea, like that of being a square—though somewhat more complicated, it is still a matter of arranging certain shapes in certain spatial relations.) Such things can be imagined in advance of being perceived, and verbal instructions can be given for producing the ideas in people's minds prior to their having perceived these things directly.

Is the idea of beauty a simple or complex idea? If it is simple, then, like the idea of red, there are no instructions one can give to enable a person to see it or identify it. There is some plausibility in holding that beauty is like that. "You either see it or you don't." If you aren't blind (or color-blind), I can show you a red object and thus produce in you the experience of color red; and if you aren't "aesthetically blind," I can show you a beautiful object and hopefully you will have the experience of beauty. Once I have placed you in a situation in which the experience is accessible to you, there is really nothing more I can do: you can lead a horse to water but you can't make him drink. "I see the beauty in the cathedral," we may say to someone with whom we are on a tour, "and if you don't see it, I'm sorry for you, you're missing a lot, but after all I can't *make* you see it." You can't make a dog or a horse see it, and apparently you can't make some people see it either. Just as a visually blind person can't see red, so an aesthetically blind person can't see beauty.

This kind of experience is somewhat familiar to us through other concepts we have already examined. We claim that a work of art is unified, and the other person doesn't see it; it is a kind of Gestalt which, after some looking or listening, one just "grasps"; suddenly after looking in vain for a time, one just "sees" it and wonders why it hadn't been evident to him before. And the same with expressive qualities such as sadness, peacefulness, tension, and stateliness. If you claim that Handel's music has a certain majesty and the other person, even after repeated hearing, claims not to "hear" it, what more can you do? You can call him an insensitive clod, but that won't help him experience it.

On the other hand, it is also plausible to say that beauty is a complex quality. If someone doesn't see the beauty of the cathedral, we may point out to him the gradual curvature of certain repeating patterns in the frescos, the angle at which the arches rise, the symmetry, and so on. This seems to show that, whatever beauty is, these perceivable qualities have *something* to do with it: that if the person sees the perceptual patterns you are trying to point out to him, he is more likely then to have the experience of beauty. This by itself doesn't show that beauty is complex; perhaps you are pointing out certain perceptual features of the cathedral *in order that* he will then experience the (simple) quality, beauty, just as a person might take you into a rose garden so that you could experience the simple quality, redness. But perhaps beauty is *itself* a complex quality, like squareness, so that in principle at least you could give instructions for perceiving it—not as easily as you could squareness, for the instructions here are easy to fulfill, but if beauty is a complex quality you should be able with the aid of instructions to help a person to experience the quality for himself, though the instructions might be ever so much more complicated and difficult to provide.

If beauty is complex, does it have the *same set of components* in every case? Can't the qualities constituting beauty be ABCD one time, CDEF another time, and EFGH another time? Let us again, consider the case of a dozen or so of the major arias from Mozart's opera *The Magic Flute*. "They are supremely beautiful," we are inclined to say when we hear them. What makes them beautiful? Among an infinity of possible tone combinations, Mozart hit upon just this combination (for this melody), and it was just this combination that made it beautiful—changing a note of it would have reduced or cancelled out its beauty. The beauty appears then to be made up of a combination of factors all coming together. Now, how can one possibly generalize about a beauty which depends on a multitude of precise conditions to come into being? Suppose that we did analyze the exact series of tone relationships in one of these arias and set it forth as the set of qualities that constitute beauty. But the very next aria would exhibit quite a different series of tonal relationships, and yet it might be just as beautiful. And even if we did find some common pattern of qualities in the Mozart arias, that pattern would desert us utterly in passages of different characters, such as the Ernest Bloch Quintet for Piano and Strings, whose dark haunting beauty is of an entirely different order. When we go outside music, the factors on which beauty depend are different yet again.

Moreover, if beauty is a complex quality, what kind of complex quality is it? (1) Is it *perceived* with the sense the way one perceives a color or a smell? Do you *see* beauty—or hear it, in the case of music? In the case of literature, what you hear (in reading aloud) or see (in looking at the page) doesn't seem to be what you appreciate, so how could you be said to either see or hear the beauty there? (2) Is beauty something *cognized* by the mind, the way you grasp the similarity of two arguments or the way you "see" that if no As are Bs then no Bs are As either? Jessop's position seems to be that beauty is grasped intellectually, since all that is demanded of us is assent to the *judgment* that something is beautiful—we need not feel any emotions, we need only grasp with our minds the fact that a certain quality is present. Or perhaps (3) beauty is something *felt:* what you see is just a precursor to something you feel, and the feeling "tells" you that the thing is beautiful: you see the contrasting colors in the painting and the placement of the masses, the perception of that does something to your feeling: you are moved in some way, and only after the feeling has been experienced are you entitled to make the judgment that the thing is beautiful.

If beauty is perceived with the senses, is it a visual quality when we see beauty in a painting and an auditory quality when we hear beauty in a piece of music? Is beauty one complex quality when seen and another complex quality when heard? The two may have features in common, such as a pattern or gestalt. But it does seem strange to say that beauty is seen or heard with the senses at all (particularly since poetic beauty seems to be neither). If the observer has normal vision and can see various features of a painting when called to his attention, how is it that (if beauty is visual) he can't see the beauty? It seems more plausible, then, to say that once certain complex qualities have been seen or heard, one either *recognizes* or *feels* the presence of beauty as a kind of *supervenient* quality. A quality is supervenient if it supervenes on other qualities: if qualities ABC are not present, then quality D, the supervenient quality, cannot appear—much as if there are no plants in a garden there can be no arrangement of the plants. But if so, it seems that the quality can supervene on a vast variety of different perceptual qualities, such as the tonal combinations in music, not to mention the expressive qualities as well, each differing from case to case.

In the light of all this, is it not possible that we are chasing a will-o'-the-wisp? Is there such an objective quality as beauty? "When we have distinguished in a painting its lines and shapes and color-tones, its structural relations, and its human regional qualities—the movement and swirl, the joyousness and vitality—is there something else left over that we have not yet mentioned, namely its beauty?"[39] And if so, where and how is it to be found?

According to one current theory, that of Guy Sircello, beauty is a complex property whose presence depends on a number of factors:

1. Things can be beautiful only with respect to properties that are capable of variations of *qualitative degree*. The vividness of a color is a matter of qualitative degree, since a color may be more vivid or less vivid, so are the vibrancy and clarity of a tone. Excluded are *nondegree* properties of such as being square, being full, being pregnant. Excluded also are properties of *qualitative* degree such as being heavy, being hot, being tall, being large: in these a numerical degree scale can easily be constructed to measure the difference of quantitative degree to which the properties are present.

2. It must not be a property of deficiency, lack, or defect. Being blemished, being deformed, being dilapidated, being unhealthy, being sallow are examples of "defect universally." There can also be defect that is relative to the kinds of objects to which they apply: "being rough (applied to skin, or a road, but not to eucalyptus bark), being shiny (applied to gabardine fabric, but not to an automobile finish), being fat (applied to adults, but not to babies), being smooth (applied to tire treads, but not to roads), being sad (applied to day, but not to music and not necessarily to people)."[40]

3. It must not be a property of the *appearance* of a lack, deficiency, or defect, such as being unhealthy looking, being sallow looking, being rotten smelling, being putrid tasting, and so on.

Any property of qualitative degree (of an object) is beautiful if it is not a property of deficiency, lack or defect, *and* is not property of the appearance of these, *and* if the property is present in that object in a very high degree.

The theory is worked out so as to include, with considerable subtlety, many hundreds of examples in both nature and art, to which the assertion "It's beautiful" is assigned, and to explain why many other things in both nature and art are not found to be beautiful.

The theory appears to be a kind of exercise in generalization. We are

[39] Monroe C. Beardsley, *Aesthetics,* p. 508.
[40] Guy Sircello, *A New Theory of Beauty* (Princeton: Princeton Univ. Press, 1978), p. 41.

presented with many cases in which something is "found" to be beautiful, and the beauty is then accounted for on the basis of these features. But what if someone sincerely believes something to be beautiful although it does not conform to the requirements given for beauty as a complex property? What if someone found a pastel color to be more beautiful than a more vivid one, even granted the precautions about context that Sircello provides? What if someone found a surface with a certain defect more beautiful than one without the defect? (It is not clear, in every case, exactly what constitutes a defect. Is the lack of a deep tan on one's skin a defect? Or perhaps its presence? Is a deep well beautiful in proportion to its darkness—darkness being a property of qualitative degree? or is darkness a defect?)

One could discuss at great length examples and possible counterexamples in connection with the theory, which space does not permit. But one question must be faced by not only this but all "objective" theories of beauty:

4. *Verification.* How is the presence of beauty to be detected? and how are we to resolve disagreements about whether it is present in a particular case?

Although redness is a simple quality, there is in fact no problem in determining whether something is red, for the sensory quality redness is correlated with a physical condition which produces the experience, and this physical condition (the emanation from the object of light waves of a certain frequency) can be verified by anyone who has the equipment and takes the trouble. It is not so with beauty. Two people can look at a painting or listen to a sonata many times, point out its features to one another and agree on them all, while yet disagreeing on whether the work of art possesses beauty. And in that case what can the one person do to convince the other? The first person, A, may simply assert that the quality of beauty is present, and the other person, B, may deny it; what comes next? Does that end the argument and begin the fight? It doesn't help for A to say that he "knows by intuition" that the painting is beautiful, for B can just as well assert that he "knows by intuition" that it is not—and so we have two conflicting intuitions with no way to check them, no way to determine which is right.

A, of course, may insist that he, being a more sensitive spirit than B, simply is aware of a quality that B is not. (But how can he show that he's more sensitive, if all the perceptual qualities pointed to by A are also perceived by B?) But this is simply an unsupported statement—that there is quality there and that A knows it, though B is looking too and doesn't see it. "It's a pity you don't see there what I do," A may say. And we may even grant that to fail to see something that's there is indeed an error of omission. But if A can accuse B of failing to see something that's there, why can't B turn around and accuse A of seeing something that isn't there—that is, of hallucinating? To see something that isn't there is as much an error as to fail to see something that is there, and this is an error not of omission but of commission. Doesn't B have as good (or bad) a case as A? "You're beauty-blind," says A; "you fail to see beauty when it's there." "You're hallucinating," says B; "you see things when they aren't there at all!'' And according to the beauty theory, who is to say which of these errors is being committed?

5. *Beauty versus aesthetic value.* There is yet another problem: the word ''beauty'' has to be stretched way out of shape to cover the whole range of qualities that people find aesthetically valuable:

> If the word ''beauty'' has any clear and restricted meaning, it does not apply, I suppose, to *Oedipus Rex*, to *The Magic Mountain,* to *King Lear,* to parts of Bartok's piano concertos, to some paintings of Rubens and Tintoretto, much less the Grünewald *Crucifixion*. These works may be powerful, grand, terrible, yes—but not beautiful. At least, the Beauty Theorist must, I think, say so. . . . Anyone who uses the word ''beautiful'' for a quality, and applies it to those objects most commonly called beautiful, will, to be consistent, have to withhold it from these works.[41]

For earlier theorists of beauty this presented no problem. Until the end of the eighteenth century the beautiful was believed to be only one of several aesthetic categories and was carefully distinguished from other ones, such as the sublime, the tragic, the comic, each with its own set of criteria. Today these have virtually disappeared as separate categories, especially under the influence of Croce, as well as the rise of new art forms which cross over the boundaries among traditional genres. Theory of the sublime has virtually disappeared today, yet it was considered as important in its day as theory of the beautiful. That which is sublime is always powerful and massive, like mountain peaks, and one feels small and powerless by comparison with it. Thomas Burnet wrote of the sublime in 1681,

> Next to the great Concave of the Heavens, and those boundless Regions where the Stars inhabit, there is nothing that I look upon with more pleasure than the wide Sea and the Mountains of the Earth. There is something august and stately in the Air of those things that inspires the mind with great thoughts and passions; we do naturally upon such occasions think of God and his greatness, and whatsoever hath but the shadow and appearance of infinity, as all things that are too big for our comprehension, they fill and overbear the mind with the Excess, and cast it into a pleasing kind of stupor and admiration.[42]

And Kant himself wrote of the sublime:

> Bold, overhanging, and, as it were, threatening rocks, thunderclouds piled up the vault of heaven, borne along with flashes and peals, volcanoes in all their violence and destruction, hurricanes leaving desolation in their track, the boundless ocean rising with rebellious force, the high waterfall of some mighty river, and the like, make our power of resistance of trifling moment in comparison with their might.[43]

[41] Beardsley, *Aesthetics,* p. 509.

[42] Thomas Burnet, *Sacred Theory of the Earth,* I, xi. First published in 1681.

[43] Immanuel Kant, *Critique of Judgment,* Meredith translation (Oxford: Clarendon Press, 1911), p.110.

Although the descriptions of these qualities were presented largely in terms of how they affect us, the view nevertheless was that they were all different properties of objects. But then aesthetic theory, which had originally centered on the properties of objects, became immersed instead in speculation on "the aesthetic" as a characteristic of our *response* to objects, and thus opened the way to aesthetic subjectivism: the view that since different persons respond to the same object in different ways, perhaps there are no such properties of objects such as beauty or sublimity, and these ways of speaking only refer to the ways in which certain objects affect us—our senses, our minds, or our emotions. We turn now to an examination of subjectivistic theories.

## B. Beauty as subjective

It is obvious that different people respond to the same objects in nature and art in different ways. The beauty theory holds that this is because there is a feature of the object—either intrinsic, like roundness, or relational, like redness—to which these are responses and that, if one truly apprehends this quality, one will respond appropriately (cognitively or affectively, or both) to the object, and that if one does not, one is failing to perceive a quality that is nevertheless "out there," just as a color-blind person fails to perceive the redness of the rose.

According to subjectivistic theories, however, statements about beauty do not describe any qualities of the object; rather, they describe our *responses* to the object; and since there is no objective quality, "beauty," sentences about beauty must be reducible to sentences about such responses.

"Beauty is in the eye of the beholder," goes an old saying. But if the beauty were literally in the eye of the beholder, it would be the eye of the beholder that was beautiful. What the statement is doubtless supposed to mean is that a thing is found beautiful or not beautiful by different people, depending on how they perceive it or "what they see in it." And this of course is true, but it tells us nothing about which theory of beauty, if any, is true.

Many writers on beauty have held views which can be classified as subjectivistic. John Ruskin (1819–1900) wrote, "Any material object which can give us pleasure in the simple contemplation of its outward qualities, without any direct and definite exertion of the intellect, I call in some way or in some degree beautiful."[44] He does not state which qualities these are—presumably there are many "outward qualities," but he does not say how they must affect the observer, except that they must not "directly" stimulate the intellect. This admits colors and sounds and simple forms, but not symbolist poetry or James Joyce novels. But, of course, one person may experience pleasure in the "simple contemplation" of an object whereas

[44] John Ruskin, *Modern Painters,* Part I, sec. 1, Chapter 6. (Many editions.)

another does not. Presumably then it is beautiful for the first person but not for the second.

Samuel Alexander (1859–1938) wrote, "In experiencing sugar as pleasant, the pleasure belongs to the mind but does not belong to the sugar. In the experience of beauty, the beauty in a beautiful object does not exist except so far as it satisfies the mind which is actually contemplating it; the pleasure in like manner belongs to the contemplating mind. . . . The difference between the work of art and the sugar is that sugar happens by its nature to please, while the beautiful is constructed so as to please."[45] (Presumably it is art, not natural beauty, which was constructed so as to please.) In both these views, it is *pleasure* that characterizes the response. "I was deeply moved but not pleased" or "I was shocked but not pleased" (in response to Picasso's *Guernica,* for example) would apparently not be beauty responses.

Curt J. Ducasse (1881–1967) wrote, "Beauty is that property of an object which consists in the capacity of the object to cause pleasure in a subject who contemplates it."[46] Again the response is pleasure. And again the theory is subjectivistic, since in response to the same object some observers feel pleasure and others do not. Ducasse adds, "It is just as natural that the same object should affect differently different minds . . . as it is that the same tepid water should feel warm to a hand that is cold but cool to a hand that is hot."

George Santayana (1863–1952) wrote, "Beauty is pleasure perceived as a quality of a thing."[47] What distinguishes aesthetic pleasures from other pleasures is that in aesthetic pleasure we project our pleasure onto the object and think of it as a property of the object. Attributions of beauty to objects involve then a kind of mistaken identity: the pleasure is in us, but since beauty is no more than pleasure felt to be a feature of the object, we attribute the beauty to the object. This definition is again subjectivistic: there is no beauty in the object, only pleasure in the subject. If one observer feels pleasure in the object and another does not, the object is beautiful for the first observer but not for the second.

"Pleasures," wrote the nineteenth-century aesthetician Henry R. Marshall, "are notably evanescent; and it cannot be claimed that there is a class of pleasures, which are permanent in themselves, that make up the aesthetic field. There are states of mind, however, which may remain pleasant for long periods in consequence of the shifting of the field of interest; other cases where an effect of permanency is produced by the fact that the mental state is always pleasant when it is presented and disappears before it becomes painful." The effect on us of beautiful objects is not so much like the effect of a single star on our vision, as upon an entire constellation of stars; when the pleasure from viewing one star wanes, our attention can shift to other stars in

[45] Samuel Alexander, *Beauty and Other Forms of Value* (New York: Crowell, 1968), p. 183. (First published 1933.)

[46] Curt J. Ducasse, *Art, the Critics, and You* (New York: Liberal Arts Press, 1944), p. 90.

[47] George Santayana, *The Sense of Beauty* (New York: Scribners, 1896), p. 39.

whose contemplation the pleasure grows. When one aspect of a work of art tires us, we become aware of others on which we can fix our attention and thus sustain the pleasure. He concludes, "That object is to be considered beautiful which produces a [psychological state] that is permanently pleasurable in revival. Each pleasure may form an element of impression in an aesthetic complex; but only those pleasures are judged to be aesthetic which (relatively speaking) are permanently pleasurable in memory."[48] But of course the theory is still subjectivistic: something can be permanently pleasurable to you but not to me.

There are several main types of subjectivist theory, each of which has certian consequences which we shall now examine.

1. *The autobiographical theory.* The simplest kind of subjectivist theory, of which all the examples just cited are cases with a special twist, is what might be called the autobiographical theory: judgments of beauty are reducible to statements about the response of an individual observer to the object. "X is beautiful," according to this view, simply means "I enjoy X" (or like X, or appreciate X) or it could mean "I enjoy X *aesthetically*" (although different people will disagree about what the qualifying adverb adds to the meaning of the sentence), or "I am *disposed* to enjoy X aesthetically" (which doesn't commit you to enjoying it at all times, only when you're in a good mood and your faculties are sharp, and so on). In all cases, however, a statement ostensibly about a property of the object (its beauty) turns out to be about a state or condition of the observer.

Several consequences of this view should be pointed out:

(a) Whether or not the statement "X is beautiful" is true is determined solely by your reaction to X. If you enjoy X at time $t_1$, then X is beautiful at that time; if you don't enjoy X at time $t_2$, then X is not beautiful at that time. If this rings strange, you can adopt the dispositional formulation: even at time $t_2$ you may be disposed to enjoy it even if at the time you are in a bad mood or asleep, if you *would* enjoy it when you are in the psychological state specified (attentive, clear in perceptual or intellectual faculties). To many this will seem a bizarre consequence: If you have enjoyed a sonata for years but don't today, surely the attribution of beauty should not change because, the sonata has not changed; perhaps its beauty has only, for the time being, "lost its savor"?

(b) If this view is true, there can never by any *disagreements* among people about beauty. If Smith says "X is beautiful," all this means is that Smith enjoys (or is disposed to enjoy) X aesthetically; and if Jones says "X is not beautiful," this means only that Jones doesn't enjoy (or is not disposed to enjoy) X aesthetically. These two statements, that Smith enjoys X and Jones doesn't, do not contradict each other. Indeed, they can both be true, and

---

[48] Henry Rutgers Marshall, *Pain, Pleasure, and Aesthetics* (New York: Macmillan, 1892), pp. 108–109.

often both of them *are* true. Nor are Smith and Jones really disputing about this, unless one of them thinks the other is lying in giving his introspective report. If Smith really disagreed with Jones on this, his appropriate remark would be, "Come on, Jones, you really *do* enjoy it, you're just saying you don't." But normally neither party believes the other is lying about his response; so there is no disagreement here—Smith admits that Jones doesn't enjoy it, and Jones admits that Smith does enjoy it. There is nothing to disagree about. They are just comparing autobiographies. And if Smith says, "Come on, Jones, you *ought* to enjoy it," he is going beyond the autobiographical theory: there is no room for "ought" here, if each person in uttering the statement "X is beautiful" is only stating that he enjoys it.

This consequence too will seem strange to many. People certainly *seem* to argue at times about beauty and other aesthetic matters; they talk and act as if they are disagreeing. If one person says that Ogden Nash's poetry is better than Shakespeare's and the other indignantly replies that this isn't so, surely he is not indignantly denying that the other fails to enjoy it: he knows that already, but thinks that the other person *should* enjoy what at the moment he fails to enjoy.

A variant of this theory, often called "the emotive theory," says that "X is beautiful" is not really a *statement* about the person's enjoyment of X: it is not a statement at all, not about the observer or the object or anything else. Rather, it is an *expression* of enjoyment or approval. (We have already referred to "'beauty'' used as a "purr word" in the previous section.) Sentences like "X is beautiful" (gorgeous, scrumptious, marvelous, etc.) are simply expressions of liking or enjoyment and *say* nothing at all. Since they state nothing, it would be inaccurate to translate these expressions into statements about enjoyment of about anything at all, since they are not statements to begin with, but expression of feelings and attitudes, like purrs, shouts, groans, cries of ecstasy, and so on.

Of course no disagreement is possible on this view either: there is no statement to disagree about, no statement that one person believes to be true and the other believes to be false, if there is no statement to begin with. It's still an autobiographical theory like the first one, but instead of *stating* that you enjoy X, you are stating nothing at all but only *expressing* your enjoyment of X (and perhaps trying to evoke a similar enjoyment in others).

It is probably true that we sometimes use sentences like "X is beautiful" to express our enjoyment of the object before us. The question, however, is: Is this *all* we are doing? When you insist that this Giorgione or this Botticelli is a more beautiful painting than one by Norman Rockwell (adorning a cover of the *Saturday Evening Post),* are you *only* expressing enjoyment or approval of the painting? Doubtless you *are* doing that; but aren't you *also* saying something else, something of this kind—that the painting is *worth* enjoying, that the other person *ought* to enjoy it, that it would be a good thing if he did enjoy it, or that enjoying Botticelli is more worthwhile or better than enjoying the Norman Rockwell? Again, there is every evidence of dispute here, and the burden of proof is surely on the person who insists that we never dispute about matters of beauty at all (not only that we never do, but that it is impossible to do so).

According to both these theories, there can be no such thing as a correct or incorrect aesthetic response to objects; you feel one way, I feel another, and that's all there is to it. And this may be admitted at once about *tastes*—when we're only comparing tastes, it is quite true that *de gustibus non est disputandum* (concerning tastes there is no disputing); but what of judgments of beauty, which don't always correspond to judgments about individual tastes?

2. *The sociological theory.* Let us turn, then, to a second kind of subjectivistic theory, what we may call the sociological theory, which translates beauty statements into statements not about an individual's response to the object, but about some group of individuals.

Suppose, for example, that one says that "X is beautiful" means the same as "*Most* people enjoy X." At least here disagreement is possible; for either it is true that most people enjoy X, or it isn't. Here at least is an objective truth. If most people enjoy X, then it follows that X is beautiful; and if you don't go along with most people in enjoying X, then it follows that X is beautiful; and if you don't go along with most people in enjoying X, then it follows that your judgment about X's beauty or lack of it is mistaken. To find out whether something is beautiful, you take a poll; and if most people (anything over 50 percent) don't enjoy X, then you who are in the minority are necessarily mistaken in believing that is.

Genuine disagreement is possible on this theory: two people can disagree about whether the majority of people (in the world today, or in the world throughout history) enjoy X, for there may be no conclusive evidence on the subject. The trouble is, however, that the disagreement seems to be about the wrong thing. Isn't disagreement about beauty one thing and disagreement about what most people enjoy another? If you consider some work of art supremely beautiful, and most people don't think so (they check "no" on the poll), do you therefore consider yourself bound to say, "Well, they're in the majority, so they must be right"? Or if a 49 percent approval becomes a 51 percent approval, does this make the judgment "X is beautiful" true when it was false before? Does a percentage point or two make the judgment "X is beautiful" true? It would, according to the theory. But if you feel strongly about your judgment of beauty, particularly if you look at the object again and again and your judgment remains the same, you are more likely to say that it is the majority who is mistaken: that it is they who fail to see things in the work of art that you see. Just as, in political democracy, the majority can be ignorant, misled, prejudiced, brainwashed, shortsighted, and in other ways mistaken, so in aesthetic matters also: a majority can be ignorant, ill-informed, insensitive here as well. You may well persist in believing that, if the majority of people don't recognize the beauty of the work, it is they who are in error and not you.

Are you really prepared to say that certain interstitial passages of music, such as recitatives, are just as beautiful musically as the Handel arias they connect? If a majority poll revealed that the poem quoted below was enjoyed by more persons than anything by Shakespeare, would you defer to majority judgment?

> Twinkle twinkle little star
> How I wonder what you are

But if this is so, then the theory that all that "X is beautiful" means is that "most people enjoy X" is mistaken. There is nothing in majority opinion by itself that renders a judgment true, other than judgment that this *is* the majority opinion. If one person can be ignorant or superficial in judgment, so can a thousand, a million, a majority.

It seems clear at least there will have to be some limitation on *who* does the enjoying—that it can't be just anyone, including people who may have seen the work just once in their lives or people without training or preparation of any kind who come to the work cold. It would seem that only *qualified* people should count in the poll. But how are we to spell out the conditions which people must fulfill in order to be considered qualified?

(a) One attempt could be "The majority of aesthetically *trained* people enjoy (or disposed to enjoy) X." This restricts the range of those voting to include only those trained in the arts. Trained how much? In the fine arts only? and in all of them? All such specifications are quite vague; and if we try to make them more precise by saying, "trained for at least one year in art school, or passed four courses in history or theory of art with a grade of B or above," all such restrictions seem arbitrary. Anyway, there are people who are *trained* in the arts on whom the training is lost: they have not aptitude for appreciation to begin with. They may know a great deal *about* the arts and their history, but they may not appreciate or even enjoy the arts that they know so many facts about. And years of training may not have succeeded in enabling them to draw or paint. On the other hand, many people without training have "picked up" appreciation on their own, often more than their duller cousins who were trained. It doesn't seem to be training that counts, but aesthetic sensitivity.

(b) So let us try saying "The majority of aesthetically *sensitive* persons enjoy (or are disposed to enjoy) X." This one sounds much better; but how is one going to specify who the aesthetically sensitive people are? In practice, much of the time, we consider those people sensitive whose preferences concur with our own.

This need not, however, be the case. One could well admit that both Igor Stravinsky and Richard Strauss were highly sensitive composers and appreciators of music, although each despised the other's work and could not bear to hear it. Your remarks in past years may lead me to believe that you are a most sensitive appreciator of the arts; and if I am convinced that you are, especially after comments of yours have helped me to appreciate certain works, then your present disagreement on the beauty of this particular work may come as a shock to me. In this case I may not doubt your sensitivity—I *may* come to believe that my judgment of the work was hasty and will probably be inclined to reexpose myself to the work again, to discover what you saw in it that I didn't. Now if not only one, but a large number, say, a majority, of people of equally demonstrated aesthetic sensitivity also gives a favorable judgment of the work, and you don't, you may well come to believe that, although you don't see in it what they see, "there must be something there," and on the basis of that faith, reverse your judgment so as to concur with theirs. And in that case your action would fall into conformity with the theory now being considered.

But on the other hand, you may still not concur. If you are a "rugged individualist" in your appreciation, you may say that it is they who are mistaken and that a majority even of aesthetically sensitive observers is not enough to render the judgment "X is beautiful" true—particularly if you can enlist a minority report from other aesthetically sensitive observers on your side.

Besides, it is difficult to isolate clearly the class of "aesthetically sensitive observers." Every art teacher knows that you can test students on the facts of art history, but it is difficult if not impossible to test them reliably on appreciation. If they say or write something about a work of art that you find fruitful in your own experience of it, that may help; but if your verdict on the work of art continues to disagree with theirs nonetheless, you will be more inclined to say something like, "While she has great sensitivity, her emphases are somehow in the wrong place, she doesn't put the whole thing together right; although she is very perceptive and insightful, her verdicts are perverse or wrong-headed," and so on. In short, even the combined verdict of a majority of aesthetically sensitive observers (at least of those *you* consider to be aesthetically sensitive) will not necessarily convince you that they must be right and that you are mistaken. A majority verdict, even of this restricted class, will not settle the matter for you. At least you will object to having the matter settled by definition as the sociological theory attempts to do.

3. *The Ideal Observer theory.* There is still another version of aesthetic subjectivism, however, which has been believed to have escaped the objections made to the previous ones: it is called the ideal observer theory (or *ideal judge*

*theory*) and is based on the concept of an "ideal observer" of a work of art. Just as an ideal judge is one who is impartial, intelligent, never whimsical or erratic in judgment, and so on, so an ideal observer in aesthetic matters is one who has certain qualifications for judging: he is aesthetically sensitive, he is intelligent, he is knowledgeable in the art-form of which the work before us is an instance, he is not given to whimsical judgments or fluctuations of taste, and so on. The verdict of anyone who fulfills all the qualifications is, by definition, the correct verdict: the merits of a work of art just *are* whatever an ideal observer says they are. (Of course, we may never know what such judgments are, since there may be nobody in the world who fulfills completely the requirements of an ideal aesthetic observer.)

The exact nature of the qualifications is, however, somewhat vague. How aesthetically sensitive must a person be? One hundred percent, one is tempted to say—but can sensitivity be dealt with in percentages? And what are to be the tests of sensitivity? (We have considered that problem already.) Must the person know art history, and if so how much? Must he have created in the arts himself, or is this not necessary? He must be impartial: but exactly what is an impartial judgment in aesthetic matters? In a court case, the impartial judge "considers all sides of a question." What is the analogy to this in aesthetic matters? The term "impartial" has its home base in legal and moral contexts; it is not clear how it applies here, as we have already seen when considering the aesthetic attitude. What aspects of works of art should he consider relevant to his judgments? How much feeling should he "put into" the work? or should he be cold and detached? "Should the ideal aesthetic observer be passionate or cold-blooded, emotional or cerebral? Poet or peasant, of the elite or the masses? In the ivory tower or in the ash can? Political or apolitical, moral or immoral? Quick to judge or slow in judgment?"[49]

In view of the vagueness of the requirements and the difficulty of how the exact specifications of the ideal observer are to be determined, the question arises, "What happens if two ideal observers were to give differing verdicts on a particular work?" "Then at least one of them would be mistaken, and thus wouldn't be an ideal observer," one is tempted to reply. But how would we know which was the genuine one? And if both of them fulfilled the requirements, how could one of them fail to be genuine? Any actual human being probably comes to a work of art with some degree of "temperamental bias," toward warm or cold, sentimental or tragic or comic, and yet without some temperamental features or other it wouldn't be a human being who was judging.

The ideal observer theory may tell us much about observers of a work of art and the qualities they must have to make the most discriminating judgments. But this tells us nothing about *the things judged,* and presumably the ideal observer will make his judgment on the basis of these. And thus the

---

[49] Peter Kivy, "The Logic of Taste–The First Fifty Years," in Dickie and Sclafani, *Aesthetics,* p. 639.

theory will seem to many persons to be, like other versions of subjectivism, about the wrong thing: it talks about the qualities of observers but not about the nature of the thing which they observe. When we talk about an ideal engineer, or a very good engineer, we never refer to his personal qualities in this way: we say simply that a good engineer is one who builds good buildings or good bridges, buildings that fulfill the specifications in the blueprints, and which are sturdily built, last a long time, and so on. A good bridge builder is someone who builds good bridges—we don't have to talk about his personal attitudes or feelings. Similarly, it would seem that a good artist is one who creates good works of art and that a good judge of art is one who gives us sound judgments. It was only because we had such trouble in finding such features of works of art that, as a move of desperation, we moved from the work of art to the observer of works of art.

What we need to have is some kind of objective grounding of our judgments, not in the qualities of the observers of art but in the qualities of the artworks themselves. We have this in the case of red, since experiences of red have as their causal basis a uniform pattern of light waves. There are other cases where we have it too, in such as examples as this from Cervantes's *Don Quixote*, as described by David Hume in his essay "On the Standard of Taste":

> It is with good reason, says Sancho to the squire with the great nose, that I pretend to have a judgment in wine: this is a quality hereditary in our family. Two of my kinsmen were once called to give their opinion of a hogshead, which was supposed to be excellent, being old and of good vintage. One of them tastes it; considers it; and after mature reflection pronounces the wine to be good, were it not for a small taste of leather, which he perceived in it. The other, after using the same precautions, gives also his verdict in favor of the wine; but with the reserve of a taste of iron, which he could easily distinguish. You cannot imagine how much they were both ridiculed for their judgment. But who laughed in the end? On emptying the hogshead, there was found at the bottom, an old key with a leathern thong tied to it.[50]

What we apparently need at this point is some analog of the key with a leathern thong. That would be an objective feature—of the wine, of the work of art—by which we could justify our judgments, the way in which the two kinsmen were justified by the qualities of the wine in their judgments about the wine.

What we need, in short, is some "objective correlative" of enjoyments. And, considering what difficulties we encountered with objectivist theories of beauty, to pin down the various and elusive sources in the object of the beauty experience, it does not seem a very promising prospect.

[50] David Hume, On the Standard of Taste," in Dickie and Sclafani, *Aesthetics,* p. 597. (Many editions.)

Aesthetic value

We began the consideration of subjectivistic theories with experiences of enjoying. Let us broaden our canvas now by speaking not of enjoying but of *valuing*.

When we enjoy a work of art, especially if we do so repeatedly on different occasions, we are inclined to attribute *value* to it; indeed, we may find it valuable in various ways even if we do not particularly enjoy it: a drama about the atrocities of a totalitarian state may not be enjoyable, but if we believe it to be well written and performed, we may nevertheless regard it as valuable. The concept of valuing is broader than is that of enjoying, just as we may attribute aesthetic value to a novel or drama even if we do not call it beautiful. Also, of course, something may have moral value, or political value, or economic value and little or no aesthetic value.

But at once we confront a familiar problem: valuing is a pretty individual matter. You may value something and I may not. If you are a collector of antiques, you presumably value antiques even though I couldn't care less about them; I may place high value on going fishing although to you it seems a waste of time. The phrase "to value it" is a kind of collective term for a variety of different things: you like it, or you desire it, or you esteem it, or you enjoy it, or you would give up quite a bit to do or obtain it, and so on. But of course the things or activities you would give up quite a bit for are not the same as the things or activities I would give up quite a bit for.

Some things we value for their own sakes, and other things we value only because we can obtain other things by means of them. The second group includes the things that are of *instrumental* value to us: we value money because by means of it we can satisfy at least some of our wants; we value a hammer because it is instrumental to conducting useful or pleasant activities like carpentry. But there are other things we value not for what they lead to but simply for themselves, such as playing games, having sex, drinking wine, swimming, attending concerts; we want these things for their own sakes, not because we can use them as a means toward some further end.

The things (in nature and art) we value aesthetically we undoubtedly value for their own sakes, although they are not the *only* things we value for their own sakes. Here as elsewhere there is endless individual variation: you may regard highly a work of art which I find unendurable. How can we ever get from individual acts or attitudes of valuing to the idea of being valuable, or *worth* valuing? Isn't the most we can do to say that this work of art is valuable *to me* (because I value it) while at the same time it is not valuable *to you* (because you don't value it)?

We do sometimes speak of value in an "objective" sense. In "You may not enjoy that course but you will find it very valuable," it is still value *to you* that is being referred to (I might not find it valuable), but there is an implication that it *really is* of value to you. Or consider, "It would be of great value to you to eat this nutritious food to build up your health, even though I admit that you don't care for it or otherwise value it." ("It's good for you even though you don't care for it.") Isn't the food of objective value, apart from the person's subjective act of valuing? Suppose the person doesn't know the food exists, or knows it exists but doesn't know of its nutritional qualities; still, isn't it valuable to him whether he knows it or not, whether he values it or not?

What the person values in this case is his health; and since he values being healthy (the end), if he is sensible he will also value the food which is a *means* toward achieving that end (even if he doesn't like it, since liking is only one way of valuing something): he may eat it because he values his health and thus adopt the means toward it, which he values in spite of its unpleasantness.

Suppose, however, that he says that he does not value his health (and maybe not his life either). Then what happens to the statement "The food is of value to you whether you value it or not"? How can the food be valuable to him if it is conducive to an end that he doesn't value? He might well assent to the statement "X (the food) leads to Y (health)," but this isn't a statement about value at all; it's just a plain empirical statement about what causes what. He could simply say "I know X leads to Y, but so what? I don't care." In other words, X (the means) is valuable only *relative* to (in relation to) Y (the end); but if the person doesn't value the end, in what way is the means nevertheless of value to him? Almost everyone values his own health and life, and thus we come to think of these as "objective values": but try to show that they are "objectively valuable" to a person who doesn't value them, and you are not likely to get far. He may still say "So what? You may consider life worth valuing, but I don't." Somewhere you have to latch onto something he himself values, and then you may get him to value other things which lead to this; but without something he values, no amount of talk about "the value" of a thing or activity will convince him.

Is there anything analogous to this we can say with regard to aesthetic value? If we say "The works of Bach are aesthetically valuable, whether you value them or not"? he can well reply "They are aesthetically valuable to you because you place a high value on them; I don't, so they are not valuable to me." "Value" is still a "to you" or "to me" characteristic, and when something is said to be "objectively valuable," it is because it is objectively related (*e.g.,* causally) to something that is valued by that person. It seems, then, that the "objective" sense of value is subsidiary to the "subjective" sense with which we began and depends for its existence and meaning on the primary sense of value, the act of individual valuing.

One's evaluations, however, often do change with time. Works of art which a person does not value, he may *come* to value, perhaps on his own, through re-exposure to the works of art, sometimes through courses in art appreciation, sometimes through having hitherto unnoticed features of the work of art pointed out to him by friends or colleagues. One may enjoy for a moment a jukebox tune if (for example) it has a catchy rhythm which one finds engaging for a few hearings, but then, since it has no more to offer, one tires of it: one has exhausted whatever resources it had to offer, and as far as that tune is concerned, the well is dry. On the other hand, there are other melodies—such as those in any of Bach's hundreds of cantatas—which one can hear over and over again with increasing enjoyment. One need not have enjoyed a work of art on first exposure: most works of classical music and drama and painting are sufficiently complex that at first they are simply bewildering, and only after repeated hearings or viewings does their power to move one shine through. And if a child likes a Mozart theme on first hearing, perhaps for its "tinkling quality," that is not usually the reason for which one returns to Mozart on the twentieth or hundredth hearing. But whatever the reason for one's returning to it—and the reasons will surely differ from one work of art to another and even more from one art-medium to another—the fact is that certain works of art in one's own experience successfully withstand the test of repeated exposure while others do not.

The test of time

It is true that *no* work of art can withstand constantly repeated exposure day after day and month after month. As a rule a person's enjoyment of a work of art increases as more of its qualities are experienced, until finally the experience reaches a kind of plateau. In some cases there is a considerable period in which there is no desire for repeated exposure at all: I value Beethoven's Fifth Symphony, but would not mind if it were put on ice for a while, since it is played so frequently; perhaps it is as great a work as his *Archduke* trio (Op. 97), but it does not seem to me so now, and this may be because I do not hear the latter as often and so it has fewer occasions on which to display its treasures. But even the works one treasures most cannot withstand constant and unremitting exposure: sooner or later "aesthetic fatigue" sets in, and one must put it aside for a time while enjoying what other, and perhaps lesser, works of art have to offer.

Moreover, there are works of art that seem to be suited not only to one's temperament but to certain periods or stages of one's life. The works of Mahler that appeal most to the young are, as a rule, the first three symphonies—direct, dramatic, full of flash and fire and high drama; only later do the more subtle wonders of the later symphonies make themselves manifest. I once was quite sure that Mahler's Third Symphony was his greatest achievement; today, however, I would make the same judgment concerning his Sixth, Ninth, and Tenth, a judgment that would have surprised me a few years ago. Then an older colleague said, "You're mistaken—Mahler's greatest work is his *Das Lied von der Erde*—only you won't appreciate that fully for some years yet. Just wait, you'll see." I still stick with my present judgment—and yet in time his prediction may be fulfilled. I cannot say what I shall value most a few years down the line.

Some works of art withstand the test of time in my experience; but of course they may not be the same ones that stand the test of time in human experience in general—that is, in the experience of that vast number of other persons who also devote a considerable portion of their time and energy to the appreciation of art. An individual's evaluations usually fluctuate through time more than that of the consensus of mankind. David Hume, in his classic essay "On the Standard of Taste," was as aware as anyone of the individual differences, through temperament and experience, in the values placed on works of art:

> One person is more pleased with the sublime; another with the tender; a third with raillery. One has a strong sensibility to blemishes, and is extremely studious of correctness. Another has a more lively feeling of beauties, and pardons twenty absurdities and defects for one elevated or pathetic stroke. The ear of this man is entirely turned toward conciseness and energy; that man is delighted with a copious, rich, and harmonious expression. Simplicity is affected by one; ornament by another. Comedy, tragedy, satire, odes, have each its partisans, who prefer that particular species of writing to all others. It is plainly an error in a critic, to confine his approbation to one species or style of writing, and condemn all the rest. But it is almost impossible not to feel a predilection for that which suits your particular turn and disposition. Such preferences are innocent and unavoidable, and can never reasonably be the object of dispute, because there is no standard, by which they can be decided.[51]

And yet, says Hume, there are works of art on which a higher evaluation is placed because they have withstood the *test of time*. Works of art in general do this better than science or philosophy:

> Theories of abstract philosophy, systems of profound theology, have prevailed during one age; in a successive period, these have been universally exploded. Their absurdity has been detected: other theories and systems have supplied their place which again gave their successors; and nothing has been experienced more liable to the revolutions of chance and fashion than these pretended decisions of science. The case is not the same with the beauties of eloquence and poetry. Just expressions of passion and nature are sure, after a little time, to gain public applause, which they maintain forever. Aristotle, and Plato, and Epicurus, and Descartes, may successively yield to each other. But Terence and Virgil maintain a universal, undisputed empire over the minds of men. The abstract philosophy of Cicero has lots its credit; the vehemence of his oratory is still the object of our admiration.[52]

"Over the long haul" there is a convergence in aesthetic judgments which, seen in historical perspective, is much greater than the convergence of judgment in science or philosophy. As we have already seen (Chapter 6), scientific theories only a few decades old are already out of date, but the art of the ancient Greeks and Egyptians is as alive today as ever. Some artists who were considered innovative geniuses in their time have been "tried in the crucible of

[51] *Ibid.*, p. 603.
[52] *Ibid.*, p. 602.

time and found wanting,'' and we wonder today why their works were so highly regarded; it is difficult today to believe when we hear a concerto by Ludwig Spohr that in his day he was considered at least the equal of his contemporary Beethoven. "Time has winnowed them out." On the other hand, there are artists who were ignored in their own day who seem to subsequent generations as the greatest of their time: during his lifetime Berlioz was ignored while contemporaries such as Meyerbeer were applauded, but today when we listen to Berlioz's *Le Troyens* and compare it with Meyerbeer's *Le Prophête,* it is difficult for us to believe that the latter could have been preferred (not that time has winnowed Meyerbeer out, but ever since his own time he has been considered a second-rate composer, at least vastly inferior to Berlioz): Berlioz was lyrically and harmonically innovative in a new fruitful way, but it took quite a few hearings to appreciate him, just as it took most of Cézanne's lifetime for students of painting to appreciate the power of his work, although every student of painting sees it (or pretends to see it) today.

The *reasons* given for placing a high evaluation on certain works of art may indeed vary from age to age, while the *fact* of the high evaluation remains: the poetry of Homer and of Virgil has been praised by critics in every generation from their day to our own, but the reasons given by Roman critics are different (somewhat, not entirely) from those given by Neoclassic eighteenth century critics and these again different from Romantic critics in the nineteenth century. The works of El Greco have been held in high esteem from his day to ours, but in his own day the reigning theory was of "art as representation," and he was praised for his excellence in the representation of human figures in a variety of situations; yet today he is praised for entirely different reasons, from the "significant form" of Clive Bell and the "plastic orchestration" of Roger Fry to the high degree of expressive quality with which he imbues not only his human figures but the entire landscapes surrounding them, for which he is praised by expressionists such as Collingwood. There is, then, considerable "relativity of reasons" but not nearly as much "relativity of judgment." Does any student of music exist who does not rank Bach with the greatest? Yet even here, in the space of two centuries, the reasons differ: sometimes it is the great emotional power of his work that is emphasized, sometimes simply his technical mastery of the medium, sometimes the great formal complexity ("mathematics in motion"), sometimes the melodic and harmonic ingenuity. But all that the "test of time" requires is that the judgment of high rank be sustained, not the reasons given for it.

One could easily say, to be sure, that each generation was simply following slavishly in the footsteps of its predecessors, making its judgments in the authoritarian shadow of the previous generation. And of course this sometimes happens: a critic may view the past with such reverential awe that he believes he would be made to look ridiculous if he disputed established judgments; or sometimes he follows them through habit or through a being in his perceptions so bound to a certain tradition that he cannot see the force of a new one in the process of being born. But it can also happen the other way 'round: a critic may be out to "get" those of the preceding generation, against whose judgments he is in rebellion—yesterday's daring is today's hidebound convention; we are still experiencing today a reaction against the literature of the Victorian era. But each generation, indeed each person, re-experiences the work of art for himself: if you have read Shakespeare, is your opinion of his work simply a deference to tradition? Do you believe his work lives today only because it has been perpetuated by generations of teachers? Is the power of his poetry not felt by *you*?

Differences, of course, remain: many listeners revere Tschaikovsky ("the emotionality is simple and direct—he gets right to your jugular"), whereas others, not denying the presence of this quality, deplore it as "unsubtle" ("he wears his heart on his sleeve," etc.). Much of this can be put down to differences in temperament, which are not *supposed* to affect one's considered judgments but often do. Shall we write this all off as lack of "aesthetic disinterestedness"? The critic, said Hume,

> must preserve his mind free from all *prejudice,* and allow nothing to enter into his consideration, but the very object which is submitted to his examination. We may observe, that every work of art, in order to produce its due effect on the mind, must be surveyed in a certain point of view, and cannot be fully relished by person, whose situation, real or imaginary, is not conformable to that which is required by the performance. . . . When any work is addressed to the public, though I should have a friendship or enmity with the author, I must depart from this situation; and considering myself as a man in general, forget, if possible, my individual being and my peculiar circumstances. A person influenced by prejudice complies not with this condition, but obstinately maintains his natural position, without placing himself in that point of view, which the performance supposes. If the work be addressed to persons of a different age or nation, he makes no allowance for their peculiar views and prejudices; but, full of the manners of his own age and country, rashly condemns what seemed admirable in the eyes of those for whom alone the discourse was calculated. If the work be executed for the public, he never sufficiently enlarges his comprehension, or forgets his interest as a friend or enemy, as a rival or commentator. By this means, his sentiments are perverted; nor have the same beauties and blemishes the same influence upon him, as if he had imposed a proper violence on his imagination, and had forgotten himself for a moment.[53]

Whether Hume is correct in explaining all the reasons for variation in judgment as due to "prejudice" is probably doubtful; at any rate, "prejudice" is a difficult thing to prove in aesthetic matters. If a critic disparages Wagner because he doesn't approve of Wagner's personal life, that is a clear case of prejudice (with regard to the music); but if one critic, temperamentally miles apart from a second, disparages a work the second one rates high because "it's too cold," whereas the second disparages another work as "too sentimental" or "too melodramatic" while the first finds the work "just right," which of them is "prejudiced"? Is a high valuation placed on "warmth of emotion" in a work of art a prejudice? Hume believed that the general criteria used in evaluating works of art (however numerous) are "universal, and nearly, if not entirely, the same in all men"; yet, he added, "few are qualified to give judgment on any work of art. . . . The organs of internal sensation are seldom so perfect as to allow the general principles their full play." But until we are told exactly what is to *count* as a "prejudice" or from what standard a critic must deviate to be rightly accused of "prejudice," the account is not really helpful in the evaluation of a critic's performance. It is all too tempting to say, "If you don't agree with me that 'cool beauty' is preferable to 'warm beauty,' you are prejudiced."

In any case, there is no doubt that certain works of art in every medium have stood the test of time, such as Rembrandt and Cézanne in painting, Chaucer and Shakespeare in English literature, and Bach and Beethoven in music. The main difficulty in using the "test of time" criterion lies with contemporary art, the art of our own time. And this is exactly what one would expect: the winnowing process of time has not yet taken place, the wheat has not yet been separated from the chaff. A new movement in art may be completely ignored by our contemporaries (if they are not yet ready for it, or if it requires too much of a change in their viewing and listening habits), or on the other hand it may seem richly innovative and hold great potential for future development, only to turn out to be a dead end or a "flash in the pan." With contemporary art, "it's too early to tell," and in this area we shall then do well to make our judgments tentative and hold final judgment in suspension, allowing time to do its work.

But if certain works of art stand the test of time and others don't, surely there must be a reason, and that reason lies in the work of art itself—not merely in the fact that observers in different eras place a high value on them, which is after all only a *consequence* of their merit, not what their merit consists in. The test of time, one might allege, is only a pointer or indicator of the presence of certain qualities in a work of art: it is because of these qualities, whatever they are, that it stands the test of time.

The instrumentalist theory

But this takes us back to our old problem: it seems impossible to find a set of qualities that can be counted as merits in all works of art, and when we do come up with a list of qualities there seems to be no way to put limits on it. Beardsley suggested three features—unity, complexity, and intensity—under which all other suggested criteria fall, but others disagree with these, or find them too vague, or wish to add indefinitely to the list (see pp. 317–29). However, he distinguishes criteria of aesthetic *criticism*—for which he suggests these three criteria—from aesthetic *value*: even if his account of critical criteria should be mistaken, and quite independently of this issue, he suggests a *theory of aesthetic value* which is applicable whatever the criteria for judging works of art may turn out to be. A work possesses aesthetic value, says Beardsley, to the degree to which it possesses the *capacity* to produce aesthetic experiences. (Of course, if you have been convinced that there are no such things as aesthetic experiences, then you will not find this theory helpful.)

To say that something is a good X is to say that it fulfills to a high degree the function of Xs—which differs from one X to another. Goodness is comparative: we speak of a good hammer, a better hammer, the best hammer in the carpentry store. Its degree of goodness depends on the degree to which it fulfills a function. Classes of things that fulfill functions are called *function classes*.

"*Chair* is a function class, and *desk chair* is also a function class, since there is a purpose that desk chairs serve better than other types. Furniture is not, I think, a function class, although it includes a number of distinct function classes; there is nothing you can do with furniture, considered solely as furniture, that you can't do as well with other things. 'This is a good piece of furniture,' then, would have to mean "This is either a good chair, or a good table, or a good sofa, or . . .'"[54] And in the same way we speak of good wrenches, good cars, good roads, good grocery stores, good colleges. We can in turn break each of these down further for special purposes: "That's a good car for hacking, but not a good car for racing," "That's a good college to go to for sports, but not much for scholarship."

But what could be meant by "good work of art" (or "good aesthetic object"—so as to include nature as well as art)? It depends on what works of art are good for, what their function is. Paintings can be used for all sorts of things, such as showing off to your guests, just as a telescope (to use Clive Bell's example) can be used for reading the newspaper, but it doesn't serve that purpose very well, and not as well as many other things could do. Are works of art a function class at all? They are, if there is something they can do that other things cannot do, or do as well. "Is there something that aesthetic objects are especially good at? Now, the sort of thing you can do with an aesthetic object is to perceive it in a certain way, and allow it to induce a certain kind of experience."[55] Such experiences are—this will come as no surprise—aesthetic experiences. Such experiences have been described on pages 358–59.

To say that something is a good work of art, then, is to say that it has a *capacity* to produce aesthetic experiences (presumably of some magnitude, since almost everything has the capacity to produce, at least in some people, some small degree of such experience). To say that X is a better work of art

[54] Monroe C. Beardsley, *Aesthetics,* p. 525.
[55] *Ibid.,* p. 526.

than Y is to say that X has a greater capacity to produce aesthetic experiences than does Y. Since works of art are here viewed as instruments for achieving aesthetic experience, this is called the *instrumentalist theory* of aesthetic value.

Is this theory subjectivistic? It may at first seem so, since like other subjectivistic theories it refers to the kind of experience the observer has. However, it also has one foot in the "objectivist" camp, for it does talk about a property of the object, its *capacity* to produce the experience. It doesn't say what that capacity is—it may be unity, complexity, and intensity, or it may be all of these and more, or it may be something else—but whatever particular qualities they may be, it is their capacity to produce aesthetic experience that makes them good works of art. The capacity is in the object, just as the nutritional quality of a food is in the food. And in both cases it is a capacity that is referred to, not the actual effects of the work of art or the food. A food may be nutritious in that it will nourish you if you eat it, although you may never eat it, so its nutritive quality is lost on you. A work of art may have the capacity to produce an aesthetic response, although you may never see the work, or look at it only fleetingly and never give it a chance to work its way with you, so the response never occurs. Gaugin's last paintings, which he burned in Tahiti, may have been great works of art, that is, would have produced aesthetic experiences if people had had a chance to see them, but since he burned them, the capacity was never fulfilled, the potentiality never actualized.

The object may have the capacity only for certain people, just as the nutritive quality of fresh eggs is not realized in people who are allergic to eggs.

> To read Baudelaire you must understand French; to listen to music, not be tone-deaf; to see paintings, not be color-blind. No doubt we could go further. Note that this is not the same problem as that of defining "competent critic," for here we are not asking for the criteria of being an expert evaluator, but only ruling out certain classes of people whom it would be useless to expose to the aesthetic object. Even after we have eliminated the impossibles, we still use the "capacity" terminology, for we cannot predict that all who understand French will derive an aesthetic experience from Baudelaire, but only that, as far as this requirement goes, they are not prevented from doing so.[56]

It takes a greater capacity to have some aesthetic experiences than to have others, depending largely on the complexity of the work of art.

> It takes a greater capacity to respond to Shakespeare than to Graham Greene, to Beethoven than to Ferde Grofé, to Cézanne than to Norman Rockwell. People outgrow Graham Greene, but they do not outgrow Shakespeare. . . . We do not say that a person has the capacity to remain unmoved by Shakespeare; this is not a capacity, but the lack of a capacity. Now the object with the greater capacity may not have its capacity actualized as often as the object with less—the heavier the sledge, the greater its force, but the fewer who can use it well. If, therefore,

[56] *Ibid.*, p. 532.

the aesthetic value of Tschaikovsky is more often had and enjoyed than that of Bach, it may still be true that the value of the latter is greater.[57]

In other words, it takes more work, or preparatory exposure to his music, to appreciate Bach, but once one does, the experience is of greater magnitude. It takes more to trigger the works' capacity, but once triggered, it pays bigger dividends. It is only to be expected that most people will be attracted to the lesser sources of aesthetic satisfaction, because less preparation is required—but if one's aesthetic experiences stop there, one pays the price of never knowing the more profound and enduring satisfactions one might have had.

If you don't enjoy a work of art which others consider great, this can be explained by saying that the work has a capacity but you have not yet "hooked in" on its capacity. But what about the opposite situation?

> When I was young I was for a time an avid reader of the Martian novels of Edgar Rice Burroughs. Recently when I bought the Dover paperback edition and looked at them again, I found that I could hardly read them. . . . If on Monday I enjoy a novel very much, and thus know that it has the capacity to provide gratification, then how can I ever reverse that judgment and say the novel lacks that capacity? If the judgment that the novel is a good one is a capacity-judgment, it would seem that downward reevaluations (that is, devaluations) are always false—assuming that the original higher judgment was based on direct experience.
> Some cases of devaluation can no doubt be taken care of without modifying the definition of "aesthetic value." The devaluation may be due to a shift in our value grades caused by enlargement of our range of experience. I might think that *Gone with the Wind* is a great novel, because it is the best I have read, but later I might take away that encomium and give it to *War and Peace*. Or the devaluation may be due to the belated recognition that my previous satisfaction in the work was a response to extra-aesthetic features. I now realize that my earlier enjoyment of detective stories was probably caused only in small part by their literary qualities, and was much more of a game-type pleasure.[58]

Does this take care of *all* cases in which I decide on reexamination that the work "isn't really that good"? (1) One might add that the work must be a reliable or dependable source of gratification: "flukes don't count." The enjoyment must be a repeatable experience. (2) What then of a person who enjoys the Burroughs novel again and again all his life, without modification of his tastes? What if the person on reading a badly written science-fiction novel "was fairly oblivious to faults of style and filled in the flat characterizations with his own imagination, giving himself up unself-consciously to the dramatic events and exotic scenery"? and that he kept on doing the same thing over and over again? In such a case we would have to say that he had

---

[57] *Ibid.,* p. 532.
[58] Monroe C. Beardsley, "The Aesthetic Point of View," in *Philosophy Looks at the Arts,* ed. Joseph Margolis (Philadelphia: Temple Univ. Press, 1979), pp. 15-16.

availed himself of a limited source of satisfaction and that, in not availing himself of other works, with greater capacities for satisfaction, he has cheated only himself. The capacity of other works was there; he simply declined to avail himself of it. What satisfaction he had was genuine enough; it's just that he could have had much more, had he put himself out a little, just as a person who eats nothing but hamburgers all his life, no matter how much he may enjoy them, is limiting the sources of gustatory satisfaction which he otherwise might have had.

"X is better than Y if it has a greater capacity to produce aesthetic experiences." But *in whom?* In the individual consumer of the work of art? or in the experience of mankind in general? Beardsley's view takes the latter course: even though the work of art may have little or no capacity to produce aesthetic experiences in you (if you are tone-deaf or color-blind, or are lacking in certain areas of your affective life which are necessary to responding to certain works of art), they are still worthwhile works of art if they have the capacity to produce such experiences in others. The more such experiences the work evokes, in varying times and places, the greater the evidence that the work has the capacity to provide them. Thus the theory fits in nicely with the "test of time" criterion already discussed.

Suppose, however, that one wishes to "go it alone." Other people's appreciation means nothing to me. *I* want to appreciate this work; and I've tried repeatedly but I can't. Perhaps it's my failing; but perhaps the work has no capacity to produce any worthwhile experiences in me, with my particular combination of experiences and temperament. And that's really all I care about. I might even pay lip sevice to other people's admiration of the work and say that it's a fine work of art, but I cannot say that from my own experience, and isn't that the only basis on which I should say such a thing? Should I, in such a situation, echo the plaudits of others and call it great, when I cannot honestly make such a judgment for myself?

This is certainly a plausible position. If I repeatedly fail to be moved when others are moved as the "Sanctus" and "Hosanna" of Bach's *Mass* is played, and I can't put it down to personal reactions (against religion or liturgy, perhaps): in spite of what others say, I cannot honestly say it is a worthwhile work. But the reactions of others, whose sensitivity and discrimination I know from my personal exchanges with them on other works, will act as a precaution and as a challenge: they will help to keep me from denigrating a work whose doors I cannot seem to unlock, and it will remain a perpetual challenge to me to attempt to unlock them through repeated attempts when there is every indication that once I did unlock them the reward would turn out to have been many times worth the effort. This is indeed the challenge put forth by all works of art which do not immediately affect one: what others do experience, you too may experience, if you but tried a little harder. The human "tragedy of waste" is nowhere more apparent than in works of art with very great rewards to deliver, but whose treasures were wasted on a person because he never really gave it a chance.

## EXERCISES

1. "Consider a surgeon performing a successful appendectomy, or an eager student listening to a brilliant lecture on medieval cosmology, or a suitably excitable person watching the sleaziest of pornographic movies. . . . The experience of the pornography consumer [to quote Mark Sagoff] could certainly beat in intensity, duration, certainty, propinquity, fecundity, purity, and extent the pleasure anyone gets from looking at a painting such as Picasso's *Guernica.*" (W. E. Kennick, in *Art and Philosophy*, p. 474.) Do you agree? If so, is it fatal to the concept of aesthetic experience or any particular formulation of it?

2. How far do you think the following comments go toward explaining the beauty of the Mozart G Minor Quintet (K. 516)? "In the first movement . . . . the first two bars balance in rhythm, but differ in curve and harmony; the third intervenes with a new figure in strong contrast; and the fourth closes the half-stanza by recalling the second. Then comes the most beautiful point of style in the whole turn. The figure of the third bar, which hitherto has only been used for contrast . . . is answered and compensated by the fifth bar, which itself leads directly into the cadence-phase. And thus every part is made vital, and differences themselves coordinated into uniformity of result." (W. H. Hadow, *Studies in Modern Music*, 1907, p. 37.)

3. In his *Elements of Criticism* (1785), Henry Home (Lord Kames) wrote, "Doth it not seem whimsical, and perhaps absurd, to assert, that a man *ought not* to be pleased when he is, or that he *ought* to be pleased when he is not?" (Vol. 2, 6th ed., p. 488.) Is there ever a point, or anything to be gained, by saying that a person shouldn't be pleased by what pleases him, or should be pleased by what doesn't?

4. "Often in watching movies of an earlier era, we *recognize* the greatness of the silent film masterpieces, but because their way of presenting things was so idealized or sentimentalized (such as the love scenes), we find them dated or mannered and we're not really *moved* by them any more; rather we *admire* them. Similarly, we see the marks of greatness in the tragedies of Aeschylus and Sophocles, but are we really moved, or touched emotionally, by the wailing of the Trojan women of Euripides?"

    Does this tend to confirm Jessop's point (in the quotations at the beginning of this chapter from his "The Definition of Beauty") that all that a work of art requires of us is the intellectual *recognition* of its beauty (or aesthetic value), not its effect on our emotions?

5. How do the following adjectives, used to describe works of art, differ in meaning from "beautiful"? (a) cute, (b) pretty, (c) charming, (d) luscious, (e) sensuous, (f) wonderful.

6. Consider other aesthetic predicates such as "intelligent," "witty," "shallow," "immature," and "smug." (See Colin Lyas, "Personal Qualities and the Intentional Fallacy," *Royal Institute of Philosophy Lectures*, 6

(1971–1972), 194–210. See also "The Goofy in Art," by Francis B. Randall, *British Journal of Aesthetics,* 11 (1971).)

7. Read David Hume's "On the Standard of Taste." Do you construe him to be defending the ideal observer theory, or doing something else?

8. The problem of *ugliness.* Is ugliness the mere absence of beauty? Bernard Bosanquet wrote, "The principal region in which to look for insuperable ugliness is . . . the region of insincere and affected art. Here you necessarily have the very root of ugliness." (*Three Lectures on Aesthetic,* p. 106.) Or Stephen Pepper: "We reach invincible ugliness when an artist assembles his materials so as to lead us to expect an imaginative integration and then by some positive action of his own directs us to another end. The end is likely to be something like popular applause, or propaganda, or a chance to make a little more money, or submissiveness to authority, or rebellion and pure cussedness, or even 'that last infirmity,' fame. For these the artist sacrifices the integrity of his work. . . . The artist himself probably had the capacity to bring his materials to aesthetic consummation. But he turned aside for an easier reward. The motive can be detected by anyone who can imaginatively follow the materials." (*The Basis of Criticism in the Arts,* p. 94.) (a) Can you render these sentences into non intentionalistic ones? (b) One consequence of this view is that art but not nature can be ugly. Do you agree or disagree and why?

9. (a) Why would you not be inclined to describe "The Royal Game" (or any work of fiction) as "beautiful" (at least not as much as a symphony or a painting)? (b) What aesthetic qualities do you think it has?

10. How would you respond to these criticisms of Sircello's theory of beauty? (From W. E. Kennick, *Art and Philosophy,* p. 637.)

   a. "Sircello wishes to exclude from the class of PQDs [properties of qualitative degree] all properties of 'deficiency, lack, or neglect'—the notorious 'privations' of ancient philosophy. But does he make clear at all what such properties are? Are wickedness, cruelty, stinginess, rudeness, effeminacy (in a man) or masculinity (in a woman), poverty, shortness (relative to the general population), inability to play basketball, or ignorance of higher mathematics such properties? How can we tell? Of course, if one is stingy then he lacks generosity; but if he's generous, then he lacks stinginess. And if he's poor, he's not rich; and if rich, not poor. So that won't do. . . Is that theory adequate or persuasive until some criterion has been provided for the recognition of such properties?"

   b. "Imagine a deep hole, perhaps a coal mine, which is very dark. Darkness is a PQD. Does it follow that the hole is beautiful with respect to its darkness? Perhaps darkness is a property of lack or deficiency—Aristotle thought it was ('darkness is merely the privation of light'). So imagine the hole being very, very deep. Depth we know is a PQD. Does it follow that the hole is beautiful with respect to its depth? Finally, imagine a man with a bulgy midriff. Bulginess is a PQD. Does it follow that his midriff is beautiful with respect to its bulginess?"

11. Suppose someone says to you, "I like all movies—good, bad, and indifferent. Every Western ever made is enjoyable to me. I like all kinds of music too—classical, rock, country western, everything." Is such a person to be envied? Can you draw any probable conclusion about such a person's concentration of attention? about his degree of aesthetic appreciation?

# SELECTED READINGS

AAGAARD-MOGENSEN and GORAN HERMEREN, eds. *Contemporary Aesthetics in Scandinavia.* Lund: Doxa, 1980.

AIKEN, HENRY D. "A Pluralistic Analysis of Aesthetic Value." *Philosophical Review,* Vol. 59 (1950).

ALEXANDER, SAMUEL. *Beauty and Other Forms of Value.* Random: Macmillan, 1933.

BARTLETT, ETHEL M. *Types of Aesthetic Judgment.* London: Allen & Unwin, 1937.

BEARDSLEY, MONROE C. *Aesthetics.* New York: Harcourt Brace, 1958. Ch. 11.

BEARDSLEY, MONROE C. "What is an Aesthetic Quality?" *Theoria,* 39 (1973).

BROILES, DAVID. "Frank Sibley's 'Aesthetic Concepts.' " *Journal of Aesthetics and Art Criticism,* 28 (1964).

BUERMEYER, LAWRENCE. *The Aesthetic Experience.* Merion, Pa.: Barnes Foundation, 1929.

BURKE, EDMUND. *A Philosophical Inquiry into the Origin of Our Ideas of the Sublime and Beautiful.* 6th edition, London, 1770.

CARRITT, E. F. *What is Beauty?* Oxford: Clarendon Press, 1931.

COHEN, TED. "Aesthetic/Non-aesthetic and the Concept of Taste." *Theoria,* 39 (1973). Reprinted in Kennick and in Dickie & Sclafani.

COLEMAN, FRANCIS X. *The Harmony of Reason: a Study in Kant's Aesthetics.* Pittsburgh: Univ. of Pittsburgh Press, 1974.

CRAWFORD, DONALD. *Kant's Aesthetic Theory.* Madison: Univ. of Wisconsin Press, 1974.

FISHER, JOHN, and JEFFREY MAITLAND, "The Subjectivist Turn in Aesthetics: a Critical Analysis of Kant's Theory of Appreciation," *Review of Metaphysics,* 27 (1974).

FREEDMAN, MARCIA. "The Myth of the Aesthetic Predicate." *Journal of Aesthetic and Art Criticism,* 27 (1968).

GOTSHALK, D. W. "Art and Beauty." *Monist,* 41 (1931).

HOGARTH, WILLIAM. *The Analysis of Beauty.* Oxford: Clarendon Press, 1955.

HUNGERLAND, ISABEL. "The Logic of Aesthetic Concepts." *Proceedings and Addresses of the American Philosophical Association,* 36 (1962-3).

HUTCHESON, FRANCIS. *An Inquiry into the Original of Our Ideas of Beauty and Virtue.* 2nd ed. London, 1726.

ISEMINGER, GARY. "Aesthetic Judgments and Non-aesthetic Conditions." *Analysis,* 33 (1972-3).

JOAD, C. E. M. *Matter, Life, and Value.* London: Oxford Univ. Press. 1929.

KANT, IMMANUEL. *Critique of Judgment.* (Numerous editions.)

KENNICK, WILLIAM. "Does Traditional Aesthetics Rest on a Mistake?" *Mind,* 67 (1958).

KIVY, PETER. "Aesthetic Aspects and Aesthetic Qualities." *Journal of Philosophy,* 65 (1968).

KIVY, PETER. *The Seventh Sense.* New York: Burt Franklin & Co., 1976.

KIVY, PETER. *Speaking of Art.* The Hague: Nijhoff, 1973. Chs. 1-3.

KIVY, PETER. "What Makes Aesthetic Terms 'Aesthetic'?" *Philosophical and Phenomenological Research,* 36 (1975).

KNIGHT, HELEN. "THE USE OF 'GOOD' IN AESTHETIC JUDGMENTS." *Proceedings of the Aristotelian Society,* 36 (1936).

LOGAN, J. F. "More on Aesthetic Concepts." *Journal of Aesthetics and Art Criticism,* 25 (1967).

LONGINUS. *On the Sublime.* Translated by Hamilton Fyfe. Various editions.

MEAGER, RUBY, "Aesthetic Concepts." *British Concepts of Aesthetics,* 10 (1970).

MORTON, BRUCE. "Beardsley's Conception of the Aesthetic Object." *Journal of Aesthetics and Art Criticism,* 32 (1974).

MOTHERSILL, MARY, "'Unique' as an Aesthetic Predicate," *Journal of Philosophy,* 1961.

NAHM, MILTON C. *Aesthetic Experience and Its Presuppositions.* New York: Harper, 1946.

OSBORNE, HAROLD. *Aesthetics and Art Theory.* London: Routledge Kegan and Paul, 1970.

OSBORNE, HAROLD. "Taste and Judgments in the Arts." *Journal of Aesthetic Education,* 5 (1971).

OSBORNE, HAROLD. *The Theory of Beauty.* London: Routledge & Kegan Paul, 1952.

PEPPER, STEPHEN. *Aesthetic Quality.* New York: Harcourt Brace, 1938.

PRALL, DAVID W. *Aesthetic Analysis.* New York: Crowell, 1936.

PRALL, DAVID W. *Aesthetic Judgment.* New York: Crowell, 1929.

PRATT, CARROLL C. "The Stability of Aesthetic Judgments." *Journal of Aesthetics and Art Criticism,* 15 (1956).

RANDALL, FRANCIS B. "The Goofy in Art." *British Journal of Aesthetics,* 11 (1971).

REID, LOUIS ARNAUD. *Meaning in the Arts.* London: Allen & Unwin, 1969. Part 2.

SCHAPER, EVA AND FRANK SIBLEY. "Symposium about Taste." *British Journal of Aesthetics,* 6 (1966).

SCHOPENHAUER, ARTHUR. *Complete Essays.* 6 vols. Crown Publishing Co. (n.d.)

SCHWYZER, J. R. "SIBLEY'S AESTHETIC CONCEPTS." *Philosophical Review,* 72 (1963).

SHIELDS, ALLAN. "The Aesthetic Object as 'Object Manque.' " *Journal of Aesthetics and Art Criticism,* 30 (1971).

SIBLEY, FRANK. "Aesthetic Concepts." *Philosophical Review,* 68 (1959). Reprinted in Dickie and Sclafani and in Kennick.

SIBLEY, FRANK. "Aesthetic Concepts: A Rejoinder." *Philosophical Review,* 72 (1963).

SIBLEY, FRANK. "Aesthetic and Non-aesthetic." *Philosophical Review,* 74 (1965).

SIBLEY, FRANK, and MICHAEL TANNER. "Objectivity and Aesthetics." *Proceedings of the Aristotelian Society,* Suppl. Vol. 62 (1968).

SIMPSON, E. "Aesthetic Appraisal." *Philosophy,* 50 (1975).

Sircello, Guy. "Subjectivity and Justification in Aesthetic Judgments." *Journal of Aesthetics and Art Criticism,* 27 (1968).

_____. *A New Theory of Beauty.* Princeton: Princeton Univ. Press, 1975.

Slote, Michael. "The Rationality of Aesthetic Value Judgments." *Journal of Philosophy,* 68 (1971).

Sparshott, Francis E. *The Structure of Aesthetics.* Toronto: Univ. of Toronto Press, 1963.

Stace, W. T. *The Meaning of Beauty.* London: Richards & Toulmin, 1929.

Stolnitz, Jerome. "The Artistic Values in Aesthetic Experience." *Journal of Aesthetics and Art Criticism,* 35 (1976).

Stolnitz, Jerome. " ' Beauty': History of an Idea." *Journal of the History of Ideas,* 23 (1961).

Talmor, Sasha. "The Aesthetic Judgments and Its Criteria of Value." *Mind,* 78 (1969).

Tsugawa, Albert. "The Objectivity of Aesthetic Judgments." *Philosophical Review,* 70 (1961).

Uphaus, Robert W. "Shaftesbury On Art: the Rhapsodic Aesthetic." *Journal of Aesthetics and Art Criticism,* 27 (1969).

Ziff, Paul. *Semantic Analysis.* Ithaca, N. Y.: Cornell Univ. Press. 1960. Chapter 6.

# Index

Works of art are indexed under the names of their authors, composers, painters, etc.

Entries in the reading lists, which occur at the end of each chapter, are not indexed.